ADULT DEVELOPMENT AND AGING

FOURTH EDITION

William J. Hoyer
Syracuse University

John M. Rybash
Hamilton College

Paul A. Roodin
State University of New York, Oswego

McGraw-Hill College

Boston   Burr Ridge, IL   Dubuque, IA   Madison, WI   New York   San Francisco   St. Louis
Bangkok   Bogotá   Caracas   Lisbon   London   Madrid
Mexico City   Milan   New Delhi   Seoul   Singapore   Sydney   Taipei   Toronto

McGraw-Hill College

A Division of The McGraw·Hill Companies

ADULT DEVELOPMENT AND AGING, FOURTH EDITION

Copyright © 1999 by The McGraw-Hill Companies, Inc. All rights reserved. Previous editions © 1985, 1991, 1995 by Wm. C. Brown Communications, Inc. All rights reserved. Printed in the United States of America. Except as permitted under the United States Copyright Act of 1976, no part of this publication may be reproduced or distributed in any form or by any means, or stored in a data base or retrieval system, without the prior written permission of the publisher.

This book is printed on acid-free paper.

1 2 3 4 5 6 7 8 9 0 QPF/QPF 9 3 2 1 0 9 8

ISBN 0-697-25301-5

Editorial director: *Jane E. Vaicunas*
Executive editor: *Mickey Cox*
Editorial coordinator: *Sarah C. Thomas*
Senior marketing manager: *James Rozsa*
Senior project manager: *Peggy J. Selle*
Production supervisor: *Deborah Donner*
Coordinator of freelance design: *Michelle D. Whitaker*
Photo research coordinator: *John C. Leland*
Supplement coordinator: *Stacy A. Patch*
Compositor: *Carlisle Communications, Ltd.*
Typeface: *10.5/12.5 Times Roman*
Printer: *Quebecor Printing Book Group/Fairfield, PA*

Freelance cover designer: *Diane Beasley*
Cover image: © *Ken Fisher/Tony Stone Images*

The credits section for this book begins on page 641 and is considered an extension of the copyright page.

Library of Congress Cataloging-in-Publication Data

Hoyer, William J.
    Adult development and aging / William J. Hoyer, John M. Rybash,
Paul A. Roodin. — 4ᵗʰ ed.
        p.   cm.
    Rev. ed. of : Adult development and aging / John M. Rybash, Paul A.
Roodin, William J. Hoyer. 3ʳᵈ ed. © 1995.
    Includes bibliographical references and index.
    ISBN 0-697-25301-5
    1. Adulthood—Psychological aspects. 2. Aging—Psychological
aspects. 3. Life cycle, Human. I. Rybash, John M. II. Roodin,
Paul A. III. Rybash, John M. Adult development and aging.
IV. Title.
BF724.5.R9   1999
155.6—dc21   98–41408
                                                        CIP

www.mhhe.com

BRIEF CONTENTS

EXPANDED CONTENTS

Preface   ix

4
ADAPTATION AND COPING   *101*

5
MENTAL HEALTH AND
INTERVENTIONS   *144*

6
PHYSICAL HEALTH   *195*

7
MEMORY, ATTENTION, AND
LEARNING   *259*

8

INTELLIGENCE AND CREATIVITY 299

9

COGNITIVE STAGES, WISDOM, AND EXPERTISE 337

10

PERSONALITY DEVELOPMENT 376

APPENDIX

DEVELOPMENTAL RESEARCH METHODS   553

PREFACE

TO THE STUDENT

*M*ost of the time, when we think about development, we think of our childhood or adolescence. However, the first 20 years of life may be only the first 25 percent of our development. For young adults, the next five, six, or seven decades are just as significant as the first two decades of life. The field of adult development and aging is new. The field is exciting for those who teach and work in this area because the knowledge that comprises the field is growing and improving. Our aim in writing this text was to communicate to you the latest, best information in a way that makes it applicable and relevant to you. Therefore, there are two perspectives to keep in mind as you go through this text. One perspective is personal. That is, the material is relevant to understanding yourself—your past and future development. The material is also relevant to understanding the changes experienced or to be experienced by your peers, friends, family members, and others. Another perspective is professional or practical. Some people are interested in the topic of this text and course because they are preparing for a career in this field as clinicians or researchers. Much of the knowledge that comprises this field derives from practical questions about how to help older adults and their families, and how to promote health and effective functioning throughout the adult years.

Because there are gains as well as losses during the adult years, we emphasize what individuals and professionals can do to promote optimal outcomes in response to everyday challenges as well as in response to diseases, declines, and losses that can occur during the adult years.

As you read this book, think about your own development. What will you be like as you grow older? This book provides an accurate picture of the awesome, complex unfolding of development during the adult years. Not only will you learn important facts about the nature of adult development, you should be able to apply these facts to your own life as you grow older. What you learn can be a guide to your future growth and development and make you aware of the opportunities and challenges that occur during the adult years.

TO THE INSTRUCTOR

Our aim in writing this text was to organize and present the most up-to-date and important research and theory bearing on the understanding of adult development and aging, and to do so in a way that would be interesting and useful to a wide range of undergraduates. We tried to present the material in a way that would engage and motivate students. In this fourth edition, we offer you and your students a clear, comprehensive, and current account of the salient issues and concerns that dominate the field. After reading this text, your students will have a keen understanding of where the field of adult development and aging has been in the past, where it is right now, and where it will be headed in the future.

We have tried to present a balanced view of the gains *and* losses that characterize psychological development throughout the adult years. Also, we have given special attention to how different aspects of psychological development may be *optimized* throughout adulthood.

A number of new pedagogical aids have been incorporated into this fourth edition to make the material more interesting as well as accessible. Each chapter opens with a chapter outline and also includes a number of boxed Research Focus inserts containing supplementary, high-interest, discussion-provoking material. All key terms are highlighted, defined, and thoroughly explained the first time they occur in the text.

AUDIENCE

This text is appropriate for all students taking a course in adult development and aging. Such courses are titled Adult Development, Adult Development and Aging (or the Psychology of Adult Development and Aging), and Adult Psychology. The level of writing is geared toward a sophomore, junior, or senior undergraduate who has completed a general introductory-level psychology course. However, the text assumes no prerequisite knowledge of psychology.

Adult Development and Aging would also be useful to instructors who teach a course in life-span development and want to use two books—one on child and adolescent development and another on adult development and aging. The text is equally appropriate for students at two-year and four-year colleges and universities.

CONTENT AND ORGANIZATION

Adult Development and Aging presents current knowledge derived from research findings and new theories and ideas about understanding adulthood and aging from an interdisciplinary, process-oriented perspective. Our focus in writing was to present material in a way that would be useful to students in terms of their own develop-

ment and to situations that they or their peers and families are likely to face in everyday life. The material is organized in terms of the biological, social, and cultural contexts in which change occurs during the adult years. The text consists of 13 chapters, each concerned with a major theme or aspect of adult development and aging. The appendix covers research methods used to investigate age-related changes.

LEARNING AIDS

This text has been written with the student in mind. There are brief as well as detailed chapter outlines, Research Focus boxes, and a comprehensive glossary. All of the terms in the glossary are printed in boldface type when they first appear to alert students to the precise meaning of key terms. Graphs, tables, and figures were constructed to clearly and concisely illustrate important research findings or to summarize facts and theories. Photographs and line drawings give visual emphasis to key concepts and events and to those people, present and past, who have advanced our knowledge of adult development and aging. Finally, at the end of each chapter, there is a detailed summary, and a list of review questions. Separate indexes for authors and subjects appear at the end of the book.

INSTRUCTOR'S MANUAL AND TEST BANK

An *Instructor's Manual and Test Bank* is available to adopters. The *Instructor's Manual* contains chapter outlines, learning objectives, classroom suggestions, internet resources, essay questions and media materials for your course. The *Test Bank* includes an expanded selection of objective test items marked as factual, conceptual, or applied to assist selection of a variety of test items. Page numbers referencing the test are provided. These test items are also available in computerized versions for both Macintosh and Windows platforms, created to make the task of writing tests and exams easier and faster.

ACKNOWLEDGMENTS

Special thanks go to Theresa Bouffard, Debbie Diment, Dayna Green, and Albert Lubarsky.

The fourth edition of this text benefited greatly from the assistance provided by colleagues through user reviews of the previous edition. For their many good ideas and helpful suggestions, we thank:

Robin K. Montvilo   Rhode Island College
Janet Kalinowski   Ithaca College
Linda M. Woolf   Webster University
Mark Mathews   University of Kansas

Morton Isaacs   Rochester Institute of Technology
J. Baeza Jr.   Southern Illinois University at Carbondale
Daniel L. Segal   University of Colorado at Colorado Springs
Cheryl R. Kaus   SUNY at Oswego
Virginia M. Spiegel   Clarke College
Harriett Amster   University of Texas at Arlington

Finally, we would like to thank our colleagues and students at Syracuse University, Hamilton College, and SUNY College at Oswego, for their constructive comments and feedback during the preparation of this fourth edition.

ADULT DEVELOPMENT AND AGING
An Introduction

INTRODUCTION

This chapter provides a foundation for the study of adulthood and aging. You will learn about some of the different ways that developmental scientists describe and explain the adult part of the human life span. In addition, you will learn about some of the fundamental controversies that are currently shaping the study of adult development and aging.

WHY STUDY ADULT DEVELOPMENT AND AGING?

People study adult development and aging for many reasons. The reasons range from wanting to understand the processes of development to wanting to directly improve the quality of life for oneself or for others. Interest in the study of adult development and aging can be categorized as: (1) scientific or factual, (2) personal, and (3) altruistic. The philosopher Habermas (1971) suggested that human action is largely motivated by precisely these kinds of concerns. First, in terms of *factual interest,* there is a desire to have an objective understanding of what happens to people as they grow older. We pursue factual knowledge because we are curious about how and why people change. How does personality or intelligence change with aging? Over the course of adulthood, is a person more likely to become wise and creative, or foolish and forgetful? Why is it that some people experience declines in cognitive function or major changes in their personality while others do not? Is aging an inherently pathological process? Can some of the negative changes associated with aging be reversed or modified? Are there some very positive aspects of psychological functioning (e.g., wisdom) that only emerge during the later years of life? Questions such as these need to be examined through precise scientific inquiry.

Second, in terms of *personal interest,* we are motivated to learn about adult development and aging because we have a selfish stake in becoming prepared for the changes, challenges, risks, and opportunities that face us as we move through adulthood and grow older. What can this field tell you about your future development and aging? Do you have any control over how you age? How can you become your best self? Knowledge of adult development and aging can be applied to one's own development. This is especially important when one considers that significant developmental change occurs throughout the entire adult life span—from the twenties onward.

A third reason for wanting to study adult development and aging is *altruistic.* We want to know how to help others. Knowledge within this domain is directly relevant in helping others to live better lives. We can assist others in the various roles of spouse, friend, confidant, adult-child, grandchild, parent, or professional by helping them negotiate the tasks and challenges of adulthood. For example, we may face the challenge of helping a close friend adjust to a new job or to a divorce. Or we may have to know how to be effective as a caregiver for a parent or grandparent with dementia. We may even want to pursue a career in psychology, medicine, or social work that involves direct service to aged individuals. Changes in the American health care system, combined with the fact that the numbers and proportions of older adults will continue to rise, have created needs within families and many employment opportunities in various health and human service professions. It is also important to mention that accurate knowledge about the myths and realities of adult development and aging provides an essential basis for helping individuals to relinquish oppressive and negative stereotypes associated with old age and aging.

WHAT IS DEVELOPMENTAL PSYCHOLOGY?

Developmental psychology has two aims. First, developmental psychology is concerned with understanding the origins and development of behavior within the individual; this focus is referred to as the study of **ontogeny** or **intraindividual change.** Although the intensive study of individual development is a primary goal of developmental psychology (Baltes, 1997; Hoyer & Rybash, 1996), relatively few studies of individual development exist. Most of the research in developmental psychology is conducted by comparing groups of individuals of different ages. Studies describing the differences between different age groups are intended to have implications for "average" individual development.

Second, developmental psychology is concerned with the study of age-related **interindividual differences.** Developmental psychologists study how different individuals develop and change as well as the factors that account for individual differences in development. Thus, developmental psychologists are primarily interested in how individuals develop and change as they grow older, and in how different people show different patterns of development and change.

With these aims in mind, we can define **developmental psychology** as the study of age-related interindividual differences and age-related intraindividual change. The main goals of developmental psychology are to describe, explain, predict, and improve or optimize age-related behavior change. We use the term *age-related* because age (or time) by itself does not give us a satisfactory explanation for development. The specific events or processes that occur during an interval of time, whether measured in hours, days, years, or decades, are the real determinants of development or aging. Time or age by itself is not a cause for change. We should also mention that *nonevents,* or the events that are not personally or directly experienced, can determine the paths of development.

That is, we might have developed entirely differently if we had lived in a different neighborhood or country, not fallen in love, attended different schools, not learned to play a musical instrument, or met different friends or teachers. Someone we know might have developed differently if we had not learned how to read or if she had not been physically injured in a car accident. We have been changed by what we have experienced, and we are different from others in part because of the developmental consequences of the events we have and have not experienced.

In the definition of developmental psychology, *behavior* is the focus of study, because psychology is the study of behavior. Psychologists conceptualize behavior broadly to include just about everything that people do. For example, social interactions, thoughts, memories, emotions, attitudes, and physical activities are all topics of study within the psychology of adult development and aging. Particular kinds of behavior are selected for study because they may be important in their own right, or because that behavior is thought to be a reliable measure of an important concept or process that cannot be measured directly.

The term **development** is reserved for changes in behavior that are known to vary in an orderly way with increasing age. Developmental change must be relatively durable and distinct from temporary fluctuations in behavior that are due to mood, short-term learning, or other factors (Nesselroade, 1991). We would not identify an infant's one-time utterance of someone's name as evidence of language development. Nor would we identify a one-time failure to recall someone's name as evidence of age-related memory deficit. Development is reversible, and the term refers to increases as well as decreases in behavior, but the changes must be relatively durable to be considered developmental change.

THEORETICAL ISSUES IN THE STUDY OF ADULT DEVELOPMENT AND AGING

The major theoretical issues in the study of adult development and aging are summarized in table 1.1. As can be seen in the table, those who study adult development and aging generally take the view that development takes place throughout the entire adult life span. In general usage, the term *development* refers to growth, such as physical maturation during the early years of childhood and adolescence; developmental psychologists who study the adult years recognize that there is development or change throughout the human life span.

Development as Gains and Losses

Although the types of changes that occur between birth and 20 years of age and the kinds of changes that occur after one's 20th birthday are quite different, development in the form of *gains* and *losses* continues to occur throughout life (e.g., Baltes, 1997; Hoyer & Rybash, 1996).

Those who study adult development and aging take the view that no age period is any more important than any other period of development. The changes that occur during the adult years are just as significant as those that occur during childhood or adolescence. For example, large changes in social maturity occur during the college

TABLE 1.1

**A Summary of Theoretical Issues in the Study
of Adult Development and Aging**

Development is a lifelong process.

No age or period of development is any more important than any other age or period of development.

Development refers to both increases and decreases, and gains and losses, in behavior.

Development is modifiable or reversible; the individual is active in determining the course of development, and there is plasticity in how an individual develops and changes throughout the life span.

Development can take many different paths, as reflected by age-related interindividual differences.

Development is multidirectional, in that there are different rates and directions of change for different characteristics within the individual and across individuals.

Developmental change can be quantitative, gradual, and continuous or qualitative, relatively abrupt, and stagelike.

Developmental changes are considered to be relatively durable, to distinguish them from temporary fluctuations due to motivation, short-term memory, or other nondevelopmental processes.

Development is contextual in that it can vary substantially depending on the historical and sociocultural conditions in which it takes place.

Development is an outcome of the interactive effects of nature and nurture; the contributions of environmental and biological influences vary for different aspects of development and for different points in the life span.

The study of development is multidisciplinary in that it involves combining the perspectives of anthropology, biology, psychology, sociology, and other disciplines.

years. One's choice of vocation has a strong impact on social and intellectual development during the adult years, and on health and happiness. Whether or not someone marries or becomes a parent has a substantial effect on many aspects of development. Perhaps we notice large changes in the attitudes, motivations, and capabilities of our parents, or grandparents, as they grow older. The point is that there are many opportunities for profound change throughout the life span.

Qualitative Versus Quantitative Change

It is also mentioned in table 1.1 that developmental change can be characterized or appear as either **qualitative,** abrupt, and stagelike or **quantitative,** gradual, and continuous. Are you basically the same person that you were five years ago, or are you basically a different person?

For example, developmental change can be considered to be qualitative when there are dramatic changes in the way the individual thinks about interpersonal relationships. Quantitative change refers to differences in amount rather than differences in kind. For example, throughout adulthood, the speed of retrieval of information from memory may gradually become slower.

Whether adult development is essentially qualitative or quantitative is both an empirical and theoretical issue. It is likely that developmental change is *both* qualitative and quantitative (Lerner, 1984).

Stagelike Versus Continuous Change

Some researchers and theorists maintain that there are identifiable stages of adult development and aging. Others maintain that no universal markers distinguish one stage of development from any other. Thus, the notion of stages of development is controversial; researchers disagree about whether distinct stages of development occur during the adult years, and they argue about the criteria that indicate the presence of stages.

A **stage theory** is a description of a sequence of qualitative changes. Stage 1 must always precede Stage 2. Additional criteria for a stage theory are that (1) each successive stage consists of the integration and extension of a previous stage, (2) the transition from one stage to another is abrupt, and (3) each stage forms an organized whole that is characterized by the occurrence of several particular behaviors or competencies. Thus, if an entire set of organized behaviors appeared rather suddenly in the course of development for most if not all individuals at a particular point in the life span, and if each new stage incorporated and extended the competencies of the previous stage, then we would have clear evidence for a developmental stage. Evidence for stages of development is quite rare, however, leading some investigators to doubt the stage concept (Flavell, 1985) and others to want to relax the criteria for defining stagelike development (Fischer, 1980; Wohlwill, 1973).

Stage theories imply an abruptness or developmental **discontinuity** between stages and **continuity** within stages. Nonstage theories imply that development is *always* continuous. This means that the same processes control psychological functioning throughout the life span. According to social learning theory, for example, the same principles operate to affect behavior throughout the life span. An individual's behavior is continually shaped over the course of development through imitation, reward, and punishment. The influence of these mechanisms results in an increase, a decrease, or stability in behavior over the life span. For example, because of changes in reinforcement contingencies, we can expect that some adults will experience feelings of depression and helplessness as they age.

The study of adult development and aging is primarily concerned with the understanding of stability as well as the gains and losses that can be observed at many points during the life span. Researchers are interested in understanding the nature of the consistencies and continuities that are evident in observations of adults across time. Although, traditionally, adulthood is characterized as a period of long-lasting continuity relative to earlier and later periods (e.g., Shanan, 1991), it is obvious that there is substantial diversity or interindividual differences among adults, as well as substantial variability within the same person across time (i.e., intraindividual change) and across tasks or situations (i.e., intraindividual differences). It is important to point out that despite the appearance of stability and continuity, it may be the case that a considerable amount of change occurs in various underlying mechanisms and processes.

Plasticity Versus Nonplasticity of Change

Another issue in the study of adult development and aging is the extent to which there is **plasticity** in behavior (Baltes, 1997; Fries, 1997). Baltes and his colleagues, in particular, have been active proponents of the notion of developmental **reserve capacity,** and they have provided a number of thoughtful discussions of the relevance of the concepts of plasticity and reserve capacity to the study of adult development and aging (e.g., Baltes, 1993; Baltes, Lindenberger, & Staudinger, 1998). There is evidence to suggest that many kinds of age-related deficits can be remediated through appropriate intervention and health promotion (e.g., Fries, 1997).

Although the reversibility of some aspects of adult development is an exciting possibility to explore, research evidence appears to support the position that reserve capacity is diminished with age in late life. That is, older adults are less able to benefit from training designed to optimize performance on cognitive tasks (e.g., Baltes & Kliegl, 1992). The significance of the notions of plasticity and reserve is in terms of the mechanisms that underlie competence and performance. Analogous to cardiovascular function, muscular efficiency, and other biological systems, age differences in behavioral efficiency arise when systems that are critical to maintaining performance are challenged by stress or other externally or self-imposed factors (Fries & Crapo, 1981; Rodin, 1986; Rowe & Kahn, 1987, 1997). Fries and Crapo (1981) reviewed evidence to suggest that reserve capacity is reduced with age across many biological systems. The concept of reserve is useful for describing adult cognitive function under stressed situations, but it may be of limited usefulness in accounting for developmental variability in everyday behavior.

Developmental psychologists are also confronted by the fact that the same individual performs differently at different times, and that any theory of adult development and aging must take account of variability in adaptive competencies. Such an approach emphasizes what the individual can do or is capable of doing under some conditions, some of the time.

Multidirectional Versus Unidirectional Change

Another theoretical issue in the study of adult development and aging has to do with the directionality of development. **Multidirectionality** refers to the observation that there are intraindividual differences in the patterns in aging. That is, individuals show stability for some types of behavior, declines in others, and improvements in still others. The developing individual might show an increase in creativity or wisdom and a decrement in some memory functions with advancing age.

In contrast to research and theory in adult development and aging, child-focused views of development, such as those of Piaget and Freud, generally assumed a **unidirectional** view of development in that all abilities were thought to show the same trend with maturation.

DETERMINANTS OF ADULT DEVELOPMENTAL CHANGE

Why do individuals change and develop as they do? Some aspects of development are universal in that they are the same for everyone. Some aspects of development are culture-specific, cohort-specific, or specific to a segment of historical time. Some aspects of development are gender-specific, and some aspects of development are entirely unique to individuals because of their particular experiences. In this section

How Have Historical Events and Life Experiences Influenced Middle-Aged Adults?

One of the most elaborate longitudinal studies—the California Longitudinal Study—provides data on individual lives over a period of almost 50 years (Eichorn, Clausen, Haan, Honzik, & Mussen, 1981). The individuals in the California Longitudinal Study, who are now in later adulthood, were born in 1920–21 and 1928–29. Thus their birthdates preceded the depression. As Glenn Elder (1981) comments:

> . . . [the] forces set in motion by the swing of boom and bust—the economic growth and opportunity of the predepression era, the economic collapse of the 1930s, and recovery through wartime mobilization to unequaled prosperity during the 1940s and 1950s—influenced the life histories of these study members in ways that have yet to be fully understood. (p. 6)

Elder describes how individuals from these two cohorts (those born in 1920–21 and those born in 1928–29), although they experienced the same historical conditions of the 1920s and 1930s, underwent these experiences at different points of development and thus were affected in very different ways. The earlier-born subjects, those in the Oakland Growth Study, were children during the prospering 1920s. This was a time of unusual economic growth, particularly in the San Francisco area. The members of this cohort entered the depression after a reasonably secure early childhood, and they later avoided joblessness because of wartime mobilization. Most of them married and started families by the mid-1940s. This historical timetable minimized their exposure to the hardships of the depression.

For the group of adults born in 1928–29, the same historical events and circumstances occurred at a different point in their development as children. Members of this group, who formed the Guidance Study, grew up in Berkeley, California. During their early childhood years, they and their parents experienced the hardships of the depression; then again, during the pressured period of adolescence, they encountered the unsettling experience of World War II. According to Elder, the hardships they experienced increased their feelings of inadequacy during the war years and reduced their chances for higher education.

Recent analyses of these data by Elder, Shanahan, and Clipp (1994) provide new insights into the potential health consequences of social disruption and social breakdown.

Table 1.A shows the ages of the Oakland and Berkeley subjects at the time of various historical events. How might some of these events and circumstances influence the lives of people—in terms of generational differences, the employment of women, and childbearing, for example? As we consider such life events and circumstances, we can see how social history shapes the lives of adults.

---

we identify three general categories of determinants of developmental change. These are (1) **normative age-graded factors,** (2) **normative history-graded factors,** and (3) **nonnormative life events.** Development occurs as the result of the interaction of these factors. Usually it is an error to attribute developmental change to only one of these factors.

Normative Age-Graded Factors

When we study young children, development appears *normative,* or similar across individuals and even cultures. It also appears that development is determined largely by a variety of normative age-graded factors. For example, the maturation and deterioration of the brain and nervous system occur at roughly the same ages in all individuals. There are also reliable age-graded changes in the speed of information processing and predictable changes in vision and hearing with aging.

TABLE 1.A

Age of Oakland Growth and Guidance Study Members by Historical Events

Date	Event	Age of Study Members	
		OGS*	GS**
1880–1900	Birth years of OGS parents		
1890–1910	Birth years of GS parents		
1921–22	Depression	Birth (1920–21)	
1923	Great Berkeley Fire	2–3	
1923–29	General economic boom; growth of "debt pattern" way of life; cultural change in sexual mores	1–9	Birth (1928–29)
1929–30	Onset of Great Depression	9–10	1–2
1932–33	Depth of Great Depression	11–13	3–5
1933–36	Partial recovery, increasing cost of living, labor strikes	12–16	4–8
1937–38	Economic slump	16–18	8–10
1939–40	Incipient stage of wartime mobilization	18–20	10–12
1941–43	Major growth of war industries (shipyards, munitions plants, etc.) and of military forces	20–23	12–15
1945	End of World War II	24–25	16–17
1950–53	Korean War	29–33	21–25

From G. Elder, "Social History & Life Experience" in Present and Past in Middle Life. Copyright © 1981 Academic Press. Reprinted by permission.
*OGS = Oakland Growth Study
**GS = Guidance Study

Normative History-Graded Factors

Some developmental influences are closely related to specific historical eras or events rather than to age. These events, called normative history-graded factors, occur at certain times in history. They produce dramatic effects on individuals who experience them—effects that may persist for a lifetime (see Research Focus 1.1). Normative history-graded factors include the pervasive and enduring effects of societal events such as wars and economic depressions on individual lives. Think of the personality differences that exist between different-aged adults. People in their thirties and forties may have different attitudes and personalities than individuals in their seventies and eighties. Why do these differences exist? Is it simply because of the different ages of these two groups of adults? Or is it because the different age groups grew up in different circumstances? In today's world, for example, the AIDS epidemic or a tough job market may have different effects on different-aged individuals.

Many people now choose to marry or begin parenting responsibilities at a later age. Medical advances and increased opportunities for family planning allow for a wider range of individual choices in many aspects of development. The timing of marriage and family decisions is also affected by work and financial situations.

Normative history-graded influences can be observed by comparing different cohorts of individuals. The term **cohort** refers to a group of individuals born at a particular time. History-graded or cohort factors have been shown to affect the level of intellectual abilities in different-aged individuals. Consider the results of the Seattle Longitudinal Study. This study began as a doctoral dissertation by K. Warner Schaie in 1956. Careful planning and design has allowed Schaie and his colleagues to distinguish the influences of age-related changes and history-graded changes over six waves of testing (1956, 1963, 1970, 1977, 1984, and 1996). For each wave of data collection, individuals ranging in age from 22 to 70 years and older were tested on measures of verbal meaning, spatial orientation, inductive reasoning, number, and word fluency from the Primary Mental Abilities (PMA) test (Schaie, 1993, 1994, 1996; Schaie & Willis, 1993). As expected, there were age-related declines for most of the measures of intellectual performance at each of the testing occasions. Considering these cross-sectional data by themselves, it appears that cognitive ability declines with age. However, when the results of different-aged individuals are examined across the six measurement intervals from 1956 to 1996, the results conclusively demonstrate that there are substantial history-graded differences in intellectual performance. These results suggest that both age and history-graded factors are responsible for differences in intellectual ability. In Schaie's study, for example, individuals born in 1910 performed worse on all of the measures of mental ability when compared with individuals born in 1917 and later. Generally, subsequent cohorts of individuals experience better schooling, greater educational opportunities, and intellectually more stimulating environments. History-graded factors influence many other aspects of psychological functioning, and the importance of distinguishing age effects and history-graded or cohort effects in developmental research cannot be overemphasized. Schaie's research design for disentangling age and cohort effects is described in detail in appendix A.

Nonnormative or Idiosyncratic Life Events

One of the most important characteristics of development during the adult years is that some changes are unique to the individual. This kind of developmental change is nonnormative or **idiosyncratic.** Idiosyncratic change is attributed to variations in experiences across a wide range of environmental or societal opportunities and constraints (e.g., Baltes, 1997; Hoyer & Rybash, 1996; Riley, 1985; Riley & Riley, 1994). Age-ordered normative change is much less evident during the adult years than during the childhood and adolescent years. Many of the individual changes and interindividual differences in adult development can be attributed to nonnormative or idiosyncratic influences rather than to general or universal patterns of adult developmental change. It is generally the case that there is a high degree of interindividual variability among adults. Thus, during adulthood, age-ordered, biological, or maturational processes are only one source of interindividual and intraindividual variability, leaving room for a wide range of environmental influences and experiences.

Many influences on adult development are nonnormative or unique to the individuals who experience them. Some nonnormative life events are common to a small proportion of same-age individuals; others affect only a single individual. Furthermore, nonnormative life events do not happen at any predictable time in a person's life. For example, winning first prize in a multimillion-dollar lottery is an event that would profoundly influence a person's behavior. However, it is only likely to happen to a small number of individuals and cannot be predicted to occur at any particular point in a person's life. Nonnormative life events, then, are usually chance occurrences.

Other examples of nonnormative events include accidents, illnesses, business failures, or the death of a young adult. Albert Bandura (1982) reminds us that nonnormative life events also include unintended meetings of people unfamiliar to one another. It is sobering to reflect that chance encounters may become critically important determinants of many aspects of our lives, including career choice and marriage. How many college students settle on an academic major because of an enthusiastic and inspiring professor they encounter by chance in an elective course? How many young men and women begin their career paths by chance? These are important and interesting research questions that have yet to be explored. The role of research in this area is not to count the frequency of occurrence of chance encounters. Instead, the aim is to examine how much choice and control we have (or do not have) over the events that affect our future development.

As shown in figure 1.1, the relative importance of normative age-graded factors, normative history-graded factors, and nonnormative life events varies across the life span. Figure 1.1 reveals that normative age-graded factors, for example, are most likely to influence development at the beginning and end of the life span. Most of the behavioral hallmarks of infancy (e.g., crawling, walking, talking, etc.) and very old age (e.g., generalized decrements in vision and attention) are probably due, to a great extent, to age-related biomaturational changes. Normative history-graded factors are most likely to produce developmental change during adolescence and young adulthood. Adolescence and young adulthood are times when an individual first constructs an understanding of society and his or her relationship to it. It seems obvious, for example, that living through the Vietnam War and the civil rights movement in the United States would have the least effect on extremely young and old individuals and the greatest effect on adults entering the mainstream of societal life. Finally, nonnormative life events may take on a gradually more powerful role in promoting developmental changes as an individual ages. This idea may account for the observation that with increasing age individual differences become progressively more identifiable. For example, there is generally more heterogeneity or interindividual variability in a group of 60-year-olds than a group of 40-year-olds. As we grow older, the continued emergence and accumulation of unique nonnormative life events helps to shape our personal lives, making individual differences more and more apparent.

Thus, we can distinguish three types of influences on adult development. These include the normative age-graded factors that have been emphasized in traditional developmental research; nonnormative life-event influences (such as winning a lottery or being abducted by a terrorist); and normative history-graded factors (such as the Great Depression of the 1930s or the Vietnam War) (Elder, 1997; Elder, Shanahan, & Clipp, 1994).

Figure 1.1 The relative influence of normative age-graded factors, normative history-graded factors, and nonnormative life-event factors in promoting developmental change at different times across the human life span.

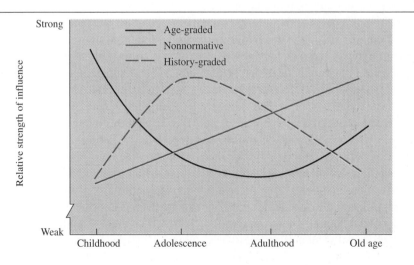

THE CONCEPT OF AGE

The concept of age is *multidimensional*. It is also the case that time since birth (or chronological age) is not always a good measure of developmental function. Some attempts have been made to assess the development of the ability to function effectively within a given environment or society, and to use **functional age** measures as replacements for chronological age. For example, an individual needs a number of skills and abilities (both psychological and physical) to function effectively as the sole occupant of an apartment—the individual has to be mobile and active to be able to shop, clean, cook, and wash as well as be able to efficiently plan and remember pertinent information. It is not surprising that some 75-year-olds are more self-sufficient than some 25-year-olds. Given the fact that chronological age is not always a good predictor of functional age, psychologists find it increasingly important to develop valid and reliable measures of a person's functional abilities. In the following paragraphs, we describe the different dimensions and meanings of age and aging.

Chronological Age

Chronological age refers to the number of years that have elapsed since a person's birth. Several psychologists (e.g., Baer, 1970) have argued that chronological age per se is *not* relevant to an understanding of psychological development; that is, a person's age in and of itself does not cause development. Age is merely a marker for the processes that change over time and influence behavior.

Both women in these photos are 80 years old. Biological and psychological aging occur at different rates for different individuals.

Biological Age

The concept of **biological age** has been defined as an estimate of the individual's present position with respect to his or her potential life span (Schroots & Birren, 1990). This concept of age involves measuring the functional capacities of an individual's vital organ system. From this perspective, age can be viewed as an index of biological health. An individual's biological capacities may be more or less vital or effective compared with those of other persons of the same chronological age.

Psychological Age

Psychological age refers to the adaptive capacities of an individual—that is, an individual's ability to adapt to changing environmental demands as compared with the adaptability of other individuals of identical chronological age. Individuals adapt to their environments by drawing on various psychological characteristics: learning, memory, intelligence, emotional control, motivational strengths, coping styles, and so on. Therefore, individuals who display a greater amount of such psychological characteristics than their chronological agemates are considered "psychologically young"; those who possess such traits to a lesser degree are "psychologically old."

Social Age

Social age refers to the social roles and expectations that people have for themselves as well as those imposed by other members of society. Consider the role of "mother" and the behaviors that accompany that role. It is probably more important to know that a woman is the mother of a 3-year-old child than to know whether she was born 20 or 30 years ago. Furthermore, individuals are often aware of being on-time or off-time with regard to social age. Some older adults, for example, act like perpetual teenagers because they consider themselves "young."

Age Profiles

Given these different dimensions of age, we can develop a comprehensive age profile for any individual. For example, a 70-year-old man (chronological age) might be in very good physical health (biological age), yet be experiencing a number of problems remembering and focusing attention (psychological age). The same man might consider himself more a "retired businessman who likes to play golf" than a "grandfather" (social age).

CONCEPT OF SUCCESSFUL AGING

Measures of biological age, psychological age, and social age are relevant to understanding what is meant by healthy development or **successful aging.** Successful aging refers to the combination of three components: (1) the avoidance of disease and disability; (2) the maintenance of high physical and cognitive capacity in the later years, and (3) continued active engagement with life (Rowe & Kahn, 1997). The concept of suc-

cessful aging is in contrast to negative views of aging. In many countries, aging is associated with disability, cognitive deficits, and loneliness. Substantial and growing evidence supports the view that the risk factors for some diseases, such as cardiovascular disease, can be modified (Sticht & Hazzard, 1995). There is also evidence showing that cognitive deficits and social disengagement are not inevitable consequences of growing older (e.g., Simonton, 1997; Verhaeghen, Marcoen, & Goossens, 1992; Willis, 1996).

CONCEPTUAL PARADIGMS FOR THE STUDY OF ADULT DEVELOPMENT

Paradigms, or "worldviews," enable researchers to construct meaningful patterns for what would otherwise be a collection of unrelated observations. Scientific activity is guided by paradigms that determine what is important to study, how it should be studied, and what kinds of theoretical ideas can be advanced on the basis of such study (Kuhn, 1962).

Paradigms are not directly testable; they are too abstract to be objectively verified or falsified. Paradigms serve to stimulate ideas, issues, and questions that *can* be tested. Thus, paradigms are *not* the same as theories. Paradigms provide a framework for generating theories, and theories generate research. Paradigms are useful if they serve this purpose, not in terms of whether they are right or wrong. Historically, psychologists have used mechanistic, organismic, and contextual paradigms to understand human development.

The Mechanistic Paradigm

According to the **mechanistic paradigm,** the individual's development is a product of environmental forces. The mechanistic model assumes that human behavior is machine-like. Machines are passive. From this view, behavior is reactive to events in life.

The Organismic Paradigm

According to the **organismic paradigm,** development is qualitative. From this view, the individual is active, planful, and strategic. The organismic paradigm shifted the emphasis from the study of simple stimulus-response relationships and quantitative change to the study of internal processes and qualitative change. Individual development unfolds in a universal, orderly sequence of stages.

The Contextual Paradigm

In recent years, the **contextual paradigm** has become predominant. The metaphor underlying the contextual paradigm is the historical event. This paradigm suggests that adults, like historical events, are ongoing, dynamic, and not directed toward an ideal goal or end-state. Furthermore, the meaning and interpretation of historical events may change, depending on the *context* or perspective from which such events are viewed. A war may be viewed as "moral" from one historical context and "immoral" from another. Similarly, the contextual model takes neither a purely passive nor a purely active view of the individual. The basic conception of this model is that an adult individual continuously influences and is influenced by the different contexts of life.

It is important to understand that context is an open-ended term that may apply at different levels of analysis. For example, the environmental context pertains to one's physical environment. The social, historical, or cultural context pertains to influences such as societal norms and the expectations of friends and relatives. Further, the biological context pertains to an individual's health and physical skills. In all of these examples, not only do the contexts have an effect upon the individual, but also the individual has an effect upon the context. To take a simple example, one's family might make unreasonable demands. When the individual begins to refuse these demands more often, it might alter the family's subsequent demands, which in turn alters the individual's responsiveness to further demands.

The contextual model serves as the foundation for a broad range of theories that address various aspects of adult development. For example, an adult's ability to remember an event depends on (1) the psychological, social, and physical contexts in which the person initially experienced the event, (2) the unique skills, abilities, knowledge, and motivation that the individual brings to the context in which he must remember, and (3) the special characteristics of the context in which the person attempts to remember. As the individual changes, and as the contexts in which she is asked to remember change, we would expect the person's memory to change as well. Thus, we could say that memory is a dynamic process involving the continual *reconstruction* of past events and experiences. Adults, therefore, seem to serve as their own "historians." They constantly revise their pasts from the perspective of the present.

One version of the contextual paradigm is the **dialectical view.** Riegl (1976) argued that individuals and the contexts of their lives are always in a state of flux; that is, adults are constantly changing organisms in a constantly changing world. From Riegel's view, the individual and society are never at rest. Riegel also believed that contradiction and conflict are an inherent part of development and that no single goal or end point in development is ever reached. The dialectical perspective stresses the inherent multidirectionality of developmental change and the wide-reaching interindividual variability observed with increasing chronological age.

New ways of thinking about a wide variety of topics in adult development and aging have emerged in recent years, and these views are largely contextual (e.g., see Baltes & Baltes, 1990; Dannefer & Perlmutter, 1990; Lerner, 1991; Sinnott & Cavanaugh, 1991). These views are partially motivated by dissatisfaction with the mechanistic and organismic preoccupation with the negative aspects of aging. There is also some dissatisfaction with the overemphasis on chronological age as the measure of development, and with the lack of emphasis on such concepts as resiliency, vitality, and adaptation in adult development and aging.

New contextual approaches to development try to take into account individual differences, gains as well as losses in function during the adult years, and the role of social interaction and contradiction or conflict in adult development. Another characteristic of new work in adult development and aging is that there is a greater emphasis than ever before on practical aspects of development. Many everyday activities in adulthood and old age are contextually based. Thinking, reasoning, and other aspects of everyday function in adulthood are not so much constrained by biological aging as they are by the contexts in which these activities take place. Primary interest is in the investigation of contextual factors that enable individuals to function effectively during the adult life span.

PARADIGMS AND ISSUES IN ADULT DEVELOPMENT

It is useful to compare the mechanistic, organismic, and contextual paradigms with respect to the issues considered earlier in this chapter. As table 1.2 shows, the organismic model is distinguished by the emphasis it places on qualitative change, distinctive stages of development, and continuity of change. It also is unique in emphasizing the importance of age-graded influences on development. One of the main differences between the mechanistic and contextual models is that the contextual model places greater emphasis on the multidirectional nature of developmental change. Another difference is the importance of history-graded influences in the contextual model. The mechanistic model emphasizes nonnormative life-event influences at the expense of all other aspects of development. The contextual model also emphasizes nonnormative influences but not exclusively; it considers history-graded influences as well as individual differences. Indeed, as indicated in table 1.3, the contextual model stresses all aspects of development. From the perspective of the contextual model, development is multifaceted and multidetermined. The contextual model, more than the others, recognizes individuals as producers of their own development.

TABLE 1.2

Overview of the Three Life-Span Models of Adult Development

Questions for Distinguishing Among Developmental Models	Models		
	Mechanistic	Organismic	Contextual
What is the underlying metaphor?	machine	cell, embryo	historical event
What is the relationship between the person and the environment?	active environment; active person	passive environment; passive person	active environment; active person
What is the focus of developmental psychology?	quantitative changes in observable behavior	qualitative changes in internal structures	person/environment transactions

TABLE 1.3

Models and Characteristics of Adult Development

Degree of Emphasis on Different Characteristics of Human Development	Models		
	Mechanistic	Organismic	Contextual
Qualitative change	Low	High	Medium
Stages of change	Low	High	Medium
Continuity of change	Low	High	Medium
Multidirectionality of change	Medium	Low	High
Reversibility of change	Medium	Low	Medium
Multiple determinants of change			
Normative age-graded factors	Low	High	Medium
Normative history-graded factors	Low	Low	High
Nonnormative life-event factors	High	Low	High
Chronological age as a useful variable	Low	High	Medium

OVERVIEW OF THE TEXT

One of the challenges for those who study adult development and aging is to construct a useful and accurate framework for describing and explaining the experiences of adult development. Some researchers focus on the factors that *constrain* development at different ages. For example, some social and cultural influences, such as restrictive sex roles and stereotypes of ageism, sexism, and racism, serve to limit opportunities for growth during the adult years and constrain individual development. Of course, there are also biological and health influences that constrain the range or nature of development during the adult years. In this text we emphasize not only the constraining factors but also the factors that are associated with *optimization* of development at different points throughout the adult life course. Furthermore, we stress the ideas that development throughout the adult years consists of a complex interplay of gains *and* losses, and that adult development and aging is characterized by a great deal of intraindividual change and interindividual variability. Throughout the text we illustrate how cultural, biological, and experiential factors influence functioning in different domains or areas of development.

DOMAINS OF DEVELOPMENT

The *biological and physical domain* refers to changes that range from simple alterations in size, weight, and other anatomical features to the genetic blueprint that places constraints on our development from conception to death. The genes we were born with still influence our adult development. Scientists are looking closely at the role genetics plays in such adult disorders as schizophrenia, dementia, alcoholism, and depression. Hormones are yet another aspect of biological makeup that play an important part in the understanding of adult development; for example, the onset of menopause in women is accompanied by significant hormonal change. Furthermore, in this text, we will pay close attention to age-related changes in the brain and nervous system. And we will describe how these changes influence psychological functioning.

The *cognitive domain* refers to the age-related series of changes that occur in mental activity—thought, memory, perception, and attention. As part of our study of cognitive development, we will explore how adults process information; how intelligence and creativity change over time; and how qualitatively new styles of thinking emerge during adulthood. We will look carefully at declines in memory during adulthood, paying special attention to the issue of how "normal" memory deficits may be distinguished from "pathological" memory deficits in older adults.

The *personality domain* in adult development usually refers to the properties distinguishing one individual from another individual. But as we will see, some experts believe that there are also commonalities that characterize individuals at particular points in adult development. One's sex-role orientation, perception of self, moral values, and sociability represent some of the aspects of personality we will discuss. You will find that it often is impossible to meaningfully present personality development in adulthood without frequently looking at the individual's interactions with and thoughts about the social world.

The *social domain* involves an individual's interactions with other individuals in the environment. Two elderly people consoling each other, a son helping his father, two sisters arguing, and a grandmother hugging her chandchild are all examples of interaction in the social world. Social development focuses on how these behaviors unfold as the individual grows older. We shall also study the contexts of social development. As we have seen in this chapter, the contexts in which adult development occurs are very important in determining behavior. Some of the most important social contexts of adult development are families, relationships, and work.

Although it is helpful to study adult development within different domains, to take it apart in order to understand it, keep in mind the importance of integrating or combining the various dimensions of human development. Biological, physical, cognitive, social, and personality development are inextricably linked. For example, in many chapters, you may read about how social experiences shape cognitive development, how cognitive development restricts or promotes social development, and how cognitive development is tied to physical development.

SUMMARY

Developmental psychology is the study of age-related interindividual differences, and age-related intraindividual change. The main goals of developmental psychology are to describe, explain, predict, and improve or optimize age-related behavior change. Some of the guiding principles of developmental psychology are:

1. Development is a lifelong process.
2. No age or period of development is any more important than any other age or period of development.
3. Development refers to both increases and decreases, and gains and losses, in behavior.
4. Development is modifiable or reversible; the individual is active in determining the course of development, and there is plasticity in how an individual develops and changes throughout the life span.
5. Development can take many different paths, as reflected by age-related interindividual differences.
6. Development is multidirectional, in that there are different rates and directions of change for different characteristics within the individual and across individuals.
7. Developmental change can be quantitative, gradual, and continuous, or qualitative, relatively abrupt, and stagelike.
8. Development is contextual in that it can vary substantially depending on the historical and cultural conditions in which it takes place.
9. The study of development is multidisciplinary in that it involves combining the perspectives of anthropology, biology, psychology, sociology, and other disciplines.

It is important to study development during the adult life span for many reasons. These reasons can be categorized as scientific or factual, personal, and altruistic.

There are multiple determinants for development during the adult years. In addition to the normative age-graded influences emphasized by traditional developmental theory, nonnormative life events (e.g., accidents and chance encounters) and normative history-graded influences (e.g., wars, social and economic conditions) also affect the course of human development.

Although chronological age does not "explain" development or change, age is an important descriptive variable in developmental research. It is possible to construct a useful age profile based not only on chronological age but also on biological, psychological, functional, and social age.

Paradigms (models) are useful for generating ideas, issues, and questions for research. Models also suggest appropriate methodological approaches for exploring these ideas, issues, and questions. In contrast to the mechanistic and organismic models, the contextual model is unique in its broad attention to all types of change and all determinants of change. Indeed, the contextual model actually seems to encompass the mechanistic and organismic models.

Development takes place within different domains. Thus, to achieve an integrative view of adult development, it is necessary to understand how the biological/physical, cognitive, personality, and social dimensions of individuals change (or remain stable) over time.

REVIEW QUESTIONS

1. Give some examples of scientific, personal, and altruistic reasons for studying adult development and aging.
2. What are the primary goals of developmental psychology?
3. Give an example of intraindividual change and interindividual variability.
4. Define the term *development.* Is development characterized by gains *or* losses? Is development reversible? What is meant by the *optimization* of development?
5. Contrast the life-span perspective of adulthood with a traditional child-focused perspective.
6. Give examples of idiosyncratic factors, normative history-graded factors, and normative age-graded factors in adult development.
7. Explain the difference between the concepts of chronological, biological, psychological,

functional, and social age. Why is it useful to make distinctions among these various dimensions of age?
8. Develop an age profile for yourself and for someone older than you (e.g., a parent or grandparent), and compare the profiles.
9. What are the purposes and functions of a paradigm? What is the difference between a paradigm and a theory?
10. Describe the mechanistic, organismic, and contextual paradigms. Which paradigm is curently generating the most important impact on research and theory on adult development and aging?
11. Give examples of the different "domains" in which adult development and aging takes place.

FOR FURTHER READING

Abeles, R. P., Gift, H. C., & Ory, M. G. (1994). *Aging and quality of life.* New York: Springer.

Baltes, P. B., & Staudinger, U. M. (Eds.). (1996). *Interactive minds: Life-span perspectives on the social foundation of cognition.* New York: Cambridge University Press.

Birren, J. E., & Schroots, J. J. F. (1996). History, concepts, and history of the psychology of aging. In J. E. Birren & K. W. Schaie (Eds.), *Handbook of the psychology of aging* (4th ed., pp. 3–23). San Diego: Academic Press.

SOCIAL AND CULTURAL DIVERSITY

> *We breathe the air of our times.*
> —Anonymous

INTRODUCTION

This chapter describes the wide range of diversity that is evident in adult populations. We examine the influences of social and cultural factors—norms and expectations—on individual development and individual differences during the adult years. We begin with a description of the current demographic characteristics of the population in the United States, and of the projected changes in the numbers and proportions of older adults. The experience of adult development and aging is different in different communities and countries, for different cohorts, and for men and women. Age roles serve as organizers for understanding social behavior and other aspects of development during the adult years.

CHARACTERISTICS OF THE ADULT POPULATION IN THE UNITED STATES

People change and cultures change—each influences the other continuously. Many changes in the composition of the American population have occurred throughout the history of the United States. In recent years, the most striking changes have to do with the size and distribution of age groups within the population and changes in the ethnic composition of the population. In terms of age distributions, the number and percentage of older adults in the United States is growing at an unprecedented rate. For example, the number of adults over age 65 in American society is expected to double in the next 40 years. In terms of ethnic composition, there is greater diversity of race and ethnicity in the United States than ever before. Ethnic and cultural diversity is evident throughout the country. For example, more foreign-born residents than nonimmigrants live in Miami and Miami Beach, Florida; in Huntington Park, Santa Ana, and Monterey Park, California; and in Union City, New Jersey. In 1990, the American population was 76 percent Anglo, 12 percent black, 9 percent Latino, and 3 percent Asian. By 2050, the population will be 52 percent Anglo, 16 percent black, 22 percent Latino, and 10 percent Asian. In the sections that follow, we first consider the "graying of America" and the "diversification of America." Then we consider the consequences of demographic trends for individual development and for social institutions such as the family, the workplace, health care, and the educational system. We begin by describing changes in the size of the older population in the United States.

THE GRAYING OF AMERICA

The phrase "graying of America" aptly describes the trend toward greater numbers and proportions of older adults in the U.S. population. As shown in figure 2.1, there were about 3.1 million Americans aged 65 and over in 1900. In the year 2000, there will be more than 10 times as many older adults—34.9 million.

Figure 2.1
Number of persons
65+: 1900 to 2030.

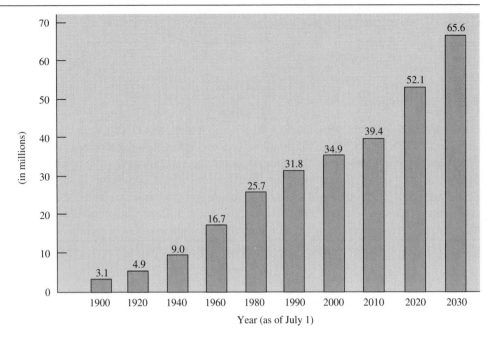

Older adults also represent a much greater proportion of the American population than ever before. Since 1900 the percentage of Americans aged 65 and over has tripled. In 1991, 12.6 percent of the population was age 65 and over, compared with 4.1 percent in 1900. As shown in figure 2.2, by 2030, 24 percent of the population will be aged 65 or older.

It is projected that the older population will continue to grow at a faster rate than other age groups. Since 1980 the older population increased by 6.1 million or 24 percent, compared with an increase of 9 percent for the under-65 population. By 2030, there will be 66 million older adults in the United States, approximately twice the present number. Older adults will comprise 21 percent of the population by 2030 (Kasper, 1988; U.S. Bureau of Census, 1990a).

The older population is getting older. The most rapidly growing segment of the American population is the *old-old,* defined as those who are aged 85 years and older. The old-old constitute nearly 10 percent of the population over age 65. By 2050, the old-old will represent 25 percent of the population (U.S. Bureau of the Census, 1990a). Between 1960 and 1990 the population of the United States aged 85 and over increased by 232 percent (U.S. Bureau of the Census, 1990a).

It is also noteworthy that the number of *centenarians,* individuals who reach their 100th birthday, has increased substantially in this century, and the number of centenarians is expected to continue to increase. In 1990, there were 36,000 centenarians (U.S. Bureau of the Census, 1990a). By the year 2080, it is expected that there will be more than 1 million centenarians.

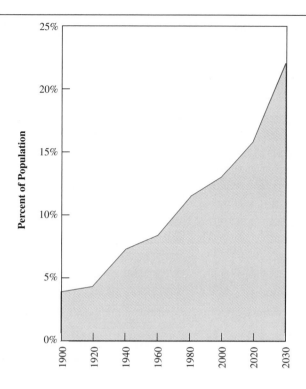

Figure 2.2
Percentage of
persons 65 or older
in the United
States, 1900 to
2030. The
percentage of
individuals 65 or
older will nearly
double in the next
30 years. *Source:
Bronfenbrenner et al.,
The State of
Americans, 1996.*

Age Structure

One of the ways to show that the United States is becoming an aging society is to examine changes in the **age structure.** Age structure refers to the percentages of men and women grouped by age decades. The top graph in figure 2.3 shows the age structure of the United States in 1955. Figure 2.3 also shows the projected age structure of the United States for the year 2010 (Taeuber, 1992). The shapes of the age distributions are quite different for different years. One of the graphs resembles a pyramid. One of the graphs looks like a rectangle. That is, comparing the age structures in 1955 and 2010, there is a trend toward equalization of the percentages of Americans within various age intervals. By the year 2010, the percentages of individuals in each period of the life course will be approximately equal.

Life Expectancy

Life expectancy refers to the predicted chronological length of one's life. Life expectancy varies from country to country, and for many countries life expectancy has increased in the twentieth century. Figure 2.4 shows the increase in life expectancy in the United States during the twentieth century. A person born in 1900 had an average life expectancy of 48 years, whereas a person born in 1990 has an average life expectancy of more than 76.1 years. In this century, average life expectancy in the

Figure 2.3 Age composition of the population: Age pyramids for selected years 1955 and 2010. (From Taeuber, C. M. [1992]. *Sixty-five Plus in America*. [Current Population Reports P23-178RV]. Washington, DC: U.S. Bureau of the Census.

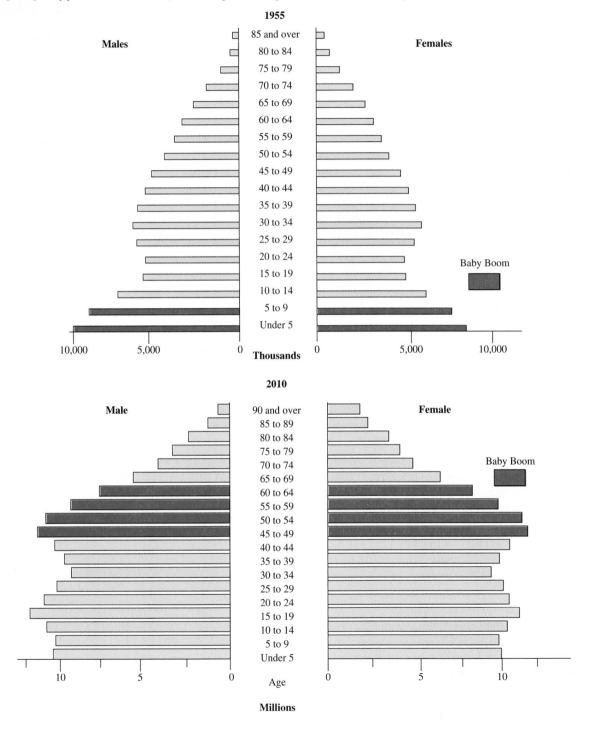

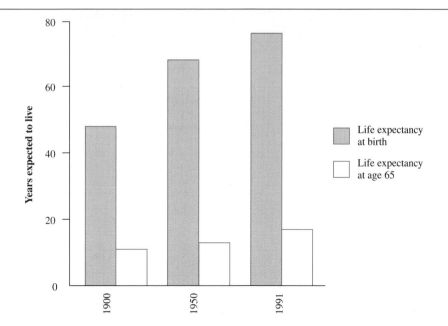

Figure 2.4 The increased life expectancy of Americans. Both life expectancy at birth and at age 65 have increased during this century. Eighty percent of Americans now live to age 65. On average, they can expect to live another 18 years after reaching age 65. *Source: Bronfenbrenner et al.,* The State of Americans, *1996.*

United States increased by 28 years. This increase in average life expectancy is greater than that seen during all of human history.

Until about 1970, most of the change in life expectancy came from improved health care in infancy and early childhood. Life expectancy for those who reached 50 years of age, in contrast, remained unchanged. More recently, however, life expectancy at age 50 has witnessed some remarkable changes. This is primarily due to improvements in the quality of health care available to today's adults. For example, during the last decade, fewer males in middle adulthood and the early part of late adulthood seem to be dying because of heart attack or stroke (National Center for Health Statistics, 1992). However, projections must be cautiously interpreted because changes in infant mortality, in the ability of individuals to resist infectious diseases, in immigration, in the quality of medical care, and in social-environmental conditions will influence the health and life expectancy of tomorrow's older adults. Research Focus 2.1, for example, describes how being overweight in adolescence affects health in later life.

The changes in average life expectancy are not uniform across race. The National Center for Health Statistics (1992) reported that between 1984 and 1986, life expectancy for blacks dropped to 69.4 years, the lowest it had been since 1982. At the same time, corresponding data for whites (males and females combined) increased to 75.4 years. This was the first time that blacks' life expectancy had declined while whites' life expectancy had risen. Whites generally have shown a pattern of living nearly six years longer than blacks, with both groups increasing in life expectancy at roughly the same rate (one year added every two and a half years since the turn of the century). A key to understanding the differential life expectancy for black men and women is to recognize that blacks are dying far earlier in young and middle adulthood.

Health in the Later Years Is Affected by Being Overweight in Adolescence

One of the major research issues in the study of adult development and aging is to understand the relationships between earlier and later development. Behavior in adolescence and early adulthood affects health in many ways throughout the adult life span.

Researchers at Harvard University have documented what people have suspected about the consequences of early obesity on health across the life span. Adverse health in the later years is associated with being overweight in adolescence. Being overweight in adolescence affects both morbidity and mortality in later life. *Morbidity* refers to the percentage or rate of disease in a group of people. *Mortality* refers to the death rate in a population group. In a recent follow-up to the Harvard Growth Study of the 3,000 children who were first measured in 1922, adolescents between the ages of 13 and 18 years who were overweight had increased morbidity and mortality 55 years later when they were old (Must, Jacques, Dallal, Bajema, & Dietz, 1992). The adolescents who were overweight when the first weight and height measurements were taken between 1922 and 1935 were more likely to experience a broad range of adverse health effects when they reached later adulthood. To make the connection between being overweight in adolescence and increased morbidity and mortality in later life, the researchers needed to take into account the more immediate adverse effects of being overweight as adults. The research showed that adult weight was a less powerful predictor of morbidity and mortality than being overweight in adolescence. Thus, being overweight in adolescence is a powerful predictor of adverse health in later life.

Black children and adults are victims of murder and violence in the streets; black males are victims of drug abuse; and blacks are more likely than whites to face limited access to medical care, poor nutrition, and substandard housing.

Sex Differences in Life Expectancy

According to 1990 Census Bureau data, females begin to outnumber males at age 25. This gender gap widens with increasing age. By age 75, about 61 percent of the population is female. By age 85 and over, 70 percent of the population is female.

Sex differences in longevity are due to a combination of social, biological, and genetic factors. Social factors include health behavior and attitudes, habits, lifestyles, and occupational styles. For example, the major causes of death in the United States, such as lung cancer, motor vehicle accidents, suicide, cirrhosis of the liver, emphysema, and coronary heart disease are more likely to strike men than women. Such causes of death are associated with habits or lifestyles. For example, the sex difference in deaths caused by lung cancer and emphysema is linked to the fact that historically men have been heavier smokers than women. Men also have fewer regular checkups by a physician than women, which reduces the opportunity for early medical treatment when needed.

To the extent that life expectancy is influenced strongly by stress at work, we would expect the sex difference in longevity to begin narrowing because so many more women have entered the work force in the last 40 years. Actually, it seems that different factors are associated with longevity and physical functioning for older men and women. Income level, educational level, and marital status are strongly associated with changes in physical functioning for men. For women, control of health was

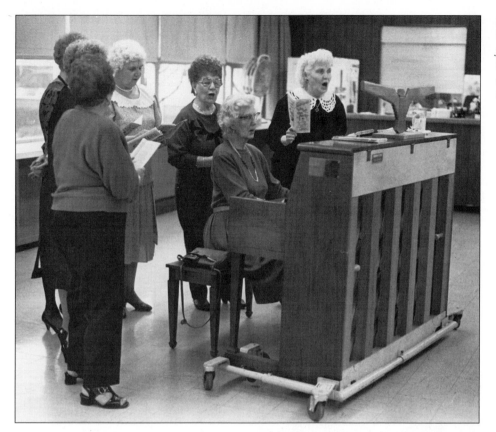

Sex differences in longevity account for the increasingly higher percentage of females in the older population.

strongly associated in one study with changes in physical functioning (Strawbridge, Camacho, Cohen, & Kaplan, 1993). Results of this study suggested that older men would do better in terms of staying healthy if encouraged to participate in structured exercise programs, and older women would do better by keeping active and doing the things they enjoy.

Biological factors also influence sex differences in longevity. In practically all animal species, females have longer life spans than males (Franceschi & Fabris, 1993). (See Research Focus 2.2 for a discussion of recent research on women's longevity.) Women have more resistance to infectious and degenerative diseases. For instance, the female's estrogen production helps to reduce the risk of atherosclerosis (hardening of the arteries). Further, the two X chromosomes women carry may be linked with the production of more antibodies to fight disease (Franceschi & Fabris, 1993).

Longevity and Life Expectancy

How long will you live? The term **longevity** refers to the number of years an individual actually lives. Longevity can be contrasted with average life expectancy, which refers to demographic projections regarding the length of life. Although life expectancy

Longevity After Menopause

From an evolutionary perspective, it is puzzling that women live as long as 40 years after menopause. Evolutionary theory has it that natural selection favors traits that enhance reproduction. According to natural selection theory, postreproductive traits in both women and men are not selected, and there is no accepted explanation to account for why people live long after their reproductive years. Humans are the only primates to have an extended life span after the last pregnancy.

Recently, Kristen Hawkes and her colleagues at the University of Utah proposed that women live past the reproductive years because grandmothers provide food that is crucial for the survival of grandchildren. By provisioning for grandchildren, grandmothers provide opportunity for boosting their daughter's availability for fertility and thereby increase the chances that her genes are passed. Daughters can breastfeed for shorter periods if grandmothers are assisting with feeding. Hawkes suggested that women who have help from their mothers can bear more babies during their fertile years than women without helpers. Hawkes and her colleagues based their theorizing on observations of 300 Hadza hunter-gatherers in the rugged hills of Tanzania. In the Hadza culture, women collect berries or dig tubers, and men hunt. The Hadza survive entirely on gathered or hunted food. These anthropologists found that children's weight gains depended on how much time their mothers had for gathering food. When mothers had less time to forage because of the caregiving demands of a new baby, the fit and hard-working grandmothers, frequently in their 60s, spent more time foraging. The weight gain of children depended on the grandmother's foraging success. Anthropologists have paid relatively little attention to the functions of grandmothers in various cultures. Confidence in the grandmother theory will depend on observations of similar patterns in other cultures.

Source: Hawkes, K., O'Connell, J. F. & Blurton Jones, N. B. (1998). Hazda women's time allocation, offspring provisioning, and the evolution of long post-menopausal life spans. *Current Anthropology, 38,* 551–557; Hawkes, K., O'Connell, J. F., Blurton Jones, N. G., Alvarez, H., & Charnov, E. L. (1998). *Proceedings of the National Academy of Sciences, 95,* 1336–1339.

Physical activity throughout the adult years is one of the predictors of longevity.

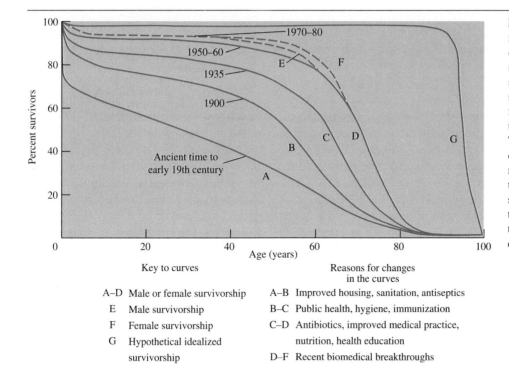

Figure 2.5 The rectangularization of the human life span. This graph shows human survivorship trends from ancient times to the present. These idealized curves illustrate the rapid approach to the rectangular survivorship curve that has occurred in the twentieth century.

Key to curves

A–D Male or female survivorship
E   Male survivorship
F   Female survivorship
G   Hypothetical idealized survivorship

Reasons for changes in the curves

A–B Improved housing, sanitation, antiseptics
B–C Public health, hygiene, immunization
C–D Antibiotics, improved medical practice, nutrition, health education
D–F Recent biomedical breakthroughs

has increased dramatically in the twentieth century, the actual upper limit of the human life span has not changed much since the beginning of recorded history.

The upper limit, or the **potential life span,** refers to the maximum age that could be attained if an individual could avoid the consequences of all illnesses and accidents. The maximum potential human life span is estimated to be approximately 110 to 120 years of age (Cristofalo, 1986; Hayflick, 1980). This means that there is a biological limit to how much benefit on longevity can be obtained by improved medical care, nutrition, and public health.

Improved health care, coupled with the fact that there is a fixed upper limit on the potential human life span, has produced changes in the survivorship curve, as shown in figure 2.5. From ancient times to the present, the curve has become increasingly more rectangular as more people reached the fullest extent of their potential life span. Further, it is generally expected that the survivorship curve will become even more rectangular in the future with continued advances in public health, nutrition, and medicine, and as more people live longer, healthier lives.

In light of some new and largely unanticipated concerns, some researchers, however, are beginning to question whether the increasing rectangularization of the life curve will ever be realized. When medical researchers and demographers put forward the notion of rectangularization of the life curve, they were optimistic that medical science would eventually succeed in conquering diseases that shorten the length of the human life span. Remarkable medical achievements, such as the eradication of smallpox, polio, and other childhood diseases by widespread vaccination, boosted optimism. Further, the potential for the universal availability of effective antibiotics, combined with national trends toward healthier lifestyles, served to support the view that people would be more likely to live to the fullest extent of their life spans.

Heart disease is the leading cause of death in the United States, and cancer is the second cause. Great strides have been made to reduce the risk and improve the treatment of these diseases. These kinds of advances have enabled many adults who have experienced heart disease and cancer to live longer than they would have in the past.

But new diseases are emerging, and "old" diseases are reemerging (Berkelman & Hughes, 1993). Certainly, by now everyone is aware of the devastating effects of human immunodeficiency virus (HIV). HIV, infection, pneumonia, and influenza are now ranked among the 10 leading causes of death in the United States. Diseases such as tuberculosis and measles, which not long ago were considered to have been practically eradicated, have reappeared as major diseases in the United States. Further, new strains of tuberculosis and other infectious diseases have developed for which there are no effective treatments. Infectious diseases are the leading cause of death worldwide, and they are the leading cause of serious illness in the United States (Berkelman & Hughes, 1993).

Predicting Longevity

What factors can be used to predict longevity? One of the most well-known studies designed to identify the predictors of life expectancy is the Duke Longitudinal Study of Aging. In this study, 270 volunteers were examined for the first time between 1955 and 1959 through a series of physical, mental, social, and laboratory tests (Palmore, 1982). At that time the adults ranged in age from 60 to 94, with a median age of 70. All were noninstitutionalized, and although it was not a random sample, the group was a mixture of males and females, blacks and whites, and different socioeconomic groups. The investigators analyzed these individuals again in 1981, some 25 years after their initial testing. Only 26 participants were still alive, and estimates of their life expectancy were made.

In the early analysis of the Duke Longitudinal data, the strongest predictors of life expectancy (when age, sex, and race were controlled) were physical function, being a nonsmoker, work satisfaction, and happiness (see, e.g., Palmore, 1982). More recent analyses of the Duke data allowed for a more precise determination of life expectancy because (1) some of the individuals alive in 1981 later died, so that their exact life span is now known, and (2) in addition to the original factors tested, a number of new ones were added to allow for more complex evaluation.

Palmore (1982) developed a mathematical model that predicted the **longevity difference** for the participants in the Duke study. The longevity difference is the difference between the number of years individuals live after initial testing and the expected number of years remaining in their lives based on age, sex, and race. Palmore's model considered both the direct and indirect effects of the variables that influence life expectancy. The variables within this model include *parents' longevity, intelligence, activities, sexual relations, tobacco and alcohol abuse, life satisfaction,* and *health.* Parents' longevity was believed to have a direct effect on longevity through genetic transmission and an indirect effect through environmental experience. Intelligence was thought to have a direct effect on survival through problem-solving and adaptive ability. Activities were thought to have a direct effect on longevity through increased physical, mental, and social stimulation and an indirect effect by means of their contribution to life satisfaction and improved health. Sexual relations were thought to have a direct effect through psychosomatic processes as well as an indirect effect through their influence on life satisfaction and health. Tobacco and alcohol abuse were predicted to have a direct effect on longevity through their effects on lung cancer, cardiovascular diseases, and other health problems and indirect effects through a reduction of life satisfaction and general health. Life satisfaction was also predicted to have a direct effect through psychosomatic processes and an indirect effect through its influence on general health. And finally, health factors were believed to have a direct effect on longevity.

Of the various predictors of longevity, the following were most important:

1. In terms of parents' longevity, only the father's age at death was significant.

2. Scores on the performance component of the Wechsler Adult Intelligence Scale were better predictors than were scores on the verbal part of this test, but intelligence predictors were significant.

3. Three socioeconomic predictors were significant: education, finances, and occupation.

4. Several activity factors were significant in predicting longevity: the number of activities requiring physical mobility; the number of organizations the individual belonged to; the number of meetings attended; the time spent reading; the number of leisure activities; and the amount of time given to daily activities and hobbies.

5. Three indicators of sexual relations were significant predictors of longevity: frequency of intercourse per week, enjoyment of intercourse in the past, and present enjoyment of intercourse.

6. Tobacco use, as measured by the daily use of cigarettes, cigars, or pipes, was a significant negative predictor.

7. Four satisfaction factors predicted longevity: work satisfaction, religious satisfaction, usefulness, and happiness.

8. Three health predictors were significantly linked with longevity. A physical-function rating was based on the individual's medical history, physical and neurological examinations, audiogram, electroencephalogram, electrocardiogram, and laboratory evaluation of blood and urine. A health self-rating was based on each individual's *own* ratings of his or her health. And a health satisfaction score was determined by an individual's agreement or disagreement with six statements, including, "I feel just miserable most of the time" and "I am perfectly satisfied with my health."

Figure 2.6
Persons 65 or older and children under 18 in the United States. Older adults will soon outnumber children under age 18. By 2040, there will be more than 5 million more individuals over the age of 65 than there are under 18.
Source: Bronfenbrenner et al., The State of Americans, *1996.*

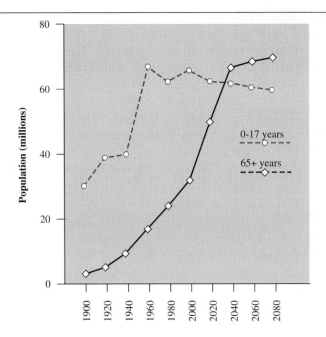

Social and Economic Impact of an Aging Population

The age structure of a society determines, in part, the allocation of its resources. Over the next several decades, larger sums will be needed to meet the needs of a progressively more aged population. One way to quantify how those who are working members of a society support those who are not working is to calculate the **dependency ratio.** In the United States, the dependency ratio is expected to drop from 4.5 in 1995 to 2.5 in 2040. This is one of the reasons that the Congress of the United States enacted policy to increase the age for receiving Social Security benefits to 67 years in 2000.

The data shown in figure 2.6 are particularly striking. In figure 2.6, it can be seen that there will be more older adults (over 65 years) than children (under 18 years) by 2040 in the United States (Bronfenbrenner, McClelland, Wethington, Moen, & Ceci, 1996).

In all societies, it is difficult to fairly distribute the economic resources needed to support the young and old (Chen, 1987; Palmore, 1990). Changing demographic trends as well as increasingly higher costs for health care pose difficult challenges for policy in the new millennium. The United States has made strides toward developing a health care system that provides for all individuals.

SOCIAL CLASS, POVERTY, AND HOUSING

In the United States, the experience of growing older is different for individuals from different social classes, races, and economic levels. One of the reasons is that if people can't afford to pay for routine dental checkups, eye exams, or physical exams, it is less likely that a health problem will be detected at an early stage. Also, economic and educational factors affect health attitudes and exposure to health information. In this section, we

African-American Women's Perceptions of Menopause and Hormone Replacement Therapy

Menopause is a life change that is related to biology, culture, and health. Women from different cultural backgrounds and ethnicities hold different views about menopause. In a recent study, a research team at Michigan State University investigated the African-American women's perceptions of menopause and hormone replacement therapy (HRT). The sample of research participants consisted of 55 African-American women who were living in a low-income housing development or who belonged to a women's group at a large urban church. The women were in average or good health and were between 46 and 56 years of age. Women discussed their thoughts and feelings about menopause in semistructured group interviews (or focus groups). The main findings were as follows:

1. Menopause was thought to be a natural transition to late adulthood or old age.

2. Menopause produced physical symptoms of bad cramps, bleeding, and hot flashes.
3. Menopause produced psychological symptoms of mood swings and negative feelings.
4. Women responded differently to the symptoms.
5. Other women and books were good sources of information about menopause.

HRT was viewed negatively by some women because of cancer risk, and positively by some women because of symptom relief.

Source: Padonu, G., Holmes-Rovner, M., Rothert, M., Schmitt, N., Kroll, J., Ransom, S., and Gladnery, E. (1996). African-American women's perceptions of menopause. *American Journal of Health Behavior, 20,* 242–251.

---

examine how the effects of social class, race and ethnicity, and economic level impact on individual development and individual differences. (See, e.g., Research Focus 2.3 to learn how African-American women perceive menopause and hormonal therapy.)

Social Class

In every culture, there is stratification by social class. Cultures differ in terms of the strictness or specificity of the prescriptions as well as the nature of the roles. In every culture, occupations vary in pay structure, prestige, and power to influence others. Thus, different individuals possess different economic resources, and individuals have different educational and occupational opportunities. Cultural differences in the methods of distribution of the rewards of society often produce inequities for different ethnicities (racism), for men and women (sexism), and for different-aged individuals (ageism). **Ageism** refers to unequal opportunities for individuals as they grow older (Atchley, 1983).

Poverty

In 1991, of the nearly 31.8 million citizens in the United States aged 65 and over, more than 3.8 million, or 12.4 percent, of the elderly were classified as poor (AARP, 1992). The definition of poverty is determined by examining the minimum income needed to sustain families of various sizes (Bould, Sanborn, & Reif, 1989). For example, in 1991 the federal poverty level for an elderly person living alone was $6,532; for an elderly couple it was $8,241. The median income of older persons in 1991 was $14,357 for men and $8,189 for women.

These figures compare dramatically with those elderly defined as affluent whose income is at least five times higher than the poverty level (Duncan & Smith, 1989). Affluent elderly couples have incomes of $41,205, while affluent single elderly individuals earn at least $32,660 (Bould et al., 1989). Women currently represent 2.3 million or 71 percent of the elderly poor in our society (Church, Siegel, & Foster, 1988).

The percentage of elderly poor would probably be much greater than statistics indicate if it included the **near poor** and the **hidden poor.** The *near poor* refers to individuals with incomes between the poverty level and 125 percent of this level. In total, 20 percent of the older population was poor or near poor in 1991. The *hidden poor* refers to those individuals who could be classified as poor on the basis of their own incomes but who are supported by relatives who are not poor. Estimates place the number of hidden poor at nearly double the rate determined by official census statistics (Bould et al., 1989). The hidden poor are cared for in the homes of family members or friends and listed in census data as part of that household. About 92 percent of those 85 years of age and older are women who live under such arrangements and are not classified as poor.

One of the socioeconomic concerns of individuals in late adulthood is the decrease in income they usually experience. Many older adults are simply unprepared for the consequences of reduced income associated with retirement from paid work. Many people expect their Social Security benefits to provide the support necessary to live comfortably in retirement, but Social Security is seldom sufficient. Yet in 1990 the major source of income for those 65 years of age and older was Social Security. Social Security accounted for 36 percent of the income of older Americans, with additional income from assets representing 24 percent, from pensions representing 18 percent, and from earnings another 18 percent, and all other assets representing 3 percent (U.S. Department of Health and Human Services, 1992). For those who are poor and living alone, Social Security represents a far more sizable percentage of income than it does for those with moderate or high incomes.

Very few older adults are prepared to handle the financial impact of long-term health care (Branch, Friedman, Cohen, Smith, & Socholitzky, 1988). Among those 75 years of age and older and living alone, 46 percent would reach poverty levels within 13 weeks of institutionalization in a skilled nursing facility. For married couples, poverty level would be reached for 25 percent of the sample in 13 weeks and for 47 percent of the sample in one year (Branch et al., 1988). Elderly couples, when compared with younger couples, have more out-of-pocket health expenditures (Rubin & Koelln, 1993).

Race is a significant predictor of poverty among the elderly. In 1992, blacks composed 34 percent of those living at poverty levels and Hispanics composed 21 percent, while whites represented 11 percent of the total population of elderly living at or below poverty levels (U.S. Census Bureau, 1995). The best predictors of poverty in old age continue to be race (black), education (no high school degree), gender (female), marital status (divorced or widowed), and city living environment (Jackson, 1988; Taylor & Chatters, 1988). (See figure 2.7 for a picture of poverty among different racial/ethnic groups and men and women during the 1980s.)

Figure 2.7 Poverty rates vary greatly among subgroups. Following are the percentages of persons aged 65 and over who were poor in 1979 and 1989, by sex, race, and Hispanic origin.

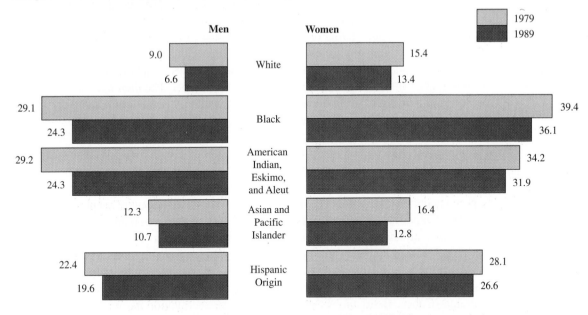

Note: Persons of Hispanic origin may be of any race. This graph is based on 1980 and 1990 U.S. census sample data.

Although some older Americans have the benefit of having accumulated substantial assets over a lifetime, for many of these individuals, their assets are not available or liquid (Church et al., 1988). It is difficult for elderly people with fixed incomes to sell their homes or assume sizable home equity loans to meet current expenses for medical care, food, clothes, and taxes.

The young-old have lower poverty rates than the old-old (Bould et al., 1989). The difference is largely due to the willingness and ability of the young-old to continue to work at either full- or part-time jobs. Among elderly Americans 65 to 71 years of age, there was only a 4 percent risk of poverty if they had been employed in any capacity for any length of time in the previous 12 months (U.S. Bureau of the Census, 1990a). For those over 75, poverty rates increase substantially as disability, the physical self-care routine, medical visits, and housekeeping demand increased time and leave minimal chances to work (Bould et al., 1989).

Housing

Although the bulk of research concerned with the living environments of the elderly has focused on special situations such as nursing homes, public housing, mobile home parks, welfare hotels, or retirement communities, the proportions of older Americans in these special living conditions are small. In 1991, approximately 20.1 million older adults lived in family homes while 9.4 million lived alone (AARP,

1992). Home ownership represents a sign of achievement among all adults, particularly the elderly (National Center for Health Statistics, 1987a).

However, the data concerned with housing quality are less positive. The U.S. Senate Special Committee on Aging estimated that 30 percent of the elderly occupy housing that is deteriorating or substandard (AARP, 1992).

Suitable living environments directly influence the morale, adjustment, sociability, and intellectual abilities of the elderly (Beland, 1987; Lawton, 1977). The immediate impact of housing is far greater for the elderly because their lifestyle centers so much more on activities in the home. Among the elderly the overwhelming preference is to maintain ownership of their own homes, assuming they are physically, mentally, and economically able to do so. Beland (1987) reported that 57 percent of an elderly sample preferred to live independently either alone or with a spouse. The remaining elderly who preferred to live with someone else and had already moved into the home of a child, relative, or friend usually had done so because of an emergent problem that prevented their independent living (Beland, 1987). In a study of rural elderly, Scheidt (1985) found that housing quality was a powerful predictor of overall mental health.

One attempt to deal with some of the problems older Americans face is to provide subsidized housing. The elderly currently compose more than 27 percent of people who reside in subsidized housing nationwide. Experts continue to debate issues such as whether housing arrangements for the elderly should be age-segregated or integrated (Cohen, Bearison, & Muller, 1987). Age segregation helps provide a defense against social rejection and social comparison. Age integration provides the opportunity for growth, insight, and understanding of different perspectives. Those older people living in single family dwellings show a distinct preference (80%) to have people of all ages in their neighborhood; however, for those living in multiunit apartments, less than 50 percent prefer age-integrated groups in such buildings, and among those living in retirement homes, communities, or attached dwellings, age-integrated neighborhoods are even less popular (AARP, 1993b). Subsidized housing will continue to be a crucial issue for those examining public policies for the elderly. As we have seen previously, race and ethnicity are factors highly predictive of which elderly adults will experience less than adequate housing.

The homeless elderly provide a grim reminder that statistics summarize human lives. Though most elderly are able to meet their housing needs in some fashion, there is a segment of our population that is not so fortunate. It is estimated that at least 27 percent of the homeless are over 60 years of age. Cohen, Teresi, Holmes, and Roth (1988) suggest that this figure is an underestimate, since many elderly homeless do not compete for shelter space, fearing beatings, abuse, and the loss of independence in such institutionalized programs. In an analysis of elderly homeless men in New York City, the use of an informal peer information and social support network helped some homeless elderly men to cope. Those who were unable to develop a support network displayed poor physical health, emotional depression, and high levels of stress (Cohen et al., 1988).

For those who are unable to live independently, those who have higher income have many more options with regard to living conditions. For example, some elderly can afford to insure themselves against long-term costs and escalating inflation, taxes, and home maintenance by enrolling in *continuity of care retirement communities*

(Branch, 1987; Cohen, Tell, Batten & Larson, 1988; Tell, Cohen, Larson, & Batten, 1987). Such individuals pay a substantial initiation or entrance fee as well as a monthly fee. The fees remain constant regardless of the medical and nursing care a resident may require in the future. Unfortunately, only a small percentage of the population can afford to consider such options.

Nursing homes may be the only alternative for older adults with serious, chronic health problems. About 5 percent (or 1.4 million adults) over 65 were residents of nursing homes in 1987 (AARP, 1992). Percentages in nursing homes increase dramatically as age increases. For example, about 1 percent of those between the ages of 65 and 74 live in nursing homes, whereas 25 percent of those who are age 85 and over reside in nursing homes.

AGEISM

Stereotypes of the elderly as nonproductive are inaccurate. Ageism, like sexism and racism, describes the prejudiced behavior of a society against older adults or negative stereotyping of the elderly (Palmore, 1990). Many older adults in the United States face painful discrimination. For example, older adults may not be hired for new jobs or may be eased out of old ones because they are perceived as incapable. Elders are sometimes avoided because they are presumed to be verbose or boring. Infirm elders are sometimes perceived as "babies with wrinkles," without sensitivity, and without regard for who they are and who they once were. The elderly are sometimes pushed out of their families by children who see them in negative ways rather than in terms of their potential to family dynamics.

One of the most serious problems facing the elderly in the United States is stereotyping. Misperceptions of aging and the elderly may be positive (idealizing old age) or negative (viewing the elderly as useless and inadequate). Table 2.1 lists some of the stereotypes.

According to Covey (1988), since the last part of the nineteenth century older people have been labeled with increasingly negative terms. Covey found terms that clearly separated old men from old women: Labels for older men included old-fashioned, feeble, and conservative, and labels for older women included bad-tempered, repulsive, and mystical. Animal terms such as "old buzzard" or "old goat" were associated with old men, while "old bird" and "old crow" were reserved for women.

AGING AND CULTURE

The cultural milieu—that is, the physical and social setting in which adults develop—has many dimensions. There is tremendous variety across cultures in terms of how aging occurs. We examine cross-cultural differences in adult development and aging.

The term *culture* refers to the behaviors, attitudes, values, and products of a particular group of people. For example, the culture of the United States, China, and the Caribbean represent different belief systems, languages, and dialects, and rituals of daily life. Always, within each culture, there are many subcultures, each with its own distinct set of behaviors and values.

TABLE 2.1
Common Misperceptions About the Elderly That Are Based on Stereotypes

Examples of Misperceptions Based on Negative Stereotypes

1. Most older persons are poor.
2. Most older persons are unable to keep up with inflation.
3. Most older people are ill-housed.
4. Most older people are frail and in poor health.
5. The aged are impotent as a political force and require advocacy.
6. Most older people are inadequate employees; they are less productive, efficient, motivated, innovative, and creative than younger workers. Most older workers are accident-prone.
7. Older people are mentally slower and more forgetful; they are less able to learn new things.
8. Older persons tend to be intellectually rigid and dogmatic. Most old people are set in their ways and unable to change.
9. A majority of older people are socially isolated and lonely. Most are disengaging or disengaged from society.
10. Most older persons are confined to long-term care institutions.

Examples of Misperceptions Based on Positive Stereotypes

1. The aged are relatively well off; they are not poor, but in good economic shape. Their benefits are generously provided by working members of society.
2. The aged are a potential political force that votes and participates in unity and in great numbers.
3. Older people make friends very easily. They are kind and smiling.
4. Most older persons are mature, experienced, wise, and interesting.
5. Most older persons are very good listeners and are especially patient with children.
6. A majority of older persons are very kind and generous to their children and grandchildren.

From S. Lubomudrov, "Congressional Perceptions of the Elderly: The Use of Stereotypes in the Legislative Process" in Journal of Gerontology, *27: 77–81. Copyright © The Gerontological Society of America.*

As a child, you began to learn the values of your community. You may have learned that some values seemed relatively constant across individuals and families, and other values were quite varied, or that your family was the same as some other families, all other families, or no other families.

In the United States, there is considerable variation in how families view parents, grandparents, and other older relatives, in part related to ethnic diversity (Bastida, 1987).

In China and Japan, older persons are venerated and encouraged to be active in family contexts and in other social roles (Kinoshita & Kiefer, 1993). Intergenerational relations are reciprocal rather than linear. **Filial piety** runs high in China; respect and homage to family and community elders is a way of life. For example, one custom permits parents to send weekly or monthly stipends to a married child. This money is not to be spent, even though it is a gift. Rather, the stipend is to be saved and safely invested so that it can be returned to the parents when they reach old age. In Japan, the elderly are more integrated into their families than the elderly in most industrialized countries. More than 75 percent live with their children, and very few single older adults live alone. Respect for the elderly in Japan is evidenced in a variety of everyday encounters: The best seats on public transportation are usually reserved for the elderly, cooking caters to the tastes of the elderly, and people bow respectfully to the elderly. However, such respect appears to be more prevalent among rural than urban Japanese and among middle-aged than young adult Japanese (Palmore & Maeda, 1985).

It is clear that, with modernization, the status and integration of elders in Japan has declined (Hashimoto, 1996; Kumagai, 1996). Tobin (1987) suggested that Western observers have idealized Japan's approach to old age. The idealization conforms to our own society's ambivalence toward the dependency experienced in old age versus that experienced at other points in the life course. Tobin noted that our idealized view of Japanese old age is exaggerated, stereotyped, limiting, and one-dimensional. Tobin suggests that there are negative aspects to Japanese aging that experts often overlook. The observance of Respect for Elders Day and the designation of subway seats as "silver seats" for the elderly and handicapped may mean that such policies are needed to ensure respect and honor toward the elderly. Similarly, although it appears that in Japan more older people live with their children than is true in the United States, the elderly may yet experience loneliness and emotional distance. Living together does not ensure reverence, respect, and belongingness. Finally, Tobin (1987) suggested that the overall percentage of parents living with children in Japan has declined steadily as modernization, housing space, and population changes have occurred. Japan is actually far behind the United States in providing housing options for elders (Kinoshita & Kiefer, 1993).

The language used to refer to Japanese old age has also evolved dramatically. Current usage gives a negative connotation to the traditional term *rojin* or *ecstasy years.* It has been replaced with the more preferable *jitsunen,* translated as the *age of harvest* or *the age of fruition* (Loveridge-Sanonmatsu, 1994).

In earlier times, when fewer individuals reached old age, the elders were granted high status in many cultures. Members of a culture may have believed that elders were imbued with special powers and wisdom. Jay Sokolovsky (1986), drawing on the work of Cowgill and Holmes (1972), identified the following seven different factors that seem to be universally associated with high status for the elderly:

1. Older people possess valuable knowledge.
2. Older persons control key family and community resources.
3. Older persons are allowed to perform useful and valued functions as long as possible.
4. There are fewer role shifts and a greater sense of role continuity throughout the life span.
5. Age-related role changes involve gains in responsibility, authority, or advisory capacity.
6. The extended family is an important residential and/or economic unit and the elderly are integrated into it.
7. Less emphasis is placed on individual ego development.

In some cultures, elders remain in their homes with friends and family regardless of health. Placing an elder in a hospital or nursing home would be unacceptable. In Hindu tradition, for example, there are four life stages (ashrams). Each stage, though distinct, produces a totality, a balance and harmony between person, nature, life forces, and one's duty (dharma). These stages apply to all but the menial caste and are centered on males. The first stage consists of the *celibate student* in adolescence and early adulthood. This is a time when a teacher provides both a home and a mentor relationship in transmitting religious knowledge. The second stage of life consists of marriage and the special obligations of a *householder,* which include bringing children into the world and involvement in family life. In traditional Hindu marriages, sons bring their wives into the paternal home, creating an extended family from which religious and cultural practices can be preserved by direct transmission to the next generation.

After the stage of householder and the establishment of family, a man is to voluntarily begin to remove himself from his family. The third life stage is that of a *hermit in the forest.* This is a time for meditating, studying, and totally absorbing Hindu religious thought and ideas. It involves living a life devoted to asceticism, self-control, and the acquisition of inner spiritual power. A man is ready for this third stage when he sees "his skin wrinkled, his hair white, and the son of his sons." The final stage is *complete separation from all worldly concerns;* the elderly man abandons all ties to family, possessions, and home. He wanders unencumbered, free to seek harmony between himself and the universe, free to find the common cord between his existence and the existence of others, both animate and inanimate. The goal of the fourth stage is to eliminate the need for spirituality, sensuality, psychological bonds, or social dimensions. The individual has no selfish needs, no real-world concerns; he waits to die. Death is blissful liberation. It is the deserved attainment of one who has led a perfect life: having committed time to religious study, having married and produced children, and having offered support and help to those in need. Given these accomplishments, his life should be in total harmony.

In India, even among the highest caste (Brahmins), few people practice or attain the goals of each of the four stages. Yet these stages provide a culturally prescribed path to follow for successful aging. They provide a direction to life, a target for maturity. Other cultures prescribe different paths. In modern technological societies, for example, productive personal achievements in the workplace are emphasized (Valliant, 1977).

AGE-RELATED CHANGES IN SEX ROLES

The term **sex role** refers to the characteristics that individuals display because of their gender. Spence and Helmreich (1978) defined sex roles as the behaviors *expected* of individuals because they are either male or female. An important aspect of being male or female is gender identity, which refers to the extent to which individuals actually take on as part of their personalities the behaviors and attitudes associated with either the male or female role. The development of sex-appropriate sex roles results in "masculine" males and "feminine" females. Although in past years researchers assessed the sex roles of masculinity and femininity as distinct categories, current researchers usually take a continuous view that is based on Bem's (1974) concept of androgyny.

Androgyny

By the mid-1970s, work by Sandra Bem (e.g., Bem, 1974) and others was helping to make clear that it was inaccurate to consider masculinity and femininity as polar opposites on a continuum. Bem (1974) reported that 30 to 40 percent of men and women have an **androgynous** sex-role identity. That is, when given a list of masculine and feminine attributes (see table 2.2) and asked to indicate how well each describes themselves,

TABLE 2.2	
Examples of Masculine and Feminine Items from Bem's Sex-Role Inventory	
Masculine Items	*Feminine Items*
Acts as a leader	Affectionate
Analytical	Compassionate
Competitive	Feminine
Forceful	Gullible
Individualistic	Sensitive to the needs of others
Self-reliant	Sympathetic
Willing to take a stand	Warm

Reproduced by special permission of the publisher, Consulting Psychologists Press, Inc., from the Bem Sex Role Inventory by Sandra Bem, Ph.D., copyright 1978.

androgynous individuals score high on both sets of attributes. Bem (1974, 1977, 1981) suggested that masculinity and femininity involve separate attributes, and that people with an androgynous identity are advantaged in psychological adjustment. The androgynous person endorses having both male traits (e.g., achievement orientation) and female traits (e.g., warmth). Having a broad range of personal attributes enables individuals to adapt competently to a wide variety of tasks and interpersonal situations.

The notion of androgyny has some limitations as it applies to the understanding of sex-role identity throughout the adult life span. Traditional sex-typed traits and behaviors are usually more characteristic of young adulthood than of middle or later adulthood, and there are several ways of interpreting *how* and *why* individuals become more androgynous as they become older (Huyck, 1990).

Several researchers have studied longitudinal changes in personality and sex-role (e.g., Chiriboga, 1982a, 1982b; Eichorn, et al., 1981; Lowenthal, Thurnher, & Chiriboga, 1975; Neugarten, 1973; York & John, 1992). In the Kansas City Longitudinal Study, Neugarten (1973) reported that older men were more receptive to their own affiliative and nurturant behavior than younger men, whereas older women were more receptive than younger women to their own aggressive and egocentric behavior. Coming to terms with the emerging dimensions of one's personality (e.g., nurturance or aggressiveness) may be one of the challenges of midlife development. With self-acceptance and integration of masculine and feminine dimensions of personality, individuals may become more adaptable in facing the challenges of growing older (Huyck, 1990).

David Gutmann's View of Sex-Role Changes During Adulthood

Gutmann (1977, 1987, 1992) suggested that a critical difference in men's and women's **ego mastery styles** is dominant in the early adult years, but that this difference shifts as adults reach middle age. *Ego mastery* refers to the style adopted in coping with self and others. It is more, however, than just how we respond or behave; ego mastery style is the underlying organization of values and beliefs that govern external behavior. Two ego mastery styles have been associated with age-related personality changes for men

Gutmann has suggested that men and women change the ways that they express mastery after the parenting years. New research suggests that individuals seek to master new "possible selves" throughout their lives.

and women: active mastery and passive accommodative mastery. **Active mastery** is typified by striving for autonomy, control, and personal competence. One shapes the external environment to fulfill one's own needs and desires. To accomplish active mastery, individuals may employ strategies centered on achievement. **Passive accommodative mastery,** in contrast, is an ego mastery style in which individuals gain control over their environments by accommodating others perceived to be in power. By accommodating the needs and desires of others, the individual gains a sense of ego mastery and control. Passive accommodation implies social sensitivity.

These two styles of ego mastery, although present in both men and women, appear to wax and wane at particular periods in the life course. According to Gutmann, active mastery generally overshadows passive accommodative mastery in younger men. By middle age, however, the two styles have shifted; passive accommodative mastery becomes the more predominant male orientation. Interestingly, Gutmann suggests that the situation is frequently reversed for women. Passive accommodative ego mastery style generally predominates women in young adulthood, whereas active mastery predominates by middle age. Gutmann's conclusions are based on observations of adults in a variety of cultures (Mayan Indian, Navajo Indian, and Middle-Eastern Druze).

Gutmann offers a socioevolutionary model for age changes in mastery style among men and women. His theory emphasizes the concept of the **parental imperative.** To ensure the biological and social survival of our species, parents must develop effective divisions of labor to manage the demands and responsibilities of childrearing. One division of labor, which has evolved over thousands of years, has given rise to the two ego mastery styles. A passive accommodative style is uniquely suited to the nurturing tasks of parenting, while the active mastery style is suited to providing the necessary economic and material support necessary for family survival. After parenting is over, middle-aged adults begin a process of sex-role reversal. The shift or transition identified by Gutmann is gradual, not abrupt. Individuals slowly recognize dimensions of their egos that have been unfulfilled and unrecognized. By middle age, men frequently become more aware of their inner selves, their dependency, social needs, nurturant dispositions, and underlying emotional lives. Corresponding changes in women are also evident by middle age.

Critics of Gutmann's theory have questioned whether the observed changes in ego mastery style in middle age are reflective of sex-role reversal or are simply a description of emergent socialization. Cool and McCabe (1983) analyzed research on a number of Mediterranean cultures and observed that women display a shift in mastery styles consistent with Gutmann's theory. However, they attributed this shift to socialization, the increased opportunity for women to control their own lives and the lives of others around them.

Carl Jung's View of Sex-Role Development in Adult Life

Carl Jung (1933) broke with traditional Freudian psychoanalytic theory to create a theory of personality development that focused on adulthood. In Jung's view, a healthy adult personality involves an equilibrium among various components, including the polarities of masculinity and femininity. The period of early adulthood is marked by a decided imbalance between the two, so that one of these components dominates to the exclusion of the other. Masculinity or femininity predominates at this time because of society's coercive sex-role stereotyping or modeling. Usually, the dominant orientation to masculinity or femininity matches one's biological sex. By middle age, however, masculinity and femininity become more balanced as males become more expressive of their feminine characteristics (e.g., nurturance), and females become more expressive of their masculine attributes (e.g., aggression). By old age, Jung suggested, a healthy equilibrium often exists in the personality components of masculinity and femininity. Older males and females see this balance in themselves and recognize their personalities as consisting of *both* masculine and feminine features.

Jeanne Brooks's View of Sex-Role Behavior and Social Maturity

Jeanne Brooks (1981), in examining data from the California Longitudinal Study (see Research Focus 1.1 in chapter 1), identified a pattern of sex-role behavior in adulthood analogous to those suggested by Gutmann and Jung. Brooks suggested that, beginning in middle age, the distinction between male and female personality characteristics becomes progressively blurred. In fact, social maturity emerges from middle age onward. *Social maturity* consists of three essential components. First is the recognition of how to live easily and comfortably with all people, both men and women. Second is the capacity to develop one's own standards and values, regardless of social stereotypes. Third is the ability to respond humanely, appropriately, and sensitively to those who, like ourselves, experience stressful life circumstances and need help coping. It is

Many older adults continue to enjoy and benefit from exercise, especially if they were physically active earlier in life. Dr. Patricia Peterson, shown here, holds a number of world running records in her age group.

Brooks's contention that from middle age onward men and women appear far more alike than different in their articulated sense of social maturity.

Conclusions about Sex-Role Changes in Later Life

Some data suggest that by middle age, males and females become increasingly aware of new or hidden aspects of their personalities and identities. Neugarten (1977), for example, described this kind of personality change as an increase in the incorporation of opposite sex role characteristics. Bengtson, Reedy, and Gordon (1985), Gutmann (1987, 1992), and others find a greater expression and acceptance of nurturance for both older men and women.

It seems that, as they grow older, both men and women become more aware of personality components that they have not previously recognized, fostered, or expressed. According to Bengtson and colleagues (1985), age-related social forces may have a profound impact on personality and sex roles.

SOCIAL DIMENSIONS OF AGING

Riley (1997) has suggested that the social dimensions of aging are best understood in terms of a conceptual framework that emphasizes *age integration* and the interplay between the developing individual and changing social structures. The meaning of aging is changing in all societies. Age integration means that societies are breaking down barriers and bringing people of different ages together. The process of age integration has consequences for the social structures in society such as the family, the community, educational institutions, and the workplace. Riley gives an example of this interplay as follows:

> There has been and will continue to be unprecedented increases in longevity. This increased longevity produces changes in the structure of family networks (e.g., there are more middle-aged adults with surviving elderly parents). The caregiving pressures on individuals lead to structural changes in society (e.g., changes in community organizations, federal regulations).

Because of the tremendous variation in cultural and ethnic backgrounds among the aged in the United States, social development must be considered within the context of different and continuously changing cultural systems (Riley, 1997; Riley & Riley, 1994). Riley and Riley have argued that social or cultural changes and changes in the patterns of people's lives are continuously changing. One lifestyle and set of activities may suit people from one ethnic background better than another. For example, social interaction with family members tends to be more frequent and important for older people of French-American background than for their Scandinavian counterparts. The Scandinavian elderly have adapted to an individualized lifestyle and may seek social integration by participation in community organizations.

There are many ways for adults to experience positive well-being and life satisfaction, and many pathways toward successful aging in American society. Some individuals age successfully by being active, and some by striking a unique balance among a variety of roles and responsibilities. However, there are also many restrictions and constraints (ageism, job discrimination) that have negative consequences for older adults.

Laura Carstensen's (1993, 1995) selectivity theory provides a useful framework for understanding social relationships across the adult life span. According to Carstensen, social interaction has three functions: (1) it is an information source, (2) it helps people develop and maintain a sense of self, and (3) it is a source of pleasure or emotional well-being. The information source and self-identity functions of social interactions wane during the later adult years because they are less important, and the emotional support function gains in significance during the later adult years (see also Carstensen, Gottman, & Levenson, 1995; Troll and Skaff, 1997).

SUMMARY

America is "graying." In 1900 about 3.1 million Americans were aged 65 and over. In 1991, the number rose to 31.8 million. By 2030, there will be 66 million older adults in the United States. Older adults, especially the old-old, represent the fastest growing segment of our population.

Although our life expectancy has increased substantially in recent years, the potential human life span has remained remarkably stable, with an upper limit of approximately 110 to 120 years. Until recently, the increase in life expectancy was mostly due to a reduction in deaths during infancy and early childhood. But in the last few decades, improved nutrition and health care have increased the chances that those reaching older adulthood will live longer. In the future, older adults are expected to have healthier, more productive, and longer lives. For reasons that are still unknown, women will continue to live longer than men. Furthermore, substantial differences in life expectancy are associated with social class, race, and ethnicity.

Increases in the numbers and percentages of older adults in the United States have profound economic and social ramifications. As the population ages and the ratios of workers to dependents become smaller, new policies for the equitable distribution of economic resources will emerge.

Aging takes place within a cultural context. One important aspect of a culture is social class. One of the major concerns of individuals in late adulthood is the decrease in income they are likely to experience. The poverty rate is higher for the elderly than for any other age group.

Aging in America carries a number of negative stereotypes. Ageist stereotypes are evident in young children who often view the elderly as inactive, lonely, and bored.

China and Japan appear to hold positive attitudes toward the elderly. However, recent social, economic, and demographic changes in these cultures have led to a decline in respect toward the elderly. Examination of various cultural definitions of aging and cultural differences in the treatment of the elderly provides important insights into values and attitudes toward aging. Knowledge of other cultures provides a basis for developing accurate views of the range of diversity in intergenerational relations across cultures.

Aging in America, as well as in most if not all cultures, is different for men and women. The nature of sex roles and how they change over the life span is highly complex. Androgyny refers to the belief that each individual's personality has both masculine and feminine dimensions. The degree to which an adult with a masculine, feminine, or androgynous sex-role orientation shows effective adjustment depends on the cultural context. Gutmann's work indicates an increase in sex-typed feminine traits in the personality profiles of older men and a corresponding tendency for older women to display an increase in sex-typed masculine traits. Riley's (1997) age integration theory provides a broad framework for understanding the complex social dimensions of aging.

REVIEW QUESTIONS

1. What is the difference between life expectancy, potential life span, and longevity?
2. Who are the old-old? Why are they an important group to study?
3. Outline the changing age structure of the U.S. population. What effects will the changing old-age and young-age dependency ratios have on society?
4. What factors seem to contribute most to longevity?
5. Discuss how sex, race, ethnicity, and social class affect life expectancy. What factors account for these differences?
6. Describe the economic hardships that many of today's elderly endure.
7. What is ageism? Trace the historical background of ageist attitudes toward the elderly in the United States.
8. How do attitudes about the aged in countries like China, Japan, and India compare to the attitudes held by Americans?
9. How do sex roles change during the adult years? What is androgyny?
10. Explain the meaning of the following terms: active mastery, passive accommodative mastery, and the parental imperative.
11. Describe Carstensen's selectivity theory.
12. Is there an optimal way to age? What evidence supports your position?

For Further Reading

Bronfenbrenner, U., McClelland, P., Wethington, E., Moen, P., & Ceci, S. J. (1996). *The state of Americans.* New York: Free Press.

Elder, G. H., Shanahan, M. J., & Clipp, E. C. (1994). When war comes to men's lives: Life-course patterns in family, work, and health. *Psychology and Aging, 9,* 5–16.

Huyck, M. H. (1990). Gender differences in aging. In J. E. Birren & K. W. Schaie (Eds.), *Handbook of the psychology of aging* (3rd ed., pp. 124–132). San Diego: Academic Press.

Kimmel, D. C. (1996). Lesbians and gay men also grow old. In L. A. Bond, S. J. Cutler, & Grams, A. (Eds.), *Promoting successful and productive aging.* Thousand Oaks, CA: Sage.

Riley, M. W., & Riley, J. W. (1994). Age integration and the lives of older people. *The Gerontologist, 34,* 110–115.

PHYSIOLOGICAL AND SENSORY PROCESSES

INTRODUCTION

In this chapter, you will learn about the biological aspects of aging. In reading this material, it is important to distinguish the processes of normal aging from the consequences of particular diseases. Although there is an increasing likelihood of poor health in later life, poor health is not the same as aging. Normal aging, or **senescence,** refers to the gradual time-related biological process during which degenerative processes overtake regenerative or growth processes. All individuals, if they live long enough, will experience senescence. In contrast, diseases associated with later life, such as Alzheimer's disease, arthritis, or cardiovascular disease, affect some individuals and not others. Although some aspects of effective biological functioning are impaired in later life, the declines associated with normal aging are relatively mild and occur gradually compared with the severity and progression of impairment associated with disease.

It is important to keep in mind that some individuals are healthy and vital in late life. Researchers make a distinction between *normal* aging and *successful* aging. One of the primary goals of medical gerontology and behavioral medicine research is to help individuals to optimize health and effective psychological functioning. To accomplish this goal, it is important to recognize both the gains and the losses associated with biological aging processes, and for individuals to build on their strengths to help compensate for losses (Baltes & Graf, 1996).

Caution is in order when interpreting the research on biological aspects of aging. Most of the available research on this topic is based on cross-sectional comparisons between young adults and elderly adults. Thus, it is impossible to distinguish between the effects of age and the effects of a wide range of cohort factors that affect health and vitality across the adult years.

WHY DO WE AGE?

We begin this chapter by raising two fundamental and interrelated questions: "What is aging?" and "Why do we age?" The former question may be answered in a rather straightforward manner. *Aging* refers to the orderly changes that occur in both physiological and behavioral function across the adult years. A conceptual distinction is made between the concepts of primary aging and secondary aging. *Primary aging,* which is the same as senescence, refers to changes that are gradual, inevitable, universal, and insidious. It also involves changes that occur in representative individuals living under representative conditions; changes associated with primary aging are not a consequence of disease. *Secondary aging* refers to the processes that affect the rate at which primary aging occurs. Intense work-related stress, prolonged exposure to environmental toxins, and the consequences of disease are examples of secondary aging factors that accelerate the rate of primary aging processes.

The latter question, "Why do we age?", is much more complex and difficult to answer. One early view, called the **wear-and-tear theory,** stated that the human body ages because it "wears out" over time because of the stresses of life. One of the difficulties for the wear-and-tear theory is that some kinds of exertion or activity, such as challenging work and vigorous exercise, are predictive of continued vitality and are essential to long life, whereas other kinds of stressful activities are detrimental to longevity (Cristofalo, 1986). Other theorists proposed that breakdowns within a particular organ system—for example, in the immune system, endocrine system, or nervous system—are responsible for aging. One major problem associated with these **physiological or system-based theories** is that it is impossible to determine if changes in a specific body system are the "cause" of aging, or the "outcome" of a basic genetic, cellular, or molecular process.

The above-mentioned theories do not explain why we should "age" before we die and why there is a "fixed upper limit" to the life span. Biologists make an important distinction between theories that explain the maximum length of the human life span and theories that explain how and why individuals experience a deterioration in particular biological and psychological functions as they approach the upper boundary of human life. Of course, the most useful and comprehensive theory would address both of these issues.

Recently, Leonard Hayflick (1996) formulated a theory of human aging that addresses both mortality and morbidity. His idea is that instead of asking the question "Why do we age?" we should ask: "Why did aging evolve?" and "What is the adaptive significance of aging?"

Hayflick opposes the belief that aging, death, and a fixed limit to the life span all have a biogenetic basis that was selected for by evolutionary mechanisms. Proponents of this view suggest that after individuals give birth to and nurture children, they would consume the resources that the younger members of their species would need to attain reproductive maturity. Thus, older individuals would become a competitive nuisance for their younger counterparts. Under this scenario, evolutionary mechanisms would have selected for genetic mutations that lead to aging, death, and a fixed life span. This argument seems very compelling. However, Hayflick points out that our animal and human ancestors did not attain old age, nor did they experience the aging process as we know it now! Human aging is a cultural invention. It occurred very recently because of improvements in sanitation and public health, medical advances, improved nutrition, and so on. Thus, our ancestors never lived long enough to participate in the process by which aging would have been selected for.

Hayflick (1996) pointed out that the key to understanding aging is the realization that evolution, since it operates on a species, not an individual, level, selects primarily for reproductive success. Species in which individuals attain reproductive age, bear children, and have their children achieve independence will flourish—other species will not. One of the best ways to ensure reproductive success is to select for organisms who have very robust vital systems that will allow them to survive environmental variations, disease, and predation. In essence, evolution would select for "overengineered" individuals with a great deal of physiological (and adaptive) reserve capacity and redundancy.

A species would increase its chance of survival by investing its resources in reproductive success rather than postreproductive longevity. Thus, Hayflick (1996) argues that evolutionary mechanisms selected for humans who reach maximum physiological vigor at sexual maturity, and that evolutionary/genetic factors indirectly selected for the upper limit of the human life span by directly selecting for reproductive success. In other words, humans (like other animals) live beyond sexual maturity because of the physiological reserve capacity and redundancy that laid the basis for their attainment of sexual maturity. During these postreproductive years, humans "age" and ultimately "die" because of breakdowns or glitches in their physiological systems that cannot be repaired in a meaningful way. Consistent with this line of reasoning is the principle of *antagonistic pleiotropy* (Rusting, 1992), which suggests that factors that enhance reproductive success may have a destructive influence later in life. The risk of breast cancer, for example, may be related to long-term exposure to estrogen, which is necessary for fertility.

One way to understand Hayflick's ideas is to think about the design of a space vehicle that will take photographs of a particular planet, say Saturn, and send the photos back to Earth. The engineers of this spacecraft would have as their fundamental goal "a vehicle that reaches Saturn." Thus, they would design a spacecraft with enough reserve capacity to reach Saturn. As Hayflick notes, the engineers would not care what happened to the craft after it passed Saturn; its goal would have been accomplished. After passing by Saturn the space vehicle would continue to move through space because of the redundancies that characterized its design. However, as time went on, the physical systems that make up the space vehicle would steadily deteriorate. Sooner or later a critical threshold would be reached at which point the physical breakdowns within the spacecraft would overwhelm its redundancies, reserve capacity, and self-repair systems. At that point it would die.

What particular breakdowns or glitches occur in the human body that lead to aging? Many of these glitches have a genetic basis. For example, the **genetic mutation theory** suggests that aging is caused by changes, or mutations, in the DNA of the cells in vital organs of the body. Eventually, the number of mutated cells in a vital organ would increase to the point that the efficacy of the cell's functioning is significantly impaired. Possible sources for these mutations may be intrinsic factors in cell division, such as chance errors in DNA replication or in the genes that specifically cause mutations in other genes. Other potential triggers of mutations are extrinsic factors such as toxins in the air, in water, and in food.

The **genetic switching theory** suggests that certain genes cease to operate or switch off, and this causes aging. Information needed to produce DNA is no longer available, so the cells atrophy (Selkoe, 1992). Eventually, genetic switching leads to cell death and the loss of organ functioning. According to this theory, there is a kind of genetic blueprint in each of the body's cells.

According to the **error catastrophe theory,** aging is caused by damage to RNA, enzymes, and certain other proteins rather than by errors in DNA. For example, if an error occurs in the RNA responsible for the production of an enzyme essential to cell metabolism, the result will be a marked reduction in cell functioning and possibly cell death. The escalating impact of the original error in the RNA is the "error catastrophe" (Orgel, 1973).

One of the most popular lines of contemporary research is driven by the **free radical theory.** This theory hinges on the fact that certain molecules within a cell display a violent reaction when they encounter oxygen. Specifically, these molecules break away from the cell and form highly reactive molecular fragments called free radicals. These free radicals, which are highly unstable, try to bind with other molecular structures within a cell. This binding process has deleterious effects on several facts of normal cell function and can damage DNA. These cellular calamities ultimately manifest themselves as the signs of aging (Selkoe, 1992).

Antiaging Interventions

Throughout the centuries, humans have tried to slow down or even stop the aging process. We want to rejuvenate ourselves, to become immortal! Primitive peoples used metaphors from nature to help them search for the secret of immortality. For example, it was observed that snakes were capable of rejuvenating themselves by shedding their skins. Thus people sought ways of ridding themselves of the confines of their outer body shell. In fact, the Greek word for old age, *geron* (from which we derive the term *gerontology*), refers to the process by which an animal sheds its skin.

Today, scientists are experimenting with a number of different techniques to prolong life. Before we discuss some of these techniques, it is important to make a distinction between the influence that a particular antiaging intervention might have on our life expectancy versus the aging process. For example, it has been estimated that the elimination of cardiovascular disease and cancer would increase life expectancy by 13.9 and 3.1 years, respectively (see table 3.1). However, we could not say with any certainty that the elimination of these diseases (along with all of the other factors listed in table 3.1) slowed the aging process unless we observed that there was a significant increase in the upper limit of the life span. This is an important point! Halting the aging processes is not the same as increasing life expectancy. To demonstrate that a particular intervention actually slowed the aging process we need to show that it increased the potential life span.

Dietary Restriction

In the 1930s researchers discovered that moderate to severe dietary restriction initiated after weaning and continued throughout the rest of life drastically increased the life expectancy of the common laboratory rat (McCay & Crowell, 1934). This finding has been replicated a vast number of times. It has also been shown that dietary restriction, even if it is not begun until middle adulthood, can extend the longevity of animal subjects (Masoro, 1984). In these studies, dietary restriction is typically defined as reducing caloric intake by 25 to 40 percent from free feeding levels while providing an adequate intake of essential nutrients and vitamins. Thus it is important to note that animals who undergo dietary restriction are "undernourished" rather than "malnourished."

It has been argued that dietary restriction increases longevity because it can delay (or even prevent) age-related pathologies in the cardiovascular, renal, and central nervous

TABLE 3.1

Gains in Life Expectancy Due to Elimination of Various Causes of Death (years), 1978

Cause of Death	Total At Birth	Total Age 65	White Male At Birth	White Male Age 65	White Female At Birth	White Female Age 65	Nonwhite Male[a] At Birth	Nonwhite Male[a] Age 65	Nonwhite Female[a] At Birth	Nonwhite Female[a] Age 65
Major cardiovascular diseases	13.9	14.3	10.6	10.1	16.4	17.4	10.6	11.2	20.3	22.1
Diseases of the heart	7.0	6.6	6.5	5.5	6.9	7.0	6.1	5.8	8.8	9.0
Cerebrovascular diseases	1.1	1.2	0.7	0.8	1.4	1.4	1.2	1.2	2.2	2.2
Arteriosclerosis	0.2	0.2	0.1	0.1	0.2	0.2	0.1	0.2	0.2	0.3
Malignant neoplasms[b]	3.1	1.9	2.8	1.9	3.1	1.7	3.4	2.6	3.3	2.0
Influenza and pneumonia	0.4	0.3	0.3	0.3	0.4	0.3	0.5	0.4	0.5	0.3
Diabetes mellitus	0.2	0.2	0.1	0.2	0.2	0.2	0.5	0.6	0.4	0.3
Motor vehicle accidents	0.6	–	0.9	0.1	0.4	–	0.7	0.1	0.4	–
All accidents excluding motor vehicle	0.6	0.1	0.7	0.1	0.3	0.1	1.0	0.2	0.5	0.2
Bronchitis, emphysema, and asthma	0.1	0.1	0.2	0.2	0.1	0.1	0.1	0.1	0.1	–
Cirrhosis of liver	0.1	0.3	0.1	0.2	0.1	0.5	0.1	0.3	–	–
Nephritis and nephrosis	0.1	–	0.1	–	0.1	–	0.1	0.1	0.2	0.1
Infective and parasitic diseases	0.2	0.1	0.1	0.1	0.1	0.1	0.3	0.1	0.4	0.2
Tuberculosis, all forms	–[c]	–	–	–	–	–	0.1	–	–	–

[a] Data for 1969–1971.

[b] Including lymphatic and hematopoietic tissues.

[c] Less than 0.05 years.

Sources: Prithwis Das Gupta, "Cause-of-Death Analysis of the 1978 U.S. Mortality Data by Age, Sex, and Race," U.S. Bureau of the Census, 1981 (unpublished manuscript); U.S. Public Health Service, National Center for Health Statistics, "U.S. Life Tables by Cause of Death: 1969–71," by T. N. E. Greville, U.S. Decennial Life Tables for 1969–71, 1, no. 5 (1975); Hayflick, L. M. (1996). How and why we age. New York: Ballantine Books, p. 99.

systems (Masoro, 1984). Furthermore, several researchers have reported that caloric restriction may have beneficial psychological outcomes. For example, Donald Ingram and his associates (Ingram, Weindruch, Spangler, Freeman, & Walford, 1987) reported that restricted-diet rats performed significantly better than a standard-diet group on a complex maze-learning task as well as a task of motor coordination. In a similar study, Campbell and Gaddy (1987) found that undernourished rats performed better than controls on three tasks of motor performance.

One shortcoming with all the preceding research is that it was conducted on rodents. However, more recent experiments by Sell and colleagues (1996) have shown that reducing caloric intake by 30 percent increased the life expectancy of two different species of monkeys. They discovered that restricted-diet monkeys had lower metabolic rates, body temperatures, and levels of pentosidine. Pentosidine is a chemical found in several parts of the body, including the skin. Importantly, it has been identified as a **biomarker** of aging, in that it is believed to be a valid indicator of the speed of the primary aging process.

Are there beneficial effects associated with dietary restriction in humans? At present, there are no scientific data that speak to this question. However, a leading gerontologist, Roy Walford, began a personal regimen of dietary restriction in 1987 when he reached middle age. It is still too early to gauge the effects of Walford's altered diet. Whatever the outcome of Walford's personal experiment, it would be difficult for the scientific community to generalize the results of a study that had one research participant who had a strong personal bias regarding the design and results of the research in which he participated. On a more objective note, it is significant that in 1996 the National Institute on Aging funded two researchers (Roberts and Mayer) from Tufts University to conduct an experiment that will determine whether restrained versus unrestrained eating in postmenopausal women affects their quality of life, physiological vigor, and longevity. Physicians, biologists, and psychologists eagerly await the result of this research. Of course, as Weindruch (1996) suggests, we all hope that understanding the biochemistry of dietary restriction will help boost longevity without increasing hunger.

Antioxidants

Recall that one of the most promising theories of aging involves the deleterious effects of free radicals on cellular function, and that free radicals are formed when components of a cell react with oxygen. To be sure, the major culprit within the free radical theory is oxygen: Oxygen makes the body deteriorate just as long-term exposure to oxygen makes metal rust. This line of reasoning suggests that the administration of antioxidant drugs might prolong life and delay the aging process.

Some antioxidants, like vitamins E and C, are contained in food. The body manufactures other antioxidants. One such antioxidant is **melatonin,** a hormone produced by the pineal gland within the brain. Melatonin binds, like all antioxidants, with free radicals before they have a chance to harm body cells. Several researchers (e.g., Pierpaoli & Regelson, 1995) have touted a whole range of beneficial effects associated

Give up the chips. Health in late life will be affected by the choices we make in young adulthood. Healthy eating habits are associated with increased longevity and reduced risk of heart disease.

with melatonin. More specifically, they have presented data that suggest that melatonin cures insomnia, lowers cholesterol, increases resistance to cancer, prolongs sexual vitality, and may reverse the aging process. This last claim is based on the finding that the administration of melatonin increases the life expectancy of laboratory mice and rats. However, as is the case with other antioxidants, it is unclear how melatonin achieves its success. Hayflick (1996) cautions, for example, that the taste of melatonin may have inhibited the food intake of lab animals. Thus, the effects of melatonin might very well be attributed to dietary restriction. He further notes that melatonin may have delayed the incidence of the diseases, especially cancers, that ultimately claim the lives of these animals without having had any meaningful effect on the aging process per se.

Sohal and Weindruch (1996) have also suggested that the amount of oxidative damage increases as an organism ages, and that oxidative stress is the major cause of senescence. More interestingly, however, they showed that restriction of caloric intake significantly lowers levels of oxidative stress and damage and increases the life expectancy of several mammals.

Lifestyle

Many scientific studies seem to confirm the obvious. Namely, if we adopt a healthy lifestyle that includes cessation of smoking, moderate alcohol consumption, reduced intake of high cholesterol foods, regular exercise, elimination of environmental stressors, and so on, we will live longer. However, as you are well aware of by now, all these interventions have an effect on life expectancy because they have disease-reducing properties, not because they have a fundamental impact on the aging process.

BIOLOGICAL AGING

In a very general way, we know what it means to age in a biological or a physical sense. We constantly observe the effects of aging in ourselves and the people around us. Scientists, however, are interested in identifying the "exact" and "specific" changes that accompany the aging process. Therefore, next we describe some of the scientific research that has looked at the changes in physical appearance that are associated with aging, and we discuss some of the changes that take place in the functional integrity in some of our most important organ systems during adulthood.

Changes in Physical Appearance with Age

One of the physical manifestations of aging has to do with changes in the appearance of the skin. Facial wrinkles and age spots become more apparent as we age. Age-related changes in the skin are largely cosmetic, since the primary functions of the skin, which involve protection of the internal organs and body temperature regulation, are rela-

Unquestionably, physical appearance continues to change as we grow older, and some changes bring on other changes—gains as well as losses. Clint Eastwood at ages 35 and 63.

tively unaffected by aging. Facial structure also changes with age. The cartilage in the nose and ears continues to grow with age, although the bones of the face do not enlarge after young adulthood. Scalp hair also grays and thins. Some men experience a form of hair loss that is genetically based. This type of hair loss, called *male pattern baldness,* begins at the temples, proceeds to the top of the head, and continues until the entire top of the head is bare (the "monk's spot").

For men, height decreases by about a half inch between 30 and 50 years and by about three-fourths inch between 50 and 70 years. The height loss for women is slightly greater and may be as much as two inches between 25 and 75 years. These changes in height are associated with postural change, compression of the cartilage in the spine, and loss of bone calcium with age.

Loss of bone calcium occurs at a faster rate for women after menopause. **Osteoporosis** is the term for the disease that involves extreme losses in bone calcium and increased brittleness. Individuals with osteoporosis are at risk for breaking bones if they fall. Osteoporosis can be detected early by a loss in height of more than one inch from one's height at age 20 (see figure 3.1). Postmenopausal women are advised to consult a physician regarding the benefits and disadvantages of estrogen replacement therapy. Risk of osteoporosis can be minimized by maintaining a properly balanced diet including daily requirements for calcium and engaging in a program of exercise on a regular basis (Nordin & Need, 1990).

With regard to height changes, it is likely that improved nutrition has had a major effect on different cohort groups. Young adults today are generally taller than young adults of just a decade ago, and part of this cohort difference is probably due to

Figure 3.1 Osteoporosis: Reducing the risk. After age 30, and especially after menopause in women, bone loss begins. Osteoporosis is an extreme form of the bone loss and mineralization that ordinarily occur with age. As bones become more brittle, fractures in the wrist, spine, and hip become more likely. Back pain, a bent spine, and loss of height also occur.

In fact, osteoporosis can first be detected by a loss of height. A decrease of more than one inch from the baseline height at age 20 is a sign that significant bone loss is taking place. The likelihood of osteoporosis can be minimized by starting as a young adult to maintain a good calcium intake, to engage in weight-bearing exercise, and to get a moderate amount of sun (in order to manufacture vitamin D), as well as by restricting alcohol intake and not smoking. After menopause, women should consult a doctor about estrogen replacement therapy and calcium supplements.

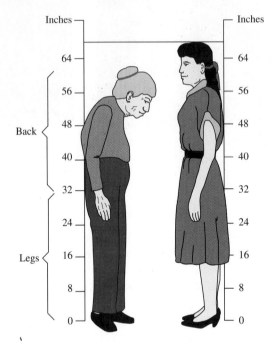

improved nutrition. The potential effects of nutrition on height are illustrated in figure 3.2 for middle-aged and older adults. This figure shows the estimated mean height for groups of middle-aged and older adults measured in 1998. The solid line indicates age differences in height. The dashed line indicates an age change for this cohort. Although these data are estimations of actual heights for these groups, they illustrate that some part of the difference we observe between different age groups for any physical measure is due to cohort factors. Methods for disentangling age and cohort influences are described in detail in appendix A.

Studies of age differences and age changes also suggest that muscle tissue gradually declines in strength, size, firmness or tone, and flexibility (Whitbourne, 1996). Age-related changes in strength and muscle tone can be attributed to tissue changes, but the extent of decline in strength depends largely on one's level of activity and exercise (Horvath & Davis, 1990; Schulz & Curnow, 1988).

Figure 3.2 This figure shows the estimated mean height for groups of middle-aged and older adults measured in 1998. The solid line indicates *age differences* in height. The dashed line indicates *age changes* for this cohort. These data illustrate two important points about physical aging. First, some part of the difference we observe between different age groups for any measure is due to cohort factors rather than age. With regard to height, improved nutrition has had a major effect on height and other physical characteristics. Second, there is a large degree of stability for individuals along some physical dimensions or for some characteristics. Do you think that the mean height of the middle-aged group tested in 1998 will decline or stay the same?

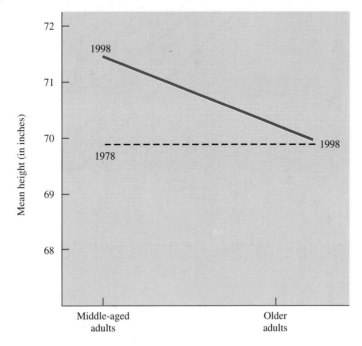

Changes in Circulation and Respiration

As can be seen in figure 3.3, all of the major biological systems of the body begin to decline during the twenties or thirties. One of the most noteworthy declines is evidenced by the circulatory system. The cells in the human body, in order to survive and to function properly, must receive oxygen and nutrients and they must have a way of disposing of waste products. The circulatory system provides for these needs. Figure 3.4 shows the four chambers of the heart, and the pattern of circulation. Although muscles of the heart become less efficient, and the arteries become less flexible and narrower, normal aging of the circulatory system does not pose a problem for most older adults. However, diseases of the circulatory system, such as heart disease, hypertension, and atherosclerosis, are serious problems for a large number of middle-aged and older adults (Elias, Elias, & Elias, 1990). Although the incidence of heart disease is decreasing, it is still the leading cause of death in the United States. Changes in health behavior as well as medical advances have helped to reduce the consequences of heart disease.

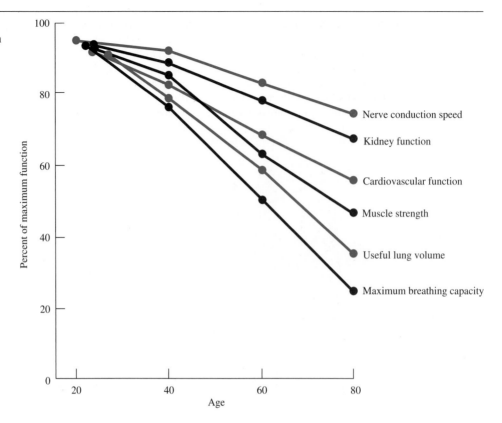

Figure 3.3
Average declines in major biological systems.

The circulatory system shares a special relationship with the respiratory system. Oxygen, which is delivered to body cells via the blood supply, is placed in the blood stream by the lungs. Starting about age 30, maximum oxygen capacity in the lungs decreases by about 5 to 10 percent per decade. Furthermore, collagen fibers begin to build up in the lungs, which makes lung tissue lose its elasticity. This means that, with advancing age, individuals experience more and more problems when performing anaerobic activities that last for more than a few seconds. For example, it is more common to see a 40-year-old Olympic weight lifter than a sprinter.

Changes in Hormone Regulation and Reproduction

There are age-related changes in hormonal regulation, due to changes in secretion patterns and in the effects of secretions on target tissues. One of the most important systems that exhibits the consequences of hormonal change with aging is the female reproductive system. The transition from the comparative regularity of the menstrual cycle during young adulthood to increased variation in the menstrual interval in middle age is due to increased variation in the length of the follicular and luteal phases of the cycle. Changes

Figure 3.4 **Circulation in the heart.** The heart is a four-chambered muscle, about the size of a fist. Each side of the heart contains two separate spaces separated by a valve. The thin-walled upper chamber is called the atrium, and the thick-walled lower chamber is called the ventricle.

Used blood returns to the heart via the vena cava, the body's largest vein, and enters the right atrium. It then flows down into the right ventricle. The ventricle contracts, forcing the blood through the pulmonary artery into the lungs, where carbon dioxide is removed and oxygen is added. The clean, oxygenated blood returns to the heart via the pulmonary veins into the left atrium and then down into the left ventricle. The powerful muscular wall of the left ventricle forces the blood up through the aorta, the body's largest artery, and into the systemic circulation. The familiar "lub-dub" sound of the heartbeat is caused by the alternating contraction (systole) and relaxation (diastole) of the chambers of the heart.

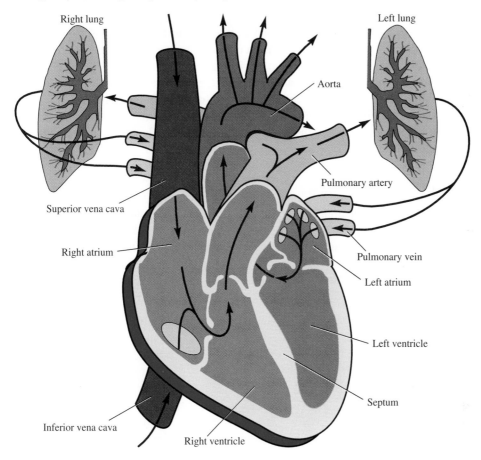

in the function of the ovaries determine the timing of the events leading to irregular cycles (Wise, 1993). Changes in anterior pituitary function are also likely to occur with aging. Age-related change in levels of follicle stimulating hormone (FSH) is one of the earliest hallmarks of reproductive aging in women. In regularly cycling women over age 45, FSH concentrations are elevated during the early follicular phase. Subsequently, FSH levels fall to normal during the late follicular phase. The mean number of follicles in the ovaries of women who are still menstruating is tenfold higher than it is in postmenopausal women of the same age. Over the entire life span, there is a continuous, exponential reduction in ovarian oocytes and follicles. By the time of menopause, there is less than 1 percent of the original reserve of oocytes and primordial follicles.

Men do not generally experience abrupt changes in fertility or other sexual functions. However, during the later adult years, reproductive impairments become more likely for men. The incidence of impotence increases, testosterone concentrations decrease, and the diurnal rhythm in testosterone levels disappears (Wise, 1993).

AGING AND SENSORY PROCESSES

We make contact with the world around us through our five primary senses—vision, hearing, touch, taste, and smell. **Sensation** refers to the reception of information by the ears, skin, tongue, nostrils, eyes, and other specialized sense organs. When we hear, for example, waves of pulsating air are sensed by the outer ear, transmitted through the bones of the middle ear to the cochlear nerve, and sent to the brain. When we see, waves of light are collected by the eyes, focused on the retina, and travel along the optic nerve to the brain. We now consider the effects of aging on vision, hearing, and other sensory processes.

Vision

Figure 3.5 shows a diagram of the human eye. Although relatively little change in visual function occurs during the early adult years, very noticeable changes in vision occur during the middle and later years. In the middle adult years, most or all individuals will experience **presbyopia,** which is exemplified by difficulties in near vision tasks such as reading. This is caused, in part, by a substantial decline in the processes

Figure 3.5 Major structures of the eye.

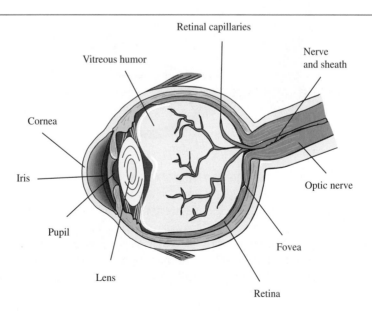

Retinal capillaries

Vitreous humor

Nerve and sheath

Cornea

Iris

Optic nerve

Pupil

Fovea

Lens

Retina

of **accommodation,** which is defined as the ability of the lens to focus on near (or far) objects and maintain a clear image on the retina (Schieber, 1992).

Although visual acuity is the most common measure of accommodation, measures of **contrast sensitivity** may provide a more accurate assessment of age-related changes in visual function (see Research Focus 3.1).

Another problem associated with the middle-aged years is an increased sensitivity to **glare.** This change in sensitivity is usually noticed after age 45. Age-related changes in glare sensitivity are largely due to changes in the lens; and indeed, the lens becomes progressively thicker, less flexible, and more opaque with age (Weale, 1986). All of these changes in the lens mean that less light reaches the retina. It has also been shown that the number of cones (color receptors) on the fovea (the center of the retina) markedly decreases between 40 and 60 years of age. Such a change has a negative influence on visual acuity (Schieber, 1992).

As we grow older, the processes involved in adjusting to changes in illumination take longer (Weale, 1986). The term *dark adaptation* refers to the adjustment involved in going from a brightly lit to a dimly lit environment.

The area of the effective visual field becomes smaller with advancing age. This means that the size or intensity of stimuli in the peripheral area of the visual field must be increased if the stimuli are to be seen. Thus, events occurring away from the center of the visual field are less likely to be detected (Cerella, 1985). Changes in the size of the visual field are due, in part, to an age-related reduction in the amount of blood reaching the eye. In fact, it has been determined that the retina of a 60-year-old receives approximately one-third of the light received by the retina of a 20-year-old (Weale, 1986). Kosnik, Winslow, Kline, Rasinski, and Sekuler (1988) surveyed a large number of adults ranging from 18 to 100 years of age about their ability to perform everyday visual tasks. The reports of the participants in this study suggested that dynamic vision (reading the moving credits at the end of a movie), and visual search (locating a particular type of cereal at the supermarket) declined very gradually with age, whereas visual processing speed (the time necessary to read a passage or recognize an object), near vision (inability to read small print), and light sensitivity (trouble seeing at dusk or sorting dark colors) declined rapidly with age.

Two of the most common pathologies of the aging eye are **cataracts** and **glaucoma** (Kline & Scialfa, 1996). A person with a cataract suffers from a lens that is completely opaque—light cannot travel through the lens to project onto the retina. Cataracts can be surgically treated by removing the lens and inserting an artificial lens. Glaucoma results from increasing pressure inside the eye, which leads to irreparable damage to the retina and the optic nerve. Glaucoma, which affects 2 percent of individuals over the age of 40, is easily detected by a simple optometric test.

Hearing

Hearing remains fairly constant during much of early adulthood and starts to decline during middle adulthood. By age 40, a specific decline in hearing can sometimes be detected. By age 50, we are likely to have problems hearing high-pitched sounds (Kline & Scialfa, 1996). Why? The reduction in the ability to hear high-pitched sounds seems

Age Changes in Contrast Sensitivity Hearing

Contrast sensitivity refers to an individual's ability to perceive visual stimuli that differ in both contrast and spatial frequency. *Contrast* is defined as the difference in brightness between adjacent areas of a visual stimulus. A black line on a white piece of paper possesses a great deal of contrast; a light grey line on a white piece of paper possesses a smaller amount of contrast. *Spatial frequency* refers to the number of cycles of bars of light (one cycle consisting of both a light bar and a dark bar of the same width) imaged within a specific area on the retina—very wide bars of light have low spatial frequencies, whereas very narrow bars of light have high spatial frequencies. Psychologists have constructed simple visual stimuli, called *gratings,* that differ in spatial frequency. See figure 3.A for an example of two simple gratings. If held at arm's length, grating A has a spatial frequency of 1 (each cycle of one light bar and one dark bar takes up one degree of visual angle on the retina); grating B has a spatial frequency of 3 (three cycles of light and dark bars are needed to take up one degree of visual angle). In other words, there are three times as many bars of light in grating B as in grating A.

Think of an experiment in which we present adults of varying ages with a number of gratings that differ in both contrast and spatial frequency. The goal of this study is to determine the contrast threshold for different-aged adults. This refers to the minimal amount of contrast needed to perceive gratings that differ in spatial frequency. By doing such an experiment, Owsley, Sekuler, and Siemsen (1983) discovered that the contrast threshold changes in a predictable manner from twenty to eighty years of age. Figure 3.B summarizes the results of this study as well as other research dealing with the topic of age-related changes in contrast sensitivity.

The area below the curve in figure 3.B represents combinations of contrast and spatial frequency that individuals can see.

Box Figure 3.A Two gratings illustrate the concept of spatial frequency.

Grating A	Grating B
Spatial frequency = 1	Spatial frequency = 3

It defines the window of human visibility. The area above the curve represents combinations of contrast and spatial frequency that are invisible to humans. In general, this figure shows that humans need a great deal of contrast to see gratings with very low or very high spatial frequencies, but relatively little contrast to see gratings of moderate spatial frequency. Furthermore, this figure also shows that, with increases in age, adults (1) need more and more contrast to see gratings with high spatial frequencies, (2) become progressively blind to higher spatial frequencies regardless of the amount of contrast inherent in a grating, and (3) display no alteration in their ability to see low spatial frequencies.

Why do you think that scientists are so concerned with the concept of contrast sensitivity in general and age-related changes in the contrast threshold in particular? To answer this question we need to consider the concept of visual acuity. When an adult goes to an optometrist for a routine eye exam, she is

---

to be caused by a breakdown of cells in the **organ of corti,** the organ in the inner ear that transforms the vibrations picked up by the outer ear into nerve impulses. Sensitivity to low-pitched sounds, on the other hand, does not decline very much in middle adulthood. The need to increase the treble on stereo equipment is a subtle sign of this age-related hearing change.

Hearing impairment becomes more serious in the later years. About 20 percent of the individuals between 45 and 54 years of age experience some hearing difficulty, but for those between 75 and 79, the percentage rises to 75 (Fozard, 1990). It has been estimated that 15 percent of the population over 65 is legally deaf. Such hearing loss is usually due to degeneration of the **cochlea,** the primary neural receptor for hearing. **Presbycusis,** which is a decline in the ability to hear high-pitched sounds, is the general term used to describe the most common age-related problems in hearing. Another specific hearing disorder of late life is **tinnitus.** This is a constant high-pitched "ringing"

Box Figure 3.B Changes in human contrast sensitivity from 20 to 80 years of age.

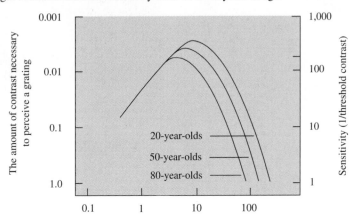

typically given a test of visual acuity. Visual acuity refers to a person's ability to perceive objects under maximum amounts of contrast. When you take your eye exam, you are placed in a dark room and the optometrist projects an eye chart consisting of black letters against a white background. Alternatively, the contrast threshold is a measurement of the minimum amount of contrast necessary to see an object. This means that a test of visual acuity would be a very liberal estimate of an adult's visual ability. For example, suppose that several older adults complain of poor vision. But when they are administered a test of visual acuity, they appear to have normal vision. This does not mean

that old people are "faking it" or that they are complaining because they want attention. Instead, it means that under conditions of reduced contrast (e.g., driving at dusk or reading in a dimly lit room), older adults may experience a pronounced difficulty in seeing. But when high levels of contrast are available, as in a test of visual acuity, they experience less difficulty in seeing.

Contrast sensitivity is a more sensitive and more meaningful measure of a person's visual ability than is visual acuity. For example, a person's contrast sensitivity seems to be a better predictor of one's ability to drive a car under conditions of reduced visibility than a person's visual acuity.

or "whistling" sound in the ears. It has been reported in nearly 11 percent of those between 65 and 74 years of age (Rockstein & Sussman, 1979). Though not unknown among middle-aged adults (9%) or younger adults (3%), tinnitus is a problem the elderly find most difficult to accept. It is distracting, virtually constant, and nearly impossible to "tune out."

With increasing age, it is more and more difficult to hear speech sounds. This effect becomes especially noticeable when processing speech sounds under noisy conditions. Corso (1981) argued that the degeneration of certain areas within the brain, as well as within the ear, may be responsible for this phenomenon. Whatever the cause, it is certain that this deficit can have a negative effect on the older adult's ability to communicate with others (Souza & Hoyer, 1996).

Many older adults use hearing aids. Recent technological improvements in hearing aids have made them more comfortable and effective, especially if they are properly

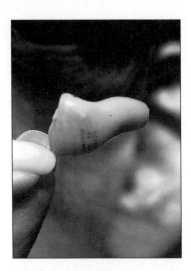 

This is the type of hearing aid that President Bill Clinton began wearing in October of 1997. Clinton, who was 51 years old at the time, complained of hearing loss ever since his days as Arkansas's governor. Note that it is virtually impossible to detect the President's hearing aid (right).

fitted by a professional. Some older adults must wear two hearing aids to correct for different degrees of hearing loss in each ear. If the aids are not properly balanced or if only one is used, the subtle differences in phase and intensity at the two ears, which enable sounds to be localized and identified, are lost. Localization of sounds helps us to attend to one conversation while ignoring another. When we don't do this well, both wanted and unwanted sounds combine and produce noise or confusion.

Deficits in hearing, like those associated with sight, may have a profound impact on an individual's sense of well-being as well as the ability to meet the demands of everyday life. Recently, Marsiske, Klumb, and Baltes (1997) examined the relationship between visual and auditory acuity and everyday functioning in a sample of 516 older adults between 70 and 103 years of age. A noteworthy aspect of this study was that the researchers measured two different facets of everyday functioning: basic living activities (e.g., eating, dressing, shopping, etc.) and discretionary social activities (e.g., socializing with friends, play cards, etc.). They hypothesized that sensory acuity would predict an individual's ability to perform basic living activities, but that intellectual and personality variables would predict the type and amount of a person's discretionary social activities. Surprisingly, Marsiske et al. (1997) found that sensory acuity explained most of the age-related variance in both aspects of everyday functioning. These results underscore the notion that sensory factors, more so than intellectual and personality variables, are powerful determinants of a person's sense of behavioral and social competence.

Taste, Smell, and Touch

Age-related declines in taste, smell, and tactile sensitivity also occur (Engen, 1977; Schiffman, 1977), although declines in these senses are not as dramatic or noticeable as those observed for vision and hearing. Declines in the sense of taste and smell affect one's enjoyment and intake of food (Whitbourne, 1996) and can also affect one's choice of diet. For example, some older adults suffer from nutritional deficiencies because of an increased desire for highly seasoned but nonnutritious "junk food."

Age-related changes in sensitivity to taste and smell affect dietary preference and may affect how much "hot sauce" we use.

The human tongue contains specialized receptors that detect four different tastes: sweet, salty, bitter, and sour. Bartoshuk, Rifkin, Marks, and Bars (1986) found that older adults were less sensitive than younger adults to all of the basic tastes. Many researchers have suggested that sensitivity to all tastes remains stable until the late fifties, when a steep decline in the ability to detect all tastes occurs (Whitbourne, 1996).

Changes in taste sensitivity are not responsible for all changes in eating behavior during older adulthood. Older adults may eat less because they don't want to bother to cook, shop, and clean up, or for other reasons such as loneliness (Schieber, 1992). Information about age-related changes in smell have been very difficult to reliably document (Engen, 1977; Whitbourne, 1996). This is because smell is one of the last senses to decline with age, and because smell is affected by a number of variables (e.g., health) that are correlated with age. Age deficits in smell may have disastrous effects. For example, Chalke, Dewhurst, and Ward (1958) reported that as many as 30 percent of adults over age 65 were not sensitive to the smell of lower concentrations of gas.

Age-related changes in touch have also been reported. Gescheider and colleagues (Gescheider, 1997; Gescheider, Bolanowski, Verillo, Hall, & Hoffman, 1994), for example, examined vibrotactile sensitivity (i.e., the ability to detect vibrations on the surface of the skin) in individuals between 8 and 87 years of age. They found substantial age-related declines in the detection of high-frequency stimulation but moderate declines in the detection of low-frequency stimulation. This suggests that certain types of sensory receptors such as Paciniam corpuscles are most adversely affected by the aging process. Corso (1977) has observed that, with aging, the touch sensitivity of the lower extremities (ankles, knees, etc.) is more impaired than that of the upper extremities (wrists, shoulders, etc.). Loss of tactile sensitivity by itself is not much of a problem for the typical older adult. It does become problematic, however, when it is combined with other severe sensory disorders.

Falling: The Leading Cause of Accidental Injury Among the Elderly

Among those over the age of 65, falling is the leading cause of accidental injury. For example, of the 200,000 hip fractures each year in the United States, more than 170,000 occur to those over the age of 65. The rate of mortality from falling increases directly with increased age and represents the seventh-leading cause of death in those over 75, surpassing even causes such as automobile accidents. About 25 percent of older people require intensive medical intervention and hospitalization from falls. Severe falls are associated with broken bones (fractures of the hip, wrist, and vertebrae), head injury, and multiple facial, skin, and hand lacerations.

Most falls occur in the homes of older people, especially in the living room or bedroom during the regular daytime routine, or while going downstairs. The institutionalized elderly are also at high risk of falling due to the many predisposing medical conditions that require institutional placement. Institutional falls are more common at night, as older people perhaps become disoriented and confused in unfamiliar surroundings. Newly admitted patients in institutions are particularly vulnerable. The causes of falling among the elderly represent a burgeoning area of research. Many studies suggest that the elderly who are most likely to experience severe injury or death from a fall are those who are just beginning to undergo physical and psychological decline and have not yet recognized their limitations. On the other hand, those elderly who are frequent fallers and have identified their problem are less likely to be seriously injured in a fall. The risk of falling has been found to be related to poor illumination, dark staircases, and loose rugs. Some of the physical conditions that contribute to falling are arthritis, loss of balance and equilibrium (presbystasis), weakness in the muscles that control coordination of the knees and ankles, impaired vision, impaired hearing (hearing provides critical feedback for walking), and diabetes (leading to reduced sensation in the legs). Several medications can even increase the risk of falling.

Why do falls lead to such severe injury in the elderly? First, because of the generalized age-related slowing of behavior, older people may not be as able as younger people to prepare themselves to break a fall. Second, the age-related phenomenon of osteoporosis, or thinning and weakening of the bones, may cause the spontaneous shattering of brittle, thinning bones (especially in the pelvis) in older people. This sudden breakage can actually cause a fall. Thus, falls can cause broken bones, and brittle or broken bones can cause falls.

Temperature, Pain, and Kinesthetic Senses

Older adults are less sensitive to temperature changes than are young adults (Schieber, 1992). Because older adults may be less able to detect changes in temperature, they are more susceptible to hypothermia, heatstroke, and frostbite. One of the age-related losses in sensory sensitivity, the sensitivity to pain, may have an advantage. Earlier studies have shown that older people are less sensitive to and suffer less from pain than do their younger counterparts (Kenshalo, 1977). Older adults tend to underreport low levels of pain and overrate higher-intensity pain (Harkins, Price, & Martinelli, 1986). Although decreased sensitivity to pain may help the elderly cope with disease and injury, it can be harmful if it masks injuries and illnesses that need to be treated. Importantly, a vast array of personality and cultural factors influence the reporting and experience of pain.

Simoneau and Liebowitz (1996) reviewed evidence that shows that the elderly are likely to have impaired kinesthesis. **Kinesthesis** refers to a person's ability to know where his or her body parts are as he or she moves through space; for example, being able to touch your nose when your eyes are closed. A reduced kinesthetic sense would make elderly adults more susceptible to falls (see Research Focus 3.2).

AGING AND PHYSICAL ABILITY

The physical skills of an individual usually peak between the early twenties and the midthirties. One of the major reasons for a decrease in physical performance during adulthood is a reduction in muscle strength. Muscular strength and the ability to maintain maximum muscular effort have both been found to decline steadily during middle adulthood. By age 30, about 70 of a man's 175 pounds are muscle. Over the next 40 years, he loses 10 pounds of that muscle as cells stop dividing and die. By age 45, the strength of a man's back muscles declines to approximately 96 percent of its maximum value, and by age 50, it declines to 92 percent. Most men in their late fifties can only do physical work at about 60 percent of the rate achieved by men who are 40. Much of this decline appears to be linked with such physiological changes as the thickening of the walls of the air sacs in the lungs, which hinders breathing, and the hardening of connective sheaths that surround muscles, which is linked with decreases in both oxygen and blood supply. All these age-related changes, because they have been identified for the most part by cross-sectional research, are confounded with a variety of other potent variables, such as changes in lifestyle and cohort differences in exercise habits. With exercise and training, individuals can reduce the rate of decline in various psychomotor and physical functions (Adrain, 1981; Rikli & Busch, 1986).

Simple actions that entail little, if any, effort are just as likely to slow down with aging as are complex behaviors that demand strength, endurance, and skill. For example, finger tapping and handwriting have been found to slow dramatically with age (Dixon, Kurzman, & Friesen, 1993). Salthouse (1985) noted that **psychomotor slowing** is probably the most reliable finding in the study of human aging. Older adults, because of the slowing of their motor performance, may be less able to adapt to the demands of a changing world than younger adults. According to Salthouse (1985):

> If the external environment is rapidly changing, the conditions that lead to the initiation of a particular behavior may no longer be appropriate by the time the behavior is actually executed by older adults. This could lead to severe problems in operating vehicles, controlling equipment, or monitoring displays. Despite some claims to the contrary . . . it appears that the speed of decision and response can be quite important in our modern automated society, and, consequently, the slowness of older adults may place them at a great disadvantage relative to the younger members of the population. (p. 401)

Although it is reasonable for individuals to expect age-related changes in health and physical functioning as they grow older, individual differences are the rule. To a very significant extent, we control our own health, and the manner by which we grow older. For example, regular exercise has many beneficial effects for the aging individual. Table 3.2 lists some of the structural changes that are associated with aging, the functional effects of these structural changes, and the beneficial or compensatory effects of exercise with regard to these changes.

The body's capacity for exercise in late adulthood is influenced by the degree to which the individual has kept his or her body physically fit at earlier points in the life cycle. It is not uncommon to find that older individuals are capable of performing in a very formidable manner compared with younger individuals (see Research Focus 3.3 for details).

TABLE 3.2

Physiological Decline Associated with Aging and the Possible Benefit of Regular Strength and Endurance Exercise

Structural Changes	Functional Effects	Effects of Exercise
Musculoskeletal System		

1. Muscular atrophy with decrease in both number and size of muscle fibers
2. Neuromuscular weakness
3. Demineralization of bones
4. Decline in joint function—loss of elasticity in ligaments and cartilage
5. Degeneration and calcification on articulating surface of joint
	1. Loss of muscle size
	2. Decline of strength
	3. Reduced range of motion
	4. Reduced speed of movement
	5. Joint stiffness
	6. Declining neuromotor performance
	7. Changes in posture
	8. Frequent cramping
	9. Gait characteristics affected:
	  a. Center of gravity
	  b. Span (height/arm length)
	  c. Stride length, speed
	  d. Width of stance
	10. Shrinkage in height
	11. Increased flexion at joints due to connective tissue change
		1. Increased strength of bones
		2. Increased thickness of articular cartilage
		3. Muscle hypertrophy
		4. Increased muscle strength
		5. Increased muscle capillary density
		6. Increased strength of ligaments and tendons

Respiratory System		
1. Hardening of airways and support tissue 2. Degeneration of bronchi 3. Reduced elasticity and mobility of the intercoastal cartilage	1. Reduced vital capacity with increased residual volume 2. Reduced O_2 diffusing capacity 3. Spinal changes lead to increased rigidity of the chest wall 4. Declining functional reserve capacity	1. Exercise has no chronic effect on lung volumes but may improve maximal ventilation during breathing exercise and breathing mechanics
Cardiovascular System		

1. Elastic changes in aorta and heart
2. Valvular degeneration and calcification
3. Changes in myocardium
  a. Delayed contractility and irritability
  b. Decline in oxygen consumption
  c. Increased fibrosis
  d. Appearance of lipofuscin
4. Increase in vagal control
	1. A diminished cardiac reserve
	2. Increased peripheral resistance
	3. Reduced exercise capacity
	4. Decrease in maximum coronary blood flow
	5. Elevated blood pressure
	6. Decreased maximal heart rate
		1. Increased heart volume and heart weight
		2. Increased blood volume
		3. Increase in maximal stroke volume and cardiac output
		4. Decreased arterial blood pressure
		5. Increase in maximal oxygen consumption
		6. Myocardial effects increased:
		  a. Mitochondrial size
		  b. Nuclei
		  c. Protein synthesis
		  d. Myosin synthesis
		  e. Capillary density
		7. Decreased resting heart rate

From Robert A. Wisewell, "Relaxation, Exercise, and Aging" in Handbook of Mental Health and Aging, edited by Birren/Sloane, © 1980, p. 945. Reprinted by permission of Prentice-Hall, Inc., Englewood Cliffs, NJ.

Aging and Peak Athletic Performance

Although peak levels of performance in running, swimming, and other athletic events is usually attained in young adulthood, age-related changes in athletic performance are much smaller than most individuals imagine. Furthermore, continued training by older athletes may help them display high levels of athletic competence in the face of age-related declines in physiological functioning (Schulz, Musa, Staszewski, & Siegler, 1994).

Ericsson and Crutcher (1990) reviewed a great deal of the research regarding age changes in swimming and running performance. These sports were chosen for analysis because (1) the distances of specific races within these sports have been fixed for approximately the last century, and (2) performance within these sports is measured objectively by specific units of time (minutes, seconds, etc.)—there is no subjective element in measuring performance in these sports, as there is in boxing or gymnastics. These attributes allowed researchers to make valid comparisons of changes in swimming and running performance from one historical era (the 1920s) to another (the 1980s).

Examination of the world records and Olympic gold medal performances in these sports from 1896 (the year of the first modern-day Olympic games) to the present revealed four major findings. First, over this time span, gold medalists and world record holders have generally achieved their feats during young adulthood, usually between 20 and 30 years of age. Second, world record and gold medal times have steadily and significantly decreased. Third, the shorter the distance of the race, the younger the age of the gold medalists and/or world record holders. Fourth, winners of shorter swimming events are becoming younger (in their early twenties), while the winners of longer running events such as the marathon are becoming older (in their late twenties to midthirties). For example, Carlos Lopes won the 1984 Olympic marathon at the age of 37.

Ericsson also examined age-related changes in maximum performance of well-trained athletes. Figures 3.C and 3.D show the best times as well as the average times achieved by swimmers between 25 and 75 years of age. Both of these figures show a decrease in performance with age. This decrease becomes more rapid, however, when the average performance of swimmers over 60 years of age is examined. Also of interest was the finding that the best performance of the over-65-year-old group equaled the average performance of swimmers about 40 years of age.

The findings of longitudinal studies by Letzelter, Jungeman, and Freitag (1986), and others suggest that athletes can maintain (and sometimes improve) their performance through middle adulthood and late adulthood. This occurs only if adults maintain (or increase) their levels of practice and training. Hagberg (1987) has argued that continued exercise is an important factor in minimizing the losses in aerobic power that are usually observed during adulthood. Aerobic power, which refers to the body's maximal ability to take in oxygen, is arguably the best predictor of performance in endurance events (e.g., long-distance running).

Box Figure 3.C Changes in the *best* race times for expert swimmers 25 to 70 years of age.

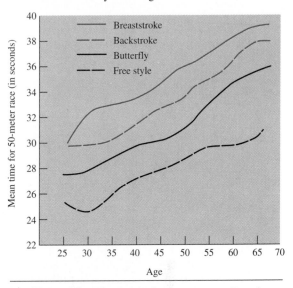

Box Figure 3.D Changes in the *average* race times for expert swimmers 25 to 70 years of age.

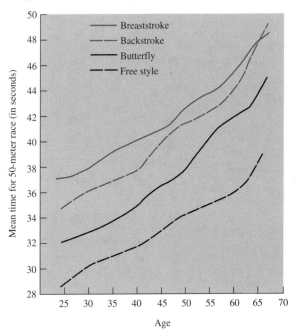

Changes in training methods are in part responsible for the steady decrease in world record times in running and swimming events over the last hundred years. Table 3.A compares the swimming times for several running events in the first modern-day Olympics that were held in 1896 and the best performances of "master" athletes in 1979. As can be seen in table 3.A there are a number of performances by master athletes that surpass the performance of these earlier (and younger) gold medalists—even in the marathon, a distance of 26 miles and 385 yards!

TABLE 3.A

Winning Times for Olympic Gold Medalists in 1896 and Best Times for Master Athletes in 1979

Event	Olympic Gold Medalists in 1896	Master Athletes in Different Age Groups in 1979			
		50-54	55-59	60-64	65-69
100m*	12.0	11.4	11.6	12.0	13.2
200m*	22.2	23.6	23.6	24.9	27.9
400m*	54.2	52.9	54.6	59.1	65.1
800m**	2:11	2:01	2:11	2:20	2:27
1,500m**	4:33	4:14	4:20	4:53	4:59
Marathon***	2:59	2:25	2:26	2:47	2:53

*event timed in seconds
**event timed in minutes and seconds
***event timed in hours and minutes
Source: Data from K. A. Ericsson, "Peak Performance and Age. An Examination of Peak Performance in Sports" in Successful Aging: Perspectives from the Behavioral Sciences, P. B. Baltes and M. M. Baltes (eds), Cambridge University Press, New York, NY.

BRAIN AGING

Age-related changes in the nervous system may have dramatic effects on the behavioral, cognitive, and personality functioning of the aging individual. Thus we turn our attention to a discussion of age changes in the human brain.

Major Components of the Brain

The major structures of the human brain along with some comments about the effects of aging on these structures are provided in figure 3.6. The **brain stem** is the oldest part of the brain. It begins as a swelling of the spinal cord and extends into the middle of the brain. It controls basic biological functions such as breathing and heart rate. The **ascending reticular activation system (ARAS),** a structure that originates within the brain stem and extends to the other portions of the brain, regulates an individual's state of con-

Figure 3.6 Age-related changes in brain structures.

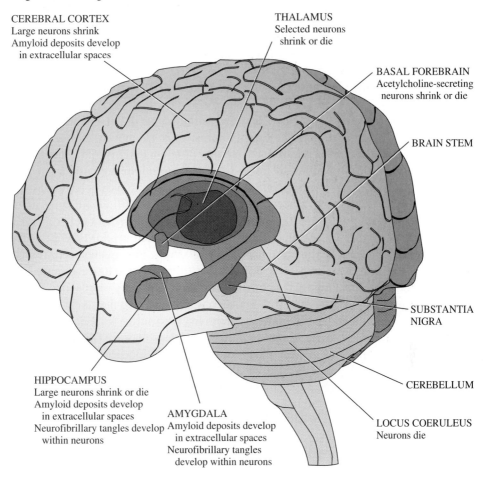

CEREBRAL CORTEX
Large neurons shrink
Amyloid deposits develop
   in extracellular spaces

THALAMUS
Selected neurons
   shrink or die

BASAL FOREBRAIN
Acetylcholine-secreting
   neurons shrink or die

BRAIN STEM

SUBSTANTIA
NIGRA

CEREBELLUM

LOCUS COERULEUS
Neurons die

HIPPOCAMPUS
Large neurons shrink or die
Amyloid deposits develop
   in extracellular spaces
Neurofibrillary tangles develop
   within neurons

AMYGDALA
Amyloid deposits develop
   in extracellular spaces
Neurofibrillary tangles
   develop within neurons

sciousness and level of arousal. Attached to the brain stem is the **cerebellum.** This structure helps maintain balance and posture and coordinate body movements. Also, memories for simple learned responses seem to be stored here (Woodruff-Pak, 1993).

The **limbic system** is a border area between the oldest part of the brain (the brain stem and cerebellum) and the newest part of the brain (the **cerebrum**). One part of the limbic system, called the hypothalamus, controls eating, drinking, body temperature, and sexual activity. Of primary interest to developmental neuropsychologists is a component of the limbic system called the **hippocampus.** A great deal of evidence suggests that the hippocampus plays a crucial role in memory processes (Schacter, 1996). Patients who suffer from amnesia and Alzheimer's disease, disorders in which memory failure is readily apparent, display significant damage to the hippocampus (Kolb & Whishaw, 1995). Furthermore, it has been suggested that biological changes in the hippocampus that accompany normal aging may be responsible, in part, for the declining memory abilities of older animals and humans (Moscovitch & Winocur, 1992; Scheibel, 1996).

The cerebrum is the largest, and evolutionarily the most recent, part of the brain. It totally covers the limbic system as well as significant portions of the brain stem and cerebellum. The cerebrum has several important features. First, it is divided down the middle into two halves or **hemispheres**—the right hemisphere and the left hemisphere. Second, the cerebral hemispheres are connected by a tract of nerve fibers called the **corpus callosum.** Third, the top covering of the cerebrum is called the **cortex.** The cortex, from the viewpoint of a psychologist, may be conceptualized as the most important part of the brain. In fact, it may be argued that it is the cortex which makes us "human" in that it has been identified as the source of personality, cognition, perception, communication, and creativity (Ornstein & Thompson, 1984).

The cortex may be divided into four different regions called **lobes,** where various psychological functions are housed. In the **frontal lobe** are basic aspects of personality and social behaviors, planning and execution of complex behavioral sequences, and control of motor movements. In the **temporal lobe** we find structures involved in the consolidation of long-term memories, the assigning of emotional properties to incoming experiences, and simple auditory sensation. The **parietal lobe** influences the construction of a spatial representation of one's body. Finally, the **occipital lobe** controls basic visual processing (Kolb & Whishaw, 1995). Despite its importance in human psychological functioning, the cortex is amazingly delicate, fragile, and thin. In fact, the cortex only consists of the top one-eighth inch covering the cerebrum.

As individuals age, they are more likely to suffer from damage or injury to the cortex. Also with aging, the brain becomes less plastic. This means that uninjured parts of the cortex are less likely to take over the functions of injured cortical areas. Damage to the elderly brain usually results from a stroke or a brain tumor. Strokes occur when brain tissue is deprived of oxygen. This deprivation may occur when a blood vessel in the brain becomes clogged, plugged, or broken. In general, damage to the left hemisphere results in **aphasia,** a breakdown or loss of an individual's language abilities. Damage to the right hemisphere, on the other hand, typically results in visual-spatial disorders. Adults with right hemisphere damage may experience **agnosia,** a failure to recognize familiar objects or faces. Or they become lost in familiar environments (even their own homes or neighborhoods) and may not be able to form a visual representation of all the objects (including their own bodies) in the left half of their visual field.

Neuronal Aging

The brain consists of a diverse array of neurons, glial cells, and blood vessels. A **neuron,** or nerve cell, is the basic unit of the brain and nervous system. Communication between neurons is responsible for all behavioral and psychological functions. Glial cells and blood vessels support, nourish, and help repair neurons. Every neuron has three major components: **soma, axon,** and **dendrites.** The axon is an elongated structure that relays signals to other neurons that are often a good distance away. The dendrites, which are typified by large branching arbors, receive signals from other neurons. The soma, or cell body, helps coordinate all of the processes that take place within the neuron. A sketch of a typical neuron is shown in figure 3.7.

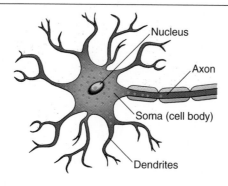

Figure 3.7 A typical neuron.

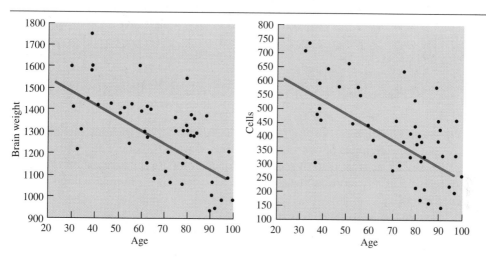

Figure 3.8 Relationship between age, brain weight, and brain cell counts.

Conventional wisdom suggests that overall brain weight as well as the number of neurons in the brain decreases with age (see figure 3.8). Reports of age-related neuronal death have been confirmed by postmortem or autopsy studies (Kemper, 1994). At the cortical level, these studies showed that neuronal loss is least likely to occur in sensorimotor areas such as occipital and parietal lobes and is most likely to be observed in those areas that control intelligence, memory, and abstract thinking, such as the frontal and temporal lobes. These studies also revealed a substantial amount of cell loss in subcortical areas, especially in certain parts of the limbic system that are central to memory, especially the hippocampus. See figure 3.9 for a photo of the dendrites of neurons in the hippocampus for different-aged individuals. Note that the conclusions derived from postmortem studies must be viewed with a great deal of caution. This is because most postmortem studies were conducted many decades ago when researchers underestimated the prevalence of Alzheimer's disease among older adults. Thus these studies may have inadvertently included many "diseased" brains in their "normal" sample (Albert & Moss, in press).

More recently, however, a number of researchers have argued that our traditional ideas concerning the severity of age-related neuronal death may be very much

Figure 3.9
Illustration of age differences in dendritic branching for healthy adults from middle age to very old age, and for an Alzheimer's patient. The illustrations are drawn from photographs of neurons from the hippocampus.

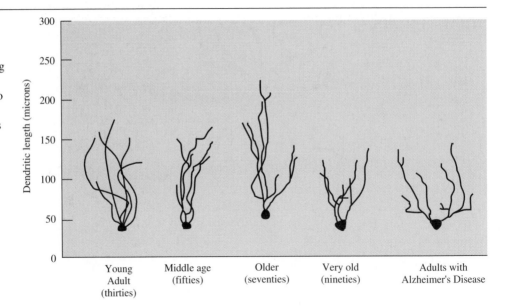

overblown (Wilkelgren, 1996). For example, Albert (1993) was one of the first to show that large numbers of neurons may shrink or atrophy, but not die, with increasing age. In fact, a great deal of recent evidence points to the conclusion that there may be little, if any, cortical neuronal loss associated with normal aging (Wilkelgren, 1996).

Neurons undergo changes in their internal architecture with aging. For example, the cytoplasm of particular cells of the hippocampus can begin to fill with tied or tangled bundles of protein filaments known as **neurofibrillary tangles.** The development of tangles during aging seems to indicate that certain proteins, particularly those of the cytoskeleton, or the internal walls of the cell, have been chemically modified in ways that impair the signaling efficiency of these neurons (Selkoe, 1992). Also, Albert (1993) has reported a large age-related decline in the amount of **white matter** (i.e., the fatty myelin sheath that surrounds and insulates long axons). Many scientists claim that age-related losses in white matter, especially in the frontal cortex, account for many of the cognitive declines older adults display (Wilkelgren, 1996).

The idea that significant numbers of cortical neurons do not die with advancing age opens up a number of exciting possibilities. For example, different types of drug therapies might be developed to prevent neuronal atrophy along with the shrinkage of white matter. This might result in increasing numbers of adults who would display enhanced levels of cognitive function into old age. As can be seen in figure 3.10, there is a massively complex network of interconnections among neurons, and there are large open spaces between neurons. With normal aging, the extracellular spaces of the hippocampus, cerebral cortex, and other brain regions gradually accumulate spherical deposits called **senile plaques** (Scheibel, 1996). These plaques are aggregates of a small molecule known as **beta-amyloid** protein. These plaques also accumulate in blood vessels in these regions of the brain.

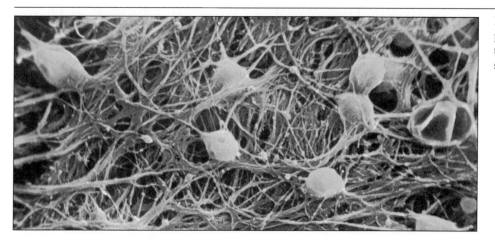

Figure 3.10 A 3-D photomicrograph of the interneuronal structure.

Another internal alteration is that neural cytoplasm in many parts of the brain becomes increasingly dotted with innumerable granules containing lipofuscin. **Lipofuscin** is a fluorescent pigment that is thought to derive from lipid-rich internal membranes that have been incompletely digested. Investigators disagree about whether lipofuscin has harmful effects on cell function.

Neurons communicate with each other by secreting chemical substances called **neurotransmitters.** Normal brain function is contingent on having normal amounts of neurotransmitters present in the brain. Too little (or too much) of a neurotransmitter may result in brain dysfunction and aberrant behavior. Scientists who study aging have focused on two important neurotransmitters: acetylcholine and dopamine. **Acetylcholine** is manufactured in the basal nucleus and travels along a cholinergic pathway to help neurons in the temporal lobe and hippocampus communicate with each other. Some researchers believe that a small reduction in acetylcholine is responsible for the memory lapses associated with normal aging, whereas a massive reduction in acetylcholine is responsible for the severe memory loss associated with Alzheimer's disease. **Dopamine** is manufactured in the cells that make up the substantia nigra and is sent along a dopaminergic pathway to neurons in the frontal cortex. Normal age-related reductions in dopamine may account for the fact that older adults cannot plan and execute motor activities (even very simple ones such as finger tapping) as quickly as younger adults. Age-related diseases which are typified by the loss of motor control, such as Parkinson's disease, are due to a massive reduction in the manufacture of dopamine.

Measuring the Aging Brain

Recent advances in brain imaging allow a noninvasive examination of the structure and function of the living human brain. The most obvious advantage of using an in vivo measure of brain aging is that we can select "healthy individuals" as research subjects. Thus noninvasive technologies help us disentangle the effects of age versus disease (or accident) on brain tissue to a much greater extent than postmortem studies.

The technique of **computerized axial tomography (CT scan)** allows a two- or three-dimensional representation of the human brain. The CT scan has revealed that the ventricles—the four cavities within the brain containing cerebrospinal fluid—enlarge with normal aging (Barron, Jacobs, & Kirkei, 1976). Some researchers (Albert & Stafford, 1988) have reported that CT changes are related to decrements in cognitive abilities.

Similar to the CT scan, but more informative, is the technique of **magnetic resonance imaging (MRI).** In this procedure, various regions of the brain are surrounded by a strong magnetic field and exposed to a specific radio-frequency pulse. Under these circumstances the stimulated brain tissue emits a signal that is transformed into an image by a computer. The MRI technique is so powerful that it can identify structural abnormalities in the brain that are as small as 1 millimeter. Recently, Naftali Raz and his associates (Raz et al., 1997) have used MRI to chart the differential aging of the human brain. The results of their research, which is depicted in figure 3.11, shows that age-related deterioration is most likely to occur in the frontal lobes and least likely to occur in posterior cortical zones. As a general rule, these findings suggest that aging is most likely to have an ill effect on higher-order executive functions and least likely to have a negative impact on basic perceptual processing.

Surprisingly, the MRI research, along with a number of more recent postmortem studies in both humans and monkeys (Albert & Moss, in press; West, Coleman, Flood, & Troncoso 1994), has established a relatively weak link between aging and reductions in the size of hippocampus. This may suggest that memory problems in older adults result from a breakdown in communication between the frontal cortex and hippocampus.

Unlike the CT scan and MRI, which depict brain anatomy, the technique of **positron-emission tomography (PET scan)** reveals the brain's actual metabolic activity by measuring changes in the amount of regional blood flow (rCBF). This is accomplished by injecting a research participant with a small amount of a radioactive isotope and determining, by the measurement of radioactive emissions, which parts of the brain

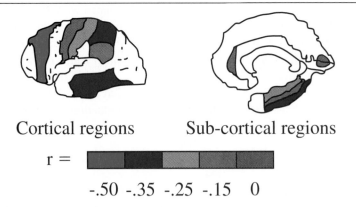

Figure 3.11
Differential aging of the cerebral cortex: A summary of MRI data. Larger negative correlations (the r values) are associated with greater amounts of deterioration in specific brain regions.

Cortical regions   Sub-cortical regions

r =

-.50 -.35 -.25 -.15   0

Differential Aging of the Cerebral Cortex:
A Summary of MRI Data

the isotope has traveled to via the vascular system. The underlying idea is that the most metabolically active parts of the brain will emit the highest levels of radioactivity. Age differences in PET data are similar to those yielded by the MRI methodology. For example, Waldemar (1995) concluded that age-related declines in blood flow are much more pronounced in the frontal cortex in comparison to the areas involved in basic sensory function, such as the occipital lobe. Grady and colleagues (1995) compared regional flow in younger and older adults when members of each age group tried to learn and remember a series of human faces. Results showed that impaired recognition performance in the older group may have been attributable to reduced flow to the frontal cortex during the encoding and retrieval phases of the experiment. Several other PET studies have documented age differences in rCBF when younger and older adults performed a variety of memory tasks. These studies will be discussed in greater detail in chapter 7.

It is also possible to measure the general electrical activity of the brain by means of an **electroencephalogram (EEG).** Research involving the EEG has yielded a number of important findings. For example, several different patterns of rhythmical electrical activity (i.e., brain waves) have been detected in the brain by using the EEG. Each of these waves has been related to a particular level or state of consciousness. The **alpha rhythm** is the dominant rhythm displayed by the brain and is linked with alert wakefulness. The alpha rhythm contrasts with the faster **beta rhythm,** which characterizes an individual during a period of focused thinking and problem solving. The **delta rhythm** is the slowest of all of the different brain waves. It appears when individuals enter the deepest, most restful component of the sleep cycle.

Bashore (1993) examined age-related changes in a particular brain rhythm called the **P300 brain wave.** The P300 is an event-related response (ERP) that occurs somewhere between 300 to 500 milliseconds after a stimulus has been presented to an individual. The onset of the P300 seems to signify that a person has recognized a stimulus and has evaluated its psychological significance. Bashore (1993) and others have shown that older and younger groups of adults differ much more on measures of physical reaction time to a stimulus (e.g., pressing a button when a particular stimulus appears on a computer screen) than to the timing of the P300 brain wave. This means that reaction-time tasks may lead researchers to overestimate the extent to which changes in central processes cause behavioral slowing in late adulthood. In contrast, the P300 data suggests that the age-related slowing of reaction time is due to decrements in peripheral processes (e.g., slower response output) in combination with the adoption of a conservative response bias (putting greater emphasis on accuracy than speed).

Another point to consider is that the brain, like any other organ in the body, may be "overengineered" in that it possesses a significant reserve capacity (just like the heart, lungs, kidneys, etc. possess a reserve capacity that is drawn upon as the individual ages). See Research Focus 3.4 for more information about this intriguing idea.

ALZHEIMER'S DISEASE

Perhaps the most devastating age-related brain disorder is **Alzheimer's disease (AD).** The symptoms of AD were first described by a German physician, Alois Alzheimer, in 1907. Alzheimer's disease is a form of **dementia** whose primary symptom is the

Brain Reserve Capacity and Aging

Earlier in this chapter, we emphasized that all of the vital organs in the human body possess a reserve capacity that we draw upon as we age. Now, we focus our attention on the idea of brain reserve capacity (BRC) as presented by Paul Satz (1993). Satz used the construct of BRC as a means of explaining interindividual variability and intraindividual change in "protection from" and "vulnerability to" cognitive impairment due to brain damage. He maintained that individual differences in BRC determine the threshold levels at which particular neurological diseases produce observable symptoms, and that BRC may be indexed by direct measures such as brain size, neuron counts, dendritic structure, brain metabolic activity, EEG patterns, and so on.

Importantly, Satz presented a wide range of evidence that showed that high levels of BRC protect older adults from the deleterious effects of neurological disorders such as Alzheimer's disease (AD). For example, consider the following study conducted by Katzman and colleagues (1988). They performed a postmortem investigation in which they counted the number of senile plaques and neurofibillary tangles in the brains of 137 residents of a skilled nursing facility. Some of these patients were diagnosed as suffering from AD (demented group), whereas another cluster of residents (the index group) was chosen for examination because they displayed preserved cognitive function—individuals in the index group scored in the top 20 percent of all the residents in the facility on various measures of mental ability. Surprisingly, the researchers found that

members of the index group displayed pronounced amounts of plaques and tangles. In fact, the senile plaque count in the index group was approximately 80 percent of that of the demented group! What could have accounted for the preserved level of cognitive function in the index group given the significant amount of brain damage they displayed? Katzman and colleagues noted that, on average, the members of the index group had heavier brains than those in the demented group. In fact, they concluded that the individuals in the index group "may have had incipient AD but . . . started with larger brains and more large neurons and thus might be said to have had a greater reserve" (p. 138).

The notion that brain size is a measure of BRC comes from recent research conducted by Willerman, Schultz, Rutledge, and Bigler (1994) that has used the technique of MRI. They showed that MRI measures of overall brain size were positively correlated with IQ test scores. Furthermore, Haier and colleagues (1988) have concluded that, based on a number of PET studies, there is an inverse relationship between neuropsychological test performance and the brain's metabolic activity. This suggests that "smart" brains expend less effort when they perform difficult intellectual tasks. Also, it has been discovered (Schafer, 1982) that individuals with high IQs are likely to exhibit large changes in EEG patterns to novel stimuli but small changes in EEG to familiar stimuli. In contrast, individuals with low IQs are not as likely to display a larger discrepancy in EEG patterns to novel versus familiar stimuli.

---

deterioration of mental functioning. Dementia represents an abnormal clinical condition. It signifies a type of mental disorder that is not part of the primary aging process. **Senility** is a term used by the general public to describe the severe mental deterioration displayed by some older adults; as used by the common person in everyday discussions, senility is nearly identical in meaning to the medical term dementia. Unfortunately, many members of the general public equate senility with senescence. They mistakenly believe and perpetuate an unfounded myth that normal aging is always accompanied by severe mental deterioration and disorganization.

Description of Alzheimer's Disease

AD is a degenerative brain disease that is the most common cause of cognitive failure in older adulthood (Selkoe, 1992). The elderly person with AD loses the ability to remember, recognize, and reason. In the final stages of the disease, the afflicted person develops profound physical as well as mental disabilities and typically needs institutional care. At present, there is no cure for this disease. It has been estimated that AD is the fourth leading cause of death for adults in the United States (Katzman, 1986) and

Since brain size and metabolic activity correlate with IQ (and IQ correlates with education level), it comes as no surprise that Satz (1993) has identified IQ and educational level as indirect measures of BRC. This is consistent with a large body of research that has shown that high IQ performance is predictive of a longer life span and reduced rates of physical illness and mental disorder (Gurland, 1981).

Satz's (1993) account of BRC represents a useful contribution to the field of neuropsychology. However, Rybash and Hoyer (1996a) have argued that there are a number of unanswered questions concerning the relationship between BRC and aging. Some of these questions are as follows:

1. Does the predictive validity of indirect measures of BRC vary by chronological age? It may be that qualitatively different indirect measures will be predictive of BRC for individuals at different points within the adult life span. Sensory function, for example, may represent a valid indirect measure of BRC for adults 85 years of age or older but not for younger adults. Consistent with this hypothesis, it has been reported that a strong connection exists between sensory acuity and psychometric intelligence among the oldest-old and that a great deal of sensory loss in advanced old age is due to deterioration at the cortical rather than receptor level (Baltes & Lindenberger, 1997; Lindenberger & Baltes, 1994).

2. Are selected indirect measures of BRC differentially predictive of symptom onset for age-related neurological disorders? Rather than exploring the predictive validity of a global indirect measure of BRC (e.g., IQ or educational level), it might be more fruitful to identify unique indices of BRC for different neurological disorders. For example, Bondi et al. (1994) showed that performance on simple memory tasks, but not more complex tasks that measured frontal lobe function (or even educational level), predicted the occurrence of AD in older adults who were family history positive for this disorder.

3. Does BRC protect an individual from the effects of "normal" aging? Satz (1993) focused on whether BRC shields an individual from age-related neurological diseases. Of central importance to cognitive researchers, however, is the question of whether BRC serves to attenuate the effects of normal aging on cognitive function.

4. Are there developmental as well as individual differences in the modifiability of BRC? It is important to determine whether certain types of individuals are most likely to benefit from intervention programs that boost BRC? For example, does the modifiability of BRC in individuals depend on such factors as age, educational level, intelligence, health status, and so on?

What other questions can you generate about the construct of BRC and aging?

---

that approximately 4 million people suffered from AD in the United States in 1996 (Marx, 1996). Given the fact that the population of the United States, as well as most Westernized societies, is gradually aging, AD will become still more prevalent in the future and the cost of caring for AD patients will rise dramatically.

In the past, it was thought that AD was a neurological disease that afflicted an exceptionally small number of middle-aged adults. Consequently, it was categorized as a type of "presenile dementia." It was believed that dementia in older adults was caused by vascular disorders such as cerebral arteriosclerosis (i.e., a hardening of the arteries that feed the brain). In the late 1960s and early 1970s, however, it was discovered that the symptoms and causes of dementia in both middle-aged and elderly adults were identical (Wurtman, 1985). Dementia in both age groups was accompanied by the same neurological abnormalities. This finding revolutionized our ideas about the prevalence and seriousness of AD. Scientists began to realize that AD in old age had been misdiagnosed and misunderstood for an extremely long time. Table 3.3 provides a recent description of some of the most up-to-date facts we know about AD as well as some of the common warning signs of AD.

TABLE 3.3

Alzheimer's Disease: Stats and Facts

A Look at the Numbers

Alzheimer's disease is a progressive, degenerative disease of the brain, and the most common form of dementia. Some things you should know about AD:

- Approximately 4 million Americans have AD. Nineteen million Americans say they have a family member with AD, and 37 million know someone with AD.

- 14 million Americans will have AD by the middle of the next century unless a cure or prevention is found.

- Alzheimer's disease is the fourth-leading cause of death among adults.

- One in 10 persons over 65 and nearly half of those over 85 have AD, and increasingly it is found in people in their 40s and 50s.

- A person with AD can live from 3 to 20 years or more from the onset of symptoms.

- AD costs society approximately $100 billion a year. Neither Medicare nor private health insurance covers the long-term type of care most patients need.

- Home care costs an estimated $47,000 annually; typically, $12,000 of the cost is paid for by insurance, and the remainder by families and other informal caregivers.

- Half of all nursing home patients suffer from AD or a related disorder. The average cost for a patients care in a nursing home is $36,000 per year, but can exceed $70,000 per year in some areas of the country.

- The federal government spent approximately $311 million for Alzheimer's research in 1995. This represents $1 for every $321 the disease now costs society. The federal investment in heart disease, cancer, and AIDs is four to seven times higher.

- More than seven of ten people with Alzheimer's disease live at home and are cared for by family and friends.

For more statistical information, contact the Benjamin B. Green-Field Library at the Alzheimer's Association at (312) 335-9602. Also try *the Alzheimer's web site*. The official web site of the Alzheimer's Association is located at *www.alz.org*.

Is It Alzheimer's?
Warning Signs You Should Know

Your wife always misplaces her keys. But last Tuesday, she couldn't remember what they were for.
Your grandfather likes to take daily strolls around the neighborhood. But four times in the past month he's gotten lost and couldn't find his way home without help from a neighbor.
Your favorite uncle can't remember your name or the names of your husband or children.

The memory loss, confusion, and disorientation described in these examples are symptoms of dementing illness. The most common dementing illness is Alzheimer's disease.

Unfortunately, many people fail to recognize that these symptoms indicate something is wrong. They may mistakenly assume that such behavior is a normal part of the aging process; it isn't. Or symptoms may develop gradually and go unnoticed for a long time. Sometimes people refuse to act even when they know something's wrong.

It's important to see a physician when you recognize these symptoms. Only a physician can properly diagnose the person's condition, and sometimes symptoms are reversible. Even if the diagnosis is Alzheimer's disease, help is available to learn how to care for a person with dementia and where to find assistance for yourself, the caregiver.

Ten Warning Signs

To help you know what warning signs to look for, the Alzheimer's Association has developed a checklist of common symptoms (some of them also may apply to other dementing illnesses). Review the list and check the symptoms that concern you. If you notice several symptoms, the individual with the symptoms should see a physician for a complete examination.

1. **Memory Loss That Affects Job Skills**
   It is normal to occasionally forget assignments, colleagues' names, or a business associate's telephone number and remember them later. Those with a dementia, such as Alzheimer's disease, may forget things more often, and not remember them later.

2. **Difficulty Performing Familiar Tasks**
   Busy people can be so distracted from time to time that they may leave the carrots on the stove and only remember to serve them at the end of the meal. People with Alzheimer's disease could prepare a meal and not only forget to serve it, but also forget they made it.

3. **Problems with Language**
   Everyone has trouble finding the right word sometimes, but a person with Alzheimer's disease may forget simple words or substitute inappropriate words, making his or her sentence incomprehensible.

4. **Disorientation of Time and Place**
   It's normal to forget the day of the week or your destination for a moment. But people with Alzheimer's disease can become lost on their own street, not knowing where they are, how they got there, or how to get back home.

5. **Poor or Decreased Judgment**
   People can become so immersed in an activity that they temporarily forget the child they're watching. People with Alzheimer's disease could forget entirely the child under their care. They may also dress inappropriately, wearing several shirts or blouses.

6. **Problems with Abstract Thinking**
   Balancing a checkbook may be disconcerting when the task is more complicated than usual. Someone with Alzheimer's disease could forget completely what the numbers are and what needs to be done with them.

7. **Misplacing Things**
   Anyone can temporarily misplace a wallet or keys. A person with Alzheimer's disease may put things in inappropriate places: an iron in the freezer, or a wristwatch in the sugar bowl.

8. **Changes in Mood or Behavior**
   Everyone becomes sad or moody from time to time. Someone with Alzheimer's disease can exhibit rapid mood swings—from calm to tears to anger—for no apparent reason.

9. **Changes in Personality**
   People's personalities ordinarily change somewhat with age. But a person with Alzheimer's disease can change drastically, becoming extremely confused, suspicious, or fearful.

10. **Loss of Initiative**
    It's normal to tire of housework, business activities, or social obligations, but most people regain their initiative. The person with Alzheimer's disease may become very passive and require cues and prompting to become involved.

The Atlanta Alzheimer's web pages were constructed by Marc Sirkin

Some of the most important findings about AD concern the types of neuronal changes that appear in patients with this disorder. Specifically, AD patients have an excessive number of senile plaques and neurofibrillary tangles. Remember that the presence of plaques and tangles represent two of the most prominent features of normal aging (i.e., senescence). This suggests that there is a quantitative, rather than a qualitative, difference between the brains of the healthy elderly and those with AD— the brains of AD patients have more plaques and tangles than those contained in normal aged brains. These plaques and tangles are spread throughout the brain but are most concentrated in the hippocampus as well as the frontal and temporal cortices (Scheibel, 1996; Scheibel & Wechsler, 1986).

AD is difficult to diagnose since a number of other biological and psychological disorders closely imitate the symptoms of AD. For example, individuals who are clinically depressed or who suffer from curable dementias display some of the same behavioral symptoms as AD patients (Heston & White, 1983; Zarit & Zarit, 1983). The only way to make a certain diagnosis of AD is by an autopsy (Whitehouse, 1993). In this procedure, brain tissue is analyzed microscopically to determine the presence and location of excessive plaques, tangles, and cell loss. Prior to a patient's death and autopsy, clinicians make the diagnosis of AD by exclusion of other causes (i.e., all other diagnoses are ruled out and nothing else is known that could explain the symptoms).

Stages of Alzheimer's Disease

In AD there seems to be a predictable, progressive decline in specific areas of psychological, physiological, and social functioning. Reisberg and his colleagues (Reisberg & Bornstein, 1986; Reisberg, Ferris, & Franssen, 1985) have developed the **Functional Assessment Staging System (FAST)** and the **Global Deterioration Scale** to categorize these losses. The advantage of such an approach is that it provides clinicians and family members with the information necessary to provide appropriate intervention and to identify the projected course of the disease. Table 3.4 contains a description of FAST along with the major clinical manifestations of AD. Note that the early stages (1, 2, and 3) are not specifically descriptive of AD. For example, stages 1 and 2 are included to inform professionals of the typical patterns seen in normal aging. Stage 3 describes an early confused state that may be characteristic of a number of possible disorders.

Causes of Alzheimer's Disease

At present, no one knows the actual cause of AD. Nevertheless, a number of different theories have been advanced to account for the development of this disease. One of the most influential theories of AD has been termed the *cholinergic hypothesis,* which states that AD is caused by decrements in the neurotransmitter acetylcholine. This theory is based on the research finding that the neurons in the hippocampus and temporal lobe are among the most negatively affected parts of the brain in AD patients, and that these brain structures employ acetylcholine as their primary neurotransmitter. Importantly, Whitehouse, Price, Clark, Coyle, and DeLong (1981) showed that there is a substantial reduction in the number of neurons in the basal forebrain that manufacture acetylcholine in patients with AD, and that the brains of individuals with AD contain significantly less acetylcholine than those of normal individuals. Beyond any doubt, the cholinergic hypothesis has generated a great deal of important research. The major drawback of this approach, however, is that it is difficult to tell whether a reduction in acetylcholine is a cause or an effect of AD.

Other researchers have put forth a *genetic hypothesis* based on the discovery that one type of AD, called early-onset familial AD (usually referred to as FAD), runs in families. In an important study, St. George-Hyslop et al. (1987) discovered that FAD is associated with a defective gene located on chromosome 21. Furthermore, Tanzi et al. (1987) found that the gene responsible for the production of amyloid (the core material of senile plaques) is also located on chromosome 21. This is interesting, since it has been well documented that nearly every individual suffering from Down's syndrome (most frequently related to extra chromosome material on the 21st pair) begins to develop the biochemical and psychological symptoms of AD by about age 40 (Kosik, 1992; Raskind & Peskind, 1992). Thus, the excessive amyloid deposition in the brain and accumulation of senile plaques in both AD and Down's syndrome patients may have a common origin—chromosome 21. This is consistent with the finding that a mutation in a gene on chromosome 21 has been found to be responsible for encoding an **amyloid precursor protein (APP).** APP is the chemical substance that underlies the manufacture of amyloid, which is the core material of senile plaques. However, as Jarvik (1987) has noted, the genes responsible for the production of APP and Down's syndrome are positioned in very different locations on chromosome 21. Thus, the specific relationship between AD, amyloid production, and Down's syndrome is still a genetic mystery.

More recently, it has been shown that mutations in the gene on chromosome 21 that manufacture APP underlie a relatively small number of cases of FAD (Selkoe, 1995). In the vast majority of instances, FAD is related to the presenilin-1 and presenilin-2 genes, which are located on chromosomes 1 and 14, respectively (Rogaev et al., 1995; Sherrington et al., 1995). In contrast, the more common, or late-occurring, form of AD seems to be related to the function of the apolipoprotein E gene, which is located on chromosome 19 (Corder et al., 1993). Thus there seem to be several genetic routes that may lead to the symptoms of AD. And, as Dewji & Singer (1996) have noted, it remains to be determined how mutations in any of the aforementioned genes can accelerate the production and formation of senile plaques that are the hallmark of AD.

One of the most fascinating longitudinal studies designed to learn more about the neurological correlates of AD is the Nun Study. Research Focus 3.5 presents information about this research project and one of its most prominent participants, Sister Mary.

Treatment of Alzheimer's Disease

Because we don't know the specific cause of AD, it has been difficult to develop a single effective treatment that cures, delays, or prevents its onset. However, it must be emphasized that since the major symptoms of AD do not appear until very late life, delaying the onset of the disease by five years could reduce the number of afflicted

TABLE 3.4

Global Deterioration Scale for Age-Associated Cognitive Decline and Alzheimer's Disease

GDS Stage	Clinical Phase	Clinical Characteristics	Diagnosis
1. No cognitive decline	Normal	No subjective complaints of memory deficit; no memory deficit evidence on clinical interview.	Normal
2. Very mild cognitive decline	Forgetfulness	Subjective complaints of memory deficit, most frequently in the following areas: (a) forgetting where one has placed familiar objects; (b) forgetting names one formerly knew well. No objective evidence of memory deficit on clinical interview; no objective deficits in employment or social situations; appropriate concern with respect to symptomatology.	Normal for age
3. Mild cognitive decline	Early confusional	Earliest clear-cut deficits; manifestations in more than one of the following areas: (a) patient may have gotten lost when traveling to an unfamiliar location; (b) coworkers become aware of patient's relatively poor performance; (c) word- and name-finding deficits become evident to intimates; (d) patient may read a passage or a book and retain relatively little material; (e) patient may demonstrate decreased facility in remembering names upon introduction to new people; (f) patient may have lost or misplaced an object of value; (g) concentration deficit may be evident on clinical testing. Objective evidence of memory deficit obtained only when an intensive interview conducted by a trained diagnostician; decreased performance in demanding employment and social settings; denial begins to become manifest in patient; mild to moderate anxiety accompanies symptoms.	Compatible with possible incipient Alzheimer's disease in a minority of cases
4. Moderate cognitive decline	Late confusional	Clear-cut deficit on careful clinical interview; deficit manifest in the following areas: (a) decreased knowledge of current and recent events; (b) may exhibit some deficit in memory of personal history; (c) concentration deficit elicited on serial subtractions; (d) decreased ability to travel, handle finances, and so on. Frequently no deficit in the following areas: (a) orientation to time and person; (b) recognition of familiar persons and faces; (c) ability to travel to familiar locations. Inability to perform complex tasks; denial is dominant defense mechanism; flattening of affect and withdrawal from challenging situations.	Mild Alzheimer's disease

Stage		Description	
5. Moderately severe cognitive decline	Early dementia	Patients can no longer survive without some assistance; patients are unable during interview to recall a major relevant aspect of their current lives; for example, their address or telephone number of many years, the names of close members of their family (such as grandchildren), the name of the high school or college they attended. Frequently some disorientation to time (date, day of week, season) or to place; an educated person may have difficulty counting backward from forty by fours or from twenty by twos. Persons at this stage retain knowledge of many major facts regarding themselves and others; they invariably know their own name and generally know their spouse's and children's names; they require no assistance with toileting or eating, but may have some difficulty choosing the proper clothing to wear.	Moderate Alzheimer's disease
6. Severe cognitive decline	Middle dementia	May occasionally forget the name of the spouse upon whom they are entirely dependent for survival; are largely unaware of all recent events and experiences in their lives; retain some knowledge of their past lives, but this is very sketchy. Generally unaware of their surroundings, the year, the season, and so on; may have difficulty counting from ten backward and, sometimes, forward; require some assistance with activities of daily living, for example, may become incontinent, require travel assistance but occasionally display ability to travel to familiar locations; diurnal rhythm frequently disturbed; almost always recall their own name; frequently continue to be able to distinguish familiar from unfamiliar persons in their environment. Personality and emotional changes occur; these are quite variable and include: (a) delusional behavior (for example, patients may accuse their spouse of being an impostor, may talk to imaginary figures in the environment, or to their own reflections in the mirror); (b) obsessive symptoms (for example, person may continually repeat simple cleaning activities); (c) anxiety symptoms, agitation, and even previously nonexistent violent behavior may occur; (d) cognitive abulia (that is, loss of willpower because individual cannot carry a thought long enough to determine a purposeful course of action).	Moderately severe Alzheimer's disease
7. Very severe cognitive decline	Late dementia	All verbal abilities are lost; frequently there is no speech at all—only grunting; incontinent of urine; requires assistance toileting and feeding; loses basic psychomotor skills (for example, ability to walk); it appears the brain no longer is able to tell the body what to do.	Severe Alzheimer's disease

From Reisberg, B., Ferris, S. H., de Leon, M. J., and Crook, T., "The Global Deterioration Scale for Assessment of Primary Degenerative Dementia" in American Journal of Psychiatry, 139: 1136–1139, 1982. Adapted with permission.

89

The Nun Study and Sister Mary

In the early 1990s, David Snowdon and other scientists at the University of Kentucky's Sanders-Brown Center on Aging began an ambitious longitudinal study of 678 nuns who belonged to the School Sisters of Notre Dame. The nuns who participated in this study lived in various parts of the United States and averaged 85 years of age (age range: 72 to 102) when the research was first initiated. All of the participants are evaluated regularly on various tasks of cognitive ability. And, upon death, each participant has agreed to donate her brain for an in-depth neuropathological examination. Thus the overarching goal of the Nun Study is to examine the relationship between cognitive ability and neuropathological evidence of AD.

One way to gain new information in a research project such as this is to analyze data from the entire sample of participants. Another strategy, however, is an intense examination of the data obtained from a single participant. Snowdon (1997) presented some very provocative findings obtained from one of the most exceptional individuals in the Nun Study—Sister Mary. Sister Mary was born in 1892 in Philadelphia to working-class parents. After graduating from the eighth grade she entered the School Sisters of Notre Dame convent in Baltimore and took her religious vows five years later. With her eight grade education she began teaching the seventh and eight grade in various schools throughout the eastern United States when she was 19 years old. After taking summer courses over a 22-year time span she received her high school diploma in 1931 when she was 41 years old. (She maintained an A average throughout her studies with her highest grade, 100, in algebra!) She retired from teaching at age 84 but continued to be active in the religious community and was very much concerned about world affairs. With regard to her "retirement" she remarked that: "I only retire at night." In 1990, at the age of 98, she decided to join the Nun Study and donate her body to science. Snowdon (1997) indicates that Sister Mary described that day as "one of the happiest days of my life."

Sister Mary was 101.1 years of age when her cognitive abilities were last assessed and she died 8 months later at the age of 101.7 years. Thus she became one of the 118 sisters whose brain tissue has been analyzed by researchers at the Sanders-Brown Center on Aging.

To grasp Sister Mary's intellectual function at 101 years of age please consult figure 3.E and table 3.B. As you can see, Sister Mary scored just as good or better than the other sisters (who were much younger and more highly educated) on all of the cognitive measures. Most interesting was her score of 27 on the Mini-Mental Status Exam. This is a remarkable score given that she was 101 years of age at the time of assessment, had less formal education than 85 percent of the other sisters in the Nun Study, and was examined less than a year before her death. (The Mini-Mental Status Exam is a brief test that is used to help make a diagnosis of AD. The average score for well-functioning, nondemented older adults is between 24 to 30.) Another point to consider is that if we consider Sister Mary's age and years of formal education relative to that of the other sisters, we would make mathematical predictions that all of her cognitive scores would be much lower than the norm. For example, table 3.B shows that we would predict Sister Mary's Mini-Mental Status Exam score should be 4!

In contrast to her excellent level of cognitive function, neuropathological examination revealed that her brain contained an astonishing number of the classic neuropathological lesions associated with AD: neurofibrillary tangles and senile plaques (for details see table 3.C). In fact, Snowdon (1997) has commented: "Although Sister Mary was not the first to live to a very old age with intact cognitive function, she may have been the first to do so in the presence of such abundant Alzheimer's Disease lesions" (p. 155). Sister Mary's low brain weight (870 grams) suggests that she did not avoid the symptoms of AD because of a large surplus of brain reserve capacity as we discussed in Research Focus 3.4. Instead, the type and location of the tangles and plaques in her brain suggests that she may have had a relatively benign form of AD. This claim is consistent with one of the major findings of the Nun Study: The best predictor of demented cognitive function is the presence of neurofilbrillary tangles in the neocortex (which were almost absent in Sister Mary's brain), whereas the worst predictors of demented

individuals by 50 percent (Marx, 1996)! Thus, scientists are extremely interested in developing drug treatment alternatives. One approach to treat some of the cognitive symptoms of AD (memory loss, confusion, and so on) involves the neurotransmitter acetylcholine. Initially, there were two variations to this approach. The first variation was based on the idea that the symptoms of AD should lessen if patients could produce more acetylcholine. This led physicians to advise patients with AD to eat foods rich in choline because choline is a food substance that the brain transforms into acetylcholine. Unfortunately, this approach has not produced any significant changes in functioning

Box Figure 3.E Age and Mini-Mental State Exam Score and best fit regression line in 678 participants in the Nun Study.
From: Snowden, D. A. (1997). Aging and Alzheimer's Disease: Lessons from the Nun Study. The Gerontologist, *37, 152.*

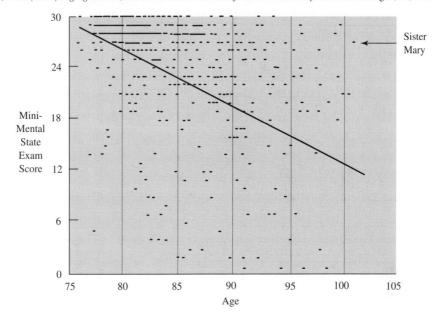

cognitive function are the presence of diffuse plaques in neo-cortex and hippocampus (which were extremely abundant in Sister Mary's brain). This leads to the more general conclusion that the most severe form of AD manifests itself in those indi-viduals with numerous neocortical tangles who possess low reserve capacity (i.e., low brain weight).

To be sure, we will learn much more about the relationship between cognitive function and neuropathological lesions as the Nun Study progresses and more data are collected and analyzed. At a more basic level, however, it seems that in order to gain more knowledge about AD, "we need more people like Sister Mary who are willing to make sacrifices. Sister Mary did not benefit directly from participating in the Nun Study, but her friends and family knew that she felt better for doing it. She was willing to lay out her life, her cognitive function, and her brain in all their details. Her only request was that we call her Sister Mary. She did not want to become a celebrity. She did not want accolades. She only wanted to help younger people who would one day reach old age. Surely there are many others who are willing to leave such a legacy" (Snowdon, 1997, p. 156).

among AD patients. More recently, the National Institutes of Health and the National Institutes of Aging have funded large-scale studies that are examining the effects of estrogen, the female sex hormone, on AD. For example, the Women's Health Initiative Study will ultimately include 165,000 women between the ages of 50 and 79 and will determine if estrogen replacement therapy initiated at menopause can prevent (or delay) the onset of AD. Note that a much smaller five-year longitudinal study already conducted by Tang and colleagues (1995) showed that 2.7 percent of older women who took estrogen developed AD compared with 8.4 percent who did not take estrogen. It

TABLE 3.B

Cognitive Function Test Scores for Sister Mary and the Other Sisters Who Died in the Nun Study

	Cognitive Test							
	Mini-Mental State Exam	Boston Naming	Object Naming	Verbal Fluency	Word List Memory	Delayed Word Recall	Word Recognition	Constructional Praxis
Sister Mary's actual score	27	9	8	8	10	5	8	9
Unadjusted mean in other sisters	17	7	7	8	10	3	5	6
Sister Mary's predicted score based on the other sisters	4	2	2	1	0	0	1	2
P-value for difference between actual and predicted score	0.01	0.05	0.05	0.09	0.09	0.03	0.02	0.02

Note: Predicted scores were adjusted for days between the exam and death, age at time of the exam, and attained education. P-value was based on the Student test, and was a test of the hypothesis that Sister Mary's scores were higher than those predicted based on the scores of the 117 other sisters who died.
Source: Snowdon, D. A. (1997). Aging and Alzheimer's disease: Lessons from the Nun Study. The Gerontologist, 37, 152.

TABLE 3.C

Alzheimer's Disease Lesion Counts and Brain Weight in Sister Mary and the Other Sisters Who Died in the Nun Study

	Cognitive Test						
	Neurofibrillary Tangles in Neocortex	Neurofibrillary Tangles in Hippocampus	Neuritic Plaques in Neocortex	Neuritic Plaques in Hippocampus	Diffuse Plaques in Neocortex	Diffuse Plaques in Hippocampus	Brain Weight in Grams
Sister Mary's actual value	1	57	3	6	179	32	870
Unadjusted mean in other sisters	11	20	15	3	92	7	1120
Sister Mary's predicted value based on the other sisters	14	22	10	1	55	4	1007
P-value for difference between actual and predicted values	0.59	0.14	0.60	0.42	0.02	0.001	0.24

Note: Predicted values were adjusted for age at death and attained education. P-value was based on the Student test, and was a test of the hypothesis that Sister Mary's values were different from those predicted based on the values of the other sisters who died. Means were based on 110 to 116 sisters (since lesion counts were not possible in some sisters because a brain infarction had obliterated a specific brain region, and brain weight was unavailable for one sister).
Source: Snowdon, D. A. (1997). Aging and Alzheimer's disease: Lessons from the Nun Study. The Gerontologist, 37, 153.

seems that estrogen facilitates the production of acetylcholine and also helps to build strong connections between neurons.

The second variation of the acetylcholine approach was based on the theory that patients' AD symptoms should dissipate if they are given a drug that inhibits the activity of acetylcholinesterase. **Acetylcholinesterase** is the chemical responsible for the synaptic absorption and deactivation of acetylcholine. The inhibition of acetylcholinesterase should allow small amounts of acetylcholine to gradually accumulate on the receptor sites of neurons. These small amounts of acetylcholine would be quickly deactivated if acetylcholinesterase production was at its normal level. Once acetylcholine levels reach a critical threshold, the receptor cell fires—and the person remembers, thinks, and reasons. William Summers and his colleagues (Summers et al., 1986) have gathered impressive results using this strategy, with the degree of success directly related to the patients' stage of AD. Summers and associates administered THA (tetrahydroaminoacridine), a drug that inhibits acetylcholinesterase, to a group of AD patients. Compared with a control group, the patients administered THA (or tacrine, or cognex as it is usually called) showed significant improvement on a number of cognitive measures. Tacrine, like other **palliative treatments,** only treats the symptoms, not the causes, of AD. It helps patients function in a more effective manner. But unfortunately, as with all palliative treatments, the underlying disease progresses and the AD patient ultimately dies. Despite the initial promise of tacrine, this drug only seems to produce beneficial results in a minority of the patients to whom it is given. Furthermore, recent clinical trials have revealed an unacceptable incidence of liver damage in some patients who have received this drug. Quite clearly, a great deal of work must be done before we can cure AD or even treat its cognitive symptoms.

Some other possible drug treatments for AD are listed in table 3.5.

TABLE 3.5		
Some Possible Drugs for Preventing or Treating Alzheimer's		
Drug	**Activity**	**Proposed Mechanism of Action**
Cognex, Aricept	Acetylcholinesterase inhibitor	Compensate loss of cholinergic neurons
Ampakines	Enhance activity of AMPA receptor	Improve memory by enhancing long-term potentiation
Prednisone, ibuprofen, other NSAIDS	Anti-inflammatory	Prevent inflammatory damage to neurons
Vitamin E	Antioxidant	Protects against free-radical damage
Premarin	Female hormone	Promotes neuronal survival
Nerve growth factor	Maintain cholinergic neurons in brain	Promotes neuronal survival
Calcium channel blockers	Inhibit calcium ion entry into neurons	Reduce calcium toxicity
Cholesterol-lowering drugs	Lower apoE4 concentrations	Prevent appE4 toxicity to neurons
Protease inhibitors	Block β-amyloid production	Prevent neuronal loss to β-amyloid toxicity

Source: Marx, J. (1996). Searching for drugs that combat Alzheimer's disease. Science, 273, 51.

The picture is somewhat brighter when one considers the noncognitive symptoms associated with AD, such as paranoia, depression, wandering, and so on. Reisberg (1987) suggests that these symptoms may be treated by using various drugs that have proven effective in psychiatric settings.

OTHER DEMENTIAS

AD is one of many different types of age-related dementias. Next we briefly describe some of these other dementing conditions.

Multi-Infarct Dementia

Multi-infarct dementia has been estimated to account for 20 to 25 percent of cases of dementia (Gambert, 1987; Zarit & Zarit, 1983). This dementia arises from a series of ministrokes in the cerebral arteries. The condition is more common among men with a history of hypertension (high blood pressure) and arises when the arteries to the brain are blocked (e.g., by small pieces of atherosclerotic plaque dislodging from the artery walls in other parts of the body and traveling to the brain). The clinical picture for multi-infarct dementia is different from that of Alzheimer's disease, since the individual typically shows clear and predictable recovery from the former versus the gradual deterioration of the latter. Symptoms may include bouts of confusion, slurring of speech, difficulty in writing, or weakness on the left or right side of the body, hand, or leg. However, after each such occurrence, rapid and steady improvement usually occurs. Each succeeding occasion leaves a bit more of a residual problem, making recovery from each new episode increasingly difficult. A relatively minor stroke or infarct is usually termed a **transient ischemic attack** (TIA). See figure 3.12 for more information about this disorder.

Mixed Dementia

In some cases, two forms of dementia coexist. For example, Alzheimer's disease and multi-infarct dementia have been estimated to co-occur in approximately 18 percent of those cases of diagnosed dementia (Raskind & Peskind, 1992); it is impossible to determine with accuracy the cause of the observed symptoms although autopsy may help to determine cause. Such cases are reasonably common and not the "medical zebras" clinicians report to their colleagues to highlight their diagnostic skills. Obviously, treatment and intervention for a person with mixed dementia presents an especially difficult challenge. Larson (1993) considers elderly people 85 years of age and older particularly likely to have mixed dementia.

Creutzfeldt-Jakob Disease

This form of dementia is infrequently encountered in clinical diagnosis. It is caused by a slow-acting virus and under rare circumstances can be infectious (Raskind & Peskind, 1992). In experimental studies, an analogous slow-acting virus has been found to be transmitted from lower animals to other primates. The analog virus in sheep produces a disease called scrapie, whose symptoms and destruction of brain tissue are similar to the

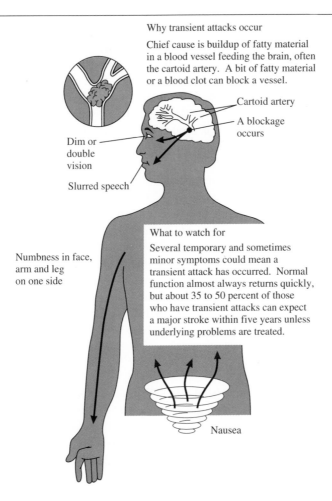

Why transient attacks occur

Chief cause is buildup of fatty material in a blood vessel feeding the brain, often the cartoid artery. A bit of fatty material or a blood clot can block a vessel.

Cartoid artery

A blockage occurs

Dim or double vision

Slurred speech

Numbness in face, arm and leg on one side

What to watch for

Several temporary and sometimes minor symptoms could mean a transient attack has occurred. Normal function almost always returns quickly, but about 35 to 50 percent of those who have transient attacks can expect a major stroke within five years unless underlying problems are treated.

Nausea

Figure 3.12
Recognizing the symptoms of ministrokes or transient ischemic attacks.

symptoms of Creutzfeldt-Jakob disease. Scrapie can be transmitted directly to chimpanzees and monkeys in laboratory investigations (Cohen, 1988). There is also evidence from work in New Guinea that another rare neurologic brain disorder, kuru, can be virally transmitted from primate to human (Zarit & Zarit, 1983). This leads to the question of whether the more common dementias such as Alzheimer's may also be the product of a virus, transmitted either from animal to human or from human to human. In the latter instance, some support for direct human-to-human transmission of Creutzfeldt-Jakob disease has been reported (Gorman, Benson, Vogel, & Vinters, 1992). The pattern of symptoms in Creutzfeldt-Jakob disease is highly variable, although central nervous system deterioration is commonly present. The rate of decline is rapid, and death ensues within two years (Raskind & Peskind, 1992). The emergence of specific symptoms and the rate of progressive deterioration in cognitive functioning, judgment, memory, and personal and social competence depends on the overall rate and extent of neuron loss in the brain, the initial level of intellectual ability, and the availability of a socially supportive and simplified environment in which to live.

AIDS Dementia Complex

This neurological disorder is characterized by progressive cognitive, motor, and behavioral loss. It arises in concert with the **acquired immunodeficiency syndrome (AIDS)** and is a predictable part of the infection (Price, Sidtis, & Rosenblum, 1988; Raskind & Peskind, 1992). **AIDS dementia complex (ADC)** is the result of direct brain infection by the human immunodeficiency virus (HIV). An HIV by-product, a protein called gp 120, is responsible for the death of neuron cells, which ultimately produces dementia. Early symptoms include inability to concentrate, difficulty performing complex sequential mental tasks, and memory loss in tasks requiring concentrated attention (reading, meeting the demands of independent living and working). Motor symptoms include clumsiness and weakness in the limbs; behavioral changes include apathy, loss of spontaneity, depression, social withdrawal, and personality alterations. As ADC progresses, mental performance becomes noticeably worse and motor behaviors become impaired. Fine motor responses weaken, walking without assistance becomes difficult, and bowel and bladder control are lost. The terminal phase is marked by confinement to bed, vacant staring, and minimal social and cognitive interaction (Price et al., 1988). Raskind and Peskind (1992) estimate that in the United States approximately 10,000 adults over 60 were diagnosed with ADC in 1992, with transmission attributable to unprotected sex or infection via contaminated blood.

Focal Brain Damage

Zarit and Zarit (1983) have suggested that the sudden emergence of selective (rather than global) impairment of specific cognitive abilities is typical of focal brain damage. Focal brain damage is not considered a dementia and is not marked by progressive deterioration. The likelihood of localized brain damage due to head trauma, stroke, or tumor is a common occurrence among young adult patients but is frequently overlooked among the elderly (Zarit & Zarit, 1983). The defining characteristic of focal brain damage is the rapid and sudden onset of limited, specific cognitive impairments. Once identified, further losses in intellectual function can be prevented with timely and appropriate intervention.

Parkinson's Disease

Tremors of the voluntary small muscle groups are the most noticeable symptoms of Parkinson's disease, a motor disorder triggered by degeneration of dopamine-producing neurons in the brain (Morgan, 1992). Other classic symptoms of Parkinson's disease include unnatural immobility of the facial muscles, staring appearance of the eyes, and the inability to initiate simple motor behaviors. This neurological disorder not only produces disturbances in psychomotor functioning but also, in about 45 percent of the cases, is associated with depression and, in 15 to 40 percent of the cases, is associated with dementia (Raskind & Peskind, 1992). The standard treatment for Parkinson's disease is the administration of a drug called L-dopa. L-dopa is converted by the brain into dopamine. It is sometimes difficult to determine the correct dosage of L-dopa. For example, if Parkinson's patients are given too much of this chemical, they may display what appear to be schizophrenic symptoms. Conversely, if young schizophrenic patients are given too much of a drug that blocks the effects of dopamine, they may develop what appear to be the symptoms of Parkinson's disease. Another treatment for Parkinson's disease involves transplanting dopamine producing neurons into the substantia nigra.

Dementia Caused by Psychiatric Disorders

The clinical picture of depression in the elderly often mimics dementia; some clinicians have even labeled depression as **depressive pseudodementia** (Kiloh, 1961; LaRue, Dessonville, & Jarvik, 1985; Zarit & Zarit, 1983). Table 3.6 presents the difference in symptoms between true dementia and depressive pseudodementia. At least 30 percent of the elderly diagnosed with dementia have been misdiagnosed and in fact have treatable depressive pseudodementia (LaRue et al., 1985). Symptoms such as apathy, psychomotor retardation, impaired concentration, delusions, and confusion in a depressed elderly person may easily be mistaken for dementia, particularly when they are accompanied by complaints of memory loss. Interestingly, clinicians observe that persons with depressive pseudodementia may complain far more about memory loss than those with true dementia. Although some studies suggest the presence of differential brain wave activity during sleep, at present, the only way of definitively identifying depressive pseudodementia from true dementia is by retrospective means (Hoch, Buysse, Monk, & Reynolds, 1992). Thus, if any of the treatments effective in helping depressives produce dramatic improvements in a person's cognitive deficits and other symptoms, then the diagnosis of depressive pseudodementia must be correct (LaRue et al., 1985). Clinicians are thus advised to treat such symptoms not as dementia but as depressive pseudodementia. Given the difficulty of diagnosing either problem prior to treatment, the scientific utility of the concept of depressive pseudodementia has been questioned. Caine and Grossman (1992) suggest that those with depressive pseudodementia sometimes may be "coaxed" into more positive cognitive functioning and

TABLE 3.6		
Depressive Pseudodementia versus True Dementia: Differential Symptoms		
	Depression	Dementia
Onset	Rapid; exact onset can often be dated	Insidious and ill-defined
Behavior	Stable; depression, apathy, and withdrawal common	Labile; fluctuates between normal and withdrawn and apathetic
Mental competence	Usually unaffected; however, may appear demented at times; complains of memory problems	Consistently impaired, tries to hide cognitive impairment
Somatic signs	Anxiety, insomnia, eating disturbances	Occasional sleep disturbances
Self-image	Poor	Normal
Prognosis	Reversible with therapy	Chronic; slow progressive decline

improved task performance through techniques such as cued recall, whereas elderly with true dementia are unable to benefit from these interventions.

Other reversible dementias may be caused by drugs, toxins, and physical illness. The sedative effects of some drugs (including alcohol) on older persons and drug-drug interactions may also contribute to memory impairment, delirium, or acute brain syndrome/reversible dementia (Cohen, 1988; Schuckit, Morrissey, & O'Leary, 1979; Zarit & Zarit, 1983). Disorders of thyroid metabolism (such as hyperthyroidism) may impair cognitive ability and represent still another reversible cause of the dementia syndrome. And almost any intracranial lesion or tumor may produce memory loss or dementia (Gambert, 1987; Zarit, Eiler, & Hassinger, 1985). Seeking the particular cause of dementia is important because treatment can be somewhat successful in at least 10 to 30 percent of the cases (LaRue et al., 1985; Smith & Kiloh, 1981).

SUMMARY

Several biological theories of aging have been proposed since there is considerable controversy about the biological causes of aging. These theories must deal with the relationship between primary and secondary aging. Current approaches to aging suggest that evolutionary mechanisms selected for reproductive vigor, which, on an indirect basis, result in the aging process as well as the upper limit to the human life span. Interventions such as dietary restriction, antioxidant drugs, and lifestyle changes may increase life expectancy. It is unclear, however, whether these interventions actually slow down the aging process.

The term *sensorimotor development* refers to the sensory systems that input information from the environment and the motor systems that enable us to perform physical actions in the environment. Vision and hearing are the two most important sensory systems in adulthood. Visual decline in late adulthood is characteristic of most individuals and can be traced to physiological changes in the visual system, including changes that limit the quality and intensity of light reaching the retina. It is important to make a distinction between visual acuity and contrast sensitivity. With increasing age, important changes take place in both contrast sensitivity and visual acuity.

Hearing usually reaches its peak in adolescence and remains reasonably stable during early adulthood, but in middle adulthood it may start to decline. Less than 20 percent of individuals between 45 and 54 years of age have a hearing problem, but for those between 75 and 79, the figure rises to 75 percent. We also become less sensitive to taste, smell, and pain as we grow older.

Motor skills usually peak during young adulthood. One of the most common measures of motor performance is reaction time. Many studies have shown that reaction time becomes gradually slower as we approach older adulthood. Decrements in reaction time may have potentially significant effects on the ability of older adults to function effectively in our complex, modern society. Experts disagree over the extent to which age-related psychomotor slowing is due to the deterioration of central rather than peripheral processes. With practice and exercise, physical abilities—even demanding physical sports—may be maintained at high levels throughout adulthood.

The human brain has three major components: the brain stem (including the cerebellum), the limbic system, and the cerebrum. The hippocampus, a structure within the limbic system, seems to be involved in the process of remembering and storing information. The cortex, the top covering of the cerebrum, is responsible for all higher-order psychological functioning. The cortex may undergo widespread or localized damage in aged individuals.

The brain is composed of specialized cells called neurons. Neurons communicate by releasing special chemical substances called neurotransmitters. It is generally agreed that we lose a large number of neurons as we grow old, but there are few precise conclusions about the psychological effects of neuronal loss. With increasing age comes an increase in the amount of lipofuscin, the number of granular particles, and the number of neurofibrillary tangles inside the neurons. Senile plaques have also been found to increase in the synaptic area between neurons.

It is possible to observe the brain in a noninvasive manner by the use of the CT scan, PET scan, or MRI. The electroencephalogram (EEG) has been used to measure the electrical output of the brain in general, and the cortex in particular. The alpha rhythm, as measured by the EEG, begins to slow as we approach older adulthood. Some psychologists have linked the slowing of alpha activity to the generalized pattern of psychomotor slowing. The delta rhythm also changes with age. Alterations in delta activity have been linked to changes in sleep patterns and sleep satisfaction among the elderly. Age-related changes in evoked brain potentials are also of interest to gerontologists. Of particular importance is the latency of the P300 brain wave.

Dementia and senescence are not interchangeable terms. The former refers to an abnormal condition of aging, the latter to the universal processes of aging. Alzheimer's disease was presented in terms of causes, diagnostic approaches, and treatment strategies. The complexities of providing home care and institutional care for patients with Alzheimer's and other cognitive dementias remain a challenge for families, service agencies, and our society.

There are many other dementing brain illnesses besides Alzheimer's disease. Unlike Alzheimer's disease, some of these disorders respond well to treatment.

REVIEW QUESTIONS

1. What does biological aging have to do with *senescence?*
2. Explain the differences between the following pairs of terms: *normal aging* and *successful aging; primary aging* and *secondary aging.*
3. Explain how evolutionary mechanisms "indirectly" selected for the aging process.
4. Discuss the effectiveness of antiaging interventions such as dietary restrictions and antioxidant drugs.
5. Describe some of the changes in physical appearance that accompany the aging process.
6. Discuss the development of sensory systems during the adult years, focusing especially on vision and hearing.
7. Explain the difference between visual acuity and contrast sensitivity.
8. Describe the changes that take place in motor performance during adulthood.
9. Compare the "peak athletic performance" of younger, middle-aged, and older adults.
10. What are the major changes that take place at the *cortical* and *neuronal* level as we age?

11. Discuss the advantages of using MRI and PET to measure the aging of the human brain.

12. Distinguish between the following terms: *senescence, senility, dementia,* and *Alzheimer's disease (AD).*

13. Discuss the pros and cons of the *cholinergic* and *genetic* approaches to understanding the cause of AD.

14. At present, what types of treatments are available for individuals with AD?

15. Compare and contrast AD with other dementing conditions.

FOR FURTHER READING

Hayflick, L. M. (1996). *How and why we age.* New York: Ballantine Books.

Pierpaoli, W., & Regelson, W. (1995). *The melatonin miracle.* New York: Pocket Books.

Restak, R. M. (1997). *Older and wiser.* New York: Simon & Schuster.

Rose, M. R. (1990). *Evolutionary biology of aging.* New York: Oxford University Press.

Snowdon, D. A. (1997). Aging and Alzheimer's disease: Lessons from the Nun Study. *The Gerontologist, 37,* 150–156.

ADAPTATION AND COPING

INTRODUCTION

In this chapter, you will learn about coping and adaptation in adulthood. We begin with a discussion of how families and caregivers cope with someone with Alzheimer's disease (AD). The different ways in which adults cope with life stresses also are examined. Individual differences in coping resources, in knowing how to cope, and in the amount and type of support are discussed as key factors in promoting effective coping and adaptation. The costs as well as benefits of stressful life events, such as caregiving, are examined. In this chapter, we also examine religion and spirituality as resources for adaptation and coping.

STRESS, COPING, AND ADAPTATION

The ability to manage stress effectively is a key factor in staying healthy during the adult years. Most older adults are in good mental health (Gatz, Kasl-Godfrey, & Karel, 1996) and capable of managing the stresses that they experience. During the adult years, individuals learn how to manage various stresses. People get better at managing stress with aging (Gatz et al., 1996). However, there are events, such as the death of a spouse, that are enormously stressful and that are likely to occur in the later years.

Stress is a physiological response to frustrating or threatening events in the environment. Threatening and frustrating events can be external (e.g., not being prepared to take an examination) or internal (e.g., thoughts about the behavior of a friend or boss), and the physiological system responds by "fight" or "flight." Part of the stress response is not having or knowing a way to respond. Three factors are helpful when faced with stressful events: (1) the person's cognitive and emotional resources for handling the event; (2) the individual's knowledge or experience that is relevant to responding effectively to the situation; and (3) the amount and type of support available to the person. Consider these factors as they apply to the demands and challenges of caring for a family member with dementia.

Coping with Alzheimer's Disease

There are profound physical, emotional, social, and financial costs associated with caring for a family member with AD (Gatz et al., 1996). Family members who provide care have been identified as the "hidden victims" of AD (Pearlin, Mullan, Semple, & Skaff, 1990; Zarit, Orr, & Zarit, 1985). Sometimes it is helpful for those who directly care for an individual with AD to participate in community support groups.

Knowing what to expect about the course of the disease is helpful to caregivers. Baum, Edwards, and Morrow-Howell (1993), for example, proposed a measurement-based approach to the management of patients with AD that emphasizes the functional strengths that remain as the disease progresses. Using the Functional Behavior Profile (see table 4.1), caregivers can focus on trying to reduce the rate at which behaviors are lost and to preserve adaptive behaviors still present (Baum et al., 1993). Activities such as listening to music or seeing photos or videos from earlier time periods may be useful for engaging the person with AD (Aldridge & Aldridge, 1992; Johnson, Lahey, & Shore, 1992; Smith, 1992).

TABLE 4.1						
Items of the Functional Behavior Profile Showing Significant Decline Between Stages of Alzheimer's Disease						
Item	0.5–1	0.5–2	1–2	0.5–3	1–3	2–3
Follows three-step command		*	*	*	*	
Learns complex tasks without difficulty	*	*	*	*	*	
Follows two-step command		*	*	*	*	*
Knows the day of the week and/or date	*	*	*	*	*	
Independently makes complex decisions	*	*	*	*	*	
Problem solves without assistance	*	*	*	*	*	
Problem solves with repeated assistance	*	*	*	*	*	
Takes responsibility		*	*	*	*	*
Finishes a task		*	*	*	*	*
Performs work that is neat		*	*	*	*	*
Concentrates on a task for a time		*	*	*	*	*
Handles tools or instruments		*	*	*	*	*
Performs fine detail				*	*	*
Performs work within a reasonable time		*		*	*	
Activities appropriate to the time of day		*	*	*	*	*
Makes simple decisions		*	*	*	*	*
Follows one-step command		*	*	*	*	*
Shows enjoyment in activity				*	*	
Socializes when others initiate				*	*	*
Participates in activities			*	*	*	
Initiates conversation with family				*	*	*
Identifies familiar people				*	*	*
Expresses self appropriately				*	*	*
Performs activity without frustration				*	*	
Makes decisions when given choices		*	*	*	*	*
Continues activities when frustrated		*	*	*	*	
Learns simple tasks without difficulty		*	*	*	*	*

From C. Baum, D. F. Edwards, and N. Morrow-Howell, "Identification and Measures of Productive Behaviors in Senile Dementia of the Alzheimer's Type" in The Gerontologist, 33: 403-408. Copyright © 1993. The Gerontological Society of America.

Respite Care

Respite care is any service that provides time away from caregiving. Day care, evening care, or brief institutionalization are examples. Respite care provides temporary relief or a break for caregivers (Hirsch, Davies, Boatwright, & Ochango, 1993; Lawton, Brody, & Saperstein, 1991). With or without respite care, the burden of providing care 24 hours a day to patients with AD takes a toll. Depression is reported in more than 50 percent of family caregivers (Hirsch et al., 1993). The experiences of caregiving for patients with AD has been highlighted in the well-known book *The 36 Hour Day* (Mace & Rabins, 1991).

Many caregivers are themselves older and frail, and they may be or become unable to provide home-based care for an older relative (Lawton et al., 1991). Cairl and Kosberg (1993) suggested that support services needed by relatives caring for AD patients in the home must be tailored to fit the type of caregiving being provided, the background and status of the caregiver, and the level of functioning of the AD patient. Targeted service interventions based on assessments of need are more effective than generic community programs (i.e., "one size fits all").

There are racial and ethnic differences in usage of respite care services and caregiver support groups. In a recent study, investigators compared African-American and white caregivers who were responsible for a relative with diagnosed dementia (Hinrichsen & Ramirez, 1992). Caregivers showed no differences in their acceptance of the demands of the caregiving role. However, African-American caregivers were less willing to consider institutionalization for their relatives and appeared to accept the distress and burden associated with the caregiving role more effectively than white caretakers. When asked to identify services that would be helpful, African Americans listed nursing care and training in physical therapy rather than respite services.

Henderson, Gutierrez-Mayka, Garcia, and Boyd (1993) implemented an AD support group for African-American and Hispanic communities. The program by Henderson et al. (1993) is outlined in table 4.2. This program demonstrates the importance of implementing an AD support group that matches the particular values of a community.

Caregiving Decisions

Families make the decision to institutionalize in different ways and at different points, but the decision is always a difficult one to make. Often the decision comes after a number of years of not managing well the increasing physical and emotional demands of caregiving. Caregivers are motivated by altruistic reasons (e.g., feelings of empathy and attachment), social norms (e.g., feelings of generational reciprocity and responsibility), and personal motives including avoidance of guilt, fear of public censure, or a sense of indebtedness (Gatz, Bengtson, & Blum 1990; Biegel, Bass, Schulz, Morycz, 1993). Yet the direct consequences of accepting the responsibility to care for an impaired or disabled relative are rarely understood until caregiving is well under way

---

TABLE 4.2

Implementation of an AD Support Group for Targeted Minorities: Basic Principles

1. Conduct Targeted Ethnographic Survey
   a. Develop a community demographic profile
   b. Develop a list of ethnic minority organizations
   c. Identify ethnic minority media
   d. Identify key community members
   e. Interview those identified as key community members
2. Train Community-Based Support Leaders
3. Announce Ethnic Specific Support Groups
4. Conduct Support Groups
5. Develop Meeting Location at Culturally-Neutral Site

From J. N. Henderson, M. Gutierrez-Mayka, J. Garcia, and S. Boyd, "A Mode for Alzheimer's Disease Support Group Development in African-American and Hispanic Populations" in The Gerontologist, 33; 409–414. Copyright 1993 © The Gerontological Society of America.

(George, 1992a, 1992b). Caregiver burden includes the negative impact on the emotional, social, and financial dimensions of caregiver (Robinson & Yates, 1994). Caregivers rarely anticipate the extent of the burden, or the diminished time and involvement in friendships, work, and leisure activities (George, 1992a, 1992b). Thus, caregivers are at risk of mental health problems such as depression (Clipp & George, 1990; Cohen & Eisdorfer, 1989; George, 1992a, 1992b).

Daughters who frequently provide much of the caregiving to their mothers when such care is needed express concern about the time constraints and anxiety about the complexity and uncertainty of the situation. Mothers who receive care express anger and helplessness about their own condition and remorse about the burden that they bring to their child (Walker, Martin, & Jones, 1992).

Following the decision to institutionalize a close relative or parent, caregivers are unburdened in terms of the extraordinary physical demands (feeding, bathing, dressing) and emotional demands (Takman, 1992). Older spouses, understandably, make the decision to institutionalize a disabled husband or wife sooner than middle-aged children will decide to institutionalize a parent or relative. Middle-aged children in comparison to older spouses are stronger and more able to deal with the physical and emotional demands of caregiving. The immediate impact of institutionalization on caregivers, freed from the day-to-day responsibilities of providing assistance to an impaired elder, is a gain of 1 hour and 47 minutes per day (Moss, Lawton, Kleban, & Duhamel, 1993). Caregivers use this gain in free time for family interaction and activities outside of the home. Institutional placement, although it brings some relief from the physical demands of caregiving, brings emotional turmoil to the extended family and the elderly person (Mace & Rabins, 1991). Once the institutionalization decision is made, it is usually viewed as a wise choice.

The steps associated with a move to a nursing home include: (1) orientation and adjustment to the new facility, (2) family and dependency concerns, (3) concerns about the quality and availability of medical care, (4) provision of tender loving care, and (5) availability of sufficient space (Stein, Linn, & Stein, 1985).

Initially, the move to an institution may produce confusion, disorientation, and withdrawal that lasts about two months (Borup, 1983; Tobin & Lieberman, 1976). Individuals who are effective at expressing their needs and preferences usually make a better adjustment than docile individuals (Simms, Jones, & Yoder, 1982; Tobin & Lieberman, 1976). The nursing home programs that receive better ratings from patients are ones that provide residents with more "tender loving care" than they had hoped to receive (Stein et al., 1986).

The Perspective of Patients with Alzheimer's Disease

What is it like to experience the losses associated with AD? Do people realize what is happening to them? What are the fears and feelings of those who are beginning to experience the symptoms of AD? A book-length narrative, *Living in the Labyrinth,* by Diana Friel McGowin (1993), provides some insights into the feelings and experiences of coping with the disease. McGowin was in her late forties when she was diagnosed with AD. In her diary, written on a computer, she described two of the earliest signs of her

mind. I will be happy to put in a word for you, if you could write down your name and other relevant details." "I don't get it," he muttered. "Your name?" I did not waver. "Diane, I'm your cousin, Rich," he said slowly. Tears began to surface in my eyes, and I embraced my cousin, whispering, "I was just trying to keep anyone from overhearing that one of my relatives is applying. Of course I'll put in a good recommendation with the personnel department. Absolutely!" It struck me that while I may forget relatives, co-workers, or the way to the restroom, I certainly could think fast enough when cornered, and come forth with a believable bluff. (McGowin, 1993, pp. 19–20)

Personal accounts such as those of Diana McGowin help to improve the management and treatment of AD through increased sensitivity. Thus far psychological studies and treatment approaches for AD have emphasized the assessment and management of functional impairments and disruptive behavior. Personal accounts suggest that more attention should be given to helping people cope with having the disease. Some programs try to build on the positive skills and abilities that remain (Sheridan, 1993). Research Focus 4.1 describes the decision about whether to tell a diagnosed person that he or she has AD.

THE LIFE-EVENTS MODEL OF ADAPTATION AND COPING

It is well known that stress and physical illness are related. Since the early work of Hans Selye (1956, 1980), researchers have examined the health risks of stressful events and of ineffective styles of managing stress. Recently, investigators have found

Natural disasters tax the coping skills of individuals throughout the life span in dramatically different ways.

that stressful events heighten hormonal and neurochemical reactions that may trigger disease and illness (Cohen & Herbert, 1996). Some psychologists have developed scales for calibrating stressful events to measure how people manage life experiences. Originally, investigators searched for commonalities in the adaptation and coping behaviors that individuals displayed. Key life events require the individual to change and adapt. A sketch of the **life-events model** is presented in figure 4.1.

Measuring Stress Through Life Events

Do some life events produce greater stress? The answer seems obvious, but there is so much variability in the meaning of events from one person to another that it is not possible to make a general list of stressful events that applies across individuals. If we could know which specific life events produced the greatest amounts of stress, then we would know when people would be at most risk of physical health and mental health problems.

Holmes and Rahe's Social Readjustment Rating Scale (see table 4.3) was developed as an index of the amount of stress associated with specific life events. Holmes and Rahe (1967) used ratings of marriage as an anchor point and assigned marriage a value of 50. Adults were asked how much readjustment would be required if each of the events listed in the table occurred in their lives. Questions were asked in relation to marriage. For example, would being fired at work require more or less readjustment than marriage? Would the death of a close friend require more or less adjustment than marriage? Looking at the life events and their readjustment scores and rankings listed in table 4.3 suggests that it is difficult to compare and quantify the amount of stress associated with particular events. In research studies, only modest relationships between the degree of stress and physical illness are reported (Aldwin, Spiro, Bosse, & Levenson, 1989; Ben-Sira, 1991). Many individuals, but not all, who have experienced stressful life events seem to show more physical and health-related problems (Cohen & Herbert, 1996; Taylor, 1990). Prolonged stress wears down the immune system, and measures of immune system function reveal the effects of prolonged stress. In one investigation of persons caring for patients with AD, reduced immune system functioning was found among caregivers and persisted more than two years after the death of the AD patient (Esterling, Kiecolt-Glaser, Bodnar, & Glaser, 1994).

Of course, not all persons react the same way to the same stressors. Some people handle stress better than others, resisting illness even in the face of highly stressful life events. Some research suggests that the **oldest-old** (85 years and older) use denial and distancing strategies more often in dealing with health concerns than individuals who are somewhat younger (Aldwin, 1994, 1995).

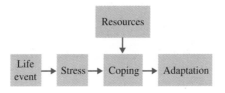

Figure 4.1 The life events model for coping and adaptation

We can ask several questions about the relationship between aging and stress. Do adults experience more or fewer stressors as they age? Are stressors experienced differently by adults of different ages? Do older people develop more effective strategies for coping with stress as they grow older? Or are older adults, when faced with stressful experiences, more easily overwhelmed?

The Social Readjustment Scale: Critique

The life-events model predicts that the more changes a person has to make, the greater the stress. Some psychologists believe the social readjustment scale places too much emphasis on such changes and the belief that change is stressful. They have also challenged the view that older adults encounter more stressful life events than younger persons, are unable to manage stress as well as younger adults, and therefore are at increased risk for health problems, illness, and disease. And, some people who face stress perceive it as a challenging opportunity, not a threat. Aldwin (1994, 1995) suggests some adults who have experienced highly stressful life events have viewed the

TABLE 4.3						
The Social Readjustment Rating Scale						
Rank	Life Event	Mean Value	Rank	Life Event	Mean Value
1	Death of spouse	100	23	Son or daughter leaving home	29
2	Divorce	73	24	Trouble with in-laws	29
3	Marital separation	65	25	Outstanding personal achievement	28
4	Jail term	63	26	Wife begin or stop work	26
5	Death of close family member	63	27	Begin or end school	26
6	Personal injury or illness	53	28	Change in living condition	25
7	Marriage	50	29	Revision of personal habits	24
8	Fired at work	47	30	Trouble with boss	23
9	Marital reconciliation	45	31	Change in work hours or conditions	20
10	Retirement	45	32	Change in residence	20
11	Change in health of family member	44	33	Change in schools	20
12	Pregnancy	40	34	Change in recreation	19
13	Sex difficulties	39	35	Change in church activities	19
14	Gain of new family member	39	36	Change in social activities	18
15	Business readjustment	39	37	Mortgage or loan less than $10,000	17
16	Change in financial state	38	38	Change in sleeping habits	16
17	Death of a close friend	37	39	Change in number of family get-togethers	15
18	Change to different line of work	36			
19	Change in number of arguments with spouse	35	40	Change in eating habits	15
			41	Vacation	13
20	Mortgage over $10,000	31	42	Christmas	12
21	Foreclosure of mortgage or loan	30	43	Minor violations of the law	11
22	Change in responsibilities at work	29			

From Journal of Psychosomatic Research, 11:213–218. T. H. Holmes and R. H. Rahe, "The Social Readjustment Rating Scale." Reprinted with permission from © 1967 Elsevier Science Ltd., Pergamon Imprint, Oxford, England.

experience as beneficial. That is, over time the event was reinterpreted as making a positive contribution to personal development by increasing the person's sense of mastery, improving coping skills and self-knowledge, creating new values and perspectives, and providing new social contacts (Aldwin, 1994, 1995).

Another criticism of the social readjustment scale is that it ignores the personal significance (context) and subjective interpretation (cognitive-emotional) of the events themselves. The scale makes no determination of different environmental resources that may be helpful in coping. For example, the death of a parent will be felt differently depending on the age and health of the parent, and will be interpreted differently by a child 16 years of age and a "child" 45 years of age. Thus, the same traumatic event may produce different levels of stress for each person. Furthermore, when faced with comparable stressful events, people do not all choose the same coping strategies and solutions. Most people examine their own coping resources and strategies in the process of deciding how to face a stressful experience (Pushkar, Arbuckle, Conway, Chaikelson, & Maag 1997).

THE COGNITIVE MODEL OF ADAPTATION AND COPING

The **cognitive model of coping** and adaptation to stress emphasizes the importance of a person's subjective perception of potentially stressful life events (see figure 4.2). It can account for individual differences in how people experience supposedly highly ranked stressful life experiences. The process of determining whether an event is stressful is called **primary appraisal.** The subjective determination of an event as stressful produces emotional reactions of tension, anxiety, and dread, while events considered nonstressful provide challenge and growth, typically leading to the emotions of hope, excitement, and joy (Lazarus & Folkman, 1984). Once primary appraisal has occurred, a person can decide how to adapt by choosing resources within themselves (emotion-focused) or within the environment (problem-focused) and determining the costs of using such resources—a process called **secondary appraisal.**

In research on stress in the adult years, Richard Lazarus and his colleagues (DeLongis, Coyne, Dakof, Folkman, & Lazarus, 1982; Lazarus & Folkman, 1984) found an inverse relationship between stressful life events and age for people aged 45 to 64. Does this mean that people experience fewer stressful life events as they age? Most elderly identify fewer life events on these lists than younger persons. The inventories may sample stressors that are more commonly encountered at earlier points in the life span (Aldwin, 1995). We cannot conclude that just because the frequency of

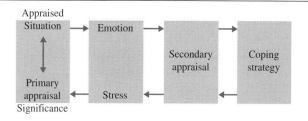

Figure 4.2
Lazarus's cognitive model of coping and adaptation

stressful life events decreases with age, older people experience less stress (Kahana, 1992). We must also consider the meaning or subjective interpretation of stress (primary appraisal). A simple frequency analysis of the number of stressful life events ignores the different coping demands of younger and older people. Older individuals, for example, may find that a single minimally stressful life event, such as leaving home for a vacation, may overwhelm them if they also have to deal with a chronic infirmity such as arthritis and nonsupportive relatives who question the wisdom of their decision to travel (Kahana, 1992). In general there is evidence that older people continue to maintain the coping abilities developed at earlier points in the life span. Although they may identify themselves as having fewer coping strategies as they grow older, their own reports identify themselves as effective at coping; they are not more vulnerable to stress (Aldwin, 1995). There is an important difference, then, between objective and subjective definitions of stressful experiences.

Daily Hassles and Uplifts: The Broken Shoelace Syndrome

Daily hassles are the little, irritating annoyances that punctuate our day-to-day existence (Lazarus & Folkman, 1984). Some hassles are relatively infrequent and random, whereas others are everyday occurrences. For example, driving in traffic or annoyances in a housing arrangement might be frequent hassles for some individuals. Lazarus and his colleagues (Folkman, Lazarus, Pimley, & Novacek, 1987; Monat & Lazarus, 1985) developed a hassles scale to evaluate the frequency and intensity of everyday stresses such as misplacing belongings, not having enough time for family, filling out forms, or breaking a shoelace. Counterbalancing such hassles are corresponding **uplifts,** or positive experiences, which we also may encounter each day (Lazarus & Folkman, 1984).

Lazarus and his colleagues found no differences between men and women in the type and frequency of hassles encountered (Folkman, Lazarus, Dunkel-Schetter, DeLongis, & Gruen, 1986; Folkman, Lazarus, Gruen, & DeLongis, 1986). Interestingly, the measurement of daily hassles is a strong predictor of a person's overall adaptation. The individual's ability to cope with hassles, in fact, is a far better predictor of morale and life satisfaction, psychological symptoms, and somatic illness than the number of major life stresses the person has endured (Lazarus & Folkman, 1984). Why might this be so? Daily hassles seem to have a stronger link with health outcomes because they evaluate proximal aspects of stress, whereas life-event rankings measure distal aspects. *Proximal aspects* are the adult's immediate perceptions of the environment, whereas *distal aspects* are more removed perceptions that may not have common meanings for all people.

In studying the daily hassles of college students, young adults, and middle-aged adults, Lazarus and his colleagues (Folkman et al., 1987; Lazarus & Folkman, 1984) found some age differences. Older people report fewer hassles than young adults, perhaps the result of the loss of specialized roles, for example, as a worker and as parental caregiver (Aldwin, 1995). Younger adults often reported more hassles than older adults in two areas: finances and work (although personal-social concerns were also problematic). Younger college students had to cope with academic and social problems— wasting time, meeting high standards, being lonely. Older adults, on the other hand, experienced hassles most often in the areas of environmental and social problems, home upkeep, and health. Lazarus's sample was essentially white, healthy, middle class, and well educated. The daily hassles of adults from other life circumstances probably vary from this pattern.

Coping and Adaptation: The Timing of Events

The extent to which individuals cope and adapt successfully to stressful life experiences is sometimes related to the timing of such events. Neugarten and Neugarten (1987) suggested that negative events produce levels of stress that are lower when experienced at predictable points in the life course than when experienced at completely unanticipated or unpredictable times. Neugarten originally provided convincing evidence that adults construct a kind of social timetable or **social clock** against which they compare their own social developmental progress; they judge the "right" age for marriage, the "right" time to have children, and the predictable time to experience losses, such as the death of a parent (most often between 40 and 50 years of age). Events that occur "on time" usually cause minimal stress, whereas those that are unexpected produce considerable stress. For example, pregnancy can be a wonderful and exciting time for a married women in her twenties or thirties; the same event can bring considerable stress to an unmarried adolescent girl or a 45-year-old woman with a demanding career and two teenagers. Similarly, changing jobs or careers can be a very different experience for a 45-year-old as opposed to a 25-year-old.

Sometimes the impact of an illness depends on when it occurs in a person's life. For example, older adults are more likely to confront cancer with less anger than younger adults. Young gay adults with AIDS often approach their extended families to ask them to accept and reconcile their identity, lifestyle, and relationships in an attempt to resolve years of isolation, distancing, and abandonment. This process of acceptance ordinarily takes decades for families to accomplish (Ascher, 1993). It is difficult for any young adult to complete such "unfinished business" with their own relatives, but imperative for those with AIDS, who might have only a short amount of time to try to bring resolution to family relationships. Persons with AIDS often work to bring acceptance before their families are ready, to resolve the conflicts between their "two worlds" (*U.S. News & World Report,* 1993). Such findings illustrate the importance of considering the personal meanings of stressful events as "off-time" events at different points in adult development.

Coping and Adaptation: Life-Threatening Illness

Shelley Taylor (1983) and her colleagues (Taylor et al., 1992; Wood, Taylor, & Lichtman, 1985) investigated a variety of illnesses to explore how people cope with life-threatening illnesses such as AIDS and breast cancer. Her work highlights the role of cognitive factors that help to give hope and a positive approach to managing these events (Rybash, Roodin, & Hoyer, 1986). Women responded to the diagnosis of breast cancer, a life-threatening illness, by undergoing a set of active distortions of reality. Of 78 women interviewed, 95 percent tried to derive a new sense of personal meaning from their illness (e.g., "I was very happy to find out that I am a very strong person"). A second theme in their coping with this life-threatening disease was an earnest attempt to gain "magical mastery" or control over their cancer. For example, many believed dietary changes, lifestyle changes, or maintaining a positive attitude would help them win their battle against the disease. A third theme was the attempt to regain feelings of self-esteem. The women selected a reference group against which to compare themselves so that they would derive a more favorable view of themselves and their disease. Thus, older women felt better off than younger women, married women felt sorry for unmarried women, and those with a poor prognosis consoled themselves that at least they were still alive. The women who coped most successfully with cancer tried to master their dilemma and take charge of their lives regardless of the probabilities and realities of their situations (Wood et al., 1985). Olivia Newton-John, popular celebrity and singer, disclosed that she had breast cancer in 1992. In her public remarks, the then 45-year-old wife and mother of a 7-year-old echoed the preceding research findings, "It really refocused my life. When you go through something like that it really puts everything else in perspective. I was trying to be everything to everybody—I was Mom, I was trying to save the world, and I was running a business. I strongly believe that illness is related to your mind and stress and your feelings."

In a similar fashion, Taylor and her colleagues (Taylor et al., 1992) reported that gay men who had tested seropositive for HIV showed "unrealistic optimism," less distress, and more positive attitudes about dying from AIDS than those who were still free of the virus. That is, the gay men who tested positive distorted the future probabilities that they indeed would develop AIDS. They were far more optimistic that they would not contract the AIDS disease, despite already harboring the virus, than a group of HIV seronegative gay men, who showed more fatalism in their perceptions. Although free of the virus, the HIV seronegative gay men believed that they had little control over the virus and the AIDS disease. Taylor suggests that unrealistic optimism is characteristic of adaptation and coping with such life-threatening illnesses. Unrealistic optimism and the active distortion of reality promote positive feelings of self-worth, the ability to care for oneself and others, a level of personal control, and the capacity to cope effectively with the stress of the life-threatening illness as well as other stresses (Taylor et al., 1992).

Coping and Adaptation: Use of Resources and Defenses

Adults use coping strategies to adapt, respond, reduce, or avoid stress. Probably, at all ages, individuals actively seek out environmental resources to enhance coping strategies or to compensate for limited or declining resources of the self (Ben-Sira, 1991; Kahana, Stange, & Kahana, 1993). Adults rarely respond passively to stress, but attempt to change circumstances when possible and seek resources and help; when they cannot cope well, they often invoke cognitive strategies to alter the meaning of stressful circumstances, as did the women with breast cancer and the men who had tested seropositive for HIV (Taylor et al., 1992). Stress has been conceptualized as having both negative and positive dimensions. Frequently, stressful situations are an opportunity for growth, a positive opportunity for questioning one's goals, priorities, and assumptions. It may lead to an enhancement in the range of coping strategies available and create a heightened sense of mastery. And, if successful, new coping strategies are developed, which can be applied in the future to different situations and stressors (Aldwin, 1995).

Individuals use defense mechanisms such as repression and denial to protect the ego from threat and anxiety. Repression and denial in particular are more likely to be adopted in response to extreme stress (Weinberger & Schwartz, 1990). George Valliant (1977), who conducted a longitudinal study of personality and coping, considers denial and distortion of reality to be at the lowest level of adult coping mechanisms. The most mature coping strategies are characterized by altruism; humor (i.e., a method of expressing emotions that is free from consequences); suppression (being optimistic in the face of problems, waiting for a desired outcome, looking for a silver lining); anticipation (planning and preparation for realistic outcomes such as death of a loved one); and sublimation (channeling unacceptable impulses and emotions into socially valued and personally rewarding activities).

In contrast to Valliant's view that denial and distortion of reality represent immature coping, some researchers consider denial to be a healthy mode of adjustment in response to specific types of stressful events (Aldwin, 1995; Taylor et al., 1992). In some studies, the oldest-old (e.g., 85+ years of age) tended to use denial and distancing to cope with health problems (Aldwin, 1995; Johnson & Barer, 1993). Denial, if used temporarily, may allow individuals to gain time to prepare themselves emotionally to face reality and to identify and access resources that may help them to cope. For example, on a short-term basis, a victim of a severe spinal cord injury may be helped by denying the extent of the injury and being optimistic that some recovery of function is possible (Kemp, 1985). However, in time, denial is usually abandoned in favor of more realistic approaches. Some denial and distortions of reality, then, may be helpful in coping, depending on the stressful event itself and the length of time these strategies are maintained. The use of positive, active distortion, however, is a different kind of defense than simple denial for those with life-threatening illness. People seem to recognize the threat they face, yet display unrealistic optimism as a way to experience feelings of control and maintain self-esteem. Taylor and colleagues (1992), for example, noted that men who were seropositive for HIV continued to engage in health-enhancing behaviors, including safe sex practices, believing that it was still within their control to defend against AIDS.

How people cope depends frequently on the type of event itself. In a recent investigation of caretaking of an older parent or relative, three dimensions or domains were identified that could produce stress: (1) the type of impairment (physical vs. cognitive-emotional), (2) the location of the caregiving (home vs. outside the home) and (3) the response to parental incompetency (regaining personal autonomy vs. relinquishing autonomy to a surrogate/guardian). Each of these three dimensions, while part of the general domain of caretaking, produced its own unique caretaking stresses and elicited unique coping responses that were related to each of these three types stresses (Albert, 1991).

Single measurements of coping may not predict how adults will react to stress across time and in various situations. Each person appears to develop a set of coping skills in response to stressors. In managing AD, for instance, the caregiver may adapt and adjust to the progressive decline of function and increased need for care by adopting new and different coping strategies over time. Folkman and Lazarus (1980) constructed a checklist of coping strategies that described how adults thought, felt, and behaved in a number of specific stressful circumstances. Using this measure, the researchers identified two basic coping strategies used by adults: **problem-focused coping** and **emotion-focused coping.** People using problem-focused coping strategies scan the external environment to attempt to obtain additional information to be more effective in solving and actively managing the stressful situation or event. Adults using emotion-focused coping strategies, on the other hand, look within themselves to identify their own behavioral and cognitive resources to help them manage the emotional tension produced by the stressful life situation. In other words, those who cannot manage the situation try to manage their response to it. Emotion-focused coping does not necessarily remove the perceived stress but, rather, helps people to manage themselves and thereby reduce accompanying emotional distress. Most people use both problem-focused and emotion-focused strategies rather than relying solely on one or the other. When coping patterns are related to age, some interesting trends emerge. Folkman and colleagues (1987) reported that

> . . . younger respondents used proportionately more active, interpersonal, problem-focused forms of coping (e.g., confronting the problem, seeking social support, planful problem solving) than did the older people, and the older people used proportionately more passive, intrapersonal emotion-focused forms of coping (e.g., distancing, acceptance of responsibility, and positive reappraisal) than did the younger people. (p. 182)

Carver, Scheier, and Weintraub (1989) suggest that the emotion-focused and problem-focused distinction made by Lazarus may be far too simple and that additional dimensions may be considered in examining age-related differences in coping. Interestingly, older adults perceive the sources of stress that they experience as potentially less controllable than younger persons (Blanchard-Fields & Robinson, 1987). Yet older adults are far more likely to cope successfully with stressors (e.g., by tailoring their coping strategies to fit the situations they believe they can control), than younger adults and adolescents, who more often employ denial and other defensive strategies (Blanchard-Fields & Irion, 1988; Blanchard-Fields & Robinson, 1987). It is more characteristic of older adults to recognize when environmental resources are needed to assist them or to help in managing a difficult situation, although mental health needs are an exception (Ben-Sira, 1991). Problem-focused coping has been identified as common among adults who have been able to see positive outcomes from some of the darkest moments in their lives. Although such events are highly stressful, these adults see such events as providing them with the impetus to grow (e.g., to meet the challenge). They used less escapism, showed less depression, and self-reported higher levels of mastery than other adults who faced similarly difficult life situations.

Coping in Action: Caring for an Older Relative

In 1997, 22.4 million households in the United States provided care for an elderly relative, compared with 7 million in 1988 (McLeod, 1997). Tensions that surround caregiving include: financial obligations, **filial responsibility,** and preservation of the personal autonomy, rights, and dignity of the older individual (Cicirelli, 1992; Wolfson, Handfield-Jones, Glass, McClaran, & Keyserlingk, 1993). When a spouse is not available, this responsibility falls on middle-aged adults; most often it is a daughter who provides for the care of her widowed mother (Baum & Page, 1991). In the caregiving role, adult children are most likely to care for a parent of the same gender; with the majority of older parents being mothers, the caregiving relationship and responsibility is assumed by daughters, following this **gender consistency model** (Lee, Dwyer, & Coward, 1993).

Providing care to an elderly parent often produces strong feelings of obligation, guilt, and resentment over the time taken from spouse and children. The popular press identifies with the stress experienced by adults with multiple responsibilities to their parents, their spouse, and their own children, labeling them the "sandwich generation." Recent analyses, however, suggest that surprisingly few adult middle-aged caregivers were found to be "sandwiched" between the multiple roles of adult caregiver to a parent and to their own children (Rosenthal, Martin-Matthews, & Matthews, 1996). In a large cross-national study in Canada the majority of middle-aged adult children did not have responsibility for providing direct care to their parents. When such responsibilities were required, they were assumed most often by daughters in their mid to late fifties who, at this point in their lives, did not have direct child-care or childrearing responsibilities. Beth Soldo (1996) has confirmed that the point in the life span when adult children begin to care for their own parents most often coincides with the launch and independence of their own adult children who are beginning their own families and work careers. Soldo (1996) notes that role conflicts for most middle-aged adults thus are few and when they do occur will most likely arise at a point later in life when one's children have left the family home.

Caregiver burden refers to the stresses associated with providing care (George, 1990b; Haley, 1991; Knight, Lutzky, & Macofsky-Urban, 1993). Research investigators have differentiated between objective and subjective caregiver burden. **Objective caregiver burden** is usually identified as a disruption in routine or expected lifestyle, which encompasses change in finances, new roles, family life, social relations, travel, and vacations. **Subjective caregiver burden** centers on the emotional reactions to caretaking, which often involve feelings of embarrassment, shame, guilt, as well as emotional overload, resentment, and exclusion (Robinson & Yeats, 1994; Vitaliano, Russo, Young, Teri, & Maivro, 1991; Vitaliano, Young & Russo, 1991). Many studies of caregiver burden have examined features of the environment as well as characteristics of the caregiver and care recipient to understand when and how to best provide specific forms of intervention to enhance caregiving and reduce stress (Seltzer, Vasterling, Yoder, & Thompson, 1997).

Wolfson and colleagues (1993) found most adults had a strong societal or moral obligation to provide for their elderly parents' financial, emotional, and physical needs. Most adult children were unable to actually provide as much support as they felt they should. However, in the case of an elderly parent moving in with an adult child, the elderly parent, despite illness or diminished finances, often provides some assistance to the extended household (Speare & Avery, 1993). Elderly parents living with their adult children do 79 percent of the housework (Ward, Logan, & Spitze,

1992) and contribute direct financial assistance to their adult children, particularly when the adult children are unmarried (Hoyert, 1991; Speare & Avery, 1993). The most common causes of elderly parents moving in with adult children are (1) inadequate finances to sustain independent living, and (2) the need for direct assistance in managing tasks of daily living.

Speare and Avery (1993) also found that it was more common for elderly Hispanic parents to move in with their adult children than for other ethnic elderly. Race and ethnicity can create an expectation for care and support that reduces the level of stress encountered in the extended family when an older parent moves in with a younger adult child (Speare & Avery, 1993).

Lerner, Somers, Reid, Chiriboga, and Tierney (1991) have shown that regardless of who provides direct care for an older parent, brothers and sisters report differential "egocentric" perceptions of their own and their siblings' contributions. Each believes individually that other siblings contribute less, derive less personal satisfaction from their contributions, and have more freedom to alter their caregiving arrangements. Perhaps even more striking in this study is the belief that other siblings would agree with the egocentric beliefs that each sibling holds about their own contributions and the relative contributions of other siblings to the caretaking arrangements.

In examining sources of stress in managing the care of a parent with dementia, Suitor and Pillemer (1993) have confirmed that although important social support is derived from friends and siblings, the interpersonal stress experienced by married daughters in their caretaking roles stems primarily from their own siblings. Another source of stress recently identified among women who assume a caretaking role is the reduction in personal income and benefits from Social Security (Kingson & O'Grady-LeShane, 1993). This effect is immediate in that women frequently have to give up work or significantly reduce their work schedules to care for an aging parent or relative. It is also seen later in the reduced Social Security benefits they receive at the time of retirement. Kingson and O'Grady-LeShane (1993) estimated this difference to result in the loss of benefits of $127 per month at retirement among women who have assumed the responsibility of caring for an older parent or relative.

L. P. Gwyther (1992) summarized the research findings of studies focused on caregiver distress, indicating "that families provide most care; that caregiving has the potential for both positive and negative outcomes (although caregiver burden, stress, and decrements resulting from caregiving tend to be the focus of most studies and interventions); that caregivers and care receivers are too diverse for simplistic, unidimensional approaches; . . . that most modest interventions to support caregivers will be subjectively perceived as satisfactory but will not produce significant changes in the multiple dimensions of burden, well-being, health, mental health or capacity to continue family care" (p. 866).

Researchers have identified three styles of coping with an ailing parent: confrontational (focusing on dealing with anger, guilt, and sadness, and attempting to bring stressful encounters with the parent to an end); denial (suppression and eventual repression of negative feelings); and avoidant (consistent suppression rather than denial or repression of negative emotions). Stephens, Norris, Kinney, Ritchie, and Grotz (1988) found both avoidance coping strategies and depression among caregivers 60 years of age and older who were responsible for the care of a spouse or elderly relative recently discharged from a rehabilitation hospital. Avoidance strategies may help people cope with the immediate impact of stress or a short-term problem. However, if employed consistently as a strategy to deal with problems of extended duration (more than six to nine months), avoidance generally produces negative outcomes (Light, Niederehe, & Lebowitz, 1994).

The caregiving role of an older relative or parent is intense and demanding; the greater the health problems and overall frailty of the older person, the more likely the caregiver experiences feelings of hostility, resentment, and guilt (Light et al., 1994). There is also a relationship between perceived burden and the care recipients' memory difficulties, inability to recognize such difficulties, and the incidence of disruptive emotions and behaviors (e.g., nighttime wandering, hallucinations). With greater perceived burden there is a higher probability of institutionalization of the older relative or parent in a health care facility or nursing home (Lawlor, 1994; Matson, 1995; Seltzer et al., 1997).

Franks and Stephens (1992) have tried to refine the concept of stress experienced in caring for an elderly parent by examining the meaning or value assigned to each of the roles (e.g., caregiver, mother, and spouse) that may be in conflict. They suggest that adult daughters will experience stress in the role of caregiver as a direct result of the degree to which each role (e.g., caregiver, mother, wife) contributes to their sense of well-being. For some daughters, role conflicts will not cause as much stress, if a particular role contributes only marginally to their sense of well-being. Thus, some roles may be more easily abandoned (temporarily) in favor of another role that contributes to their well-being (Franks & Stephens, 1992). The role conflict between mother and caretaker for an older parent may not be as stressful if the role of mother is not a highly valued component of one's well-being.

It is also important to note that the experience of stress in caring for elderly adults is by no means restricted to adult children. Investigators have also found that the impact of caregiving and the effects of stress extend to the entire family system (Fisher & Lieberman, 1994). Lieberman and Fisher (1995), for example, studied the effects that chronic illness (e.g., AD and vascular dementia) had on the spouses, adult children, and the spouses of the adult children. Although there was a significant relationship between the severity of the chronic health problems presented by the family member receiving care and the stress experienced by the primary caretaker, this was also true for the remaining family members. All family members are affected by the "cascading effect" of chronic illness.

Caregiving in the home influences everyone in the family to some degree. Other studies of the impact of caregiving on the larger family suggest that some positive outcomes may coexist along with stress or burden. Beach (1997) documented specific benefits for a sample of older adolescents who were living with a parent, grandparent, or aunt/uncle with AD who received care in the immediate family. Adolescents developed increased empathy for older adults, a greater closeness or bonding between themselves and their mothers who were providing the caregiving, an increase in sibling sharing and common activities, a more selective choice of peers (e.g., those who were empathic and understanding of the commitment to provide care in the home to a relative with AD), and enhanced communication effectiveness with peers.

Health care professionals who provide direct services and supervision in community programs such as respite and day care for those with AD also experience high levels of stress. Regular staff who provide services for the elderly in nursing homes, hospitals, and extended care facilities are similarly affected (Biegel & Blum, 1990; Chappell & Novak, 1992; Montgomery, Kosloski, & Borgatta, 1990). Chappell and Novak (1992) report that nursing assistants in a long-term care institution for the elderly were found to experience significant stress, defined as burden, burnout, and perceived job pressure. The importance of providing specific training to help the nursing assistants cope with elderly residents with cognitive impairment was a major variable in reducing job-related stress. Support from family and friends also provided nursing assistants some help in reducing perceived job pressures and burnout.

COPING EFFECTIVELY WITH STRESS

The general level of success most adults have in managing stress shows the unique resiliency of human beings. There are individuals who are able to maintain their efficacy and effectiveness while coping successfully with complex, demanding, and emotionally challenging life situations. For example, in managing the burden of AD, many caregivers, while enduring the stress associated with caregiving over many years, cope successfully with their own feelings and use social/environmental resources to assist them. Farran (1997) notes the "majestic serenity, calmness, and sense of 'being at peace' with what they are doing and experiencing" (p. 250). From examining successful coping in such situations, experts today question whether caregiving has been portrayed in an overly negative way. There are newer, more positive models to represent coping with caregiver burden. They can also help to direct intervention in the future by examining the background, context, and personal characteristics of caregivers who have managed their "burden" well. Newer models will add to our understanding of the essential resources needed for successful adaptation to the caregiving role, and the subjective and objective appraisals which are used to cope effectively.

Coping Effectively with Stress: The Value of Social Support

In some research on informal caregivers of the elderly (e.g., relatives), the value of social support has been confirmed. Debate continues regarding the importance of the number of people who provide support versus the type of social support that is provided (Vitaliano et al., 1991; Lawton, Moss, Kleban, Glicksman, & Rovine, 1991). It has been suggested that social support serves the informal family caregivers of the elderly as a buffer, protecting them against some of the more difficult stresses of coping with a chronic situation that is difficult to manage. Families appear to be able to maintain their caretaking of a frail or ill older parent in the home primarily through social support (Gwyther, 1992; Thompson, Futterman, Gallagher-Thompson, Rose, & Lovett, 1993).

In one study, different types of social support were compared to determine those most effective in reducing the burden of caretaking on family members (Thompson et al., 1993). Engaging in social interaction for simple fun and recreation was measurably superior to other forms of social support in helping family members manage the stress of caregiving to an older relative. Other types of social support, such as direct aid, physical assistance, emotional support, and validation of self-esteem, were ineffectual in reducing the stress associated with chronic caregiving to an elderly relative in the home. The data suggest that caregivers should engage in regular pleasant activities with friends and other relatives to best manage the chronic stress of their roles in the extended family and the burden of their complex and demanding roles (Thompson et al., 1993).

The value of the social environment in promoting effective coping, however, can be overstated (Taylor, Repetti, & Seeman, 1997). When the assistance provided by others robs the caregiver or the care recipient of the opportunity for independence, mastery, and self-sufficiency, the risk of dependency, depression, and helplessness can increase. In such situations the health status of the care recipient can be compromised, and declines can be documented (Taylor et al., 1997). Unfortunately, the presence and availability of a close and supportive social network does not consistently lead to lowered levels of stress among caregivers nor to greater incidence of recovery among those facing chronic illness (Bolger, Foster, Vinokur, & Ng, 1997; Coyne & Fiske, 1992).

Coping with Alzheimer's Disease: Caregivers' Appraisals of Efficacy

Gignac and Gottlieb (1996) studied a group of 87 family caregivers of older adults with AD. Using the cognitive model of coping developed by Lazarus and colleagues, they identified various types of cognitive appraisals of caregivers' personal efficacy in coping with a family member with AD, the stability of such appraisals, and the overall frequency of such appraisals. They identified 12 basic efficacy appraisals that were employed by family caregivers in managing the person with AD across five separate domains: problem-solving, regulating emotional distress, protecting self-esteem, managing social interactions, and self-development. The 12 types of cognitive appraisals of coping efficacy are specified in table 4.4. These data revealed that 5 of the 12 basic efficacy appraisals were associated directly with caregiver distress or well-being: non-efficacious coping outcomes, no coping options, no control, improved ability to cope, and means/ends insights. Interestingly, there was variability in the caregivers' assessments of their individual efficacy in coping with a relative with AD. Stability in self-assessment of efficacy was determined by how successful the interactions with their older relative were at the time of evaluation.

The research by Gignac and Gottlieb (1996) suggested that caregivers focus on very broad goals in determining their ways of coping with a relative with AD. Coping efficacy was directly related to an individual's subjective appraisal of success or failure. In managing the most upsetting problems, caregivers tended to use "making meaning" and humor as tactics for managing their own emotions. Emotional management of distress and burden has been recognized as a key to efficacy in previous interventions. When disruptive actions associated with AD occur (e.g., noxious habits, confusion, aggression, and nighttime disruption), caregivers need to be educated to attribute these problems to the disease, not to the volition of the patient.

Using longitudinal data collected from 456 respondents, Skaff, Pearlin, and Mullan (1996) observed that differences in the sense of mastery were related to changes in

TABLE 4.4

Types of Appraisals of Coping Efficacy

Type	Illustrative Quotations
Efficacious coping outcomes: appraisals of efficacious coping outcomes.	"I've tried everything, but that seems to work." "And that makes it a little better." "This has really helped my situation."
Nonefficacious coping outcomes: appraisals in inefficacious coping outcomes.	"But with not much result." "It doesn't do any good." "But it just doesn't register."
No coping options: appraisals that nothing further can be done to manage stressor demands.	"I don't know what to do." "There's nothing I can do." "I'm just helpless."
Control appraisals: appraisals of the control the respondent can exercise over the stressor or his or her emotions.	"I'm more able to control things now." "I'm fortunate enough to be able to control any upset feelings."
No-control appraisals: appraisals that the respondent is not able to control the stressor or his or her emotions.	"I guess it's a situation that I can't control."
Less stressors reactivity: appraisals that the respondent is able to tolerate the stressor.	"But I'm getting used to that now." "It doesn't upset me like it used to."
More stressor reactivity: appraisals that the respondent is unable to tolerate the stressor.	"I never get used to it." "I just can't get used to the idea of my mother sitting there."
Depletion of energy: appraisals of diminished energy.	"Trying to cope with it all, it's tiring me out." "As much as I love them, it is wearing." "You get to the point where you don't even try."
Improved ability to cope: appraisals of improvements in coping.	"I'm more reasonable than I used to be." "I've learned to cope with it." "The more you know about the disease, the more [you are able] to understand him."
Coping self-criticism: appraisals of shortcomings in coping.	"I should know better." "I realize I should have done something or said something different." "I haven't been able to handle it too well, I guess."
Means/ends insights: appraisals of the relationship between coping efforts and their outcomes.	"Because she gets really upset if I yell at her." [Changes subject] "So she can start thinking about something else." [Hold onto hands] "So he doesn't pull the waitress's arm."
Strategic planning: appraisals of the costs entailed in different coping efforts.	"I wouldn't say anything to hurt her feelings." "You don't *want* her to feel guilty, you know." "Otherwise, you're going to have a frustrating time your whole life here."

From Gignac, M., & Gottlieb, B. 1996, Caregivers appraisals of efficacy in coping with dementia. Psychology and Aging, 11(2), 214–225.

the caregiving role. A sense of mastery emerged directly as the result of the lengthy career of caregiving. Mastery was not considered to be a stable personality trait. Skaff and colleagues (1996) also found three distinct patterns related to mastery among the caretakers. For those relatives who continued to care consistently for a family member with AD, the sense of mastery declined steadily; for those who decided that they could not provide adequate care and placed their relative in a full-time institutionalized care facility, the sense of mastery remained unchanged (e.g., at the level it was just prior to placement). The only group for whom the sense of mastery was found to increase was for those who had experienced the death of their relative and thus the end of their caretaking careers (Skaff et al., 1996). There are transitions that occur among caregivers who derive a sense of mastery and efficacy in response to the changing nature of their experience in coping with a family member with AD. The career of care provider is a dynamic one with multiple trajectories throughout an extended period of time. In some cases this time period may encompass a decade or more and caregivers themselves showing increased difficulties in meeting the needs of the older person as they grow older and the physical demands for care increase.

Coping Effectively with Stress: The Beneficial Effects of Caregiving

The benefits of caregiving include gains in personal efficacy and mastery from the role of caregiver as well as enhancement of well-being and self-worth (Kramer, 1997a). Caregivers, for example, express positive feelings about their ability to assist a relative, their selflessness in choosing to do so, and their willingness to forgo other interests (Kramer, 1997a). Caregiving has also been reported to increase feelings of pride and personal achievement, enhance meaning, and heighten the sense of closeness and warmth between caregiver and care recipient (Farran, 1997; Kramer, 1997a).

It is only through the use of multiple outcome measures that positive benefits have been identified (Kramer, 1997a; Miller & Lawton, 1997). Perhaps most intriguing is the possibility that there may be differential predictors for caregiver burden and caregiver benefits. The literature reviewed by Kramer (1997a) suggests that motivational differences in assuming the role of caregiver, attitude, and ethnicity are all predictive of benefits. For instance, both white and black caregivers show satisfaction in being able to assume the role of provider and positive affect in doing so (e.g., indicators of mental health and well-being are enhanced) (Lawton, Rajagopal, Brody, & Kleban, 1992). White caregivers derived benefits when their motivation for assuming the role of caregiver included maintaining family traditions, showing mutual aid, concern, and reciprocity; however, benefits for black caregivers were not predictive from these motivations (Kramer, 1997a). In a number of studies, satisfaction with the caregiving role was related to the care recipient's level of day-to-day independent functioning, assessed through inventories such as **activities of daily living (ADL)** (Kramer, 1993a, 1997a). Burden and depression are predictable from caregivers' difficulties in managing the care recipient's behavioral symptoms, the length of time engaged in the caregiving role, prior history of the relationship between caregiver and care recipient, and the level of stress created by the care recipient's limitations in day-to-day independent functioning (Kramer, 1993a, 1993b).

Figure 4.3 A conceptual model of caregiver adaptation.

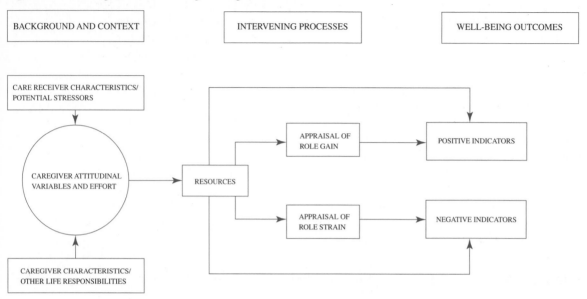

Figure 4.3 describes Kramer's conceptual model of some of the predictors of caregiver burden and caregiver gains. The model takes into account the influences of background and context variables including (1) care recipient characteristics: the severity of the illness, capacity for self-care, cognitive abilities, disruptive actions, awareness of memory impairment; (2) caregiver demands; and (3) caregiver attitudes: motivation for helping, value in helping, and goals for helping. The intervening processes in the model include those identified as resources external to the caregiver, chiefly social support and organized community services including adult day care and respite care (in-home and out-of-home). Intervening processes also include resources within the individual such as coping style and adaptiveness, personal control, appraisal of efficacy, health status, knowledge, and resiliency. Kramer's model accounts for the relationship between strong social support and caregiver gains, and for the relationship between reduced support and perceptions of increased caregiver burden. The model also accounts for poor or declining health among caregivers leading to negative outcomes, increased strain, and higher incidence of depression (Kramer, 1997a).

In reviewing 29 studies of the positive aspects of caregiving, Kramer carefully noted some of the methodological weaknesses in this type of research. These include the use of heterogeneous samples that "lump together" different groups of caregivers (e.g., spouses, adult children, relatives, and friends), the paucity of studies studying gender effects and specifying type of relationship (e.g., husband vs. wife caregiving, adult male child vs. adult female child caregiving), the failure to recognize caregivers are at different points in their caregiving careers, and an overreliance on cross-sectional and quantitative data (see Research Focus 4.2 for a perspective on caregiving to spouses by husbands). There has also been a problem in developing a clear and

Wives with Dementia and Caregiving by Husbands

The majority of studies of caregiving have focused on those who most often provide direct intervention and services: women. This is certainly the case for spousal care among the frail elderly. Deriving principles and predictors of both caregiver burden and benefit/gain from studies may have over-sampled women and may not generalize to today's cohort of older men engaged in caregiving for their wives (Harris, 1995; Kramer, 1997b). Only relatively recently has gender been a focus in studies of caregivers (Harris, 1995). The role of spousal caregiver may be differently experienced: emotionally, cognitively, and socially by husbands when compared to wives. It is not clear whether women experience or express greater feelings of burden from caretaking than men; however, males have been found to experience depression in caring for their wives with Alzheimer's disease. Males who are caregivers to a spouse with Alzheimer's disease are in poorer overall health than men who are not caregivers (Fuller-Jonap & Haley, 1995). When compared with women, older males appear to have differential needs for and differential responses to available services both in the community and from friends and relatives.

Based on interviews with husbands, Harris (1995) identified four types of caregiving roles assumed by spouses whose wives suffered from AD: Worker, Labor of Love, Sense of Duty, and At the Crossroads. The Worker role found husbands modeling their spousal caregiving after their work role. They established small offices in their homes to manage the disease in terms of HMO, Medicare, and Blue Cross paperwork as well as keeping careful track of bills, payments made, and scheduled medical visits. The Labor of Love role described husbands who cared for their wives out of love and devotion, not duty. Husbands continually talked about the love they felt in providing care for their wives. The Sense of Duty role was characterized by husbands who felt highly responsible, conscientious, and committed to the caretaking role; they would never abandon their spouse. Finally, the group of husbands "At the Crossroads" were in the initial period of coping with their wives' disease and were in crisis. They were exploring options for their wives' care as well as beginning to develop a routine system for managing regular caretaking needs associated with AD.

Kramer (1997b) examined the various predictors of positive gain and negative burden experienced by 74 husbands engaged in the role of caregiver for their wives with dementia. Qualitative studies in the past have suggested that most husbands are reluctant to share their inner feelings with others and try to bear up as long as possible with the role and burden of caretaking. While stoic and reserved, husbands have identified their own feelings of "pride, gratification, satisfaction" in managing the caretaking role. Kramer's cross-sectional study revealed specific stressors, background characteristics of the husbands, and availability of resources that were predictive of husbands' perceptions of gains

Box Figure 4.A Buffering effect of duration of illness and satisfaction with social participation on strain in husbands caring for wives with dementia.

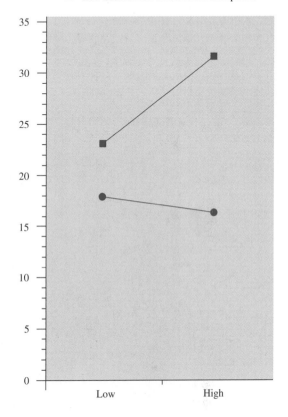

Duration of caregiving

and losses in providing care to their wives. As in other research, the length of time in the caretaking role and the degree of memory difficulties and problem behaviors of the care recipient were predictive of negative burden or role strain. Husbands who experienced higher levels of strain were in poorer health, less satisfied with their level of social interaction, and relied more on emotion-focused coping strategies. Box figure 4.A shows clearly one of the most important results of the regression analysis: The longer husbands were in the caretaking role and the more satisfied they were with their level of social participation with family and friends, the less role strain or burden experienced. And husbands also showed positive gain predicted from their satisfaction with social participation, higher levels of health, and the greater use of problem-focused coping strategies.

Interestingly, the only personal or background characteristic predictive of caregiver burden for husbands was health status of the caregiver. When predictors of positive gain in the role of caregiver were examined, a different picture emerged. Husbands' level of education was inversely related to positive outcomes of the caretaking role. Those with lower levels of education derived the highest benefits. The relationship suggesting that lower education is predictive of perceptions by husbands that they have derived positive outcomes from the caretaking role with their wives has been confirmed in two other studies, one with white adult children as caregivers and one with African-American caregivers (Miller, 1989; Picot, 1995). However, Kramer (1993b) did not obtain this result in an earlier study of wives who were caregivers. It is argued that perhaps the role of caregiver is devalued by more educated husbands when compared with their own previous type of employment (Kramer, 1997b). Or, alternatively, husbands with less education may establish lower levels of expectations for their success than wives in the caregiving role. Males appear to place significant value in the caretaking role as a purposeful, direct, and instrumental activity (e.g., it provides a concrete direction for action).

When the management and personal care of Alzheimer's patients becomes too complex and burdensome, nursing home care is sought by most families.

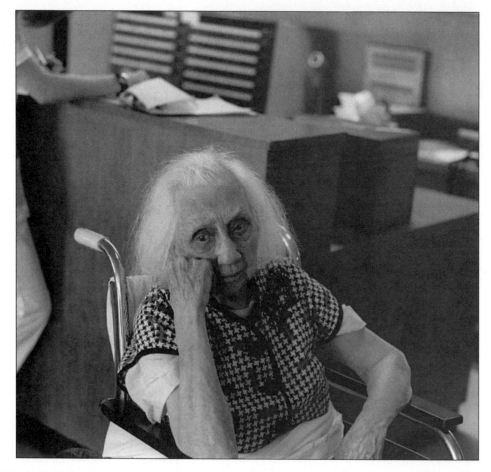

unambiguous definition of both independent and dependent measures in this research, which makes it difficult to compare studies. Finally, the richness and meaning of the caregiving role is often missing in simple quantitative indicators of caregiver gain or loss. The positive value of caretaking is highlighted in qualitative research studies. Caregivers identify positive benefits from caregiving that include: (1) past memories of meaningful relationships with the recipient, (2) feelings of appreciation from the recipient, (3) efficacy and satisfaction with the quality of care they provide, (4) positive relationships with the larger social system, and (5) enhanced feelings of self-worth, mastery, and individual growth as a person. Clearly the gains derived from the role of caregiving include both knowledge and skills as well as emotional or affective enhancements (e.g, growth in self-knowledge, self-awareness, and well-being).

Coping Effectively with Stress: Cognitive Variables

In examining how stressful life events are dealt with by adults of different ages an important set of cognitive variables has emerged according to Willis (1996). Older adults may have an advantage in resolving stressful life situations. When compared with younger persons, older individuals have developed efficient and, in some ways, more effective cognitive problem solving throughout their lives. For example, in a well-controlled study, older adults were presented a hypothetical medical illness and asked how they would resolve it. From a description of symptoms, older persons recognized the severity of the hypothetical illness far earlier than middle-aged adults (Leventhal, Leventhal, Schaefer, & Easterling; 1993). And when the illness was determined to be "serious," they sought medical attention much earlier than middle-aged adults. Middle-aged adults delayed seeking treatment far longer than the older age participants, despite descriptions highlighting growing pain arising from the hypothetical medical condition. Both age groups had equal access to medical care and equivalent knowledge regarding the level of severity of the hypothetical medical condition for which treatment might be sought (Willis, 1996). In another study, older women presented with a hypothetical medical crisis were able to arrive at a treatment decision more quickly than either young or middle-aged women.

Cognitive appraisal is helpful in managing the stress of the caregiving role. Seltzer, Greenberg, and Krauss (1995) noted that problem-focused strategies have been found to be more "proactive" in helping to control stress. Cognitive appraisal leads caregivers to take direct action and is related to positive affect and positive outcomes, particularly for males attempting to manage disruptive behaviors in care recipients. Some cognitive strategies such as wishfulness and stoicism are related to depression and negative affect in caregivers (Schulz & Williamson, 1994; Williamson & Schulz, 1993). And, emotion focused coping by adult caretakers tends to be predictive of negative mental health outcomes such as higher levels of anxiety and depression (Kramer, 1997b). Depression is also related to the repetitive use of simple strategies to control disruptive behaviors such as memory deficits, wandering, repetitive actions. Repeated reliance on simple control strategies such as physical intervention or shouting leads to exhaustion and a sense of failure among caregivers. These strategies ultimately prove fruitless and inadequate in reducing the unwanted behaviors (Kramer, 1997b; Williamson & Schulz, 1993).

Coping Effectively with Stress: Personality, Social Interaction, and Well-Being

In a classic longitudinal study, Marjorie Fiske (1980) assessed the balance between inner resources and deficits among men and women at different stages of the life course, the relationship between resources and deficits, and the individual's sense of well-being. Looked at separately, inner resources and deficits are related to life satisfaction in an entirely rational fashion. People with the most resources (such as the capacity for mutuality, growth, competence, hope, and insight) tend to be satisfied with themselves and their lives; those with deficits (psychological symptoms, including anxiety, hostility, and self-hatred) are the least satisfied. But these expected results were found among fewer than one-third of the people studied. Among the other two-thirds, a combination of many positive and negative attributes seemed to increase the individual's sense of well-being.

Well-being and physical health among the elderly have been found to be related (Angel & Angel, 1995). Those elderly with better health status are able to initiate and sustain more contacts with their families than those in poorer health (Field, Minkler, Falk, & Leino, 1993). Depression leads to reduced involvement with the social environment. It is a common outcome coexisting with a variety of physical illnesses: arthritis, cancer, chronic lung disease, neurological diseases, and heart conditions (Angel & Angel, 1995; Katon & Sullivan, 1990). Well-being is enhanced with higher levels of social interaction and is lowest among adults who have no close confidants and no regular companions (Kramer 1997b, Thomae, 1992). Field and colleagues (1993) hypothesized that a feeling of closeness between healthier elderly and their families is possible through the mechanism of reciprocity (i.e., mutual giving and receiving of social, tangible, and emotional support). Reciprocity is less likely among family members and the elderly who are in poorer health than among those in better health (Field et al., 1993). This result was also recently confirmed in a cross-cultural investigation among the rural elderly in China (Shi, 1993). Elderly Chinese with greater resources such as health, income, and education were more likely to provide rather than receive assistance in their family social support networks; exchanges were most often in the form of emotional support and/or behavioral assistance (Shi, 1993).

Friendships established earlier in life are frequently maintained through the later years. The degree of contact reported by older persons with friends and family is nearly comparable to the levels of earlier ages (Field & Minkler, 1988). Age by itself is not as good a predictor of the type and frequency of social interaction when compared with more powerful variables such as gender, ethnicity, and social class (Antonnuci & Akiyama, 1991a). However, social networks were found to contract around age 70 and then increase dramatically as direct help with daily activities from family members became necessary, most typically near age 85.

Ryff and Keyes (1995) identified six unique dimensions of well-being: (1) positive relations with others, (2) self-acceptance, (3) purposeful life or sense of meaning, (4) autonomy, (5) environmental mastery, and (6) continued personal growth. There are distinctive age trajectories identified for each of these six structural dimensions. Figure 4.4 shows that two components of well-being, environmental mastery and positive relations with others, increase with age, whereas two other components, personal

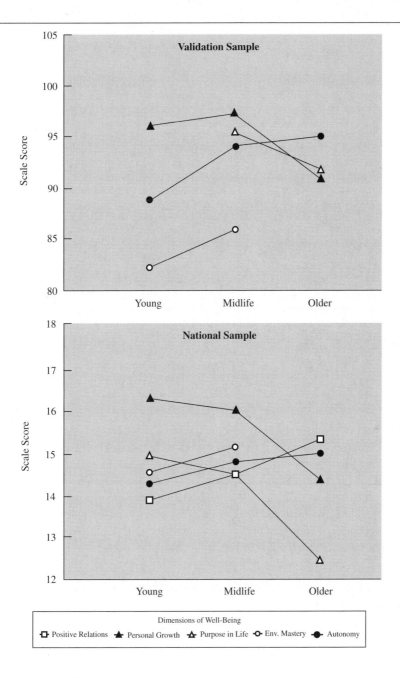

Figure 4.4 Self-ratings on the six dimensions of well-being for young, middle-aged, and older adults. The top graph shows scores from the original sample. Scores are based on a 20-item scale ranging from 20 to 120. The bottom graph shows scores from a national sample. Scores are based on a 3-item scale ranging from 3 to 18. Only results showing significant age differences are graphed. *Source: Ryff, C. (1995). Psychological well-being in adult life.* Current Directions in Psychological Science, *4(4), 99–104.*

Well-Being and Happiness

The search for factors that promote well-being and happiness comes from outside the traditional theories of psychology. Most psychological theories have focused on the origins of mental disorders, psychological problems, anxieties, and adjustment difficulties. It was assumed that the absence of such issues led to well-being, positive outcomes, and overall happiness. The absence of pathology, however, does not guarantee well-being and a positive emotional state.

David G. Myers (1993), in his book *The Pursuit of Happiness: Discovering the Pathway to Fulfillment, Well-Being, and Enduring Joy,* has approached this field from a totally different perspective. His understanding of contemporary research suggests that well-being and happiness are highly related to four positive traits: (1) high self-esteem, (2) optimism, (3) outgoing personality, and (4) strong belief in the ability to control and master the environment. Well-being has also been related to exercise and positive physical self-image, to the presence of a warm supportive social network of friends, a nurturing marriage, religious commitment and spiritual faith, and the ability to establish realistic expectations and attainable personal goals. To this list Myers adds the importance of deriving meaning and personal satisfaction from work, friendships, and family relationships. It is critical to be well matched in these areas to derive a sense of well-being and happiness.

The sense of well-being does not show much change across the life span. Well-being and happiness are relatively impermeable to culturally sanctioned methods that are supposed to enhance them. For example, studies do not find that financial success leads to greater happiness.

The sense of well-being and happiness does appear to be modifiable according to Myers.

1. When adults are encouraged to behave and speak as if they were happy, optimistic, positive, and in control, they begin to change their basic attitudes and enhance their sense of well-being and personal happiness. Act happy and you will become happier.

2. Live in the present and savor every moment, regardless of whatever else might be occurring in other spheres of life or what may be in store in the future.

3. Enjoy what you do, especially your work. Become totally invested in work or hobbies that match your personal skills, individual talents, and unique interests.

4. Develop a sense of mastery by establishing a timetable for accomplishing small goals that lead ultimately to those very important larger goals of life. The feedback and success experience are important to help maintain the direction and enthusiasm.

5. Begin or continue to be involved in regular exercise to maintain physical health.

6. Engage in the process of downward comparison, which allows people to appreciate what they have and what they have accomplished. Comparing oneself with those who are in worse situations helps focus on the positive features of one's life.

7. Emphasize and make time for close personal relationships, both family and friends.

8. Rekindle the importance of one's spirituality and religious faith.

Source: Myers, D. G. (1993). The pursuit of happiness: Discovering the pathway to fulfillment, well-being, and enduring personal joy. New York: Avon Books.

---

growth and purpose in life, show significant declines as individuals move into old age. Ryff (1995) also reports gender differences on two components of well-being. Women at all ages were found to have higher levels of positive relations with others and higher levels of personal growth than men. This may, in part, explain why social support is one of the more critical dimensions contributing to well-being and lower levels of stress among elderly women. As Kramer (1997a) notes, well-being is no longer considered a single unitary construct but is multidimensional. Examine Research Focus 4.3 for additional insights into the construct of psychological well-being.

The Search for Meaning: Cognitive Distortion, Social Comparison Processes, and Mastery

The attempt to make sense of our lives influences the cognitive appraisal of stressful encounters and the choice of coping strategies. It is part of the continuous existential search for understanding, mastery, and control of difficult situations (Skaff et al., 1996;

Willis, 1996). The cognitive-affective struggle we call coping has important implications for health, well-being, psychological functioning, competence both at work and at home, and successful interpersonal relationships (Taylor et al., 1997).

Adaptation and coping are important ingredients in understanding the adult's subjective experience of stressful events. Recently, psychologists studying coping and adaptation in the elderly have begun to question how older people are able to maintain positive self-esteem, feelings of control, and a sense of mastery in the face of an increasing number of forced changes and losses (Brandtstadter, Wentura, & Greve, 1993). Lachman and her colleagues (Lachman & Burak, 1993), for instance, provide support for the notion that older adults continue to maintain a strong belief in their ability to control the external environment. A strong belief in personal control is positively related to other areas of psychological functioning, physical health, and cognitive-intellectual achievements (Lachman & Burak, 1993; Rodin, 1990). Older adults make choices regarding those areas of life that they can still manage and forego areas in which they no longer have as much control. This is, of course, in contrast to younger adults who have minimal control over life tasks such as schooling, work, or residential location (Brim, 1992; Lachman & Burak, 1993). In this sense, older adults adjust aspirations, relinquish goals, lower expectations, and readjust priorities as developmental changes occur (Lachman & Burak, 1993). In the face of age-related developmental change they maintain a positive view of self and their own sense of personal control.

In one account (Brandtstadter et al., 1993), the success of adults in adjusting and coping with the cumulative losses in old age and corresponding threats to self-esteem lies in their use of accommodative and assimilative processes. **Accommodative processes** allow older adults to disengage and lower their aspirations from goals that they cannot attain. Accommodative processes become more important with advancing age, since they are relevant to the adjustment and coping process as well as to the self-evaluation and reprioritizing of goals in old age. **Assimilative processes** direct older adults' instrumental behavior, actively engage them, and encourage them to strive to achieve personally derived goals and priorities. Assimilative processes imply a directed, intentional activity that prevents or reduces the developmental losses in domains that are central to the older person's self-esteem and personal identity.

It is in the interplay of these two processes that older adults are able to maintain both a sense of control and a positive view of self (Brandtstadter et al., 1993). Figure 4.5 shows that the interplay between assimilative and accommodative processes contributes to the maintenance of self-esteem across the life span. Based on results of cross-sectional comparisons from 1,256 participants, the figure shows little difference between age groups in their perceived self and their desired self. Thus, although older adults recognize losses in different domains, they are able to promote a positive view of self. Brandtstadter and colleagues (1993) note that self-evaluations in the later years remain virtually unaffected by actual or perceived age-related developmental losses. The data in figure 4.5 show self-evaluations for each age cohort, measured by the difference between actual and desired self, to remain about the same. That is, among successive age cohorts, perceived self-deficits do not increase with age, regardless of real or perceived declines in function (Brandtstadter et al., 1993; Ryff, 1991).

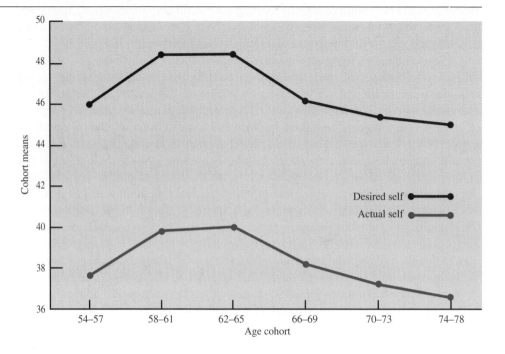

Figure 4.5 Age differences in ratings of desired self and of actual self (sum scores). By accommodating normative self-conceptions, self-esteem can be stabilized despite perceived developmental losses.

The complementary dual processes of assimilation and accommodation compose **life management,** or the process by which older persons help to protect the aging self. Older persons are able to manage stress and preserve a positive view of themselves based on subjective interpretations of developmental gains and losses. The process of life management offers one explanation of effective coping (e.g., positive self-evaluation and enhanced well-being) despite the adverse effects of developmental changes as older persons age. Life management is not, however, a process of active denial and repression; older persons are well aware of changes and losses that occur. Rather, positive self-evaluations are derived through active processes such as assimilative and accommodative modes of coping. Brandtstadter and colleagues (1993) also have begun to apply this model to help us understand how older people preserve their sense of control. They suggest that personal control may simply be a lowering of aspirations or devaluing goals that are difficult to attain. This process leads to stability or enhancement of the older person's sense of personal control (Brandtstadter et al., 1993; Brandtstadter & Renner, 1992).

In addition to life management, older adults also make use of other coping and adjustment processes such as **social comparisons** to maintain a stable and positive view of self in the face of age-related change (Gibbons & Gerrard, 1991; Ryff & Essex, 1991). Based on a hypothesized need for self-appraisal, adults compare themselves with other people to evaluate how they are doing, especially when situations are ambiguous or when external standards of performance are lacking (Heidrich & Ryff, 1993). In two separate studies, Heidrich and Ryff examined the role of social comparison processes in a large sample of elderly women. Those women who were in poor physical health more frequently engaged in social comparison processes; yet, surprisingly, the results of such frequent comparisons with others led these women to have more positive mental health and better coping. The more frequently social comparisons were utilized, the more positive the mental health of the women, even among those in the poorest of physical health. The primary mechanism employed by the older women was *downward comparison* in which they evaluated themselves against a group of women who experienced poorer physical health than themselves. The process of downward comparison has also been reported previously among individuals attempting to cope with life-threatening illnesses (Heidrich & Ryff, 1993; Taylor & Lobel, 1989).

Heidrich and Ryff (1993) not only found that elderly women's social comparisons resulted in self-enhancement and improved mental health, they documented those areas in which downward comparisons were utilized: physical health, coping with aging, and level of activity. All of these domains are ones in which loss or declines are likely to emerge in old age and document that downward comparisons indeed serve a self-enhancing function. Two areas in which upward comparisons were reported involved friendships and physical appearance. It was hypothesized that elderly women were motivated in these domains by a continued need for self-improvement, with upward social comparisons motivating them with particular role models or serving an inspirational function (Heidrich & Ryff, 1993).

Even in the most difficult of caregiving that extends for lengthy periods of time, individuals can find meaning in their caregiving activities, derive a sense of purpose, and identify a social support network (Farran, 1997). Caring for a loved one provides an opportunity for caregivers to seek meaning, value, and positive outcomes from the experience. The **search for meaning** is part of the human condition. It is identified in existential philosophy, humanistic psychology, and popularized by authors, such as Harold Kushner in *When Bad Things Happen to Good People*. Meaning and understanding comes from within the person, from their prior histories, and from their own value system (Farran, 1997).

Autonomy and Control

Mental health experts have recognized the importance of providing the elderly with a sense of control and autonomy. Older persons need to do all that they can to remain in charge of their lives. Preservation of mental and physical function, positive affect, and decreases in dependency are the direct results of supportive but not overly intrusive assistance (Seeman, Bruce, & McAvay, 1996). Older people encounter many circumstances that limit their sense of autonomy and control. These include physical impairments, reduced economic resources, and change in residence (Seeman et al., 1996).

In some studies, researchers have observed that genuine concern and love may lead a caregiver or human service professional to do too much for an older person. There are risks to having spouses, relatives, and friends assume too much responsibility for those faced with disability, illness, and even dementia. Too much helping may unintentionally produce decreased physical function, anxiety, lowered motivation, depression, greater dependency, loss of a sense of control and autonomy, reduced feelings of well-being and life satisfaction, and deficits in cognitive and motor performance among the elderly (Taylor et al., 1997). In a study of elderly over the age of 85, Johnson and Barer (1993) found that coping and a sense of control were associated with a high degree of well-being. Most of the elderly's coping strategies were directed at specific problems and these were identified by narrowing the social and physical boundaries of their environments. The elderly in this study appear to have redefined themselves (e.g., their long-term survivorship, health status, physical functioning) and moved from a future-oriented to a present-oriented time frame to produce a greater sense of control.

When control and autonomy are given to residents of nursing homes and other institutions, beneficial outcomes are routinely found. Beneficial interventions include providing choice over the timing of a move in living arrangements; providing options for residents to select in their nursing home environment; giving residents control over the length and timing of student volunteer visits; and having residents care for pets and plants (Langer & Rodin, 1976; Rodin, 1986). These interventions have been reported to improve health, emotions, subjective well-being and satisfaction, activity levels, eating, and sleeping. Encouraging control and autonomy also means discouraging well-intentioned caregivers from **infantilizing the elderly**—treating them as cute children rather than dignified adults. Overprotecting and infantilizing robs the elderly of their dignity, self-worth, mastery, and sense of achievement.

Coping with Loss of Autonomy and Personal Control: Driving and Aging

One of the most important signs of autonomy and control is the freedom afforded adults who can drive a car (Campbell, Bush, & Hale, 1993). For individuals in our society, driving provides the ability to maintain an independent lifestyle whether residing in a rural environment or an urban center. Among the cohort of older people today, men, in particular, associate driving with independence and are most reluctant to forgo their driving privileges (Campbell et al., 1993; National Research Council, 1992). Scharff (1991) notes, however, that there will be a growing number of elderly women in the coming years who also associate driving with personal freedom and independence. Persson (1993) reported the following communication from an interview with an older man: "Driving is a way of holding on to your life. I was 94 years old, and it was like losing my hand to give up driving." When asked to identify what older people missed most about being able to drive, they responded most often with the following three words: *independence, convenience,* and *mobility* (Persson, 1993). Walker (1991) projected cohort differences among today's elderly drivers and those who will become 65 years of age in the coming decades: More and more women reaching old age will routinely possess a driving license and will have had many years of experience behind the wheel. Only a few decades ago, most elderly drivers were males; women who held driving licenses were small in number, often learning to drive later in life. In one recent study, nearly 40 percent of adults over 65 had never driven a car (Marottoli, Ostfeld, Merrill, Perlman, Foley, & Cooney, 1993). By the year 2000, drivers 55 years of age and older will comprise 28 percent of the driving population and by 2050 will comprise 39 percent of all drivers (Malfetti, 1985; Persson, 1993).

Society is concerned about the safety of older drivers because of the increased likelihood of impairments in physical, visual, and cognitive capacities (Campbell et al., 1993). There is no unified approach to assessing the driving skills of older individuals, nor is there agreement regarding the use of the results of vision screening tests currently required by all states for an older person's license renewal (Persson, 1993). Investigators have found that the physical skills necessary for safe driving decline dramatically by age 75 (Persson, 1993). However, even in late middle age there is evidence that driving is problematic. The National Research Council reported that for adults 65 to 74, vehicular crashes are the leading cause of accidental death and the second leading cause (next to falls) for adults 75 and over (Persson, 1993). Studies have shown that with increasing age older drivers have difficulty in reading signs, particularly at night (Kline, Ghali, Kline, & Brown, 1990; Kline et al., 1992). The Canadian government has recommended a ratio of letter size to distance be established for road signs in recognition of this problem for older drivers and recommended the creation of minimum levels of illumination for signs at night (Charness & Bosman, 1990). When visual images or pictorial signs are used instead of lettered signs, no age differences are reported among younger, middle-aged, or older drivers (Kline et al., 1990).

Visual acuity and peripheral vision show loss beginning in the fifties, and it becomes more difficult to engage in **dual-processing tasks.** Driving demands this type of complex task performance in which physical and visual-cognitive processing of complex and dynamic information is required, such as that required in yielding the right of way at an intersection (Kline et al., 1992; Persson, 1993). In one investigation, drivers from 22 to 92 years old were surveyed to evaluate any visual difficulties they encountered in routine driving tasks (Kline et al., 1992). There was a relationship with age such that older drivers experienced more problems with routine tasks: unexpected vehicles, vehicle speed, dim displays, windshield problems, and sign reading. These data, plotted as a function of age, are presented in figure 4.6 and suggest that the declines in visual functioning reported in other studies are related to the perceived experiences of older drivers. Kline and colleagues (1992) also found these data in figure 4.6 were related to the types of automobile accidents most frequently found among older drivers.

The decision to stop driving completely is a difficult one for older persons to make. Campbell and colleagues (1993) found that nearly 50 percent of those drivers who had ceased driving completely, despite the vast majority maintaining a valid license, identified medical reasons for their decision. Specific factors in their decision to stop driving included visual impairments (macular degeneration, retinal hemorrhage), deficits in functional ability (e.g., the ability to physically carry through other daily living tasks), Parkinson's disease, stroke and stroke-related residual paralysis or weakness, episodes of losing consciousness, and Alzheimer's disease (Campbell et al., 1993; Gilley et al., 1991; Kline et al., 1992; McLay, 1989).

There are people diagnosed with AD who continue to drive for many years. They usually drive slowly, avoid heavy traffic, and easily get lost. Persuading people with AD who wish to drive that they must stop is difficult; often families enlist the support of doctors, lawyers, insurance agents, or close friends. At times families have taken away the keys to the car, hidden the keys, disabled the vehicle by disconnecting the

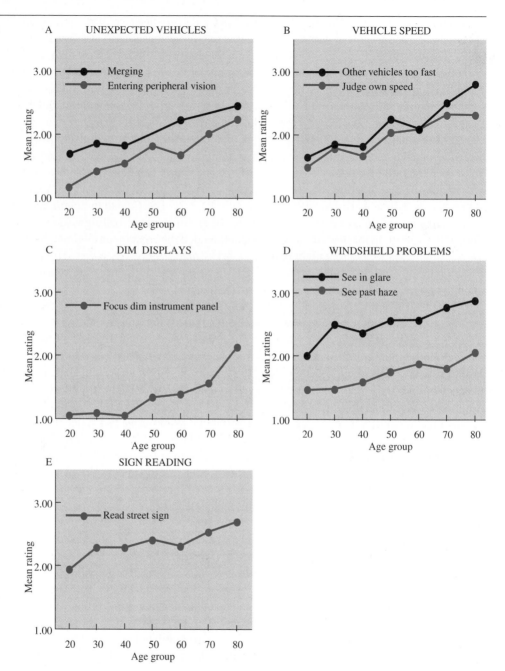

Figure 4.6 Mean reported difficulty on visual driving tasks as a function of age.

battery or starter, or notified the police or motor vehicle agency to see about suspension of the person's license. Now, many states are requiring doctors to report suspected diagnoses of AD to the motor vehicle agency responsible for issuing driving licenses (*Harvard Mental Health Letter,* 1995a, 1995b). The rate of traffic accidents is high for older drivers with Alzheimer's disease with a reported 20 times the average number of accidents per mile compared to adults of similar ages without the disease (*Harvard Mental Health Letter,* 1995a, 1995b).

Marottoli and colleagues (1993) confirm that some older adults may decide to stop driving based on their own assessment of their abilities, their age, the presence of neurologic disease, cataracts, and other limiting disabilities. However, social and economic factors also play a role (Campbell et al., 1993; Marottoli et al., 1993). Among a group of older drivers (Marottoli et al., 1993), 40 percent had stopped driving within the past six years due to physical or visual impairment, increased physical disability, and social factors (economics and retirement). Though all of these factors combined to predict total cessation of driving, the single best predictor of driving cessation was a social factor, "no longer working." In another investigation, Persson (1993) asked elderly adults to identify the reasons for their having stopped driving. The reasons included: advice from a physician, increased anxiety while driving, trouble seeing pedestrians and other cars, medical conditions, and advice from family and friends.

Persson (1993) reports that among older adults still driving, 42 percent drive more than 5,000 miles per year. Those who drive more than 5,000 miles have higher incomes, are still employed, most often male, and relatively younger and less disabled than older adults who drive less miles or do not drive at all (Marottoli et al., 1993). Other studies suggest that older drivers voluntarily adjust their driving habits in terms of frequency, length of trips, speed, time of day (e.g., daylight hours rather than evening), miles driven, and avoid peak traffic or superhighways (Kosnik, Sekuler, & Kline, 1990; Marottoli et al., 1993). Although older individuals can and do make the decision to stop or reduce their driving themselves, little research has examined how the elderly perceive their own driving skills. Some studies report that older drivers individually believe that they are both safer and more skilled than other drivers of a similar age (Persson, 1993). It is interesting that older individuals apparently ignore factors related to safety such as hearing loss or cognitive difficulties in making assessments of their own driving skills and abilities. One of the respondents in Persson's investigation jokingly remarked, "I can barely hear, barely see, and barely walk. Things could be worse though. At least I can still drive." Perhaps this reflects a bias in the sample of respondents typically surveyed, that is, community-residing and ambulatory older adults (Campbell et al., 1993). The point in much of the research is that while most older adults voluntarily decide to stop driving, there is evidence that many elderly individuals with identical problems and circumstances believe that they still can continue and indeed do so, often in the face of physical health problems. For example, consider the presence of medical conditions such as **syncope** (pronounced sin-co-pea) (losing consciousness). Florida, along with 13 other states, requires patients with this condition to have a 12-month driving suspension. Yet, a recent analysis revealed that 65 percent of those older people with syncope continued to drive (Campbell et al., 1993).

It remains difficult to limit the independence and autonomy of older drivers even when conditions appear to warrant cessation of driving privileges. Yet, it should be clear from the national statistics on automobile accidents that older persons are increasingly at risk with a higher rate of accidents than any other age group, except teenagers (Insurance Institute for Highway Safety, 1992). Persson (1993) found that the advice of a physician to stop driving is one of the most authoritative voices to which older adults are sensitive. Thus, physicians can play a critical role in managing this problem. Adults must realize that with increased age there truly are concomitant declines in some of the basic skills and abilities needed to be successful in the complex task of driving a car.

RELIGION, SPIRITUALITY, AND COPING

Until recently most gerontologists tended to overlook the importance that religion plays in the lives of older persons. In a Gallup poll, 76 percent of persons 65 years of age and older identified religion as a "very important" part of their lives, while an additional 16 percent indicated that religion was "fairly important" to their lives (McFadden, 1996; Princeton Religion Research Center, 1994). In an earlier survey, 52 percent of the respondents over age 65 reported that they attended religious services weekly, 27 percent read the Bible two to three times each week or more, and nearly 25 percent prayed at least three times daily (McFadden, 1996). Most ethnically identified and minority elderly report having a high level of religious attendance and religious commitment. The overall health and mental health needs of the elderly must recognize the spiritual needs of the elderly in planned activities and intervention programs (McFadden, 1996).

Spirituality and Religion

There is considerable variability in how investigators have defined and measured spirituality and religion. McFadden (1996) differentiates between functional and substantive definitions of religion. The former highlights the role of religion in giving meaning to life and the unknown as well as providing direction for behaviors leading to social control or psychological support. Substantive definitions of religion focus on the link between a higher power and human existence. Spirituality itself is also difficult to define conceptually. Some experts consider **spirituality** to be the motivational and emotional cause of the human **search for meaning.** The spiritual dimension usually refers to an individually experienced connection to a higher being (McFadden, 1996). There is an emotional dimension to spirituality, a "felt" experience that provides a sense of connectedness and transcendence.

Obviously religion and spirituality are not the same but represent two separate multidimensional concepts for which a variety of measures can be derived. Most studies employ cross-sectional designs and offer little insight into the patterns of religious belief, commitment, spirituality, and practices of individuals over time. Religion appears easier to measure quantitatively through church or synagogue attendance or degree of religious belief when compared with the complex components involved in assessments of spirituality. Traditional research methods may not be sensitive to dimensions of spirituality that may require in-depth individual interviews to assess the meaning persons have derived from their religious faith and commitment (Thomas & Eisenhandler, 1994).

Spirituality, Health, and Coping

Spiritual feelings and beliefs appear to be related to health. Adults report spirituality contributes to enhanced feelings of well-being, inner emotional peace, and satisfaction with life (Marcoen, 1994). Spirituality and participation in formal religious services are regularly identified in the lives of many centenarians. Older adults who attend religious services regularly and participate in the formal structures of an organized religion show improved health status, reduced incidence of chronic diseases, and more effective coping with stress (Hoeger & Hoeger, 1995). According to some religions, illness can be seen as a "test of faith" or punishment for sins and may even underlie the health-promoting behaviors of elderly (McFadden, 1996). The importance of social support as well as the act of giving to others in times of need have been identified as part of the reason that spirituality and religious participation have a positive influence on health.

For the elderly, spirituality is one mode of connecting themselves to God (McFadden, 1996). Spirituality has been linked to hopefulness among nursing home residents (Gubrium, 1993) and underlies the use of prayer by older persons coping with illness and terminal diseases (Bearon & Koenig, 1990). Spirituality has been identified as the most frequently addressed topic of home hospice visits with the terminally ill, with death anxiety a distant second (Reese & Brown, 1997). Hospice programs need to consider this important dimension in their service delivery and intervention programs. In another study of hospice patients' coping with their terminal illness, those with greater spiritual strength and ego strength were best able to buffer their response to their upcoming death. Spiritual and ego strength helped hospice patients overcome their fears of death, view themselves as "whole," and affirm death as a new, challenging, and transformational experience (Kazanjian, 1997).

Religion, Health, and Coping

Among adult populations, religion serves an organizing function. It helps individuals to derive meaning, a sense of purpose, and a coherent framework for their lives (Argyle, 1994; Ellison, 1991, 1994; Krause, 1995a). There is mounting evidence that religion and psychological well-being are represented by a U-shaped model. That is, psychological well-being is highest among those who have high religious beliefs or those who have no religious commitment; those adults with a moderate commitment to their religious beliefs showed the greatest psychological distress (Krause, 1995a; Ross, 1990). Religion has been linked consistently to longevity, improved health status (e.g., reduced risk of cardiovascular disease and less hypertension), higher self-esteem, and improved psychological well-being (Simons-Morton, Greene, & Gottlieb, 1995; McFadden, 1996). Adults with the least educational attainment (e.g., those from lower social classes) had the highest degree of religious participation. And older adults with the lowest levels of self-worth had the least religious commitment (Krause, 1995a).

There are competing views to explain the beneficial effects of religious involvement in the promotion of well-being and enhanced subjective health status. Religion serves older persons as an anchor providing not only continuity to earlier periods in their lives but also stability as "individuals begin to disengage from other roles and formal institutional involvements due to retirement, declining health, or other reasons" (Levin, Markides, & Ray, 1996, p. 461). Religion has also been reported by older persons to serve as the strategy that is most frequently chosen to help them cope (McFadden, 1996). Older adults consistently report that prayer and faith are the most frequent and most effective strategies adopted (McFadden, 1996).

A church, mosque, or synagogue provides elderly congregants access to social services and a number of deeply personal and emotionally satisfying benefits: hopefulness, preservation of self, forgiveness, and reconciliation with God (Koenig, 1995; Levin et al., 1996, Tobin, 1991). Religion serves as a significant buffer against many of the stressors encountered by older persons. We must remember that the family may not be the only, or the most important, source of social support for older adults (Grams & Albee, 1995). Spiritual support refers to the general enhancement of older persons' coping derived from their participation in organized and nonorganized religious activities, their seeking or receiving pastoral care, and their belief in a compassionate higher spiritual being who cares for all human beings (McFadden, 1996). In fact religious institutions serve older persons not only as sources of social support in times of stress but also as social outlets by channeling volunteer efforts in direct community service work that benefits needy others (Grams & Albee, 1995).

Religion and Diversity

Religious participation serves the diverse populations of ethnic and religious older persons especially well. Investigators have repeatedly noted the special significance that religion and religious attendance have on the well-being and life satisfaction of older persons from ethnically diverse backgrounds (Levin et al., 1996). Religion serves to connect such older persons to the cultural traditions and values of their own parents, grandparents, and other relatives; it is an especially valued resource as disengagement from other roles, retirement, and losses due to health occur (Post, 1992). While religion offers continuity and "hope" to most practicing older adults, it helps those from diverse backgrounds in particular to gain a sense of control over their lives (Levin et al., 1996; Koenig, 1995). In Mexican-American as well as black older populations, religious participation plays a major role in well-being. Among a sample of older Mexican-Americans and among black Americans, overall subjective health, well-being, and life satisfaction were found to be directly related to religious attendance. For older Mexican Americans regular religious attendance provided important connectedness to both family and cultural traditions. The church, its membership and its ministers are sought for social support in both times of joy as well as family life cycle events associated with loss and conflict (Levin, Chatters, & Taylor, 1995; Levin et al., 1996).

Religion, for some experts, plays a major role in meeting the health and mental health needs of many ethnic and religiously diverse populations. For example, these needs for Hispanics are initially met by the social supports offered through the community (e.g., the family, the church, neighbors and friends). The value of such primary group support for Hispanics is often used to explain their underutilization of programs such as health clinics. **Alternative resource theory** is one of the major explanations for the underutilization of community services, including mental health, which researchers have identified in Hispanic populations. Hispanics turn initially to their families or to the church to help solve their problems before turning to secondary support groups, community services, or institutional programs provided by local, state, or federal governments (Rogler, Malgady, & Rodriguez, 1989). The inability of family or religious institutions to help them cope is a cultural stigma indicative of failure. Certainly with these central values, Hispanic elderly and their families coping with health and mental health problems will exhaust their family and religious social support systems before professional care institutions and community agencies are sought. In a recent study, foreign-born older Mexican Americans were more likely to reside in the home of their adult children when compared with those born in the United States. Factors related to the decision to reside with an adult child were mutual help, economic needs, and declining health (Angel, Angel, McClellan, & Markides, 1996).

Religion and Aging

There is little consistent support for the view that religious commitment and religious practice change with increasing age (McFadden, 1996). Some studies report an increase in religious faith and practice with increasing age, whereas others report stability from early adulthood to older age. Certainly, to investigate the meaning of one's religious faith across time, a longitudinal strategy must be adopted rather than the more common cross-sectional approaches that have been employed to date (McFadden, 1996). Most persons appear to be content in old age with their level of spirituality, faith, and time commitment to their religion, although a surprising 35 percent would like to be able to spend more time in religious pursuit (DeGenova, 1992). It has been suggested that there may be a relationship between the documented changes in mature thinking (e.g., postformal thought, wisdom, awareness of multiple perspectives, integration of cognitive and emotional realities) and various developmental views of spirituality such as the growth of faith, resolution of religious dilemmas and value conflicts, and spiritual questioning (Fowler, 1981; Oser, 1991; Oser & Gmunder, 1991; Sinnott, 1994). Sinnott (1994) finds that spirituality can be understood best from a cognitive developmental perspective. She suggests that the ability of adults to recognize they coexist at both a physical and spiritual level requires **postformal operational thought.** Thus, not all older individuals who seek spirituality will necessarily realize their goal, since postformal thought itself is not a universal style of thinking for all adults.

SUMMARY

The ability to cope and adapt to life is an important feature of adult development. We have illustrated reactions and adjustments of individuals with a diagnosis of AD. The dilemma of whether to tell a person who has been diagnosed with Alzheimer's about their condition was also discussed. We have also explored the importance of respite care for patients with Alzheimer's and their caregivers, both family and health care staff. One view of stress focuses on the impact of life events, attempting to determine the relative severity of the stresses. However, other experts believe that simply rating stressors does not accurately predict adaptation and adjustment. Lazarus and his colleagues believe that how the individual cognitively perceives and understands events is far more significant than a rating of the severity of the stress caused by a life event. They have identified the importance of primary appraisal in the determination of an event as stressful. Secondary appraisal refers to the choice of resources to be utilized in stress management and includes both problem-focused resources (e.g., those in the external environment) and emotion-focused resources (e.g., those within the person). Additional support for the cognitive view is found in the concept of daily hassles and uplifts.

Some experts believe that adaptation is best understood by examining the timing of significant life experiences. Neugarten and her colleagues, for example, report that off-time events are more likely to be experienced as stressful than events that are predictable or on-time. Recent studies have confirmed the importance of cognitive distortion and unrealistic optimism as effective coping strategies for people facing life-threatening illnesses such as cancer or AIDS. The care of an older relative demands effective coping by caregivers who, in line with a gender consistency model, are typically middle-aged daughters.

Middle-aged adult children face complex burdens in caregiving. They try to maintain some pleasures, interests, and social interactions without sacrificing all of their time and resources. Too much intervention or caregiving beyond what is truly needed can make care recipients dependent on others and lead to depression and hopelessness. The importance of social support in times of stress was highlighted for both caregivers and for the elderly themselves. When Alzheimer's patients remain at home with relatives, respite care provides valuable relief from round-the-clock caregiving; minorities do not readily seek respite care programs.

In examining adaptation by adults throughout the life span we have discussed the importance of the search for meaning, the preservation of personal control and autonomy, the maintenance of a positive view of self, and contributions to a continued sense of mastery. Different life management processes designed to accomplish these goals were identified and the interplay of accommodative and assimilative processes in maintaining a positive view of self was examined. The special significance of driving as a part of autonomy and mastery also was examined. Newer studies of the process of caregiving were reviewed. This research documents the beneficial outcomes of caregiving and the positive impact of the role for the caregiver. Gender differences in caretaking were assessed and the often overlooked contributions of husbands in helping manage a wife with AD were detailed.

Finally we explored the importance of spirituality and religion in the lives of older persons, paying special attention to the impact on health and adaptive processes. Spirituality and religion play an especially important role in the lives of older adults from ethnic and racially diverse backgrounds. It may account for their reluctance to seek support such as respite care from the larger community consistent with alternative resource theory.

REVIEW QUESTIONS

1. Discuss two major views of stress.
2. Outline Lazarus's basic ideas about stress and coping.
3. Distinguish between accommodative and assimilative processes as they apply to coping and life management. Give an example of each process.
4. Describe an off-time event and an on-time event and indicate how timing influences stress.
5. Describe some of the coping strategies used by women facing a diagnosis of breast cancer.
6. Describe the differences in coping by gay men diagnosed as seropositive with HIV and those still seronegative. What are the motivations underlying AIDS patients seeking family reconciliation?
7. Describe the role of respite care in families dealing with AD. What are the immediate consequences of caregiving within such families?
8. Provide a "patient's perspective" on AD. How is this perspective related to the concepts of stigma and disruption of self-image?
9. What are the benefits of caregiving to those who provide such care?
10. Define *caregiver burden* and identify some of the factors that reduce this type of stress.
11. What are the differences between emotion-focused and problem-focused coping?
12. Discuss the concept of well-being and its relationship to coping and development.
13. Describe the roles of religion and spirituality in the lives of elderly persons. How can they reduce the impact of stress and enhance health?

FOR FURTHER READING

Edwards, A. J. (1993). *Dementia.* New York: Plenum.

Gray, D. D. (1993). *I want to remember: A son's reflection on his mother's Alzheimer's journey.* Wellesley, MA: Roundtable Press.

Hersen, M., & Van Hasselt (Eds). (1998). *Handbook of clinical geropsychology.* New York: Plenum.

McGowin, D. F. (1993). *Living in the labyrinth: A personal journey through the maze of Alzheimer's disease.* New York: Delacorte Press.

Rubenstein, R. L., & Lawton, M. P. (1997). Depression in long-term and residential care: Advances in research and treatment. New York: Springer.

Willis, S. L., Schaie, K. W., & Hayward, M. (Eds.). (1997). Societal mechanisms for maintaining competence in old age. New York: Springer.

MENTAL
HEALTH AND
INTERVENTIONS

INTRODUCTION

Some people have difficulty coping with the demands and complexities of everyday life. In this chapter, you will learn about methods for optimizing or promoting effective psychological functioning. Breakdown in coping strategies and loss of the ability to adapt are the indications of a psychological disorder. There is a shortage of professionals trained to work with the mental health needs of the elderly, and the elderly, in turn, must see that they can and do benefit from various therapeutic mental health interventions that improve their coping, adaptation, and overall mental health. Mental health care must also be affordable and available. For example, Medicare currently provides a lower percentage reimbursement for mental health care than for physical care. As improvements in the variety, accessibility, and availability of mental health interventions are made, the quality of care for adults and the elderly in society will be enhanced (Lebowitz & Niederehe, 1992).

MENTAL HEALTH AND AGING

Despite the importance of meeting the mental health needs of older adults, many needs are unmet in the United States and in most countries (Eisdorfer, 1993; Kiesler, 1992). Currently less than 3 percent of Medicare funding is being used to support mental health. A significant number of nursing home admissions and hospitalizations among the elderly relate directly to mental health disorders; yet, a minimal amount of outpatient treatment (e.g., individual therapy, group intervention) is being provided to those 65 years of age and older, a situation that has persisted for decades (Eisdorfer, 1993).

Mental health refers to the absence of mental disorders, and to the ability to deal effectively with life events. Although the absence of adjustment difficulties is part of the definition of good mental health, the definition includes positive characteristics of adaptation and coping (Butler, Lewis, & Sunderland, 1991). Positive indicators of mental health include a range of coping and adaptation skills: a generally accurate perception of reality, a sense of personal mastery, capacity for independence, and positive self-esteem. Mental health competencies also include successful social relationships, a productive orientation to life and work, self-direction, and a focus on self-actualization. Since older adults are more likely than younger adults to have some type of physical illness, the interweaving of physical and mental health problems is more likely to occur in later adulthood than in younger adulthood (Deeg, Kardaun, & Fozard, 1996).

Aging itself has not been found to be related to an increase in mental health disorders. Gatz and colleagues (1996) estimated that about 22 percent of older adults (65+) may be classified as having a mental disorder defined within the categories of the *Diagnostic and Statistical Manual of Mental Disorders of the American Psychiatric Association (DSM-IV)* (American Psychiatric Association, 1994). This percentage, which includes both cognitive impairments such as dementia as well as emotional disorders such as depression, is identical to that reported by the National Advisory Mental Health Council (1993) for all adult age groups and is also consistent with that reported by Kazdin and Kagan (1994) for children and adolescents under 18 years of age (i.e., 17–22%).

Beyond any doubt, societies must address the mental health needs of the growing population of older adults. Growing older does not necessarily increase the risk of mental health problems, but the numbers of older adults are increasing in most countries. It has been reported that the wide variety of life circumstances of older adults creates a large amount of interindividual variability in mental health. For example, in some individuals, mental distress may increase with age because of the death of friends and loved ones and the onset of chronic illness; other older adults may show improvements in mental health as the strains caused by an unbearable job or caring for ill parents come to an end. Aldwin and colleagues (1989) concluded that

> rather than asking whether mental health changes with age, perhaps we should ask what patterns of change are characteristic of different groups of adults, and what are the antecedents and consequences of long-term change or stability in mental health? In this manner we can begin to understand the process of "successful" aging. (p. 305)

The **diathesis-stress model** describes the relationship between challenging life events (stress) and the individual's degree of frailty or vulnerability (diathesis). Figure 5.1 shows the diathesis-stress model and highlights the relationships between life-event stressors and individual vulnerabilities. The threshold point is when stresses exceed the individual's capacity to handle them.

Older adults with mental health problems are those who may have had (a) the same disorder at one or more earlier points in development, (b) a problem in earlier development that blossoms into a more serious mental disorder as the individual ages, or (c) no evidence of any mental health problem earlier in development but one that appears de novo in late life. Some authors suggest that in terms of psychological diathesis, older adults may be less vulnerable than younger adults. For example, some research suggests that older adults coping with physical illness show less anger, fear, or shame than younger persons. Older persons may have developed more successful strategies to cope with illness over their own lives or perhaps have adjusted their expectancies to accept such problems (Deeg et al. 1996). Other investigators suggest that the severity of certain stressors such as the loss of spouse,

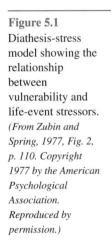

Figure 5.1
Diathesis-stress model showing the relationship between vulnerability and life-event stressors.
(From Zubin and Spring, 1977, Fig. 2, p. 110. Copyright 1977 by the American Psychological Association. Reproduced by permission.)

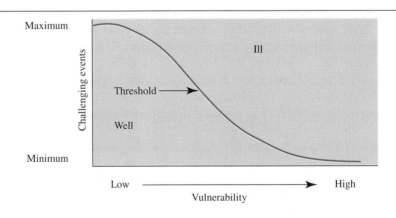

retirement, or relocation may be much harder on older persons than younger persons. However, other research suggests that younger adults experience a greater number of negative events overall than the elderly. Chronic stress leading to mental disorders such as depression is far more characteristic of younger adults than among the elderly (Gatz et al., 1996; George, 1992). The risk of depression does not increase with advancing age unless special physical conditions or medical problems occur or unless analyses are restricted to the oldest old (Gatz et al., 1996). Even the patterns of depressive symptoms seen in the elderly are somewhat unique when compared with those of younger adults. Perhaps biological diathesis may increase with advancing age.

UTILIZATION OF MENTAL HEALTH SERVICES

Compared with younger adults, fewer older adults use mental health services. It has been suggested that older people today hold many stereotypical views and inaccurate beliefs about mental health treatment and diagnoses (Davies, Sieber, & Hunt, 1994; Dick & Gallagher-Thompson, 1996; Harel & Biegel, 1995).

For example, elderly people may associate treatment with institutionalization in a hospital or psychiatric center or with labels like "nervous breakdown." They often assume that treatments for mental disorders such as depression are not generally successful. They may be embarrassed by mental health problems, believing that such disorders should be hidden from family and friends or that the person with a disorder should be isolated from the community. Those who fear that such disorders leave a stigma on other family members may consider mental health problems as a sign of genetic weakness. Older persons have not been socialized to self-disclose or discuss personal adjustment issues openly; they frequently believe that their own problems are not serious enough to warrant attention. They may assume that all therapeutic intervention is based on intensive, expensive, and long-term individual clinical therapy. They may assume that mental health centers and mental health professionals are only for those who are highly disturbed, for example, those who are "ready for the loony bin" or "crazy" (Dick & Gallagher-Thompson, 1996).

With such stereotyped understanding of mental health, older persons expect little success from mental health treatment and may be unaware of new and effective clinical advances or innovative services. Many older adults have difficulty recognizing symptoms of mental health problems in others and in themselves (Davies et al., 1994; Robbins, Locke, & Reiger, 1991). Adults over the age of 65 generally report fewer mental health problems throughout their lives when compared with younger adults (Robbins et al., 1991). Although fear of self-disclosure may be responsible, in part, for underrecognition and underutilization of mental health services, other possibilities remain. Padgett, Patrick, Burns, and Schlesinger (1995) note that older persons may have poor memory for such incidents and a lower level of acceptance of diagnostic labels indicative of mental disorders. Mental health professionals are concerned about older persons because evidence suggests that there are higher mortality rates for those with serious and untreated mental health disorders (Davies et al., 1994).

Harel and Biegel (1995) note that attitudes toward mental health services vary greatly depending on the ethnic community, gender, and age cohort to which individuals belong. In an ethnically diverse culture like our own there will be a projected greater need for broader mental health services in the coming years (Aponte & Crouch, 1995). The prediction arises from the fact that **ethnic elderly** populations historically have been at lower socioeconomic levels, in poorer health, underemployed or nonemployed for significant periods in adult life, and recipients of fewer benefits in retirement. These demographic factors are associated with increased mental health needs among ethnically diverse elderly. These older adults already do not take advantage of the available intervention services provided by local, state, and federal government. Women from ethnically diverse backgrounds seem to be more likely to use mental health services more frequently than men from similarly diverse cultural backgrounds (Rivers, 1995).

Some investigators have suggested that being both old and a member of an ethnic subculture results in extra vulnerability for health and mental health problems; however, others have questioned whether such "double jeopardy" applies to all ethnic elderly (Padgett, 1995). Considerable effort needs to be given to removing the barriers and obstacles that affect utilization of mental health services by elderly from various ethnic populations. However, careful study also needs to be directed at when and how mental health services are currently accessed by elderly from diverse ethnic populations. Mental health disorders have quite different defining behavioral symptoms and are treated differently within each ethnic subculture (Rogler & Cortes, 1993). Psychologists need to be sensitive to the operational definitions of mental health problems in different ethnic subcultures to understand the meaning and significance of unique presenting complaints and symptoms. This understanding is crucial to the development of culturally appropriate treatment plans and subsequent successful functioning within specific ethnic communities (Dinges & Cherry, 1995; Rogler & Cortes, 1993).

Mental Health and Ethnicity

The importance of understanding the relationship of psychological disorders and ethnic aging is being addressed, in part, by educating mental health professionals about the values, beliefs, and cultural assumptions of specific ethnically diverse aging populations. There is considerable emphasis on training, program design, and service delivery for mental health professionals. And, there is increased education in ethnic communities as to the importance and benefits of mental health intervention. Ethnic populations cannot be stereotyped and treated the same since the success of any clinical treatment depends on each therapist's ability to establish trust, build relationships, develop empathy, and listen sensitively to clients as individuals, free from personal prejudice and bias. Successful intervention requires mental health professionals who are caring, who are compassionate, who are curious, who seek to discover the unique individuality of every client. Sensitivity embraces a willingness to understand the culture, values, and background of the client seeking treatment (Wohl, 1995).

Ethnic group membership implies, on the one hand, identification and participation in the unique attributes of that subculture, its heritage, and its values. Yet, there are wide individual differences in the centrality of **ethnic identity** across subcultures and correspondingly sharp differences in acculturation and assimilation to the majority society within each subculture (Wohl, 1995). Various indexes are used to mark acculturation, such as preferred language, number of years in the United States, age at which migration occurred, ethnic self-identification, or degree of contact with members of other ethnic groups (Rodriguez & O'Donnell, 1995). At least for elderly Hispanics, such indexes are significant because those who are most acculturated access mental health services at higher rates than those who are less acculturated (Rodriguez, 1987; Rodriguez & O'Donnell, 1995; Starrett, Todd, & DeLeon, 1989). The low rates of using mental health services by ethnically diverse populations of elderly has also been linked by Rogler and colleagues (1989) to two major explanations: alternative resource theory and barrier theory.

Alternative resource theory, as discussed in Chapter 4, is one of the major explanations for the underutilization of community services, including mental health. There is a wide range of social organizations or primary group structures that are available to older persons in ethnic subcultures; these will be accessed first, before other formal organizations such as community mental health agencies are consulted. It is only when culturally accepted interventions (e.g., alternative resources) have failed that older persons reluctantly seek professional mental health services. Hispanics, for example, turn initially to family, friends, religious leaders, spiritualists, or folk healers to help solve their psychological problems before turning to secondary support groups, community services, or institutional programs provided by local, state, or federal governments (Rogler et al., 1989). Hispanic culture places a high value on the mutual help provided by the nuclear and extended family. **Mutual help** according to Rogler and colleagues (1989) is an obligatory norm sustained by both guilt and gratitude. Guilt is felt if one should fail to help a relative who is in need, while gratitude is experienced in being helped by one's relatives. Certainly with these central values, Hispanic elderly and their families coping with health and mental health problems exhaust alternate resources such as family or religious support, before professional mental health agencies are sought.

Specific Hispanic cultural values that also lead to underutilization of community mental health services include: (1) *confianza,* or the value of trust in a person more than in an organization; (2) *personalismo,* or the value of the immediate personal relationship with friend/family more than an unknown impersonal mental health institution; (3) *respeto,* or the value of respect owed to one's elders; (4) *verguenza* and *orgullo,* or the sense of shame and the value of pride; and (5) *machismo,* or the pride in manliness and the difficulties in admitting personal defects and weakness (Rodriguez & O'Donnell, 1995; Rogler et al., 1989). Professional community mental health services appear to be a last resort, among those who are least acculturated. Traditionally, in a Hispanic community, a person with mental health disorders is stigmatized, if he or she cannot be helped informally. Persons needing formal help are seen as having lost ties to their family and to their Hispanic community; their social value within the community is significantly reduced (Angel & Angel, 1995).

For elderly Puerto Ricans living in New York City, alternative resource theory has been found to underlie the importance of family social support in lowering stress and reducing the rate at which professional mental health services have been utilized (Rodriguez & O'Donnell, 1995). Having natural community resources such as social support can be helpful; however, they do not necessarily take the place of needed mental health services among older Puerto Ricans. Social support may delay the search for professional intervention services, may not be as effective as professional intervention in treating mental health disorders, and may take a heavy toll on the caregivers who provide such support. In one study, among older Puerto Ricans the best predictor of those seeking community mental health services was the ability to subjectively identify a need for professional services (Rodriguez & O'Donnell, 1995).

Another alternative resource that has been identified in Hispanic cultures is the use of **folk systems** to heal people with mental and physical disorders. Three distinctive Hispanic cultures within the United States have been identified, each with its own unique view of mental and physical illness and appropriate treatment: *espiritismo* in Puerto Rican subculture, *santeria* in Cuban subculture, and *curanderismo* in Mexican American subculture. Each shares the following common features:

1. The cause of illness and misfortune is external to the individual and is mostly spiritual.
2. Group participation in healing rituals is often preferred to individual sessions.
3. The individual with the disorder is treated as if within a family or community.
4. Morality is both a cause of illness and a condition for recovery and healing.
5. Healing depends largely on nonverbal and symbolic interactions (Koss-Chioino, 1995, p. 146).

In simplistic terms, the cause of physical, mental, emotional, and interpersonal problems is due to forces outside the person and outside of the person's awareness. To bring relief there must be a resolution of forces that threaten the ideal balance between the person, the environment, and the spirits or cosmos. Healing in this sense is seen as bringing harmony and equilibrium to the person (Koss-Chioino, 1995). Knowing what is out of balance is determined by the healer, with little or no input from the client. As acculturation proceeds the use of folk healing decreases among each of these three Hispanic groups.

Barrier theory hypothesizes that institutional obstacles within the mental health system itself are responsible for underutilization of available services by ethnic minorities. Barriers are also perceived in service delivery. Consider the perceptions of Hispanic elderly seeking mental health treatment who identify community agencies as impersonal, in conflict with their basic cultural traditions, and discriminatory in discouraging the use of Spanish language. There are also basic values within Hispanic culture which turn persons away from any agency perceived to be part of a distant, large bureaucratic system and not part of the immediate face-to-face social supports of the community (Rogler et al., 1989). Barrier theory is not necessarily in conflict with alternative resource theory. Experts believe that current needs for mental health services are high among ethnic elderly (Angel & Angel, 1995). Culture, class, and language all appear to be barriers to utilization. Barriers also include the following (see Harel & Biegel, 1995; Vasquez & Han, 1995):

1. Overt discrimination and prejudice
2. Lack of bicultural understanding among professionals in mental health centers
3. Professionals speaking only English

4. Socioeconomic differences between therapist and clients
5. Geographic inaccessibility to mental health services located outside of the ethnic community
6. Lack of transportation to mental health centers providing services
7. Lack of health insurance and/or income to cover the cost of treatment
8. Lack of ethnic minority mental health professionals or role models
9. Physical and social isolation of the ethnic community itself

Other barriers to full utilization of mental health interventions by ethnically diverse elderly include a lack of education and awareness of mental health, mental health services, and the value of counseling as a way of problem solving (Vasquez & Han, 1995). In some subcultures there are specific restrictions against discussion of personal problems with nonfamily members. And some ethnic subcultures have a unique understanding, language, definition, and representation of mental health symptoms.

Explanations for the underutilization of community mental health services by older black adults have centered on alternative resource theory, limited availability of services, and institutional barriers. In time of need, alternative resources are sought first. These include extensive social supports provided by the immediate and extended family network, friends, and by community institutions like the black church and black clergy (Aponte & Barnes, 1995; Miller, 1992; Padgett et al., 1995). A number of barriers limit utilization of mental health services by older black adults. For example, the small number of appropriate professional black role models on staff of community mental health agencies suggests that the agency is biased, prejudiced, and discriminatory in attitude, treatment, and service delivery. With few black mental health professionals on staff, it appears that perhaps the community mental health needs of the community are being ignored. Economic barriers suggest that with less income and insurance coverage for mental health services, many ethnic populations, including black Americans, are less likely to seek and receive professional treatment. However, it may be that the type of mental health services sought by older black adults differs from that of older whites. In one investigation equal access to mental health services was available to black and white federal workers who received identical health and mental health insurance coverage. Black and white adults over the age of 55 utilized inpatient health and mental health services at equal rates. Yet, older blacks were less likely to make use of mental health outpatient services, as measured by frequency of number of visits to the agency, than similarly aged older whites (Padgett et al., 1995).

Access and Ethnicity

Research on the rate at which older ethnic populations access mental health services appears to mirror the lower overall rate for elderly persons in the United States (Padgett, 1995). For example, Barney (1995) noted that within a recent 6-month period approximately 7.1 percent of a Native American population of older persons accessed some mental health services, a figure that is nearly identical to that for national surveys of non–Native American older persons. The best predictor of utilization of mental health services by older Native Americans living on a reservation was their subjective self-assessment of perceived need. However, for those living in urban settings, the degree of mental impairment was the best predictor. Reservation-dwelling elderly have a choice of traditional spiritual healing or standard mental health approaches; those residing in urban settings have only the latter. As Barney noted, "traditional healing, as an option, may assist reservation elderly in having more control over their own self-perceived need for 'treatment'; thus explaining why this variable was so strong in predicting mental health service use for reservation elders and so weak in predicting service use for urban elders" (Barney, 1995, p. 210). Older Native Americans on reservations perceive themselves to be more isolated, a reality based on the reduced availability of traditional social support and the decline of the extended family network as younger persons move away to live or to work. Elderly Native Americans living on reservations may be more at risk for psychological disorders as a result and appear to be in greater need of mental health services today than in the past. Those older Native Americans residing in urban settings may be more knowledgeable about mental health agencies and in closer geographical proximity to such services than those residing on a reservation (Barney, 1995).

Comparisons of the rate at which older blacks and whites seek mental health services are rare (Padgett et al., 1995). The assumption has been that underutilization of mental health services for older black Americans should mirror that found for younger black adults. Black Americans facing mental health problems are underrepresented in both inpatient hospitalization programs and outpatient community mental health programs (Padgett et al., 1995).

There has been considerable research on the type of mental health disorders that cause elderly from different ethnic populations to seek services. Regardless of specific ethnicity, elderly from diverse backgrounds seek help from their family or their immediate social network first. Social supports for older persons with mental health problems are readily available and accessible within most ethnic subcultures (Aponte & Barnes 1995; Thompson, Walker, & Silk-Walker, 1993). When primary social supports prove inadequate or ineffective in managing the disorder older persons from ethnically diverse backgrounds usually seek specific mental health treatment. Older persons from diverse backgrounds, however, are not as likely to access outpatient services as they are inpatient services. Inpatient treatment is usually appropriate for mental health disorders that are fairly serious. Harada and Kim (1995) found that 89 percent of older Asians and Pacific Islanders utilizing mental health services sought direct inpatient care. The presenting mental health disorders were severe and required constant monitoring. Mental health referrals for Asians and Pacific Islanders were usually made by health care agencies. In contrast, however, older Vietnamese clients were most often referred for mental health treatment by family, friends, or social agencies. Elderly Vietnamese clients were referred for less severe mental health problems (e.g., adjustment disorders) than other Asians and Pacific Islanders. The older Vietnamese clients also stayed longer in treatment than other older Asian and Pacific Islanders (Harada & Kim, 1995). Depression was the most common presenting problem for older Koreans, Chinese, Japanese, and Filipinos seeking treatment in mental health agencies. They were most often referred by social service or health agencies rather than families or friends (Harada & Kim, 1995).

MENTAL HEALTH AND PSYCHOLOGICAL DISORDERS

In the past, psychologists have often overlooked mental health issues in the elderly. With growing interest in this segment of society, special attention has been devoted to the more common psychological disorders experienced by the elderly, such as depression, anxiety, and alcoholism.

The Incidence of Clinical Depression

The incidence of depression reported among older adults varies widely since different methodologies, samples, nationalities, and criteria have been employed in research studies (Anthony & Aboraya, 1992; Koenig & Blazer, 1992; Raskind & Peskind, 1992). There is some agreement that about 4 to 7 percent of the elderly overall experience **clinical depression** serious enough to require intervention (Anthony & Aboraya, 1992). The incidence of clinical depression in community-residing adults over the age of 65 is 1 to 4 percent, which is lower than that found for other age groups (Dick & Gallagher-Thompson, 1996; Gatz et al., 1996). However, specific subgroups of older individuals show rates of clinical depression that are quite high (e.g., 10–15%). For example, clinical depression is often a corollary condition among older persons with serious health problems and quite common among the frail elderly (Dick & Gallagher-Thompson, 1996). Futterman, Thompson, Gallagher-Thompson, and Ferris (1995) found the lowest incidence of clinical depression among community-dwelling older residents, followed by older adults with health problems severe enough to warrant outpatient care, and highest among elderly receiving residential care.

Cross-sectional age comparisons with respondents 18 to 90 years of age reveal that clinical depression is at its lowest level in middle age and reaches its highest level in those over the age of 80 (Mirowsky & Ross, 1992). Contributing factors to the steady increase in clinical depression across the later part of the life span include losses in marriage, employment, economic well-being, health, status, and personal control (Mirowsky & Ross, 1992). In some studies of older couples it appears that depressive behavioral symptoms in one spouse are likely to result in depressive behavioral symptoms in the other (Tower & Kasl, 1995). And the closer the preexisting emotional relationship between spouses, the greater the similarity in clinical depression and specific depressive behavioral symptoms. The multiple mechanisms underlying these findings may include, but are not limited to, mate selection, emotional contagion, and common environmental influences (Bookwala & Schulz, 1996). Among institutionalized elderly populations, in particular, deteriorating health and associated increases in clinical depression have been found to be predictive of death (Parmelee, Katz, & Lawton, 1992).

Previous studies relating the incidence of clinical depression to age are subject to criticism. Some have used a very narrow age range of older persons (e.g., 65–75), a small number of older respondents (e.g., 75+ years of age), or a measure of age that combined all individuals over the age of 65 into a single group for analysis (Kessler, Foster, Webster, & House, 1992). Other investigators have based their conclusions on nonrepresentative samples (e.g., given the high rate at which older research participants exclude themselves from research participation). Sometimes the very phenomenon that is being investigated (i.e., clinical depression), may lead older adults to refuse to participate in research. Without representative samples, there will be consistent underestimates of the incidence of clinical depression in the elderly as well as greater difficulty in the search for significant correlates of depression itself (Thompson, Heller, & Rody, 1994).

The highest rates of depressive *symptoms* appear among those older than 65; yet the frequency of clinical depression as a psychiatric diagnosis (e.g., see table 5.1) is highest among those 25 to 65 years of age. The rate of depressive symptoms among older community-residing elderly has been reported to be from 9 to 30 percent (Dick & Gallagher-Thompson, 1996). Many common myths suggest that depression is a "normal" part of aging; as a result, it is often ignored, underreported, and untreated. Yet depression remains the most common mental health diagnosis in old age (Dick & Gallagher-Thompson, 1996). Each year 1 of every 1,000 older persons becomes hospitalized for major depression with a resultant hospital stay of about two weeks at a cost of about $6,750 (Callahan & Wolinsky, 1995). Though coping with loss is a part of the culture of growing old, it is not uniquely restricted to the later part of the life span and may occur at any age; clinical depression demands intervention whenever it is encountered.

Diagnosis of Clinical Depression

The clinical diagnostic criteria of depression in the *DSM-IV* are presented in table 5.1. Clinical depression in old age may be more difficult to diagnose than in younger persons for several reasons. First, it is manifest somewhat differently in older and younger populations. Clinical depression among the aged is most often marked by "diminished interest in things around them, fatigue, difficulty with waking early in the morning and not being able to get back to sleep, complaints about their memory, thoughts about death, and general hopelessness" (Gatz et al., 1996, p. 368; also see Feifel, 1990; Kastenbaum, Feifel, Rosenberg, & Lule, 1995).

A pattern of depressive symptoms termed the **depletion syndrome** has been identified among the elderly that is manifestly different from the depressive symptoms seen in younger persons (Newmann, Engel, & Jensen, 1991). Depletion syndrome is characterized by lack of interest and feeling that everything is an effort. It has been identified diagnostically as a minor depression (Blazer, Burchett, Service, & George, 1991). However, the current *DSM-IV* does not recognize so-called minor depression (American Psychiatric Association, 1994). Some experts disagree that depletion syndrome is truly indicative of clinical depression; they note that there are many adjustments that produce disappointments, anxieties, and motivational difficulties that should not be taken as evidence of clinical depression. The depletion syndrome is useful in describing many of the motivational difficulties older adults have in getting things initiated or completed. It also underscores the reports by the elderly that routine daily tasks become increasingly exhausting and difficult to complete. The depletion syndrome also is descriptive of the loss of interest and enjoyment in things that older people formerly found rewarding.

A second factor making it difficult to diagnose clinical depression in the elderly is that both older persons as well as other family members usually disregard depressive

Symptoms of Depression: Diagnostic Criteria for Major Depressive Episodes

A. Major depressive episode: Five (or more) of the following symptoms have been present during the same two-week period and represent a change from previous functioning; at least one of the symptoms is either (1) depressed mood or (2) loss of interest or pleasure. Note: Do not include symptoms that are clearly due to a general medical condition or mood-incongruent delusions or hallucinations.

1. Depressed mood most of the day, nearly every day, as indicated by either subjective report (e.g., feels sad or empty) or observation made by others (e.g., appears tearful). Note: In children and adolescents, symptom can be irritable mood.
2. Markedly diminished interest or pleasure in all, or almost all, activities most of the day, nearly every day (as indicated by either subjective account or observation made by others).
3. Significant weight loss when not dieting or weight gain (e.g., a change of more than 5% of body weight in a month), or decrease or increase in appetite nearly every day. Note: In children, consider failure to make expected weight gains.
4. Insomnia or hypersomnia nearly every day.
5. Psychomotor agitation or retardation nearly every day (observable by others, not merely subjective feelings of restlessness or being slowed down).
6. Fatigue or loss of energy nearly every day.
7. Feelings of worthlessness or excessive or inappropriate guilt (which may be delusional) nearly every day (not merely self-reproach or guilt about being sick).
8. Diminished ability to think or concentrate, or indecisiveness, nearly every day (either by subjective account or as observed by others).
9. Recurrent thoughts of death (not just fear of dying), recurrent suicidal ideation without a specific plan, or a suicide attempt or a specific plan for committing suicide.

    B. The symptoms cause clinically significant distress or impairment in social, occupational, or other important areas of functioning.

    C. The symptoms are not due to the direct physiological effects of a substance (e.g., drug abuse, a medication) or a general medical condition (e.g., hypothyroidism).

    D. The symptoms are not accounted for by bereavement; that is, after the loss of a loved one, the symptoms persist for longer than two months or are characterized by marked functional impairment, morbid preoccupation with worthlessness, suicidal ideation, psychotic symptoms, or psychomotor retardation.

From the American Psychiatric Association: Diagnostic and statistical manual of mental disorders, fourth edition, *Revised, pp. 161–163. Washington, DC: American Psychiatric Association, 1994. Reprinted by permission.*

symptoms, believing that they are normal for anyone who reaches old age (Blazer, 1993; Dick & Gallagher-Thompson, 1996). The oft-held assumption among the elderly themselves and their families is that depressive symptoms are a natural consequence of growing older, reflecting the accumulation of many personal losses (spouse, job, friends, family, housing) and the steadily increasing physical and medical health problems that are encountered in old age (Weiner, 1992). More than 50 percent of all older persons believe that manifestations of clinical depression remain a "normal" part of aging and a natural response to the typical medical illnesses and expected losses associated with growing old (Katz, 1997).

    A third factor contributing to the difficulty of diagnosis is that older persons may not have well-developed strategies for self-assessment, and fail to recognize depression by how they feel. Compared with younger adults, the elderly are less likely to identify themselves as being depressed or feeling "down" (Gallo, Anthony, & Muthen, 1994). For example, older adults often report negative feelings to other family members and their physicians in metaphorical terms: (1) cognitive complaints such as worthlessness, demoralization, hopelessness, despair; and (2) somatic complaints such as difficulties sleeping, low energy, weight loss, intestinal disorders, appetite decline, aches and pains, and nervousness (Blazer, 1993; Dick & Gallagher-Thompson, 1996). Alternatively, it may be that there are age differences in the nature of depression itself, both in how it is experienced and in how it is manifested (Gatz et al., 1996).

Fourth, clinicians find it difficult to identify depression in older persons using the criteria in the *DSM-IV* appropriate for mood disorders (Blazer, 1994). Analogously, research investigators who have studied age and the incidence of clinical depression have also found inconsistency in published reports due to the variety of scales used to screen or identify symptoms in older populations. The inclusion of many items with a strong somatic component is biased against the elderly, who are far more likely to report symptoms in this domain than are younger persons (Kessler et al., 1992).

Weiner (1992) has confirmed a final difficulty in the diagnosis and treatment of depression in the elderly. Today's cohort of elderly may be embarrassed to seek treatment for depression and reluctant to admit such personal difficulties to others due to shame, guilt, and fear of public knowledge. The elderly today often hold inaccurate beliefs that mental health issues are highly stigmatizing, incurable, and a mark against one's entire family. A unique characteristic of untreated depression in the elderly is the significantly higher risk of suicide when compared with younger adults with this disorder (Gatz et al., 1994).

As mentioned, self-assessment of psychological disorders such as clinical depression is difficult for older persons and this, in part, accounts for the fact that fewer older persons are treated for this condition than should be (Davies et al., 1994). The decision to seek treatment has been conceptualized as following a series of steps beginning with the conceptual understanding of mental health and the identification of a psychological disorder, followed by direct observation and recognition of specific mental health symptoms, and concluding with a decision to take action or not (Davies et al., 1994). With treatment, older people find, as do younger persons, that the manifestations of clinical depression (e.g., feelings, thoughts, and behaviors) improve or even disappear. Effective treatments for both older and younger adults include intensive, brief therapy; drug treatments; or some combination (Davies et al., 1994).

The diagnosis of depression is sometimes difficult to determine since the criteria listed in table 5.1 are not adjusted for age. It is often quite complicated trying to separate depression from the typical age-related physical changes and symptoms that occur in the elderly. Dick and Gallagher-Thompson (1996) note that many symptoms of depression in the elderly are similar to age-related health complaints: difficulty sleeping, poor appetite, cognitive difficulties with memory, coping with loss, bereavement and grief, and side effects of various medications. Also recall from chapter 3 that it is hard to separate mild dementia from depression because they share common behavioral patterns, for example, difficulty with memory, attention, and concentration. Generally, dementia is characterized by slow onset and generally deteriorating functioning, whereas depression is more sudden and clearly noticeable to others as a change in personality (Dick & Gallagher, 1996).

Risk Factors and Stress-Buffering Effects

Tower and Kasl (1995) noted that with increasing age the risk factors for depressive symptoms increase: poor health, loss of relatives and friends due to death, financial stress, and so on. Yet the actual occurrence of depressive symptoms shows a U-shaped relationship across adulthood with a drop in middle age and a return to higher levels only among the oldest-old. Tower and Kasl (1995) suggested that a **stress-buffering effect** could account for the U-shaped relationship between depressive symptoms and age, despite the clear increase in the number of risk factors leading to depression as people get older and older. Stress-buffering effects include social support from a spouse, the extended family, the social network of close friends, and community organizations. These can all help to reduce the impact of risk factors for depression as well as other negative life events. Stress-buffering effects reduce the likelihood that multiple risk factors will lead to an increase in clinical depression or depressive symptoms.

Stress-buffering effects can also enhance effective coping in older people. Mittleman and colleagues (1995) have shown the overall benefits of psychosocial support in reducing depression among a group of spousal caregivers and the immediate families of Alzheimer's patients. The stress-buffering effect of psychosocial support was evident by the eighth month of intervention. Multifaceted psychosocial intervention was provided that included family counseling, ad hoc counseling whenever needed, and social support through targeted discussions with spouses facing similar problems. Caregivers clearly showed significantly less depressive symptoms than control caregivers without such intervention.

Clinical Depression, Functional Disabilities, and Chronic Disease

Older adults may experience depression as a result of stressors, such as chronic physical illnesses, that limit their functioning and cause specific functional impairments (Zeiss, Lewinsohn, Rohde, & Seeley, 1996). There is support for a relationship between certain kinds of functional disabilities, the presence of pain, and depressive symptoms in older persons. Williamson and Schulz (1991) found that community-residing people over the age of 55 identified limitations in nine activities—self-care, care of others, eating habits, sleeping habits, doing household chores, going shopping, visiting friends, working on hobbies, and maintaining friendships—in association with the degree of pain or discomfort they reported experiencing throughout the previous week. Older persons who reported the highest levels of pain were also those who identified the most limitations across these nine areas and, not surprisingly perhaps, were also the most depressed. Although other studies have conclusively shown a link between chronic pain and depression, these studies have been conducted with institutionalized elderly. In the more-restricted environment of the nursing home, functional disability was not found to play a role in the incidence of depression (Parmelee, Katz, & Lawton, 1991). However, when community-residing elderly were investigated, a clear relationship was found among functional disability (i.e., the nine areas identified), level of pain experienced, and depression (Williamson & Schulz, 1991).

Physical illness is one of the strongest risk factors for depression (Gatz et al., 1996). Individual diseases by themselves do not appear to predict depression among the elderly (Zeiss et al., 1996). Clinical depression has also been found to be a predictable but not inevitable outcome of chronic disease (Beckman, Kriegsman, Deeg, & Van Tilburg, 1995; Deeg et al., 1996). Studies have reported that some older persons make a better adjustment to later-onset chronic disease if they have developed coping skills over their lifetime to deal with stressful events. Older persons who expect to have to deal with chronic diseases as a part of their own aging and are not as deeply disturbed or clinically depressed by such problems (Deeg et al., 1996). Apparently the more severe the chronic disease and the more life-threatening it is, the more often clinical depression is found. In one investigation, the rate of clinical depression among older adults in medical settings was reported to be 15 percent (Reifler, 1994). The coexistence of clinical depression with chronic disease suggests greater functional disabilities and higher rates of mortality than is found among elderly with the chronic disease alone (Sullivan, 1995). Thus the treatment of clinical depression among older persons with chronic disease may well have positive benefits not only in terms of mental health but also for maintenance of functional abilities (Deeg et al., 1996).

Coping with chronic disease, as we have seen in chapter 4, can lead to depression among those who provide direct care (e.g., caregiver burden and distress) as well as among other family members. And in one investigation of caregivers, depressive symptoms were found to continue even after the older relative for whom they provided care had died. Bodnar and Kiecolt-Glaser (1994) found comparable levels of depressive symptoms among both those currently providing direct care to a relative with dementia and those who had done so but had stopped due to the death of the relative. Both groups showed depressive symptoms that were significantly higher than controls who were not and had never provided care to a relative with dementia.

Clinical Depression and Alzheimer's Disease

Among the newer challenges facing clinicians today is the treatment of clinical depression in older persons with Alzheimer's disease (AD). The coexistence of depression and AD is common and in the early phases of the disease may add "excess" disability in terms of day-to-day functioning (Teri, 1996). Depression is also highly likely in older persons diagnosed with other mild levels of cognitive disability. And depression is increasingly likely among family members who provide direct care and supervision for a relative with AD. Some research shows that depressive symptoms in the care recipient are mirrored in the persons who provide care; the more depression in the care recipient, the greater the depression among caregivers (Teri, 1996). It is not that depression is contagious but rather it adds so much to the burden of caregiving, often serving to negate rewards and recognition for the love and concern of caregivers. In one study, caregivers of depressed patients with Alzheimer's experienced greater depression and burden themselves than caregivers who provided care for nondepressed patients with Alzheimer's (Pearson, Teri, Wagner, Truax, & Logsdon, 1993). In another study, spouses caring for a husband or wife with AD showed greater depression when their own adaptability and lack of flexibility in defining their spousal role was identified

Treatment of Depression in the Elderly

Many elderly who are depressed do not seek or receive help. Older adults with depression are at risk of suicide. Elderly men have the highest rate of suicide. Suicide rates are highest for individuals who have encountered a moderately severe episode of depression for the first time and have seen a physician in the month before their death.

Participants at a conference on depression concluded that the available statistics on the incidence of depression in older adults are underestimates. The reported incidence rates are 5 percent for individuals living in the community and 20 to 25 percent among nursing home residents. Nearly one-third of all widows and widowers evidence signs of bereavement depression in the first month following the death of a spouse, and half of these individuals continue to show signs of depression throughout the next twelve months. Experts considered a change in the *DSM-IV* to include a special diagnostic category of depression in the elderly. They hope that with better diagnosis we can increase the proportion of depressed elderly who actually receive treatment, which currently stands at only 10 percent. Conference attenders concluded, based on the extant literature, that treatment of elderly persons with major depression should include antidepressant drugs over a 6- to

12-month period. Similarly, there was weak endorsement of a controversial treatment for depression, electroconvulsive shock therapy, based on research evidence supporting its effectiveness in treating depressed elderly persons. Experts noted that "psychosocial treatments can also play an essential role in the care of elderly patients who have significant life crises, lack social support, or lack coping skills." To date, few comparisons between treatments based on drugs versus psychotherapy have been conducted with populations over the age of 65; for example, less than 25 well-designed studies have evaluated drug treatment versus psychosocial treatments. The questions remaining to be answered are: (1) Why have so few studies been conducted comparing the effectiveness of psychosocial therapies versus other treatments? and (2) When can we expect outcome studies to indicate which of the various psychosocial interventions (e.g., counseling, cognitive therapy, etc.) work best in treating depression in the elderly and prevent its recurrence? Conference participants discussed whether the funds provided by drug companies to evaluate their products may have contributed to the imbalance in research on treatment approaches for depression (Adler, 1992).

(Majerovitz, 1995). With effective treatment there will be a reduction in those aspects of depression that limit functioning in the patient with Alzheimer's and a corresponding improvement in caregiving burden.

Treatment of Clinical Depression

Treatment for clinical depression in older adults can be complex since there are often valid reasons for feeling depressed. And, as family and friends can verify, depressed people are difficult to be around, unusually dependent, withdrawn, and demanding. Clinically depressed people generally discourage social contact from the very people who can be most supportive. Thus, families and caregivers need assistance, and depressed older adults need interventions that will mobilize their resources while recognizing their concerns as valid.

The treatment of clinical depression in older persons has shown effective results with brief psychotherapy based on cognitive or behavioral models, with drug interventions, and with both forms of treatment concurrently. Research Focus 5.1 discusses recommendations for treatment of clinical depression in the elderly. Combined drug and psychotherapy produced the most improvement in older persons treated for clinical depression, while drug treatments alone had the poorest results. Surprisingly, older persons whose clinical depression was treated with brief (e.g., 4 months) psychotherapy alone or with combined individual psychotherapy and drug treatment

Creative Achievement, Eminence, and Psychological Disorders

Experts examining psychological adjustment and coping processes have noted that frequently, but not always, those who make unique and outstanding contributions in their fields are burdened with psychological disorders. Some believe that mental turmoil helps to feed the creative process (Ludwig, 1996). For example, it is curious that many of the musical geniuses of the past two centuries suffered from bouts of manic-depression, or bipolar affective disorder. DeAngelis (1989) examined the suffering and personal anguish this mood disorder brought to those in the creative arts. Talented composers such as George Frederic Handel, Hugo Wolf, Robert Schumann, Hector Berlioz, and Gustav Mahler suffered the cyclic effects of intense periods of activity or mania, which probably contributed to their immense musical productivity and creative compositions. Yet their corresponding bouts of debilitating depression, leading at times to suicidal thoughts or behaviors, also affected these composers.

The following diary excerpts and letters reveal how difficult it was for these composers to cope with their manic-depressive episodes. Berlioz, for instance, described his two moods as "the two kinds of spleen; one mocking, active, passionate, malignant; the other morose and wholly passive." Schumann likened his mood swings to two imaginary people, the first "impulsive, widely energetic, impassioned, decisive, masculine, high-spirited, and iconoclastic; the other gentle, melancholic, pious, introspective, and inwardly-gazing." According to musicologist Robert Winter, Gustav Mahler recognized the emergence of the condition as early as age 19, writing, "I have become a different person. I don't know whether this new person is better; he certainly is not happier. The fires of a supreme zest for living and the most gnawing desire for death alternate in my heart, sometimes in the course of a single hour."

Is manic-depression a prerequisite to creative expression in the arts? Are all creative people likely to experience manic-depression? Though many creative people in music, writing, and the visual arts have experienced manic-depression, the percentages rarely exceed 66 percent in any of the samples selected for study. However, even more modest estimates that 25 to 50 percent of a sample of creative persons experience and/or have been treated for manic-depressive disorders represents a "disproportionate rate of affective illness in the highly creative," according to Kay Jamison of Johns Hopkins University of Medicine. However, not all persons who are creative, talented, and gifted in the arts experience manic-depressive disorders. Nor are all those with manic-depression necessarily creative.

Current research and theory suggests that manic-depression stems from biological factors that are expressed psychologically. The condition is apparently triggered when an environmental stressor primes the pump and the affective disorder begins its inevitable progression. The most effective treatments are based on a combination of psychotherapy and the use of lithium, a drug used to level extreme moods. But researchers estimate that fewer than two-thirds of the more than two million adults with manic-depression are diagnosed or treated. Many of these untreated adults are elderly.

Other types of psychological disorders have been observed in creative persons of achievement. Ludwig (1996) identified a sample of 1,000 deceased twentieth-century persons who were prominent in their fields. Their eminence was identified from data on reputation, public recognition, breadth of creative achievements, originality, foresight, influence in their fields, and so on. Those in the creative arts were more likely to experience psychological disorders at some time in their lives—or more than 72 percent. Those in social, business, and investigation professions showed disorders on average 39 to 49 percent of the time. The most common psychological disorders among artists, composers, entertainers, and writers were depression and alcoholism. Actors and those involved in performance had high rates of drug abuse, while poets were more likely to show evidence of manic-depression and psychoses. Suicide attempts were most often reported among actors, writers of fiction, poets, and musical entertainers. According to Ludwig (1996), across all fields in the creative arts, achievements that relied on precision, reason, and logic were less likely to be associated with psychological problems than achievements

showed nearly identical, positive results (Dick & Gallagher-Thompson, 1996; Thompson, Gallagher-Thompson, Hauser, Gantz, & Steffen, 1991). At present it appears that brief clinical treatment using behavioral approaches or cognitive approaches alone are equally effective in treating older persons with clinical depression (Gallagher-Thompson & Thompson, 1995). There is also a place for the use of psychoeducational programs that combine both group therapy and education.

that tapped into emotional expression and subjective experience. For example, poets and writers of fiction showed higher rates of adjustment disorders than those who wrote nonfiction. Among those creative artists in adulthood who reached levels of eminence in adulthood, more than one-third experienced severe psychological problems by adolescence; two-thirds showed difficulties in adulthood. Their mothers were likely to have suffered from alcoholism, drug abuse, depression, and psychoses; their fathers more often were alcoholic. Eminence in other areas such as science, academics, or politics was not associated with higher probabilities of psychological difficulties either in adolescence or adulthood. Ludwig points out that higher rates of psychological disorders among creative artists does not mean that mental turmoil is a necessary precondition for creative achievement. There were similar levels of creativity and eminence among those in the arts who were stable and those who were less so. Eminent people who experienced emotional difficulties in Ludwig's sample included Virginia Woolf, Ernest Hemingway, Eugene O'Neill, Paul Gauguin, and Robert Lowell. Those who were free from difficulties included Albert Einstein, Niels Bohr, Camille Pissaro, Margaret Mead, George Gershwin, and Orville Wright.

Although some believe that turmoil can spur creativity and creative expression, others recognize that the mental anguish associated with psychological disorders can be very limiting to one's achievement and productivity. Ludwig did note that psychological disorders can indirectly lead to a state of perpetual "uneasiness" and tension that is released through creative productivity. Those who are stable emotionally, however, may generate their own uneasiness by identifying problems that require creative solutions. Both sources of creative achievement produce an individual who is highly motivated, focused, and able to concentrate for long, long periods of time on their work. There is a sense of total commitment to the productive process of creativity, an exclusivity to their work, and a timelessness to the enterprise. This process has been identified as a state of "flow" by University of Chicago psychologist Mihaly Csikszentmihalyi and is descriptive of that process in which individuals lose all sense of time as they become fully absorbed by their work. It is not restricted to those adults who suffer from psychological disorders or unique to only certain fields.

Ludwig identified eight factors that distinguished the lives of those who had achieved exceptional achievement and eminence from those who were less eminent. Those at the top showed: (1) early signs of giftedness; (2) special parenting and mentoring; (3) contrariness—disrespect for traditional beliefs and customs; (4) capacity for solitude; (5) physical vulnerability, particularly likely in childhood to be seen as frail, sickly, or having a physical disability; (6) personal seal or professional signature to clearly mark their individuality, talent, and accomplishments, such as Walt Disney's identity linked to cartoon characters, Picasso's signature on paintings, or Charlie Chaplin's image as the Little Tramp; (7) drive for dominance through self-confidence; and (8) psychological uneasiness leading to restlessness, impatience, and a strong drive for achievement and personal accomplishment. As Ludwig concludes, those with the highest attainments among people of eminence, whether they experienced psychological disorders or not, did not bring contentment and peace of mind. Their successes did not satisfy them for very long. Since few eminent people showed all eight background factors, Ludwig suggests that the search for a relationship between emotional disturbance and creative artistic achievement will be complex and subtle. Mental disorders by themselves do not necessarily prove helpful or destructive to the process of creative achievement. "Other personal attributes and circumstances determine the capacity to exploit inner tensions in the service of creative achievement" (Ludwig, 1996, p. 6).

From T. DeAngelis, Mania, Depression, and Genius: Concert, Talks Inform Public about Manic-Depressive Illness, *APA Monitor, 20* (1): 1, 24. Copyright 1989 by the American Psychological Association. Reprinted by permission.
A. M. Ludwig, Mental Disturbance and Creative Achievement, *Harvard Mental Health Letter,* March (1996), 4–5. Copyright 1996 by Harvard Mental Health Letter. Reprinted by permission.
A. M. Ludwig, (1995). Resolving the creativity and madness controversy. N.Y.: Guilfod Press.

Psychoeducational programs employ a specific "curriculum," which presents essential information for older persons along with an opportunity to discuss the presenting problem experienced by group members. A clinical leader encourages active, focused discussion in a supportive environment. Older persons (e.g., those with depression) are encouraged to share their feelings and concerns with each other and the clinical leader. Although not exclusively a prevention approach, psychoeducational programs are helpful for elderly spouses caring for a husband or wife with dementia (Dick & Gallagher, 1996). Many antidepressants are available to treat depression in the elderly and these are generally highly effective, once appropriate dosages and side effects are determined. The more common antidepressants include the older monoamine oxidase inhibitors, tricyclic antidepressants, and the newer selective serotonin reuptake inhibitors such as Prozac (Blazer, 1993). Older persons with depression have responded best to brief psychotherapy, and drug therapy, in combination.

Suicide

The major consequence of undiagnosed and untreated depression is an increased incidence of suicide among people of all ages. (See Research Focus 5.2 for a discussion of the occurrence of suicidal ideation and other psychological disorders among creative people.) Among the elderly, clinical depression is frequently ignored or accepted as the natural consequence of aging (Katz, 1997). In fact, older people with clinical depression are at higher risk for successfully carrying out suicidal wishes when compared with other age groups. They commit 17 percent of all suicides yet comprise only 11 to 12 percent of the population. Estimates suggest that one of every six elderly with severe depression actually brings about their own death (Koenig & Blazer, 1992). Statistics also reveal that nearly 25 percent of those who commit suicide are older than 65, with rates of 18 per 100,000 for those 65 to 74; 22 per 100,000 for those 74 to 85; and 19 per 100,000 for those 85 and older (Church et al., 1988). Figure 5.2 presents the incidence of suicide as a function of age. One of the major goals of a U.S. Public Health

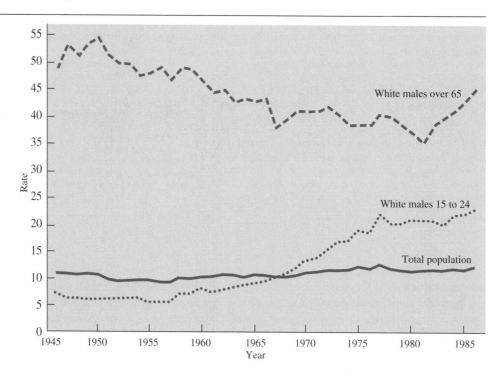

Figure 5.2 Total and white male suicide rates for ages 15 to 24 and 65 and over per 100,000 population: 1946 to 1986.

Service project, Healthy People 2000: National Health Promotion and Disease Prevention Objectives, is to reduce the suicide rate in older persons (Kaplan, Adamek, & Geling, 1996; National Center for Health Statistics, 1993). The four greatest risk factors related to suicide among the elderly include: (1) living alone, (2) being male, (3) experiencing the loss of a spouse, and (4) failing health. There is no evidence that the rate of suicide increases following retirement. Among older white males the suicide rate is nearly seven times that of older white females, although the incidence of clinical depression is more prevalent among females than males.

Ethnicity and Suicide   Mental health professionals who focus on aging have examined in the relationship of suicide to ethnicity. Suicide is a more probable outcome of untreated depression among older adult white males, but not among Asians, Hispanics, or blacks (Conwell, 1994; McIntosh, Santos, Hubbard, & Overholser, 1994). Recent surveys show that white males 65 years of age and older have a suicide rate of 42.7 per 100,000 versus a national rate of 12.2 (Kaplan et al., 1996; McIntosh, 1995). Analysis by race reveals that white males aged 85 or older have three times the rate of suicide of African-American males in the same age group (Koenig & Blazer, 1992). As figure 5.3 suggests there are different patterns of suicide among white and black American older males, with elderly females showing rather low rates among both races. Whereas older white men show the largest age-related increase in suicide, black American men show two peaks, one in later life beginning at age 80 and one in younger adulthood from age 20 to 35 (Katz, 1997).

Turnbull and Mui (1995) have suggested that the lower rates of suicide among older black American men may be due to selective mortality or to better coping skills among this population of hardy "survivors," given the differential life circumstances that have separated this cohort of elderly males from their white counterparts. Older black American men, by virtue of their survival, are representative of a group that has succeeded in managing stress and discrimination in their earlier years, although for some experts they often appear to have done so by "acculturation" to the social realities of a white-dominated society. Blacks over the age of 75 show a **crossover effect.** Although they are at higher risk for death at earlier ages, black Americans who manage to live into old age represent a select group of hardy survivors whose life expectancy is higher when compared with those of similar age from other races (Padgett, 1995). Black suicide is highest in urban areas of our society and lowest in the South where blacks' population density is the highest (Conwell, 1995; Group for the Advancement of Psychiatry, 1989). Investigators speculate that regional differences may relate to the significant role of community institutions in the South, particularly the black church and the black family network, which hold older persons in high esteem and are important in rural southern areas.

Native American peoples represent more than 302 separate tribal identities; therefore, it is difficult to make generalizations about mental health issues such as suicide among this diverse ethnic group. The Navajo of the Southwest for instance consider that death due to suicide will lead to bad luck and illness in the future for all family survivors and any others who were directly associated with the death (Holmes & Holmes, 1995). Navajo suicide rates are the lowest among Native Americans, with only

Figure 5.3 (a) Total incidence of white male and white female suicide for ages 15 to 24 and 65 and over by year. *Source: NCHS Products site; http://www.cdc.gov/nchswww/products/pubs/msvr/supp46*

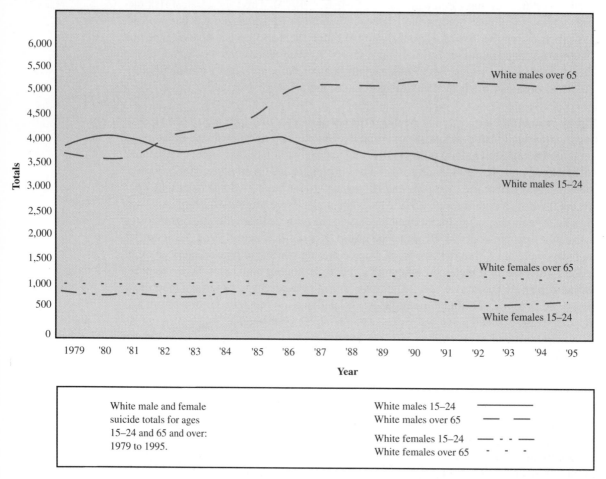

12 suicides per 100,000 population. This is dramatically low when compared with Intermountain Native American tribes (Blackfoot, Shoshone-Bannock, and Shoshone-Paiute), which reveal a suicide rate of almost 100 per 100,000 population (Group for the Advancement of Psychiatry, 1989). Among the Inuit peoples of Northwest Canada, the Yukon, and Alaska it has been well documented that high suicide rates among the elderly are the direct result of cultural acceptance of the practice. When infirmity and disability limit the contributions of the elderly to Inuit society or make the traditional nomadic lifestyle difficult to follow, older persons themselves, as well their society, recognize that they have become a burden and make suicide an acceptable response. Suicide may also emerge as a response to the death of a close relative or loved one among the Inuit. According to Inuit religious belief, through death, especially a violent one, a person can become reunited with family and loved ones (Group for the Advancement of Psychiatry, 1989).

Figure 5.3 (b) Total incidence of black male and black female suicide for ages 15 to 24 and 65 and over by year. *Source: NCHS Products site; http://www.cdc.gov/nchswww/products/pubs/msvr/supp46*

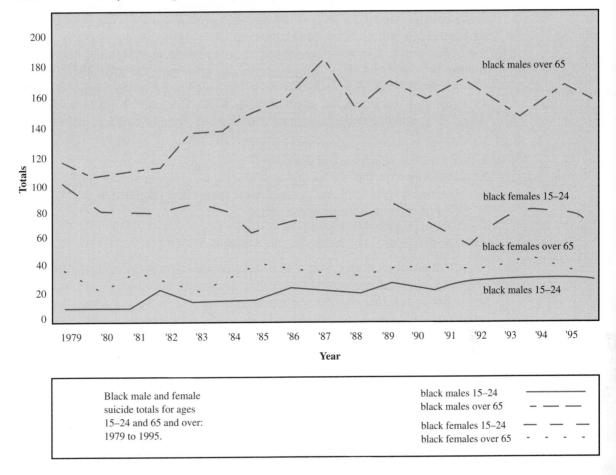

Recognition and Treatment of Suicide Risk Suicide among elderly persons is directly related to the incidence of depression (Katz, 1997; Kennedy, 1996). Clinical depression can be successfully treated; however, when left untreated and undiagnosed in older persons, it creates a much higher risk of suicide than when untreated and undiagnosed in younger adults. Since many ethnic and racial groups are reluctant to access community-based mental health services, family members, friends, and neighbors play a critical role in recognizing the signs of depression and helping older persons to seek treatment. Many depressive episodes in late life are the direct result of medical conditions, chronic health problems leading to functional impairment, and disabilities. Unfortunately, more than 50 percent of all older persons believe that depression is a "normal" part of aging and a natural response to typical health problems associated with growing old (Katz, 1997). They see no reason to seek treatment for what they assume to be inevitable declines associated with growing old.

In racial and ethnically diverse populations of older persons, the physical symptoms of depression will be brought to the attention of physicians and other health care professionals first. They can help to identify depression and to encourage treatment before suicide is attempted. Suicides among the elderly are sometimes preceded by clear signals that, unfortunately, are largely ignored (Katz, 1997; Koenig & Blazer, 1992). Since older people are usually more likely to be successful in committing suicide than younger persons, intervention must be directed at preventing the attempt itself (Katz, 1997; Kennedy, 1996; Koenig & Blazer, 1992). Mental health professionals must look for signs of extreme despair, overwhelming helplessness, and hopelessness in the elderly. The signs appearing among at-risk individuals, regardless of age, include:

1. Extreme mood or personality changes
2. Discussion of suicide and death
3. Preoccupation with the futility of continuing the struggle of daily living
4. Giving cherished personal possessions to friends and relatives
5. Disturbances in sleeping and/or eating
6. Severe threat to identity and self-esteem
7. Death of loved ones and/or long-term friends

Without a social support network to monitor depressive or presuicidal feelings on a regular basis, suicidal thoughts among the elderly easily become actions. It is important to have physicians, mental health professionals, and caregivers discuss with one another possible suicide plans that have been shared with them by an older person so that they can help monitor and prevent an older person from carrying them out (Koenig & Blazer, 1992). Suicide techniques used by older people are somewhat more passive than those used by younger groups. Koenig and Blazer (1992) suggest that suicide rates in the medically ill, who often successfully employ passive techniques, may not be accurately reflected in current estimates. Other techniques include starvation, single-car automobile accidents, failure to take needed medications, mixing medications, combining medications with dangerous drugs such as alcohol, or overdosing on prescription medications (Church et al., 1988). Suicides by firearms is the most prevalent active method of suicide among older white males (Kaplan et al., 1996). They reported the most significant predictors of suicide due to firearms to include: (1) being married, divorced, or widowed; (2) residing in a nonmetropolitan area; and (3) having less than a high school education. White males over the age of 85 years were more likely to use firearms in attempting suicide; however, those between 65 and 84 years were more likely to actually commit suicide using firearms (Kaplan et al., 1996).

Alcoholism

Among today's elderly Americans, the excessive use of alcohol is the most common drug abuse problem, excluding tobacco use (Atkinson, Ganzini, & Bernstein, 1992). Congressional reports estimate that 2.5 million older persons have alcohol-related disorders (U.S. House of Representatives, 1992). Among this population, widowers over the age of 75 have the highest incidence of alcoholism of any group within our society (Glass, Prigerson, Kasl, & Mendes de Leon, 1995).

In recent years, experts have concurred that the incidence of alcohol-related problems in the elderly has been regularly and consistently underestimated (Adams & Waskel, 1993; Caracci & Miller, 1991). In one study, a group of new admissions to a hospital was screened for alcoholism. Positive identification of alcoholism was reported among 27 percent of adults under 60 years of age and 21 percent among those 60 years of age and older. The cost of hospitalizations and alcohol-related problems amounts to more than $60 billion each year (Dupree & Schonfeld, 1996). In another investigation of alcohol-related hospitalizations, the rate per 10,000 individuals aged 65 years of age and older was reported to be 54.7 for men and 14.8 for women. It has been estimated that up to 50 percent of residents in nursing homes have problems related to alcoholism (AARP, 1993a, 1993b; U.S. House of Representatives, 1992).

Current statistics suggest that alcoholism among white older Americans is higher than that of African Americans, Hispanics, and Asians (Aponte, Rivers, & Wohl, 1995). There is also evidence that within minority populations older adult African Americans have higher rates of alcoholism than other minorities (Atkinson et al., 1992; Curtis, Geller, Stokes, & Levine, 1989). However, investigators continue to emphasize that socioeconomic status plays a significant role in alcohol abuse among older adults who have had to cope with poverty, underemployment or unemployment, discrimination, and substandard housing over a lifetime (Aponte et al., 1995).

Older adults generally show symptoms of alcoholism similar to those found among younger persons (e.g., amount consumed, alcohol-related social and legal problems, alcohol-related health problems, behavioral signs of drunkenness, and self-recognition of alcohol problems). The U.S. House of Representatives report found that 15 percent of people over the age of 60 had the equivalent of four or more drinks per day. However, some age differences between older and younger alcoholics have been reported (Curtis et al., 1989; Freeman, 1992). For instance, older adults are not likely to be seeking or receiving treatment. In a national survey, less than 4 percent of the clients in alcoholism treatment programs were over the age of 55 (Dupree & Schonfeld, 1996). And in another study, only 10 percent of alcoholics receiving treatment for their condition were over age 60, with a gender difference showing far more males than females seeking help (Rivers, Rivers, & Newman, 1991). Demographic surveys indicate that older men are two to six times more likely than older women to be alcoholic (Atkinson et al., 1992). Older women appear to begin abusing alcohol at a point much later in life than men. Older males turn to alcohol abuse, while older women seem more at risk for abusing prescription drugs (Dupree & Schonfeld, 1996).

With increasing age, the body becomes less able to tolerate the effects of alcohol. As people age there is a decrease in lean body mass, a lower volume of water in the body, and reduced blood flow; taken together, these changes suggest greater sensitivity to alcohol and higher levels of blood alcohol concentrations (Dupree & Schonfeld, 1996). Given the increased biological sensitivity of older persons to drugs, intoxication with alcohol may occur at lower levels of consumption; additionally, older persons more often than younger persons more readily self-report alcoholism (Atkinson et al., 1992). Paradoxically, statistics reveal that with increasing age, beginning at age 50, the number of people classified as alcoholics decreases. Those who develop alcoholic behaviors in early adulthood **(early-onset alcoholism)** often do not survive to reach middle or old age, or they develop multiple health problems that force them either to abstain or cause their early death (Atkinson et al., 1992). However, among those who continue to abuse alcohol, the rate of alcoholism holds between 4 and 10 percent (Department of Health and Human Services, 1990). Early-onset alcoholics who reach old age are beset with a variety of physical health problems, including liver damage, high blood pressure, heart disease, and alcohol-based organic brain syndrome. The latter condition, called **Korsakoff's syndrome,** is marked by behavioral disorientation, confusion, delusions, and irreversible memory disorder. Patients with Korsakoff's syndrome have an inability to remember new facts and events for more than a few seconds (anterograde amnesia) and have basic difficulties with temporal discrimination, spatial organization, abstraction, and initiative (Eberling & Jagust, 1995). Alcohol-based organic brain syndrome is related to the destruction of brain cells and reduced metabolism in the frontal cortex and parietal cortex. There is a correlated incidence of malnourishment, vitamin deficiency, and inadequate protein. Alcoholics typically forgo basic nutritional needs in favor of gratifying their substance dependency (Eberling & Jagust, 1995).

Like all substance abuse treatments, the goals for intervention with elderly alcoholics are to attain stabilization or reduction in alcohol consumption, to treat coexisting psychological problems, and to establish appropriate social intervention (Atkinson et al., 1992). Higher rates of success are reported with treatment in this older population, in contrast to that reported among young adult alcoholics (Liberto, Oslin, & Ruskin, 1992; Lichtenberg, 1994). And both **late-onset alcoholism** (emerging in middle-to-late life) as well as early-onset alcoholism that extends into later adulthood show generally positive outcomes with treatment interventions designed for older adults or those over 50 years of age (Dupree & Schonfeld, 1996; Lichtenberg, 1994). Late-onset alcoholism accounts for between one-third to one-half of all elderly alcoholics (Liberto et al., 1992; Welte & Mirand, 1995).

The existence of late-onset alcoholism was disputed for many years. The phenomenon, however, has been confirmed in many studies. It may emerge in one of three forms: (1) as an increase in consumption over earlier periods in development, (2) as a relapse reflective of earlier patterns of overuse, or (3) as a first-time phenomenon. The incidence of drinking problems for the first time among those 60 years of age and older has been reported in studies across a wide range, with rates varying between 29 percent to 68 percent. Late-onset alcoholism appears to be more common among older women than older men and is also associated with higher socioeconomic status. This form of alcoholism is underdiagnosed by professionals and ignored by family members and friends (Atkinson et al., 1992; Dupree & Schonfeld, 1996; Lichtenberg, 1994).

The **tension-reduction hypothesis** serves as one explanation for why problem drinkers turn to alcohol (Glass et al., 1995; Krause, 1995b). Alcohol is a way of managing tension created by negative life events and chronic stress. Those with limited coping skills and social resource deficits are likely to use alcohol to manage tension (Brennan & Moos, 1992; Moos, Mertens, & Brennan, 1993). Support for the hypothesis can be found in studies with young adults, but the results are equivocal when older adults are the target of investigators (Glass et al., 1995; Krause, 1995b). Research Focus 5.3 provides a recent study of the tension-reduction hypothesis.

Life Events and Alcohol Use:
Tension-Reduction Hypothesis

In a three-year prospective longitudinal study, the tension-reduction hypothesis was explored with 2,487 community-residing persons 65 years of age and older (Glass et al., 1995). Each person's baseline alcohol consumption was identified at the beginning of the study and then 11 different negative life events common to the experience of older persons were monitored over the next 36 months to determine their effect on drinking. The negative life events included the loss of a close friend who moved away from the area, the death of a close relative, having a close relative become sick or injured, being the victim of a crime, hospitalization, or a nursing home stay. Heavy drinkers, light-moderate drinkers, and nondrinkers were all included in the population sample.

The major finding of the study was that initial baseline level of alcohol consumption determined the impact of only certain specific negative life events on drinking. Most important, not all negative life events had the same effect on alcohol consumption. There were interactions between initial level of alcohol consumption and the type of negative life event. Some negative life events, such as dealing with a sick or injured relative, caused an increase in drinking among those who drank heavily, yet had no effect on those who were light drinkers. Other negative life events, such as being hospitalized or being the victim of a serious crime, were associated with a decrease in drinking, regardless of initial level of alcohol consumption. These results were moderated still further depending on gender. When taken together, these data offer only moderate support for the tension-reduction hypothesis as an explanation for alcoholism among older persons.

In a related study Krause (1995) found some support for the tension-reduction hypothesis as a factor in alcohol consumption in the elderly. The salience or importance of the role in which stressors were encountered was the major determining factor leading to increased alcohol consumption. Alcohol did reduce tension or lower stress by helping to buffer the older person from stressors arising in roles that were not very important to older persons. However, in roles that were highly salient, alcohol was found to increase stress and tension for the elderly (Krause, 1995).

The data showing gender differences obtained by Glass and colleagues (1995), however, are consistent with other studies showing that men and women react differently to negative life events (Glass et al., 1995). Women appear to react more strongly to negative life events that affect their social network while men react more strongly to negative life events that involve their work or have an impact on their finances (Conger, Lorenz, Elder, Simmons, & Xiaojia, 1993). The data also show that one-third of the men and one-half of the women abstained from drinking completely for at least one year during the study's duration. It was hypothesized that abstinence for a 12-month period was most likely related to medical treatments, medications that could not be taken with alcohol, and illnesses that required hospitalization, and extensive nursing home care. Perhaps most interesting, given current national concern for alcoholism in the elderly, is the data from Glass and colleagues (1995) that showed that overall alcohol consumption declined over baseline over the three years of the study, regardless of the initial level of alcohol consumption. Key negative life events, however, were found to delay this general decline in alcohol consumption among the elderly.

Older alcoholics are more likely to have adopted cognitive and behavioral avoidance responses as a way of coping and managing life stress (Moos, Brennan, Fondacaro, & Moos, 1990, 1992). Avoidance is linked to a higher incidence of problem drinking, more depression, more physical symptoms, and lowered self-confidence (Dupree & Schonfeld, 1996). Older adults with prior incidents of alcoholism in their developmental history are more likely to experience recurrence of the syndrome when faced with stressors in late life (Atkinson et al., 1992; Liberto et al., 1992). Interestingly, late-onset alcoholism has been reported to be related to chronic, multiple stressors, rather than a direct consequence of one specific stressful life event such as loss of a spouse, relocation, or presence of a physical disability or life-threatening illness (Dupree & Schonfeld, 1996; Liberto et al., 1992; Welte & Mirand, 1995).

Many health care professionals do not make referrals, even if the alcoholism is suspected to be a problem. They believe that such identification is worse for an older person than the occurrence of alcoholism itself. They accept an older person's refusal of help and denial of any mental health problems (Lichtenberg, 1994; Marion & Stefanick-Campisi, 1989). Such acceptance of the problem is particularly likely in Hispanic populations, where symptoms of alcoholism such as frailty, depression, senility, or unsteadiness are taken to be "normal" aging (Lopez-Bushnell, Tyra, & Futrell, 1992). However, it is important to distinguish different utilization of alcohol among various Hispanic populations and their risk for alcoholism. Cuban American males, for example, have shown in both middle age and older age a tendency to continue their low rates of alcoholism, which is not the case for Mexican American or mainland Puerto Rican males (Black & Markides, 1994).

Among the more innovative interventions recently suggested for elderly alcoholics is the use of an age-specific group treatment program with an older peer counselor/ facilitator present. The older peer serves as a model of recovery and provides ongoing encouragement for those willing to try to make positive, permanent lifestyle changes. Group treatment using peer counselors as "coaches" has been found to be successful for older adults with alcohol dependency who are facing the multiple loss of loved ones and friends, unresolved grief, severe loneliness, social inactivity, and resentment over their life situation (Kostyk, Lindbolm, Fuchs, & Tabisz, 1994). Other treatment approaches for elderly alcoholics include those also appropriate for younger adults, such as Alcoholics Anonymous, social support, individual behavior modification, insight therapy, and self-management. There are also programs designed to train older alcoholics in "drink refusal," in assertiveness, and in developing alternative management strategies to deal with tension and anxiety to reduce their incidence of alcoholism. However, it is important to recognize that the success of therapeutic treatments with the older alcoholic requires working at a slower pace, avoiding direct confrontation, and developing special sensitivity to the coexistence of clinical depression and social isolation (Schonfeld & Dupree, 1996). Through training in coping and self-management skills, it is possible to discourage alcoholism, encourage abstinence, and give responsibility back to the older person who has been abusing alcohol. There are also specific programs designed to help older persons who relapse. They emphasize increasing self-monitoring and self-assessment to know when to call for help (Dupree & Schonfeld, 1996). Consider the six recommendations for treatment of the older alcoholic derived by Dupree and Schonfeld from their extensive review of contemporary research studies (1996):

1. Emphasize age-specific group treatment with supportive approaches and minimal "confrontation."
2. Focus on negative emotional states (e.g., depression, loneliness, overcoming personal losses such as death of friends and family, health status, and lowered self-concept).
3. Develop resources to rebuild social support systems.
4. Employ staff with a decided commitment to and extensive experience with the elderly.
5. Develop links with aging and medical services to receive appropriate referrals and to direct older people as necessary.
6. Create a therapeutic environment with an appropriate pace and content that fits the elderly client.

THERAPEUTIC INTERVENTION WITH ETHNIC ELDERLY

The need to know the backgrounds, values, and assumptions that clients bring to the therapeutic treatment is clear when examining the ethnic elderly. Therapists are well advised to understand older clients from different ethnic traditions before developing intervention strategies and to help with overall case-management decisions.

Ethnic Sensitivity

Aponte and Barnes (1995) reviewed the importance of intervention strategies that recognize and incorporate the broad differences that affect major ethnic groups in the United States. Membership in an ethnic group does not mean that all such individuals share homogeneous characteristics, values, and attitudes. Trimble (1989) originally identified the term **ethnic gloss,** which refers to the tendency to try to make ethnic groups (e.g., blacks, Asians, Hispanics, and Cubans) appear more homogeneous than they actually are. Ethnic categories can obscure individual differences among those who fit the category. Hispanic group membership, for example, may refer to people who have come from the Caribbean such as Puerto Rico or Cuba, from specific countries of South America, Central America including Mexico, or from Spain. Not only do such different origins lead to different values, they also may reflect different levels of acculturation to Western society. Some families voluntarily choose to become immigrants; others arrive as refugees, migrating under involuntary conditions and experiencing harsh conditions and significant stress; still others have established roots for many generations and are indigenous; and others may immigrate temporarily (e.g., foreign students or workers from other countries). Despite the appearance of commonality based on ethnicity, each individual is at differential risk for psychological problems (Aponte & Barnes, 1995; Berry & Kim, 1988). The field of psychology has too often ignored individual differences among people with similar ethnic backgrounds. People with different acculturation, different migration histories, and different socialization experiences are not likely to be the same, regardless of their shared cultural identity. Thus, it is difficult to develop general mental health recommendations and treatment approaches for older persons from apparently similar ethnic backgrounds (Aponte & Barnes, 1995). Despite common ethnic membership, each person seeks "to understand themselves, their culture, other cultures and the majority culture" (Aponte & Barnes, 1995, p. 24).

Case Management

Ethnic elderly clients most often present themselves to health and mental health professionals with diverse symptoms that could stem from any of a number of mental health disorders (Grant, 1995). Some individuals prefer to share their complaints with physicians, rather than with mental health professionals. This can delay appropriate diagnosis and make treatment both challenging and complex (Grant, 1995).

Historically, clinical intervention with the elderly has not been a highly valued role among mental health professionals, and until recently, few ethnic role models were involved in the delivery of mental health services (Grant, 1995). Ethnic elderly who are particularly likely to need treatment services are those who have had adjustment difficulties in the past or whose demographic profiles suggest vulnerability for adaptation, for example, financial restrictions, health problems, and lack of health care insurance (Grant, 1995). Some older persons find it increasingly difficult to manage stress as new coping demands emerge in later life. Mental health professionals are encouraged to pay specific attention to the role of culture and social environmental factors in understanding the symptoms presented for resolution by ethnic elderly.

Cultural differences mean that some ethnic populations do not conceptualize mental health disorders as based on "internal psychological" processes. Among some ethnic groups mental health disorders are expressed primarily through health symptoms and physical complaints (Grant, 1995). Older persons in particular may show symptoms that have special significance for their culture. Psychologists must develop sensitivity to the meaning of these symptoms and carefully review the adaptive coping of elderly from diverse backgrounds in their everyday environments. Functional assessments involving the analysis of physical health parameters, cognition, activities related to independent daily living such as self-care, and social interactions may be confounded by symptoms of psychological disorders for ethnically diverse elderly (Grant, 1995). It is important to understand how ethnic differences in symptom expression can influence such assessments before drawing conclusions regarding functional impairment.

Treatment Concerns: Individual Therapy

Professional mental health workers are not equally effective in working with different ethnicities. Consultation with others who are knowledgeable about the ethnic identity and culture is one way to build cultural sensitivities. Successful interventions require multilevel and broad-based consultation to develop a full appreciation of the multiple factors in the culture, community, and social network that may be contributing to a mental health disorder. Therefore, intervention with ethnic elderly often requires professionals from different agencies and disciplines working together in teams to bring about treatment success (Markides & Miranda, 1997; Uba, 1994).

Individual therapy has been successful in helping older people from diverse cultural backgrounds cope more effectively with adjustment disorders, depression, and anxiety (Grant, 1995). There are basic treatment assumptions in Western models of individual therapy, however, that may not be adapted to the backgrounds of older ethnic minorities. These treatment assumptions include: the primary focus on the person; the expectation of open verbal, emotional, and behavioral sharing between client and therapist in an intimate relationship; the adoption of an analytic, linear model of causation in identifying problems and creating solutions; and the tendency to see inner, emotional functioning as separate from physical life (Aponte & Barnes, 1995; Sue, 1998, 1981; Sue, Fujino, Hu, Takeuchi, & Zane, 1992; Sue, Zane, & Young, 1994; Uba, 1994). Therapeutic intervention is also problem-focused, time-limited, and empowering to the client. It is vital for therapists not only to understand these assumptions but to clarify them when treating older persons from diverse ethnic backgrounds (Aponte & Barnes, 1995). For example, what cultural beliefs does the client hold regarding mental illness and its symptoms or behavioral manifestations? What cultural biases are held regarding emotional self-expression and gender differences? What beliefs influence access to mental health services? What expectations govern time in therapy and treatment outcomes? For instance, Asian Americans have difficulty placing themselves, their needs, and their individual treatment ahead of family or community (Aponte & Barnes, 1995; Uba, 1994). Recently, Asian-American therapists were asked to identify the most important cultural values they would like other therapists to know in conducting therapy with Asian-American clients. The results of this survey, in descending order of importance, appear in table 5.2. The therapists were also asked to identify the ethnic-specific problems, values, and concerns that therapists should know in treating Asian-American clients. These data appear in table 5.3

Sensitive and culturally aware therapists recognize the discomfort that certain ethnic subgroups will experience in therapy. Without such sensitivity and awareness clients may perceive the therapist as lacking in care and concern, empathy, and understanding—factors that can lead to the decision to end treatment long before successful intervention has been achieved (Aponte & Barnes, 1995). Clients and therapist may have rather different goals and definitions of success (Grant, 1995, Uba, 1994).

TABLE 5.2

Most Important Cultural Values for Therapists to Know About

Importance of family
Shame and guilt
Respect for people based on their status and roles
Styles of interpersonal behavior
Stigma associated with mental illness
Restraint of self-expression
Orientation toward group
Achievement
Sense of duty and obligation
Expectations that follow from different roles

Note. Data in table are based on Matsushima and Tashima (1982).

TABLE 5.3

Important Ethnic-Specific Problems Therapists Need to Know About

Immigration experiences (presumably including traumas experienced prior to leaving Asia)
Cultural conflicts in lifestyle and values
Importance of family issues
Racism
Conceptualizations of mental health and attitudes toward mental health services
Behavioral styles and norms
Language
Ethnic identity
Intergenerational problems

Note. Data in table are based on Matsushima and Tashima (1982).

Thus, therapists must be prepared to be far more active with older ethnic minority clients in order to maintain them in treatment for sufficient periods of time. The passive strategies common to most listening therapies run the risk of being perceived as disinterest (Grant, 1995). It is vital that intervention be broad based so that in addition to individual psychological counseling, biological, medical, nutritional, and social interventions are utilized. This may require educating clients to the availability of services and helping them to access appropriate intervention. Therapists must be prepared to work with the broader social network of the client, including friends and multiple generations in the family, to enlist their support and so that they can provide appropriate intervention to extend the benefits of individual therapy (Grant, 1995; Uba, 1994).

Treatment Concerns: Group Therapy

Group therapy for older ethnic populations seeking mental health services must be sensitive to clients' specific concerns in seeking treatment. The following guidelines developed by Vasquez and Han (1995) have been designed to help professionals implement group therapy. These principles are appropriate for any group, including those directed at caregivers overwhelmed by the burden of dealing with an older patient with Alzheimer's or targeted to older persons experiencing specific types of adjustment or coping disorders.

1.   Focus on each group member's strengths. Therapeutic intervention may overemphasize problems; ethnically diverse clients may assume more responsibility for creating their problems and for solving their difficulties than other clients. Positive evaluation of ethnic minorities' personal strengths and functioning will help build self-esteem.

2.   Promote empowerment of group members. Group leaders need to create opportunities for participants to begin to trust their individual emotions and direct observations. Many ethnically diverse clients, particularly older women, appear to have had little opportunity to have their feelings, perceptions, and understandings validated. They benefit from support that helps them express their opinions and exchange their views with others.

3.   Promote skills of communication and assertiveness. Help participants to develop communicative effectiveness, appropriate assertiveness, and build connections with others in the group. These skills will generalize to other areas and enhance the ability of older persons from ethnically diverse backgrounds to express a personal view, to indicate a personal preference, or to negotiate strong differences of opinion between close family members.

4.   Facilitate expression of negative feelings. Through group membership and regular meetings with the same people there is an emphasis on connectedness, cooperation, and face-to-face relationships. Many ethnic subcultures discourage negative emotions. Clients may have some difficulty in group settings expressing negative emotions to others (e.g., anger and hostility, conflicts, disapproval). Group settings provide an opportunity to learn how to recognize and express these emotions when they occur in other settings.

The challenge of bringing individual or group therapies to the lives of ethnically diverse adults lies in overcoming cultural values that are incompatible with the process and goals of traditional treatments.

5. Promote focus on the here and now. Living with the reality of today, the emotions that are immediately felt, and current coping concerns is useful. Clients can explore how current issues are related to their unique past experiences, particularly ones that have challenged ethnically diverse group members' self-esteem such as prejudice, discrimination, and bias.

6. Focus on sociocultural issues. Help people see the contribution of forces outside of themselves that have contributed to their development: sociocultural factors, environmental factors, politics, power, and economics.

Treatment Concerns: Language

Language differences for a number of ethnic groups in the United States can have an impact on both the decision to access mental health services as well as on treatment effectiveness or outcomes. In the most recent U.S. census data there were more than 17.5 million people over the age of 5 who spoke Spanish and another 4.5 million whose primary language was Asian or one from the Pacific Islands. Mental health professionals often show a negative bias regarding those whose speech is not English. They tend to evaluate such persons as being more disturbed and as having greater pathology and more difficulty expressing affect (Aponte & Barnes, 1995). The decision to leave treatment before successful outcomes have been attained can often be traced directly to the perceived effectiveness of both verbal and nonverbal communication between client and professional. Important questions to consider are the following: Are bilingual clients using their preferred language?, Does the clinician understand the cultural expressions conveyed by critical words in English?, and Does symptom expression truly convey the depth of feeling and psychological experience of the client to the clinician (Westermeyer, 1993)? Many older clients belonging to diverse subcultures have identified language differences between themselves and therapist as one of the primary causes of perceived bias underlying their decision to terminate treatment (Uba, 1994; Westermeyer, 1993).

Treatment Concerns: Bias and Prejudice

There are of course many obstacles to seeking and staying in treatment among culturally diverse older people in addition to language. Many of these stem from an older person's long personal history of discrimination with the majority institutions in our society (Aponte & Barnes, 1995; Jones, 1990; Priest, 1991). One often-mentioned barrier to seeking mental health treatment among older black Americans is healthy **cultural paranoia.** This describes the hostility, suspicion, and distrust of mental health programs as well as other community-based services associated with white majority culture. Improving access to mental health services does not automatically lead to better treatment or the end of prejudice. And, similarly, reducing many of the barriers to mental health utilization does not automatically improve outcomes for older persons from ethnically diverse backgrounds. In one study, the overall impact of **ethnic matching,** that is, linking clients to a professional with similar ethnic characteristics as themselves, resulted in a decrease in premature dropout among clients receiving therapy, but it did not result in better treatment outcomes (Sue et al., 1992; Sue et al., 1994). Professionals who provide treatment to adults from ethnically diverse cultures must also recognize the strong fear of becoming stigmatized among those populations seeking mental health services. Many such concerns are justified given studies that have shown that ethnicity and race are predictive of client misdiagnosis, reduced mental health services, inappropriate treatments, and service provided by the least-seasoned among the professional staff (Adams, 1990; Aponte & Barnes, 1995; Sue, 1998).

Improvements in Service Delivery

Older persons from diverse backgrounds have needs for mental health services that are not being met. Both alternative resource theory and barrier theory explain, in part, the restricted access to mental health services by older ethnic populations. Working from a community-based approach, Harel and Biegel (1995) have developed a set of principles that, in theory, should help to enhance access to mental health services for older adults from ethnically diverse backgrounds. These include encouraging access long before crises occur, matching cultural differences and community resources, and developing a system delivery that is sensitive to the needs of older ethnic populations. Examine each of the following seven principles that identify changes in mental health **service delivery** to directly address the special concerns of older ethnic populations:

1. Link the mental health system and ethnic communities. For example, leaders from various ethnic communities can become part of planning teams that develop mental health programs and services.

2. Develop outreach services specifically to serve the needs of older ethnic diverse elderly.

3. Disseminate information about benefits and services available. For example, use bilingual materials to appropriately and actively encourage professionals from the ethnic community to take a visible role in leadership positions.

4. Reduce the barriers to mental health services among elderly from ethnically diverse backgrounds.

5. Reduce attitudinal barriers of agency professionals that work against elderly from culturally diverse backgrounds.

6. Enhance mutual support and coping resources among informal caregivers providing social support to ethnic elderly. This will enhance the opportunity to access professional mental health services when appropriate.

7. Help to identify the at-risk population of community-dwelling elderly from diverse ethnic backgrounds, for example, those who are unaffiliated in the community and without social support (Harel & Biegel, 1995).

A DEVELOPMENTAL PERSPECTIVE ON INTERVENTION

Psychological problems can be related to age if they are brought about by internal and external events that are likely to occur at certain points in adult development. As identified earlier in chapter 4, most adults carry an "expected timetable" of normal life events and experience minimal distress when life events seem to occur as anticipated. Much of the information regarding anticipatory events is transmitted by observation (e.g., within the extended family, from the social network of neighbors and friends, and from the mass media). Some may regard this information as a form of "preventive intervention" since it allows adults to prepare for their own future and plan ahead to avert problems. When events are off-time, occurring earlier or later than anticipated, when the events cause larger than expected functional impairments, or when they require coping and adaptation far beyond the ability of the individual to manage, then interventions become necessary. Available resources include both formal and informal social support and one's own inner resources. As we age our own coping resources may change. A woman widowed at 65 may profit from the many years of coping with life changes and manage a loss well. She may have developed strengths and skills that were absent when she was 40.

Problems and resources may also be age-related because of particular cohort effects. For example, women today will be far more economically self-sufficient in adulthood and old age than were their mothers and grandmothers. In the past, many women were delayed until middle age to achieve some measure of economic self-sufficiency and autonomy through work, often after children were launched. They entered their retirement years never having worked, having only worked part-time, or being employed far fewer years than men. As a result, this cohort of women had fewer retirement benefits, less Social Security, and fewer available resources. They were uniquely different from today's generation of women, most of whom have chosen to work from early adulthood through middle age and beyond. Cohort differences also emerge in the willingness to define personal problems in terms of mental health and the willingness to self-disclose such problems to others. As mentioned, older adults in our society, unlike younger persons, seldom define a personal problem in terms of mental health issues and consequently they are not as likely to seek mental health services (Padgett, 1995). The way that individuals define problems influences the kinds of intervention they seek. The need for mental health services among older adults is likely to increase when today's current cohort of young and middle-aged adults reach old age.

Before examining various intervention options, consider the more salient issues in adult development that follow and some of the ways that mental health interventions can be developmentally appropriate.

Intervention in Young Adulthood

The main goal of intervention in young adulthood is promoting positive development. Young adults face many developmental challenges that can have lifelong consequences—clarifying personal values and goals, selecting and preparing for a career, and satisfying needs for intimacy and parenting. In addition, young people renegotiate their relationships with parents as they establish themselves in adult commitments and accept adult responsibilities.

Those who move from high school directly to the world of work enter young adulthood at earlier ages than those who attend college and thus may experience somewhat different strains. College is often a time to explore career and intimacy options; yet, today's young adults seem to continue such questions well beyond college as the launch into the adult world is extended into the late twenties and early thirties. The following list represents questions that apply to young adults. Of course, many of these questions apply to making changes at any age.

1. What is motivating the search or change?
2. What are my needs, wants, and interests?
3. What do I like to do? What do I like to learn?
4. What is available? What are the opportunities?
5. What are my abilities and skills?
6. What preparation do I need?
7. What are my priorities?
8. What are my short-term and long-term goals?
9. What are the benefits and costs of my alternatives?
10. What is the best alternative?
11. What do I need to do to carry out my goal?
12. What is my first step?

One risk for young people is that they can be overwhelmed by the pressures involved in the choices they make. For example, young women without a spouse or partner, who decide to parent small children, often experience significant stress, whether or not they combine parenting with outside employment. Another risk is that young adults may not settle on any choices in work, love, or personal values that they can honor. As a result, they reach middle age without having established themselves as adults by failing one of the most important developmental tasks of young adulthood.

Intervention in Middle Adulthood

During the transition in to middle adulthood it is common for people to reexamine the choices made in young adulthood: goals, vocation, mate, lifestyle, geographical location. Levinson (1996) suggested that early in life we develop a dream of how life is supposed to be and then in midlife we reexamine the dream, either affirming it or rejecting it for another. It appears that **life dreams** may be constructed without much information about what is required to carry them out. An adolescent may decide to be a TV sports announcer, a physical therapist, a software company president, or a travel agent without really knowing the true costs and benefits of such choices. Even young adults may not fully appreciate the long-term consequences of career and mate selection. In middle age there is a strong need to use one's remaining time well, to do the right things, and make the right decisions while there is time left. Thus, one important area for intervention in middle adulthood is midlife transitions and the intense self-study that accompanies such transitions. Few men and women are able to realize their life dreams and "have it all," and attain the multiple goals of successful career or challenging occupation, children, and marriage. At least for the cohort of 35- to 45-year-old women in Levinson's study, most felt their life dreams were not met. About half of the 45 women in Levinson's intensive study had sought mental health services by the time they reached middle age. They saw that the effort to combine marriage, motherhood, and full-time career had been a partial or massive failure. In other words, a different dream or "new basis for living" needed to be invented from middle age onward for such women.

In time, most adults master the transition of midlife and derive a sense of control over the more important decisions that affect them. They carry a sense of substantial responsibility over family and work. At this point in development there is often an expansion of life goals and priorities to include more affection and compassion in men and more assertiveness and autonomy in women. Marriage relationships may be revised and redefined and work may, for some, become a place to mentor others. After the earlier years of work that are focused on competition, getting ahead, and increasing leadership, many middle-aged employees get tired of the pace and these goals and shift to the next generation who will follow them in the company or organization. With middle age also comes the launching of children from the home, watching some return for a while, caring for grandchildren and aging parents. The strains of this developmental period are greatest when the individual feels blocked from making desired changes or is forced to make changes they do not endorse. Interventions make it possible for individuals to match their goals and their ambitions with opportunities. Obviously people enter midlife with unique developmental histories, which can promote successful transitions or can bring about problems in adjustment. Erik Erikson suggests that successful resolution of prior developmental tasks makes the transition in midlife more likely to be successful, whereas prior problems lead to less success within this developmental period.

Intervention in Late Adulthood

Later life is marked by change for which some intervention is helpful, appropriate, and, in some cases, absolutely necessary. The greatest danger is in providing too much intervention, long before it is really called for, thus robbing older individuals of a sense of autonomy and sense of personal control in their lives (Tiffany & Tiffany, 1996). Of course, the other side of the coin suggests that there are older people who need specific interventions that are not available, not affordable, or not recognized as essential for them to maintain their independence. More people now enter their later years in generally better health than did previous cohorts. The elderly are no longer heavily involved in full-time employment and are free from concerns about parenting. This "young-old" segment of our populations faces the challenge of these remaining years wondering how to make the most of this period of life. Generally, older persons who remain involved in activities that are meaningful to them show higher morale and well-being and are more adaptive than those who cannot replace their involvements and middle-age roles and responsibilities. Options for the young-old include giving more time and energy to volunteer activities, spiritual growth, continuing education, hobbies and recreation, travel, and part-time employment. The latter activity is important to recognize in describing the retirement careers of older persons. Mutchler, Burr, Pienta, and Massagli (1997) have noted that while a single retirement from a career or work role (a so-called crisp exit) is assumed to be normative in society, more than one-half of all older persons in a recent study experience repeated exits and returns to the labor market (so-called blurred transitions). The most common reason for reentry to the workforce is to sustain or enhance a particular standard of living.

Older couples married for many years may use this period to revitalize their relationship or deal with problems that have been put aside during the middle years. Many individuals during later life need to cope with the illness or death of a spouse, adjust to their own chronic illness, and so on and seem to benefit from interventions that provide social support and group discussion with others facing similar circumstances. The loss of a lifelong partner does not mean that one's social needs must end; some survivors choose to date and some remarry. Those who remarry, as well as extended family members, can benefit from counseling and group discussion to make this late life transition successful. In later life we also see older persons trying to deal with the divorces and remarriages of their own children and grandchildren.

Interventions may be called for to help older persons who face declining health. Some health concerns lead to restrictions in activities, some of which can be permanent if associated with chronic conditions. We see the elderly residing at home, moving in with their children, and moving to supportive living arrangements (e.g., assisted living, transitional living services, or nursing homes). Some have emotional problems and suffer from dementia and other conditions that leave them needing either community-based intervention provided at home or requiring their relocation to a group or institutional living arrangement. Recall that approximately 50 percent of those 85 years of age and older (the oldest-old) have Alzheimer's disease. Although no one can prevent such conditions, specialized intervention strategies can enhance physical and mental health at earlier periods of development or reduce the impact of more serious disorders that arise in later life. Such interventions include education, exercise, nutrition; eliminating behaviors that compromise health; and increasing behaviors that promote mental health such as early diagnosis and treatment of disorders. By taking an aggressive approach to intervention, improvements in the quality of life in old age can be made; for example, successful treatment of depression in young adulthood will mean improved opportunities as individuals enter their later years. Of course, therapeutic approaches for older persons can be just as successful as those for younger persons. But, as noted earlier in this chapter, older persons are not as likely to seek or receive treatment for mental health disorders. Older adults are at risk since they must redefine themselves and their social roles, and adapt to change, as spouses, friends, and coworkers die and as they themselves face retirement, reduction in income, and threats to health (Pettibone, Van Hasselt, & Hersen, 1996). Depression and adjustment disorders are the common mental health concerns of older persons and successful therapeutic treatments are available.

Understanding Intervention Options

Intervention can take many forms. It is important to recognize that before any intervention occurs, the problem to be addressed must be defined. Exactly how the problem is conceptualized and who defines it is, in part, a question of power. There may be several "stakeholders" involved in problem definition and conceptualization—those who most directly experience the problem, those who are called upon to assist in the intervention, and those who are financially responsible for the intervention. Adult children may have great difficulty admitting that an aging parent has problems serious enough to require intervention. They may fear having to become more intensely involved in daily contact with the parent, may harbor unresolved conflicts with the parent, may fear the decision to move a parent to a group living arrangement, and may become anxious over the loss of the parent. Parents may be similarly reluctant in their definition of the situation, believing that it is not serious and does not require outside help. Often such power struggles result in inaction; thus, when intervention is sought, the problem may have become quite disabling with serious consequences. Once the problem has been defined, it is important to examine the presumed cause or causes. This often requires the services of professionals who help in assessment or diagnosis and provide a clear understanding of the typical developmental course of the problem, considering what might happen with or without intervention. One of the best ways to determine causation is to examine the outcomes of intervention. **Probable causes** for depression in old age may be assessed through the effectiveness of individual therapies such as drug treatments and brief psychotherapy. If the problem improves as a result of the intervention provided, then its probable cause has been identified.

Through intervention we can enhance the meaning and enjoyment of all periods in the life span, including old age. Examine table 5.4, which summarizes in outline form the variety of goals, techniques, settings, and change agents involved in intervention across the life span. We will briefly explore each of these dimensions.

Goals of Intervention

Four general goals of intervention are identified in table 5.4, and any particular intervention may entail one or more of these. Goals may be short term or longer term; however, there is a tendency for interventions with the elderly to emphasize short-term goals in that interventions sought are often focused on symptom relief and halting or

TABLE 5.4
A Framework for Intervention Options

GOALS
  Alleviation
  Compensation
  Enrichment
  Prevention

TECHNIQUES
  Clinical Intervention/Therapy
  Education and Training
  Psychopharmacology
  Service Delivery
  Ecological Interventions
  Legislating Social and Behavioral Change

SETTINGS
  Home
  Work
  Institution
  Community
  Society

CHANGE AGENTS
  Self
  Family Members
  Friends
  Paraprofessionals
  Professionals
  Administrators
  Lawmakers/Governmental Leaders

slowing further decline or loss. Resources for intervention are always scarce, limited in terms of availability and financial cost. Professionals and politicians continue to debate such matters in the field of health care access and service.

Alleviation   One goal is to alleviate or remove an identifiable problem. If an older person is having difficulties with anxiety, for example, a therapist may establish a goal of reducing this feeling in the client. Treatment interventions may involve drugs or individual or group therapy with a goal of alleviating or reducing the anxiety of the client.

Compensation   A second goal may be to compensate for losses contributing to the problem. For example, if a person experienced some brain damage due to a stroke, a plan to simplify the individual's living environment might be seen as necessary to permit continued independent functioning.

Enrichment   This intervention establishes a goal of bringing the level of functioning above that ordinarily seen. Clinical therapy in psychology may have a goal for clients of enhancing their self-acceptance, self-fulfillment, and self-actualization. Some therapists may establish a goal of enhancing interpersonal flexibility so that an older adult may function more effectively and comfortably in social settings, adjust better to institutional living, and create greater intimacy from interpersonal relationships.

Prevention Some interventions are designed to prevent problems from occurring or recurring. Prevention programs work best when there is reasonably good information about the factors that place individuals or groups at risk for certain kinds of problems. For example, the risk of developing cancer is heightened among those who smoke, and prevention programs are designed to discourage younger persons from choosing this behavior and to help those who have started smoking to receive support and techniques to help them to stop. Or interventions can be designed to slow down the rates of decline; for example, improved diets and regular exercise may help middle-aged adults or those in old age to preserve a range of physical health. Most psychological problems are not so easily addressable, although health-promoting behaviors seem to fit this model quite well.

Kinds of Functioning

Within any particular area the kind of functioning defined as problematic or pathological may change with age. Shifting definitions reflect unique and personal expectations about what is normal and what is appropriate for individuals at different ages. Older persons often turn to health care professionals, relying on their practical experience and clinical expertise to help determine whether the level or range of functioning is representative of other people at a certain age or whether there is pathological aging. Using age-appropriate definitions of functioning makes it difficult to apply simple rules of thumb (e.g., functional assessment of the degree of interference with everyday functioning) because each age expresses a wide range of acceptable and appropriate behaviors and abilities. Older persons themselves are quite understanding of such latitude, sometimes tolerating significant pain and discomfort as a "normal" part of aging; yet, younger people when faced with similar problems may seek and obtain intervention without question.

Symptoms

The symptoms used to identify problems change with age. For example, the symptoms of depression in older persons are somewhat different from those in younger persons. Elderly persons often present a high incidence of somatic complaints that are frequently mistaken for physical illness (so-called masked depression), show psychomotor retardation, difficulty with memory, and usually deny their depressed mood. They tend not to report everyday symptoms such as difficulty sleeping, feeling tired, being anxious, feeling down, and having impaired attention, wrongly believing that these are the normal consequences of being old (Turnbull & Mui, 1995). Clinicians sensitive to these symptoms in the elderly offer an opportunity for open discussion and encourage exploration of treatments. If the symptoms are ignored as "just old age" or treated as illness-related, there may be further decline and further difficulty in problem resolution.

Techniques of Intervention

A wide range of different interventions are possible. The specific intervention and its application are limited only by the imagination and resources of the intervener. Since professionals tend to develop expertise with only a few specialized techniques, intervention programs can often be enhanced by combining the special perspectives and skills of several intervention specialists.

Psychopharmacology   The **psychopharmacology** technique refers to the use of medications that alter the individual's biological state to attain a desirable goal. The administration of drugs suggests that the cause of the problem lies in the biological sphere and remedies are so developed. Physicians, usually psychiatrists, are authorized to prescribe drugs, and they must monitor their direct and indirect effects. The government controls access to such controlled substances and requires written documentation (e.g., a medical request on a prescription) before administration of these powerful drugs can occur. We know that drugs have different effects on people of different ages. As people grow older there are physiological changes in metabolism and absorption rate as well as decreased drug transport due to reduced arterial flow (Salzman & Nevis-Olesen, 1992). Many professionals are wary of the side effects of drugs, cautious regarding the interactive effects that drugs have on each other, concerned about the long-term effects of drugs, and sensitive to each individual's unique reaction to the same drug and dosage level. Drugs do not activate new behaviors; rather, they serve to alter the rate and quality of ongoing behavioral processes.

Clinical Therapy   Clinical intervention depends on the interpersonal relationship between client and professional to restore or enhance functioning. As we have seen earlier in this chapter, there are specific Western assumptions regarding clinical therapy, which include the presence of an intimate, confiding relationship and verbal exchange as well as an agreement to work to change some features of the recipient of the treatment (i.e., the client). The length of the relationship, the treatment goals, the content of interaction, and the style of interaction may differ from one specific type of therapy to another. Outcomes of clinical therapy have been found to vary as a function of client characteristics, therapist characteristics, and the setting itself. Therapeutic clinical approaches with the elderly include both individual and group intervention and may be combined with psychopharmacologic treatments.

Education and Training   Another major technique of intervention uses education and training to alter or prevent maladaptive behavior. Information about problems that may lie ahead or that are currently being experienced is provided, with the expectation that the individual will use the information in beneficial ways. Specific coping skills needed for successful adaptation may be taught directly to those participating in psychoeducational programs. Other examples can be found in classes and seminars designed to help people prepare for retirement. These programs typically provide information about the needs of retirees: health care, money management, social contacts, marital relationships. The goal is to provide some anticipatory

fied the long-term risks of providing too much social support. Social support initially can reduce chronic financial strain and reduce depressive symptoms, but over time it is associated with increased psychological distress among care recipients. Social support can also prove problematic if it is provided with great reluctance or if it is absent and truly needed. Caregivers may lose their patience or become domineering, abusive, and highly critical as their caregiving careers extend over many months and years. Newsom and Schulz (1996) noted greater impaired functioning among older persons with limited social supports (e.g., those with fewer contacts with friends, fewer contacts with family, and less objective direct aid).

Krause (1995) has suggested, then, that there are limits to the value of social support for the elderly and that any stress-buffering effects are moderated by the care recipient. Ideally the elderly must determine for themselves the interventions that they need, when they are needed, and who should provide them. Krause also suggests that effectively managing the environment is best accomplished by those older persons who do not first turn to others for help but who rely on their own personal resources to cope. Therefore, social support is critical in helping older persons cope well, but older persons must feel that they are in control of it. Knowing that there are others to help, if needed, gives rise to risk taking, personal mastery, and autonomy in the elderly. The subjective perception of support was more predictive of depressive symptoms among older persons than the actual objective measure of support provided. Those who subjectively perceived their support to be low not only had more depressive symptoms they also had decreased **life satisfaction** (Newsom & Schulz, 1996).

Institutional Intervention: Reducing Disruptive Behaviors

Older persons living in institutional settings such as health care facilities, assisted living environments, and nursing homes are involved in many forms of intervention. Some programs of intervention are designed to increase specific targeted behaviors to foster as much autonomy, awareness, and control as possible, whereas others are focused on reducing behaviors that are disruptive or problematic, such as wandering, disruptive vocalization, physical aggression, or unwillingness to walk (Burgio, Cotter, & Stevens, 1996).

Historically, the occurrence of disruptive or problematic behaviors among institutionalized individuals with dementia was largely controlled through psychoactive medications. The long-term use of psychoactive drugs can result in some difficult and irreversible side effects in the elderly. Based on these issues as well as humanizing and improving the overall quality of care in nursing homes throughout the United States, the Omnibus Budget Reconciliation Act of 1987 prohibited psychoactive drugs alone from being used to control disruptive behaviors in nursing home residents (Burgio et al., 1996). There must be attempts to employ psychosocial and environmental interventions.

One of the oldest environmental interventions is the application of **behavior therapy** to manage disruptive or intrusive responses in the elderly. Behavior therapy uses positive rewards for appropriate behaviors and nonrewards for inappropriate behaviors directly in the environment. The environment is carefully analyzed to see what rewards are reinforcing and maintaining the disruptive behaviors: staff attention, withdrawal from an unwanted activity, escape from responsibility (Burgio et al., 1996). Rewards are applied contingently for appropriate behaviors, particularly those that are incompatible with the unwanted problem behaviors. There is extensive training of staff and a concerted effort to be consistent in shaping the desired behaviors.

Another commonly found intervention strategy developed to help control disruptive behaviors in older persons in institutional settings is **reality orientation.** The essential feature of this approach is that the elderly are reminded of where they are and the present situation (e.g., day, month, year, residence) through cues in their immediate environment and the direct encouragement and reminders of staff. The goal of such intervention is to help older residents become more aware of their environment and their own place in it. There are few well-controlled studies to examine the effectiveness of this approach to managing disruptive behaviors (Burgio et al., 1996).

Reminiscence therapy implies a specific sensitivity to the life memories of older persons in institutions. Its primary feature is to encourage older persons to remember their past and reflect on their own unique life memories and experiences; older persons are encouraged to resolve lifelong conflicts and other **unfinished business.** Reminiscence therapy is often part of the treatment approach taken with patients with Alzheimer's, who are given opportunities and encouragement to reminisce in an organized, focused manner. This intervention reduces agitation, confusion, and wandering by helping institutionalized elderly understand and accept themselves, by permitting them freedom to "be" in the institution, and by accepting them and their experiences as they are (Burgio et al., 1996). By giving patients with Alzheimer's permission to live more in the past than the present, reminiscence therapy provides a greater sense of well-being and security. Programs based on reminiscence therapy have extensive reminders of the past, for example, music, posters, furniture, magazines, and appliances.

Milieu therapy is concerned with improving the quality of older persons' interactions with the physical, social, and emotional world in which institutional residents currently live. Milieu therapy can also benefit confused or forgetful elderly by modifying the living environment of the institution. Rooms are highly individualized, doors to each room may have a distinctive color, and there may be special colored pathways marked by arrows on the floor of the hallways designed to assist residents in negotiating the residence and reducing confusion, wandering, and getting lost (Burgio et al., 1996).

Therapeutic Benefits of Pets for Institutionalized Elderly

Pet therapy is an intervention directed at nursing home residents to enhance their overall functioning by increasing their sense of autonomy, responsibility, and control. It is intervention designed to increase social participation among institutionalized elderly since it leads to expanded contact with other staff and residents. It also gives residents the opportunity for independent self-expression, creativity, and productive participation in a structured activity. Pets are assigned to individual residents during regular days each week through so-called pet visitation programs. Alternatively, pets may be specifically assigned directly to a residential ward, floor, or unit.

The goal of pet therapy programs is to encourage contact and involvement between pet and the elderly, which will generalize to the larger social environment (e.g., other residents, staff, and family members). Pets offer one solution to dealing with loneliness and improving self-esteem among elderly residing in nursing homes (Burgio et al., 1996; National Institutes of Health, 1988). Haughie, Milne, and Elliot (1992) have shown that nursing home residents become more spontaneous, animated, and talkative during the time they care for and visit with a pet. And residents become more aware of their environments in preparing for the regular visit of the pet and in providing routine care. For severely depressed residents, pets reduce anxiety, elicit responses (such as care and stroking) when the human environment has been rejected, provide physical reassurance, and help maintain reality, even among those who are terminally ill (Brickel, 1985; Haughie et al., 1992). In nursing homes, pet visitations two or three times each week helped break the cycle created by institutionalization: helplessness, hopelessness, dependency, and despair. Institutionalized older people become less depressed, become more communicative, and evidence higher rates of survival than controls who do not participate in such programs (Haughie et al., 1992; Langer & Rodin, 1976; National Institutes of Health, 1988). Some institutions have maintained cats or dogs for a considerable time for this purpose. Others have developed similar programs using tropical fish, or feeders that attract wild birds. There are some concerns with pet visits in institutions, including residents' allergies, fear of certain types of animals, injuries due to scratches or bites, and jealousy if a pet has a special affinity for and spends more time with some residents rather than others (Brickel, 1986; Burgio et al., 1996).

Therapeutic Benefits of Pets for Community-Residing Elderly

For the widowed or single individual, pets can play a therapeutic role by allowing pet owners to organize each day (Soares, 1985). Routine pet care may also help to increase the number of interactions between the pet owner and other people (Brickel, 1986; Miller, Staats, & Partlo, 1992). Miller and colleagues (1992) found among a group of 250 pet owners (50 to 90 years old) that pets provided far more uplifts than hassles; older pet owners were happier, more self-confident, and more responsible than those without pets. Additionally, pets served slightly different roles for older men and women. Women more than men reported pets to be associated with uplifts, freedom, and positive use of leisure time. Men, on the other hand, associated pets with decreases in social interaction as well as with hassles over time and money (Miller et al., 1992).

Pets may help to meet the dependency needs and increase the responsiveness of the elderly. Pets also provide a concrete anchor for those whose lives have undergone major change or loss. Pets may even serve as family substitutes, providing comfort and support to those experiencing the negative consequences of aging: death of loved ones, sickness, and feelings of loneliness (Brickel, 1986; Tucker, Friedman, Tsai, & Martin, 1995). Some research suggests that the ability to care humanely for pets gives meaning, purpose, and a sense of control over one's environment to the elderly. And caring for pets provides a sense of independence for elderly adults who can take care of something rather than be taken care of by others. Pets have also been shown to have positive health benefits in

The value of pet therapy for the elderly has many dimensions, including the general enhancement of social responsiveness to other elderly residents and staff.

other areas (National Institutes of Health, 1988). The reciprocity involved in pet care leads elderly adults to avoid becoming wholly dependent on others (Miller et al., 1992).

However, the long-term benefits to owning pets among community-residing older adults are not so clear. In one investigation, adults who cared for a pet over a 14-year period were not found to have improved health, health-promoting behaviors, perceived health, or lowered mortality risk when compared with those without such human-pet interactions (Tucker et al., 1995). Perhaps the reported positive benefits of pets in other studies are restricted to populations in which there has been a uniquely stressful event or to special populations such as the institutionalized elderly. In one classic study, owning a pet was the best predictor of survival one year after leaving a coronary care unit in the hospital. Of 53 pet owners, only 6 percent died within one year, whereas of 28 individuals who did not own pets, 28 percent died within the same period. Pets provided a regularity and predictability in routine care that gave a sense of order to these heart attack patients' lives (Friedmann, Katcher, Lynch, & Thomas, 1980). It has been reported that even having a small aquarium with goldfish or other minimal-care pets helps to reduce the owners' blood pressure and anxiety and to increase leisure satisfaction (Tucker et al., 1995).

Legal Intervention: Judgments of Competence and Incompetence

In dementia patients the **competence** to make good decisions is often impaired. When a person's competence to function independently becomes a concern, a formal legal hearing is required; often a psychiatrist or clinical psychologist is asked to evaluate the person and share the professional judgments with the court. Competence is always linked to a specific type of task, decision, or judgment, for example, competence to make medical decisions, competence to consent to psychological evaluation, or competence to execute legal matters such as deciding to marry or to complete a will (Haldipur & Ward, 1996; Pruchno, Smyer, Rose, Hartman-Stein, & Henderson-Laribee, 1995). A legal determination of competence is similarly specific (e.g., competent to make health care decisions such as refusing admission to a nursing home but incompetent to distribute personal assets through a will). The difficulty for the courts is how to balance individual differences in intellect, ability, and personal values (e.g., what is important, good or in one's own interest) with a minimal "threshold" of competence in judgments. There are no absolute, value-free, objective standards for judging competence—each case must be evaluated individually (Haldipur & Ward, 1996).

Competence cannot be called into question every time older persons refuse a medical treatment or exercise their freedom based on their unique personal value system, which may differ from that of other family members. Rather, competence can only be questioned if a judgment appears to be "irrational." For instance, the competence of an elderly person to make medical judgments can be questioned when there has been a refusal to accept standard treatment for a life-threatening condition and the specific treatment refused has minimal side effects, is proven effective, and its refusal will likely lead to irreparable harm and even death (Haldipur & Ward, 1996). Growing concern for the issue of competence can be traced to legislation in the Nursing Home Reform Act and Omnibus Budget Reconciliation Act of 1987, which mandates that nursing home residents participate in decisions about their own care unless they are judged incompetent according to the standards established in the states in which they reside (Pruchno et al., 1995).

Most legal determinations of competency address the following threshold cognitive standards according to Appelbaum and Grisso (1988): (1) ability to communicate a choice, (2) ability to understand the information about a treatment decision, (3) ability to appreciate the situation and its consequences, and (4) ability to manipulate the relevant information rationally. Irrationality in medical settings may find older persons focused on the here and now, fearing pain in certain treatments, and believing themselves invulnerable (e.g., capable of beating the odds without treatment) (Haldipur & Ward, 1996). This suggests incompetence to render medical decisions. Some question whether existing standards for competence may be skewed toward cognitive capacity with affective issues nearly absent (Bursltajn, Harding, Gutheil, & Brodsky, 1991). Depressed persons, for example, may be unable to see the benefits of treatments, may identify with the risks only, and may harbor strong feelings of worthlessness, believing their own lives are not worth living (Haldipur & Ward, 1996). Similar affective factors may underlie the reluctance of an older person to decide to move to a nursing home. While older persons may not wish to move, the decision can be rationally framed in terms of the improvements likely to be derived in the older person's current level of functioning, improvements in the level of care, and reduced demands on family caregivers to sustain the older person in present living arrangements (Haldipur & Ward, 1996).

The appointment by the courts of a **guardian** or a conservator is rare and reserved for only the most serious of situations when older persons are unable to provide day-to-day care for themselves or their property. Guardians are appointed by the courts to make substitute decisions for those judged not competent to make decisions for themselves (Wilber & Reynolds, 1995). Most guardians appointed by the court are from the immediate family and often have served as a caregiver. Those who become guardians often experience role strain, burden, personal sacrifice, and overwhelming demands (Keith & Wacker, 1993, 1995; Wilber, 1997). Haldipur and Ward (1996) note that the courts require documentation that there are functional deficits in basic mental or physical capacities that make decisions regarding money management, property, and health care questionable (Pruchno et al., 1995; Smyer, 1993). Some older persons, as a safeguard against the possibility that they may become incompetent and have a guardian appointed by the courts, choose in advance a specific family member or trusted friend who has **durable power of attorney.** A person with durable power of attorney can make substituted judgments for an individual if they become incompetent; "durable" simply means that the authority to act on behalf of the older individual continues throughout the time of the incompetence and is not revokable without cause (Haldipur & Ward, 1996). There has been considerable concern about the obligations and priorities to the primary beneficiary (e.g., the ward), when a guardian has been appointed (Schmidt, 1995; Wilber, 1997). These benefits have not been well studied to date, and guardianship remains the intervention of last resort, since all authority for independent decisions is transferred to a surrogate (Wilber, 1997; Wilber & Reynolds, 1995).

A final area of competency of concern to the elderly and their families is that of **testamentary capacity,** or the competence to execute a will. Many individuals postpone a will until late in life (Haldipur & Ward, 1996). They often need to change the basic document as situations and their own circumstances change. Changes, called **codicils,** are recorded and legally documented but not always widely shared with other relatives. It is only upon the death of the individual that these changes become known, and the codicils then may serve as the basis of challenges by dissatisfied family members. These challenges are often based on the mental competence of the older person to have made the changes in a will or on the possibility that the changes were made under undue influence (Haldipur & Ward, 1996). Three conditions are used to assess the mental capacity to complete a will: (1) an individual must be able to understand that a will is being created, (2) an individual must know the extent of the property and assets being distributed, and (3) an individual must understand who will benefit from the execution of the will being created (Haldipur & Ward, 1996). The competence of older persons to make decisions that affect them, their participation in such decisions, and the issue of guardianship will all continue to be important matters in the future.

SUMMARY

Because of projected increases in the numbers of older adults in most countries, there will be increased needs for mental health services. The incidence of mental health disorders among older adults mirrors that for other age groups throughout the life span.

Mental health has been defined as the absence of psychological disorders. Positive attributes of mental health, however, can also be used to characterize adaptation and coping. Physical illness and chronic health problems are often linked to mental health disorders such as depression. The diathesis-stress model explains the relation between challenging life events (stress) and individual vulnerabilities (diathesis) based upon an individual's biological status, genetic predispositions, and psychological profile. Older adults are less likely to identify themselves as needing mental health intervention and will rely on informal support from family and community. There are cultural and ethnic differences in the extent to which elderly seek mental health services when primary social supports prove inadequate or ineffective. The lower rates of utilization of mental health services by Hispanics and blacks in the United States has to do with reliance on family and community and barriers to treatment.

An extensive review of depression among older adults was presented. Depression is the most common mental health disorder in old age. Sometimes the causes and symptoms of depression are different for different age groups. The depletion syndrome has been identified with "minor" depression. Treatments for depression include medications and brief psychotherapy. Incidence of depression and suicide varies among different ethnicities. Untreated depression may lead to suicide. The highest rates of suicide are for older white males. Late-onset alcoholism is an underrecognized and undertreated problem for older adults in the United States.

Clinicians are becoming increasingly aware of the importance of ethnic differences in working with older adults. The management of individual clients requires understanding of cultural values, beliefs, and language. Behavioral symptoms may take on quite different meanings in special ethnic cultures. The treatment concerns of older ethnically diverse clients were explored in both individual and group treatment situations. The special issues of language differences and basic treatment assumptions in Western models of therapy were considered for older adults from diverse cultural backgrounds. Overcoming bias, prejudice, and long-held stereotyped perceptions of community mental health agencies remain challenges among racially and ethnically diverse populations of society. Improvements in access and treatment intervention were considered especially important.

A developmental intervention framework was presented to help increase the possibility of producing a positive outcome in the lives of adults. Interventions can take many forms appropriate to the age and life changes with which persons must come to terms. Young adults appear to need assistance with commitments to work, to intimate relationships, and to personal values. Middle age shows commitments established in early adulthood being reassessed and coping with new dimensions of gender. Among the young-old there is a shift away from full-time employment and parenting responsibilities to developing meaningful use of time and energy. The experience of loss, particularly of a spouse, requires major redefinition of one's life; there may be dating, remarriage, or learning to live alone. Intervention requires identification and definition of the problem to be faced. A variety of successful intervention strategies are available. The options must fit the goals, techniques, settings, and change agents appropriate for each problem and the available resources. Interventions may be designed to alleviate problems, to compensate for losses, to enrich existing functioning, or to prevent problems. Some interventions have multiple goals.

Illustration of interventions with the elderly were presented, including community-based intervention evaluating social support, institutional intervention evaluating disruptive behaviors, and intervention using pet therapy in both institutional and community residences. Finally, legal intervention was considered from the perspective of mental competence to make health care decisions, appointment of a health care proxy, and execution of a will. The issue of guardianship and its appropriateness was also considered within the framework of legal intervention.

REVIEW QUESTIONS

1. Identify at least two aspects of depression that make it difficult to diagnose and treat in older adults.
2. What is the relationship between depression and suicide in the later years? Why does this relationship exist?
3. Identify some of the specific risk factors associated with depression and with suicide among older adults.
4. List some of the barriers to mental health access and service treatment for ethnically diverse elderly.
5. What is the distinction between early-onset and late-onset alcoholism?
6. List some of the cultural assumptions in traditional Western clinical therapy that may make traditional psychosocial treatment difficult for older adults from ethnically diverse backgrounds.
7. What are the strengths and weaknesses of alternative resources in the cultures of ethnically diverse older adults?
8. Outline the structural organization of the many and varied interventions that may be employed across the adult life span.
9. What are some of the more effective ways of intervention when trying to reduce the occurrence of disruptive behavior in institutionalized elderly?
10. Discuss the goals of intervention.
11. What benefits have been specifically identified with pet therapy among both institutional and community-residing elderly?
12. What is the legal basis for the judgment of competence to make health care decisions versus competence to execute a will?

FOR FURTHER READING

Blazer, D. (1997). *Emotional problems in later life: International strategies for professional caregivers* (2nd ed.) New York: Springer.

Burlingame, V. S. (1995). *Gerocounseling: Counseling elders and their families.* New York: Springer.

Carstensen, L. A., Edelstein, B. A., & Dornbrand, L. (Eds.). (1996). *The practical handbook of clinical gerontology.* Thousand Oaks, CA: Sage.

Facio, E. (1996). *Understanding older chicanas: Sociological and policy perspectives.* Thousand Oaks, CA: Sage.

Padgett, D. K. (Ed.). (1995). *Handbook on ethnicity, aging, and mental health.* Westport, CT: Greenwood Press.

Richman, J. (1993). *Preventing elderly suicide: Overcoming personal despair, professional indifference, and social bias.* New York: Springer.

Uba, L. (1994). *Asian Americans: Personality patterns, identity, and mental health.* New York: Guilford Press.

Zarit, S. H., & Knight, B. G. (1996). *A guide to psychotherapy and aging.* Washington, DC: American Psychological Association.

Zimny, G. H., & Grossberg, G. T. (1998). *Guardianship of the elderly: Psychiatric and judicial aspects.* New York: Springer.

PHYSICAL HEALTH

INTRODUCTION

In this chapter, you will learn about the effects of aging on physical health. Both assessment and intervention strategies are examined. The economics of health care is a growing concern for older adults and for public policy makers in our society. It is essential to understand how health care will be financed in the future and the threats to current Social Security programs such as Medicare and Medicaid. Increasingly, older persons must face decisions about health care. When they require services, they question what health care intervention should be provided, where it should be received—home care, hospital care, assisted living, or nursing home—who will provide it, and how will it be financed. The cost and availability of nursing home or long-term care is a major issue for older persons. Although some elderly experience impairments in the later years, health care in the United States emphasizes rehabilitation and preservation of autonomy.

This chapter also explores the importance of a number of health-promoting behaviors, the risk of heart disease and cancer, and the changing nature of physical health status among older persons. The benefits of health-enhancing interventions are highlighted wherever possible. The important role of rehabilitation, exercise, and health intervention in helping older persons to cope with health-compromising problems associated with normal aging is also presented.

MEETING THE HEALTH CARE NEEDS OF THE ELDERLY

Public policy has increasingly focused on identifying programs that must be developed or enhanced to meet the health needs of older adults in the United States (Gottleib, 1992). Women will compose a larger and larger segment of the elderly population as will ethnically diverse elderly, who are also projected to grow by more than 5 percent within the next thirty years (Gottleib, 1992). Older women and elderly from ethnically diverse cultures are adversely affected in terms of access to health care. Census reports indicate that 40.6 million Americans or 15.4 percent of our total population lacked health care insurance in 1995, an increase of 2 million people over the previous year (U.S. Bureau of the Census, 1997). Women, for example, have fewer financial resources the longer they live, and health care consumes an increasingly larger portion of their income. One consequence is that women become more and more dependent both on their own children and the health care system to meet their medical, social, and physical needs (Gottleib, 1992; Soldo & Agree, 1988). Analogously, many elderly from diverse ethnic backgrounds continue to reveal the accumulated effects of socioeconomic disadvantage and routinely encounter financial, social, and cultural barriers to health care (Gottleib, 1992). They reach retirement and old age in poorer health than other segments of society (Padgett, 1995).

It is difficult for older persons to meet the increased costs of health care given the typical decline in yearly income of 30 to 50 percent following retirement (Gottleib, 1992; Soldo & Agree, 1988). Health care costs are partially covered by Social Security income and Medicare. Some elderly are able to meet the gap in their health care coverage with personal savings, others rely on private insurance coverage (*Medigap policies*). Still other older persons depend on special appropriations through government-sponsored programs designed for low-income elderly.

Developing simple comprehensive programs to ensure adequate health care is exceedingly difficult given the disparities in income among the elderly (Gottlieb, 1992). Further, public policy regarding health care must consider the mechanisms for continued funding of programs given both the escalating cost of providing health care and the increasing number of enrollees. The anticipated growth in the *dependency ratio* (a larger number of older adults needing support from a smaller number of workers) may mean shifting some of the costs of health care programs directly back to those who utilize program services, that is, the elderly themselves (Gottlieb, 1992). Many program changes are possible and will be debated throughout the next decade. However, programs that emphasize health promotion and health prevention are more effective and less expensive than programs that deliver health care services after illness or disability arise. With improved health as individuals age, there is less need for costly intervention, greater derived benefits in terms of overall psychological, social, physical functioning, life satisfaction, and perceived quality of life (Gottlieb, 1992).

The needs of the elderly and the provision for intervention services are important dimensions of health and psychological well-being that must be addressed. A goal of intervention programs is to enhance and preserve independent functioning throughout the later years, that is, **optimization.** Programs rely heavily on the concept of **functional assessment,** that is, determining the basic abilities necessary for adequate functioning in our society. Different interventions to preserve independence are possible at different functional levels. Functional abilities deemed important in assessments include physical health, mental health, complex cognitive skills, and social roles (Kemp & Mitchell, 1992). Figure 6.1 shows one hierarchical model of functional abilities.

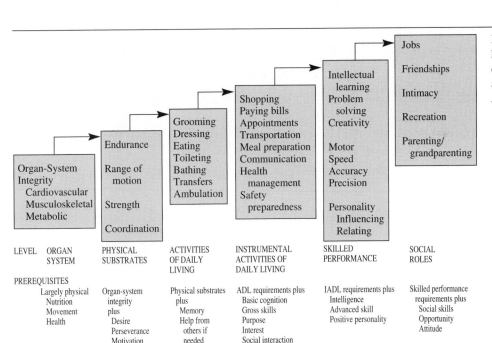

Figure 6.1 A hierarchical model of functional abilities. *(Kemp & Mitchell, 1992)*

A number of factors have restricted the application of useful interventions to the older adult population. First, psychologists and other health care workers must be encouraged to work with the elderly, and the elderly must see that they can and do benefit from various types of therapeutic intervention. Second, health care and mental health care must be made both affordable and widely available. Third, the number of health care professionals who are interested in working with the elderly must be increased (e.g., geropsychologists, physicians, nurses, social workers, physical therapists) to improve intervention services and enhance the quality of care for the elderly (Lebowitz & Niederehe, 1992). Perhaps this goal could be accomplished, in part, by advocating that courses on aging be part of undergraduate and graduate programs in fields such as psychology, human services, nursing, the allied health care professions, and sociology. If students find the study of the field of aging and gerontology interesting and challenging, they may become committed to a career working with the elderly. On the McGraw-Hill Developmental Psychology website (www.mhhe.com/developmental) you will find further discussion of specific careers in applied gerontology referenced under the cover of this book.

Functional Assessment of Health

More older adults today are healthier than ever before, although aging is associated with declines in health. Figure 6.2 shows the proportion of healthy and disabled adults projected over the next two decades. Older adults report fewer sick days compared with previous

Figure 6.2
Disabled versus healthy adults over age 65. *Source: Manton, Coraer, & Staliard, 1993: Riley & Riley, 1994.*

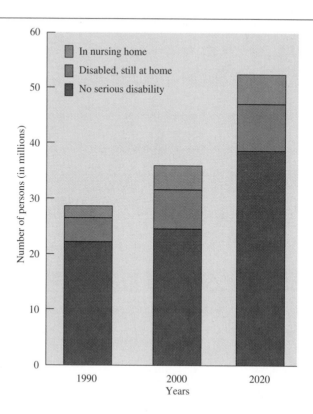

generations, spend fewer weeks in the hospital, and have fewer physical and mental disabilities and limitations. The number of days in which activities are restricted because of illness or injury increases with age, averaging thirty-one days per year (Lentzner, Pamuk, Rhodenhiser, Rothberg, & Powell-Griner, 1992; Manton, Corder, & Stallard, 1993).

The assessment of older persons' health status is an important factor in determining their capacity to live independently and a critical variable in determining the nature and timing of intervention services. Many older individuals live successfully without much intervention or assistance and others do so despite serious illness and physical restrictions. Psychologists recognize that self-assessments by older persons of their own functioning can be biased and distorted. Some people err in the direction of enhancing self-functioning to avoid relocation and to maintain their autonomy; others overemphasize losses in physical health and seek assistance far beyond that which is really needed (Kart, Metress, & Metress, 1992).

To better gauge the practical aspects of the physical skills necessary for self-care and maintenance of functional health, gerontologists developed **activities of daily living (ADL)** scales for older adults. The activities assessed include: bathing, dressing, toileting, getting in or out of a bed or chair, walking, getting outside of the home or apartment, and feeding oneself. The activities just listed are ordered toward increasing dependency; for example, bathing is the most common limitation among older persons, and the inability to feed oneself indicates the most severe restriction in physical functioning (Kart et al., 1992). Identification of specific deficits in the elderly creates an opportunity for environmental intervention to optimize independence and physical functioning as seen in figure 6.3. Most studies show a relationship between

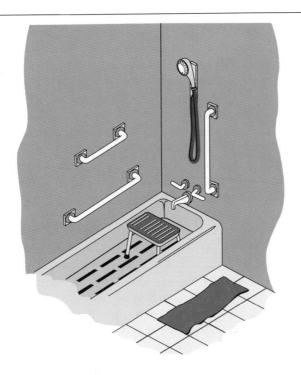

Figure 6.3 An older person's ability to continue using a bathtub can be enhanced through the installation of such features as a hand-held shower, grab bars, a bench-type seat, nonskid strips on the bottom, and lever-type control handles.

health status or physical functioning as assessed by ADL and demographic variables. Those who are oldest, female, live in poverty, are nonwhite, and come from rural regions of our country show the most restrictions in ADL. Nearly 90 percent of adults up to age 64 show no restrictions in ADL, compared with 50 percent of those over the age of 85 (Kart et al., 1992).

Another comprehensive assessment of autonomous functioning has also been developed, the **instrumental activities of daily living scale (IADL).** This assessment subsumes personal self-care as well as more complex dimensions of functioning: preparing meals, going shopping, managing money, using the telephone, doing light housework, and doing heavy housework (Kart et al., 1992). The IADL tasks are more complex, multidimensional, and physically demanding than ADL tasks. Functional declines are more likely to appear in assessments of the IADL than ADL. For example, nearly 33 percent of those over the age of 85 reported four or more limitations in IADL tasks. Limitations in multiple IADL tasks predict that persons will be house-bound, in need of significant levels of assistance on a regular basis, and at high risk for relocation to an institutional living arrangement (Kart et al., 1992).

In a recent study, Rudberg, Parzen, Leonard, and Cassel (1996) reviewed a national sample of more than 5,000 community-residing older adults to see whether functional limitations as measured by the number of restrictions in ADL were related to or predictive of death. The results indicated that although death was predictable from age alone, it was not predictable from knowing the number of impairments in ADL. When the number of functional limitations was held constant, death was predicted by increasing age. For example, women aged 70 to 79 who had difficulty in three activities of daily living had a 21 percent probability of dying within two years, whereas those aged 90 or older with the same number of functional impairments had a 52 percent probability of dying within two years. Interestingly, gender differences were found for similar amounts of functional restrictions. The risk of dying was greater for men than for women with similar functional impairments (i.e., limitations in one or more ADL). Older persons without any functional impairments generally have predictably higher life expectancy than those with functional restrictions in ADL. And for those with functional restrictions in ADL, it was possible to predict the length of time (i.e., in two-year periods) before additional restrictions would appear. The significance of this study lies in being able to estimate specific services needed and the average length of time for assistance for older adults with functional restrictions. Declines in functional abilities are predictable from data on the typical age of onset and the typical course of diseases (e.g., heart disease, diabetes).

Although women live longer than men, women are more likely to be in poorer health than men in their later years. In Lentzner et al.'s (1992) study, for example, women were 40 percent less likely than men to be fully free of restrictions in ADL and were 70 percent more likely to have been severely restricted in the last year of life. Women are more responsive to symptoms of their illness than are men (Hickey, Akiyama, & Rakowski, 1991). In Lentzner et al.'s (1992) study, being unmarried dou-

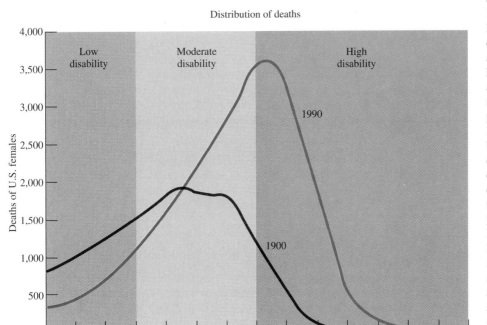

Distribution of deaths

bled the chances of being severely restricted for both men and women; those who also smoked or abused alcohol showed greater functional impairments.

One implication of these findings is that health care costs will increase substantially in the future because greater numbers of adults will reach old age and will require costly medical services. Of those age 85 and over, 50 percent will be severely restricted in their last year of life. As can be seen in figure 6.4, disability levels are greater in older adults over age 85 because people with heart disease, cancer, and other diseases are living longer than ever before (Olshansky, Carnes, & Cassel, 1993). On the other hand, some evidence suggests that disability rates among the elderly are declining when compared with the growth of this segment of the population (see figure 6.2). Although the population of 65-year-olds increased by 15 percent between 1982 and 1989, the chronically disabled elderly population increased by only 9 percent during this same period (Manton et al., 1993).

Perceptions of Health

Two perspectives dominate thinking about health and perceptions of how adults live and enjoy their years. First, the world of older adults is one that must be understood from their perspective, their sensitivities, and their references—that is, what brings them pleasure; maintains their sense of integrity and responsibility; and preserves their sense of self-worth, individuality, and uniqueness. Second, it is critical to avoid equating successful living among the elderly exclusively with the preservation of autonomy. Success cannot mean continuing a lifestyle exactly as it was earlier in life. Many experts have decried this model of equating old with young, which leads to an overemphasis on sameness and the labeling of even the slightest deviation as increased vulnerability and dependence (Smyer, 1995).

Most older adults are in fairly good health and live a lifestyle that in many ways reflects the continuation of the pathways and choices they made when they were younger. Most older persons live independently in their own homes or apartments and function as part of a community (Smyer, 1995). Cohler (1992) noted that:

> The reality of aging in our society is that most older adults remain as healthy through their mid-seventies as they were at younger ages, equally active and often still working. Even those who retire during their sixties may expect to spend as much as one-third of their lives after retirement, living within a modified-extended multi-generational family system often encompassing five generations.
>
> Finally, at least until their mid-seventies, most older adults enjoy the same continued good health as had characterized their earlier adult life. Less than ten percent of adults over age sixty-five live in residential care, and most older adults enjoy independent living through oldest age. (p.19)

Older individuals usually show some increase in health-related problems as they age. Of all the factors predictive of how individuals will adjust to aging and predictive of subsequent mortality, health is the most powerful (Rodin & McAvay, 1992). Among persons 62 years of age and older, perceived health declines with the onset of new illnesses and the associated increase in the number of visits to physicians for care and/or preexisting illnesses that worsen (Rodin & McAvay, 1992). Among older adults, perceived health is also predicted by higher scores on tests used to measure depression and by lower scores on a life satisfaction index.

Studies of the trajectories of chronic disabilities suggest that factors such as poor self-concept, lower self-perceived health status, depressive symptoms, or the presence of multiple chronic diseases accelerates the rate of functional declines. Those with more negative perceptions have increased mortality, independent of the severity of the disease. And, as might be expected, with each new disease or medical emergency, older persons who already have a chronic illness experience greater functional losses than those facing these illnesses initially (Deeg, Kardaun, & Fozard, 1996).

Health can be defined in many ways: number of illnesses, chronic conditions, disabilities, number of restrictions or limitations, physical pain, emotional status, or cardiovascular capacity, to cite but a few of the most common. More older adults are healthy than disabled, as can be seen in figure 6.2 (Manton et al., 1993). In 1990, 28 percent of older persons assessed their health as fair or poor, compared with 7 percent for persons under 65 years old. There were no differences between men and women in health self-ratings, but there were racial differences. Older blacks were more likely to rate their health as fair or poor (40%) than were older whites (27%).

ECONOMICS OF AGING AND LONG-TERM HEALTH CARE

The "graying of America" (Kausler & Kausler, 1996) finds people living 20, 30, and 40 years past retirement. Some senior organizations have been effective in influencing health care policy. Older adults are concerned about whether they will be able to live independently or whether they will require in-home assistance or have to move to an institution. Many older adults are concerned about the availability of financial resources needed to meet their health care needs. Who will pay for costs of health care? Many older adults pay attention to the politics of health care cost containment and access (e.g., will benefits be capped for individuals, will health maintenance organizations limit access to controversial treatments, will they deny coverage for newer "experimental" treatments, will they offer high-cost interventions such as transplants to only those who have the resources to pay for them). Some gerontologists study the economics of growing old. They have found escalating health care costs for products, delivery, and service as well as fees for more thorough testing of patients and the availability of more comprehensive care and services.

Social Security and Health Care

Today Americans are focused on the economic survival of Social Security and its four component trust funds: (1) Old-Age Survivors Insurance, (2) Disability Insurance, (3) Hospital Insurance Trust Fund—Medicare Part A, and (4) Supplementary Medical Insurance—Medicare Part B. Health care experts and politicians question the capacity of the Social Security program to expand to meet the projected growth of eligible recipients beginning with the retirement of the baby boomers. Most experts predict the current system will exhaust all of the financial resources in its four trust funds by the year 2030 unless changes are made (Burkhauser, Couch, & Phillips, 1996). And Medicare is likely to be the first casualty, perhaps within the next decade (Gavin, 1997). Medicare spent more than $163 billion in 1994 and is projected to see expenditures continue to grow at a 10 percent rate through the year 2004 (National Academy on Aging, 1995).

Social Security is the federal government's income and insurance program for those who have worked a minimum of 10 years in jobs that earn credit and accumulate benefits. Social Security represents a significant source of income for more than 36 percent of the elderly (National Academy on Aging, 1996). In 1995, 141 million persons were working in jobs covered by Social Security, but not every worker is a part of Social Security (National Academy on Aging, 1996). All eligible workers must contribute to Social Security based on a percentage of their earnings. Workers, or survivors if the worker dies, receive benefits upon retirement. Although retirement benefits can be accessed beginning at age 62, they are reduced in proportion to what would have been received at age 65.

In December 1995, 26.6 million retired workers were drawing benefits from the Old Age and Survivors Insurance Trust. The average monthly benefit was $720 for these workers. Benefits are based on each worker's highest average earnings. Today eligible workers contribute 5.26 percent of their earnings to the Old Age and Survivors Insurance Trust and 0.94 percent to the Disability Insurance Trust. There is a fixed limit established on the maximum contribution that is assessed. The Hospital Insurance Trust Fund (Medicare Part A) has no maximum limit on workers' earnings, which are assessed at its rate of 1.45 percent. Benefits that retirees receive are tax free as long as individuals do not exceed certain limits.

Since health care costs represent an increasing burden to those older adults on fixed income, it is important to understand how Social Security programs, both income and hospital coverage, help to meet these costs. For example, in 1994 older persons in the United States living outside of a nursing home spent $2,519 on health care costs, representing 21 percent of their average yearly income (Teachers Insurance and Annuity Association [TIAA], 1996). For a significant segment of older Americans, federal programs are the only means to meet the costs of long-term nursing care. Estimates are that in the 25 years between 1993 and the year 2018 the number of nursing home residents will increase from 2.2 to 3.6 million, health care services offered in private homes will increase from the current 5.2 million to 7.4 million elderly, and the costs associated with these changes will increase from $76 billion to $168 billion. While there are more than 2.2 million beds available for elderly in nursing homes today, there are slightly more than 100,000 places for adult day care, chiefly for those with dementia (Somers & Beatrice, 1994). How will these increasing needs and costs be met?

Pensions

Having a yearly pension from an employer, in addition to Social Security benefits, has a significant impact on the financial well-being and health care of an older adult (Burkhauser & Salisbury, 1993; Lillard, Rogowski, & Kington, 1997). In several European countries, such as Sweden, Germany, France, Great Britain, and the Netherlands, and in Australia, nearly all older persons receive a substantial pension and subsidized health care, which are provided at government expense. In the United States, by comparison, pensions provided by private employers are modest and available to only a relatively small group of older adults (Quinn & Smeeding, 1993). Thus, fewer retirees in the United States receive comparable levels of support to that of retirees in these six other countries. And although Social Security gives older adults a base of financial support from the federal government, it leaves many individuals in retirement to live a meager life if this is all they have to draw upon.

Increasingly, people are beginning to anticipate the need for multiple levels of support to sustain them into old age. Table 6.1 identifies the combination of traditional "passive" economic supports available to older people, which include Social Security, pensions, earnings, and assets. There is considerable disparity in such passive sources of income as a function of both marital status, ethnicity, and race. As table 6.1 shows, Social Security is the single most important source of income for retirees. According to Snyder (1993), unmarried older African Americans derived more than 70 percent of their total retirement from Social Security, Hispanics more than 74 percent, and whites, 54 percent). Many married women, in particular, discover that the death of a spouse may mean the end of supplemental pensions and other types of income supports. Often pensions and other benefits such as health insurance are available to former employees until they die but do not necessarily transfer directly to a spouse. Postretirement health

TABLE 6.1

Sources of Passive Income for Retirees by Marital Status, Gender, Race, and Hispanic Origin

Income Share and Amount	White	Black	Hispanic
Married Men and Their Wives			
Total number (in thousands)	521.2	40.3	12.5
Median amount	$18,240	$11,980	$12,700
Total income	100.0%	100.0%	100.0%
Social Security	34.5	44.1[a]	42.4[a]
pensions	19.9	23.3	10.4[a,b]
earnings	19.8	25.1[a]	31.0[a]
assets	21.1	3.6[a]	10.0[a]
other	4.7	3.9	6.2
Married Women and Their Husbands			
Total number (in thousands)	335.1	21.8	7.9
Median amount	$17,780	$10,790	$13,040
Total income	100.0%	100.0%	100.0%
Social Security	37.3	48.3[a]	44.9[a]
pensions	16.2	21.7[a]	19.4
earnings	24.5	24.6	25.9
assets	18.0	2.0[a]	8.3[a]
other	4.0	3.4	1.5[a]
Unmarried Men and Women			
Total number (in thousands)	239.0	41.5	11.3
Median amount	$9,940	$5,570	$5,210
Total income	100.0%	100.0%	100.0%
Social Security	40.3	53.8[a]	52.9[a]
pensions	18.8	14.4	12.6[a]
earnings	14.0	21.8[a]	17.9
assets	20.0	3.6[a]	9.1[a]
other	6.9	6.3	8.5

Source: data from Richard V. Burkhauser and Dallas L. Salisbury (eds.), Pensions in a Changing Economy, Copyright © National Academy on Aging, Department of Health and Human Services, Washington DC; and data from new Beneficiary Survey, 1982.
[a]significantly different from whites at the 0.95 level of confidence.
[b]Significantly different from blacks at the 0.95 level of confidence.

insurance is a significant benefit that can increase the value of a pension; it is a type of deferred compensation offered by some companies to workers who have remained on the job for many years (Lillard et al., 1997).

Hospital Care and Home Health Care

When major health problems strike older people, they often require medical or short-term nursing to care for an acute condition. Nursing home care and reimbursement guidelines are linked to current health care policies designed to contain hospital and medical costs. National health care policy requires that each patient with a specific medical condition, or **diagnostic related group (DRG),** conform to the average cost and length of treatment in a hospital comparable to other patients with this condition. Hospitals receive federal support for each patient in a specific DRG based on this average. If some patients require longer stays or more complex treatment, the hospital must absorb the differential in cost between the patient care provided and that reimbursed by federal programs such as Medicare (Church et al., 1988).

Treating patients within the norms of the DRGs for comparable conditions is difficult. Hospital stays and medical costs above DRG averages must be subsidized by the hospital, corporation, and physician; those under the averages qualify for the standard reimbursement. With the rise in the use of DRGs to control hospital reimbursements, there is increasing interest in discharging older persons more rapidly into home care, nursing homes, and other institutional arrangements (Harvard Health Letter, 1995). The result is that patients are now discharged as soon as practically possible and sent home or to a nursing home facility. The most commonly treated medical conditions among nursing home residents include circulatory diseases (40%); mental disorders and various forms of dementia (20%); endocrine, nutritional, and metabolic diseases (6%); and neoplasms including cancer (2.5%). Nearly one-third of residents have also lost bladder control (Schnelle, McNees, Crooks, & Ouslander, 1995). Urinary incontinence among nursing home residents remains one of the primary risk factors for skin breakdown and infections that lead to costly treatment and further hospitalizations (Beck-Sague, Banerjee, & Jarvis, 1993; Schnelle et al., 1995).

Home health care has become an attractive alternative to nursing home or hospital care. Home health agencies provide sophisticated intervention; they train patients and family members to monitor and provide services such as tube feedings, intravenous antibiotics, physical therapy, and respiratory therapy. The economic incentives for home health care are clear. Whereas hospital charges may total nearly $1,800 per day, home care with a single daily nursing visit costs about $90 and is usually covered by private insurance or Medicare (Harvard Health Letter, 1995). Unless an older patient requires extensive intervention throughout the day and evening or is suffering from Alzheimer's disease, home care is preferable to hospital or nursing home care. There are often so many home health services being arranged that a specialized hospital staff member is assigned the role of "discharge planner." These professionals focus on determining the services older adults need, and they arrange for community resources to meet these needs. Working with multiple agencies, they coordinate visits and schedule services to coincide with patients' return home and recovery.

Many adults still think only of nursing homes as an alternative for intervention services and do not realize the range of choices that exist. With an average cost of $36,000 per year nationwide, nursing home costs are expensive. In some urban areas in the Northeast, nursing homes can cost more than twice this amount (Jasen, 1993). Adult children cannot always take time away from their work and personal responsibilities to help make arrangements and supervise the care of a parent who requires assistance with routine, day-to-day personal needs. Many live hundreds or thousands of miles from their aging parents. Professional **geriatric care managers** can be hired to develop a plan of intervention services and identify appropriate service agencies in the community for each older client. They assess the medical, social, emotional, nutritional, and physical status of the client as well as the current residence, the client's ability to function independently, their functional level, and financial situation. They identify alternative living arrangements, if needed, and appropriate interventions for an older parent within the financial restrictions of the family (Jasen, 1993).

Assisted Living

Assisted living is another alternative to nursing home residence for many frail elderly who have difficulty with routine ADL and IADL skills. Assisted living, a new concept based on maintaining as much freedom and independent living as possible among older adults, brings direct intervention and services to the elderly in an apartment-type setting based on identified needs. Assisted living is costly but certainly less costly than nursing home care. In some ways it fits the call for interventions that

Nursing homes vary in the kinds and quality of services they offer.

foster *successful aging* or aging for which there is a sufficient amount of support to produce positive day-to-day functioning. Rather than accept "usual aging" with losses assumed to be difficult to reverse, the model of successful aging employs environmental interventions and services that permit older people to maintain their independence and functioning despite age-related declines (Smyer, 1995). Baltes and Baltes (1990) have suggested using biological criteria (length of life, biological health), psychological criteria (mental health, absence of pathology), and positive dimensions of personal autonomy and control (cognitive and social efficacy, productivity, life satisfaction) to mark the positive outcomes of interventions that produce "successful aging" (Smyer, 1995). These dimensions are more informative than simple assessment of the ADL or IADL inventories to mark changes in an older person's life.

Elderly persons in assisted living reside in generally new, modern apartments with a small kitchen area and separate bathroom. Residents have meals together in a single dining area and have the option of participating in group activities in large common living spaces. The average assisted living costs for rent and basic services in the Northeast is $2,900 per month, and subsidies for the poor are sometimes available (Kindleberger, 1996). Residents contract for additional services such as help with bathing, dressing, or other routine tasks; the typical services needed by older persons cost about an additional $1,000 each month (Kindleberger, 1996). Residents in assisted living are generally happier than those in nursing homes, and the cost per month is usually less. Assisted living is not easily within the reach of most older persons (Kindleberger, 1996). Massachusetts, for instance, recently built an assisted living complex with almost half of its 69 apartments set aside for low-income elderly. Low-income residents qualified for up to $1,000 of Medicaid funding to help with their expenses; however, even when linked with Social Security Supplemental Income benefits of $500 to $700 each month, these low-income residents did not really live well in assisted living housing and could not afford all of the services that might have helped them (Kindleberger, 1996).

Converting existing apartments to assisted living is not a simple matter of adding physical features such as walkways or changing bathrooms to accommodate the elderly. Assisted living facilities must also provide social services and other kinds of assistance and intervention to permit the elderly to age successfully in their new residences (Kindleberger, 1996).

Long-Term Care

The elderly who, through illness or accident, require long-term care experience significant economic hardships. **Long-term care** includes medical intervention, social support services, and personal care assistance to help chronically ill or disabled elderly cope with basic day-to-day activities. Long-term care in the past was referred to as custodial care. The day-to-day care activities with which older persons need assistance include personal care such as dressing, bathing, toileting, and walking. Some long-term care is delivered in the home and includes help with cooking, shopping, or feeding. Other long-term care is provided in specialized centers such as those offering physical rehabilitation, supervised adult day care for a person with Alzheimer's disease, community-based visiting nurse programs, home health aide services, or respite programs for those with Alzheimer's disease and their families. Table 6.2 illustrates the differences between long-term care and acute care, using an example of the treatment and delivery of services to an older person who has experienced a stroke. As is true for any impairment, the goal of long-term care is to help the older person regain skills and maintain as much independent functioning as possible. Table 6.3 shows that with advancing age among adults over 65, there is an increasing probability that some long-term care services will be required; estimates are that nearly 60 percent of adults will require such services at least once in their lives (TIAA, 1992).

The cost of long-term care for the elderly is substantial, and many people have little knowledge of the economics involved until such services are needed. Figure 6.5

TABLE 6.2

Types of Care

This chart shows the possible types of care given to someone who has suffered a stroke. It illustrates the differences between acute care and long-term care.

	Acute Care	Long-Term Care
Care objectives	Improve patient's ability to function	Maintain patient at current level of function
Where care is received	Hospital and rehabilitation unit	At home
Who provides care	Physicians, nurses, therapists	Family member, home health aide
Type of care	Medication, X rays, IV feedings, physical therapy	Help with bathing and dressing, shopping and housework
Length of care	4 weeks in hospital and rehabilitation	Ongoing
Who pays for care	Medicare and private supplemental insurance	Patient most likely pays out of pocket

From Long-Term Care—A Guide for the Educational Community. Copyright © 1992 Teachers Insurance and Annuity Association (TIAA).

TABLE 6.3

Percentage of Persons over 65 Years of Age Reporting Difficulty with Selected Personal Health Care Activities

Age	Personal Care Activity						
	Bathing	Dressing	Eating	Transferring	Walking	Getting outside	Using toilet
65 years and over ..	9.8	6.2	1.8	8.0	18.7	9.6	4.3
65-74 years	6.4	4.3	1.2	6.1	14.2	5.6	2.6
65-69 years	5.2	3.9	1.2	5.3	12.2	4.9	2.2
70-74 years	7.9	4.8	1.1	7.1	16.6	6.6	3.0
75-84 years	12.3	7.6	2.5	9.2	22.9	12.3	5.4
76-79 years	9.8	6.4	2.1	7.5	19.5	9.9	4.1
80-84 years	16.8	9.7	3.2	12.4	29.0	16.8	7.8
85 years and over ..	27.9	16.6	4.4	19.3	39.9	31.3	14.1

Source: National Health Interview Survey, National Center for Health Statistics, 1984.

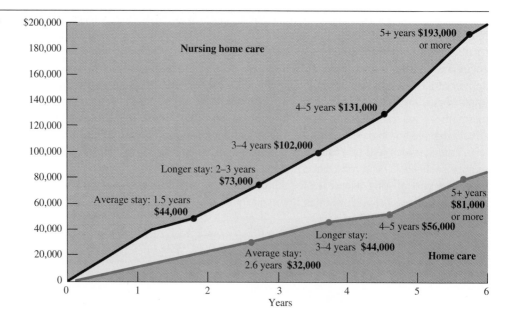

Figure 6.5 How much does long-term care cost? Expected cost of long-term care.

compares the typical costs incurred for long-term home care and long-term nursing home care over a six-year period. Note that the costs for these services vary somewhat across service providers and in different regions of our country. They are projected to increase year by year due to inflation.

Long-term care is most frequently delivered in nursing homes. With an expected annual rise in nursing home costs of 5 percent per year due to inflation, an institution charging only $86 a day will be charging more than $230 in 20 years (National Association of Insurance Commissioners, 1993). The typical nursing home stay is about 75 days, but long-term care needs may require a six- to seven-year stay or even longer. Who pays for such services? Medicare and Medicaid are federally subsidized programs that provide some of the basic health care coverage older people need. Ordinarily these programs do not cover the complete costs of long-term care as seen in figure 6.6. It is important to understand how Medicare and Medicaid differ from each other and the eligibility criteria established for program enrollees.

Medicaid

Medicaid is a federal insurance program that provides matching funds to the states to pay for the medical care of lower-income elderly over the age of 65 who are at or near the level of poverty. Medicaid is provided to states only if minimum basic benefits are offered, although individual states may establish restrictions on the types of services offered and the level of support offered to older persons (Gottleib, 1992). Medicaid typically covers about two-thirds of the cost of the medical health services of poor elderly, including some psychiatric services (Liska, Obermaier, Lyons, & Long, 1995).

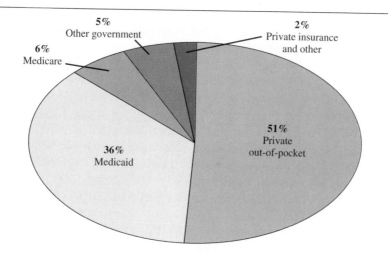

Figure 6.6 Long-term care costs. *Source: Data from Select Committee on Aging, U.S. House of Representatives, June 1991.*

5%
Other government

6%
Medicare

2%
Private insurance
and other

51%
Private
out-of-pocket

36%
Medicaid

If older people have significant assets, of course, Medicaid cannot help with long-term care expenses. However, when such assets are depleted due to long-term care costs and reach a minimum level, a process called **spending down,** older people become eligible for Medicaid. In 1997 the spouse of a person receiving Medicaid payments was restricted to $1,976 per month in income and $79,020 of assets, excluding the couple's home. Data from national studies suggest that at the time of nursing home admission, about 35 percent of the elderly qualify for Medicaid, about 15 percent will qualify within the first 12 months by spending down, and another 10 percent will qualify after the first year of spending down (LifePlans, 1990). More than a third of the Medicaid funds for poor elderly were used to provide long-term care, including community-based services, home health care, nursing, and individual personal care (Burwell, 1996; Weiner, 1996). Elderly adults received more than 60 percent of all Medicaid funds assigned for nursing home care (Weiner, 1996). In one study, nearly 70 percent of all nursing home residents were covered either fully or partially from Medicaid funds (Weiner, 1996). Experts believe some modifications in the structure and coverage of Medicaid must be made to preserve it financially (Weiner, 1996).

Medicare

Medicare is funded from the Hospital Insurance Trust Fund–Part A of the Social Security system. It provides some support, but not complete coverage, for medical services for any individual over age 65. More than 31.8 million people were covered by Medicare in 1994, including not only the elderly but also any individuals with end-stage renal disease and disabled younger persons who pay a monthly premium for coverage (Gottlieb, 1992; National Academy on Aging, 1995). Medicare has no fee or premium for those eligible and covers hospitalization for each illness up to 150 days, less deductibles, as long as the older person requires medical treatment. There are no limits to the number of hospital stays that will be covered as long as 60 days has elapsed between discharge and readmission. Medicare will also cover nursing home services (a maximum of a hundred days) for each medical condition as long as a physician has "prescribed" such services (Gottlieb, 1992; Health Care Financing Administration, 1996).

Medicare is designed to deal with acute illnesses or accidents, not chronic conditions that require intervention. The only home care covered by Medicare is for that related directly to recovery from an acute illness. A physician must file a written recovery plan for the patient including needed home health services (Health Care Financing Administration, 1996). The elderly person is assumed to be house-bound, under the direct care of a physician who has provided a written plan for intervention and recovery, requires only intermittent skilled nursing or other therapy (e.g., speech therapy, physical therapy, or occupational therapy). Services must be provided by a certified home care agency (Mannix, 1993).

For an additional monthly premium of $42.50, extended hospital coverage benefits are available to older persons under a voluntary Supplemental Medical Insurance–Part B program. Basic covered services are reimbursed at 80 percent of allowable charges, less a $400 per year deductible (National Academy on Aging, 1995; Health Care Financing Administration, 1996). Nearly 98 percent of those who are eligible for Hospital Insurance–Part A also elect extended coverage under the Supplemental Medical Insurance–Part B program. The Part B Trust Fund was created from general revenue from the federal government, monthly premiums, and the trust fund interest. Medicare remains the leading insurance provider in the United States, accounting for 28 percent of all hospital payments and 20 percent of all physician payments (Gottleib, 1992; National Academy on Aging, 1995). In 1997 there was a deductible for each inpatient hospital stay ($760) and a daily copayment ($190) for hospital stays extending for 61 to 90 days. Coverage for hospitalization beyond three months is limited to 60 additional days in a lifetime (Health Care Financing Administration, 1996).

Physicians receive reimbursement from Medicare based on customary, prevailing, and reasonable rates established by the government. Reimbursement rates for physician services are an integration of (1) the typical costs of similar services by physicians in a community, (2) the lowest cost of specific services, (3) the charge of specific services by other physicians, and (4) historical review of charges for similar services (Gottlieb, 1992). There are no limits on medical or surgical benefits for Medicare recipients (e.g., lifetime costs, costs per illness, or number of visits for treatments). Inpatient psychiatric coverage is set at a lifetime maximum of 190 days and outpatient psychiatric services, until very recently, were restricted to those provided under the direct supervision of a physician. Currently, clinical social workers and psychologists may receive direct reimbursement as independent providers, although Medicare only covers half of the costs for outpatient mental health. Skilled nursing care directly related to the condition for which hospitalization occurred is covered completely for the first 20 days and for the next 80 days with a $92 per day copayment. Skilled nursing and intravenous medical care are covered in a home setting only if prescribed by a physician and directly related to the condition for which hospitalization was required (National Academy on Aging, 1995). Nearly all hospice care for the terminally ill is covered for up to 210 days, including home care services, some prescription drugs, and counseling (Health Care Financing Administration, 1996).

Long-Term Health Care Costs

Long-term care refers to intervention provided to adults who cannot take care of themselves and need assistance with routine IADL or ADL. Many adults erroneously believe that Medicare or Medicaid will meet both their hospital and nursing home needs (TIAA, 1992). Ordinarily Medicare does not cover an older person's long-term health care needs, since it excludes personal home care services as well as nursing care, regardless of whether it is provided in a hospital or in a nursing home (National Academy on Aging, 1995; TIAA, 1992). Some states have permitted private insurance companies to fill in the missing coverage with **Medigap policies.** These policies, for an additional fee, provide coverage for home-based personal care and other health expenses not covered or not fully covered by Medicare (Mannix, 1993; Health Care Financing Administration, 1996). For example, Medicare does not cover the cost of prescription drugs, routine physicals, hearing aids, eyeglasses, or nonsurgical dental care (National Academy on Aging, 1995). Kington, Rogowski, and Lillard (1995) found that 44 percent of the elderly required dental services in one 12-month period and only 13 percent had dental insurance to meet even part of the costs. One of the most underutilized covered services in the Medicare program has been treatment for psychiatric disorders; the costs for such services for the elderly totaled less than 2.5 percent of program expenditures (Gottlieb, 1992).

By the time adults reach age 65 there is a 40 percent chance that they will need some long-term care intervention (Balch, 1997). Private long-term care insurance is available to reduce the direct costs of such services, but it can be costly. Less than 10 to 20 percent of today's population of older persons can afford such costly premiums, and most policies are beyond the reach of those at or near poverty levels (Weiner, 1996). Table 6.4 shows comparative costs for one national insurance company. Like most policies, the younger the age at which insurance coverage is purchased, the lower the cost. A policy is nearly three times more costly for someone 79 years of age to purchase than for a 65-year-old (Coronel & Fulton, 1995; Weiner, 1996). Insurance policy costs also vary considerably based on coverage as seen in table 6.4; better policies with higher lifetime benefits cost three times more than basic policies. A standard long-term care policy with a high deductible, no inflation protection, modest $100 per day coverage, and 90-day wait period is only half the cost of a premium policy. Compare this coverage with the data in figure 6.5 (p. 210), which illustrates comparative national costs for nursing home care, in-home care, and a typical long-term care scenario, which includes four years of home care and an additional two years of nursing home care (TIAA, 1992).

Insurance companies may not accept those most likely to use nursing home services—older people with prior illnesses, prior nursing home utilization, and chronic disabilities. Many policies may specifically exclude disorders such as Alzheimer's disease or require that nursing care must be continual and supervision necessary to protect the

TABLE 6.4

Long-Term Care Insurance Costs

Premiums for each plan are based on age at the time the policy is issued.

	Plan A-96	Plan B-96	Plan C-96
Lifetime Benefit Maximum	$109,500.00	$182,500.00	$255,500.00
Nursing Home Daily Benefit Maximum	$100.00/day	$100.00/day	$100.00/day
Home Health Care/Adult Day Health Care Daily Benefit Maximum	$50.00/day	$50.00/day	$50.00/day
Waiting Period	90 days	90 days	90 days

Illustration of Long-Term Care Insurance Costs

Age	Plan A-96 Quarterly	Plan B-96 Quarterly	Plan C-96 Quarterly	Age	Plan A-96 Quarterly	Plan B-96 Quarterly	Plan C-96 Quarterly
25	$23.97	$28.02	$29.83	55	109.05	127.74	135.37
26	25.35	29.63	31.52	56	115.83	135.68	143.71
27	26.70	31.21	33.23	57	122.62	143.61	152.08
28	28.07	32.82	34.91	58	132.72	155.37	164.42
29	29.43	34.40	36.59	59	142.79	167.10	176.76
30	30.80	36.01	38.30	60	152.89	178.85	189.08
31	32.16	37.59	39.99	61	162.97	190.59	201.43
32	33.53	39.19	41.67	62	173.07	202.34	213.77
33	34.88	40.78	43.35	63	188.47	220.40	232.72
34	36.26	42.38	45.06	64	203.85	238.43	251.67
35	37.61	43.96	46.74	65	219.25	256.49	270.59
36	40.19	47.00	49.96	66	234.63	274.52	289.54
37	42.77	50.01	53.17	67	250.04	292.58	308.49
38	45.34	53.04	56.38	68	273.22	320.02	337.39
39	47.94	56.08	59.57	69	296.43	347.49	366.28
40	50.52	59.11	62.79	70	319.61	374.93	395.15
41	53.09	62.12	66.00	71	342.82	402.40	424.05
42	55.67	65.16	69.21	72	366.00	429.84	452.95
43	58.58	68.58	72.83	73	405.92	477.56	503.11
44	61.49	71.99	76.46	74	445.83	525.28	553.28
45	64.37	75.41	80.08	75	485.72	572.97	603.45
46	67.27	78.83	83.70	76	525.63	620.69	653.61
47	70.18	82.25	87.32	77	565.55	668.40	703.78
48	73.88	86.58	91.91	78	628.46	745.17	784.42
49	77.58	90.92	96.50	79	691.41	821.96	865.04
50	81.28	95.28	101.12	80	754.33	898.73	945.68
51	84.97	99.61	105.71	81	817.27	975.52	1026.30
52	88.67	103.95	110.30	82	880.19	1052.29	1106.95
53	95.46	111.88	118.67	83	961.42	1153.06	1211.97
54	102.24	119.81	127.00	84	1042.62	1253.85	1316.97

person or others (TIAA, 1996). Finally, most policies provide a fixed daily rate of reimbursement (e.g., indemnity) rather than meeting the costs of services required. The reimbursement rates in a standard policy ordinarily do not increase year by year to take inflation and the generally escalating costs of nursing home stays into account. When people purchase policies 10 to 15 years in advance of their use, they often discover that their own projections of nursing home costs are far below current charges (Coronel & Fulton, 1995; Weiner, 1996).

In practice, however, only 4 to 5 percent of older people have purchased long-term health care insurance, most often when they are close to retirement (Weiner, 1996). Among retirees, wealth is the best predictor of whether they carry separate long-term care insurance protection. Older black Americans, women-headed households, and those with less education tend not to purchase supplemental coverage. Interestingly, health status is not related to the decision to buy private health care insurance (Lillard et al., 1997). Lillard and colleagues (1997) reported that many elderly fortunate enough to have private long-term care insurance were provided policies by the companies from which they retired as a reward for long, continuous employment.

To reduce Medicare expenditures on long-term care, the government has periodically considered a range of incentives to encourage individuals to purchase private long-term care insurance. Incentives being considered include tax benefits for the cost of purchasing individual policies, allowing greater assets to be held for elderly who have purchased policies, and offering employer-sponsored policies to current, younger workers (Weiner, 1996). The government has also considered meeting the growing Medicare funding gap through increased payroll taxes, shifting contributions from the other Social Security Trust Funds, increasing premiums from $42.50 to $67, instituting a small $5 copayment for services, and contracting with managed care systems and health maintenance organizations for services (National Academy on Aging, 1995). Other alternatives are being discussed, including raising the age of eligibility for Medicare from 65 to 67, requiring higher-income retirees to pay higher premiums, reducing reimbursement rates to specialty physicians, freezing hospital reimbursement rates, and permitting older persons special tax-free medical savings accounts to purchase private medical/health care insurance (Gavin, 1997).

Medicare and Medicaid programs can only reimburse accredited nursing homes (i.e., homes that have passed federally mandated inspections) and home health care agencies that are regularly and systematically reviewed by governmental agencies. Investigative reports of nursing home abuses in the past have reinforced the need for vigilance and careful monitoring. Not more than a decade ago more than one-third of the skilled nursing homes investigated were found to be seriously deficient in at least one major area and, therefore, not eligible for this reimbursement. Many nursing homes, however, do not have major deficiencies in service delivery; they simply cannot meet the minimum requirements for availability of physicians, pharmacists, and various rehabilitation professionals (e.g., occupational and physical therapists). Reviews also ensure compliance with Public Law 100-203, which includes patients' rights to privacy, access to information (open access to medical files), a lifestyle in keeping with the resident's mental and physical capacities, safety, and maintenance of personal items (Haber, 1987).

COGNITIVE IMPAIRMENT AND ENVIRONMENTAL INTERVENTION

Physical disabilities among the elderly usually trigger standard types of environmental intervention to preserve autonomy. However, comparable interventions to address cognitive impairments in older adults show far less agreement among mental health professionals. The goal of intervention that addresses cognitive impairment is to strengthen independent function, preserve self-worth, and limit family exposure to the burden of caregiving.

Community and Home Care

Not all older persons will need the specialized services provided by an institutional environment. George (1992) has emphasized the significance of understanding the timing and access of specialized home care and community services for the cognitively impaired elderly. Sommers, Baskin, Specht, and Shively (1988), for instance, originally reported that following discharge from a state mental hospital, older adults without sufficient social support and also a high degree of cognitive impairment were most likely to enter nursing homes rather than community-based alternatives. Based on this and other work, George (1992) identified two general hypotheses to explain the relationship between decisions to access community and home care living arrangements for cognitively impaired older persons. The *substitution hypothesis* is based on the premise that formal services will be used by older persons whose informal support system (e.g., friends, family) is unable or unwilling to provide sufficient help. Communities offer replacement services directly to the impaired elderly when social supports are lacking. Another form of substitution consists of *respite services* that permit the continuation of informal assistance from social networks such as family to delay institutionalization as long as possible or avoid it completely (George, 1992).

Alternatively, the *supplementation,* or linking, hypothesis places the formal services required to help the cognitively impaired elderly as secondary to the contributions provided by family members (George, 1992). Caregivers may target specific supplementary formal services for the impaired older adult for which caregivers are not trained or able to provide, so-called task differentiation. Or caregivers may simply link the impaired older adult to appropriate formal programs and services. George (1992) suggests the need for further research to understand the conditions under which substitution versus supplementation choices are made by family members providing care to a cognitively impaired older person. Although some investigations of the elderly have explored this concern in the area of physical disabilities, no comparable research has explored cognitive impairments. Some studies suggest, however, that family caregivers can actually be trained to access specific direct community services for the cognitively impaired elderly as well as intervention programs such as respite care, social support groups, and case management training programs to help the caregivers themselves (Greene & Monahan, 1987). In general, such training and intervention appears to decrease the risk of institutionalization of care recipients, although not all studies show that accessing formal services reduces the likelihood of institutional placement (George, 1992).

Delivering prepared food (Meals on Wheels) is a service found throughout communities in our society.

Environmental Design for the Cognitively Impaired Elderly

Regnier and Pynoos (1992) developed a set of 12 principles to enhance the institutional settings and home environments in which cognitively impaired elderly, such as those with AD, live. These principles can help professionals responsible for the architecture, interior design, and aesthetics of institutions focus on critical dimensions of the immediate environment that are known to influence both the behavior and quality of life of cognitively impaired older persons. For example, the "L" design or "toe-to-toe" placement of beds shown in figure 6.7 provides more privacy for residents than placing the beds side by side. And when cognitively impaired residents with AD are able to see their bathroom and toilet from bed, incidents of incontinence are significantly reduced (Brink, 1993; Regnier & Pynoos, 1992). Such principles are outlined and briefly discussed in table 6.5 (for a more complete account see Regnier & Pynoos, 1992, pp. 763–792). It is hoped that cognitively impaired elderly will continue to experience better, safer, and more secure environments to optimize their capacity for independent living.

Wandering and Cognitive Impairment

Institutional and home care for cognitively impaired elderly must also address the difficulties and the safety concerns that are associated with wandering. Wandering is a common problem among older persons with dementia and a special burden on those providing home care (Martino-Saltzman, Blasch, Morris, & McNeal, 1992). In the past, caregivers and nursing homes were permitted to use physical restraints and even psychopharmacologic drugs to reduce wandering, but these methods, when used indiscriminately, violate the legal rights of older persons as well as their humanity and dignity (Namazi, 1994). The U.S. Veterans Administration considered wandering "so imprecise as to defy definition." Wandering includes "pacing, trying doorknobs, entering other people's rooms, talking about going 'home,' attempting to leave or leaving an institution against advice, getting lost on a walk, or simply talking in a way that someone considers disoriented." In one investigation, nursing home residents

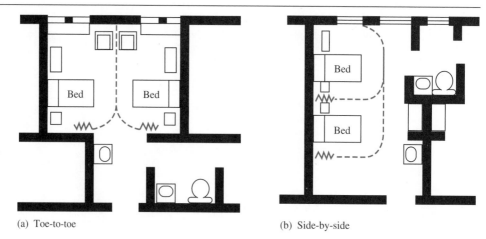

Figure 6.7 Two basic room configurations are commonly utilized in skilled nursing facilities today. (a) Two-bed room, toe-to-toe, (b) two-bed room, side-by-side. Configuration (a) provides more privacy.

(a) Toe-to-toe   (b) Side-by-side

TABLE 6.5

Twelve Environment-Behavior Principles for Cognitively Impaired Older Persons

Privacy: *Provide opportunities for a place of seclusion from company or observation where one can be free from unauthorized intrusion.* Privacy may be illustrated by having one's own room and the time to be away from others, free from unnecessary surveillance.

Social Interaction: *Provide opportunities for social exchange and interaction.* For cognitively impaired individuals, social interaction can be therapeutic and even the wide corridors of institutions can become "streets" for social activity, viewing others, and opportunities for friendly exchange.

Control, Choice, and Autonomy: *Promote opportunities for residents to make choices and control events that influence outcomes.* Older persons need to have a sense of control and mastery over the environment in which they live.

Orientation and Way Finding: *Foster a sense or orientation within the environment that reduces confusion and facilitates way finding.* Provide an environment that is easy to negotiate and easy to understand for those with cognitive impairments.

Safety and Security: *Provide an environment that ensures each user will sustain no harm, injury, and undue risk.*

Accessibility and Functioning: *Consider manipulation and accessibility as the basic requirements for a functional environment.* Utilize environmental features that are easy to manipulate (doors, windows) and require simple decision choices.

Sensory Aspects: *Changes in visual, auditory, and olfactory senses should be accounted for in environments.* Plan to meet the needs of older residents to sustain social and successful physical interaction with their environment such as providing sufficient audition and illumination.

Stimulation and Challenge: *Provide a stimulating environment that is safe but challenging.* Stimulating environments minimize boredom and passivity and challenge the older person to maintain their alertness and awareness.

Familiarity: *Environments that use historical reference influenced by tradition can provide a sense of familiarity and continuity.* Encourage the use of personal objects, particularly in new settings, to provide the older impaired individual a familiar frame of reference and a sense of continuity regarding the self.

Aesthetics and Appearance: *Design environments that appear attractive, proactive, and noninstitutional.* Avoid appearance of living conditions that depersonalize and stigmatize residents; build on residential models to humanize and individualize the living experiences.

Personalization: *Provide opportunities to make the environment personal and mark it as the property of a single, unique individual.* Maintain self-identity through individualizing the space that the individual occupies; demonstrate the older person's uniqueness.

Adaptability: *An adaptable or flexible environment can be made to fit changing personal characteristics.* With flexibility environments can be adapted to the changes encountered by the elderly to permit them to "age in place" rather than to have to move to new settings; this permits redesign within existing structures, for example, to enhance safety. An illustration of such an environment is found in figure 11.14, which displays the relatively simple but essential adaptations necessary to help the cognitively impaired older adult successfully, and with as much autonomy as possible, negotiate the risk of bathing.

From V. Regnier and J. Pynoos, "Environmental Intervention for Cognitively Impaired Older Persons" in Handbook of Mental-Health and Aging, ed. Copyright © 1992 Academic Press, Orlando, FL.

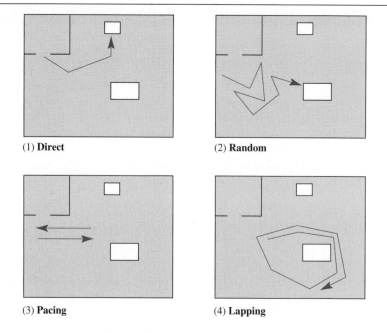

Figure 6.8 Travel patterns of nursing home residents identified as wanderers and nonwanderers. Lapping was more common among wanderers.

(1) **Direct**   (2) **Random**

(3) **Pacing**   (4) **Lapping**

with dementia and identified as wanderers were compared with a group of residents in the same nursing home who were not wanderers. Martino-Saltzman et al. (1992) identified four types of travel patterns, which may be seen in figure 6.8, based on their analysis of more than 10,000 events that were video-recorded in the nursing home over a one-month period, 24 hours each day. Although developed from a small sample of dementia residents, the results summarized in table 6.6 suggest that with more severe dementia, direct patterns of travel were less frequent, and lapping was significantly more common. The groups primarily traveled independently within the nursing home for specific or directed reasons.

Pacing and its relationship to cognitive impairment in the elderly has also been reported by others (Cohen-Mansfield, Werner, Marx, & Freedman, 1991). Pacing, when examined across a 24-hour period of study, was found to increase most dramatically in the evening hours from 7:00 to 10:00 P.M., consistent with other observations of **sundowning** in dementia patients. The peak for nondirective travel was 7:15 P.M. and table 6.7 shows the distribution of nondirective travel (e.g., random, pacing, and lapping) across the day and evening hours.

These findings suggest that the overall travel of wanderers, particularly those with severe dementia and the difficulties presented to nursing homes may be overestimated (Martina-Saltzman et al., 1992). With the greater likelihood of lapping, it may be desirable to design and utilize structured or protected walking environments given the need for patients to engage in such autonomous behaviors. Regnier and Pynoos (1992) describe an institution that has incorporated AD wandering gardens that provide to "restless patients" the chance to walk unencumbered in a safe, controlled area. And other institutions have found effective techniques to permit wandering by dementia

Table 6.6

Characteristic Wandering Patterns among Nursing Home Residents with Different Levels of Dementia

	Mild/No Dementia	Moderate Dementia	Severe Dementia
Pattern of Travel			
Direct	94.7%	92.5%	72.0%
Random	0.2%	1.0%	1.7%
Pacing	1.5%	0.0%	0.03%
Lapping	3.6%	6.5%	26.0%

Adapted from Martino-Saltzman, Blasch, B. B., Morris, R. D., and McNeal, L. W. (1992). Travel behavior of nursing home residents perceived as wanderers and nonwanderers. The Gerontologist, 31 (5), 666–672.

Table 6.7

Percentage of Nondirective Independent Travel Events at Selective Time Periods for Nursing Home Residents with Various Levels of Dementia

	Level of Dementia		
Time Period	Mild/None (n = 12)	Moderate (n = 11)	Severe (n = 9)
10 pm–4 am	4%	1%	31%
4 am–7 am	2%	13%	26%
Breakfast	2%	5%	19%
9 am–12 noon	2%	7%	31%
Lunch	4%	5%	15%
2 pm–5 pm	7%	6%	32%
Dinner	4%	8%	23%
7 pm–10 pm	15%	12%	31%
Total	5%	7%	28%
Total excluding meal times	7%	8%	31%

patients, including disguising emergency exits (e.g., placing cloth covers matching the color of the walls on tamperproof doorknobs). Restricting visual accessibility helps reduce exiting behaviors. These visual barriers, used singly or in combination, were effective in redirecting wandering in one institution without compromising safety and fire codes (Namazi, 1994).

Restraints

In view of safety and legal concerns, most nursing home staff understandably take a very conservative approach to control wandering using electronic monitoring, drugs, or physical restraints. In 1989, as many as 40 percent of nursing home residents were restrained for part of each day to beds, chairs, or wheelchairs by lengths of cloth tied at the waist, hips, chest, arms, or legs. This practice had declined to about 22 percent

The Use of Restraints in Nursing Homes

The use of restraints in nursing homes is controversial and but one of many practices under which nursing home residents receive federal protection under a bill of rights, established in 1987 under the Omnibus Budget Reconciliation Act. Although penalties for nursing homes that fail to comply are still evolving, the bill of rights currently specifies that residents have the right to a physician, to be informed about treatment, to refuse treatment, to complain without fear of reprisal, and the right to be free of restraints (Brink, 1993). Investigators (Burton et al., 1992; Miles & Irvine, 1992) suggest that many considerations govern the use of restraints by staff. Schnelle, Simmons, and Ory (1992), for example, reported that staff failed to provide release from physical restraints (wrist, mittens, vest, and geri-chairs) among nursing home residents who were perceived by them to be verbally aggressive, physically aggressive, and generally unpleasant. The continuous use of restraints for any extended period must be monitored carefully. Restrained residents require as much as 15 percent more time from nursing home staff than those who are unrestrained, and restraints over extended periods limit independence such as toileting and may contribute to painful pressure sores (Brink, 1993). Miles and Irvine (1992), using an ex post facto analysis, reported that the ultimate risk inherent in using restraints continuously without supervision and without regular monitoring in nursing homes was death. Their analysis revealed that death was most likely to occur to a nursing home resident who was female, about 81 years old, and diagnosed with dementia. Miles and Irvine (1992) estimated that about 1 in 1,000 nursing home deaths could be linked directly to the use of restraints and advocated a dramatic reduction in their use; they suggest short-term use of restraints only to ensure medically necessary therapy for acutely ill, delirious older persons. From their analysis of case records, a composite scenario has been developed to illustrate the way in which restraints can accidentally cause death:

A nurse or aide applies a vest or strap restraint. While unobserved for ten minutes to several hours the patient slides off the bed or chair so that the restraint bears her weight and prevents her from sliding further down to a weight-bearing surface. She is confused and unable to use her arms or legs to return to a safe position in her bed or chair. Her weight, transmitted through the restraint, creates a force about her chest. As she struggles, the restraint gathers, thus concentrating the pressure around her chest. She asphyxiates, usually because she cannot inhale, less often because the restraint slides up and gathers to act as a ligature on her neck. (Miles & Irvine, 1992, p. 765)

An illustration of such a situation is provided above.

Miles, S.H. and Irvine, P. (1992) Deaths caused by physical restraints. *The Gerontologist, 32 (6),* 762–766.

by 1992, according to the American Health Care Association (Brink, 1993). Advocates have justified the use of restraints to protect residents from falling, to maintain needed medical treatment, to control wandering, and to protect staff and other residents from aggressive behaviors. Burton, German, Rovner, Brant, and Clark (1992) studied the use of restraints among elderly persons admitted with "mental illness" to a nursing home facility. The more severe the cognitive impairment and the more difficulty in managing independent daily living skills, the more likely staff were to employ physical restraints. There were also clear differences in the use of restraints among the eight nursing homes studied, with high-use institutions tending to restrain persons who needed assistance in walking and low-use homes not engaging in this practice. Burton et al. (1992) suggest that it is staff attitudes that predominately account for differences among high- and low-use nursing homes; in high-use homes, staff try to protect residents from falling and are quick to provide assistance with daily living tasks such as walking and dressing. They report considerable latitude in staff adoption of the use of physical restraint rather than mandated policies of the nursing home (Burton et al., 1992). It is important to understand the variables that predict adoption of restraints in institutional care facilities and the risks/benefits associated with their use. Research Focus 6.1 provides some insights on these issues.

HEALTH AND BEHAVIOR

The fact that physical functioning and health are at their peak in early adulthood is in some ways a risk. Young adults do not notice any immediate negative consequences of poor diet, alcohol abuse, stress, smoking, and lack of exercise. It is difficult to take better care of one's health when the consequences of choices are many decades away. Nine out of 10 people between the ages of 17 and 44 view their own health as good or excellent. Relative to older adults, young adults have few chronic health problems. If young adults are hospitalized, it is usually because of an accident or for childbirth (National Center for Health Statistics, 1992).

Verbrugge and Jette (1994) have noted that the health care community itself is particularly interested in eliminating specific risk factors that accelerate the rate of decline in illness or chronic diseases and promoting behaviors that can delay, reverse, or even prevent the occurrence of illnesses. Healthy life choices can help people reach old age in the best of physical condition. And aging can be slowed and premature death associated with chronic illnesses prevented (Deeg et al., 1996). The following sections discuss some of these risk factors and interventions. There is a national effort to mobilize people of all ages to become aware of the importance of lifestyle, behavior, and individual choice in promoting good health and longevity. (See Research Focus 6.2.)

Exercise

The overall benefit of regular exercise has been emphasized for more than 50 years by physicians and other health care professionals. Regular exercise is advocated in recent national surveys and in a major report from the surgeon general (U.S. Public Health, 1996). In the most recent analysis it has been shown that any moderate exercise (e.g., sufficient to burn 150 calories per day) provides important health benefits. Americans are encouraged to think differently about the type of exercise that can improve their overall health. Everyday activities such as walking the dog, washing a car, climbing stairs, and gardening can reduce the risk of heart disease, high blood pressure, cancer, and diabetes as much as those that involve intense participation such as jogging or aerobic exercise classes. Activities must be engaged in regularly and at a brisk rather than leisurely pace in order to be effective. However, analyses of the typical American lifestyle shows that despite more than 30 years of trying to persuade the nation of the benefits of exercise, the government has been rather unsuccessful—60 percent of adults living in the United States do not exercise regularly and of this number 25 percent do not exercise at all.

Possible Selves: The Fear of Poor Health

Karen Hooker and Cheryl Kaus (1994) investigated how adults create a framework in which their own behaviors are linked directly to their health. The study was based on the pioneering work of Markus and Nurius (1992) on *possible selves:* a future view of our self-identity representing a desirable goal in terms of what we might like to become or an undesirable goal or fear of what we might become. Markus and Nurius believe that possible selves provide individuals with heightened motivation to action to either realize those positive goals we seek for our "self" or to avoid becoming what we fear for our "self." The construct of possible selves implies that individuals can shed images that no longer fit the reality of aging (e.g., accepting accumulated losses). As such, possible selves have been closely related to positive adjustment, since they help to preserve well-being (Markus & Nurius, 1992) and a sense of personal integrity (Ryff, 1991). Possible selves are both causes of action (Karoly, 1993) and a source of direction in later development (Hooker & Kaus, 1992). Possible selves represent the individual's embodiment of actual life goals (definition of possible selves) and behaviors (actions) that will help attain these goals.

The 84 young adults (24–39 years old) and 87 middle-aged adults (40–59 years old) in Hooker and Kaus's study indicated whether they had positive images of a healthy self in the future (e.g., "hoped-for selves") as well as negative images of an unhealthy self (e.g., "feared selves"). In the results obtained by Hooker and Kaus (1994) middle-aged respondents indicated significantly more health-related selves than did young adults.

Both young and middle-aged adults did not seem to be considering healthy possible selves as much as unhealthy possible selves. In other words, the goal for individuals was primarily to avoid a possible self replete with health problems and health deficiencies. Similar responses have been reported among middle-aged persons (Cross & Markus, 1991; Leventhal, Leventhal, & Schaefer, 1992, 1993). Carol Ryff (1991) also noted that fear of declining health and well-being dominated older adults' views of possible selves. In this regard, "dread" directs middle-aged individuals to adopt health-enhancing behaviors (actions), e.g., "I do not want to have these events occur to me." Indeed, when Hooker and Kaus assessed goal-oriented activities and other self-regulatory variables, they found that there were two types of significant predictors of health behaviors: (1) actions that were taken to avoid feared health-related selves, and (2) a person's perception or belief that they were capable of preventing such "dreaded" selves. Leventhal, Leventhal, and Schaefer (1992, 1993) noted that though middle-aged and younger adults are similar in their fear of health threats, older adults are more likely to have adopted a greater number of health preventive behaviors. In fact, in an earlier study (Hooker & Kaus, 1992), older adults reported to have both feared and hoped-for health-related selves. Remaining at issue for future research is the identification of those possible hoped-for health-related selves that may promote specific types of health preventive behaviors, particularly for young and middle-aged adults (Hooker & Kaus, 1994; Leventhal, Leventhal, Schaefer, & Easterling, 1993).

Promoting the enhanced health benefits of even moderate exercise is designed to encourage sedentary adults to become active without the need for a highly intense, vigorous, and organized formal program. The government will undertake a massive effort over the next 10 years to educate people about the dangers of not exercising. The Centers for Disease Control and Prevention allocated more than $10 million in 1997 to promote the benefits of physical activity and exercise. Most research suggests that the more exercise, the longer the exercise regimen, and the more intense the workout, the better the overall impact on health. However, some moderate exercise is better than no exercise at all.

Physical competence is a concept that combines both physical fitness and expertise, that is expertise derived from practice. It is used to assess the impact of physical exercise and training (Stones & Kozma, 1996). It is difficult for scientists to obtain valid measures of physical competence across people of different ages (Stones & Kozma, 1996). In the case of the oldest-old it may be difficult and often very expensive to bring them to an exercise laboratory for precise assessments. There also may be potential safety or health risks inherent in the age group being studied that may make

Physical exercise and regular training activities can promote strength, muscle mass, and endurance for adults from the twenties through the nineties, no matter when they are initiated.

such measurements inadvisable (Stones & Kozma, 1996). And, of course, some tasks may simply be impossible for certain populations such as the frail elderly (Stones & Kozma, 1996). When research investigators have to change tasks from one age group to another, it becomes difficult to compare performance; there is no single index of physical competence that can be applied universally to all persons throughout the life span, regardless of age (Stones & Kozma, 1996). Common measures used in research to assess physical function are an index of independent activities of daily living and simple tests of physical fitness such as grip strength, endurance capacity, or trunk flexibility. *Functional age,* or more precisely psychophysical fitness, requires field-based assessments of four variables: flexibility, balance, vital capacity, and digit symbol memory (Stones & Kozma, 1996).

The overall benefits of exercise have been found for the cardiorespiratory system, strength, and strength endurance (Stratton, Levy, Cerqueira, Schwartz, & Abrass, 1994). Some studies have even found generalized improvements in cognitive/neuropsychological performance with exercise programs lasting only a few weeks or months (Stones & Kozma, 1996). For example, in one study, nursing home residents in their eighties improved their cognitive performance on a semantic memory task by 20 percent over baseline with a simple physical exercise program (Stones & Dawe, 1993; Stones & Kozma, 1996). However, the overall benefits of sustained physical exercise, or **chronic exercise,** on cognitive performance is not so convincing. Stones and Kozma (1996) speculate that perhaps it is easier to demonstrate the benefits of short-term exercise programs on psychomotor competence and cognition in older adults because the participants are often very poorly fit at the outset of the studies. In such samples it may be easier to demonstrate the immediate benefits of exercise with a single intervention session or from those lasting only a few days or weeks. Gains in physical health, however, are subject to "a law of diminishing returns, with the extent of gain varying negatively with the baseline level" (Stones & Kozma, p. 349).

Investigators have noted that physical inactivity relates directly to a decrease in aerobic exercise capacity in older men and women (Spina, Miller, Bogenhagen, Schechtman, & Ehsani, 1996). Reversing the process through aerobic exercise is accomplished by different physiological mechanisms in men and women. In men, improvements in cardiac function increased aerobic exercise capacity primarily by changes in the left ventricle of the heart, leading to stronger blood flow volume at each heartbeat and improved filling of the ventricle itself. For women, improved cardiac function was the result of increased oxygen transport through the arteries and veins (Spina et al., 1996).

Attitude, Disease, and Psychoneuroimmunology

There has been consistent interest by medical experts, psychologists, and health care professionals in the role of attitude in promoting disease and wellness. Cohen and Herbert (1996) reviewed some of this research within the context of a simple model (see figure 6.9). According to the model, a person's psychological state can trigger a set of neurological, hormonal, and behavioral responses that can directly alter the functioning of the immune system. **Psychoneuroimmunology** is the study of those multifaceted changes in the central nervous system and immune system that heighten or lower a person's susceptibility to disease and recovery from disease. The immune system protects the body from potential damaging or fatal bacteria, viruses, fungi, and parasites that cause disease through activation of immune system cells (e.g., white blood cells, antibodies) that circulate regularly in the blood.

The effects of psychological stress on reducing the effectiveness of the immune system have been shown in studies with rheumatoid arthritis. **Rheumatoid arthritis** is an autoimmune disease characterized by swelling of the joints and marked over time by degeneration of cartilage in the affected joints and loss of joint function. Adults coping with stressful life events and without a strong social support network appear to be more susceptible to the onset of this disease and more prone to flare-ups of symptoms (Cohen & Herbert, 1996).

A great deal of work on psychoneuroimmunology has focused on the possible psychological triggers that might depress immune system function and lead to cancer. By and large the results are not consistent, perhaps in part because research has failed to recognize that cancer is not a single disease entity and that stress or depression as predictors are not stable attributes of individuals but change as the individual ages and as the disease progresses or slows down (Cohen & Herbert, 1996). Two general types of studies have been conducted: (1) prediction of who will develop cancer among a population of older persons free of the disease, and (2) prediction of those who have longer mortality following a diagnosis of cancer. Some studies do show a tendency for cancer patients to have longer survival with positive rather than pessimistic attitudes toward life and their disease. Other

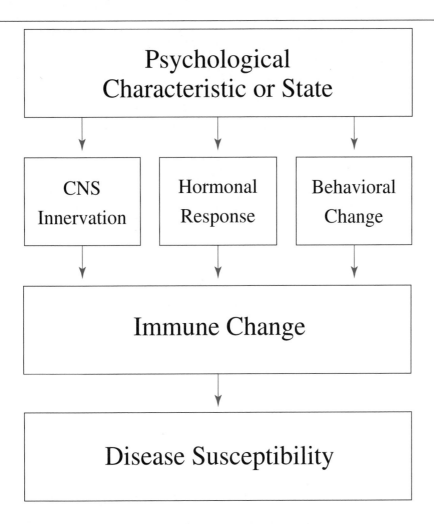

Psychological Characteristic or State

| CNS Innervation | Hormonal Response | Behavioral Change |

Immune Change

Disease Susceptibility

Figure 6.9
Pathways through which psychological factors might influence onset and progression of immune system–mediated disease. For simplicity, arrows are drawn in only one direction, from psychological characteristics to disease. No lack of alternative paths is implied. *From: Cohen, S. & Herbert, T. B. (1996). Health Psychology: Psychological factors and physical disease from the perspective of human psychoneuroimmunology. Annual Review of Psychology, 47, 113–142.*

studies show the same results for mortality when access to social support is readily available. However, the relationship of mortality to positive attitude and access to social support appears to hold for younger adult cancer patients, 40 to 59 years of age, but not for older adults with the disease (Cohen & Herbert, 1996; Schulz, Bookwala, Knapp, Scheier, & Williamson, 1996). In addition, social isolation itself has been reported to have a more negative impact on survival for women with cancer than it does for men (Cohen & Herbert, 1996; Reynolds & Kaplan, 1990). The effects of other psychological variables such as the degree of depression or optimism expressed by cancer patients generally does not show effects on either mortality or disease onset (Cohen & Herbert, 1996).

Cancer

Cancer is not a single disease but a group of different diseases that share a common feature: rapid and uncontrollable growth of abnormal cells resulting in the formation of a cancerous or malignant tumor. Unless the growth of the malignant tumor is halted through some treatment or combination of treatments, death will occur. Malignant tumors can easily spread or metastasize to other sites and organs because cancerous cells travel throughout the body via blood and lymph systems circulation. Scientists are focusing on why the normal process of cell division suddenly goes awry and produces cancer cells that multiply uncontrollably. They have found genetic links in certain kinds of cancers as well as defects in genetic codes—some that cause cell division to speed up and some that fail to limit cell division. One mechanism, *angiogenesis,* permits small tumors that have been dormant to grow larger and larger by promoting growth of the blood vessels, nutrients, and blood supply surrounding the tumor. Researchers do not know what triggers angiogenesis to the point of overcoming other processes that formerly kept the tumor under control. A number of effective cancer treatments use antiangiogenic drugs or angiogenesis inhibitors, which can slow blood vessel growth and thereby eliminate or reduce tumor size. These new discoveries include interleukin-12, angiostatin, and alpha-interferon and are often part of the multiple, combined treatments used ("Stopping Cancer in Its Tracks," 1995).

If a malignancy is detected early, before any cancer cells have had a chance to migrate or metastasize to other body organs, the treatment success by **oncologists** (physicians who specialize in cancer treatment) is quite high. In 1997, for example, nearly 1,382,400 persons were newly diagnosed with cancer; yet, more than half will be cured and only 44 percent will die of the disease (Cancer Facts and Figures, 1997). The American Cancer Society estimates that about 33 percent of all adults will develop cancer at some point in their lifetime. Following heart disease, cancer is the second leading cause of death in the United States. Currently more people die from lung cancer than any other type. More than 10 million new cancer cases have been diagnosed since 1990; current statistics show that one of every four deaths in the United States is from cancer (Cancer Facts and Figures, 1997). Figure 6.10 shows the age-adjusted death rates due to different types of cancers for men and women from 1930 to 1993. The expected distribution of new cancers for men and women, as well as the different types of cancers leading to death, for 1997 are summarized in figure 6.11.

There are three major classes of cancerous tumors. They are identified by the type of cells responsible for their genesis. The most common malignancies are called *carcinomas.* They arise from the epithelial layers or outside layers of the cells of the body: the skin, the outside layers of glands (e.g., breast, uterus, prostate), outside layers of respiratory tract and lungs, the urinary tract, and the gastrointestinal tract (e.g., colon, rectum, stomach, and mouth). *Sarcomas* are malignant tumors that develop from cells of the connective and fibrous tissue of the body (e.g., bone, muscle, and cartilage). *Lymphomas* are cancers that arise in the lymph nodes or infection-fighting system of the body. Leukemia is a cancer that arises in the bone marrow, resulting in the overproduction of mutant white blood cells and the reduction of red blood cells. The abnormal white blood cells cannot effectively protect the individual from infection and disease; the loss of red blood cells produces anemia and tiredness since oxygen transport is compromised (Insel, Roth, Rollins, & Peterson, 1996).

Breast Cancer   The most common cancer among women in the United States is breast cancer. If all women lived to age 85, recent statistics indicate that one in nine women

Figure 6.10(a) Age-Adjusted Cancer Death Rates,* Males by Site, US 1930–1993.

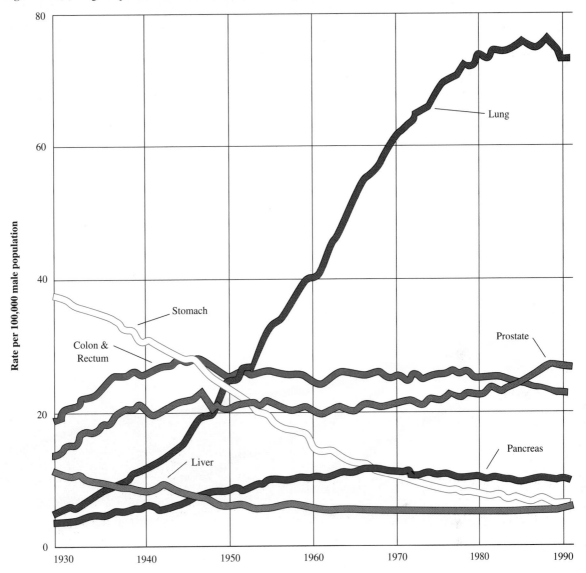

Rates are per 100,000 and are age-adjusted to the 1970 US standard population.
Note: Due to changes in ICD coding, numerator information has changed over time. Rates for cancers of the liver, lung, and colon and rectum are affected by these coding ranges. Denominator information for the years 1930–1959 and 1991–1993 is based on intercensal population estimates, while denominator information for the years 1960–1989 based on postcensal recalculation of estimates. Rate estimates for 1968–1989 are most likely of a better quality.
Source: Vital Statistics of the United States, 1993.   *©1997, American Cancer Society, Inc.*

Figure 6.10(b) Age-Adjusted Cancer Death Rates,* Females by Site, US 1930–1993.

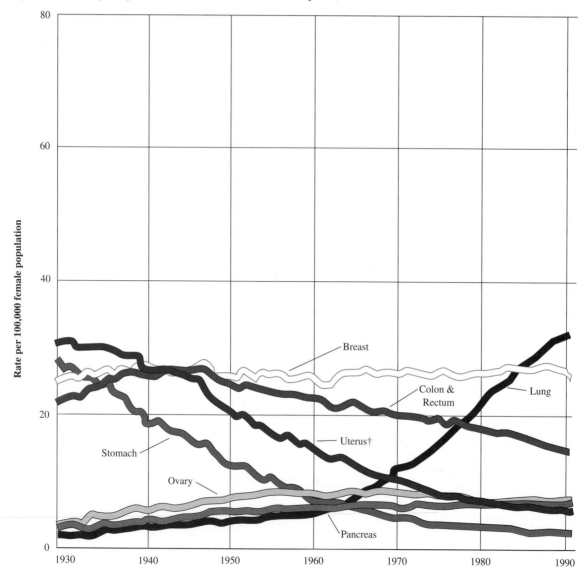

*Rates are per 100,000 and are age-adjusted to the 1970 US standard population.

†Uterine cancer death rates are for cervix and corpus combined.

Note: Due to changes in ICD coding, numerator information has changed over time. Rates for cancers of the ovary, lung, and colon and rectum are affected by these coding ranges. Denominator information for the years 1930–1959 and 1991–1993 is based on intercensal population estimates, while denominator information for the years 1960–1989 based on postcensal recalculation of estimates. Rate estimates for 1968–1989 are most likely of a better quality.

Source: Vital Statistics of the United States, 1993.

©1997, American Cancer Society, Inc.

Figure 6.11 Leading Sites of New Cancer Cases and Deaths—1997 Estimates*

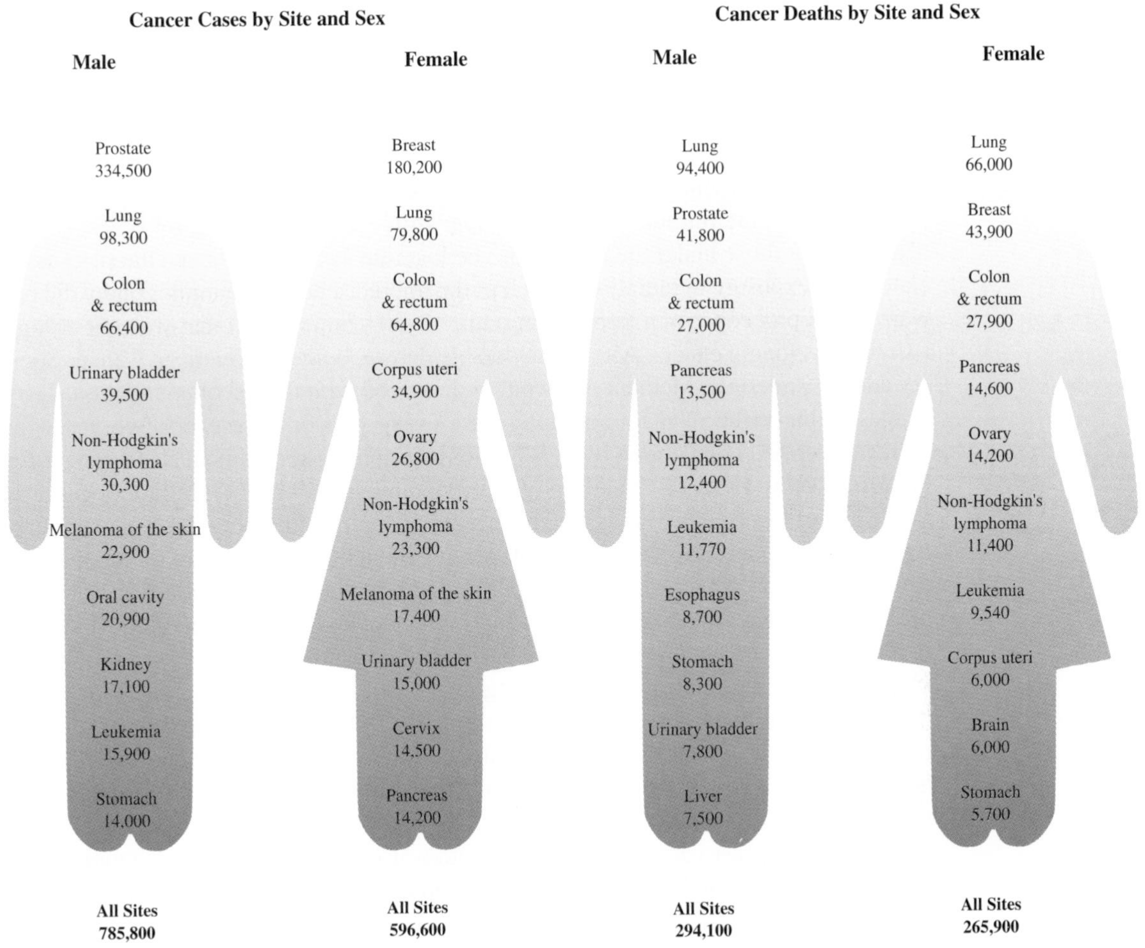

Cancer Cases by Site and Sex

Male	Female
Prostate 334,500	Breast 180,200
Lung 98,300	Lung 79,800
Colon & rectum 66,400	Colon & rectum 64,800
Urinary bladder 39,500	Corpus uteri 34,900
Non-Hodgkin's lymphoma 30,300	Ovary 26,800
Melanoma of the skin 22,900	Non-Hodgkin's lymphoma 23,300
Oral cavity 20,900	Melanoma of the skin 17,400
Kidney 17,100	Urinary bladder 15,000
Leukemia 15,900	Cervix 14,500
Stomach 14,000	Pancreas 14,200
All Sites 785,800	**All Sites 596,600**

Cancer Deaths by Site and Sex

Male	Female
Lung 94,400	Lung 66,000
Prostate 41,800	Breast 43,900
Colon & rectum 27,000	Colon & rectum 27,900
Pancreas 13,500	Pancreas 14,600
Non-Hodgkin's lymphoma 12,400	Ovary 14,200
Leukemia 11,770	Non-Hodgkin's lymphoma 11,400
Esophagus 8,700	Leukemia 9,540
Stomach 8,300	Corpus uteri 6,000
Urinary bladder 7,800	Brain 6,000
Liver 7,500	Stomach 5,700
All Sites 294,100	**All Sites 265,900**

*Excluding basal and squamous cell skin cancer and in situ carcinomas except bladder.
American Cancer Society Surveillance Research, 1997.

©1997, American Cancer Society, Inc.

could expect to have a diagnosis of breast cancer. Statistics also indicate that 1.6 million women have the disease, and that there may be as many as 1 million undiagnosed cases. According to the American Cancer Society, there were more than 182,200 new cases of breast cancer in women in 1995. Nearly 80 percent of women with breast cancer survive for at least 5 years following initial diagnosis, the 10-year survival rate is 65 percent, and the 15-year survival rate is 56 percent (Frieswick, 1997). The incidence of breast cancer is less in black women than in white women, yet more black women die of breast cancer. The risk of breast cancer doubles every five years between ages 30 and 45 and the risk increases by 10 to 15 percent for each five-year interval beyond 45. Most breast cancer is found in women over 50 (80%); when women 40 and older are included, the rate of occurrence is 90 percent. There is some evidence that younger women who are premenopausal have less favorable survival statistics, given the higher rate of reoccurrence of the disease (de la Rochefordiere, Asselain, & Campana, 1993).

Risk factors for breast cancer include increased age, genetic family history, high-fat and low-fiber diet, sedentary lifestyle, obesity, alcohol consumption, oral contraception, early menstruation, late menopause, extended exposure to postmenopausal estrogens, recent use of oral contraceptives, never having children or having a late-in-life first childbirth (Cancer Facts and Figures, 1997). Although early detection is a key to successful treatment of cancer, the National Cancer Institute issued a controversial opinion against the routine use of **mammography** (X-ray screening for breast cancer detection) for those under the age of 50. The Institute's experts believed the risks associated with exposure to radiation as well as the impreciseness of mammography did not warrant the procedure in a population (e.g., 40–50 years of age) that was not at high risk for developing cancer. After considerable debate, both the American Cancer Society and the American Medical Association disagreed with this recommendation. They suggested the value of mammography once every year or once every two years for women over 40. For women over 50, mammography is recommended to screen for breast cancer as a part of a yearly physical. Mammography is not infallible regardless of the age of the woman; however, those aged 50 years and older who have regularly received mammography have a 20 to 40 percent reduction in the risk of dying of breast cancer (Kerlikowske et al., 1993). At all ages, early diagnosis is critical to surviving breast cancer (Kerlikowske et al., 1993). The American Cancer Society urges women to conduct their own self-examination each month; mammography misses some 10 to 15 percent of breast cancers (Breast Imaging, 1995).

Treatment of breast cancer is determined by the specific characteristics of the malignant tumor, whether it has metastasized, patient preferences, and the age and health of the woman. Without metastasis to lymph nodes, breast cancer treatments show that 97 percent of women survive at least five years (Cancer Facts and Figures, 1997). Treatment for breast cancer may involve removal of the tumor and the lymph nodes under the arm (**lumpectomy**), removal of the breast itself (**mastectomy**) and the lymph nodes, and/or administration of radiation, chemotherapy, or hormone therapy. Usually some combination of treatments is suggested. Surgeons and oncologists continue to debate when lumpectomy or mastectomy is advised. Some studies suggest that with small breast tumors, survival rates with lumpectomy followed by radiation treatments are the same as those following mastectomy and radiation (Posner & Wolmark, 1994).

Older and younger women differ in the processing of information related to diagnosis and treatment decisions involved in breast cancer. Older women arrive at treatment decisions more quickly than younger women. Young women tend to focus on detailed information and bottom-up processing; older women tend to approach information with a balanced problem-solving approach, seeking information within the context of their expertise and choice of treatment alternatives (Meyer, Russo, & Talbot, 1995; Sinnott, 1989). Older women (65–88 years of age) generally sought less information before making a treatment decision for breast cancer. Interestingly, in the preceding research studies, the actual treatment decisions made by younger and older women were virtually identical. Younger women (18–39 years of age) tended to seek more information and sought more detail before coming to a resolution regarding treatment.

Women face a nexus of psychological reactions to the diagnosis of breast cancer, some lasting for the rest of their lives. The initial diagnosis is met with disbelief, shock, anger, and denial. In time there is an acceptance and a desire to conquer the illness. Feeling in control is empowering to women. Developing a "fighting spirit" against the disease, creating a sense of control, hopefulness, and personal responsibility seem to be related to women's success in the battle against breast cancer. These factors have been found to be related, in part, to the successful management of the disease, its treatment, and a higher quality of life (Cohen & Herbert, 1996; Frieswick, 1997). In a longitudinal study of mortality, Greer (1991) first showed that women with a "fighting spirit" were more likely to live longer than other breast cancer patients who maintained a "stoic acceptance" or hopeless/helpless attitude regarding the disease and their recovery. In a related study, Phillips, Todd, and Wagner (1993) reported that among Chinese Americans facing breast cancer, those who believed they were "ill-fated" and "gave up" did not live as long with the disease as those who did not hold these beliefs and who accepted the possibility that they could be successfully cured of the disease. The conclusions from this emerging research, however, are somewhat complex since age appears to play a role in the results. It also appears that optimism and pessimism provide differential prediction of treatment outcome and must be evaluated separately for clear and unambiguous conclusions of their efficacy in promoting survivorship (Schulz et al., 1996).

Every woman facing breast cancer must cope with some degree of helplessness and anxiety; the disease is proof of one's mortality and vulnerability. There is also a deep sense of loss—the potential loss of one's future, the fear of missing out on the continued growth and development of family members, and the loss of a breast if surgery is required. Mastectomy causes the loss of a critical element of gender identity and can lead to a profound sense of loss of basic sexuality. Clinical psychologists and psychiatrists regularly help women with breast cancer who feel depressed and unattractive after surgery. Some women seek reconstructive breast surgery, although no reconstruction can ever replace the breast that has been lost (Frieswick, 1997). In some cases, depending on the ensuing treatments that will follow and patient characteristics, certain reconstruction procedures can be performed at the time of mastectomy (Cancer Facts and Figures, 1997).

Research suggests that the quality of a woman's primary relationship with a partner or husband can help in coping with the diagnosis and treatment of breast cancer. In some intervention programs, support is given to both the patient and her significant other (Frieswick, 1997). Breast cancer patients are encouraged to share their emotions and not try to protect other loved ones in their families. Patients in particular are helped to express their concerns, deep emotions, and basic fears. One program at Harvard University's Brigham and Women's Hospital offers 10 sessions in a "Partners in Coping" program. It helps couples work on and improve coping strategies such as communication, listening, intimacy, sharing responsibilities, child care, and living with breast cancer itself. The disease puts strains on partners and their relationships; poor relationships get worse and strong relationships are challenged. Couples need to speak openly and honestly about their concerns to help each other in the process of adjustment. Since strong social support is so important to improving quality of life for those with cancer, the American Cancer Society offers women with breast cancer an opportunity to talk to a volunteer who has survived the disease in its "Reach to Recovery" program. Often the physical recovery from mastectomy, radiation, and chemotherapy can proceed far more rapidly than a woman's emotional adjustment (Frieswick, 1997). With every checkup throughout each passing year it is common for survivors to experience anxiety that their cancer has reappeared.

Prostate Cancer   The most common cancer among men is prostate cancer. This carcinoma affects the prostate gland, which lies at the base of the bladder. In 1997 more than 334,500 new cases were reported in the United States (Cancer Facts and Figures, 1997). Cancer of the prostate is increasingly more common as men age; 80 percent of diagnoses are made in those over the age of 65, and African-American men have a particularly high incidence of the disease with a 66 percent higher rate than that for white males. Some experts believe that nearly every male over the age of 80 has the disease, but the rate at which it grows and threatens survival can be quite slow. One out of every 11 males will be diagnosed with prostate cancer in their lifetime (Cancer Facts and Figures, 1997).

As with other cancers, early detection is a key to successful treatment. Many men with prostate cancer have no noticeable symptoms. A yearly physical should include a routine rectal examination to permit a physician to monitor the size of the prostate gland and the presence of smaller tumors on its surface. In some cases ultrasound tests detect extremely small malignancies in the prostate. A blood test that assesses the level of **prostate specific antigen (PSA)** can be very helpful in providing early warning for cancer. This blood test is recommended by the American Cancer Society for all men over age 50 and for those over 40 if they have a family history of the disease or are African American. A single PSA reading is not as helpful diagnostically as a series of readings over a number of years to help determine whether there is cause for concern (Insel et al., 1996). PSA testing has improved early detection of prostate cancer by more than 25 percent since 1986 ("PSA Debate," 1995). Note that a condition unrelated to cancer of the prostate—*benign prostatic hypertrophy (BPH),* or enlargement of the prostate—naturally occurs with aging. BPH can cause difficulty in urination, interrupted urine flow, frequent urination, reduction in the flow of urine, and difficulty in emptying the bladder fully.

Treatment for prostate cancer is most effective when there has been no metastasis beyond the gland, and current statistics suggest a five-year survival rate of 99 percent under such conditions. Overall survival rates are about 87 percent; 41,800 men died from prostate cancer in 1997. The mortality rates are twice as high for African-American males (Cancer Facts and Figures, 1997). Various treatment options are available, including chemotherapy, implanting radioactive pellets in the gland, laser surgery, destruction of tumors by selective freezing or high heat, hormone therapy, surgery to remove the prostate, or radiation to shrink it. Men are understandably concerned about any treatment for prostate cancer since some of the treatment options are associated with an increased risk of incontinence and sexual impotence. For example a common surgical procedure to remove the prostate, *transuretheral resection (TUR),* may result in cutting the nerves responsible for establishing an erection in nearly 40 percent of such cases. Many older men in their late seventies and eighties may be advised by their physicians to simply live with prostate cancers that are slow growing and not an imminent threat to their survival, rather than be exposed to unnecessary risks from surgery, chemotherapy, or radiation. Physicians find "watchful waiting" appropriate for older men with early-stage tumors (Cancer Facts and Figures, 1997; "PSA Debate," 1995).

Lung Cancer   In the United States, lung cancer remains the leading cause of death of all of the various forms of cancer. Nearly 160,400 persons died from lung cancer in 1997, and there were 178,000 new diagnoses of lung cancer the same year (Cancer Facts and Figures, 1997). The American Cancer Society has identified the single most significant risk factor in this disease: cigarette, cigar, and pipe smoke. Lung cancer has clear early warning signs, which include a persistent cough, pain in the lungs or chest area, and frequent bouts of bronchitis. Only 15 percent of lung cancers are detected early and there is a five-year survival rate of 48 percent in such cases. Surgical removal of the carcinoma if it has not metastasized is the most common treatment. Surgery often involves removal of one or more of the lobes of the lung (lobectomy) and follow-up treatment with radiation or chemotherapy. Since detection usually occurs very late in the disease, metastasis is commonly encountered and chemotherapy and radiation are needed in combination with surgery. Statistically, overall survival rates for five years or more for those with lung cancer are only about 14 percent (Cancer Facts and Figures, 1997).

Human Immunodeficiency Virus and AIDS

Another threat to the health of adults and the elderly is AIDS. Health care professionals are concerned with the growing number of elderly persons (50 years of age and older) who suffer from AIDS. There is neither a vaccine nor a cure for AIDS. Therefore, preventing the transmission of the virus that causes AIDS, the human immunodeficiency virus (HIV), is the primary goal of public health programs. Not every person exposed to the virus develops AIDS, although Cohen and Herbert (1996) note that poor nutrition, continued drug abuse, and repeated HIV exposure can accelerate the progression of the disease. Psychoneuroimmunologic factors that heighten the immune system function and promote disease resistance and survival include acceptance of the disease and the presence of a strong emotionally supportive social network (Cohen & Herbert 1996). Other factors studied such as presence of depressive symptoms, degree of current stress, and negative affect have not been related to disease progression and immune system function.

Older adults may be more likely than younger adults to become HIV-infected and to develop the symptoms of AIDS for three reasons (Catania et al., 1989). First, the efficacy of the immune system declines with age. Older adults have a shorter HIV incubation period than younger adults (5.8 years versus 7.3 years, respectively). Second, older adults—more so than younger adults—are likely to be the recipients of blood transfusions, which increases the risk of infection through contaminated blood. Third, postmenopausal women are likely to experience the thinning of the cells of the vaginal wall. Since AIDS is transmitted by sexual contact, the deteriorating vaginal walls of the older woman provides more potential sites for HIV infection. Although AIDS is generally thought of as a young adult disease that affects mainly males, there are more than 100,000 HIV-infected middle-aged and older adults (Stall, Catania, & Pollack, 1988).

Weight Control and Physical Activity

Being overweight is a critical health problem in adult development, and those who are more than 20 percent over ideal body weight are defined as **obese.** More than one-third of adults in our society are identified as obese, nearly 9 percent higher than that reported in the early 1960s (Manley, 1996). The greatest risk of being overweight is seen in adults 25 to 34 years old (Williamson, Kahn, Remington, & Anda, 1990). For people who are 30 percent or more overweight, the probability of dying in middle adulthood increases by 40 percent. Obesity increases the likelihood that an individual will suffer a number of other ailments, including hypertension, diabetes, circulatory problems, and kidney and digestive disorders.

Weight gain is a consequence of reduced rates of **metabolism** (i.e., the rate at which calories are burned) with advancing age. Eating the same amount of calories per day as adults age results in accumulated body weight. To avoid weight gain, adults must either eat less as they age or exercise more (e.g., to burn the calories that are consumed). And, most important, they must continue these changes throughout their lives for permanent success in weight management.

As adults age there are significant changes in body composition. The total amount of fat stored in the body increases and is typically stored in abdominal tissue for men and women. The increase in body fat from early adulthood to age 85 is approximately 18 percent for men and 11 percent for women (Evans, 1995b). Recently Baumgartner, Stauber, McHugh, Koehler, and Garry (1995) documented this pattern for adults 65 to 80 years of age and for men 80+ years old. Interestingly, women over 80 years of age showed a significant decrease in body fat, which the authors hypothesize was related to reduced calorie intake. In general the data show that as people age they tend to adopt a more sedentary lifestyle but continue to eat as they did when they were younger, with increased preferences for both sweetness (e.g., sugars) and saltiness to liven up or enhance the flavors of foods.

Nutritional needs are determined by body size, level of physical activity, and rate of metabolism, but relatively little is known about age-related changes in nutritional needs. These factors were assessed in a nursing home population in Italy composed of predominantly frail elderly women, none of whom was being treated for depression. General results showed that reduced quantity of food intake was predictive of mortality in a 28-month follow-up study of survivorship. Careful monitoring of the quantity of food consumed is thus a useful early indicator of overall health. Intervention strategies focused on food intake, rather than nutritional value per se, may serve to improve health and survival among the frail elderly in nursing homes (Frisoni et al., 1995).

Diet centers, quick weight loss programs and other magic cures are likely to produce long-lasting effects in fewer than 5 percent of adults. To change eating behaviors at any point in the life span, people must commit to change their entire lifestyle—permanently (Hafen & Hoeger, 1994). It is unfortunately difficult for people to alter long-standing eating patterns. Beginning a diet to help prevent disease and enhance health is not a simple matter of following a set of recommendations for a few weeks or months. Weight control requires a lifetime commitment.

In some recent research the advantages of reduced calorie intake in promoting longevity in animal species has been documented (Weindruch, 1996). It will likely be a decade or more before we can conclude anything definitive about humans and caloric restriction, although there is no question that reduced calorie diets promote longevity in species such as the laboratory rat, spiders, and guppies. Weindruch (1996) suggests that the mechanism most likely at work is at the cellular level, specifically the **mitochondria,** which are the "power plants" of cells. In creating energy, mitochondria release **free radicals** (reactive molecules with an unpaired electron); free radicals will rapidly and indiscriminately oxidize or destroy other electrons. Some biological theories of aging hypothesize that the accumulation of free radicals accelerates the process of aging. As the cells themselves become less efficient and as more free radicals are produced, the body's tissues and organs become compromised, deteriorate, and become less able to respond to the demands imposed on them. Research with animals suggests that a restricted calorie diet and the reduced production of free radicals may slow down the rate of aging itself. Does a low-calorie diet increase the efficiency of the mitochondria so that fewer free radicals are produced?

Recent studies have demonstrated the long-term benefits on health and longevity for those who are physically active and not obese (e.g., Paffenbarger, 1993; Sandvik & Erikssen, 1993). Paffenbarger and his colleagues showed that maintaining average body weight and making other healthy lifestyle choices (such as quitting smoking and exercising) were associated with lower mortality for middle-aged and older men in the United States and Norway.

Heart Disease and Lifestyle

Heart disease is the leading cause of death for women and men. Heart attacks are more common in middle adulthood than in old age and more common in men than in women up to age 65. Nearly one-third of women over the age of 65 have evidence of heart disease. Women have been found to be at increasingly high risk of dying of a heart attack. Black women are 1.4 times more likely than white women to die of a heart attack (American Heart Association, 1992). The statistics show that compared with women, men are more likely to experience heart attacks, more likely to have them earlier in life (e.g., in middle adulthood), and more likely to survive heart attacks. Women are less likely to survive a heart attack and more likely to experience another.

The heart and coronary arteries begin to show change in middle adulthood. Under comparable conditions of stress, the heart of a 40-year-old can pump a much smaller number of liters of blood per minute (23) than the heart of a 20-year-old (40). Older persons may experience difficulties with the heart muscle itself. The heart muscle loses its elasticity and ability to pump blood throughout the body as people age. When the muscle can no longer easily pump the blood, fluids may accumulate in body tissues and the lungs. If this persists it can lead to pneumonia and ultimately death. This condition, *congestive heart failure,* is common in older people and treated with drugs to increase the strength of the beating heart muscle and diuretics to reduce the amount of fluids in the body (Harvard Health Letter, 1995).

The **coronary arteries** that supply blood to the heart narrow during middle adulthood, and the level of cholesterol in the blood increases with age (average at age 20, 180 mg/dl; at age 40, 220 mg/dl; at age 60, 230 mg/dl). Cholesterol begins to accumulate on the artery walls, which themselves begin to thicken. Total cholesterol remains a risk factor for heart attacks for middle-aged and older adults. However, the presence of good cholesterol (high-density lipoprotein [HDL]) reduces the risk of death due to heart disease just as the presence of bad cholesterol (low-density lipoprotein [LDL]) increases the risk of death due to heart disease. Total cholesterol readings that are high (e.g., above 240 mg/dl) are associated with a high risk of dying from heart disease for middle-aged men and women, but in older populations are predictive of higher risk only for women. Heart attack risk for adults at all ages is best predicted by an analysis of the ratio of total cholesterol to HDL cholesterol (e.g., total cholesterol divided by HDL). A ratio of 4.5 or lower is highly desirable (Harvard Health Letter, 1995).

With increasing age the arteries increase the pressure on the arterial walls, which in turn pushes the heart to work harder to pump blood and makes a stroke or heart attack more likely. **Atherosclerosis,** or coronary artery disease, refers to the buildup of fatty deposits called plaque on the arterial walls. One consequence of this process is high blood pressure (**hypertension**), usually evident by middle adulthood. High blood pressure is also related to personal stress, obesity, diet, and family history. Without treatment, high blood pressure can cause a break in the artery wall (aneurysm) and lead to death. If the arteries continue to narrow, a blood clot or small piece of plaque may prevent blood from reaching vital organs. A heart attack, or **myocardial infarction,** occurs when one of the coronary arteries to the heart is deprived of blood, causing irreversible destruction of the heart muscle. The neurological equivalent of a heart attack is a **stroke,** characterized by the death of brain cells (Harvard Health Letter, 1995). A stroke can occur if a blood vessel supplying the brain itself is blocked; consequences can be nominal or severe.

Lifestyle, as well as diet, physical condition, stress, and family history, are risk factors for heart disease. One intriguing theory relates individual behavior styles to either a high risk (**Type A**) or a low risk (**Type B**) of heart disease (Friedman & Rosenman, 1974). The Type A behavior style is excessively competitive, accelerates the pace of ordinary activities, is impatient with the rate at which most events occur, often thinks about doing several things at the same time, shows hostility, and cannot hide the fact that time is a struggle in life. By contrast, the Type B behavior style is typified by the absence of these behavioral tendencies. About 10 percent of the individuals studied were clearly Type A or Type B styles, although most people were various mixtures of the two. It is interesting to note that high achievement and Type A behavior style seem also to be related (Friedman & Rosenman, 1974).

Stephanie Booth-Kewley and Howard Friedman (1987) reviewed 83 different studies investigating the relationship between behavioral lifestyle (Type A versus Type B) and coronary heart disease. Their analysis revealed that Type A behavior is reliably related to the incidence of heart disease. However, they discovered a somewhat different profile of the Type A behavioral style predictive of heart disease than the one originally outlined by Friedman and Rosenman. Specifically, they concluded that "the true picture seems to be one of a person with one or more negative emotions: perhaps someone who is depressed, aggressively competitive, easily frustrated, anxious, (or) angry . . ." (Booth-Kewley & Friedman, 1987, p. 358). An "angry" or "hostile" personality was related not only to heart disease but also to general health and disease (Friedman & Booth-Kewley, 1987).

Health and Coping with Illness

The probability of developing disease or chronic illness increases with advancing age. A majority of individuals who reach the age of 80 will likely have some type of health impairment. This is simply part of normal or usual aging, which can be distinguished from unusual aging or successful aging with regard to health. It is very rare to find anyone over the age of 80 or 85 who is completely free from disease or illness (Baltes & Baltes, 1990).

Heart disease and cancer are the most serious health concerns in late adulthood. Other diseases, such as arthritis, can severely limit physical functioning, mobility, and the quality of life of older adults. Almost two of every five people between the ages of 65 and 75 have some impairment that limits their physical functioning. After age 75, the rate rises to three of every five persons. Some of the most common chronic conditions that compromise the health of the elderly are arthritis (38%), hearing impairments (29%), vision impairments (20%), and heart conditions (20%). Studies of sex differences in health indicate that elderly women are more likely to have a higher incidence of arthritis, hypertension, and visual problems but are less likely to have difficulty with hearing than men.

Individuals differ in how they cope with the effects of disease and chronic illness. Taylor (1983) emphasized the importance of meaning, mastery, and self-enhancement in adapting to life-threatening illnesses. For example, Taylor found that women who had breast cancer adapted more successfully if they were somehow able to create an explanation for their cancer, if they were able to have or perceive some control over their disease, and if they were able to maintain or restore their self-esteem. Taylor and colleagues (1992) also have demonstrated how optimism affects coping, psychological distress, and the high-risk sexual behavior of men at risk for AIDS. Howard Leventhal and his colleagues (Leventhal, Leventhal, & Schaefer, 1992, 1993) have studied individual differences in how people think about their illnesses. These investigators examined the cognitive factors that are involved in people's representation and understanding of illness. A person's representation of illness, whether accurate or not, will affect the emotional reactions to the illness and the coping and appraisal process (Folkman et al., 1986). As we have seen already in this chapter, there are a number of studies examining different diseases that suggest that individuals who are more optimistic cope more effectively with illness. The best approach for optimizing health throughout the adult years, including coping with disease and chronic illness, is to use optimistic attitudes to manage our own behavior and emotions effectively (Rodin, 1986). Mental health experts also have recognized the importance of providing the elderly with a sense of control and autonomy. Without individual control, human beings experience emotional distress, depression, lowered motivation, reduced feelings of well-being and life satisfaction, and deficits in cognitive and motor performance (Rodin, 1986; Tiffany & Tiffany, 1996).

HEALTH PROMOTION AND WELLNESS

Individuals are responsible for their own health status through active, direct, and deliberate behavioral practices (Simons-Morton, Greene, & Gottlieb, 1995). Adults accept responsibility for their health by making choices and adopting lifestyles designed to promote effective functioning. Socioeconomic status is related to health because the health choices people make are related to income and education (Benson, 1997).

Diet and Nutrition

Proper nutrition combined with dietary restriction produces beneficial effects with regard to life expectancy, biological integrity, and behavioral ability. The definition of a proper diet for Americans encourages eating a low-fat, high-fiber, low-salt, low-sugar, and moderate-calorie regimen. There are guidelines and recommendations from various government agencies that center on the Food Guide Pyramid (U.S. Department of Agriculture, 1992). The pyramid assumes that a specific number of servings across six different food groups each day is necessary to promote health:

1. Bread-cereals-pasta-rice (6–11 servings)
2. Vegetables (3–5 servings)
3. Fruits (2–4 servings)
4. Meat, poultry, fish, beans, eggs, nuts (2–3 servings)
5. Milk, yogurt, and cheese (2–3 servings)
6. Fat, oils, sugars (minimal, no recommended servings)

An adult following this diet and the recommended serving sizes would consume about 1,600 calories per day. Many companies that manufacture and process foods have adopted the food pyramid guidelines as part of their compliance with federal laws requiring packages to disclose nutritional content (i.e., serving sizes and the percentage by weight of fat, saturated fat, cholesterol, protein, dietary fiber, and sodium). Adults are not forbidden to eat specific foods all of the time. Rather the guidelines suggest that there must be a balance in what is eaten over many days, weeks, and months. Adults are encouraged to select a wide variety of different foods from among the pyramid's six groups. They work toward preserving a reasonably health body weight with a diet that limits cholesterol to 300 to 500 milligrams a day, restricts fats to no more than 30 percent of total calories, and keeps both saturated fats and sugars to a maximum of 10 percent of total calories each. Currently Americans consume a diet with nearly 34 percent of calories from fat. The American Heart Association (1995) is even more stringent, recommending that no more than 10 percent of the calories consumed each day come from saturated fat. Hidden fats appear in meats, processed foods, oils, butter, dairy products, and certain vegetarian sources such as seeds, nuts, avocados, and tropical oils: coconut and palm. Americans are reducing their total fat intake in a variety of ways. They substitute leaner choices of meats or fish, use steaming or broiling to cook their foods rather than deep fat frying or cooking with oils or butter, and increase the consumption of fruits, vegetables, legumes, grains, and carbohydrates while reducing the amount of meats, processed foods and dairy products (Insel et al., 1996). A healthy diet includes sufficient vegetables, fruits and grains to help reach the goal of eating 20 to 35 grams of dietary fiber a day for maximum protection against cancer.

Most younger adults are unlikely to believe that good nutrition is essential for their own health in later adulthood. Health and diet usually become major concerns in middle adulthood. Middle adulthood is characterized by an increasing awareness of gradual losses in optimal physical functioning and health. The negative results of poor nutrition usually do not show up for many years and there are no observable effects to signal escalating difficulties until a major illness strikes. It is only when a disease or other threat to one's health occurs that people show a willingness to change their behaviors.

Diets high in cholesterol and fat are associated with heart disease and cardiovascular disease, the number one cause of death in the United States (National Center for Health Statistics, 1992). A diet rich in saturated fats such as those contained in meats and dairy products appears to increase cholesterol, one of the key risk factors in promoting heart disease. Cholesterol and a high fat intake in the diet are also related to a higher incidence of colon cancer (Hafen & Hoeger, 1994; Willett, Stampfer, Colditz, Rosner, & Speizer, 1990). Adults who fail to maintain a diet with sufficient fiber also increase their risk of cancer (Cancer Facts and Figures, 1997).

There are even some studies linking short-term, reversible mental impairments in the elderly (acute brain syndrome) with inadequate amounts of such nutrients as vitamin B_{12}, folic acid, and niacin (Masoro, 1988).

Diet and Health Risks

Diet has been linked to increased risk of high blood pressure, cancer, and, as already discussed, heart disease. The addition of salt to processed foods such as cereals, breads, and processed meats is a potential hazard to older persons who already have high blood pressure as well as a risk factor in younger adults who may develop the disease. Yet, despite warnings about limiting salt intake from processed foods and prohibitions about adding extra salt to foods at the table, many older persons appear to ignore medical advice and use salt to enhance the flavor of their foods. They do not seem to be able to place the medical risks of elevated blood pressure ahead of their taste sense and taste preferences. Diets with high salt consumption are not good for hypertension and can lead to heart disease, artherosclerosis, and an increased risk of stroke (Simons-Morton et al., 1995). Elevated blood pressure is also a consequence of being overweight, a significant health risk for older persons.

A diet high in saturated fats has been implicated in the development of cancer of the colon, breast cancer, and prostate cancer. The American Cancer Society estimates that between 10 to 70 percent of the deaths from cancer could be prevented by modification in diet, especially cancers of the stomach, the colon, breast, and lung (Simons-Morton et al., 1995). To reduce the risk of certain types of cancer, recent guidelines developed by the American Cancer Society in the fall of 1996 warn against eating red meat and drinking alcohol. By the year 2000 cancer is expected to be the leading cause of death as heart disease declines. Heart disease today contributes directly to more than 500,000 deaths each year, one-third of which are related to diet, one-third related to smoking, and one-third related to genetics, work, and other causes (American Cancer Society, 1996).

To reduce the risk of cancer (especially respiratory cancers and those of the gastrointestinal tract) current guidelines suggest a diet high in fruits, vegetables, fiber, whole grains, minimal consumption of high-fat foods, especially those from animal sources;

careful monitoring of weight; limited or no consumption of alcohol; and moderate physical activity of 30 minutes or more each day (American Cancer Society, 1996). These guidelines differ from those of the U.S. government, which permits, for example, one to two drinks of alcohol per day, eating lean red meat in moderation, and the limited consumption of high-fat processed meats (e.g., those cured with nitrates and high levels of salt). The American Cancer Society finds high-fat foods contribute to high levels of obesity as well as increases in colon, rectal, prostate, endometrial, and kidney cancers and, for postmenopausal women, breast cancer. Thus, the Cancer Society recommends other sources of protein such as beans, seafood, and poultry (American Cancer Society, 1996).

Exercise and the Consequences of a Sedentary Lifestyle

The beneficial effects of regular and consistent aerobic exercise on aging and longevity have been documented for more than four decades. A sedentary lifestyle is one of the major risk factors in the development of heart disease and is a controllable risk factor. Other controllable risk factors include being overweight (defined as 30% over recommended levels), stress, smoking, and psychological factors such as personality type and the ability to trust others (American Heart Association, 1996). Adults who engage in at least 30 minutes of regular exercise nearly every day are at significantly reduced risk of developing heart disease. The type of exercise is far less important when considering a person who has been sedentary then the regularity of the exercise (Evans, 1995b). Even routine activities such as housecleaning, mowing the lawn, climbing stairs, or walking can enhance cardiovascular fitness and increase longevity. Those persons who are the most fit live the longest (Evans, 1995b). The body is quite responsive in adapting to the demands of exercise. The principle of **progressive overload** describes the process of improving fitness by gradually and progressively increasing the amount of exercise that is demanded. And it is clear that fitness can be lost as demands on the body are reduced, a principle called **reversibility of fitness** (Fahey, Insel, & Roth, 1997).

The positive benefits of regular exercise in promoting longer life are identifiable for adults at virtually any age. The greatest enhancement of life expectancy is found from regular exercise. Exercise does not have to be continuous or sustained, although this is ideal, but can be intermittently engaged in throughout the day (Evans, 1995b). To improve physical fitness and quality of life significantly, however, the American College of Sports Medicine recommends at least 20 minutes of sustained aerobic exercise (e.g., that which boosts heart rate) three to four times each week. Many older adults plan for specific exercise time in their daily routine, such as jogging, cycling, or swimming. Exercise has many beneficial effects, which include stress reduction, lowering of blood pressure, increasing the "good" type of cholesterol (i.e., HDL), and weight control (Insel et al., 1996).

Physical exercise has different consequences depending on which outcome investigators have selected to study. For example, to improve physical fitness and quality of life more sustained and vigorous exercise is needed than is necessary to improve life expectancy (Evans, 1995b). Moderate-intensity physical activities can fit every individual's lifestyle and preference. For example, a brisk walk simply means that an adult could walk two miles in 30 to 40 minutes (Evans, 1995b).

The President's Council on Physical Fitness and Sports has endorsed the summary statement appearing in table 6.8. This statement supports a preventative approach

TABLE 6.8

Summary Statement

—SUMMARY STATEMENT—

Workshop On
Physical Activity and Public Health

Sponsored By:
U.S. Centers for Disease Control and Prevention
and American College of Sports Medicine

In Cooperation with the President's Council on Physical Fitness and Sports

Regular physical activity is an important component of a healthy lifestyle—preventing disease and enhancing health and quality of life. A persuasive body of scientific evidence, which has accumulated over the past several decades, indicates that regular, moderate-intensity physical activity confers substantial health benefits. Because of this evidence, the U.S. Public Health Service has identified increased physical activity as a priority in Health People 2000, our national health objectives for the year 2000.

A primary benefit of regular physical activity is protection against coronary heart disease. In addition, physical activity appears to provide some protection against several other chronic diseases such as adult-onset diabetes, hypertension, certain cancers, osteoporosis, and depression. Furthermore, on average, physically active people outlive inactive people, even if they start their activity late in life. It is estimated that more than 250,000 deaths per year in the U.S. can be attributed to lack of regular physical activity, a number comparable to the deaths attributed to other chronic disease risk factors such as obesity, high blood pressure, and elevated blood cholesterol.

Despite the recognized value of physical activity, few Americans are regularly active. Only 22% of adults engage in leisure time physical activity at the level recommended for health benefits in Healthy People 2000. Fully 24% of adult Americans are completely sedentary and are badly in need of more physical activity. The remaining 54% are inadequately active and they too would benefit from more physical activity. Participation in regular physical activity appears to have gradually increased during the 1960s, 1970s, and early 1980s, but has plateaued in recent years. Among ethnic minority populations, older persons, and those with lower incomes or levels of education, participation in regular physical activity has remained consistently low.

Why are so few Americans physically active? Perhaps one answer is that previous public health efforts to promote physical activity have overemphasized the importance of high-intensity exercise. The current low rate of participation may be explained, in part, by the perception of many people that they must engage in vigorous, continuous exercise to reap health benefits. Actually the scientific evidence clearly demonstrates that regular, moderate-intensity physical activity provides substantial health benefits. A group of experts brought together by the U.S. Centers for Disease Control and Prevention (CDC) and the American College of Sports Medicine (ACSM) reviewed the pertinent scientific evidence and formulated the following recommendation:

Every American adult should accumulate 30 minutes or more of moderate-intensity physical activity over the course of most days of the week. Incorporating more activity into the daily routine is an effective way to improve health. Activities that can contribute to the 30-minute total include walking up stairs (instead of taking the elevator), gardening, raking leaves, dancing, and walking part or all of the way to or from work. The recommended 30 minutes of physical activity may also come from planned exercise or recreation such as jogging, playing tennis, swimming, and cycling. One specific way to meet the standard is to walk two miles briskly.

Because most adult Americans fail to meet this recommended level of moderate-intensity physical activity, almost all should strive to increase their participation in moderate or vigorous physical activity. Persons who currently do not engage in regular physical activity should begin by incorporating a few minutes of increased activity into their day, building up gradually to 30 minutes of additional physical activity. Those who are irregularly active should strive to adopt a more consistent pattern of activity. Regular participation in physical activities that develop and maintain muscular strength and joint flexibility is also recommended.

This recommendation has been developed to emphasize the important health benefits of moderate physical activity. But recognizing the benefits of physical activity is only part of the solution to this important public health problem. Today's high-tech society entices people to be inactive. Cars, television, and labor-saving devices have profoundly changed the way many people perform their jobs, take care of their homes, and use their leisure time. Furthermore, our surroundings often present significant barriers to participation in physical activity. Walking to the corner store proves difficult if there are no sidewalks; riding a bicycle to work is not a option unless safe bike lanes or paths are available.

Many Americans will not change their lifestyles until the environmental and social barriers to physical activity are reduced or eliminated. Individuals can help to overcome these barriers by modifying their own lifestyles and by encouraging family members and friends to become more active. In addition, local, state, and federal public health agencies; recreation boards; school groups; professional organizations; and fitness and sports organizations should work together to disseminate this critical public health message and to promote national, community, worksite, and school programs that help Americans become more physically active.

The American College of Sports Medicine and the U.S. Centers for Disease Control and Prevention, in cooperation with the President's Council on Physical Fitness and Sports, released this statement July 29, 1993, at the National Press Club in Washington D.C.

From Summary Statement: Workshop On Physical Activity and Public Health, sponsored by U.S. Centers for Disease Control and Prevention and American College of Sports Medicine, Sports Medicine Bulletin, 28(4), 7. Reproduced by permission.

to disease and the enhancement of an individual's lifestyle, health, and overall fitness. Corporations know that a healthier workforce is more productive, less likely to make medical claims, and less often out of work (Peters, 1996). Less than 55 percent of companies with 750 workers or more offered corporate fitness programs in 1985; yet by 1992 more than 83 percent provided this option to their workers (Peters, 1996). Promoting wellness for corporate America makes good sense financially in other ways as seen in the comparisons between high-risk and low-risk workers provided in table 6.9 show. The highest cost differences among low-risk and high-risk workers appear for the categories: (1) drinking alcohol, (2) physical health, (3) life satisfaction, and (4) physical activity. Carrier Corporation has built one of the largest business-based wellness centers for employees in the nation. The 40,000-square-foot center has a track for running, jogging, or walking on an upper level, which overlooks a fully equipped, high technology fitness area, with machines such as treadmills, weight-lifting

---

TABLE 6.9

Some Workers Cost More

High-risk employees—those who use tobacco, abuse alcohol, don't exercise and are at risk because of other factors, such as age—cost companies considerably more in medical claims each year. Here's a comparison of health-claim costs for high-risk and low-risk workers.

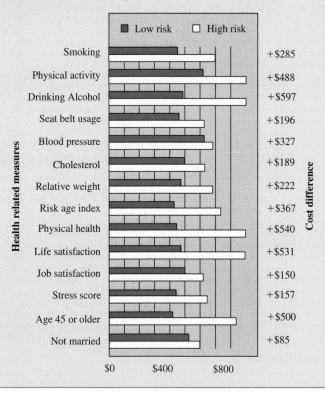

Source: University of Michigan Fitness Research Center
Syracuse Herald American, Sunday Sept. 29, 1996, p. 5.

machines, and steppers (Peters, 1996). Preventing illness rather than providing costly health care to employees who develop illnesses can improve the bottom line. For example, each heart bypass operation that can be prevented will save $30,000 to $35,000 in medical insurance claims. Thus the economic impact of a sedentary lifestyle is a primary concern to big business and insurance companies as health care costs, which topped $800 billion in 1993, continue to escalate (Hafen & Hoeger, 1994). Clearly, fitness and wellness (i.e., prevention) is more cost-effective than bearing the higher costs of treatment once employees become ill.

Measurement of health and physical function is complex. Many standard methods are available, depending on the physical system one is interested in assessing. For instance, the overall cardiovascular endurance of individuals can be determined by assessments of their overall aerobic capacity, or **maximal oxygen uptake (VO$_2$max).** Table 6.10 provides standard values of VO$_2$max levels for adult men and women as well as a method—running 1.5 miles—for estimating an adult's individual aerobic capacity from performance. The higher the oxygen consumption per minute, the more effective

TABLE 6.10

Cardiorespiratory Fitness Classification

Age (years)	Maximal Oxygen Consumption (ml/kg/min)				
	Very Low	Low	Moderate	High	Very High
Women					
Under 29	Below 24	24–30	31–37	38–48	Above 48
30–39	Below 20	20–27	28–33	34–44	Above 44
40–49	Below 17	17–23	24–30	31–41	Above 41
50–59	Below 15	15–20	21–27	28–37	Above 37
60–69	Below 13	13–17	18–23	24–34	Above 34
Men					
Under 29	Below 25	25–33	34–42	43–52	Above 52
30–39	Below 23	23–30	31–38	39–48	Above 48
40–49	Below 20	20–26	27–35	36–44	Above 44
50–59	Below 18	18–24	24–33	34–42	Above 42
60–69	Below 16	16–22	23–30	31–40	Above 40

Determining Maximal Oxygen Consumption Using the 1.5 Mile Run/Walk Test

1. Convert your running/walking time from minutes and seconds to a decimal figure. For example, a time of 14 minutes and 25 seconds would be 14 + (25/60) or 14.4 minutes.

2. Insert your running time in the equation below, where

   T = running time (in minutes)
   $$VO_{2max} = (483 \div T) + 3.5$$

   For example, a person who completes 1.5 miles in 14.4 minutes would calculate maximal oxygen consumption as follows:

   $$VO_{2max} = (483 \div 14.4) + 3.5 = 37 \text{ml/kg/min}$$

Source; Preventive Medicine Center, Palo Alto, Calif., and a survey of published sources. As published in Fahey, Insel, & Roth, 1997.
Source: G. A. Brooks and T. D. Fahey, Fundamentals of Human Performance (New York: Macmillan, 1987).

the cardiovascular system and the greater the overall endurance (Hafen & Hoeger, 1994). The use of a standard 1.5-mile test requires that it be conducted *only* under a physician's supervision for men over age 40 and for women over 50, and *only* after adequate aerobic training (e.g., six weeks) prior to taking the test. The test is simple—it consists of an "all-out" determination of the time it takes an individual to complete a full 1.5-mile run. From this information it is then possible to determine an individual's fitness classification. Acceptable cardiovascular endurance is indicated by scores at the upper end of average, good, and excellent. Scores in the poor, fair, and lower range of average would benefit from training and fitness programs. Recall that there are some changes with age that are not modifiable through exercise. The heart pumps less blood with advancing age and the maximum heart rate also declines with increased age (Fahey et al., 1997).

Age and Fitness: Is It Ever Too Late to Exercise?

The basic variables used to assess the physical fitness of an individual include cardiovascular endurance, muscular strength and endurance, muscular flexibility, and body composition (weight and percentage of body fat). Physical exercises and training that are designed to promote or enhance fitness can be successful at any age, and the benefits derived include functional health as well as cognitive and emotional well-being. In some studies sustained exercise was found to trigger the release of important neurotransmitters responsible for boosting alertness, to improve cerebral blood flow, and to improve cognitive performance as measured by reaction time, short-term memory, and nonverbal reasoning skills (Fahey et al., 1997; Rogers, Meyer, & Mortel, 1990).

Current research suggests that older men and women can improve their cardiovascular endurance, strength, and flexibility as a result of training that specifically targets increased physical activity. Hoeger and Hoeger (1995) note that the effectiveness of such interventions with the elderly depends on the initial level of fitness and the type of activities chosen for training. Kasch, Boyer, VanCamp, Verity, and Wallace (1990) have estimated that one-third of the loss in VO_2max from middle age to old age is the direct result of aging itself, while two-thirds of this loss comes from physical inactivity and a sedentary lifestyle (Hoeger & Hoeger, 1995). Improvements in VO_2max among older persons can be documented with extended training. However, although such gains require a longer time to produce, the gains accomplished are comparable to those seen in younger persons. Research Focus 6.3 presents an analysis of the rate of normal decline in biological aging in physical systems among gifted older athletes.

Similarly, older persons up to 90 years of age have been found to improve their strength with regular and sustained training programs. Results of training programs to improve strength can often be shown in a matter of a few weeks, even among nursing home residents. It is not necessary to undertake intense weight training to achieve beneficial results. Programs that last for 10 to 15 minutes and are repeated a few times each week seem sufficient to produce beneficial results. As in all intervention programs for the elderly, care should be directed at choosing activities that do not cause a large increase in blood pressure or place an undue strain on the heart (Hoeger & Hoeger, 1995).

Insel and colleagues (1996) recently summarized some of the benefits of exercise for the elderly (p. 312): (1) increased resiliency and suppleness of arteries, (2) better pro-

How Fast Do We Age? Exercise as an Indicator of Biological Decline

The degree to which declines in assessments of physical function reflect true biological aging processes in adulthood has been debated for many years. Bortz and Bortz (1996) examined this basic question from an unusual perspective. They suggested that many studies which have documented declines in physical functional capacities (e.g., cardiovascular, respiratory, kidney, sarcopenia and muscle strength) do not really reflect age or biological factors per se but are more the result of disuse and atrophy due to physical inactivity and a sedentary lifestyle. The majority of the participants in past studies were themselves typical sedentary adults, rarely in top physical shape, and rarely involved in regular exercise.

To assess the effects of biological processes on the rate of decline in physical function in adulthood, the investigators made use of the outstanding national records attained by a special cohort of adult Masters athletes 35 years of age and older who were "free of the artifacts of disease and disuse. . . ." Adult Masters are older athletes who have, by virtue of their accomplishments in special sports, maintained their major body systems as well as anyone else of similar age. They are in superb shape as evidenced by national recognition for their athletic success. Using the established national records by elite Masters athletes from 35 to 85+ years old, three endurance events were compared across age. The events examined were the marathon, 100-meter run, and 2,500-meter individual rowing. Results showed declines with advancing age in Masters record performance. The declines for each of the three events approximated a .5 percent decline per year from age 35 to age 65. After age 65, however, the rate of decline accelerated, perhaps due to more rapid physiological decay or the result of reduced participation. Although the analysis of record times from an elite subsample of Masters athletes may not be representative of the population of older adults as a whole, the rate of change itself was assumed to be identical to that of non-athletes of similar age.

These data were consistent with other cross-sectional studies showing losses of .3 percent per year in timed swimming speed events (Whitten, 1992), equivalent to an 11 percent decline in performance overall from 35 to 65 years of age. Masters record holders in field events (e.g., shotput, high jump, javelin throw) showed even faster rates of loss with advancing age than those in running events. The data reported by Bortz and Bortz (1996) also closely approximate the estimated biological decline of 0.5 percent in VO_2max obtained by Kasch, Boyer, VanCamp, Verity, and Wallace (1990) with athletes 35 to 70 years of age participating in several different events. And the studies also match the reported decline of 0.5 percent per year identified by Schaie (1994) for cognitive/intellectual loss across the life span.

Bortz and Bortz (1996) noted that a rate of biological loss of 2 percent per year in physical function has routinely been estimated from previous research with adults, for example, those who were not highly trained athletes. This figure does not appear to be that great a difference from the 0.5 percent found in this investigation with records from highly trained athletes. However, if these rates are compared cumulatively after two or three decades, the differences in physical function between highly trained athletes and more typical older adults should be quite striking. Bortz and Bortz have helped clarify the contribution of biological factors in the decline in physical function in adulthood.

tection against heart attack and enhanced probability of surviving a heart attack should one occur, (3) sustained capacity of lungs and respiratory reserves, (4) weight control through reduction of fat tissue, (5) maintenance of physical flexibility, balance, agility, and reaction time, (6) significantly preserved muscle strength, (7) protection from ligament injuries, dislocation, strains in the knees, spine, and shoulders, (8) protection against osteoporosis, (9) increased effectiveness of the immune system, and (10) maintenance of mental agility and flexibility, response time, memory, hand-eye coordination.

Strength Training

Evans and other experts suggest that the single most important exercise to actually reverse the process of aging is **strength training** (Evans, 1992; Liebman, 1995). Most healthy adults at any age can enhance their lives through exercise and strength training, reducing the likelihood of injuries and the impact of chronic diseases. Experts have noted that by increasing muscle strength through regular exercise, even the oldest-old can show benefits. The simple fact remains that strength training is the only way to stop muscle atrophy (Liebman, 1995). From the twenties through old age, research has confirmed that if you are not building muscle you are losing muscle (Liebman, 1995). Strength training requires resistance against a mass or load in order to produce muscle contractions.

Strength training and physical exercise may reduce the severity of chronic conditions, in some cases eliminating entirely hypertension, obesity, arthritis, and diabetes. Simple strength training coupled with walking can reduce symptoms of chronic conditions, increase mobility, increase range of motion, and assist in weight reduction (Liebman, 1995). Evans (1995b) reported that with only three months of strength training, older adults increased the calories they burned by 15 percent, which led to a loss of body fat.

Among sedentary middle-aged and elderly adults, inactivity produces a "stiffness" in the joints with advancing age. This stiffness may cause poor or unnatural posture, leading to chronic back pain, but may be somewhat relieved through regular stretching programs and strength training that helps persons to expand their range of motion (Fahey et al., 1997). For older persons, increased strength and elasticity of tendons and joints as well as reductions in the stiffness of muscles have been found with strength-training programs (Liebman, 1995). Similarly positive results emerge in stretching programs designed to help older persons recapture some of the body's **flexibility,** defined as the ability to move the joints through their full **range of motion.**

The documented gains of exercise and training for the physical health of older adults has benefits in other areas. People engaged in strength training and stretching programs begin to feel better, have enhanced mobility, increased energy and endurance, and show improvements in their sleep (Cox, 1997). Those who are physically fit report enjoying a higher quality of life, experience better overall health, and are able to improve their functional health status. And, of course, with psychological (i.e., cognitive-emotional) and physical gains there is a higher probability of maintaining autonomy and living independently among older adults (Hoeger & Hoeger, 1995). Examine the suggestions in Research Focus 6.4 to see how adults may better prepare for their entry into old age.

Muscle Atrophy: Sarcopenia

One of the most generally recognized and predictable physical consequences of aging is skeletal muscle mass atrophy, or **sarcopenia** (Baumgartner et al., 1995). The term *sarcopenia* means loss of skeletal muscle mass and is derived from two words: *sarco* or "flesh" and *penia* or "reduction in amount or need" (Evans, 1995a). Health experts have explored the phenomenon of skeletal muscle mass atrophy in old age extensively, because it is one of the chief causes of decreased muscle strength as people grow older. The effects of sarcopenia explain, in part, the reduced mobility, limitations in ADL, physical restrictions in lifestyle, and physical disabilities commonly seen in old age. Loss of muscle mass makes even the simplest tasks of daily living—such as climbing a flight of stairs, doing yard work, or getting up from a chair—difficult or impossible. Sarcopenia is found in all muscle groups and implicated in upper body and arm weakness, postural stoop and balance, as well as increased difficulties in walking and general mobility (Evans, 1995a).

Preparing for a Longer, Healthier Life

Preventive actions that adults can take to prepare for their later years and prolong their health, independence, wellness, and sense of well-being include the following 10 *biomarkers* developed by Evans, Rosenberg, and Thompson (1991).

1. Muscle Mass. The rate at which adults lose muscle mass accelerates after the age of 45, although muscle mass begins to shrink far earlier in development. By using the muscles, pushing them to the limits of their capacity, they can grow no matter at what age specific exercises such as weight lifting are begun. With even a moderate program, older persons can increase muscle mass by 10 percent and show a corresponding increase in strength of 200 percent (Evans, 1992). A program of weight lifting to increase muscle mass would take about three to four months before significant improvements in strength were attained.

2. Strength. By 30 years of age, and even earlier for some individuals, muscle cells and the nerves that provide connections to contract the muscles themselves begin to be lost. To regain strength, physical exercise such as weight training must be initiated.

3. Basal Metabolism Rate. The number of calories burned at rest drops by 100 calories per decade starting at age 20. Older persons need less oxygen to fuel their smaller muscle mass. By building up muscle mass in older persons there will be a corresponding increase in the calories burned.

4. Body Fat Percentage. It is possible to reduce the amount of body fat each adult carries. When we examine aging, it is a fact of American life that we show a steady increase in body fat. Reducing calories can be a significant way to lose fat, but unless adults also

exercise, there will be a reduction in muscle mass as a consequence of calorie reduction.

5. Aerobic Capacity. An increase in aerobic capacity is one of the most significant markers of enhanced life expectancy.

6. Blood-Sugar Tolerance. By maintaining high tolerance through exercise and a high-fiber and low-fat diet, there is less body fat overall and an increase in the muscle response to insulin. With low tolerance there is a higher risk of heart disease and diabetes.

7. Cholesterol/HDL Ratio. The lower the ratio of high-density lipoprotein (HDL) to low-density lipoprotein (LDL) and total cholesterol in the blood, the less risk of heart attack and coronary artery disease. The recommended ratio is 4.5 or lower; overall cholesterol should be lower than 200 mg/dl. Proven techniques that can increase HDL include regular exercising, losing body fat, and stopping smoking.

8. Blood Pressure. Some research has shown that regular exercise increases blood volume, which lowers the risk of high blood pressure.

9. Bone Density. Weight-bearing exercise (e.g., walking, jogging, running, or bicycling) can reduce the rate at which adults and the elderly lose bone.

10. Body-Temperature Regulation. Older persons show heightened susceptibility to dehydration and injuries caused by heat or cold. Aerobic exercise, however, can improve one of the ways the body regulates temperature e.g., the ability to sweat.

BioMarkers—The 10 Determinants of Aging You Can Control (1991) by William Evans and Irwin H. Rosenberg, with Jacqueline Thomson. Simon & Schuster, New York, by permission.

Interventions are particularly important, since studies reveal that strength training can reduce the rate of muscle atrophy, preserve the level of current functioning, or reestablish greater muscle mass. Even among the oldest-old, muscle mass and strength that has been lost can be regained through training. Muscle atrophy can be reversed and muscles retrained in a matter of a few weeks or months through regular exercise programs.

Sarcopenia is often attributed to normal aging, but it appears to be more a function of lifestyle changes as people age and become more sedentary. The data suggest that functional independence and overall mobility can be enhanced through targeted activities such as exercise and strength training and thereby improve the level of overall functioning in older persons, especially in frail elderly and institutionalized elderly. Sarcopenia may also underlie the decrease in functioning associated with many age-related chronic diseases (Evans, 1995a). In the sections that follow we will examine the role of sarcopenia in falls, fractures, walking or gait velocity, and balance.

Balance and Postural Stability

Maintaining a sense of balance for younger persons is a smooth, coordinated, and effortless function in which the sensory and motor systems dynamically work together. Falls may occur among older adults when their sensory perceptual system is impaired, when they plan their movements inaccurately, or when they initiate an inappropriate motor response (Simoneau & Leibowitz, 1996). During the aging process the vestibular organs show progressive deterioration, which makes it more difficult for older adults to sense awareness of head position, body position, and bodily motion in space (Simoneau & Leibowitz, 1996). It is also more difficult to make postural corrections when the vestibular sensory system functions less adequately in old age.

The visual system provides feedback to assist in controlling balance and postural stability. On the one hand it is a system designed to alert a walking person to potential environmental threats and hazards and on the other hand it gives feedback about spatial orientation (e.g., the location, orientation, and movement of the body in the environment) (Simoneau & Leibowitz, 1996). The aging visual system can also have a potential negative effect on postural stability and contribute to incidents of falling through reduced light transmitted to the retina, reduced visual acuity, and slowed responsiveness to rapid changes in illumination. Falling may also be more likely with reduced sensitivity to the position of the joints and their movement as well as overall muscle strength and muscle mass (e.g., sarcopenia) (Simoneau & Leibowitz, 1996).

Considerable evidence indicates that postural stability is more effortful for older persons (Simoneau & Leibowitz, 1996). Older persons when standing display more sway or body movement than do younger adults. Some studies have found body sway can predict the risk of falling in older adults; however, increases in body sway do not always indicate difficulty with balance and postural stability. For some investigators, bodily swaying is seen to be a natural consequence of development in the later years (Patala, Frank, & Winter, 1990). McIlroy and Maki (1996) have highlighted the special compensatory short, quick lateral stepping that older people use to regain their balance if they begin to trip, fall, or encounter an unexpected loss of balance. That is, older persons (65–81 years old) take a few short steps to the side in order to regain their balance when confronted with a sudden and unexpected motion, controlled experimentally, which threatens their stability. This is in contrast to younger adults (22–29 years old) who, when faced with a similar threat, regain their balance without the same corrective measures as older persons.

Balance requires lower extremity strength and is affected by sarcopenia (Wolfson, Judge, Whipple, & King, 1995). Balance as a dynamic process is also influenced directly by gait speed and vice versa. When balance is unsteady, other factors may also play a role in restricting an older person's mobility, independence, and functioning. These include the fear of falling, pain, joint impairment, visual difficulties, and reduced sensation (Brown, Sinacore, & Host, 1995). The sense of balance is involved in lifting and carrying. When the sense of balance is not functioning well, it restricts an older person's range of movement and functioning. Figure 6.12 shows the direct consequence of sarcopenia on other muscle groups (e.g., back and thoracic muscles) that compromises balance. From this figure we can see how sarcopenia is related to the

Figure 6.12
Tracings of
photographs. When
this woman with
scapulo-thoracic
muscle weakness
brings her arm
forward, her
thoracic kyphosis
increases, and her
center of mass
moves forward.
The shift in center
of mass is even
more pronounced
when the person is
holding something.
Thus, scapulo-
thoracic weakness
can increase the
risk of falling.
Source: Brown, M.,
Sincore, D. R. &
Host, H. H. (1995)
The Relationship of
Strength to Function
in the Older Adult.
*Journals of
Gerontology Series A,
50A,* (special issue),
55-59. Reprinted by
permission.

sense of balance and the postural adjustments that are required in bending, moving, and lifting. It is understandable how fear of losing one's balance and falling can become a preoccupation for some elderly.

Falls

It has been estimated that one in three persons over the age of 65 and two of five persons over the age of 80 fall at least once each year (Simoneau & Leibowitz, 1996). Falls frequently lead to restrictions in daily activities, loss of confidence, loss of autonomy, and a higher likelihood of nursing home placement (Burker et al., 1995). Fear of falling is the most common fear among community-residing elderly persons (Burker et al., 1995; Downton & Andrews, 1990; Walker & Howland, 1990). According to one study, among community-residing elderly about 33 percent harbor this concern (Burker et al., 1995). Statistics on falling incidents are haphazard and often confined to falls that cause significant physical injury such as fractures. Falling is the sixth leading cause of death in the elderly and remains the leading cause of injury-related death in those 75 years of age and older (Burker et al., 1995; Tinetti, 1990).

Intrinsic risk factors for falling are the result of normal aging or disease such as cognitive, sensory, neurological or musculoskeletal deficits (e.g., those associated with sarcopenia). Muscle atrophy leading to declines in strength appears to underlie both balance and gait and is directly related to falling incidents. Generally, falls are more likely when lower muscle strength is weak and mobility impaired. However, there has not been any quantitative determination of the amount of muscle strength needed to maintain good balance and appropriate gait velocity (Wolfson et al., 1995). Other intrinsic risk factors include disability of the knees, legs, ankles and foot, gait and balance abnormalities, poor vision, and disease (Simoneau & Leibowitz, 1996; Tinetti, 1990). Among the elderly who experience dizziness, the fear of falling is very high, with nearly half of a sample (47%) expressing this concern (Burker et al., 1995). Three factors predicted a fear of falling among elderly with dizziness: (1) difficulties with ADL (e.g., reduced independence), (2) higher scores on a symptom depression scale, and (3) stability when standing with feet together (Burker et al., 1995).

Most falls in older persons are the result of tripping, slipping, or side effects from medications. Extrinsic risk factors that heighten the probability of falls include medications (sedatives or psychoactive drugs), alcohol, and environmental hazards such as loose throw rugs, snow, ice, and poorly illuminated stairs. Incorrect use of assistance devices for walking such as canes or walkers also contribute significantly to the incidence of falls in the elderly. The intrinsic and extrinsic risk factors associated with falls are additive and any intervention that can reduce or eliminate one of the factors may lead to a significant reduction in the probability of falling (Simoneau & Leibowitz, 1996; Speechly & Tinetti, 1990). The injuries associated with falling include fractures, with hip fractures among the most common, and other associated soft tissue injuries.

The fear of falling is usually greatest among those elderly who have already fallen and been injured or who have had a close friend or relative who has died from a fall (Simoneau & Leibowitz, 1996; Tideiksaar, 1989). Thus the aftermath of a falling incident for an older adult may be psychological trauma expressed through anxiety, hesitancy, avoidance, and generalized decreased mobility. Efforts to overcome fear of falling involve direct intervention (physical training and emotional support) as soon as possible after the fall as well as a host of preventative approaches. Individuals with a history of falling are at high risk of falling again. Early screening for risk factors so that appropriate interventions can be established to address specific deficits (e.g., strength, balance, vision) are currently being developed. The Frailty and Injuries: Cooperative Studies of Intervention Techniques (FICSIT) provided a series of training experiences and interventions to reduce the risk of falling among the elderly. The program included training to improve strength, endurance, balance, and other physical skills; wearing hip protection devices; monitoring the environment for hazards; providing direct instruction; and nutritional intervention. The results appear quite promising (Ory et al., 1993). A review of the appropriateness of current medications, dosages, and their interactions is also an important part of reducing the risk of falling. And, an evaluation of the immediate environment to ensure adequate lighting in hallways—especially stairwells—availability of grab bars in bathrooms, railings in the hallways and stairs, use of appropriate footwear, and removal of loose area rugs is also recommended to reduce the risk of falls in the elderly (Simoneau & Leibowitz, 1996).

Prevention of Falls and Fractures

Older persons and the frail elderly experience sarcopenia as a function of increased age, muscle disuse, disease, and an increasingly sedentary lifestyle (Evans, 1995b). Institutionalized and frail elderly are particularly at risk. Atrophy of muscle mass and decreasing muscle strength leads to a corresponding increased risk of falls and fractures. However, exercise programs targeted to specific muscle groups related to strength, balance, stability, and endurance can significantly reduce the risk of falling. Even among the frail elderly, recovery of function through reversibility of sarcopenia is possible through resistance/strength-training programs. In an institutionalized population aged 87 to 96 years old, significant improvements in leg strength and quadriceps muscle size were found with only an eight-week program of training. The participants also improved their gait speed and functional mobility. Such gains once established can be maintained with minimal programming, for example, as little as once a week of strength-training exercise (Evans, 1995b).

Strength training, which helps stability and balance as well as strength, can lower the risk of hip fractures due to falling by 30 to 40 percent (Cox, 1997). Various types of strength or resistance/weight training reduce the risk of fractures in some groups of older persons such as postmenopausal women who have adopted a sedentary lifestyle (Evans, 1995b). Strength training appears to increase bone density in postmenopausal women as well as reduce likelihood of falls and subsequent risk of bone fractures among those who have osteoporosis. Fractures due to falling are more likely among the elderly who have poor balance, poor gait, and reduced lower extremity leg strength (Liebman, 1995).

Through disuse the muscles used to run, climb a flight of stairs, get out of a chair, or even just stand will atrophy. Rebuilding important muscle groups can be accomplished and in so doing an older person's independence and sense of control can be enhanced as well. It is not any easier to get older persons to exercise than it is younger persons. However, with adequate training older adults, both men and women, show comparable gains to those of younger adults with similar strength training programs (Evans, 1995b). Nelson and colleagues (1994) worked with postmenopausal women 50 to 70 years old in a resistance/weight-training program with intervention consisting of only two training sessions per week for 12 months. Compared with a sedentary control population, the women in the training program showed increased bone density, muscle mass, and strength as well as an improved sense of balance and higher overall levels of physical activity. These improvements significantly reduced the risk of falling and subsequent fractures. Generally the greater the intensity of the exercise program, the greater the benefits (Evans, 1995b). And, not surprisingly, benefits will decline and disappear unless some program continuity is maintained. Evans (1995b) concludes that exercise can minimize and even reverse many dimensions of physical frailty for virtually all elderly.

Gait Velocity

The autonomy of older persons is challenged by threats to their mobility, especially limitations in walking (Simoneau & Leibowitz, 1996). Some challenges may be alleviated through exercise and strength training while others are psychological and appear less responsive to exercise. Judge, Davis, and Ounpuu (1996) identified normal aging with a reduction in **gait velocity** (walking speed) for most elderly. Gait velocity reduction is, in part, the result of a shortened step length among the elderly when compared with younger adults. There is also a corresponding loss of power from decreased ankle flexion at the "push-off" phase of gait, which is the result of shortening or reduction of the flexion of the ankle itself. This is recognized more simply as flat-footedness in the appearance of the elderly as they walk (Simoneau & Leibowitz, 1996). Reductions in gait velocity are also characterized by an increase in the time at which both feet are on the ground simultaneously, a decrease in the length of the step taken, and an increase in stride width. Others have found that a loss of strength in the leg muscles (quadriceps and hamstring) coupled with declines of other lower extremity muscle groups interact to cause reduction in gait speed (Brown et al., 1995). This is a particularly common occurrence among those older persons with arthritis. There is also a power loss due to muscle atrophy and reduced ankle flexion, which some elderly counteract with an increase in power directly from hip flexion. One way to increase gait speed, then, could come from exercises that strengthen ankle flexor muscles and increase leg strength by targeting muscles of the lower extremities in weight training (Judge et al., Ounpuu, 1996).

There are many reasons for a reduction in gait velocity beside sarcopenia and reduced ankle flexion. These usually are related to the older individual's stability, postural balance, and concern for personal safety (Simoneau & Leibowitz, 1996). In one study, less than 1 percent of people aged 72 or older showed normal walking speed (about four feet per second) that would permit them to cross the street at intersections in the time allowed by stoplights (Langlois et al., 1997). In another investigation of factors associated with reductions in gait speed among the elderly, Buchner and his colleagues (1996) identified three expected predictors of reduced gait speed in a sample of 152 community-dwelling older adults (68–85 years old). These predictors were: (1) leg strength, (2) maximal aerobic capacity (VO_2max), and (3) body weight. Surprisingly however, a psychological variable—an indicator of depressive symptoms—was also strongly related to gait speed. It seems likely that declines in physical health status can have a direct impact on depressive symptoms and these factors together can contribute to slowness in gait velocity (Buchner et al., 1996).

Gait speed itself is predictive of institutionalization, mortality, and physical functioning in general since it is highly correlated with both strength and aerobic capacity in older adults (Buchner et al., 1996). Changes in gait velocity are correlated with reductions in the ability of older adults to live independently, to be active and fully mobile, and to function adequately in the various activities of daily living.

Rehabilitation

Rehabilitation is a growing field devoted to appraising, intervening, and ameliorating the effects of disabilities. Most of the disabilities experienced by older adults are chronic and have little chance of being cured. They include conditions such as stroke, Parkinson's disease, osteoarthritis, rheumatoid arthritis, multiple sclerosis, diabetes, coronary artery disease, and cancer, as well as conditions occurring early in development such as mental retardation or cerebral palsy. A disability (1) is caused by a physical injury or exists as the result of a physical or mental illness, (2) produces long-term interference in day-to-day function, and (3) produces a clear disruption in a person's typical style of social or physical response to the environment (Kemp, 1985).

The underlying theme of rehabilitation is the concept of *normalization,* meaning that as much as possible every citizen, regardless of age and disability, is entitled to participate fully in every aspect of life. Thus, intervention is designed to maximize individual functioning and promote independence, personal autonomy, self-worth, and positive self-concept. In implementing this approach, rehabilitation programs for the elderly face a variety of challenges. Older adults often have multiple chronic illnesses as well as mental disorders such as depression. Health professionals and the elderly themselves frequently hold negative attitudes toward older people (ageism), perhaps because of their slower rate of progress as compared with younger persons in rehabilitative programs. The goals of rehabilitation for younger people include improving functioning to enable a person to lead an independent, community-based lifestyle with social supports from friends and family, but the goals are somewhat different for the elderly. With severe arthritis, heart disease, or stroke, an older person may not be able to resume independent living. A rehabilitation program for an elderly person may be more concerned with preserving some degree of independence in a supervised residence (Kemp, 1985).

Failing health and increased disabilities are among the predictors of suicide among the elderly. Disabilities often emerge without any warning and without any opportunity to develop coping resources to deal with them (Kemp, 1985). Some experts believe a series of adjustments or phases are experienced when a disabling condition suddenly strikes. The initial phase is one of *shock,* when the total impact of the disability is not yet fully understood. Next, a phase of *defensive retreat* emerges, in which the individual realizes what has occurred. The individual is terrified as he or she seeks to cope. Often, primitive defense mechanisms are adopted in this stage; the person may deny and regress to protect against the fear, anxiety, and depression that arise from the reality of the disability. As we have seen earlier in this text, individuals under stress frequently distort reality; older adults, for instance, may believe a disability was not correctly diagnosed or will not be permanent. Such beliefs may continue for many months or even years. Final recognition of the reality of the disability and its permanence occurs during the *acknowledgment* phase. The final phase, *adaptation,* reflects the attempt to face the difficult challenges the disability presents—becoming as well integrated as possible into the mainstream of social action (Kemp, 1985).

For some elderly adults, the emergence of a late-onset disability may not neatly follow the progressive pattern just outlined; rather, the disability may represent just one more loss in a lengthy string of other loss experiences (Kemp, 1985). Whereas the presence of high-functioning role models (e.g., athletes with diabetes) helps the younger adult to look ahead, older individuals have few such role models. Older adults may compare their current functioning with a disability to their previous functioning without the disability. Such comparisons frequently produce negativism and depressive reactions (Kemp, 1985).

Rehabilitation goals for older persons, then, center on both normalizing and preserving functional integrity within the limits of the disability. Rehabilitation requires a variety of contextual assessments, including the current family situation; other social supports; type of home environment; perception of the disability by the person, relatives, and friends; and a variety of other personality, cognitive, and emotional evaluations. It is important to examine the person's view of the rehabilitation goals as well as their motivation for improvement. Baltes, Neumann, and Zank (1994) have also implicated the value of working directly with staff in promoting independence and reaching rehabilitation goals with institutional-residing elderly. They identified a strong tendency for staff to feel helpful and instrumentally supportive of residents by providing help and assistance. Such "dependency support," however, was not consistent with many of the rehabilitation needs of the elderly; specifically, those elderly who developed or maintained a higher level of independence were often ignored by institutional staff. With an educational program for staff emphasizing behavioral modification, facts about aging, and improvements in basic communication skills, a decrease in staff dependency support and a corresponding increase in staff independence support of residents was documented. With this background, intervention in the forms of therapy, family involvement, and staff training can help improve the ability of the disabled older adult to function both in the community and in institutional environments (Baltes et al., 1994).

SUMMARY

The promotion of health for adults and elderly is a societal priority as increasing numbers of people live longer. The elderly face complex questions of health care financing, their ability to access services, and the survival of the Social Security system itself, specifically Medicare and Medicaid. Adults today are entering old age in better health when compared with their cohorts from earlier years. Optimization for those older people who do need intervention services helps to preserve their autonomy and independent functioning. Assessment of older persons' functioning is based on activities of daily living scales (ADL) and more complex dimensions of functioning using the instrumental activities of daily living scale (IADL). The greater the limitations in ADL or IADL, the more intervention services required and the higher the probability of institutionalization. Those who have difficulty coping with chronic disease show poor self-concept, depressive symptoms, and lower perceived health status. Although women live longer than men, women generally are in poorer health than men in their later years. Socioeconomic status, ethnicity, and race are also related to health.

Health care costs represent an increasing burden to those older adults on fixed income. Higher costs for health care are based in part on the escalating costs of products, delivery, and service, a greater number of people living to old age, and the greater availability of newer diagnostic tests and procedures. The financial viability of Social Security—Medicaid and Medicare—to meet these increased costs is a concern for today's elderly. The eligibility and reimbursement policies in each program have been reviewed. Medicaid is designed to meet the medical care needs of older adults living at or near poverty. Medicare provides federal insurance for older adults needing medical services and/or hospitalization. Social Security will not cover all of a retiree's basic medical expenses, nor will it necessarily cover long-term home care or nursing home costs. The elderly increasingly are recognizing that they need multiple sources of support to help them in old age, not just Social Security, Medicare, Medicaid, and extended hospital coverage benefits. Some are fortunate enough to carry a pension into retirement to help them financially. Many purchase private Medigap insurance policies to assist with medical expenses not covered by Medicare, and some purchase long-term care insurance to meet the cost of nursing home or in-home care should they become chronically ill or disabled and need help with basic day-to-day activities. Cognitively impaired elderly may receive care at home or in an institutional environment. Key features of environmental design for the cognitively impaired residing in an institution were presented. The phenomena of wandering among cognitively impaired adults and their patterns of pacing or agitation especially in early evening (sundowning) was examined. The use of restraints to control cognitively impaired adults has become less frequent in nursing homes.

The health consequences of behavior were reviewed. Beneficial effects of both moderate and intense exercise are found for adults at all ages: cardiorespiratory system, strength, strength endurance, and cognitive measures. Psychophysical fitness and physical fitness are the basic indicators of intervention success from exercise and training programs. Heart disease and cancer are the leading causes of death in the United States. Attitude, control/autonomy, social support, and a "fighting spirit" can help people cope successfully with cancer. Psychoneuroimmunology is the study of those multifaceted changes in the central nervous system and immune system that heighten or lower a person's susceptibility to disease and recovery from disease. Based on age and gender considerations, weight control, regular exercise, and belief in mastery are effective in reducing the health risk of heart disease, cancer, and chronic illness.

The importance of lifestyle, proper diet, and nutrition were evaluated in terms of health promotion and health prevention. The consequences of a sedentary lifestyle on the cardiorespiratory system were reviewed and key health problems were identified such as artherosclerosis, myocardial infarction, stroke, and congestive heart failure. The value of strength training in overcoming the natural process of sarcopenia or muscle atrophy was considered in detail. Strength training and intervention can prevent or reverse the effects of muscle atrophy at any age with virtually any population, including the frail elderly. The relationship of muscle atrophy to balance, postural stability, and the occurrence of falls was examined. Preventing falls in the elderly can be accomplished by a careful review of both intrinsic and extrinsic factors. Gait velocity is important to understand since it is directly related to mobility and ultimately an older person's sense of autonomy and perceived independence. Finally, rehabilitation of disabled elderly was considered both theoretically and practically. Rehabilitation is a vital intervention strategy for the elderly.

REVIEW QUESTIONS

1. Discuss optimization of the later years in terms of the health needs of the elderly. What are some of the basic considerations that must be recognized in service delivery?

2. Outline the features of long-term care and the current funding mechanisms available for older persons receiving such treatment.

3. What is the difference between Medicare–Part A, Medicare–Part B, and Medicaid? What is the significance of spending down in these two programs?

4. Given the escalating costs of long-term care and the eligibility requirements currently in effect, develop a justification appropriate for the purchase of private long-term care insurance versus a justification appropriate for failing to purchase this form of insurance.

5. Discuss the principles of environmental design applicable for older persons with cognitive impairments.

6. How do institutions balance their responsibilities and older person's right to freedom and personal

independence? Discuss the special issues of restraints and wandering.

7. What is the relationship between rehabilitation and normalization? Discuss the challenges facing individuals responsible for implementing rehabilitation services for the elderly.

8. Explain how diet, nutrition, and exercise in middle age are related to health maintenance and health promotion both at middle age and in old age.

9. Discuss the evidence related to the risks of cancer and heart disease. What is the role of psychoneuroimmunologic factors in these diseases and the effectiveness of subsequent treatments?

10. How can older people best deal with the phenomenon of sarcopenia? What is the relationship of sarcopenia to balance, posture, gait velocity, and the risk of falling?

11. What are the benefits of moderate and intense exercise? Discuss the value of chronic exercise in overall health promotion.

12. Discuss the risk of falling in the elderly. What is the relationship of falling, exercise, and sarcopenia?

FOR FURTHER READING

Abeles, R. P., Gift, H. C., & Ory, M. G. (1994). *Aging and quality of life.* New York: Springer.

Binstock, R. H., Cluff, L. E., & Von Mering, O. V. (1996). *The future of long-term care.* Baltimore: Johns Hopkins University Press.

Bond, L. A., Cutler, S. J., & Grams, A. E. (1995). *Promoting successful and productive aging.* Thousand Oaks, CA: Sage.

Dandekar, K. (1996). *The elderly in India.* Thousand Oaks, CA: Sage.

Dixon, R. A., & Backman, L. (1995). *Compensating for psychological deficits and declines: Managing losses and promoting gains.* Mahwah, NJ: Lawrence Erlbaum.

Haber, D. (1994). *Health promotion and aging.* New York: Springer.

Harel, Z., & Dunkle, R. E. (1995). *Matching people with services in long-term care.* New York: Springer.

Seltzer, M. M. (1995). *The impact of increased life expectancy: Beyond the gray horizon.* New York: Springer.

Spiriduso, W. W. (1995). *Physical dimensions of aging.* Champaign, IL: Human Kinetics.

Wilber, K. H., Schneider, E. D., & Free, W. (1996). *Long-term care financing.* New York: Springer.

MEMORY, ATTENTION, AND LEARNING

7

INTRODUCTION

Consider an older man driving to the supermarket to buy some groceries. While driving to the store he asks himself, "I know I have to buy orange juice, dish detergent, and lettuce, but what are the two other items my wife wanted me to buy?" After finding some of the items he was supposed to buy, the man is standing in a checkout line when an elderly woman walks past him. Upon seeing the woman he experiences the following thought, "I'm certain that I met this woman a couple of weeks ago, but I don't really remember where, and I can't remember her name." After leaving the supermarket, he roams the parking lot and repeatedly asks himself, "Where did I park my car?" He locates his car and begins the drive home, and says to himself that, "I can't remember things as well as I did when I was younger." And, he begins to wonder if his memory problems are "normal" or if his forgetfulness signals the onset of dementia.

What are your reactions to the preceding scenario? Do all older adults experience these kinds of memory failures? Do older persons experience a global deterioration of all aspects of memory? Or are only particular kinds of memory losses associated with aging? How do factors such as health or intelligence influence memory function? What types of age-related memory loss, if any, are predictive of the onset of dementia? In this chapter we address these issues.

SELF-CONCEPTIONS OF AGE-RELATED MEMORY LOSS

One way to determine the degree to which memory is impaired by aging is to merely ask older individuals to rate the quality of their memory, to estimate the frequency to which they suffer from memory failures in everyday situations, and to predict how they would actually perform on an objective memory test. Self-ratings of memory performance are measure of metamemory. **Metamemory** refers to the self-appraisal or self-monitoring of memory. It gauges how well we understand the efficacy of our own memory. In their review of the literature on this topic, Hess and Pullen (1996) pointed out that older adults have a much more negative view of their memory ability than younger adults, report more memory failures in real-life contexts than younger adults, and expect to perform much worse on laboratory tasks of memory compared with younger adults. You probably aren't surprised by these findings. In fact, you probably assume that older individuals have intact metamemory skills since they possess an accurate self-perception that their memory has weakened over time. However, what is surprising (and very important) is that Hess and Pullen (1996) showed that, among the elderly, no relationship exists between self-reports in the frequency of everyday memory complaints and objectively measured memory performance on laboratory tasks. Self-appraisals of memory function in real-life contexts do not predict performance on objective tests of memory!

Why is there no relationship between self-reported memory failures and the actual memory performance in older individuals? What could account for this apparent glitch in older adults' metamemory? Hess and Pullen (1996) offer four possible solutions to this puzzle. First, it may be the case that self-perceptions of everyday

Have you ever had difficulty remembering where you parked your car at the mall? As we get older, we pay more attention to encoding such things as where we park as a way of avoiding memory failures.

memory failures are confused with age-related changes in physical and/or mental health status. This idea is reinforced by a wealth of research that shows that deficits in vision, hearing, and overall health status as well as the incidence and severity of depression are all related to the frequency of self-reported memory complaints among the elderly. Second, older adults (and their relatives and health care providers) tend to overestimate the amount of memory problems they experience in everyday life. Older adults seem to be more aware of their memory failures than younger adults, and they are more likely to become anxious about minor forgetfulness in comparison to their younger counterparts. Exaggerated concern about memory failure is especially likely to occur in novel or stressful situations. In other words, older adults may possess a number of "ageist" attitudes and stereotypes that distort their metamemory skills. Third, everyday memory tasks may draw on different skills and mind-sets than do laboratory tasks. Everyday tasks occur within ecologically valid and familiar circumstances. Laboratory tasks are administered in very artificial and unfamiliar settings that older people have no experience with. Fourth, self-report measures may, in actuality, assess the complexity of an individual's psychosocial environment rather than his or her memory. For example, Rabbitt and Abson (1990) argued that memory in older adults (say in their late fifties to early seventies) continues to function effectively in very demanding environments. These older adults continue to work, to coordinate busy family schedules, and so on. Under such circumstances, individuals might be overly concerned about memory failures and might worry about them too much. Alternatively, people in their eighties and older have less complicated lives where memory lapses are less noticed. Thus, memory problems would be less of a concern and underreported in the oldest-old.

Another important reason why self-reports of memory complaints do not predict actual memory performance is that peoples' naive ideas about the structure, function, and organization of human memory may be inaccurate. Laypersons typically think of memory as a large filing cabinet that stores diverse pieces of information for later retrieval. They equate remembering with conscious recollection of the past. And they assume that the major function of memory is to provide a fully detailed and precise reproduction of previous events and experiences. These kinds of intuitions, according to current theory and research, are ill-founded.

A better way to approach the topic of memory is to take a *multiple memory systems* point of view (Schacter, 1996; Schacter & Tulving, 1994; Squire & Knowlton, 1995). This chapter is organized from this theoretical perspective. Multiple memory systems theory suggests that the human brain may be decomposed into a number of different memory systems, each of which possesses a different fundamental goal, achieves its goal via the implementation of qualitatively different psychological operations, and is physically instantiated in different neural structures or circuits. At the most basic level, a distinction is made between **short-term memory** and **long-term memory.** More important, several different long-term memory systems have been identified.

Short-Term Versus Long-Term Memory

More than 100 years ago, the famous psychologist William James (1890) pointed out the differences between primary memory and secondary memory. James identified *primary memory* with conscious awareness of recently perceived events. *Secondary memory* was identified with the retrieval of events that left consciousness. James's ideas about the differences between primary and secondary memory were derived from his own introspections, but now a similar distinction is supported by a great deal of experimental evidence. Today a host of theoretical approaches to human memory incorporate a distinction between primary, or short-term memory, and secondary, or long-term memory.

An example of one such a model is presented in figure 7.1. The model includes a system of sensory stores or buffers in addition to short-term and long-term stores. Note that figure 7.1 indicates processes that transfer information from one store to another. Transfer from sensory to short-term memory entails attention, whereas transfer from short-term to long-term memory requires rehearsal and elaboration. The

Figure 7.1 A generalized three-stage model of memory.

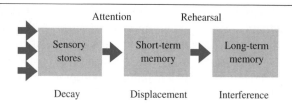

model also hypothesizes three different types of forgetting that correspond to the three memory stores. Forgetting from sensory stores is thought to result from simple decay; information is lost (within less than a second) simply as a function of time. Forgetting from short-term memory is thought to result from displacement in that new information bumps out old information. Forgetting from long-term memory results from interference between memory for one piece of information and other information learned previously or subsequently. Indeed, many investigators believe that interference does not destroy information in long-term memory but simply impairs the retrievability of information from long-term memory.

Are there age differences in short-term memory? One way to answer this question is to examine the capacity of short-term memory in both younger and older adults. For many years, psychologists have known that the capacity of short-term memory for younger adults is approximately seven pieces of information (Miller, 1956). Do older adults have the same capacity limitation? One way to answer this question is to give younger and older adults a digit- or letter-span task. In forward span tasks, individuals are given lists of numbers or letters of the alphabet and are asked to repeat the sequence. The key to this procedure is that the lists vary in length from 1 to say 12 items. A tremendous amount of research has shown that digit and letter span are hardly, if at all, affected by aging (Craik, 1977; Craik & Jennings, 1992). For example, consider the findings of Botwinick and Storandt's (1974) study of age differences in memory span for letters (see table 7.1). The measure of short-term memory span was the number of items a person could repeat in order without error. Note that memory span was only about one letter shorter for 70-year-olds than for 20-year-olds.

In contrast to the results of simple tests of memory span, it should be noted that age differences are evident on more demanding measures, such as backward span (Craik & Jennings, 1992). In backward-span tasks, the person is asked to recall the items that were presented in the reverse order.

Working Memory   Alan Baddeley (1986, 1994) suggested that traditional short-term memory tasks such as digit or letter span are overly passive and simplistic. Consequently, he coined the term **working memory** to refer to the more dynamic aspect of

TABLE 7.1					
Memory Span for Letters Presented Auditorily					
Age (Years)					
20s	30s	40s	50s	60s	70s
Span					
6.7	6.2	6.5	6.5	5.5	5.4

From Jack Botwinick and Martha Storandt, Memory-Related Functions and Age, 1974. Courtesy of Charles C. Thomas, Publisher, Springfield, Illinois.

short-term memory. One way to understand the concept of working memory is to think of a desktop. During the course of a day, new pieces of information (memos, reports, work requests, and so on) constantly accumulate on an individual's desk. Throughout the workday, the individual has to determine (1) which information is the most important, (2) which pieces of information on the desktop require further processing, (3) which processing strategy to use, and (4) which pieces of information are cluttering up the desktop and should either be discarded or saved. Thus, by analogy, a working memory task requires an individual to simultaneously select, coordinate, and process incoming information.

Baddeley (1994) theorized that working memory consists of three major components: a central executive, an articulatory loop, and a visual scratch pad. The central executive is responsible for making decisions about "what" information is processed in working memory and "how" that information is processed. For example, the central executive helps you remember what you need to buy at the supermarket. It may accomplish this goal by devising an elaborate encoding procedure that involves the assistance of the other parts of working memory. If you need to buy strawberries,

Complex everyday tasks require divided attention. Age-related declines in divided attention performance have been attributed to a number of factors, including limited processing resources, an additive increase in task complexity, and the costs of having to switch attention from one task to another.

chicken, milk, and cereal, the central executive may devise a strategy whereby it instructs the visual scratch pad to develop a mental image of "a chicken sitting down to a breakfast of strawberries, milk, and cereal." Or, it may instruct the articulatory loop to rehearse the sentence "Chickens like milk and strawberries on their cereal" as you drive to the store.

Age-related deficits in working memory, especially in the effectiveness of the central executive, may have far-reaching consequences. A breakdown in the central executive means that an older person cannot keep her mind on a particular task (cannot inhibit intrusive thoughts and distractions) and cannot manipulate the contents of working memory to solve a complex problem. Consider the following working memory task that typically yields a substantial age difference in performance favoring younger adults: Individuals listen to a tape recording of a list of words that correspond to "things you can drink" (e.g., coffee, soda, water, milk, etc.); and, at the same time, they see another list of words presented one at a time on a computer screen that correspond to "things you can eat" (e.g., pizza, spinach, crackers, apple, etc.). The participants are told to ignore the auditory words but remember the visual words. Immediately after the presentation of both word lists, participants are told to repeat the visual words beginning with the word that represents the item you would be most likely to eat if you were on a diet (e.g., *apple*) and ending with the word that represents the item you would be least likely to eat if you were on a diet (e.g., *pizza*). Older adults would perform poorly on this task because they must selectively attend to some information (the visual words), ignore other information (the auditory words), and manipulate the visual words held in working memory according to a specific rule (how healthful is each food item).

Furthermore, it has been suggested that age differences in long-term memory are the result of the central executive's decision to use ineffective strategies when it encodes (or retrieves) information from long-term memory. For example, instead of using one of the previously mentioned strategies to remember our shopping list of strawberries, chicken, milk and cereal, an older adult may try to remember a list by simply repeating to herself the words on the list or by forming a mental image of the words on the list.

Memory Search   Besides being better at manipulating the contents of working memory, younger adults are faster than older adults in searching or scanning the contents of short-term memory (e.g., Fisk & Rogers, 1991). Memory search is measured by presenting a person with a set of items (usually digits, such as 6, 3, and 9) to hold in memory. Then another digit (e.g., 9) is presented, and the individual's task is to decide whether the digit matches one of the digits in the memory set. Memory sets of varying lengths are used, and as might be expected, reaction times increase (answers are given more slowly) as the length of the memory set increases. Figure 7.2 shows the results from one study (Anders, Fozard, & Lillyquist, 1972) that compared the speed of short-term memory search for individuals in early, middle, and late adulthood. Note that longer memory sets produced longer reaction times, and that the slope (i.e., the steepness) of the reaction-time curve is greater for individuals in middle and late adulthood

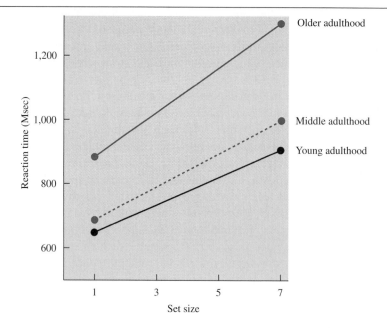

Figure 7.2 Mean reaction times as a function of age and set size.

than for those in early adulthood. This difference in slope indicates that the two older adult groups scan through lists of items in short-term memory at a slower pace than younger adults.

Spatial Processing Visual-spatial processing in short-term memory also becomes slower as we grow older (Cerella, 1985; Cerella, Poon, & Fozard, 1981; Hoyer & Rybash, 1992b; Johnson & Rybash, 1993). In Cerella's studies, younger and older adults were shown a capital letter at different degrees of tilt. Sometimes the letter was in the normal plane, and sometimes the letter was reversed from left to right (reflected). The task was to decide as quickly as possible whether each letter was normal or reflected. Participants made judgments by pressing one of two response keys. The latencies, or how long it takes to make these responses, were longer as the degree of tilt increased. This effect of tilt on response time suggested that adults mentally rotate the tilted letters to upright before making their judgment (see figure 7.3). Cerella et al. (1981) examined age-related differences in the speed of mental rotation. The results of this study are shown in figure 7.4. Note that the latencies grow longer with greater departures from vertical orientation; this supports the idea that response time is a measure of the amount of mental rotation required. Note also that the slope or steepness of the line relating orientation to latency was greater for older adults. This pattern suggests that the process of mental rotation is slower in older adults than younger adults.

Rotating a mental image is a very complex endeavor. For example, before a mental image can be mentally manipulated or rotated, it must be generated, and once it is generated it must constantly be maintained or refreshed during the rotation process.

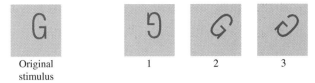

Figure 7.3
Examples of the
stimuli employed in
an imagery task
examining mental
rotation.

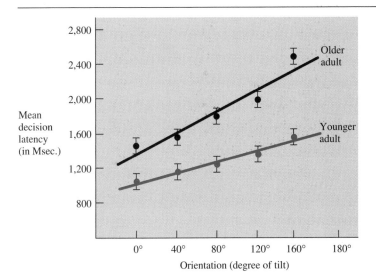

Figure 7.4 Mean
decision latency for
young and old
adults as a function
of stimulus
orientation.

Johnson and Rybash (1993) described a series of experiments that showed that aging
has a more detrimental effect on the processes involved in image maintenance than the
processes associated with image generation.

DIVISIONS OF LONG-TERM MEMORY: MULTIPLE MEMORY SYSTEMS

As we have just seen, older adults are at a significant disadvantage when they are
required to quickly and accurately manipulate the contents of short-term memory. On
the other hand, older adults perform as well as younger adults when they are given tasks
that require them to passively report the items within short-term memory system. Thus
we cannot come to any sort of simplistic conclusion as to whether short-term memory
is spared or impaired by age.

What about the effects of age on long-term memory? Long-term memory is typically defined as the retrieval of information that was processed more than one minute
ago, or the retrieval of information that has left consciousness. For many years, psychologists were certain that long-term memory underwent a significant deterioration
across the adult years. This "fact," as we have previously noted, is certainly consistent

Figure 7.5 A tentative memory taxonomy. *Source: Squire, L. R., & Knowlton, B. J. (1995). The organization of memory. In H. Horowitz & J. Singer (Eds.), The mind, the brain and the CAS: SFI studies in the Sciences of complexity, Vol 22 (pp. 63–77) New York: Addison Wesley.*

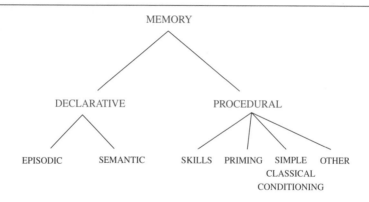

with one of the most common self-perceptions among the elderly: "I can't remember as well as I did when I was young."

Within the past decade, research in cognitive neuroscience has radically changed our understanding about the nature of human memory. Psychologists such as Endel Tulving, Daniel Schacter, and Larry Squire contributed to the development of the multiple memory systems theory of long-term memory (Schacter, 1996; Schacter & Tulving, 1994; Squire, 1994; Squire & Knowlton, 1995). Collectively, they have argued (see figure 7.5) that long-term memory consists of two major systems, which are both functionally and neurologically distinct: declarative memory and nondeclarative memory. **Declarative memory** involves the conscious recollection of the past. When people use their declarative memory system they "remember that" something has happened in the past. In fact, declarative memory is responsible for the remembrance of previous events that can literally "be declared." An example of declarative memory would be: "I remember that the first car I ever drove was a 1966 Ford Mustang."

Nondeclarative memory, in contrast, reveals itself by the influence that past events have on a person's current behavior. When people use their nondeclarative memory system they "remember how" to do something because of the beneficial effect of past experience. An example of nondeclarative memory would be: "Remembering how to drive a car."

Figure 7.5 shows that there are a number of major subdivisions of declarative and nondeclarative memory. In the next several sections of this chapter, we will discuss the affects of aging on these different memory systems.

EPISODIC AND SEMANTIC MEMORY

Episodic memory refers to the conscious recollection of the specific details of previous events. Most importantly, episodic memory is accompanied by a sense of remembering, pastness, and autonoetic awareness (Tulving, 1993; Wheeler, Stuss, & Tulving,

1997). *Autonoetic awareness* is the feeling that a remembrance actually happened to us. It is a type of "self-awareness" that indicates that we are mentally reexperiencing a specific event from our personal past.

Try to remember the first time you flew in an airplane. If you can mentally transport yourself back in time and personally reexperience the way the inside of the plane looked as you located and moved toward your seat, the mannerisms of the flight attendant and person who sat next to you on the plane, what you saw (and how you felt) when you looked out the window as the plane cruised through a cloud bank, and so on, you are experiencing the output of your episodic memory system.

Semantic memory refers to the remembrance of acquired knowledge about the world. Semantic memories are not accompanied by any of the phenomenological characteristics that mark episodic memories. When we remember something via the semantic memory system, we literally do not feel as if we are remembering anything from our personal past. This is because our semantic memories are accompanied by a sense of *noetic awareness*—the feeling that we are aware that we possess certain pieces of information and that this information is objective rather than subjective in nature.

To illustrate the salient features of semantic memory, let's return to our example of a person trying to remember his first airplane flight. Say that our hypothetical individual can remember that his first flight was on November 12, 1988, from New York City to Chicago on American Airlines Flight #238, that he sat in seat 24A, and that he flew on a nice sunny day. At the same time, however, let's assume that he has no personal recollection of actually being on the airplane and cannot remember the personal experiences he had during the flight. This person would be experiencing a semantic, but not an episodic, memory.

A great deal of neuropsychological data points to the validity of the distinction between episodic and semantic memory. Tulving, Hayman, and MacDonald (1991) studied a brain-injured patient named K. C. who displayed a severe amnesia for all of the episodic, but not the semantic, memories he acquired during the course of his life. After his brain injury, K. C., who loves to play chess, can still remember how to play chess, can remember the fact that his father taught him to play chess, and can remember that he played chess with his father on several occasions, but K. C. cannot remember a single instance from his personal life in which he actually played a game of chess! Also, when asked "What was the saddest day in your life?," K. C. replied it was the day of his brother's funeral. Yet, despite his ability to remember when and where his brother's funeral took place, K. C. cannot remember actually being at this sad event.

Other research by Tulving (1989) used the technique of positron emission tomography (PET) to distinguish between the episodic and semantic memory systems. These experiments have shown that areas in the frontal cortex become activated when individuals retrieve episodic memories, whereas more posterior brain regions become activated during the recall of semantic memories.

Cognitive psychologists have devised an interesting technique for studying age difference in episodic and semantic memory. See Research Focus 7.1 for details.

The findings described in Research Focus 7.1 provide clear evidence that episodic, but not semantic, memory is negatively affected by age. In the next few sections, we provide other examples of how aging affects these two memory systems.

Age Differences in Remembering Versus Knowing the Past

Endel Tulving (1993) has proposed that when we experience an episodic memory we feel as if we *remember* something, but when we experience a semantic memory we feel as if we *know* something. An interesting paradigm that has been used to understand the differences that arise in remembering versus knowing the past has been developed by Gardiner and colleagues (Gardiner & Java, 1990; Gardiner & Parkin, 1990). In this methodology, each participant is given a recognition task for a list of common words or faces. Then the participant is required to classify each of the items that he claims to have recognized as an item that he remembers (**R response**) or knows (**K response**) was on the study list. Using this technique, it has been shown that increasing the length of the study-test interval and making participants divide their attention during study has a detrimental influence on the frequency of R responses. Yet these manipulations have no influence on K responses. These data are important in that they reinforce the idea that R and K responses reflect the operations of different memory systems.

Parkin and Walter (1992) used the preceding paradigm to examine age differences in the episodic and semantic memory. The results of their research are shown in figure 7.A. This figure shows that when younger and older adults are matched on overall recognition accuracy, younger people make more R than K responses, but older individuals make more K than R responses! Furthermore, Parkin and Walter (1992) found that the elderly participants tendency to display a decrement in R responses was related to poor performance on a neuropsychological test of frontal lobe function.

The data reported by Parkin and Walter support the contention that, as a result of frontal lobe dysfunction, older individuals experience a deficit in episodic memory that is compensated for by a reliance on semantic memory. How could this pattern of impairment and preservation affect the everyday life of the typical older adult? It might be the case that when events, persons, or things from the recent past are considered, older

Box Figure 7.A Experiment 1: Recognition as a function of response type in a group of older subjects and a group of younger subjects matched on overall recognition accuracy. *Source: Parkin, A. J., & Walter, B. M. (1992). Recollective experience, normal aging, and frontal dysfunction. Psychology and Aging, 7, 293.*

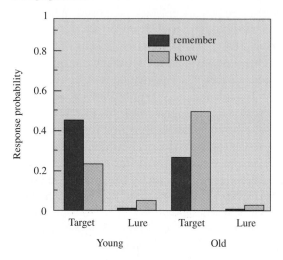

individuals live in a psychological world that is characterized by rather fuzzy and ill-defined recollective experiences. These experiences may be predominated by vague feelings of "familiarity" and "just knowing." In contrast, it might be the case that memories from the very distant past (childhood and adolescence) may be processed on more of an episodic basis. Thus the older person might remember the past, but just know about the present.

Recall and Recognition

Episodic memory can be measured using a variety of measures, including **recall** and **recognition.** Both of these tasks make use of the same study items—say a list of 20 common words. In a recall task, research participants would be instructed to say or write down as many of the 20 study items as possible without any hints or clues. A recall score is calculated by subtracting the number of intrusion errors (i.e., the false recall of words that were not on the list) from the number of items that were correctly recalled.

In a recognition task, participants would be presented with all of the 20 study items along with another 20 distractor items that were not on the study list and are

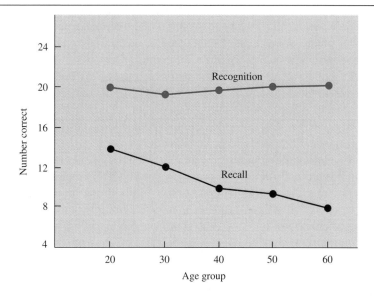

Figure 7.6
Recognition and recall scores as a function of age.

asked to indicate which of the 40 words were presented at study. Recognition ability is determined by subtracting the number of "false alarms" (i.e., the number of items that were not on the study list that were mistakenly identified as on the study list) from the number of "hits" (i.e., the number of items on the study list that were correctly identified).

Results of a classic experiment by Schonfield and Robertson (1966) that contrasted the recall and recognition ability of different-aged adults are presented in figure 7.6. The lower line shows that there is an age-related decline for recall. In contrast, the top line indicates that recognition is relatively unimpaired by aging.

Why should aging have a detrimental effect on recall but not recognition? It could be argued that recall and recognition tap the efficacy of the episodic and semantic memory systems, respectively. When performing a recall task, most participants try to think back to the study session and try to "remember" words that they actually studied. When performing a recognition test, however, participants may be guided by feelings of familiarity rather than recollection. Thus, when given a recognition task, an individual can look at a test item and have the vague feeling that he "knows" the word was on the list even though he can't actually remember studying it.

Another reason why recall is harder than recognition is that good recall performance may demand that individuals engage in rather complex processes when learning (or encoding) the information that they must subsequently remember. Three types of encoding processes appear especially important: organization, semantic elaboration, and mental imagery.

Effective **organization** of information means that individuals categorize study items in some conceptual manner. In experiments within this line of research (Backman, Mantyla, & Herlitz, 1990; Hultsch, 1971), participants are given instructions to sort (or organize) a number of words by categories. Other individuals are merely told to remember words. They are not given instructions to organize the study items in any particular way. When recall of the study material is tested, it has been found that older adults perform much worse than younger adults in the no organization condition; whereas age differences in the organization condition are minimized. Furthermore, younger adults tend to recall just as many items regardless of whether they are told to organize (or not organize) them at study, whereas older adults recalled substantially more items when they were required to use an organizational strategy. This pattern of results suggests younger, but not older, adults spontaneously use complex organizational strategies when they study to-be-remembered material.

Semantic elaboration entails the embellishment of a study item by linking it to some piece of conceptually-related information. Smith (1977) required adults to study a list of words under three different conditions. Adults in the no-cue condition were shown a list of words (e.g., *apple, yellow, horse,* etc.) and instructed to learn it. Those in the structural-cue condition saw each word on the list along with its first letter (*apple*—A). In the semantic-cue condition, the participants saw each word on the list along with a category the word belonged to (*apple*—fruit). Age-related differences in recall appeared in the first two conditions. The young group (aged 20 to 39) had the best recall, the late adulthood group (aged 60 to 80) showed the poorest recall, and the middle-aged group (aged 40 to 59) was intermediate. However, in the semantic-cue condition, recall was approximately equal in all age groups! These findings suggest that an age-related decline in recall can be eliminated by incorporating semantic elaboration of the words to be recalled at the time of study.

Another process that is known to affect long-term memory performance is **mental imagery.** One study (Mason & Smith, 1977) focused on the recall of individuals in early, middle, and late adulthood. Those in the imagery condition were instructed to form mental images for each word on a list, but those in the control condition were given no instructions to aid recall. Imagery instructions did not affect recall in the early- and late-adulthood groups but did improve recall in the middle-adulthood groups. Indeed, middle-aged adults in the imagery condition performed as well as young adults, though in the control condition they fell below young adults. Again, these results indicate an age-related deficiency in recall memory that can be eliminated through appropriate learning procedures. In this case, however, the learning procedure effective with middle-aged adults was not effective with elderly adults.

In summary, the research suggests that organization, elaboration, and imagery might be less efficient or less likely to occur in old age, and that with appropriate techniques, older adults can overcome or at least reduce deficits in recall. Most puzzling, of course, is the question of why older people don't use the rather simple strategies to help them remember.

Source Memory

Source memory is the ability to remember the context (i.e., the exact time and/or place) in which a particular piece of information has been learned. Remembering that "last Saturday evening at 8:00 while you were cooking dinner in your kitchen your best friend telephoned to say that she is moving to California" is an example of a source memory. In contrast, remembering that "your best friend is moving to California," but being incapable of remembering how and/or when your learned this information is an example of fact memory.

Traditionally, memory for source has been measured by presenting subjects with fictitious facts (Bob Hope's father was a fireman) or obscure facts (Bingo is the name of the dog on the Cracker Jack box). At a later date, individuals are given a recall test (What was the occupation of Bob Hope's father?) or recognition test (Bob Hope's father was a: (1) policeman, (2) fireman, (3) baker, (4) mechanic) for the factual information. And they are asked to provide information about when and/or where they learned each fact that they correctly recalled or recognized (How did you first learn that "Bob Hope's father was a fireman"? Did you read it in a magazine?, Hear about on TV?, etc.). Problems with source memory are observed when individuals can remember a fact but are incapable of remembering the exact context within which they first learned it.

Using this methodology, researchers (Janowsky et al., 1989) have found that neurological patients with damage to frontal cortex display pronounced source memory deficits despite the fact that their ability to recall or recognize factual information is just as good as control subjects. It has also been shown (Craik, Morris, Morris, & Loewen, 1990; McIntyre & Craik, 1987; Schacter, Kasniak, Kihlstrom, & Valdiserri, 1991) that elderly adults are more likely to commit more source errors than younger adults—even when younger and older individuals are matched on the amount of fact memory! Furthermore, the magnitude of source error rates among the elderly is related to their performance on neuropsychological tests that measure the integrity of frontal cortex.

Consider the following scenario in order to grasp some of the real-life consequences of a breakdown in source memory. A younger and older adult walk through a supermarket checkout line and notice the following headline on a tabloid newspaper: "Wearing a copper bracelet will cure insomnia." A few days later, both of these individuals remember the fact that they recently became aware of the claim that a copper bracelet is a valid treatment for insomnia. Since the younger adult has intact source monitoring skills, he dismisses this claim as nonsense because he read about it in a non-credible source. The older adult, because he possesses poor source memory skills, remembers that he heard about the advantages of wearing copper bracelets by listening to a world-renowned physician who was interviewed on a very credible TV news program. Consequently, the older person throws away his insomnia medication and begins wearing a copper bracelet.

Usually, it is not commonplace to directly ask an individual to recall the source of a particular piece of information. Thus, assessing source memory via the traditional methodology may yield an overly liberal estimate of an individual's ability to monitor a source within real-life contexts. Source monitoring usually takes place implicitly as a component of some ongoing cognitive activity. This indirect and unintentional form of source memory may have the greatest impact on everyday behavior and decision making.

Because traditional tests of source monitoring may not generalize to situations outside of the laboratory, Larry Jacoby and his colleagues (Jacoby, Kelley, Brown, & Jasechko, 1989) developed an alternative methodology—the Fame Judgment Task. In this paradigm, research participants are required to read a series of nonfamous names, such as Bruce Hudson. Then they are shown a list of names and are asked to indicate which of the names are famous. Items consist of previously presented nonfamous names (e.g., Bruce Hudson), nonfamous names that the participants were not previously exposed to (e.g., Shawn Johnson), and famous names (e.g., John Milton). Individuals are reminded that all of the names they previously read were nonfamous and that some of these names may appear on the current list. If a person consciously recollects that a name on the list was previously read, the name should be judged "nonfamous" without hesitation. Alternatively, if a person fails to remember that a name appeared on the reading task, but is nevertheless familiar with the name due to its prior exposure, the name might mistakenly be judged "famous." A misattribution of fame to a previously presented nonfamous name is defined as a source error. Thus, the Fame Judgment Task allows an experimenter to determine if, in the absence of conscious recollection, an individual can monitor the source of the familiarity that accompanies a test item.

Dywan and Jacoby (1990) found that elderly adults are much more likely than younger adults to display heightened source error rates on the Fame Judgment Task. In other words, they were much more likely than college students to claim that "Bruce Hudson" is, in fact, a famous person. Thus older adults were not able to use their conscious recollection of when and/or where they last saw the name "Bruce Hudson" to oppose the effects of familiarity and prevent the occurrence of a source error.

Dywan and Jacoby (1990) offered several instances of how an inability to monitor source on an implicit basis might affect an older adult's ability to function in everyday life. For example, sitting down to play cards with a group of friends may serve as a cue for an older adult to remember a funny story from her distant past. Telling the story the first time at the card table might have the unconscious influence of making the story pop into her mind during future card games with her friends. If her conscious memory for telling the story does not oppose her unconscious tendency to repeat it, she may retell the story countless times to her card-playing companions.

First Memories and Infantile Amnesia

Until now, we have discussed age differences that are found on laboratory studies of memory. In these experiments, participants are given lists of arbitrary items to learn and their memory is tested shortly afterward. This research, while important, may not tell us very much about how aging affects the everyday or personal aspects of human memory.

When people are asked to remember a real-life experience, they are engaging in an autobiographical memory task. For example, can you remember your high school graduation or the last time you ate a pizza? One of the most important functions of autobiographical memory is to allow each of us to become our own personal historian. We are continually engaged in the process of writing, editing, and updating the story of our own life (Nelson, 1993).

An individual's first recallable autobiographical memory usually comes from the middle of the fourth year of life. Psychologists have coined the term **infantile amnesia** to describe the fact that the typical adult cannot remember life experiences from the first three and one-half years of life. Psychoanalysts, such as Sigmund Freud, speculated that infantile amnesia was caused by the repression of traumatic sexual experiences. This hypothesis lost credibility because the vast majority of infants do not experience the types of horrific experiences that were postulated by Freudian theory. Later on, it was assumed that infantile amnesia was caused by the neurological immaturity of the declarative memory system (Moscovitch, 1986). Without an "up-and-running" declarative memory system there could not be conscious recollection of the past. Several lines of more contemporary research, however, have made it clear that the declarative memory system is operative within the first year of life (McKee & Squire, 1993). Nowadays it is believed that the offset of infantile amnesia is linked to the development of a rudimentary sense of self or self-consciousness that emerges during the fourth year of life. It seems that we cannot remember events from our early life until we develop a "self" that is capable of experiencing (and remembering) those events (Howe & Courage, 1993; Nelson, 1993; Usher & Neisser, 1993; Webster & Cappeliez, 1993). This theoretical perspective suggests that cognitive functions such as memory share a very intimate relationship with basic personality and social processes.

The vast amount of research on infantile amnesia has employed children, adolescents, or younger adults as participants. Not much is known about the first memories of elderly persons. Do older adults have earlier- (or later-) occurring first memories in comparison to younger adults? What types of psychological variables predict the age of younger and older adults' first memories? To address these issues, Rybash and Hrubi (1997) conducted two studies that examined the roles played by intellectual and psychodynamic factors in the first memories of younger and older individuals. They found that the relationship between IQ test scores and age of first memories was identical for members of both age groups. That is, younger and older adults who scored above average on various facets of IQ had earlier first memories than individuals who displayed below-par performance. This replicated earlier research by Rabbitt and McInnis (1988) that showed that "smarter" older adults tend to have earlier first memories.

In contrast, Rybash and Hrubi (1997) found that psychodynamic factors affect younger and older adults' first memories in different ways. They reported, in line with previous research on life review and reminiscence, that the need to reminisce about the past to prepare for death was more typical (as well as more adaptive) for older than for younger adults. Importantly, they showed that reminiscing for death preparation was negatively related to age of older adults' first memories, but positively related to age of younger adults' first memories. It makes sense that older adults who think about the past to prepare themselves for death would have deeper, richer, and earlier memories of their childhood in comparison to those who do not reminisce for this purpose. These individuals may be facing the final portion of the life span with a sense of ego integrity (Erikson, 1968). Alternatively, it may be that younger individuals who have a developmentally inappropriate way of reminiscing have a difficult time gaining access to their personal past.

Another point to consider is that the elderly participants in the Rybash and Hrubi (1997) research reported first memories that occurred later in life (approximately 4 years of age) than did younger adults (approximately 3.5 years of age). This finding could reflect a genuine age difference in the ability to remember the personal past, or a conservative bias in older adults' willingness to estimate the age of their earliest memory. Whatever the basis for this age difference, it should be emphasized that Rybash and Hrubi measured the narrative rather than the historical truth about the exact age at which participants' first memories actually occurred (cf. Bruner, 1986). Rybash and Hrubi argued that the retrieval of early memory is a constructive process that represents the interaction of diverse processes that operate according to similar (or different) rules across different developmental periods.

Not all remote memories from the distant past are autobiographical. Bahrick, Bahrick, and Wittlinger (1975) investigated memory for high school classmates after a long interval. The research assessed face recognition, name recognition, and name-face matching. Free recall of names and cued recall of names in response to faces were also evaluated. The participants differed in the number of years that had elapsed since their high school graduation (from three months to 47 years since graduation). Figure 7.7 shows that recognition and matching performance were nearly constant (and nearly perfect) up to a retention interval of 34 years. Adults in their midfifties were performing about as well as 18-year-olds. In contrast, the recall measures, particularly free recall, showed clear evidence of age-related decline that began shortly after graduation. Of special interest is the steady drop in free recall from the 3-year interval (adults about 21 years old) to the 47-year interval (adults about 65 years old). Also note that Bahrick and his colleagues have found similar results when they have measured long-term retention of academic information (e.g., geography and foreign language) that adults learned in high school. How do these findings relate to the laboratory-based research that we described earlier?

Vivid Memories and the Reminiscence Bump

Joseph Fitzgerald examined age differences in different aspects of autobiographical memory. Fitzgerald and Lawrence (1984) presented older adults with a series of 40 common words. Each participant was required to think of a specific autobiographical memory that would trigger each word. The results of this study revealed that participants were most likely to remember events that had just occurred rather than those that had occurred years ago. In fact, most of the autobiographical memories reported by the subjects happened within a few years prior to testing. In another study, Fitzgerald (1988) asked a group of older adults (approximately 70 years of age) to write a paragraph describing three different vivid or **flashbulb memories.** Participants were told that a flashbulb memory is an exceptionally vivid, detailed, and long-lasting mental image of a personally experienced event. Participants wrote about vivid memories that occurred at any time over the course of their lives. Finally, Fitzgerald also asked the

Figure 7.7 Recognition and recall of names and faces of high school colleagues.

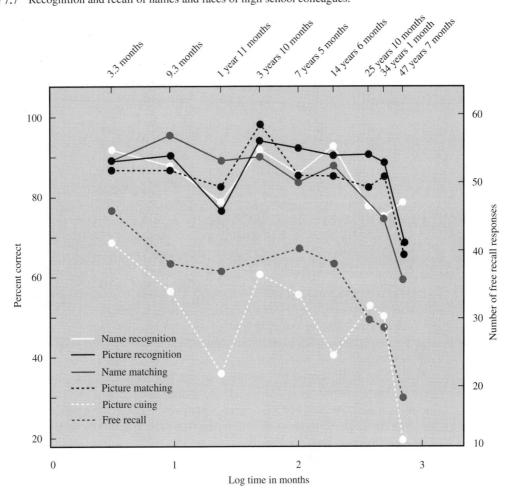

older adults to rate each vivid memory on several dimensions. These dimensions included personal importance, national importance, frequency of rehearsal, and intensity of emotional reaction.

Unlike the data collected in the Fitzgerald and Lawrence (1984) study, Fitzgerald's (1988) study showed that vivid memories do not exhibit a normal retention function. Participants were very unlikely to recall vivid memories from middle adulthood or old age. Instead, these older adults were most likely to recall vivid memories from their late adolescence and early adulthood. The tendency for older adults to recall more vivid memories from this time period has been called the **reminiscence bump** (see figure 7.8). The data for the study were collected shortly after the *Challenger* explosion; yet, none of the participants included this event in their list of vivid memories. Some of the older adults' vivid memories possessed a great deal of personal importance and were steeped in emotion (e.g., a soldier remembering his friends dying in combat, and

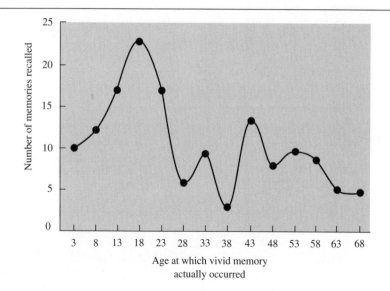

Figure 7.8 Older adults' retention of vivid memories.

a mother remembering the birth of her child). However, most of these vivid memories did not have personal import, nor were they highly emotional.

Why does the age distribution of vivid memories manifest a reminiscence bump rather than a normal retention function? Fitzgerald (1988, 1996) speculated that adolescence and young adulthood may represent that period of the life span when we are in the process of forming unique personal identities. We may use this period as a marker or anchor from which to begin the story of our adult psychological selves. Thus, because of the special status we attach to the experiences of youth, we may be likely to have vivid memories from this period of our lives. Fitzgerald (1988, 1996) also suggests that because we live in a youth-oriented society, a rich storehouse of vivid memories from youth would allow older adults to maintain contact with a point in the life span when they were young, healthy, and had their lives in front of them.

Jansari and Parkin (1996) offered an explanation of the reminiscence bump that complemented the one proposed by Fitzgerald. They suggest that there is a bias, in an unconstrained recall task, to report first-time memories ("The first time that X happened to me was when . . ."), and there may be an overabundance of first-time memories from late adolescence and young adulthood.

It has also been suggested that older adults have a much more difficult time forming flashbulb memories than younger individuals. For example, Cohen, Conway, and Maylor (1994), who worked with a large sample of individuals from the United Kingdom, showed that 90 percent of younger adults, but only 42 percent of older adults, had flashbulb memories for an event of great national importance—the surprise resignation of British prime minister Margaret Thatcher. These results are intriguing because in the vast number of instances, older adults who experienced flashbulb memories scored the same as older adults who did not experience flashbulb memories on several encoding and rehearsal variables surrounding the prime minister's resignation (e.g., How much did you think about her resignation?, How surprising was her resignation?, How intense was your reaction to her resignation?, How interested are you in politics?, etc.). In fact, both groups of older adults scores' on these questions were essentially identical to younger adults who possessed flashbulb memories! Thus the low incidence of vivid memories among the older adults could not have been caused by low levels of rehearsal, interest, or reactivity. Cohen et al. (1994) speculated the neurological factors that underlie age differences in source memory (i.e., the inability to remember the exact contextual details of a given piece of information) may also be responsible for age-related deficits in forming flashbulb memories.

False Memories

If older adults are less capable of remembering events that actually occurred, are they also more likely to remember events that never happened to them? Recently, the issue of false memories has become an extremely controversial topic. There have been several cases chronicled in both the print and electronic media in which adults have experienced "recovered memories" of childhood traumatic events such as being the victim of sexual abuse or witnessing a murder. On the basis of these recovered memories a wide range of individuals, including family members, priests, and day-care workers, have been accused (and convicted) of serious crimes (Loftus & Ketcham, 1994).

Many recovered memories are, in actuality, *false memories* that were implanted in the minds of individuals by unscrupulous psychotherapists (Loftus & Ketcham, 1994). Consequently, scientists have become very interested in developing methodologies that help members of the health care and legal communities distinguish true from false memories, and in determining the extent to which different groups of people, especially young children and elderly adults, are susceptible to the false memory effect.

One of the best ways to study the production of false memories has been popularized by Roediger and McDermott (1995). If you were a participant in their research, you would listen to lists of common words such as *nurse, sick, health, hospital, office, cure, operation, medicine,* etc. Then you would be asked to recall as many of the words as possible. (Close your eyes and try to recall the list items as accurately as you can.) The key to this methodology is that Roediger and McDermott selected a false target word that was not presented on the list but was strongly associated with list items. For the previously mentioned list, the false target word was *doctor.* Roediger and McDermott (1995), who did their original research with college students, found that a large percentage of the participants had false memories in that they confidently claimed that they had vivid memories of listening to the false target item on the study list. (Did you recall reading the word *doctor* in your textbook?) In fact, college students were given 12 word lists to study and the typical student displayed, on average, false memories for 5 of the 12 lists!

What psychological mechanisms are responsible for this false memory effect? One line of reasoning suggests that hearing a list of words such as *nurse, sick, health, hospital,* and so on makes an individual think of semantically related words such as *doctor.* When given a recall task, the individual can remember the word *doctor* but cannot remember if he heard it on the list or thought about it in his mind. In other words, a person's false memory of having heard the word *doctor* is a source memory error.

If false memories constitute source errors, we would expect that older adults would be more likely than younger adults to display memory distortions. To test this hypothesis, Rybash and Hrubi (1997) presented college students, elementary school children, and elderly adults with the words used by Roediger and McDermott. Right after some of the lists were presented, participants were asked to "generate" words that were related to the list items but were not on the list. The purpose of this generate condition was to prevent false memories by making the person think of the target item (doctor) and reinforce the notion that the target item was not on the study list. Compared with a baseline condition, the generate condition reduced the incidence of memory distortions in the young adults but had no beneficial effects on either the children or the elderly.

These results, along with data from several other paradigms (see Cohen & Faulkner, 1989), lead to the conclusion that older individuals are more likely than younger individuals to experience memory distortions, and that older people may not be as credible in giving eyewitness testimony as their younger counterparts. However, as Schacter (1996) cautions, this general conclusion does not mean that any particular younger eyewitness is always more reliable than any particular elderly eyewitness. Put somewhat differently, individual differences within age groups may be larger than overall differences between age groups.

NONDECLARATIVE MEMORY

Nondeclarative memory does not involve the conscious recollection of past events, or previous knowledge. Remembering on a nondeclarative basis involves a person "being able to do something very effectively" because of the beneficial effects of past experience. Being able to drive a car is an example of a nondeclarative memory. Your ability to sit behind the wheel of your car, start the engine, manipulate the brake and accelerator pedals, turn the wheel, and so on, as you drive to your friend's house depends on your ability to retrieve information from your nondeclarative memory system. Yet, while you are in the process of driving the car, you don't feel as if you are remembering anything (e.g., your driver's education class), and you don't experience any sense of pastness—you just feel as if you are doing something.

Several different types of everyday activities depend on nondeclarative memory, especially perceptual-motor skills. Activities within this category include (besides driving) playing golf, playing a musical instrument, using a word processing program, tying your shoelaces, and so on.

One way to better understand the general distinction between declarative and nondeclarative aspects of memory is to consider the distinction between "memory as object" versus "memory as a tool." See Research Focus 7.2 for details.

Memory as an Object Versus Memory as a Tool

What is the difference between an object and a tool? This seems to be a simple and trivial question. An object is something that could be looked at, inspected, held onto, and so on. A tool, in contrast, is something that could be used to perform some sort of function or task. This distinction notwithstanding, it is important to realize that a particular "thing" could be both an object as well as a tool. For example, a hammer is certainly an object. You can hold it in your hand, see it, weigh it, and so forth. At the same time, a hammer is a tool. You can use it to pound a nail. A hammer becomes an "object of inquiry" versus a "tool to be used" because of the circumstances we find ourselves in. When we go to the hardware store for the intention of buying a hammer, the hammer becomes an object. When we repair a roof that has been damaged in a wind storm, the hammer becomes a tool.

What does the object-tool distinction have to do with memory? The answer to this question is clear. Our everyday, intuitive conceptualization of memory is that it is an object. A memory, it would seem, is an experience that takes place in our mind. It is something that may be inspected, analyzed, and attended to. If you remember what you did last 4th of July, your memory is an object of inquiry within your conscious mind. Beyond any doubt, the objectlike aspect of memory diminishes with age. Older adults have greater difficulty than younger individuals in deliberately retrieving and inspecting bits of their past lives.

Darlene and James Howard (1996), suggest that the tool-like properties of memory are much less obvious—but just as important—as its objectlike characteristics. To illustrate this

point Darlene Howard gives an example of showing one of her most favorite films, which had a rather fuzzy and garbled soundtrack, to a psychology class. As she watched the film, she had no trouble hearing what the main characters were saying. However, the college students in her class had great difficulty deciphering what they heard. What was responsible for this effect? Was her hearing better than that of her students? Was she sitting closer to the speaker system than her students? (The answer to both of the questions is a definite, "No!") She suggests that since she had seen the film several times before, she was using her memory of film's soundtrack to help her comprehend what she heard. The students could not do this because they were being exposed to the film for the first time. Most important, she was using her memory of the film in an unintentional and automatic way. In fact, she was unaware that she was remembering anything at all when she listened to the film. She had the illusion that she was "hearing" the sound when she was actually "remembering" it. This shows how memory may be used as a tool for performing some current task that seems totally unrelated to memory. Memory of the past may facilitate perception of the present!

(As an analog to Howard's experience, do you think that a song you have heard several times in the past seems to be louder and easier to understand than a song that you've heard for the first time? Why is this so?)

Does the tool-like quality of memory decline with age? Read the section on "implicit memory and aging," especially the research on age differences in priming, to find the answer to this important question.

Priming and Implicit Memory

The most popular way of studying nondeclarative memory in the laboratory is by assessing participants' performance on various types of priming tasks (Schacter & Buckner, 1998). In a **priming task,** individuals are asked to identify or make judgments about stimuli that were (or were not) presented during an earlier phase of an experiment. Priming is demonstrated if exposure to items during a study phase results in enhanced performance (e.g., reduced latency of response or increased accuracy of response) relative to control items during a test phase. Consider the following procedure that typifies the priming format. Participants study a list of familiar words such as *motel.* Later they are presented with three-letter stems for items on the study list (mot____ , motel) and an equal number of word stems for items (matched for length and frequency) that did not appear at study (sha____ , shape) and are instructed to: "Complete as many stems as possible with the first letters that pop into mind that spell valid words." Priming is demonstrated if more stems are completed correctly for study items than control items. This task, referred to as *word-stem completion,* provides a measure of **implicit memory** because individuals are not directly asked to complete test items with words from the study list. Their memory for the study items is assessed in a rather indirect or sneaky manner.

On the other hand, **explicit memory** tasks are those in which an individual is instructed to deliberately recollect a previous event. Traditional tests used in memory research such as recognition, recall, and cued-recall are measures of explicit memory. In a cued-recall task, for example, participants are shown a series of three-letter stems for items that were presented (mot____) or not presented (sha____) at study and are asked to complete as many stems as possible that spell words from the study list and to guess on stems for which they cannot produce studied words. Explicit memory, which draws on the resources of the declarative memory system, is demonstrated if more stems are completed for study items than control items.

Psychologists have become very excited about the distinction between explicit and implicit memory for two reasons. First, a wealth of evidence shows that brain damage has dramatically different effects on how well individuals perform implicit versus explicit memory tasks. For example, neurological patients who suffer from amnesia display no memory whatsoever for lists of common words when they are tested by explicit tasks, yet these same individuals display robust levels of performance when they are tested by implicit tasks. The finding that amnesics perform exceptionally well on priming tasks, despite the fact that these individuals are unaware that they are remembering on an indirect basis, has led some psychologists to categorize implicit memory as memory without awareness. Second, when non-brain-injured individuals are considered, it has been demonstrated that various independent variable have differential effects on implicit versus explicit tasks. For example, consider an experiment in which participants encode common words (e.g., *sharp*) in a shallow ("Is there an e in this word?") or a semantic ("Is this word the opposite of dull?") manner. It has been discovered that semantic encoding facilitates explicit memory more than shallow encoding. In contrast, these two encoding procedures have the same effect in implicit memory. Furthermore, it has been shown that a long delay in the study-test interval (e.g., one week) will significantly reduce individuals' performance on explicit tasks but will have no effect on their performance on various implicit tasks.

This evidence points to the conclusion that implicit and explicit tasks reflect the operation of structurally distinct memory systems that are associated with different brain regions (Schacter, 1996; Schacter & Tulving, 1994; Squire & Knowlton, 1995). All these researchers would agree that performance on explicit tasks is controlled by the declarative memory system, which has its neurological basis in the hippocampus, frontal cortex, and diencephalon. The issue of which brain regions control performance on implicit tasks is a much more complex and controversial issue. Daniel Schacter (Schacter 1994, 1996) has argued that priming is regulated by posterior neural regions that process information about physical/surface (but not the semantic) features of words and objects. He has labeled these brain areas the Perceptual Representation System (PRS).

AGE DIFFERENCES IN IMPLICIT MEMORY

One implication of the growing body of research suggesting that memory systems can be experimentally dissociated in normal and brain-injured populations is that a comparison of younger and older adults' performance on implicit and explicit tasks might help us achieve a better understanding of the stabilities and losses that characterize the aging of human memory. For example, it might be the case that aging has an influence on memory that is identical to the one associated with amnesia: A person's ability to perform explicit tasks is impaired, but her ability to perform implicit tasks is spared.

Rybash (1996) reviewed the vast literature that has addressed the issue of how normal aging, neuropathological aging (e.g., Alzheimer's disease [AD]), and neurological dysfunction (e.g., amnesia) affect different types of implicit memory. He found that performance on priming tasks that are highly perceptual, depend solely on posterior brain regions such as PRS, and make minimal retrieval demands are not impaired by normal aging, AD, or amnesia. An example of such a priming task is called *word naming*. In this task, a person reads a list of common words such as *motel* that appear one at a time on a computer screen, and the experimenter measures the exact number of milliseconds that it takes to read each item. At another time (e.g., one hour, one day, or one week), the participant is required to read another list of individual items, half of which were read at study (*motel*) and the other half were not (*shape*). Priming is measured by comparing the speed at which the participant reads study versus control words. The fact that aging, AD, and amnesia have no ill effect on some types of priming opens up the very exciting possibility that psychologists might develop memory rehabilitation programs for brain-injured or demented individuals that are based on implicit memory (Camp, Foss, O'Hanlon, & Stevens, 1996).

On the other hand, it seems that aging has a slight, but statistically significant, effect on a person's ability to perform priming tasks such as word-stem completion. These tasks seems to draw on both conceptual as well as perceptual factors, possess a strong retrieval component, and are controlled by the interaction of anterior and posterior brain centers. It is interesting to note that patients with AD, but not amnesia, also perform in a subpar manner on word-stem completion tasks.

Based on the available evidence, Rybash (1996) concluded that the performance of older adults across a wide range of priming tasks is more similar to the performance of patients with AD than it is to the performance of individuals suffering from amnesia. This suggests that amnesia does not serve as an adequate model for understanding age-related changes in human memory, and that the memory changes associated with AD and normative aging are united by a common thread. These conclusions do not necessarily mean, of course, that AD represents an acceleration of the normal aging process, or that normal aging is inherently pathological.

One drawback associated with priming task methodology is that implicit memory performance may be contaminated by explicit memory, especially in non-brain-damaged individuals. This means that when performing a word-stem completion

Process Dissociation Procedure

The priming methodology, even though it has yielded a wealth of important data, possesses a serious drawback. Individuals may, on either a voluntary or involuntary basis, use their explicit recollection of a study list when they are performing a priming task. Thus their explicit memory may contaminate their implicit memory. At the same time, it is possible that unconscious memory processes may influence a person's behavior on an explicit memory task!

How can we eliminate the unwanted influence of conscious recollection on implicit tasks, and unconscious recollection on explicit tasks? Larry Jacoby (Jacoby, 1991; Jacoby, Yonelinas, & Jennings, 1996) has proposed a very novel approach to this problem. He developed a technique called the **Process Dissociation Procedure (PDP)** that estimates the degree to which conscious and unconscious (or automatic) factors independently contribute to performance on any conceivable memory test. The key to the PDP is a comparison of individuals' performance on inclusion and exclusion versions of a particular memory task. In an inclusion task, conscious and unconscious processes work in concert with each other because participants are asked to respond with items that appeared at study. In an exclusion task, however, conscious and unconscious processes work in opposition to one another because participants are asked to respond with items that did not appear at study. Comparing the degree to which individuals respond with studied items on an inclusion task vis-à-vis an exclusion task via a series of standard equations yields separate estimates of conscious and unconscious influences on memory.

For example, say a group of individuals learns a list of common words such as *motel,* and their memory is tested by having them complete word stems such as mot____ . In the inclusion condition, participants are told to complete the stem with a word they remember from the study list and to just guess if they cannot remember a word from the study list. Given these instructions, pretend a person does what we tell him to do. He completes the stem as *motel.* Why? Jacoby suggests that the response *motel* could have occurred because the person consciously recollected *motel,* or because the person unconsciously recollected *motel* but experienced a failure of conscious recollection.

In the exclusion condition, participants would be told to complete the stem with a word they remember was not on the study list. Given these instructions, say a person does what we tell him not to do. He completes the stem as *motel.* Why? Jacoby argues that response *motel* could have occurred because the person unconsciously recollected *motel* but experienced a failure of conscious recollection.

Given these assumptions, we can estimate the strength of conscious recollection by subtracting the probability of producing study items on the inclusion tasks from the probability of producing study items on the exclusion task [Conscious Recollection = Inclusion − Exclusion]. And we can estimate the strength of unconscious recollection by dividing the probability of producing study items on the exclusion task by the failure of conscious recollection [Unconscious Recollection = Exclusion / (1-Conscious Recollection)].

Research using the PDP has consistently shown that older adults display lower levels of conscious recollection than younger adults (Jennings & Jacoby, 1993, 1997; Rybash & Hoyer, 1996b; Rybash, DeLuca, & Rubenstein, 1997; Rybash, Santoro, & Hoyer, in press. However, it remains unclear as to whether age differences obtain in unconscious contributions to memory.

One of the most exciting aspects of the PDP approach involves detecting age- and disease-related memory deficits (Jacoby, Jennings, & Hay, 1996; Jennings & Jacoby, 1997). For example, telling the same story to a friend on more than one

task, some individuals may deliberately try to remember words from a study list in order to complete word stems, whereas other persons may unintentionally recall study items when they are attempting to complete word stems under implicit instructions. Furthermore, it could be argued that the age difference favoring younger adults on priming tasks like word-stem completion is an artifact of developmental changes in voluntary (or involuntary) conscious recollection favoring younger adults. Research Focus 7.3 provides information about an ingenious approach to studying "memory without awareness" that is very different from the priming paradigm.

TABLE 7.A

Estimated Strength of Conscious and Unconscious Memory Processes for Repeated Items in the 3 and 12 Lag Conditions

	Conscious Processes		Unconscious Processes	
	Lag 3	Lag 12	Lag 3	Lag 12
Younger Adults	.90	.83	.64	.66
Older Adults	.71	.51	.67	.74

occasion (i.e., unnecessarily repeating yourself) certainly represents a failure of memory. However, we would be much more concerned about an individual who repeats the same story after five minutes than a person who repeats himself after an interval of five weeks.

How capable are older adults at detecting and avoiding unwanted repetition? What role do conscious and unconscious memory processes have in promoting (or avoiding) repetition? To address these issues, Jennings and Jacoby (1997) conducted an experiment in which younger and older participants studied a list of words. Then the participants were given inclusion and exclusion versions of a recognition task that contained previously studied words as well as control words that were not on the original study list. Most important, some of the control words only appeared once on the memory tasks. In contrast, other control words were repeated after 3 or 12 intervening test items occurred. (These items were said to be in the 3 and 12 lag conditions, respectively.) On the inclusion task, participants were instructed to say yes to study items and repeated control items, and no to nonrepeated control items. On the exclusion task, participants were instructed to say yes to study items and no to repeated and nonrepeated control items. This methodol-

ogy allowed Jennings and Jacoby to compute the estimated strength of conscious and unconscious contributions to memory for repeated control words at each lag condition.

The results of the experiment (as shown in table 7.A) were very clear-cut. Namely, age differences in unconscious processes were not found at either lag interval. However, older adults were much less likely to consciously recollect that a control item was repeated during the test phase of the experiment, even when only three words intervened between the repetition of a control word. This suggests that older adults repeat themselves because of a failure to consciously use recollection to oppose the unconscious tendency toward repetition—not because unconscious processes, by themselves, are more powerful in the elderly. (Note that Ste-Marie, Jennings, & Finlayson [1996] found this same pattern of performance in younger brain injured adults.) A final observation is that older adults exhibited profound deficits in conscious recollection compared with the younger adults. This suggests that previous reports of spared recognition memory in older individuals was probably due to the contaminating influence of unconscious memory processes on conscious recollection.

CONCLUSIONS ABOUT AGING AND MEMORY

There are no simple, sweeping conclusions that can be made about the relationship between memory and aging. We have seen, for example, that researchers have sought to distinguish between different types of: memory systems (declarative versus nondeclarative; episodic versus semantic), memory tasks (explicit versus implicit), and memory functions (object versus tool). It seems that older adults are at a distinct disadvantage when they perform explicit tasks for recently acquired information that focus on the objectlike properties of memory that are controlled by the declarative memory system. Explicit memory for events from the distant past, however, seems to hold up remarkably well with aging. Likewise, older adults perform almost as well as younger individuals when they are given implicit tasks that draw upon the tool-like aspects of memory that are controlled by the nondeclarative memory system.

Besides age-related changes in some aspects of memory performance, there are changes in the subjective dimension of memory. The younger adult's memory of a past experience is accompanied by a sense of remembering, whereas the older person's recollections of the past is marked by feelings of knowing. Another way to think of the relationship between memory and aging is to draw a distinction between memory processing and memory knowledge (Perlmutter, 1980). As we have seen, aging is associated with a decline in the speed and efficiency of the processes responsible for establishing new memories. This decline, however, does not affect the amount of knowledge already stored within memory, which is available for use in many different tasks. Thus, age-related declines may be restricted to tasks in which a person's prior knowledge is not used. Tasks that capitalize on previously learned information may show no age-related declines; indeed, on such tasks older people may even outperform young adults. The distinction between memory processing and knowledge is similar to the distinction between fluid and crystallized intelligence (discussed in chapter 8), and to the theory of encapsulation (discussed in chapter 9). A final point to consider is that there are vast individual differences in memory that have to do with differences in acquired knowledge and skills. Almost everyone has a rich foundation of knowledge in several areas of work, sports, hobbies, or entertainment. For healthy individuals, access to such knowledge is unaffected by aging. Mr. Stephen Powelson, a 76-year-old retired accountant, for example, has almost finished memorizing all 15,693 lines of Homer's Iliad in ancient Greek. Mr. Powelson has visited a number of college campuses to recite the lines of the Iliad before audiences of classics professors and their students ("Taking the Iliad on the Road," 1994). Many of the young adult students who hear Mr. Powelson have to change their stereotypically held view about memory aging. Individuals maintain their ability to use well-learned knowledge, strategies, and skills throughout middle age and into old age (Rybash, Hoyer, & Roodin, 1986). Tests of factual knowledge (e.g., vocabulary or events of the news) typically show no decline from young adulthood to old age (Perlmutter, 1980).

ATTENTION

Probably too much emphasis is given to the study of memory, and too little emphasis is given to the study of the processes of attention and learning, and how these processes affect the encoding and retrieval of information. The term *attention* refers to the capacity or energy necessary to support information processing (Plude & Hoyer, 1985). That the attentional capacities of humans are limited is evident when observing a wide variety of cognitive activities, including alertness, and in situations in which we are required to select or distinguish between relevant and irrelevant information or handle multiple sources of information simultaneously. The two aspects of attention that are most affected by aging are selective attention and divided attention (e.g., Hartley, 1992; Madden & Plude, 1993).

Selective Attention

Selective attention refers to the ability to distinguish relevant from irrelevant information. Selective attention is required when we are trying to concentrate on something we are reading while trying to ignore information that is irrelevant or interfering such as loud or unpleasant music.

In the laboratory, researchers frequently use *visual search* tasks to study age-related differences in the factors that affect selective attention. In a visual search task, the participant decides if the target item is present in displays containing different numbers of distractor items. Typically, older adults are more affected by the amount of distractor information than are younger adults (Madden & Plude, 1993). It has also been reported that older adults are at a disadvantage when the target can appear anywhere in the display to be searched, and the task is to find or localize the target (Plude & Hoyer, 1986). Age differences are smaller or nonexistent in *filtering tasks,* in which the target item is always in the same location, and the person's task is to identify the item in the presence or absence of distractor information. Thus, it is well established that there are age-related declines in the ability to attend to relevant information while trying to ignore distracting information (Connelly & Hasher, 1993; Hasher, Stoltzfus, Zacks, & Rypma, 1991; Kotary & Hoyer, 1995; Plude & Hoyer, 1986).

Divided Attention

It has also been reported that there are age-related declines in divided attention (Madden & Plude, 1993; McDowd & Birren, 1990). **Divided attention** deficits are evident when there are problems in simultaneously processing multiple sources of information. In other words, doing two things at once, or having to pay attention to two things at the same time, would probably be more difficult for older adults than for younger adults. Generally, when we have to do two or more tasks at once, our performance on each of the tasks suffers; for example, when it might be difficult to track two conversations at the same time, or to concentrate on what we are reading while also listening to an interesting conversation. Divided attention deficits may be responsible for the difficulties that older drivers experience in some situations. For example, driving a car in heavy traffic in unfamiliar surroundings while looking for a specific road sign is an example of a real-life divided-attention task (Ponds, Brouwer, & Van Wolffelaar, 1988). Although it is frequently reported that there are age-related deficits in divided attention (e.g., Hartley, 1992; McDowd & Craik, 1988), older adults are not any worse than younger adults in relatively simple divided-attention situations (McDowd & Birren, 1990) or when initial age differences in nondivided attention are taken into account (Salthouse & Somberg, 1982). It can be concluded that age-related differences in divided attention emerge when performance in complex tasks is assessed, but age-related decrements are negligible when simple and relatively automatic tasks (such as those employed by Somberg and Salthouse) are used. In fact, McDowd and Craik suggested that overall task complexity, rather than the requirement to divide attention per se, may account for age-related performance decrements on divided-attention tasks. The ability to ignore or inhibit irrelevant information affects our performance in many kinds of tasks. One of the primary hypotheses in cognitive aging is that age decrements in inhibitory processes can account for many aspects of aging and cognitive functioning (e.g., Hartley, 1992; Hasher & Zacks, 1988).

Limited Attentional Resources

Age-related differences in attention have been described in terms of limitations in *general-purpose processing resources.* Although several kinds of evidence suggest that there are age-related limitations in processing resources, researchers must be careful to avoid circular explanations of aging phenomena. That is, age differences should *not* be attributed to a decline in some resource or capacity that cannot be measured. Perhaps the strongest evidence to suggest an age-related decline in processing resources comes from comparisons between **effortful information processing,** which is thought to draw on limited attentional capacity, and **automatic information processing,** which presumably does not draw on limited attentional capacity. In a study by Plude and Hoyer (1986), young and elderly women searched for two or four target letters in computer displays composed of one-, four-, or nine-letter arrays. Half of the women in each age group were placed in a *varied-mapping condition;* they looked for different target letters on different trials. The remaining women were included in a *consistent-mapping condition;* they looked for the same letters on all trials. There is good evidence that practice on the consistent-mapping procedure results in automatic processing, or processing that is independent of other demands on limited attentional capacity. Interestingly, Plude and Hoyer found only very small age-related differences in the consistent-mapping condition. In contrast, the varied-mapping condition, which demanded effortful processing, produced a large deficit in the elderly participants. The results support the contention that there are age-related differences in effortful processing, but no age differences or only small differences in the efficiency of automatic processing (see also Fisk & Rogers, 1991; Plude et al., 1983).

LEARNING

Pronounced age differences have been reported for many types of learning (e.g., see Hoyer & Lincourt, 1998; Kausler, 1994). For example, in an early study by Thorndike, Bregman, Tilton, and Woodyard (1928), right-handed young adults between the ages of 20 and 25 years and right-handed older adults between the ages of 35 and 57 years were given 15 hours of practice writing left-handed. Large age differences were found in the rate at which writing speed improved with practice. Recent studies of the effects of age on training of word processing skills have also revealed that the rate of learning is slower for older adults than for younger adults (e.g., Czaja & Sharit, 1993).

Recent studies addressing the processes that might account for age-related differences in learning have examined the effects of practice on the development of skilled cognitive performance (e.g., Fisk, Cooper, Hertzog, Anderson-Garlach, & Lee, 1995; Fisk, Hertzog, Lee, Rogers, & Anderson-Garlach, 1994; Hertzog, Cooper, & Fisk, 1996). The emphasis in this extensive work by Fisk, Hertzog, Rogers, and their colleagues has been to demonstrate that different mechanisms are involved in

Did I take my pills today? Older adults frequently rely on a mnemonic aid of some sort, such as a time-coded pill box, to help them keep track of complicated medical regimens.

memory search and visual search, and that these mechanisms show different age trends (but see Cerella, 1991). Younger and older adults show large and roughly equal gains as a result of consistent practice in memory search tasks. However, older adults and younger adults do not show equivalent gains, and older adults do not develop an *automatic attention response* to consistently mapped items in visual search tasks. Fisk, Hertzog, Rogers, and their colleagues suggested that the same learning mechanism, *memory set unitization,* operates effectively for both younger and older adults in memory search, whereas visual search, even with consistently mapped stimuli and responses, involves age-sensitive mechanisms that are different than those in memory search.

In other studies of adult age differences in learning, it has been reported that there is an age-related deficit in associative learning. That is, older adults require more presentations to learn and remember simple associations. Also, an age-related deficit in memory-based learning and in developing cognitive skills has been reported (e.g., Lincourt & Hoyer, 1996; Lincourt, Hoyer, & Cerella, 1997).

EXPLAINING THE EFFECTS OF AGING ON MEMORY, ATTENTION, AND LEARNING

We now turn our attention to three different approaches that have been developed to explain age-related memory deficits: biological, information processing, and contextual. Each of these approaches attempts to understand the aging of memory from a very different perspective or level of analysis. Consequently, these approaches should be viewed as necessarily antagonistic. A truly balanced understanding of age-related memory change is based on a researcher's ability to see the connections among these different perspectives.

Biological Approach

The **biological approach** maintains that age-related memory deficits may be traced to the deterioration of the brain. As we have already mentioned in chapter 3, several structural changes at the neuronal level, such as senile plaques and neurofibrillary tangles, accompany the aging process. Also, concentrations of neurotransmitters, including acetylcholine, diminish with age. These changes, along with cell death and atrophy, occur in varying degrees throughout the brain but are especially prominent within the frontal cortex. In fact, healthy older adults often make the same types of errors on neuropsychological tests as patients who suffer from frontal lobe damage.

There are several ways in which age-related deterioration of the frontal cortex explains the most prominent losses in explicit memory displayed by older adults. For example, Moscovitch (1994) has proposed that the hippocampus and frontal cortex are involved in the automatic retrieval and strategic retrieval of declarative memories, respectively. Automatic retrieval occurs when an individual is presented with a specific environmental cue such that a memory "spontaneously" pops into a person's mind. For example, seeing an ad in the newspaper for an Italian restaurant may automatically trigger off the recollection of the last time you and your friends had a pizza together. Strategic retrieval occurs when a person is not provided with any external cues or aids to jog their memory. In other words, individuals must develop an effortful strategy whereby they try to retrieve a particular memory. For example, you would have to develop a strategy to find the memory that answers the following question, "When was the last time you had a pizza with your friends?" This helps explain why age-related differences are greater in recall than recognition memory. The former task calls for strategic retrieval, whereas the latter could be performed by automatic retrieval.

The development of a strategy or a search mechanism that helps retrieve a declarative memory is a conscious, "on-line," and deliberate activity that calls for sustained attention and a steadfast goal-orientated focus. In other words, generating and using a successful retrieval strategy may be conceptualized as a working memory task that places great demands on the central executive. As you would guess, the frontal cortex (not the hippocampus) regulates this aspect of working memory (Fuster, 1991; Schacter, 1996).

Recently, Schacter, Savage, Alpert, Rauch, and Albert (1996) used the PET methodology to examine some of the claims made by Moscovitch. These researchers found that blood flow increased to frontal lobes when individuals tried to search for a memory (strategic retrieval), whereas blood flow increased to the hippocampus when a memory was actually recollected (associative retrieval). Furthermore, their data showed that older adults showed less activation of frontal cortex during strategic retrieval than did younger adults. Age differences in blood flow to hippocampus were found to be minimal. This suggests that age differences in memory are found when strategic retrieval is called for, and that age declines in the frontal cortex underlie age differences in strategic retrieval.

Another important aspect of the frontal cortex is that it is responsible for coding information about the context (e.g., the time and place) within which events occur (Schacter, 1996; Squire, 1987). The most salient age-related memory deficit associated with this aspect of frontal lobe function is a breakdown of source memory.

On a more positive note, several aspects of nondeclarative (or implicit memory) do not exhibit age-related declines. This is because the Perceptual Representation System, which underlies performance implicit tasks and is located in posterior cortical regions such as occipital lobe, is largely unaffected by the aging process (Schacter, 1996).

Information-Processing Approach

The **information-processing approach** emphasizes the kinds of cognitive processes involved in performing different kinds of memory tasks. That is, some researchers have focused on the nature of age differences in the encoding, storage, and retrieval aspects of memory (Craik, Govoni, Naveh-Benjamin, & Anderson, 1996). Encoding refers to the registration or pickup of information. Storage refers to the retention of information in memory. Retrieval refers to finding or using information in memory. From a memory processing perspective, researchers are trying to understand the factors that are associated with age differences in the efficiency of encoding, storage, and retrieval. Interestingly, there is a large amount of evidence to suggest an age-related encoding deficit, and an equally large amount of evidence to suggest an age-related retrieval deficit. An **encoding deficit** suggests that elderly persons are less capable of engaging in the organizational, elaborative, and imagery processes that are helpful in memory tasks. A **retrieval deficit** implies that older adults cannot develop the strategies that would help them find stored information.

Current research using the PET methodology has increased our understanding of the nature of encoding and retrieval processes. For example, Nyberg, Cabeza, and Tulving (1996) have shown that younger adults display a very specific pattern such as blood flow increases in the left and right frontal cortex during encoding and retrieval, respectively. Interesting, several researchers (Cabeza et al., 1997; Grady et al., 1995) have consistently shown that older adults exhibit more diffuse and unorganized patterns of neural activation during encoding and retrieval. This suggests that aging is associated with both encoding and retrieval deficits.

Another line of research within the information-processing perspective is illustrated by the work of Tim Salthouse (1992, 1996, 1997). Salthouse has examined the influence of mediating variables that are correlated with age on memory performance. Salthouse's research strategy is illustrated in figure 7.9.

The three circles in figure 7.9 signify age, the mediating variable, and memory performance. Of crucial importance are the two areas of overlap: a and b. A represents the extent to which age is related to memory performance independent of the mediating variable; whereas b represents the extent to which performance on the mediating variable is related to memory performance independent of age. In other words, this

Figure 7.9 Venn diagram showing the logic of using the correlational method to determine common variance among age, memory, and a mediating construct. The overlap in circles represents shared variance. *Source: Smith, A. D., & Earles, J. K. L. (1996). Memory changes in normal aging. In F. Blanchard-Fields & T. M. Hess (Eds.), Perspective on cognitive change in adulthood and aging (p. 210). New York: McGraw-Hill.*

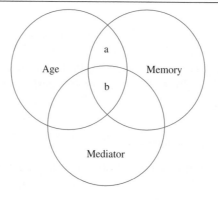

a = Proportion of variance in memory associated with age but not mediated by mediator

b = Proportion of age-related variance in memory performance mediated by mediator

methodology allows us to determine if, after we control for the mediating variable, age still shares a significant relationship with memory.

Smith and Earles (1996) reviewed several studies that used the above-mentioned technique to examine the relationship between age and memory performance. They concluded that noncognitive mediators such as years of education and self-reported health status did very little to attenuate the relationship between age and memory. However, when cognitive mediators were considered, a very different picture emerged. For example, Anderson and Earles (1996) reviewed several studies that showed that age differences in both working memory and free recall are mediated by processing speed (i.e., the ability to perform very simple cognitive operations like matching abstract symbols to different numbers ($+ = 3$, $* = 7$, $\approx = 4$, etc.). And, as you will see in chapter 8, a great deal of the relationship between age and various facets of IQ performance may be mediated by perceptual speed. It seems that performance on measures of perceptual speed give us clues about the basic efficacy of the mind and brain.

Contextual Approach

The **contextual approach** suggests that age differences in memory be explained by understanding the relationship between the characteristics of the memory task and the characteristics of the individual performing the task. Many characteristics of the person apart from age can determine performance in memory tasks. These characteristics include: attitudes, interests, health-related factors, intellectual abilities, and styles of learning.

Craik, Byrd, and Swanson (1987) performed an experiment that was inspired by the contextual approach. They studied memory ability in three groups of elderly people who ranged from 64 to 88 years of age. Group 1 consisted of highly intelligent and relatively affluent individuals. Group 2 was composed of individuals somewhat lower in intelligence and socioeconomic status who were actively involved in the community. Group 3 consisted of individuals of lower intelligence and socioeconomic status who were not involved in community or social affairs. Furthermore, Craik et al. studied a group of college students matched on verbal intelligence with the first group of elderly participants. All participants received lists of words to remember. The participants differed, however, in the number of cues (i.e., contextual support) they were given at encoding and/or retrieval. Some participants were provided cues when they were initially presented with each word on a list (e.g., "a type of bird—*lark*") but not during recall. Other participants were given this cue during recall but not during presentation; others were cued during both presentation and recall; and still others were not cued during either presentation or recall. The extent of age-related differences in memory was found to depend on the amount of support offered in the task and the characteristics of the persons performing the task. Among the participants who received the greatest degree of support (cued presentation and cued recall), all of the elderly groups with the exception of group 3 (low IQ, low socioeconomic class) performed just as well as the college students. Among the participants who received an

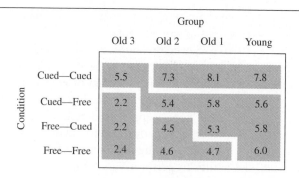

Figure 7.10 Word recall scores grouped into four levels of performance.

	Old 3	Old 2	Old 1	Young
Cued—Cued	5.5	7.3	8.1	7.8
Cued—Free	2.2	5.4	5.8	5.6
Free—Cued	2.2	4.5	5.3	5.8
Free—Free	2.4	4.6	4.7	6.0

intermediate amount of support (noncued presentation and cued recall), only the first elderly group performed as well as the college students. When participants were not provided with any support (noncued presentation and noncued recall), the college students performed better than all of the elderly groups. Figure 7.10 illustrates the different levels of performance for the participants.

NORMAL VERSUS PATHOLOGICAL MEMORY LOSS

Until now we have focused mainly on the description of age differences in cognition in healthy adults. Older adults who are in good health and who do not have any debilitating disease usually exhibit only minor declines in their everyday cognitive functions. As individuals age, however, some diseases that produce memory loss and deficits in other aspects of cognitive function are more likely to occur. For example, AD, which produces progressive and severe memory and attentional losses is more likely to occur in late life than in midlife.

It is important to differentiate normal memory loss from memory loss due to AD and other kinds of dementia. The nonpathological loss of memory in the normal elderly has been labeled as **benign senescent forgetfulness.** This type of memory impairment is benign because it does not interfere with a person's ability to function in everyday life. Some adults notice a decrease in memory ability as early as 50 to 60 years of age, although it is more common to become aware of memory problems after 60 years of age. In many instances, the elderly become very concerned about their self-recognized memory loss. They want to know if their failing memory is normal for their age or a sign of an abnormal disease process. Schacter (1996) has given some general advice about how to distinguish normal from pathological memory loss. He stated that, ". . . the next time you forget where you put your car keys, you need not worry that you are headed for Alzheimer's. Nor do you need to become concerned the next time you fail to come up with the name of a friend that feels like it is on the tip of your tongue. But if you forget that you possess a car or you can't remember your own name, then there is clearly cause for concern" (p. 285).

Read (1987) identified at what points memory problems can occur in information processing. First, Read suggested that the ability to recall events from the recent past can be negatively affected by (1) lack of attention to or a difficulty in understanding what has happened (an encoding deficit), (2) a failure to store the event, or (3) difficulty retrieving events already stored in memory. Second, Read argued that the benign memory loss observed in normal elderly adults is caused by a combination of mild deficits in encoding and retrieval, not by an inability to store information. Third, he suggested that among elderly adults with depression, poor memory performance stems from both encoding and retrieval deficits that are more severe than those found in the normal elderly. Depressed individuals, for example, may be so preoccupied that they do not expend the effort to encode new information in a meaningful way; and even if they encode and store information, they make little effort to retrieve it. Fourth, Read argued that in AD the major cause of memory loss is the brain's inability to store information. Memory loss in patients with AD should persist, therefore, even if they engage in meaningful encoding processes and are given the utmost support during retrieval. Note that Read does not deny that adults with AD experience severe deficits in both encoding and retrieval. Rather, the thrust of Read's argument is that storage deficits are unique to patients with AD.

A distinction can be made between apparent memory deficits and genuine memory deficits (Grober & Buschke, 1987). **Apparent memory deficits** are memory problems resulting from the use of ineffective encoding and retrieval strategies. Apparent memory deficits can be overcome by inducing individuals to process information in an effective way or by providing individuals with effective retrieval aids. **Genuine memory deficits** are memory problems that persist even after individuals have carried out effective encoding and retrieval activities. In other words, genuine memory deficits are largely irreversible (Grober & Buschke, 1987). In contrast, nondemented individuals (both normal elderly and depressives) would be more likely to experience apparent memory deficits than genuine memory deficits. See Research Focus 7.4 for more information about how Grober and Buschke distinguished between apparent versus genuine memory deficits.

Hart, Kwentus, Hamer, and Taylor (1987) reported that depressed elderly patients, but not patients with AD, displayed better memory scores when they were given support while encoding and retrieving information. This finding is consistent with the idea that memory loss in depressed individuals is more apparent than genuine, and that depressives are more likely to display better memory when they are placed in a supportive context. Even with the extra help, however, depressed patients were found, on the whole, to remember less than the normal elderly.

Another important distinction between normal elderly and depressed elderly centers around the different response bias displayed by both of these groups (Niederehe, 1986). Depressed elderly people have been found to display a conservative response bias on memory-recognition tasks. When they are unsure about a test item, the depressed elderly are likely to respond, "I can't remember," whereas normal elderly individuals are more likely to take chances and guess. In fact, Niederehe (1986) has argued that differences in response bias may be the single most important characteristic in differentiating normal from depressed elderly. More information about the differences between dementia and depression is presented later in the text.

Memory Abilities in Normal and Demented Elderly

Ellen Grober and Herman Buschke (1987) developed a methodology that distinguishes between genuine memory deficits and apparent memory deficits. In the controlled-learning component of their paradigm, groups of normal and demented elderly were given a list of 16 common items drawn from different conceptual categories. The items were presented four at a time on four different sheets of paper. Each item was presented as a picture (e.g., a bunch of grapes) with the name of the item boldly printed above the picture (e.g., GRAPES). The participants were given the name of a conceptual category (in this case, "fruit") and were told to point to and name the picture on the card that corresponded to the category. After identifying all four items on a sheet of paper, the participants were given an immediate recall task in which they had to recollect the names of the four items they had just identified. If a participant could not recall the items, the sheet of paper was re-presented, the identification procedure was repeated, and the participant was given another chance to recall the item. This entire procedure was repeated again if necessary. Then, the remaining 12 items (four items drawn and labeled on three different sheets of paper) were presented, identified, and recalled in the same manner. All of these controlled-learning procedures ensured that the participants attended to all of the items, briefly stored the items, and could immediately recall the items.

Twenty seconds after the controlled-learning phase was over, the participants were given three separate recall trials for the entire 16 items. Each recall trial consisted of two distinct tasks: a free recall task and a cued-recall task. During the free recall task, participants were allowed two minutes to remember as many of the 16 items as possible. In the cued-recall task, participants were provided with conceptual cues for the items they did not remember in the free recall task. (For example, a researcher might ask, "What was the type of fruit pictured on the card?") Two different types of recall scores were obtained for each participant: a free recall score and a total recall score.

Box Figure 7.B Free recall (open circles) and total recall (closed circles) of sixteen unrelated pictures by normal elderly adults and by elderly patients with dementia. Total recall is obtained by adding items from cued recall to the number remembered from free recall. *Source: Data from E. Grober and H. Buschke, "Genuine Memory Deficits in Dementia" in Developmental Neuropsychology 3:13–36, 1987.*

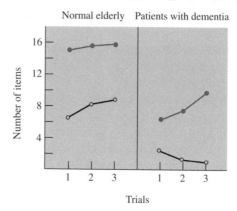

The free recall score represented the number of items retrieved without cues on each trial. The total recall score consisted of the total number of items recalled on each trial by both free recall and cued-recall methods.

Grober and Buschke (1987) reasoned that the total recall score should provide a valid estimate of the total number of items stored in memory and potentially available for recall. Thus, a participant's total recall score, rather than free recall score, should be a better predictor of whether he or she belonged to the normal or demented group.

SUMMARY

In this chapter, we have described age-related changes in memory. The capacity of short-term memory does not undergo significant change with age. However, age-related deficits in working-memory tasks and in the speed of short-term memory search have been reported. Older adults perform more poorly than young adults on tasks of long-term memory, especially when episodic rather than semantic memory is tested. Memory in the elderly is more robust when it is measured by implicit rather than explicit memory tasks.

When older adults are instructed to use efficient encoding strategies, older adults show an improvement in their ability to remember. Age-related differences in memory are unlikely to occur when older adults draw upon previous knowledge to help them

Box Figure 7.C Free recall (open circles) and total recall (closed circles) by (A) a normal 89-year-old man, (B) a normal 87-year-old woman, and (C) an 86-year-old woman with Alzheimer's disease. *Source: Data from E. Grober and H. Buschke, "Genuine Memory Deficits in Dementia" in Developmental Neuropsychology 3:13–36, 1987.*

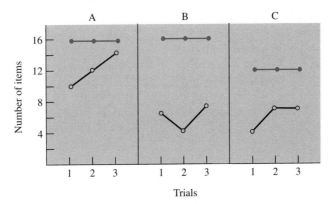

The results of the study were straightforward. First, as can be seen in box figure 7.B, free recall dramatically underrepresents the amount of learning and memory that has taken place in both the normal and demented groups. Box figure 7.B also shows that the normal group, because they had near-perfect total memory scores, had stored all 16 test items. The demented group, on the other hand, stored only about one-half of the 16 items.

From the evidence illustrated in box figure 7.B, it appears that knowledge of either a participant's free or total recall score should be equally useful in predicting if he is demented. The data portrayed in box figure 7.C, however, indicate this is not the case—total recall is better than free recall at distinguishing normal from demented elderly. More specifically, box figure 7.C

shows the free and total recall scores of three participants. Graph A represents the scores of an 89-year-old normal participant who had exceptionally good free recall. Graph B represents the scores of an 87-year-old normal participant who had an average range of free recall scores. Graph C represents the scores on an 86-year-old patient with AD whose free recall scores are almost identical to those shown in graph B. The normal participants (A and B) had perfect total recall scores, while person B and the demented person (C) had identical free recall scores but differed in total recall. In other words, total recall proved to be a better indicator of dementia because normal elderly, but not demented patients, displayed near-perfect performance on the total recall score regardless of their free recall scores.

remember. Researchers try to explain age-related changes in memory using three perspectives. The biological perspective suggests that the age-related deterioration of the brain causes decrements in memory. The information-processing perspective suggests that age-related changes in memory are the result of strategy differences for encoding and retrieving information. The contextual perspective stresses the relationship between the task, the person, and the environment.

With aging, there may be a normal decline in the ability to remember information. This type of benign senescent forgetfulness does not seriously affect an older adult's ability to function in everyday life. Psychologists have developed behavioral techniques that help distinguish normal from pathological memory loss.

REVIEW QUESTIONS

1. Discuss the accuracy of older adults' self-perceptions of their memory.
2. Compare and contrast short-term and working memory. What type of memory is more likely to be affected by aging?
3. In general, what are the major assumptions of multiple memory systems theory?
4. Describe the differences between declarative and nondeclarative memory, episodic and semantic memory, and implicit and explicit memory.
5. What types of memory systems and/or memory tasks are spared (or impaired) by aging? What factors are responsible for the observed pattern of age-related preservation (or impairment) in memory?
6. Why are psychologists interested in comparing the performance of younger versus older adults on priming tasks?
7. Explain the advantages associated with using the "Process Dissociation Procedure" in the study of memory aging.
8. Compare and contrast the biological, information-processing, and contextual approaches to the study of age-related memory changes. Is one of these perspectives more useful or valid than the others?
9. What is benign senescent forgetfulness?
10. Explain the differences between the memory impairments that occur in the normal elderly versus those that occur in someone who has a dementia such as AD.

FOR FURTHER READING

Howard, J. L., & Howard, D. V. (1996). The aging of implicit and explicit memory. In F. Blanchard-Fields & T. M. Hess (Eds.), *Perspectives on cognitive change in adulthood and aging* (pp. 221–254). New York: McGraw-Hill.

Jacoby, L. L., Jennings, J. M., & Hay, J. F. (1996). Dissociating automatic from consciously-controlled prosesses: Implications for the diagnosis and treatment of memory disorders. In D. J. Herrmann, C. L. McEvoy, C. Hertzog, P. Hertrel, & M. K. Johnson (Eds.). *Basic and applied memory research: Theory in context,* (Vol 1, pp. 161–193). Hillsdale, NJ: Erlbaum.

Rybash, J. M. (1996). Aging and implicit memory: A cognitive neuropsychological perspective. *Developmental Neuropsychology, 12,* 127–178.

Schacter, D. L. (1996). *Searching for memory: The brain, the mind, and the past.* New York: Basic Books.

Smith, A. D., & Earles, J. L. (1996). Memory changes in normal aging. In F. Blanchard-Fields & T. M. Hess (Eds.), *Perspectives on cognitive change in adulthood and aging* (pp. 192–220). New York: McGraw-Hill.

INTELLIGENCE AND CREATIVITY

> *In the desert there is no sign that says, Thou shalt not eat stones.*
> —Sufi Proverb
>
> *Intelligence is what makes people hungry to know.*
> —Anonymous

INTRODUCTION

This is the second of the three chapters that focus on adult cognitive development. In this chapter we consider the **psychometric approach,** a measurement-based view that has sparked debate on the definition and assessment of intelligence. How and why does intelligence change during adult years? We summarize the research examining the effects of physical health and generational (or cohort) influences on adult intelligence. In this chapter, we discuss the relationship between scores on intelligence tests and performance in everyday situations. Next, we examine creativity. We examine the differences between creativity and intelligence and chart the developmental course of creativity over the adult years. Last, we examine the relationships between aging, intelligence, education, and work. How do age-related changes in intelligence affect occupational productivity during the adult years?

THE PSYCHOMETRIC APPROACH

The term *psychometric* literally means "the measurement of the mind." Psychometricians construct and validate various tests that measure a number of relatively enduring characteristics of the individual. It seems safe to say that the greatest emphasis in psychometric research has been placed on the measurement of human intelligence. Before we summarize the main results of the studies of age-related changes in intelligence, however, we try to describe what intelligence is, and how it is studied.

The Nature of Intelligence

Intelligence is a concept that is easy to understand but hard to define. The word *intelligence* is derived from the Latin words that mean "to choose between" and "to make wise choices." But how can a researcher objectively measure if an individual has made a wise choice? Is there a measurable as well as meaningful definition of intelligence?

One of the questions concerning the nature of intelligence is whether it is a single or unitary ability or a collection of a number of independent mental abilities. In the earlier part of this century, Charles Spearman (1927) argued that intelligence was a single ability that an individual could apply to any task. Spearman called this unitary ability the **g factor**—g—for "general capacity." Spearman assumed that because of the g factor, an individual performs at roughly the same level of proficiency regardless of the type of task he or she is doing. A college student with a high level of g would demonstrate excellent grades in most or all of his or her courses. The notion that intelligence is best conceptu-

TABLE 8.1

The Primary Mental Abilities

Verbal comprehension: The principal factor in such tests as reading comprehension, verbal analogies, disarranged sentences, verbal reasoning, and proverb matching. It is most adequately measured by vocabulary tests.

Word fluency: Found in such tests as anagrams, rhyming, or naming words in a given category (e.g., boys' names or words beginning with the letter *T*).

Number: Most closely identified with speed and accuracy of simple arithmetic computation.

Space (or spatial orientation): May represent two distinct factors, one covering perception of fixed spatial or geometric relations, the other manipulatory visualizations in which changed positions or transformations must be visualized.

Associative memory: Found principally in tests demanding rote memory for paired associates. There is some evidence to suggest that this factor may reflect the extent to which memory crutches are utilized. The evidence is against the presence of a broader factor through all memory tests. Other restricted memory factors, such as memory for temporal sequences and for spatial position, have been suggested by some investigations.

Perceptual speed: Quick and accurate grasping of visual details, similarities, and differences.

Induction (or general reasoning): Early researchers proposed an inductive and a deductive factor. The latter was best measured by tests of syllogistic reasoning and the former by tests requiring the subject to find a rule, as in a number series completion test. Evidence for the deductive factor, however, was much weaker than for the inductive. Moreover, other investigators suggested a general reasoning factor, best measured by arithmetic reasoning tests.

From Macmillan Publishing Company, Psychological Testing, *6th ed., by Anne Anastasi. Copyright © 1988 by Anne Anastasi.*

alized as a single, general ability was also held by Alfred Binet. Binet was the French psychologist who developed the first intelligence assessment in 1906. Today, Spearman and Binet would be likely to conceptualize intelligence as a very general and abstract computer program. This program would be so general that it could be applied, with the same degree of success, to any problem it was called upon to solve. Other psychologists have suggested that intelligence consists of a number of separate, independent mental abilities. This position was originally advocated by Thurstone (1938), who proposed that there are a small number of **primary mental abilities.** For Thurstone, these primary mental abilities were verbal comprehension, word fluency, number, space, associative memory, perceptual speed, and induction or general reasoning. These abilities are described in table 8.1. K. Warner Schaie adapted Thurstone's test for use with older adults, and the **Schaie-Thurstone Adult Mental Abilities Test** (Schaie, 1985) has been used in many studies of adult intellectual development. Applying the computer analogy, Schaie would take the view that intelligence consists of a number of separate computer programs, each designed to carry out a particular kind of task.

Some psychometricians have even gone a step further than Thurstone and Schaie. They believe there are more basic components of intelligence than these psychologists originally envisioned. Ekstrom, French, and Harman (1979), for example, have isolated 29 separate mental abilities. And Guilford (1959, 1967) has argued for the existence of an astonishing 120 independent components of intelligence!

John Horn (1982; Horn & Noll, 1994) pointed out that a model based on a large number of mental abilities (e.g., 29 or 120) is too unwieldy. He suggested that it is difficult, if not impossible, to represent a large number of mental abilities in an internally consistent, parsimonious, coherent, and empirically sound fashion. For this reason, Horn has argued for the existence of two highly abstract components of intelligence that subsume the various primary mental abilities. These two abstract components are crystallized intelligence and fluid intelligence. **Crystallized intelligence** roughly represents the extent to which individuals have incorporated the valued knowledge of their culture. It is measured by a large inventory of behaviors that reflect the breadth of culturally valued knowledge and experience, the comprehension of communications, and the development of judgment, understanding, and reasonable thinking in everyday affairs. Some of the primary mental abilities associated with crystallized intelligence are verbal comprehension, concept formation, logical reasoning, and induction. Tests used to measure the crystallized factor include vocabulary, simple analogies, remote associations, and social judgment.

Fluid intelligence represents an individual's "pure" ability to perceive, remember, and think about a wide variety of basic information. In other words, fluid intelligence involves mental abilities that are not imparted by one's culture. Abilities included under the heading of fluid intelligence are seeing relationships among patterns, drawing inferences from relationships, and comprehending implications. Some of the primary mental abilities that best reflect this factor are number, space, and perceptual speed. Tasks measuring fluid intelligence include letter series, matrices, and spatial orientation. It has been suggested that fluid intelligence represents the integrity of the central nervous system (Horn, 1982). See figure 8.1 to gain a better understanding of the differences between crystallized and fluid intelligence. This figure contains a number of sample tasks that measure both of these types of intelligence.

Self-Conceptions of Intelligence

In the previous section, we examined different views about the structure of intelligence. What seems to be lacking in the psychological literature, however, is a thorough examination of peoples' intuitive beliefs about intelligence and how different facets of intelligence change across the adult years. One of the first empirical studies to address this topic was conducted by Heckhausen, Dixon, and Baltes (1989). These researchers presented 102 adults between the ages of 20 to 85 with a list of 358 adjectives that characterized a broad range of intellectual (intelligent), personality (skeptical), and social (friendly) attributes. With each of these three categories there were approximately equal numbers of desirable (wise) and undesirable (forgetful) traits. Participants were asked to rate (1) the extent to which each attribute is expected to increase at any period from 20 to 90 years of age; (2) the extent to which an increase in an attribute is desirable; and (3) the age at which the increase in a specific attribute begins and ends. Increases in desirable and undesirable traits were characterized as developmental gains and losses, respectively. Results (see figure 8.2) reflected the common theme that gains outweighed losses except for the oldest-old. Contrary to the negative aging stereotype, these data reflect a fair amount of optimism about the nature of adult developmental change. More interestingly, the oldest participants in this study (aged 60–85) were more likely than younger and middle-aged adults to view adult development as a complex multifaceted process, which, in itself, is an indicator of cognitive sophistication.

Fluid intelligence

Matrices Indicate the figure that completes the matrix.

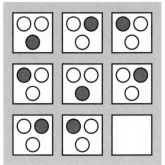

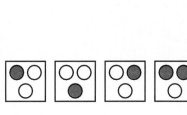

Figure 8.1
Examples of test
items that measure
fluid and
crystallized
intelligence.

Letter series Decide which letter comes next in the series.
A   D   G   J   M   P   ?

Topology Find the figure on the right where the dot can be placed in the same
relation to the triangle, square, and circle as in the example on the left.

Crystallized intelligence

Analogies Fill in the blank.
Atom is to _____ as cell is to organism.

Remote associations What one word is well associated with the words *bathtub,
prizefighting,* and *wedding*?

Judgment You notice that a fire has just started in a crowded cafe.
What should one do to prevent death and injury?

Somewhat similar findings have been reported by Berg and Sternberg (1992). They required groups of young (aged 22–40), middle-aged (aged 41–59), and older adults (aged 60–85) to rate a list of 55 behaviors (is inquisitive, acts responsibly, displays good vocabulary, etc.) in terms of which each behavior was representative of an individual of either 30, 50, or 70 years of age who possesses exceptional intelligence. Results showed that participants in all three age groups perceived intelligence as characterized by three independent dimensions: ability to deal with novelty, everyday competence, and verbal competence. Furthermore, all participants rated behaviors indicative of everyday competence and verbal competence to be more representative of 50- and 70-year-olds than 30-year-olds, whereas behaviors reflective of ability to deal with novelty showed the opposite developmental trend.

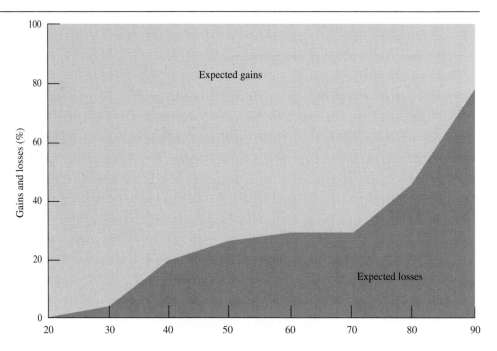

Figure 8.2 Age-related pattern involving 163 psychological attributes: expected gains (increase in desirable attributes) and losses (increase in undesirable attributes) across the adult life span. *Source: Data from Heckhausen, Dixon, & P. Baltes, 1989.*

Overall, it seems that adults have a rather multidimensional and optimistic conceptualization of intellectual change. Psychometricians would be wise to develop standardized instruments that capture the intellectual gains, especially those involving everyday competence in interpersonal affairs, as well as the losses that accompany the aging process.

The Measurement of Intelligence

It is one thing to develop a theory of intelligence and another thing to develop a valid and reliable test or measure of intelligence. A psychometrician must consider several factors in developing an intelligence test. First, it is important to realize that intelligence does not really exist! Intelligence is a **hypothetical construct** rather than a real entity. It is not possible, for example, to look inside the brain of an individual and see the amount of intelligence she possesses in the same way that one can look inside a refrigerator to see the amount of food stored there. This means that psychometric tests must measure intelligence indirectly by examining performance on tasks that depend on the generation and application of intelligent behavior.

A second factor psychometricians must consider, since intelligence cannot be directly measured by any psychometric test, is that intelligence test performance is influenced by many factors other than intelligence. These factors include personality characteristics, motivation, educational background, anxiety, fatigue, and so on. Despite the influence of these extraneous factors, however, psychometricians still assume that intelligence tests primarily measure intelligence.

TABLE 8.2

Subtests of the WAIS

Verbal Scale

Information: Answer questions about general information. For example, who is John Glenn? Or, name five classical or modern famous painters and five classical or modern famous musicians or composers.

Comprehension: Answer questions about social circumstances, or explain the meaning of proverbs or quotations. For example, explain why there is a legal drinking age. Explain what it means when people say, "Don't count your chickens before they hatch."

Arithmetic: Solve simple arithmetic word problems. If Paul has $20.00, and he buys two sandwiches that cost $5.97 each, how much change does he receive?

Similarities: Explain how two things or concepts are similar. For example, describe in what ways are a pencil and a tree alike.

Digit span: Listen to a series of numbers, then repeat the numbers in the same order in which they were presented (forward span), and in the reverse order in which they were presented (backward span).

Vocabulary: Define the meanings of words. For example, what does "perfidious" mean?

Performance Scale

Digit symbol substitution: Write down symbols that are paired with numbers using a key or code showing the pairings of symbols and numbers. The person's score is the number of symbol substitutions completed in 90 seconds.

Picture completion: Identify a missing part of a picture.

Block design: Arrange blocks having different patterns of colors to form a design that is identical to a design shown by the examiner.

Picture arrangement: Arrange a set of cards into a logical sequence.

Object assembly: Arrange cut up pieces to form a familiar object.

Note: The examples are intended to illustrate the types of questions that appear on the WAIS subtests, are not actual questions from the WAIS.

A third consideration for psychometricians to remember in developing an intelligence test is that it is necessary to present individuals with a wide variety of tasks to evaluate whether intelligence is a single ability such as a g factor or a number of independent abilities. This is why contemporary intelligence tests consist of a number of different scales or subtests. One of the most commonly used tests to measure adult intelligence is the **Wechsler Adult Intelligence Scale (WAIS).** This test consists of 11 subtests. Six of the subtests compose a verbal scale. These subtests include general information, digit span, vocabulary, arithmetic, comprehension, and similarities. The items on this scale require a strong language component. The remaining five subtests make up a performance scale. The subtests on this scale include picture completion, picture arrangement, block design, object assembly, and digit symbol substitution. On this scale, a person is required to make a nonverbal response (e.g., arranging a number of pictures in a logical sequence so as to tell a story) after a careful appraisal of each problem. Table 8.2 contains a brief description of all of the subtests on both the verbal and performance scales of the WAIS.

Another thing to consider in developing intelligence tests is that although we can construct tests that possess a large number of subtests, this does not necessarily mean that each subtest measures a different aspect of intelligence. Each subtest might measure the same mental ability, the g factor for example, but in a different way. To determine whether the various subtests of an intelligence test are measuring a single ability or a number of special abilities, researchers developed the technique of factor analysis. **Factor analysis** (discussed later in appendix A) is a statistical procedure used to determine how scores on a large number of tasks intercorrelate (or fail to intercorrelate) with one another. Using the method of factor analysis, Thurstone discovered the different primary mental abilities. Cattell and Horn also used factor analytic procedures to discern the difference between crystallized and fluid intelligence.

Finally, it is important to understand how a person's IQ score is calculated. The first intelligence tests were constructed solely for children and young adolescents. On these tests, IQ was computed by multiplying the ratio of mental age to chronological age by 100 ($IQ = MA/CA \times 100$). A child's mental age was measured by the items passed on the IQ test. For example, if a child passed all of the items that a typical 6-year-old could pass but could not pass any of the items solved by children 7 years of age and above, a mental age of 6 years was assigned to that child. Then the child's IQ could be computed by determining the ratio between mental age and chronological age and multiplying by 100. For example, if the child with a mental age of 6 is 6 years old chronologically, the child's IQ is 100 ($IQ = 6/6 \times 100$). Thus, an average IQ, regardless of the age of the person tested, is always 100.

Psychometricians discovered that it was very easy to classify the mental ages of children. However, the concept of mental age broke down when applied to adults. It is relatively easy to develop questions that distinguish between children with mental ages of 6 and 7, but it is impossible to develop questions that distinguish between adults with mental ages of 66 and 67. The IQ formula used for children could thus not be used to determine adult intelligence. To resolve this problem two approaches were taken. The first approach, which is no longer used today, was to assign a mental age of no greater than 16 to adults' IQ test items. This approach wrongly assumed that little, if any, development in intelligence occurs beyond midadolescence. The second approach, the one adopted by contemporary psychologists, is to determine an adult's IQ by comparing the number of correct answers a person achieves on the whole test to people of the same chronological age. A score of 100 is arbitrarily assigned to those performing at the average for their age group, while IQs greater or less than 100 are assigned according to the degree of statistical deviation from this average.

Using this scoring system, it is possible for different-aged adults to perform in a manner identical to one another yet receive radically different IQ scores. To take a simple example, suppose that the average 25-year-old can pass 65 questions on an IQ test while the average 75-year-old can pass 45 questions on the same test. Thus, a 25-year-old who passed 55 questions would be assessed to have a below-average IQ, while a 75-year-old who passed 55 questions would be assessed as having an above-average IQ. This discovery leads to an interesting question. What should we pay closest attention to when we conduct research on developmental changes in adult intelligence? Should we focus on the raw scores (the total number of questions correctly answered) obtained by different-aged adults or on the adjusted IQ scores (the comparison of the raw score to the average score for a particular age group) for different-aged adults? It seems that examining raw scores would provide more valuable information about developmental changes in test performance than examining the adjusted scores (the IQ scores). Significant changes in test performance would most certainly be obscured if we focused attention on the IQ scores alone.

DEVELOPMENTAL CHANGES IN INTELLIGENCE

There is no doubt that the raw scores that adults obtain on intelligence tests decline with age. However, the age at which decrements in IQ test performance first begin, as well as the magnitude of the decline, depends on the research design employed to measure developmental change. In this section we compare the results of various cross-sectional and longitudinal studies of adult intellectual development. Overall, we will see that declines in intelligence (1) occur much later than was earlier thought, (2) affect a smaller number of individuals than was earlier thought, and (3) affect a smaller number of intellectual abilities than was earlier thought.

Cross-Sectional Studies

Initially, a number of cross-sectional studies (Garret, 1957; Jones & Conrad, 1933; Wechsler, 1939) showed that raw or unadjusted scores on intelligence tests decreased with age. Decrements in test scores began in late adolescence and early adulthood (at about 20 years of age) and steadily continued over the remainder of the life span. These results suggested that intelligence peaked in early life, and this conclusion was not at all surprising to the psychologists of this era. At this point in time, you will remember, psychologists held a child-focused perspective on developmental change that assumed that adulthood can only be characterized by the decline of intellectual abilities.

A few researchers began to notice that adults displayed a steeper rate of decline on some types of intellectual tasks in comparison to others. For example, Wechsler (1958, 1972) and Siegler (1983) reported that with increasing age, the scores on performance subtests of the WAIS declined more rapidly than the scores on the verbal subtests. It should be noted, however, that performance subtests are speeded while verbal subtests are nonspeeded. A speeded subtest is one in which individuals must make their responses as quickly as possible, while in a nonspeeded test, individuals are allowed to take their time answering items. These data suggest that speed of responding may underlie the poor performance of the elderly on nonverbal tasks. However, many older adults continue to perform poorly on the performance subtests of the WAIS even if given unlimited time to respond (Botwinick, 1977).

The conclusion that various components of intelligence decline at different rates has been illustrated, rather nicely, by a study conducted by Schaie and Willis (1993). These researchers administered a battery of tasks that measured the primary mental abilities of inductive reasoning, space, number, verbal comprehension, speed perception, and associative memory to 1,628 community-dwelling adults between 20 to 90 years of age. The results of this study are depicted in figure 8.3. Three findings are noteworthy.

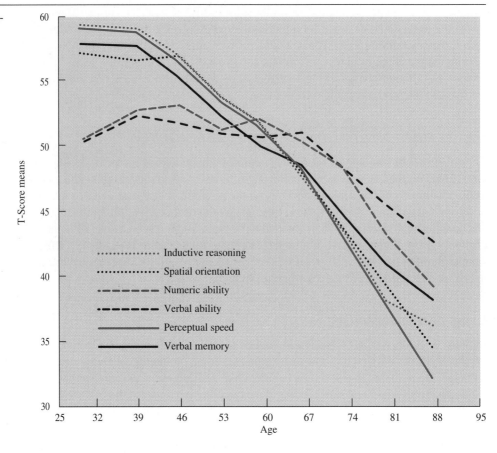

Figure 8.3 Cross-sectional age differences in several primary mental abilities.

First, there are age-related decrements in all of the primary mental abilities. Second, verbal comprehension is least affected by age, whereas perceptual speed is the most affected by age. Third, after midlife, performance on the different mental abilities becomes more variable.

Similarly, when the developmental changes in crystallized and fluid intelligence are analyzed in a cross-sectional manner, an interesting pattern emerges. With advancing age, crystallized intelligence shows increases up until the sixth decade of life (Horn, 1982, Horn & Donaldson, 1976). On the other hand, fluid intelligence exhibits a steady decline beginning in early adulthood. The net effect is that the increases in crystallized intelligence tend to cancel out the decreases in fluid intelligence. Therefore, if one did not make a distinction between crystallized and fluid abilities, one would conclude that intelligence, as a general ability, remains relatively stable until the onset of late adulthood. Figure 8.4 contains a schematic representation of the relationship between crystallized intelligence, fluid intelligence, and general intelligence.

In summary, cross-sectional research seems to indicate that intellectual and physical development follow the same pattern of steady decline—a pattern of irreversible decrement. Furthermore, it has been consistently shown that scores on non-

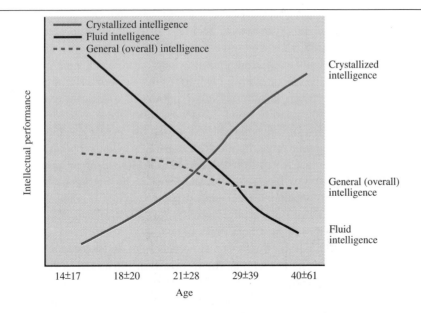

Figure 8.4 Age-related changes in crystallized intelligence, fluid intelligence, and general intelligence from adolescence to older adulthood.

Within the figure:
- Crystallized intelligence
- Fluid intelligence
- General (overall) intelligence

Intellectual performance (y-axis)

Age (x-axis): 14±17   18±20   21±28   29±39   40±61

verbal or fluid abilities display an earlier, steeper decline than scores on verbal or crystallized abilities. The tendency for nonverbal abilities to deteriorate more rapidly than verbal abilities has been referred to as the classic aging pattern (Botwinick, 1977). How can we understand this phenomenon? John Horn and colleagues (Horn, 1982; Horn & Donaldson, 1976) have proposed that crystallized intelligence is spared by age because it reflects the cumulative effects of experience, education, and acculturation, whereas fluid intelligence is impaired by age because of a gradual age-related deterioration of the physiological and neurological mechanisms necessary for basic intellectual functioning.

Longitudinal Studies

Longitudinal studies offer a very different impression of adult intellectual development than cross-sectional studies. A number of longitudinal studies were initiated during the early 1920s. It was at this time that incoming groups of college freshmen in the United States were administered intelligence tests on a routine basis. Psychologists kept track of these individuals as they grew older, retesting them at different intervals during adulthood. Surprisingly, the participants in these longitudinal studies showed an increase in IQ test performance up to approximately age 50 (Owens, 1966). After age 50, these gains were usually maintained or sometimes evidenced a small decline (Cunningham & Owens, 1983).

In one longitudinal study, Schwartzman, Gold, Andres, Arbuckle, and Chiakelson (1987) analyzed the intelligence test scores of a group of 260 men. These men were first administered intelligence tests when they were army recruits during World War II. Forty years later, the men were retested. At the second testing, the participants were approximately 65 years of age. They had completed, on average, nine years of formal education. One of the interesting twists of this study was that at the 40-year retesting, the men were given the intelligence test under two different conditions: a normal-time condition in which participants were given the standard amount of time to answer the test questions, and a double-time condition in which participants were given twice as much time to answer the test questions. Overall results showed a slight decline in test scores under the normal-time condition but a reliable and significant improvement in scores in the double-time condition! IQ gains were most likely to occur in those portions of the test that measured verbal abilities (e.g., vocabulary), while losses in IQ appeared in essentially nonverbal abilities (e.g., spatial problem solving). Three other findings are especially noteworthy. First, individual differences in IQ scores remained very stable over the 40-year time span. Second, gains in IQ were more highly associated with the number of years of formal education the men had attained than with their ages at the retesting. Third, self-reported activity levels and personal lifestyle differences were related to IQ scores at both times of testing.

One way to compare the results of cross-sectional and longitudinal studies of adult intellectual change is to examine the information illustrated in figure 8.5. The cross-sectional data indicate that adults show a peak in verbal ability at 35 years of age, followed by a significant decline thereafter. The longitudinal data, on the other hand, show that verbal ability peaks at about age 55. In addition, the longitudinal data exhibit only a very small decline up until 70 years of age, while the cross-sectional data show a more dramatic and earlier rate of decline.

One of the most informative investigations of adult intelligence is the Seattle Longitudinal Study (SLS) of K. Warner Schaie and his associates. This investigation used a sequential research design (i.e., a combination of both cross-sectional and longitudinal methods of data collection). The study began in 1956 when 500 participants between 22 and 70 years of age were administered the Primary Mental Abilities Test. These individuals, along with new groups of individuals, were retested at seven-year intervals in 1963, 1970, 1977, 1984, and 1991. Overall, this research project, which consists of six cross-sectional studies and one longitudinal study covering a 28-year period, has tested more than 5,000 individuals. A large number of published reports

Figure 8.5 A comparison of the results of cross-sectional and longitudinal studies investigating the relationship between age and verbal intelligence.
Source: Data from K. W. Schaie and S. L. Willis, 1986.

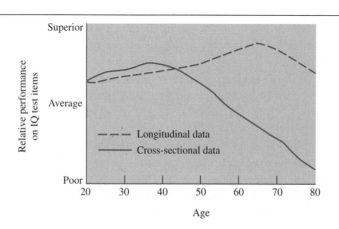

have summarized the outcomes of the SLS (Schaie, 1979, 1983, 1994, 1996; Schaie & Hertzog, 1983, 1985; Schaie & Labouvie-Vief, 1974; Schaie & Willis, 1996). Generally, the cross-sectional comparison exhibited the typical pattern of decline across all of the different primary mental abilities. These comparisons support the irreversible decrement model of intellectual aging. The longitudinal findings, however, tell a different story. They indicate that intelligence test scores either increase or remain stable until approximately age 60, when a small decline becomes evident. The results from one of the first reports of this investigation are illustrated in figure 8.6. This figure, based on the findings of Schaie and Labouvie-Vief (1974), compares the cross-sectional data collected in 1963 (black lines) with the cross-sectional data collected in 1970 (colored lines). The longitudinal data is signified by the dashed lines connecting the black and colored lines.

Two other reports (Hertzog & Schaie, 1988; Schaie, 1990) based on the SLS are especially important. Hertzog and Schaie (1988) examined the relationship between the mean stability of intelligence (e.g., the extent to which the average intellectual performance of a group of 70-year-olds differs from the average performance of a group of 50-year-olds) and the covariance stability in intelligence (e.g., how individuals perform compared with their agemates at 50 versus 70 years of age). Participants were between 22 and 70 years of age at the beginning of the study. They were tested three times over a 14-year period on five different primary mental abilities. Results showed

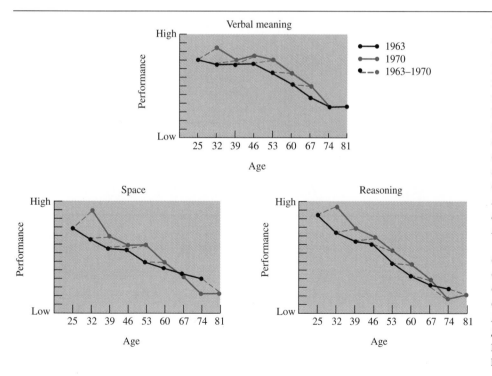

Figure 8.6 A comparison of cross-sectional and longitudinal findings concerning the relationship between age and intelligence based on the data obtained by Schaie and Labouvie-Vief (1974). *Source: Data from K. W. Schaie and G. Labouvie-Vief, "Generational Versus Ontogenetic Components of Change in Adult Cognitive Behavior: A Fourteen-Year Cross-Sequential Study" in* Developmental Psychology, *10:305–320, 1974.*

that the mean stability of the participants' performance was affected by age. The youngest participants displayed progressively higher levels of performance, middle-aged adults showed stability of performance, and older adults displayed a significant linear decline in performance—a decline that seems to take place for the majority of individuals somewhere between 55 and 70 years of age. On the other hand, all of the participants displayed exceptionally high levels of covariance stability across the 14-year period during which they were tested. These data provide substantial evidence for normative age-related changes in the mean stability of intelligence and the maintenance of individual differences in intellectual performance throughout the adult years.

Schaie (1990) examined the effects of age on the mental abilities of verbal meaning, spatial orientation, inductive reasoning, number, and word fluency. Longitudinal data were collected on individuals from ages 53 to 60, 60 to 67, 67 to 74, and 74 to 81. Table 8.3 reveals that, as age increased, participants were more likely to display a decline on any specific mental ability. More important, only about one-third of the participants showed a significant decline on any ability between 74 to 81 years of age. Likewise, table 8.4 shows that very few individuals showed global intellectual decline. For example, at age 60, about 75 percent of the participants maintained their performance on at least four out of five primary mental abilities. This level of maintenance

TABLE 8.3

Proportion of Individuals Showing a Decline in Specific Intellectual Abilities

Intellectual Ability	Age 53 to Age 60	Age 60 to Age 67	Age 67 to Age 74	Age 74 to Age 81
Verbal Meaning	15.2	24.8	26.8	35.7
Spatial Orientation	21.1	27.0	29.6	32.6
Inductive Reasoning	14.0	26.5	23.6	27.9
Number	17.2	26.2	26.2	31.8
Word Fluency	23.6	28.4	27.5	37.2

Source: Data from K. W. Schaie, "The Optimization of Cognitive Functioning in Old Age: Prediction Based on Cohort-Sequential and Longitudinal Data" In P. B. Baltes and M. Baltes (Eds.), Longitudinal Research and the Study of Successful (Optimal) Aging, Cambridge University Press, Cambridge, England, 1990, pp. 94–117.

TABLE 8.4

Proportion of Individuals Showing Decline in Intellectual Abilities

Number of Abilities	Age 53 to Age 60	Age 60 to Age 67	Age 67 to Age 74	Age 74 to Age 81
None	41.3	26.7	24.3	15.5
One	35.3	35.1	37.7	37.2
Two	17.0	22.0	21.8	24.8
Three	4.8	10.3	11.3	14.0
Four	1.2	5.0	3.9	6.2
All Five	0.5	0.8	1.1	2.3

Source: Data from K. W. Schaie, "The Optimization of Cognitive Functioning in Old Age: Prediction Based on Cohort-Sequential and Longitudinal Data" in P. B. Baltes and M. Baltes (Eds.), Longitudinal Research and the Study of Successful (Optimal) Aging, Cambridge University Press, Cambridge, England, 1990, pp. 94–117.

was also found for slightly more than half of the 81-year-olds in the sample. Also, only 2 percent of the participants showed a decline on all five abilities between 74 to 81 years of age. Finally, it was discovered that no participants displayed constant intellectual decline on all five primary mental abilities over the 28 years during which data were collected! Overall, these results suggest that constant, linear, and all-pervasive intellectual decline is more mythical than real. More positively stated, these data show that a significant percentage of individuals maintain most of their intellectual abilities well into old age.

All of the research we have reviewed, until now, has focused on the relationship between age and intelligence. We want to know if individuals become more (or less) intelligent as they grow older. A related question, of course, is whether we as a society become more (or less) intelligent as we move through time and undergo the effects of sociohistorical change. Research Focus 8.1 provides some very interesting data pertaining to this issue.

FACTORS RESPONSIBLE FOR DEVELOPMENTAL CHANGES IN INTELLIGENCE

Several investigators have suggested that intellectual decline results from the deterioration of the central nervous system. Without doubt, age-related changes in the brain have a significant impact on adult intellectual functioning. However, these changes alone cannot account for the pattern of results researchers found, nor can they adequately explain the individual differences that dispute the claim of universal biologically based loss. In this section, we discuss a variety of factors that may have a profound impact on intellectual performance during adulthood.

Cohort Effects

Why do cross-sectional studies paint a more pessimistic picture of adult intellectual change than longitudinal studies? The answer may be that in cross-sectional studies, age-related differences are confounded with cohort differences. **Cohort** means the generation one is born into, or the year of one's birth.

In a cohort-sequential analysis of the data from the Seattle Longitudinal Study, Schaie (1979, 1983, 1994, 1996) discovered that adults' intellectual performance changed as a function of both age and cohort. Figure 8.7, adapted from Schaie's (1994) data, illustrates the profound influence of cohort effects on five different primary mental abilities. This graph represents the IQ test performance of individuals from 12 successive birth cohorts (1889 to 1966). Notice the multidirectional manner in which the abilities change. The graph shows that inductive reasoning, verbal meaning, and spatial reasoning have increased in a linear manner over time. Number ability seems to have peaked with the 1924 cohort and declined since then. Finally, word fluency declined steadily until the 1938 cohort; since then it has displayed a slight upward movement.

Gisela Labouvie-Vief (1985) has called attention to the fact that performance on tasks of fluid intelligence (e.g., space) is not immune to cohort effects. Even measures

Societal Changes in Intelligence

You have probably heard many social critics lament the fact that the United States, along with other major industrialized nations, are "dumbing down" because of the deleterious effects of the media and popular culture. In support of this viewpoint, one only has to examine the decline of SAT (Scholastic Aptitude Test) scores over the last several decades and the constant refrain that academic standards have taken a tumble—today's "Johnny" can't read, write, and do mathematics as well as his predecessors. Despite these popular stereotypes, you may be surprised to know that the average IQ score has increased dramatically over the course of this century (see box figure 8.A). In fact, the average 20-year-old tested in the 1990s scores about 15 points (or one standard deviation) higher than the typical 20-year-old tested in the 1940s. This startling fact, first discovered by James Flynn (1984, 1987, 1996), has been dubbed the **Flynn Effect.**

Remember how IQ scores are constructed. Raw scores may vary from age group to age group, but the average scores for individuals within any particular age group is always set at 100 IQ points. The same logic applies to the Flynn Effect. As can be seen in box figure 8.A the average IQ score over the last 70 years has been a constant 100. However, the raw scores that underlie IQ test performance have risen substantially. It is the increase in raw IQ scores that constitutes the Flynn Effect.

Consider the fact that psychologists make a distinction between IQ test items (or subscales) that measure crystallized versus fluid intelligence. What aspect of intelligence (crystallized or fluid) do you think forms the basis of the Flynn Effect? Most probably, you answered "crystallized," since this dimension of intelligence seems most likely to be affected by schooling and life experience. Surprisingly, generational changes in measures of fluid intelligence are responsible for the Flynn Effect! This aspect of intelligence, which measures abstract reasoning and raw processing speed, is much less likely to be affected by schooling than crystallized intelligence. In fact, the IQ gains associated with the Flynn Effect have not generally been accompanied by gains in school achievement.

Psychologists Ulric Neisser and colleagues (Neisser et al., 1996) considered several possible explanations for the Flynn Effect. First, there are striking differences in the nature of everyday life for successive generations of individuals. Today, life is much more fast-paced and more dependent on the use of technological devices than it was in the past. Perhaps the increased demandingness of everyday life is related to gains in IQ. Second, better nutrition and health care may have boosted IQ. Third, changes in IQ may reflect increasingly higher levels of

Figure 8.A The Flynn Effect. *Source: Flynn, J. R. (1987). Massive IQ gains in 14 nations: What IQ tests really measure. Psychological Bulletin, 101, 171–191.*

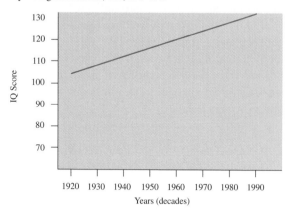

educational attainment among parents. For example, Steven Ceci (1991) has noted that, in general, the number of parents attending college has increased by 70 percent from 1970 to 1990, whereas the number of minority parents attending college has jumped by 350 percent over the same time span. These data are consistent with the finding that the average difference in IQ scores between blacks and whites in the United States has been reduced by half since 1970. Fourth, given the dramatic gains in measures of fluid intelligence over the last several decades, it may be that fluid intelligence isn't really intelligence at all. Maybe fluid intelligence merely represents some sort of minor abstract problem-solving ability. For example, Neisser and colleagues (1996) noted that in 1952 about 0.4 percent of the individuals tested in the Netherlands had IQs that were indicative of genius (an IQ of 140 or greater), whereas in 1982 approximately 9.1 percent of the Dutch population had IQ in the same range when their performance was scored by the 1952 norms. Flynn (1987) suggested that if IQ truly reflects intelligence, then the Netherlands should be experiencing an unrivaled cultural renaissance.

Most of the research on the Flynn Effect has focused on college-aged individuals. Do you think that the IQ of older adults has also increased during the last 80 years? We touch on this topic at a later point in this chapter when we discuss the issue of "cohort" (or generational) changes in IQ.

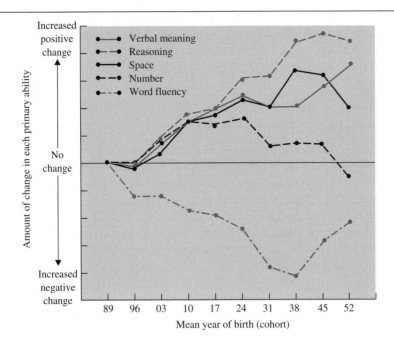

Figure 8.7 Cohort changes in the primary mental abilities.

of fluid intelligence do not assess the pure information-processing abilities of the human mind; they are influenced by cohort differences in environmental and social influences.

Cohort effects on intellectual development can be relatively negative or relatively positive. Paul Baltes (1987) described three different ways in which cohort differences can boost intellectual performance: in terms of education, health, and work. First, successive generations have received increasingly more formal education. Educational experience has been positively correlated with IQ scores. Second, each succeeding generation has been treated more effectively for a variety of illnesses (e.g., hypertension) that are known to have a negative impact on intellectual performance. Third, changes in the work life of more recent generations have placed a much stronger focus on cognitively oriented labor. Many of our grandfathers or great-grandfathers may have been farmers or manual laborers. Today, we are more likely to find jobs in service fields, such as emergency medical assistants, paralegal aides, or computer operators. This increased emphasis on cognitively oriented occupations most assuredly modifies and enhances intellectual abilities.

Selective Dropout

The **selective dropout** of participants may mean that longitudinal studies provide an overly optimistic view of adult intellectual change. The concept of selective dropout is based on the idea that as information is gathered during a longitudinal study it becomes harder and harder to keep one's original sample of participants intact. Specifically, participants who are unhealthy, unmotivated, or who consider themselves to be performing poorly on an intelligence test are not likely to return for repeated testing. As a longitudinal study progresses, a positively biased sample of participants is thus likely to evolve. This biased sample consists of adults who tend to do well on measures of intellectual functioning—that is, those who are highly educated, successful, motivated, and healthy.

Health

It seems obvious that individuals who are in good physical health can think, reason, and remember better than those in ill health. Even 20-year-old college students may find it difficult to concentrate during an exam if they are ill with the flu or some other illness. The problem for developmental researchers, of course, is that older adults are much more likely to suffer from chronic illness than younger people are. The relatively poor health of the elderly population can bias both cross-sectional and longitudinal studies. The older the population studied, the greater the number of persons with limiting health problems (Siegler & Costa, 1985).

Developmental psychologists must concern themselves with two interrelated issues. First, they must recognize that health may become much more of a determinant of intellectual functioning as individuals move through the life span (Siegler & Costa, 1985). Second, they must try to develop methodologies that separate the effects of aging from the effects of disease on psychological abilities.

Research has shown that the incidence of hypertension (high blood pressure) is related to a decline in intellectual abilities. Wilkie and Eisdorfer (1971) discovered in a longitudinal study that hypertension was linked to decreases on the WAIS for adults over age 60. Schaie (1990) found that hypertension was a better predictor of the intellectual performance of older adults than was a measure of overall health status. Schultz, Elias, Robbins, Streeten, and Blakeman (1986), in a longitudinal study of middle-aged adults, reported that nonhypertensive participants displayed increases in performance on the WAIS, whereas hypertensives showed no significant change in performance on the WAIS. Another longitudinal study conducted by Sands and Meredith (1992) showed that hypertension predicts performance on certain aspects of intelligence independent of the contributions of age, education, and gender.

At a more general level, recent studies have investigated the degree to which a healthy lifestyle influences intellectual abilities. Hultsch, Hammer, and Small (1993) found that, for a sample of adults between 55 and 86 years of age, self-reported health status, alcohol and tobacco use, and level of participation in daily activities predicted performance on a wide range of mental abilities. More specifically, Hultsch et al. (1993) discovered that these measures were better predictors of fluid rather than crystallized measures of intellectual function, especially for older participants. In a related study, Hill, Storandt, and Malley (1993) charted the effects of a yearlong aerobic exercise program on a group of 87 sedentary older adults. They reported that long-term exercise increased cardiovascular fitness and morale and prevented an age-related decline in verbal memory for the participants in their study.

Likewise, Schaie and Willis (1996) reviewed a number of recent studies that have highlighted the complex relationship between IQ and health-related behavior. In general, these studies showed that adults who scored high on various measures of IQ were very likely to have healthy diets that excluded sodium and fat and to engage in a number of self-initiated health practices, such as exercise, use of seat belts, regular medical checkups, and so on. These relations held true even when participants' ages and their educational achievement were taken into account.

One important aspect of an individual's overall health status is his or her level of sensory function. See Research Focus 8.2 for a discussion of some recent research that has focused on the relationship between adults' ability to see and hear vis-à-vis their IQ scores.

Terminal Drop

Closely associated with selective dropout and health status is the notion of terminal drop. **Terminal drop** refers to the tendency for an individual's psychological and biological abilities to exhibit a dramatic decrease in the last few years prior to death. Terminal drop occurs when individuals die of chronic illnesses that drain them of their strength, energy, and motivation. Most older people die of chronic diseases rather than accidents or injuries. Chronic diseases reduce older adults' capacities for clear thinking, undivided attention, and mental effort. As a result, their scores on cognitive tasks drop off dramatically (Kleemeier, 1972; Riegel & Riegel, 1972). Given the greater number of older versus younger adults being tested near their deaths, the intelligence test scores of older adults are much more likely to reflect terminal drop than the test scores of younger adults. Thus, the declines in intelligence revealed in cross-sectional and longitudinal studies may be, at least in part, a statistical artifact caused by terminal drop.

White and Cunningham (1988) have examined the relationship between distance from death and adults' scores on tests of vocabulary, numerical facility, and perceptual speed. They found that vocabulary scores were most likely to decline in the years just prior to a person's death. Thus, terminal drop may be limited to those abilities (such as vocabulary and other verbal abilities) that are usually the least affected by age.

Processing Speed

As mentioned previously, one of the most ubiquitous findings in developmental psychology is an age-related slowing of behavior and information processing. If the slowing of cognitive processing is one of the major hallmarks of aging, could it be the case that a decrement in processing speed is the primary determinant of intellectual decline in older adulthood? This hypothesis was examined in a study by Lindenberger, Mayr, and Kliegl (1993). They administered measures of processing speed (e.g., the digit symbol substitution task) as well as tasks of fluid (reasoning and associative memory) and crystallized intelligence (knowledge and verbal fluency) to 146 individuals between 70 to 103 years of age. Results showed that negative age differences on all of the measures of crystallized and fluid intelligence were mediated through age differences in speed of processing. In other words, the amount of variability in individuals' performance due to age per se was exceptionally small, whereas the variability in performance due to speed by itself, and speed in combination with age, was exceptionally high. It is interesting to

Sensory Acuity, Intelligence, and Aging

It seems obvious that how well we can see, hear, touch, taste, feel, and smell has no relationship whatsoever to our intellectual prowess. To prove the obvious, a number of researchers have shown that sensory ability is, in fact, independent of cognitive functioning.

Ulman Lindenberger and Paul Baltes (Baltes & Lindenberger, 1996; Lindenberger & Baltes, 1994) noted, however, that previous research and theory on the topic of sensory functioning and intelligence has been conducted from the perspective of a developmental approach that focused on middle-aged adults. Thus they wondered if sensory functioning and intelligence might be strongly related in very old individuals (those between 70 to 100 years of age). They based their hunch on Baltes's (1987) claim that there may be fundamental discontinuities in the correlates of cognitive functioning at different times during the adult life span. For example, Lindenberger and Baltes agree that there is nothing to suggest that sensory acuity would be related to intelligence in a group of healthy 20-year-olds. However, they offer two hypotheses as to why these variables might share a powerful relationship during advanced old age. The sensory deprivation hypothesis suggests that age-related declines in cognitive functioning reflect the cumulative effects of reduced high-quality sensory stimulation in the oldest-old. It is difficult, if not impossible, for very old individuals to maintain their cognitive ability and engage in intellectually stimulating activities if they cannot see and hear well. The common cause hypothesis, on the other hand, maintains that deficits in sensation and intelligence in advanced old age are the end result of a third (or common) factor—the physiological deterioration of the brain. It is reasonable to assume that negative brain changes lead to impoverished cognitive performance. However, it seems just as intuitive to believe that changes in visual acuity are caused by deleterious changes in the eye. In contrast to this point of view, recent research has shown that a great deal of the age-related deterioration of visual acuity is caused by changes at the level of the brain, not just the eye!

To explore these ideas Lindenberger and Baltes (1994) tested 156 older adults who were part of the Berlin Aging Study. The average age of the individuals in this research was 85 years and the range was 70 to 103 years of age. All participants were given 14 different tasks that measured five basic intellectual functions: speed, reasoning, memory, knowledge, and fluency. Furthermore, they were also administered standard measures of visual acuity (Snellen reading task) and auditory acuity (auditory threshold for pure tones).

The data were analyzed by a complex statistical technique called *structural equation modeling*. This methodology allows a researcher to construct a graphic representation of the probable causal pathway between a number of variables, all of which may be correlated with each other. As can be seen from box figure 8.B, age was correlated with visual and auditory acuity. More important, visual and auditory acuity were related to intelligence. Thus the pathway between age and intelligence was mediated by sensory acuity. In fact, when taken together, visual and auditory acuity account for 93 percent of the age-related variability in intellectual task performance!

In another study (Baltes & Lindenberger, 1996) involving 680 individuals between 25 and 103 years of age, these researchers showed that the average proportion of individual differences in intellectual functioning related to sensory function increased from 11 percent in adulthood (25–69 years of age) to 31 percent in old age (70–103 years of age). In fact, Baltes and Lindenberger (1997) have even shown that sensory function is a better predictor of intellectual ability than sociobiographical variables such as occupational prestige and years of education.

What are the implications of the exceptionally powerful link between sensory and intellectual functioning in very old adults? Baltes and Lindenberger (1997) offer several provocative sug-

note that speed of processing was highly related to performance on the knowledge tasks even though these measures were untimed! Lindenberger et al. (1993) suggested (see figure 8.8) that age affects speed of processing, which negatively affects general intellectual ability, which, in turn, affects performance on individual tasks. Finally, the absence of a differential relationship between speed of processing and performance on crystallized versus fluid tasks suggests that age differences in speed may be responsible for a dedifferentiation or convergence of intellectual ability in advanced old age. Also, these findings reinforce Salthouse's (1997) claim that any legitimate theory of cognitive aging must address the centrality of age-related changes in the speed of basic processing and how age changes in processing speed affects higher-order cognitive processes.

Figure 8.B Age, IQ, and Sensory Activity *Source: Lindenberger, U., & Baltes, P. B. (1994). Sensory functioning and intelligence in old age: A strong connection. Psychology and Aging, 9, 348.*

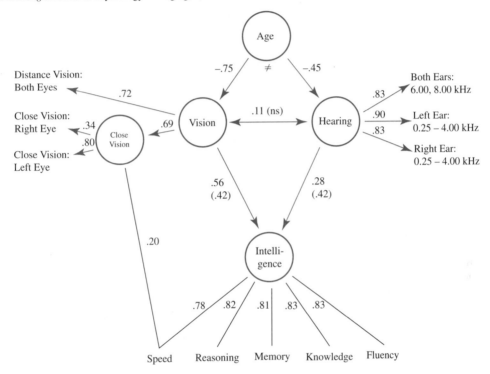

gestions about the outcome of their research. Most interestingly, they speculate that ". . . the assessment of visual and auditory acuity is 'transformed' into a task of cognitive func-tioning with advancing age " (p. 352). Thus the standard clinical assessment of sensory function may provide a great deal of insight into the operations of the aging mind.

Mental Exercise and Training

The idea that mental abilities can be improved by training, experience, or exercise has intrigued psychologists for many years. The enhancement of mental abilities via training is consistent with Baltes's (1987) notion of the plasticity of adult intellectual development. The concept of plasticity suggests that older adults have substantial cognitive reserve capacity and that training makes use of untapped reserve (Baltes, Sowarka, & Kliegl, 1989). Baltes and Kliegl (1986) and Willis (1985) hypothesized, for example, that older adults have little everyday experience with test items that measure fluid intelligence. But they also assumed that older adults possess the reserve capacity to raise their levels of performance on fluid-intelligence tasks. These researchers found that

*Health status is
a major factor
affecting
intellectual
functioning.*

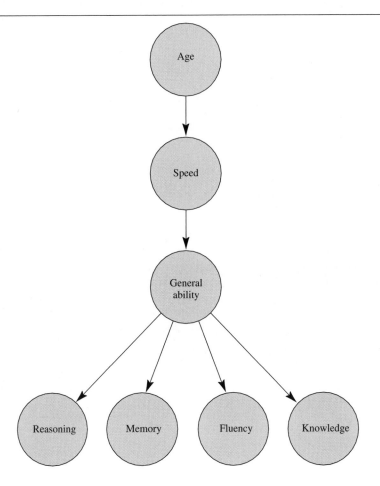

Figure 8.8
Schematic relationship between age, speed of processing, intelligence, and the primary mental abilities in old age.

older adults between 60 and 80 years old who were exposed to a program of cognitive training exhibited performance levels on fluid tasks that were comparable to the performance levels of a group of untreated younger adults. Baltes et al. (1989) have even shown that older adults can train themselves to become more proficient in tasks of fluid intelligence. However, Dittmann-Kohli, Lachman, Kliegl, and Baltes (1991) discovered that boosting the fluid intellectual abilities of older adults did not increase their perceived intellectual self-efficacy in real-life situations.

Nancy Denney (1984) suggested a distinction between unexercised ability (the level of performance that can be expected if the individual has had no exercise and/or training on a specific ability) and optimally exercised ability (the level of performance expected if the individual has received optimal exercise and/or training). The region between the two abilities in figure 8.9 represents the degree to which mental exercise and/or training can affect abilities. Of course, exercise or training can accumulate over a long period of time, even years or decades. Thus some types of ability might be essentially unexercised for many young adults but optimally exercised for middle-aged adults. Such abilities should not decline from young adulthood to middle adulthood. Indeed, they might even improve.

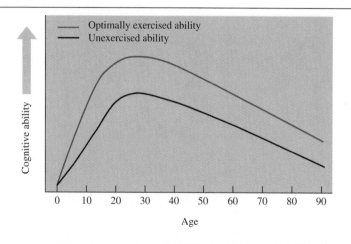

Figure 8.9 The hypothesized relationship between age and both unexercised ability and optimally exercised ability. *From: Nancy Wadsworth Denney, "Aging and Cognitive Changes" in* Handbook of Developmental Psychology, *edited by B. J. Wolman, © 1982, p. 819. Prentice-Hall, Inc., Englewood Cliffs, N.J.*

TABLE 8.5
Factors That Reduce the Risk of Intellectual Decline During Older Adulthood
Absence of cardiovascular and other chronic diseases
Favorable environment mediated by high socioeconomic status
Involvement in complex and intellectually stimulating environment
Flexible personality style at midlife
High cognitive status of spouse
Maintenance of high levels of perceptual processing speed

From K. W. Schaie. (1993). The Seattle longitudinal studies of adult intelligence. Current Directions in Psychological Science, *2, 171–174.*

Willis and Schaie (1986), along with Schaie, Willis, Hertzog, and Schulenberg (1987), found that older adults can, with training, show significant gains on different primary mental abilities. Moreover, gains in specific primary abilities derived from the training programs were found to generalize to other tasks measuring the same mental ability. These researchers discovered, therefore, that increases in intellectual ability associated with training studies go beyond merely teaching the test or changing the ability that is trained.

These results are especially significant in light of the criticisms leveled at training studies by Donaldson (1981). He suggested that training programs designed to improve fluid intelligence may provide misleading results. More specifically, he argued that fluid abilities themselves become "crystallized" with extensive training. Thus, successful intervention programs transform a fluid ability into a crystallized ability. This speculation seems less credible given the results obtained by Baltes and Schaie and their associates.

Finally, even though training programs may significantly boost the fluid abilities of older adults, it is important to realize that training has a much more beneficial effect for younger than older adults. It is certainly possible to teach older adults to display better performance on some components of intelligence in comparison to untrained younger adults. But, all things being equal, younger adults show greater gains from training than do their older counterparts. See table 8.5 for a general summary of the factors that K. Warner Schaie believes reduce the risk of intellectual decline during later adulthood.

INTELLIGENCE AND EVERYDAY PROBLEM SOLVING

At first glance, there seem to be a number of reasons why IQ test scores are poor indicators of an individual's ability to deal with the demands of everyday life. First, several of the items in IQ tests—such as defining unusual words, solving arithmetic problems, arranging pictures in a particular sequence, and so on—seem to have little in common with the problems adults face in real life. Second, many of the performance items on IQ tests are speeded in nature. This puts older adults at a disadvantage given the phenomenon of psychomotor slowing. Their responses are slower than those of the typical younger adult. Third, older adults are not as accustomed as younger adults to taking tests and as a result may be more anxious and/or cautious. Fourth, older adults seem to be less motivated than younger adults to take IQ tests seriously and to perform at their optimal levels. Fifth, the original goal of IQ tests was to predict school success or failure among groups of children and adolescents. This goal seems to possess little meaning when applied to older individuals.

Despite the preceding factors, many psychologists have found that scores on various psychometric intelligence tests are somewhat predictive to real-life problem solving. Willis and Schaie (1985; Schaie & Willis, 1993), for example, administered a test of the seven primary mental abilities to older adults along with a variety of everyday intellectual tasks: reading street maps and bus schedules, interpreting the information found on medicine bottles, filling out a Medicare form, comprehending Yellow Page advertisements, and so forth. They found that performance across all of the everyday tasks was related to performance on tasks that measure both crystallized and fluid intelligence, although the relationship was somewhat stronger between everyday competence and performance on the fluid tasks. The power of this finding is reinforced by a recent finding from the Seattle Longitudinal Study. Specifically, Schaie (1996) showed that performance on crystallized and fluid tasks predicted everyday functioning seven years later.

One potential shortcoming of the aforementioned research is that it involved printed stimulus materials. This motivated Diehl, Willis, and Schaie (1995) to perform a study in which they observed older adults performing everyday tasks (e.g., using call forwarding on a telephone, preparing a meal, etc.) in their home. Diehl et al. found that performance on the everyday tasks was strongly related to performance on measures of fluid intelligence.

Cornelius and Capsi (1987) investigated the relationship between aging and the implicit and explicit dimensions of intelligence. Implicit theories of intelligence (Sternberg, 1985) refer to people's commonsense beliefs about intelligence and how it develops. Explicit theories, in contrast, are concerned with formalized psychometric notions about what intelligence is and how it is best measured. It has been found that implicit views place a heavy emphasis on the practical or social aspect of intelligence. Practical or social intelligence involves sizing up situations, admitting mistakes, determining how to achieve goals, and so on. These types of abilities are not measured by the

Older adults, unlike college students, are often unfamiliar with standardized tests and testing situations.

items found on traditional IQ tests. Cornelius and Capsi's (1987) study assessed the relationship between practical intelligence and measures of crystallized and fluid intelligence. Their study consisted of two phases. In phase 1, these researchers developed a measure of practical intelligence called the Everyday Problem-Solving Inventory. This test consisted of 48 problems within six different social areas such as managing domestic issues and resolving interpersonal conflicts between family members, friends, and coworkers. Phase 2 involved the administration of the Everyday Problem-Solving Inventory along with measures of crystallized intelligence (the Verbal Meaning Test) and fluid intelligence (the Letter Series Test) to groups of young, middle-aged, and older adults. The results of this study, illustrated in figure 8.10, indicate that performance on the Everyday Problem-Solving Inventory and the Verbal Meaning Test increased with age, while performance on the Letter Series Test decreased with age. Furthermore, a modest correlation was found between scores on the Problem-Solving Inventory and both the Verbal Meaning Test and the Letter Series Test. Finally, it was discovered that familiarity with problems on the Everyday Problem-Solving Inventory was not related to scores on this measure.

These results suggest that practical problem solving, an important component of people's implicit or social view of intelligence, may be somewhat distinct from traditional measures of fluid and crystallized intelligence. The results also seem contrary to

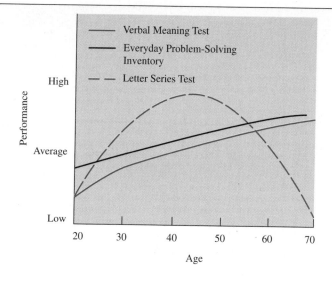

Figure 8.10 An illustration of age-related changes on the Everyday Problem-Solving inventory, the Verbal Meaning Test, and the Letter Series Test. *Source: Data from S. W. Cornelius and A. Capsi, "Everyday Problem Solving in Adulthood and Old Age" in Psychology and Aging, 2:144–153, American Psychological Association, Washington DC, 1987.*

Denney's (1984) position that older adults perform better on measures of practical intelligence because they have much more experience in solving these problems. More positively, the results of this study support the viewpoint advocated by Paul Baltes and his associates (Dittmann-Kohli & Baltes, 1988; Dixon & Baltes, 1986). These investigators suggested that practical or social intelligence increases with age and has little in common with traditional psychometric measures of intelligence.

One important aspect of everyday functioning that would seem to demand a blend of both analytic and practical intelligence is job performance. Research Focus 8.3 provides some information concerning the speculation that intelligence is related to occupational success.

CONCLUSIONS ABOUT ADULT INTELLECTUAL CHANGE

One of the major goals of this chapter was to answer what seems to be a relatively simple question: What happens to intelligence as one ages? As we have seen, however, there is not a simple answer to this question. Cross-sectional studies show a more dramatic and steeper rate of intellectual decline than longitudinal studies.

Cross-sectional studies, because they are likely to be contaminated by cohort effects and terminal drop, are likely to paint an overly pessimistic picture of adult intellectual change. Longitudinal and sequential studies indicate that intelligence remains stable (or actually increases) until approximately 60 years of age, after which a slight decline may be observed. This conclusion seems most valid, however, for healthy, well-educated adults. Furthermore, the findings of longitudinal studies may be contaminated by selective dropout.

We have also seen that different types of intelligence show different patterns of change over age. Crystallized and verbal components of intelligence seem to increase

Intelligence and Occupational Success

Initially, intelligence tests were designed to predict academic success (or failure) in school-aged individuals. In their extensive review of the psychometric literature, Neisser et al. (1996) concluded that IQ tests have achieved this goal remarkably well. The average correlation between IQ test performance and school grades is +.50. What else should IQ test performance be a good predictor of? Doesn't it seem reasonable that IQ should be related to the type of job a person takes during adulthood as well as the degree to which an individual succeeds within her occupational life? After all, IQ is related to education success. And we would hope that school success should predict occupational success. Again, Neisser et al. (1996) have commented that IQ test scores possess a great deal of predictive power along these lines. For example, individuals with blue-collar jobs (e.g., truck drivers) typically have IQs of about 100, whereas white-collar workers (e.g., physicians) have IQs that are substantially higher, approximately 125. Also, job performance within a variety of occupations, as measured by supervisor ratings, productivity, work quality, and so on, correlates about +.50 with IQ scores. In effect, IQ scores may be the best "single predictor" of job success. However, as Neisser et al. (1996) have cautioned, other characteristics of the individual—such as motivation, personality, and interpersonal skills—probably play just as important, or perhaps even more important, a role in predicting occupational success in comparison to IQ.

Psychologists are just beginning to understand the complex relationship between IQ and occupational success. Cognitive psychologist Earl Hunt (1995) has put forth one of the most interesting perspectives on this relationship. The crux of Hunt's argument is that there is a nonlinear, rather than a linear, relationship between IQ and job performance (see box figure 8.C). As can be seen from the figure, a linear relationship is one that is characterized by a straight line—a specific distance on one axis of the graph is not identical to the distance on the other axis of the graph. A nonlinear relationship is one that is characterized by a curved line—a specific distance on one axis of the graph is not identical to the distance on the other axis of the graph. The figure, which illustrates nonlinearity, suggests that increases in IQ have a negligible effect on job performance. Hunt (1995) presents a great deal of evidence that suggests that, "In economic terms it appears that the IQ score measures something with decreasing marginal value. It is important to have enough of it but having lots of it does not buy you that much. My regrets to Mensa but that's the way things are" (p. 362). Put somewhat differently, Hunt suggests that having a certain level of IQ is important for getting into an occupation as well as the speed at which one learns the basics of that occupation. However, once the rudiments of an occupation have been mastered it seems that motivational, interpersonal, and experience-based factors—not IQ—drive job performance.

Hunt's ideas, which are backed up by a great deal of empirical research, have far-reaching societal implications. For example, the controversial book *The Bell Curve,* written by Herrnstein and Murray (1994), contains a number of policy statements concerning the relationship between minority hiring and worker productivity that are based on the premise the IQ and job performance share a linear relationship. Do you have more faith in the practice of affirmative action hiring given the fact that the relationship between job performance and IQ is nonlinear? Also, think of the productivity of older persons who may have worked in the same occupation for several decades. Would you predict a strong relationship between IQ and job performance in these individuals?

Figure 8.C "Curvilinear" relationship between IQ and job preference. *Source: Hunt, E. (1995). The role of intelligence in modern society.* American Scientist, 83, *361.*

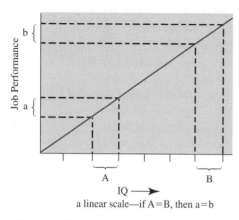
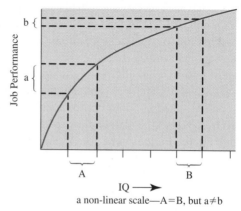

with age, while fluid intelligence as well as performance measures of intelligence decline with age. Despite these predictable patterns of age-related change, there is a great deal of plasticity in adult intelligence. It is possible to train adults to increase their scores on intelligence tests, even on tasks that measure fluid abilities. But training effects are larger for younger than older adults.

The finding that fluid intelligence can be boosted among older adults is important within the context of Earl Hunt's (1993) remarks about the productivity of older workers. For example, he noted that older people are not adept in performing jobs in which they must make quick decisions, recognize stimuli embedded in a noisy background, and keep track of several pieces of information at once. However, these are the kinds of tasks at which computers excel. Thus, older (as well as younger) workers who possess the skills necessary to perform highly speeded perceptual-motor tasks run the risk of being replaced by machines. On the other hand, machines are not capable of dealing with the "novel" problems that arise in any industry or occupation. Hunt maintained that fluid intellectual abilities are needed to solve these types of problems. He also suggested that understanding why fluid intelligence declines during middle adulthood and how this decrement may be prevented and ameliorated will be of major economic necessity. Hunt's message to the employers (and employees) of the twenty-first century is rather straightforward, "The simple fact is that fluid intelligence will be in demand. Crystallized intelligence is only of use in a crystallized society" (Hunt, 1993, p. 597).

Finally, we reported that traditional measures of intelligence are modestly related to measures of practical or social intelligence during adulthood. This finding does not mean that traditional tests are invalid measures of intelligence. Rather it suggests that psychometricians need to develop a more differentiated theory (and tests) of intelligence—a theory that does full justice to the broad array of intellectual abilities manifested by adults as they age. Research Focus 8.4 presents the basic ideas that underlie some new theoretical viewpoints about the nature of human intelligence theory.

CREATIVITY

What is it about someone like Thomas Edison that made him able to create so many inventions? Was he simply more intelligent than most people? Did he spend long hours toiling away in private?

Surprisingly, when Edison was a young boy, his teacher told him he was too dumb to learn anything! There are many examples of unnoticed creative genius in early development (Larsen, 1973): Walt Disney was fired from a newspaper job because he did not have any creative ideas. Winston Churchill failed one year of secondary school. Consider the following comments made by John Lennon: "People like me are aware of their so-called genius at ten, eight, nine. . . . I always wondered, 'Why has nobody discovered me?' In school, didn't they see that I'm more clever than anybody in this school? Why didn't they put me in art school? Why didn't they train me? I was different, I was always different. Why didn't anybody notice me?" (quoted in Gardner, 1983, p. 115).

One of the reasons that creative ability is sometimes overlooked is because we have such difficulty in defining and measuring creativity.

New Conceptions of Intelligence

Howard Gardner and Robert Sternberg have developed two unique theories that challenge the traditional psychometric views concerning the measurement and meaning of intelligence. In this research focus we outline the basic tenets of these theories.

In a controversial book entitled *Frames of Mind,* Howard Gardner (1983) proposed a **Theory of Multiple Intelligences.** This theory suggests that there are different human intelligences, each of which is localized in a different area in the brain. The different intelligences identified by Gardner are linguistic intelligence, logical-mathematical intelligence, spatial intelligence, musical intelligence, bodily-kinesthetic intelligence, and personal intelligence. Each of these different intelligences makes use of a different symbol system through which individuals represent or structure experience. For example, experience can be symbolized through words; logical-numerical relationships; visual images; tones, pitches, or rhythms; body movements; and so forth. Furthermore, Gardner maintains that only the first three of the preceding intelligences are measured on traditional IQ tests. Gardner's criteria for identifying specific types of intelligences include: (1) each intelligence can be independently represented in the brain and destroyed by damage or injury to a localized brain site; (2) exceptional individuals, child prodigies, and idiot savants may exhibit extraordinary performance in one form of intelligence but moderate or poor performance in other forms of intelligence; (3) each intelligence has a unique developmental history; (4) each intelligence consists of a core set of operations that are automatically triggered by particular types of experiences or information; (5) each intelligence has an evolutionary history; (6) the existence of each intelligence can be demonstrated by laboratory experiments and psychometric research; and (7) each intelligence possesses its own unique symbol system.

The vast majority of the research on Gardner's theory (see Gardner, 1993b) has been directed toward children, especially within the context of educational policy. Unfortunately, Gardner's theory has not been assessed fully in adult and/or aged populations. Based on the extant psychometric literature, however, we might expect that logical-mathematical and spatial intelligence would decline with age, whereas linguistic and personal intelligence might remain stable (or perhaps increase) with age.

Similar to Gardner's notion of personal intelligence is Daniel Goleman's (1995) concept of **emotional intelligence.** Emotionally intelligent people are aware of the needs, feelings, and motives that operate in themselves and in others. More important, they can effectively manage their emotional states (and those of others) to achieve a number of desirable goals. Consequently, they may have tremendously successful professional careers despite the fact that they may not possess extremely high levels of "academic smarts." Researchers need to determine how best to measure emotional intelligence and how emotional intelligence interacts with more traditional notions of intelligence.

Robert Sternberg (1985, 1988) has put forth a **Triarchic Theory of Intelligence.** This theory suggests that intelligence consists of three independent facets: analytic, creative (or insightful), and practical (or street smarts). The analytic aspect of intelligence refers to any individual's ability to process information and solve problems. This component, according to Sternberg, is very closely related to traditional psychometric conceptualizations of intelligence. Put somewhat differently, Sternberg argues that psychologists have all but ignored the creative and practical aspects of intelligence.

To get a feel for Sternberg's theory, think of the following individuals who are about to enter college. Tom's strength is analytic intelligence. He has extremely high SAT scores and gets very good grades in college, but he is not considered to be a "great student" by his professors. George's forte is creative intelligence. His SAT scores and grades are just about average, yet he amazes his professors by sudden flashes of insight and brilliance. They wonder why such a gap exists between his grades and the quality of his ideas. Sam possesses a great deal of practical intelligence, which we might think of as common-sense or street smarts. His grades, along with his insight, are average. However, he is very well liked and "noticed" by all of his professors. After graduation, he is offered a much better array of job opportunities than either Tom or George.

One of Sternberg's most important goal is to develop adequate measures of creative and practical intelligence. Note that problems that measure analytic intelligence are clearly defined, have a single correct solution, and are somewhat divorced from everyday experience, whereas tasks that measure creative and practical intelligence possess the exact opposite set of characteristics. How could you possibly develop and score measures of creative and practical intelligence?

Sternberg, Wagner, Williams, and Horvath (1995) have adopted the following strategy to assess practical intelligence within the area of business management. They have developed a number of vignettes that describe various problems that arise in real-life business situations and ask the participants in their research (actual managers) to rank order a number of possible solutions to each vignette. (Note that the quality of these solution is determined by the ratings assigned to them by individuals who are excellent managers.) This research has shown that scores on the questionnaires are relatively independent of performance on traditional IQ tests, yet performance on the questionnaires correlates very highly with measures of actual job performance.

Sternberg's theory is especially important when one considers that practical intelligence may become increasingly important to individuals as they journey through the adult life span.

Georgia O'Keeffe is an example of someone who maintained artistic creativity in older adulthood.

Definition and Measurement of Creativity

The prevailing belief of psychologists who study creativity is that intelligence and creativity are not the same. Just think about it: If intelligence and creativity were identical, there would be no reason to make a distinction between them! We could choose one of these terms—intelligence or creativity—to describe the same phenomenon.

Distinguishing between creativity and intelligence is a difficult task. David Ausubel (1968) has emphasized that creativity is one of the most ambiguous and confusing terms in psychology. He believes the term *creative* should be reserved for people who make unique and original contributions to society. Surely a list of creative individuals, from this point of view, would include Marie Curie, Charles Darwin, Thomas Edison, Georgia O'Keeffe, Pablo Picasso, and William Shakespeare— they possessed creative genius, or **exceptional creativity.** The world we live in has been shaped and influenced by the creative acts of these individuals. Several other researchers (e.g., Mumford & Gustafson, 1988; Simonton, 1988, 1990, 1997) have also agreed that psychologists should focus their attention on the study of exceptional creativity.

Robert Weisberg (1986) argued that it is important to understand ordinary creativity. **Ordinary creativity** refers to the creative behavior of "ordinary" adults in "ordinary" real-life situations. People we interact with everyday show their creativity in how they respond in conversations, in how they work, in how they dress, or in how they live on a small budget.

Divergent thinking, one of the dimensions of intelligence according to J. P. Guilford (1967), is a kind of creativity. **Divergent thinking** refers to the ability to produce many different answers to a single question. In contrast to divergent thinking, **convergent thinking** refers to the ability to derive the one correct solution to a problem. For example, there is one correct answer to the question, How many quarters can you trade for 60 dimes? This question calls for convergent thinking. But there are many possible answers to the question, What are some of the possible uses for a coat hanger? This question requires divergent thinking.

Rebok (1987) suggested that the generation of novel ideas (divergent thinking) should be viewed as a necessary but not sufficient condition for creativity. Creativity depends in part on possessing a critical amount of knowledge about a particular domain. For example, it would be impossible to be a creative composer if one did not know much about musical composition. Researchers interested in creativity should simultaneously assess an individual's thinking style and the degree of knowledge he or she possesses within a particular domain. This suggestion may be especially important for understanding creativity in older adults. As individuals age, they develop a substantial base of knowledge through their activities and experience.

Another way of understanding creativity is based on Csikszentmihalyi's (1997) ideas about the relationship between discovery or creativity and autoetelic activities. *Autoetelic activities* are those we do purely because we enjoy them, not because we have to do them, and not because of external rewards such as money or prestige. A writer who creates a wonderful poem, a play, or a novel for its own sake, regardless of salary or fame, is working creatively. For example, you might love to write poems, or play tennis, or play music, or swim in the ocean. The creative process is more likely to be engaged when you are doing an activity that is autoetelic. The creative process can occur authentically when we are involved in autoetelic activities. For Thomas Edison, for example, discovering the principles and applications of electricity was probably autoetelic.

Developmental Changes in Creativity

Because there are different levels of creativity, ordinary and exceptional, this section consists of two parts. First, we discuss age-related trends in exceptional creativity—the creative accomplishments of well-known people in various fields of specialization. Second, we discuss age-related differences in ordinary creativity. This form of creativity has been measured by administering psychometric tests of creativity to individuals representative of the general population.

TABLE 8.6	
Some Creative Accomplishments of Older Adults	
Accomplishment	*Age*
George Bernard Shaw writes his first play	48
Sophocles writes *Oedipus Rex*	75
Sigmund Freud writes last book	83
Benjamin Franklin invents the bifocal lens	78
Claude Monet begins the Water Lily series	73
Michelangelo creates St. Peter's and frescoes the Pauline Chapel	71–89
Mahatma Gandhi launches the Indian Independence Movement	72
DeGaulle returns to power in France	68
Frank Lloyd Wright completes the Guggenheim Museum	91

Exceptional Creativity

Many examples demonstrating that older adults can be exceptionally creative can be mentioned. Some examples are given in table 8.6. Lehman (1953, 1960) and Dennis (1966, 1968) conducted some of the earliest and most influential research on age-related changes in exceptional creativity in adulthood. Lehman (1953) charted the ages at which adults produced highly creative works that had a significant impact on their fields. As shown in figure 8.11a, the quality of productivity was highest when such individuals were in their thirties and then gradually declined. Lehman argued that approximately 80 percent of the most important creative contributions are completed by age 50. In fact, he concluded that ". . . genius does not function equally throughout the years of adulthood. Superior creativity rises rapidly to a maximum which occurs usually in the thirties and then falls off slowly" (Lehman, 1953, pp. 330–331).

Unlike Lehman (1953), Wayne Dennis (1966) studied the total productivity, not just the superior works, of creative people in the arts, sciences, and humanities who lived long lives. He discovered (see figure 8.11b) that the point at which creative production peaked in adult life varied from one discipline to another. For example, in the humanities, people in their seventies appeared equally creative as people in their forties. Artists and scientists, however, began to show a decline in creative productivity in their fifties. In all instances, the twenties was the least productive age period in terms of creativity.

Dennis (1968) also examined the creative output of famous scholars, scientists, and artists who lived until at least 80 years of age. Dennis discovered that, on the average, the sixties was the most creative decade in the lives of these individuals! Thirty-five percent of the total output of scientists was produced after age 60—20 percent while they were in their sixties and 15 percent while they were in their seventies. Famous inventors produced more than half of their lives' work after age 60. Approximately 20 percent of the total output of artists was achieved after age 60. In a study of Nobel laureates in science, it was found that the average age at which they published their first major paper was 25.

Figure 8.11
(a) The percentage of superior output as a function of age. This generalized curve represents a combination of various fields of endeavor and various estimates of quality. *Source: Data from Lehman, table 34, 1953;*
(b) The percentage of total output as a function of age. The humanities, sciences, and arts are represented by the means of several specific disciplines. *Source: Data from Dennis, table 1, 1966.*

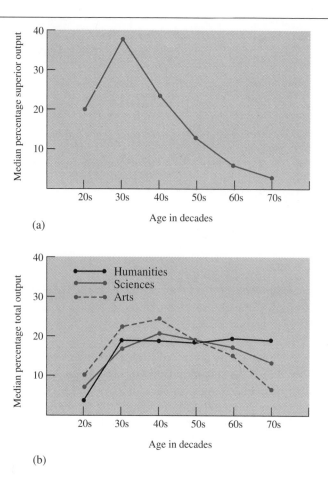

(a)

(b)

Furthermore, all of the laureates in this study who were past 70 continued to publish scholarly papers in scientific journals. Therefore, by relaxing the criteria for defining exceptional creativity (i.e., by examining the total creative output of individuals, not just their best work), we see that creativity may not decline as early as Lehman (1953) suggested. It seems as if individuals who are bright and productive in early and middle adulthood have a good chance of maintaining their creativity in older adulthood. This conclusion is consistent with Simonton's statement that the most creative individuals "tend to start early, end late, and produce at above-average rates" (1988, p. 253).

Over (1989) examined the relationship between age and exceptional creativity by analyzing the percentage of both high- and low-impact articles published by scientists at different ages. He discovered that young scientists published more high-impact and low-impact works than older scientists. This finding is consistent with Simonton's (1990) conclusion that the "periods in a creator's life that see the most masterpieces also witness the most easily forgotten productions . . . the 'quality ratio,' or the proportion of major products to total output per age unit, tends to fluctuate randomly over the course of any career. The quality ratio neither increases or decreases with age" (p. 323).

Ordinary Creativity

What happens when we administer psychometric tests of creativity to "typical" as opposed to "exceptional" groups of aging individuals? Does ordinary creativity show a pattern of age-related change? One of the first scientific studies on this topic was conducted by Alpaugh and Birren (1977). Their cross-sectional sample consisted of 111 teachers between 20 and 84 years of age. These individuals were administered the WAIS as well as a battery of psychometric tasks that measure creativity. Within this well-educated sample, scores on the WAIS remained stable across adulthood. However, scores on the measures of creativity peaked at 30 and declined thereafter.

In another study, Ruth and Birren (1985) tested 150 persons enrolled in adult education classes in Finland using several psychometric tests of creativity and several measures of crystallized and fluid intelligence. Participants in this study were between 25 and 75 years old. Results indicated that performance on the creativity measures declined with age. The great majority of this decline, however, was found to occur between young and middle adulthood. No age-related differences were found on the measure of crystallized intelligence; but scores on the fluid tasks were found to decline with age. One of the major problems associated with the Alpaugh and Birren (1977) and Ruth and Birren (1985) studies is the use of a cross-sectional methodology. In comparison, Schaie and Hertzog (1983), in a longitudinal study on aging and creativity, discovered that only one aspect of divergent thinking (word fluency) declined with age. Unfortunately, the results of this study are clouded by the fact that the word fluency task was highly speeded. This may have placed the older adults at a greater disadvantage than the younger adults.

In one of the most comprehensive studies of aging and creativity, McCrae, Arenberg, and Costa (1987) combined cross-sectional, longitudinal, and cross-sequential methods of data collection. Their research, a component of the Baltimore Longitudinal Study of Aging, involved testing 825 well-educated men at regular intervals between 1959 and 1972. The men ranged from 17 to 101 years old. All of the participants were administered several different divergent-thinking tasks. These tasks involved (1) associational fluency—the ability to provide synonyms for specific words; (2) expressional fluency—the ability to write sentences with words beginning with certain letters; (3) ideational fluency—the ability to name objects in specific classes; (4) word fluency—the ability to write words containing a designated letter; and (5) consequences—the ability to imagine unusual, novel outcomes for particular situations. The participants were also administered the vocabulary test from the WAIS.

Results indicated that scores on the measures of creativity and the WAIS were distinct from each other. This is surprising, given the fact that the vocabulary test and all of the measures of creativity were verbal in nature. Furthermore, all the different methods of data collection and analysis (cross-sectional, longitudinal, and cross-sequential) revealed that scores on the measures of creativity declined with age. Based on these results, McCrae et al. (1987) concluded that creativity, like fluid intelligence, declines with age. However, the correlations between age and performance on the measures of creativity, although statistically significant, were in the modest range ($-.10$ to $-.30$). Also, McCrae and his colleagues administered the tests of creativity under standardized conditions with strict time limits, a procedure that may be especially disadvantageous to older participants.

Perhaps the complex and somewhat confusing nature of developmental changes in creativity may be best understood by approaching creativity from a contextual perspective. A contextual view suggests that a number of psychological and social changes may influence creativity during adulthood. In a discussion of life-span creativity, Jean and Michael Romaniuk (1981) provide an example from the academic world of how incentives for productivity may influence an individual's creativity. Tenure and the pressure to publish may affect creative accomplishment. Shifts in career interests and activities, such as transferring from research to administrative activity, individual shifts in priorities concerning career goals and job security, and attention to refining earlier creative accomplishments may influence creativity. And the opening of new research fields, along with the saturation of existing fields, may also influence creative accomplishments.

At a more general level, it would seem that as people age they may become less interested (due to internal as well as external pressures) in the creation of new ideas. Alternatively, they may become more interested in reflecting on the meaning of the knowledge that has already been created and on using that knowledge to help them come to grips with the meaning of their own lives and to help their culture evolve in an adaptive manner. Thus, as Simonton (1990) has suggested, with age, the desire to be creative may be replaced with the need to be wise. This viewpoint is consistent with Simonton's (1988) observation that older individuals occupy positions of power and leadership within a number of social, political, and religious institutions, whereas younger adults are more likely to create new institutions and to revolutionize existing ones. For example, a typical pope of the Roman Catholic Church assumes his position at approximately double the age at which Jesus of Nazareth ended his ministry. This seems to support Hall's (1922) position that ". . . men in their prime conceived the great religions, the old made them prevail" (p. 420).

In summary, we have seen that creativity is an elusive concept, one that is difficult to define, measure, and chart. It seems that exceptionally creative individuals may continue to function in a creative manner well into middle and late adulthood. In fact, many creative people do some of their best work late in life. The need to be creative, however, may decline with advancing age for a variety of psychosocial as well as intrapersonal reasons.

Genius

In today's world, there are large numbers of exceptionally creative and highly intelligent adults. However, there seems to be something above and beyond creativity and intelligence—genius. What factors are responsible for the development of genius? At what age can genius first be identified? Until what age can genius be maintained? At present, many developmental psychologists are attempting to answer questions such as these. For example, in a book entitled *Creating Minds* (1993a), Howard Gardner has analyzed the lives of seven geniuses of the modern era: Einstein, Freud, Picasso, Stravinsky, T. S. Eliot, Mahatma Ghandi, and Martha Graham. What can we learn about "genius" by studying these individuals?

First, it should be recognized that intelligence and creativity are a necessary but not sufficient condition for the development of genius. Second, geniuses are not content with solving problems. They relish the enterprise of **problem finding.** As Begley (1993) observed, Freud's genius was not evident in his interpretations of dreams; rather, it was Freud's genius that recognized the significance of dreams for understanding human motivation. Third, geniuses seem to approach their work with a combined sense of childlike enthusiasm and obsessiveness. Geniuses work hard and they gain their fundamental insights by asking questions that are childlike in nature. For example, Einstein wondered about space and time (things that the average adult may have thought about as a child) from the point of view of a scientist. Fourth, geniuses seem to synthesize different modes of thought to produce their work. Composers, for example, often maintain they can see music, whereas painters often remark that they experience sounds as visual symbols. Fifth, there seems to be a critical amount of knowledge that a person must possess about a certain domain to make a geniuslike contribution. Too much knowledge and too much time spent thinking about the same problem may be just as antagonistic to genius as too little knowledge and too little thought. This may account for the fact that genius is a phenomenon of young and middle adulthood. The child may be prodigious. The older adult may be wise. But the individual who creates a major revolution in art, science, or literature is likely to be in her twenties or thirties.

SUMMARY

The psychometric approach emphasizes a measurement-based orientation to the study of adult intellectual change. Psychometricians differ on the issue of whether intelligence is a general ability or a constellation of separate abilities. Intelligence, from the psychometric perspective, is assessed by the use of standardized tests. One of the most widely used tests to assess adult intelligence is the Wechsler Adult Intelligence Scale (WAIS). This test contains both verbal and performance scales. Different types of developmental studies have reflected different patterns of age-related changes in intelligence. Cross-sectional studies show that intelligence declines sharply from early adulthood onward. Longitudinal studies, on the other hand, indicate that intelligence remains stable until late adulthood, when it may undergo a slight decline. Verbal intelligence is likely to improve with age, while nonverbal or performance components of intelligence are likely to decline with age. Put somewhat differently, crystallized intelligence has been found to increase with age, but fluid intelligence seems to decrease with age. Several factors appear to contribute to the observed age-related changes in intelligence. These factors include cohort effects, selective dropout, health status, reduced processing speed, and terminal drop. It has been shown that adults who actively exercise specific mental abilities, or who receive special training in specific abilities, do not display significant age-related decrements in those abilities.

Research on developmental changes in exceptional creativity suggests that in the arts and sciences, creative thought may peak in the forties, whereas in the humanities, creativity maintains itself well into the early part of late adulthood. Regardless of when creativity reaches its peak, research shows that for the majority of individuals, creative output continues throughout midadulthood to later life. Research designed to study everyday creativity in typical individuals has shown a modest, but statistically significant, decline in divergent thinking over the adult life span. This research, however, may be marred by various methodological problems (including the speeded nature of standardized tests of creativity).

REVIEW QUESTIONS

1. What does the term *psychometric* mean?
2. Explain how psychometricians determine the IQs of different-aged adults.
3. What does it mean to say that intelligence reflects the operation of a single g factor? Have researchers obtained data supporting the g factor theory?
4. Explain the difference between crystallized and fluid intelligence. How do these different forms of intelligence change over time?
5. Explain the different results obtained by cross-sectional versus longitudinal studies of adult intellectual change.

6. Explain how cohort effects, selective dropout, health status, and terminal drop influence IQ test scores.
7. Discuss the concepts of mental exercise, plasticity, and cognitive intervention in late adulthood.
8. Describe two different approaches to the study of creativity and explain what you think is the best way to measure it.
9. Trace the developmental course of creativity during adulthood. How do developmental changes in "exceptional" creativity differ from those in "ordinary" creativity?

FOR FURTHER READING

Blanchard-Fields, F., & Hess, T. H. (Eds.) (1996). *Perspectives on cognitive change in adulthood and aging.* New York: McGraw-Hill.

Gardner, H. (1993). *Creating minds.* New York: Basic Books.

Goleman, D. (1995). *Emotional intelligence.* New York: Bantam Books.

COGNITIVE STAGES, WISDOM, AND EXPERTISE

INTRODUCTION

The information presented in the preceding chapters indicates that some degree of cognitive decline is an inevitable aspect of aging. There are no measures of intelligence, learning, or memory for which older adults reliably outperform younger adults. Research stemming from the information-processing and psychometric perspectives seems to reinforce one of the most common images of adult cognitive development—as you age, you become less intelligent, less able to learn, less attentive, and less able to remember.

But some older adults have the extraordinary mental characteristic referred to as wisdom. **Wisdom** is a particular mental quality associated with the cognitive abilities of some aged individuals but not with younger individuals. With the attainment of wisdom, older people are able to blend personal history and important information from the past to resolve a current problem (Clayton & Birren, 1980; Dittmann-Kohli & Baltes, 1988). Those considered to possess wisdom combine reflective abilities such as self-analysis and introspection along with affective components such as empathy, gentleness, and peacefulness. Wisdom is more than the sum total of an elderly person's cognitive abilities; it is composed of reflection, affect, and knowledge. Certainly, traditional psychometric and information-processing approaches have little, if anything, to say about the development of wisdom during older adulthood.

Which is the more valid image to hold of the cognitive abilities of the older adult? Are the elderly forgetful, inattentive, unintelligent, and foolish; or wise, knowledgeable, and sage? To help you make a meaningful choice between these two contrasting images, this chapter describes the stage theory approach to the study of adult cognitive development. Stage theories stress the idea that new, more sophisticated ways of thinking emerge during adulthood.

We begin this chapter with a description of Piaget's theory of cognitive development, paying special attention to Piaget's description of formal operations. This stage was originally thought to be the final, most advanced stage of cognitive development. Next, we consider newer research that has sought to identify a stage of cognitive development beyond formal operations. This stage, which only emerges during the adult years, has been referred to as postformal operations. We review the basic characteristics of postformal thinking especially as it applies to social cognition—the manner in which people understand and resolve the interpersonal problems characteristic of everyday life.

Then we discuss the encapsulation model of adult cognitive development. This model, developed by John Rybash, William Hoyer, and Paul Roodin, integrates and extends the different theoretical perspectives (the psychometric, information-processing, and developmental stage theories) that bear on the topic of adult cognition. We illustrate the basic tenets of the encapsulation model by describing recent research dealing with aging and cognitive expertise, and the growth of wisdom during the adult years.

STAGE THEORIES OF ADULT COGNITIVE DEVELOPMENT

People often say, "He's in a stage," or "She's going through a phase," when describing someone's development. However, it is important for researchers to be precise when describing stage-based sequences of developmental changes. Developmental psychologists use a set of criteria to identify and define stages of development.

Characteristics of Cognitive Stages

Traditionally, psychologists have argued that a true set of cognitive stages must satisfy five different criteria: invariant movement, qualitative change, hierarchical integration, universal progression, and structured wholeness.

The notion of **invariant movement** suggests that individuals must pass through a single, unchangeable sequence of stages during development. For example, if a stage theorist maintains that cognitive development consists of a four-stage sequence, then individuals must move through the stages in order: stage 1 → stage 2; stage 2 → stage 3; stage 3 → stage 4. It would be impossible to skip stages, or to regress backward through the stages.

The concept of **qualitative change** suggests that at each different stage an individual actively constructs a completely different set of highly abstract, internal, and generalizable rules that are used to represent and understand reality. These thought structures are assumed to be as different from one another as apples are from oranges. Thus, stage theorists assume that mental development involves the growth of qualitatively different ways of thinking about the world. In other words, a stage theorist would argue that a person's intellectual functioning is determined by the manner in which the individual understands reality, not by the quantity of information the individual possesses.

Hierarchical integration implies that each stage in a developmental sequence should be viewed as an incorporation as well as an extension of the stage that preceded it. This means, for example, that stage 3 in a cognitive sequence has its basis in the thought structures laid down in stage 2. It also means that stage 3 extends the structures laid down in stage 2.

The idea of **universal progression** suggests that all individuals in all cultures progress through a set of stages in the same invariant sequence. A valid stage theory must apply to all individuals, regardless of social class, race, ethnicity, educational level, or culture.

The criterion of **structured wholeness,** which may be the most controversial aspect of stage theories, implies that individuals can only understand reality one stage at a time. This means, for example, that if an individual is at stage 2 within a particular cognitive developmental sequence, she will find herself thinking about every issue or problem she might potentially confront from the perspective of that stage. In other words, a person would not be expected to reason about mathematical problems from the perspective of stage 4 and interpersonal problems from the perspective of stage 2; such an inconsistency would violate the concept of structured wholeness.

PIAGET'S STAGE THEORY

Beyond any doubt, Jean Piaget (see Piaget, 1970; Piaget & Inhelder, 1969) has formulated the most important and far-reaching stage theory of cognitive development. He identified four stages of intellectual development: the sensorimotor stage, the preoperational stage, the concrete-operational stage, and the formal-operational stage. The **sensorimotor stage** lasts from birth to about 2 years of age and is synonymous with the period most people refer to as infancy. Piaget (1954) argued that infants cannot think about the world by means of internal mental symbols (such as words, visual images, etc.). Instead, infants can only represent objects or events by external body movements.

During the **preoperational stage,** which begins at about 2 years of age and lasts until 7 years of age, children can form internal mental symbols. At this stage, however, preoperational children have a great deal of difficulty in distinguishing between internal mental symbols and the objects or events they stand for. For example, mental symbols can represent concrete or imaginary events and objects. Thus, children in this stage have a great deal of difficulty distinguishing the real from the imaginary. In the preoperational stage, children's thinking may also be irreversible. This means that they do not understand that every action has an opposite action that is the reverse of the original. For example, preoperational thinkers have difficulty grasping the idea that addition is the reverse of subtraction. Thus, they do not understand that the best way to solve the following subtraction problem: $? - 7 = 1$ is to transform it into an addition problem: $7 + 1 = ?$.

In the **concrete-operational stage,** which lasts from approximately 7 to 12 years of age, children and young adolescents can distinguish between mental symbols and real-life events or objects. Thus, children at this stage understand that Santa Claus is not a real person. Also, individuals begin to think in a reversible manner. Not only can concrete thinkers understand the complementary relationship between addition and subtraction, they can understand a relationship from different or reversible points of view. For example, when shown two pairs of sticks, the concrete thinker can understand that (1) if the red stick is taller than the blue stick ($R > B$), and (2) the blue stick is taller than the green stick ($B > G$), then the red stick must be taller than the green stick ($R > G$). Put another way, the concrete thinker is able to reason that "If the blue stick is shorter than the red stick but taller than the green stick, then the red stick must be taller than the green stick."

Concrete thinking has its limitation. Consider, for example, the following problem: "Imagine there are three girls walking down the street. Of these three girls, Mary is taller than Jane but shorter than Susan. Who is the tallest of the three?" This problem is very similar to the stick problem, but the stimuli in the former problem were concrete (they were actually seen and touched) while the stimuli in the latter task were hypothetical (they had to be imagined). Piaget maintained that it is only during the fourth and last stage of cognitive development, the stage he termed **formal operations,** that individuals can reason about hypothetical, abstract relationships.

FORMAL OPERATIONS

The stage of formal operations, which according to Piaget emerges somewhere around early adolescence to midadolescence, has occupied an important place in the study of adult cognition. The importance of formal operations lies in the fact that it represents Piaget's view of mature adult cognition.

Characteristics of Formal Operations

Piaget and his associate Barbel Inhelder (Inhelder & Piaget, 1958; Piaget & Inhelder, 1969) have discovered three important characteristics of formal thinking:

1. A reversal in the relationship between reality and possibility
2. An ability to think in a hypothetical-deductive manner
3. A capacity to think about the nature of thinking

With regard to the first of these characteristics, Piaget suggested that a concrete thinker's understanding of reality consists of a series of generalizations based on specific, real-life experiences. At the level of concrete operations, therefore, real experiences are more important than possible (or hypothetical or abstract) experiences. Formal thinkers, however, are capable of creating a reversal in the relative importance they attach to real versus possible experiences. This reversal allows formal thinkers to think logically about verbal propositions. Verbal propositions may be regarded as pure ideas. The truth value of a verbal proposition depends on its logical relationship to other propositions, not on its relationship to concrete, real-life events. Thus, formal thinkers can reason about contrary-to-fact ideas and experiences. For example, think about the following problem: Would the weather be any different if snow was black, not white? A concrete thinker would probably argue that this is a silly problem because in real life, snow is not black. Formal thinkers, on the other hand, can rise above the constraints of reality. They understand that even though snow is not black, it is nevertheless logical to conclude that if snow was black the weather would change because the temperature would change (if large portions of the earth's surface were covered by a black substance, the earth would become hotter because the dark surface would absorb heat).

The concept of hypothetical-deductive thinking means that formal thinkers are capable of reasoning like scientists. They can create abstract hypotheses and then test the validity of these hypotheses by observing the results of well-controlled experiments. Thus, scientific thinking is deductive in that it proceeds from the general (the abstract hypothesis) to the specific (creating a single experiment designed to test the theory).

The notion of thinking about thinking means that formal thinkers can ponder the meaning and significance of their mental experiences from multiple points of view. For example, an individual at the formal operational stage can think, "I want to be married," and can then generate a number of hypothetical explanations of the meaning and significance of that thought from his point of view as well as the point of view of others (e.g., parents). The ability to think about thinking accounts for the fact that adolescents and adults often become armchair psychologists who find it intriguing to analyze their own mental activity as well as the thoughts and feelings of others.

Measurement of Formal Operations

Inhelder and Piaget (1958) invented several different types of tasks to determine whether an individual has reached the stage of formal operations. In this section we discuss two of these tasks: the proportional-thinking task, and the isolation-of-variables task. A *proportional-thinking* task refers to a type of problem that can only be solved if an individual approaches a mathematical problem by using simple arithmetic (a con-crete-operational strategy) or by using algebraic reasoning (a formal-operational strat-egy). For example, consider the following:

> A psychologist takes a cup, dips it into the large bowl filled with beans, and pulls out 80 beans. Next, she takes a felt-tipped pen and places a large X on each of the 80 beans. She puts the marked beans back into the bowl and randomly mixes the beans. Then she dips the cup back into the bowl and extracts another sample. She discovers that there are 75 beans in the cup and that 15 of the 75 beans have an X on them. What would you estimate the total number of beans in the bowl to be?

A concrete thinker, using simple arithmetic, might answer 140 (adding the 60 unmarked beans in the second sample to the 80 marked beans in the first sample). A formal thinker, using algebraic reasoning, would say 400 (if one-fifth of the beans from the second sample were marked, it is logical to assume that one-fifth of the total num-ber of beans were obtained on the first sample. Therefore, if 80 is one-fifth of the total number of beans, there are 400 beans because $5 \times 80 = 400$).

In the *isolation-of-variables* problem, a person must determine which of a large number of variables produces a specific outcome. One of the most widely used prob-lems of this type is the pendulum task in which a participant is asked to determine the factor(s) influencing the speed at which a pendulum swings back and forth. These fac-tors include the length of the pendulum string, the weight of the object placed at the end of the string, the height at which the pendulum is released, and the force with which the pendulum is pushed.

Participants are given a pendulum apparatus that comes with two different strings (a long string and a short string) and two objects of different weights that can be placed on the ends of the strings (a heavy weight and a lighter weight). Given the materials at their disposal, the participants are told to do as many experiments as they need to solve the problem. This task measures formal operational thinking because it requires partic-ipants to behave like scientists. They must develop a theory about what controls the oscillation of the pendulum and then perform the crucial experiments to test the theory. Only at the stage of formal operations do individuals approach this problem in a scien-tific and systematic manner; that is, they evaluate each of the potential factors one at a time (keeping all of the other factors constant). Using this approach, they discover that the length of the string, not any of the other factors, determines the speed of oscillation.

Research on Formal Operations

Piaget (1972) assumed that individuals begin to develop formal operational thinking skills at about 11 years of age and that they fully complete the transition from concrete to formal operations at no later than 15 to 20 years of age. A great deal of research has examined Piaget's assertions about the age at which individuals attain formal reason-ing. Surprisingly, it has been discovered that a significant percentage of young adults, middle-aged adults, and older adults do not attain the stage of formal operations. Fur-thermore, it has been shown that being able to solve one type of formal-thinking task does not guarantee that a person will be able to solve another type of formal-thinking task (Berzonsky, 1978; Brainerd, 1978). For example, adults who are able to solve an

Complex logical problem solving remains a salient feature of adult thinking.

isolation-of-variables task are not necessarily capable of solving a proportional-thinking task, and vice versa.

Overall, the available research seems to indicate that the earliest point in development during which formal operational thinking may appear is early adolescence to midadolescence. But this does not mean that all individuals begin thinking in a formal manner at this time; nor does it mean that all individuals will ultimately reach formal operations. These findings have forced psychologists to reconsider Piaget's conception of formal operations.

Reconceptualizing Formal Operations

As you may have recognized, the tasks Piaget constructed for assessing formal thought focus on problems from the fields of mathematics and physics. Without the prerequisite educational background and cultural experience, many adolescents and adults are at a distinct disadvantage when given these tasks.

In an important paper published in 1972, Piaget modified his view on formal operations. Piaget argued that the stage criteria of structured wholeness may not apply to formal operations. He maintained that based on aptitude, educational experience, motivation, professional specialization, and other factors, adults may develop formal thinking in some, but not all, areas. For example, an experienced garage mechanic may use formal reasoning to diagnose (and correct) the problem with a faulty automobile engine, but the same mechanic may have a concrete understanding of a critically ill patient's right to refuse medical treatment. On the other hand, a physician may reason at the formal level when thinking about problems involving medical ethics, but the same physician may continue to use concrete thinking to figure out why the family car keeps stalling.

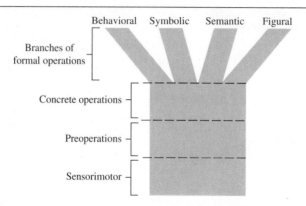

Figure 9.1 An illustration of Berzonsky's branching model of formal operations.

Branches of formal operations

Concrete operations

Preoperations

Sensorimotor

Behavioral Symbolic Semantic Figural

The behavioral branch involves an understanding of interpersonal and intrapersonal psychological processes.

The symbolic branch involves the ability to represent and manipulate arithematic and algebraic symbols.

The semantic branch involves the representation and manipulation of ideas within a verbal medium.

The figural branch involves the representation and manipulation of ideas and concrete objects within a visual medium.

One of the more interesting extensions of Piaget's (1972) modified view of formal operations has been articulated by Michael Berzonsky (1978). He proposed that Piaget's theory can be conceptualized as a tree (see figure 9.1). The first three stages of the theory make up the trunk of the tree. The formal operational stage represents the branches. These branches, which are based on Guilford's (1967) ideas about the different dimensions of intelligence, represent the areas within which an adult could develop formal-thinking skills. As you can see, it is possible to develop formal reasoning in any of a number of different domains (e.g., reasoning about interpersonal relations; reasoning about art, music, and literature; reasoning about mathematical or scientific issues; and so forth).

Critique of Formal Operations

Formal operational thinking provides a powerful, but somewhat limited, mode of thought. In this section, we discuss six limitations of formal thinking as identified by Rybash, Hoyer, and Roodin (1986).

1. Formal operations overemphasizes the power of pure logic in problem solving. This limitation is expressed in the following passage:

    Reason reveals relations within any given context. . . . But there is a limit. In the end, reason itself remains reflexively relativistic, a property which turns reason back upon reason's own findings. In even its farthest reaches, then, reason will leave the thinker with several legitimate contexts and no way of choosing among them—no way, at least, that can be justified through reason alone. If he still is to honor reason he must now also transcend it; he must affirm his own position from within himself in full awareness that reason can never completely justify him or assure him. (Perry, 1968, pp. 135–136)

2. Formal operations underemphasizes the pragmatic qualities of real-life cognitive activity. Labouvie-Vief (1984) reinforced this point when she noted that upon entry into adulthood, ". . . there is a concern with the concrete constraints of real life or the refusal to sever cognition from its affective, social, and pragmatic ties" (p. 159).

3. Formal thinking is only suited for the problems that call for scientific thinking and logical mathematical analysis. Piaget assumed that the goal of the cognitively mature adult was to reason like a scientist or a mathematician. Consequently, he did not examine how cognition is applied to real-life social or interpersonal problems. In connection with this point, Flavell (1977) maintained, "Real problems with meaningful content are obviously more important in everyday human adaptation (than abstract, wholly logical problems), and it is possible that these are the kinds of problems our cognitive apparatus has evolved to solve" (p. 117).

4. Formal operations is geared for the solution of closed-system, well-defined problems. A closed-system problem is one in which a person determines how a limited number of controllable and specific variables produce a specific and reliable outcome. For example, in the pendulum task, a series of miniexperiments helps to determine how a limited number of controllable and specific variables influence the oscillation of a pendulum. Closed-system problems are also well defined in that they have a single, correct solution (it is the length of the string that controls the oscillation of the pendulum). Real-life problems, in contrast, are open to the extent that they are characterized by an unlimited number of uncontrollable, fuzzy variables (see Basseches, 1984; Koplowitz, 1984). For example, a woman must consider an infinite number of constantly changing variables when deciding whether to pursue a business career or take time off from business when having a child. Furthermore, open-system problems are ill-defined because they emerge from changeable and uncontrollable variables and do not have a single correct solution (there is no one correct solution, e.g., to the woman's problem about whether to pursue her career or take time off when she becomes a mother).

5. Formal operations does not recognize the relative nature of knowledge and the need to adopt multiple frames of reference. Thinking from a relativistic standpoint has been referred to as "intersystemic thinking" by Gisela Labouvie-Vief (1982). She argued that intersystemic thinking ". . . reveals the basic duality of logical truth. This realization initiates a movement from logical absolutism to logical relativism. . . . Much as truth now is relativistic, one's actions must be singular and particularized. The erosion of logical certainty throws the self explicitly back on its own resources" (Labouvie-Vief, 1982, p. 182).

6. Formal thinking places a greater emphasis on problem solving than on problem finding. This means that formal thought is best suited for generating and testing hypotheses that aid in the solution of closed-system, well-defined problems. Problem finding, in contrast, represents the ability to generate new questions that arise from ill-defined problems (Arlin, 1975, 1984). It reflects the ability of

adults to ask novel questions about themselves, their work, and the events that surround them. Arlin (1984) observed that the essence of problem finding was described by Wertheimer (1945). Wertheimer suggested that "the function of thinking is not just solving an actual problem but discovering, envisaging, and going into deeper questions. Often in great discovery the most important thing is that a certain question is found" (p. 46). Problem finding is observed in particular scientific fields at particular times when faulty assumptions are challenged by new discoveries and questions.

POSTFORMAL COGNITIVE DEVELOPMENT

The shortcomings of formal thinking have set the stage for a major conceptual revision of Piagetian theory. It is now assumed that a unique form of thinking, called **postformal operations,** emerges during the adult years.

Characteristics of Postformal Thinking

Diedre Kramer (1983) identified three basic features of postformal reasoners. First, postformal thinkers possess an understanding of the relative, nonabsolute nature of knowledge. Second, postformal thinkers accept contradiction as a basic aspect of reality. For example, a physicist might come to understand light as being both waves and particles, or an individual might realize that his feelings about another person cannot be described in terms of love or hate alone, but by the simultaneous existence of these apparently contrasting emotions. Third, postformal thinkers are capable of dialectic reasoning. They possess an ability to synthesize contradictory thoughts, emotions, and experiences. Instead of viewing a contradictory situation as a choice between alternatives, the postformal reasoner views it as a call to integrate alternatives. See Research Focus 9.1 for Michael Basseches's (1984) conception of dialectic thinking.

In addition to the insights offered by Kramer (1983), we suggest that postformal thinkers adopt a contextual approach to problem solving. That is, they solve problems by continuously creating new principles based on the changing circumstances of their lives—rather than by applying a set of absolute principles or standards across all contexts and circumstances. This may be especially true when adults reason about the ill-defined problems characteristic of everyday social life. Furthermore, postformal thinking seems to be domain-specific in nature. This means that adults develop postformal thinking within some, but not all, areas of knowledge. Finally, postformal thinking may be more directed toward problem finding than problem solving.

RESEARCH ON POSTFORMAL THINKING

William Perry (1968) was one of the first researchers to address the topic of postformal thought. He conducted a longitudinal study in which he questioned university students about their educational and personal experiences. Perry found that first-year students approached various intellectual and ethical problems from a dualistic (formal) perspective. These students assumed that any problem or ethical dilemma could have

Basseches's View of Dialectic Thinking

Michael Basseches's (1984) view of postformal thought focuses on the means by which the adult thinker envisions reality as a multitude of relationships or systems that continuously change over time. Furthermore, Basseches proposed that the adult thinker comprehends these constantly changing systems in a constantly changing world through the principle of the dialectic. The term *dialectic* refers to an understanding of how transformations occur through constitutive and interactive relationships.

Relationships are constitutive in that the elements of a relationship are created by the whole relationship they make up. The whole relationship could not exist, however, without its component parts. Therefore, it is both the relationship that creates the elements and the elements that create the relationship. Relationships are also interactive: They are characterized by mutual (or reciprocal) influence. In other words, the components of a relationship are changed by one another to the same extent that they change one another.

Let's look at an illustration that contrasts formal thinking with dialectic or postformal thinking. This example, which is drawn from Basseches (1984, pp. 26–27), deals with the topic of marriage and the problems that could arise between husband and wife.

A formal thinker would probably view the partners of a marriage as two individuals, each of whom possesses a number of fixed and stable traits. The traits that characterize the husband's personality exist independently of those that characterize the wife's personality, and vice versa. Therefore, the marriage of these individuals represents a connection between two elements (husband and wife) that have a separate existence outside of the relationship they are entering. These two sets of fixed traits should give rise to a relationship that remains fixed and stable over time. Marital problems from a formal perspective might develop for two reasons. First, they could result from a permanent flaw or shortcoming in either the husband's or

wife's personality (e.g., one of the marriage partners made a bad choice—he or she picked a mate with a totally incompatible personality). Second, it could be that neither of the partners was intrinsically flawed; their marriage developed problems because in some cases the interaction of the personalities of two good people proves to be problematic (e.g., they were two nice people who just weren't meant for each other).

A dialectic thinker would view the elements of any relationship as being in a state of constant flux. Therefore, the traits of the man and the woman who enter the marriage are not regarded as stable and permanent over time. More important, it is assumed that the traits of both husband and wife could not exist independently of one another. The traits of the man as a husband are influenced by his relationship with his wife, and vice versa. In other words, marriage is a constitutive relationship in which the elements of the relationship are totally interdependent on each other. Furthermore, dialectic thinkers view marriage as an interactive relationship, a relationship in which the elements of the relationship (husband and wife) mutually change and are changed by each other. Finally, a dialectic thinker would regard marital problems as the result of a relationship that has evolved in an increasingly maladaptive manner. The negative interactions have consequences for the whole of the relationship—the marriage—and the negative interactions have consequences for the growth of the individuals in the relationship (the husband and wife who create and are created by the relationship). Viewing a problematic relationship from this perspective allows husband and wife to avoid blaming each other as the cause of the problems. It also allows them to value their relationship as something that was meaningful at some point in its growth and evolution. The crucial question the dialectic thinker asks is, "How does our marriage need to change in response to the changes it has brought about in both of us?"

---

only one correct answer, and that it was the task of authority figures (in their case, perhaps, professors) to teach them the correct answer. In time, they began to realize the inherent subjectivity of experience. This led the students to conceptualize all knowledge and value systems—even those espoused by authorities—as relative and nonabsolute. At this level, the students felt as if they were adrift in an ocean of uncertainty. They thought that any problem could be approached from a variety of viewpoints, each of which seemed to possess equal merit and validity. Finally, some students reached a developmental level, termed *contextual relativism,* that indicated postformal thinking. They still understood the relativity of knowledge, but they were no longer overwhelmed by it. These students became committed to a self-constructed intellectual and ethical point of view in which they both accepted and transcended relativity.

Karen Kitchener and Patricia King (1981) have investigated the relativistic nature of adult thinking with their reflective judgment model. This model postulates the existence of a series of seven stages, each characterized by a set of assumptions upon which individuals justify their beliefs about reality and knowledge. Table 9.1 contains a brief description of each of these stages. Several researchers (King, Kitchener, Davison, Parker, & Wood, 1983; Kitchener & Wood, 1987) have discovered that individuals systematically pass through these different stages from adolescence to middle adulthood. To date, this model has not been extended to research involving the elderly.

Jan Sinnott (1981, 1984, 1989) maintained that relativistic thinking can be directed at several different intellectual domains (e.g., the physical sciences or mathematics). But she contended that it is easiest to understand the relativistic nature of post-formal reasoning within the area of interpersonal reality. Specifically, she applied the term *necessary subjectivity* to describe relativistic thinking within the area of interpersonal relations. Necessary subjectivity means that when adults solve interpersonal problems, they are guided by the premise that subjectivity, or mutually contradictory frames of reference, is a basic characteristic of interpersonal reality. This contrasts with the typical view of physical reality, in which subjectivity is considered to be faulty thinking and eliminated from problem analysis. To examine the relativistic nature of

---

TABLE 9.1

Stages in Kitchener and King's Reflective Judgment Model

Stage 1: Belief in the absolute correspondence between reality and perception. Therefore, beliefs require no justification because to observe reality means to know reality.

Stage 2: Belief in the existence of an objective reality and absolute knowledge of this reality. It is the role of authority figures (e.g., professors) to know and transmit objective knowledge. Therefore, personal beliefs are justified by their correspondence to the beliefs of authorities.

Stage 3: Belief that authorities may be temporarily unaware of particular types of absolute knowledge. It is also assumed that while such missing knowledge will ultimately be obtained, it is permissible to believe in what "feels right" to the self.

Stage 4: Belief that there is an objective reality that can never be known with certainty. Therefore, all knowledge, even knowledge possessed by authorities, must be conceptualized as relative to the individual's point of view.

Stage 5: Belief that not only is knowledge subjective or relative, but that all of reality is subjective or relative as well. Since reality and knowledge of reality can only be understood through subjective interpretation, understanding is contextual and cannot be generalized.

Stage 6: Characterized by the belief that even though all knowledge is subjective, some forms of knowledge may be more valid than others. This claim is based on the premise that there are principles of inquiry which generalize across contexts.

Stage 7: Characterized by the belief that knowledge is the result of critical inquiry. Valid knowledge claims may be made by evaluating the work of many individuals over a long period of time. The process of critical inquiry, however, may give rise to fallible knowledge. Therefore, all knowledge claims must remain open to reevaluation vis-à-vis the formulation of new theoretical paradigms and the accumulation of new data.

From K. S. Kitchener and P. M. King, "Reflective Judgment: Concepts of Justification and Their Relationship to Age and Education" in Journal of Applied Developmental Psychology, 2: 89–111. Copyright © 1981 Ablex Publishing Corporation, Norwood, NJ. Reprinted with the permission of Ablex Publishing Corporation.

adult cognition, Sinnott (1984) presented a group of adults between 26 and 89 years of age with a variety of problems designed to detect the presence of formal thinking and relativistic thinking. The results showed that older adults were more likely to use relativistic thinking to deal with real-life rather than abstract problems. Younger participants were more likely to solve all types of problems by adopting a nonrelativistic, formal mode of thinking.

Rakfeldt, Rybash, and Roodin (1996) examined the relationship between postformal thinking and the ability to profit from psychotherapy. The participants in this study were adult, first-admission patients in a psychiatric hospital. It was discovered that patients who displayed relativistic thinking tended to have a more efficacious understanding of themselves, their disorders, and their relationships with others. These patients also seemed to take an active role in their healing. In contrast, patients who adopted an absolute (i.e., formal) perspective seemed to make less significant therapeutic gains. Formal thinkers believed it was the duty of authority figures—their psychiatrists—to discover the "true" disorder they suffered from, and treat the disorder while the patients adopted a passive stance. Rakfeldt et al. concluded that relativistic thinking allows patients to better understand the complexities and paradoxes of their psychiatric disturbances as well as the choices and options open to them within the therapeutic encounter.

Arlin (1984, 1989) studied postformal thinking in a group of young adult artists, all of whom performed equally well on measures of formal thought. Differences between artists who were classified as either formal or postformal in their cognitive orientation were related to their answers to questions such as, "Could any of the elements in your drawing be eliminated or altered without destroying its characteristics?" The formal-thinking artists viewed their works as fixed, unalterable, and finished, while the postformal artists viewed their works as changeable and unfinished. Arlin suggested that the more creative artists were postformal thinkers who (1) did not adopt a single, fixed, and absolute view of their work, (2) accepted the idea that their work could evolve and change over time, and (3) actively tried to find new perspectives from which to view their work.

Kramer, Kahlbaugh, and Goldston (1992) developed an objective measure of postformal reasoning called the Social Paradigm Belief Inventory (SPBI). This test consisted of several statements about social, interpersonal, and intrapersonal issues, each of which was written in absolute, relativistic, and dialectic versions. Participants were required to choose the one version that best captured their viewpoint on a particular issue (see table 9.2 for an example of a test item, and table 9.3 for some of the basic assumptions that underlie absolute, relativistic, and dialectic thinking). Kramer et al. (1992) administered the SPBI to subjects within five age groups: college students (aged 17–20) to older adults (aged 60–83). Results, which are illustrated in figure 9.2, indicated that statements which espoused a simplistic, absolute orientation were uniformly rejected by participants within each of the five groups. Importantly, it was discovered that as age increased, participants were more likely to endorse dialectic statements and less likely to choose relativistic ones. Furthermore, participants' responses on the SPBI were found to be unrelated to verbal intelligence and several personality variables such as dogmatism, tolerance of ambiguity, and social desirability. These findings suggest

TABLE 9.2

Examples of Absolute, Relativistic, and Dialectic Statements on the Social Paradigm Belief Inventory

Absolute Statement: Change comes from the outside. It is for the most part forced on us by job changes, financial circumstances, and the like.

Relativistic Statement: Change comes from the inside. It comes from a change in outlook on things; no matter what happens on the outside you can always alter your view of things and you will be different.

Dialectic Statement: Change comes neither from the inside or the outside. It comes from an interaction of natural changes the person goes through with changes in the environment and how these changes are seen by the person.

From D. A. Kramer, P. E. Kahlbaugh, & R. B. Goldston, "A Measure of Paradigm Beliefs about the Social World" in Journal of Gerontology: Psychological Sciences, 47: 189. Copyright © 1992 The Gerontological Society of America.

TABLE 9.3

Basic Assumptions of Absolute, Relativistic, and Dialectical Perspectives on Personal and Social Issues

Perspective	Basic Assumptions
Absolute	Belief in the inherent stability of all things. Individual seen as passive in environmental influence of behavior. Causality is seen as linear, deterministic, and universal. Belief in absolute, universal principles and ideals. Belief in validity of one-sided solutions. All phenomena and knowledge are seen as inherently noncontradictory.
Relativistic	Decision making on pragmatic, rather than absolute criteria. Change is basic to reality. Every person, relationship, system, or situation is unique. Unpredictability and indeterminism are central to reality. Contradiction is seen as a primary feature of reality.
Dialectical	All phenomena imply their opposites. Emergence characterizes systems, whereby the whole defines the parts; all life is systemic. Development occurs via increasingly adapted forms. All change is characterized by reciprocity, where a change in any one part affects the whole system.

From D. A. Kramer, P. E. Kahlbaugh, & R. B. Goldston, "A Measure of Paradigm Beliefs about the Social World" in Journal of Gerontology: Psychological Sciences, 47: 189. Copyright © 1992 The Gerontological Society of America.

that relativistic thinking may be the first component of postformal thought to emerge during late adolescence/early adulthood, and, with age and experience, dialectical thinking replaces relativistic thinking as the main characteristic of mature thought.

Conclusions About Postformal Cognitive Development

Clearly, some adults are capable of conceptualizing reality in a postformal manner. Furthermore, the postformal cognitive orientation displayed by these adults is very different from the formal orientation displayed by adolescents. Postformal thinking seems to

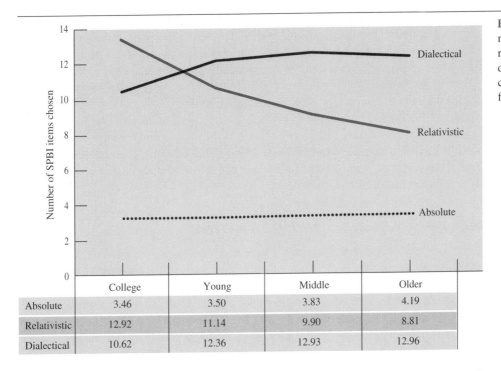

	College	Young	Middle	Older
Absolute	3.46	3.50	3.83	4.19
Relativistic	12.92	11.14	9.90	8.81
Dialectical	10.62	12.36	12.93	12.96

Figure 9.2 The number of absolute, relativistic, and dialectical items chosen as a function of age.

be a necessity if adults are to truly appreciate the complexities of both physical and social reality. It would be a mistake, however, to believe that all adults display all of the characteristics of postformal development.

Reasoning about social matters clearly occupies a central role in post-Piagetian attempts to identify the levels or stages of postformal cognitive development. Indeed, one characteristic of all of the Piagetian revisionists described in this chapter is the dominant theme that adult cognition involves the interchange of the individual with his or her social world. Reasoning about the social and interpersonal world is termed **social cognition.** Clearly, our social cognitions are a pervasive aspect of our lives.

There continues to be a great deal of controversy concerning the characteristics of postformal reasoning. Some psychologists believe that postformal thinking reflects a genuine stage of cognitive development well beyond formal operations (Commons, Sinnott, Richards, & Armon, 1989). With regard to the stage issue, Lamberson and Fischer (1988) have made a distinction between optimal level and functional level. *Optimal level* refers to the best or highest level of stagelike performance a person can achieve under ideal conditions. *Functional level* refers to a person's stagelike performance under normal, nonoptimal conditions where the individual is offered little environmental support. Lamberson and Fischer argued that it is only possible to observe genuine stages of development if we measure an individual's optimal level, not his or her functional level. They also suggest that we focus our attention on an individual's developmental range—the gap between the person's optimal and functional levels. Other psychologists have suggested that developmental changes in thought beyond formal operations, even when measured under optimal conditions, may not meet the criteria that define genuine cognitive stages. Rybash et al. (1986), for example, argued that postformal development may be best understood as a set of styles of thinking (relativistic, dialectic, etc.) that emerge during adulthood rather than a true stage.

Finally, several developmental psychologists have expressed reservations about the need for the stage concept itself. For example, Brainerd (1978), Gelman (1979), and Gardner (1983) have commented that the cognitive performance of children and adolescents is so inconsistent and variable that it is difficult to embrace the existence of a set of stages that comprise cognitive development. Certainly, adult cognitive performance may reflect even greater individual variability and inconsistency due to the accumulation of different experiences.

ADULT COGNITION: AN INTEGRATION

In the last three chapters of this text, we have reviewed theory and research that bears on the different approaches to the study of adult cognition: the psychometric approach, the information-processing approach, and the stage approach. Each of these different approaches provides valuable information and perspective about the nature of adult cognitive development. However, each of these different theoretical views focuses on a different aspect of cognition, and each has a number of major limitations. In this section, we describe a perspective on adult cognitive development proposed by John Rybash, William Hoyer, and Paul Roodin (1986). This approach, referred to as the encapsulation model, integrates and extends the basic features of the traditional approaches to the study of adult cognition.

The Encapsulation Model

The **encapsulation model** makes the fundamental assumption that cognition consists of three interrelated dimensions: processing, knowing, and thinking. *Processing* refers to the way in which various mental abilities and/or capacities are used to process (encode, store, and retrieve) information. *Knowing* refers to the way in which extant knowledge aids in information processing and problem solving. *Thinking* refers to an individual's understanding or perspective on the knowledge that she has accumulated during her development. Unfortunately, these three facets of cognition have been examined in relative isolation from one another by psychologists interested in the study of adult cognitive development.

Adherents of the information-processing and psychometric approaches have explored processing. In general, researchers working within these traditions have viewed adulthood as a period of negative developmental change. They have concluded that adults become less adept at general problem solving because they process reduced amounts of information in a progressively slower and less efficient manner.

Knowing has been the primary focus of the cognitive-science perspective on cognition. The dominant concern within this tradition has been with the growth and representation of knowledge and with the development of artificial intelligence software systems (see Gardner, 1985; Waldrop, 1984). Cognitive scientists assume that intelligent problem solving has its source in the size and breadth of the individual's knowl-

Advanced intellectual skills remain functional in highly specific domains throughout adult life.

edge base rather than in the power of the individual's generalized mental abilities (fluid intelligence), mental capacities (attention, memory), or internalized thought structures (postformal thinking). Research conducted within the context of this approach is essentially nondevelopmental. It has been suggested (Charness, 1988), however, that research within the cognitive-science tradition has important implications for the study of adult cognitive development. Adulthood is the portion of the life span during which individuals develop domain-specific cognitive expertise. Thus, older adults are likely to display sophisticated cognitive performance in the areas of specialization within which they have developed an expertlike knowledge base. Read Research Focus 9.2 to gain a better understanding of the cognitive-science approach to the study of cognition.

Developmental changes in thinking have been the focus of theory and research inspired by traditional Piagetian theory. Neo-Piagetian theorists have viewed adulthood as a period of positive developmental change marked by the transition from formal to postformal styles of thinking. Postformal thinking permits adults to view reality in relativistic and dialectic terms. Such thinking styles provide the necessary basis for the solution of both well- and ill-defined problems and the discovery of new perspectives from which new problems may be identified. The postformal approach certainly has its merits. Postformal theorists, however, appear to paint an overly optimistic picture of aging. They fail to acknowledge the cognitive losses and declines that play a salient role in development during the middle and later years of adulthood.

The Cognitive-Science Approach

Rybash, Hoyer, and Roodin (1986) noted that psychologists studying cognitive development during adulthood are faced with an apparent paradox. Research based on psychometric and information-processing theory indicates a deterioration of generalized cognitive ability with age, while everyday observation of adults within their occupational roles, social interactions, and hobbies indicates that with increasing age comes stability (and sometimes even enhancement) of cognitive performance.

An important line of research that bears on the resolution of this paradox is represented by the cognitive-science approach to the study of cognition. This approach suggests that intelligent problem solving lies in the possession and utilization of a great deal of specific knowledge about the world. Waldrop (1984), in tracing the influence of the cognitive-science approach on the study of artificial intelligence (AI), comments: "The essence of intelligence was no longer seen to be reasoning ability alone. More important was having lots of highly specific knowledge about lots of things—a notion inevitably stated as, 'Knowledge is power' " (p. 1280). Thus, in contrast to the earlier approaches (such as the psychometric and information-processing perspectives) that represented human problem solving as a generalized mental process, capacity, and/or ability, contemporary cognitive scientists suggest that problem solving in adulthood requires expert knowledge.

Importantly, expert performance has been found to be domain-specific and independent of generalized mental abilities. For example, Chase and Simon (1973) and de Groot (1965) carried out a number of groundbreaking studies on chess experts and novices. These researchers found that chess experts (i.e., grand masters) could reconstruct the positions of approximately 25 chess pieces arranged in a real game configuration on a chessboard after having seen the display for only five seconds; novice players, on the other hand, could only remember the positions of about six or seven pieces. When the same 25 pieces were arranged in a random configuration on a chessboard, both the experts and the novices remembered the positions of the same number of pieces—approximately seven. Furthermore, experts and novices were not found to differ from each other with regard to generalized measures of memory span and short-term memory. And expert players did not evidence a superiority in

general intellectual ability as measured by IQ test performance. It seems safe to conclude that chess experts have exceptionally good memories for positions of pieces on a chessboard when the arrangement conforms to a real game because of the vast amount of specific knowledge they possess about game configurations of chess pieces. In fact, it has been estimated that chess experts have stored, in long-term memory, approximately 40,000 different game configurations!

Ceci and Liker (1986) investigated the ability of gamblers to handicap horse races. The individuals in the study were avid horse-racing enthusiasts who went to the racetrack nearly every day. Ceci and Liker gave all these participants an early form of a racing sheet. This allowed the gamblers to study the past performances of the horses that would be competing in all 10 races the next day at a real racetrack. The researchers asked the men to pick (1) the favorite in each of the 10 races, and (2) the top three finishers in each of the 10 races in the correct order. The men's selections were compared with the post-time odds for the horses in each race as well as with the actual order of finish for each race. Based on their analysis, Ceci and Liker identified 14 "experts" and 16 "nonexperts." The experts selected the horse with the best post-time odds in 9 out of the 10 races and the top three horses in at least one-half of the races. The nonexperts performed much more poorly. The experts were found to use very complex mental models to make their selections. These models took into account the interaction of about seven different variables: the horse's times during the first and last quarter-miles of a race, the quality of the horses it had competed against in the past, the jockey riding it, and so on. In comparison, the nonexperts used very simplistic models to make their picks.

Most surprisingly, Ceci and Liker found that the experts and nonexperts did not differ on a number of variables that would seem to be good predictors of their handicapping skill. For example, these two groups did not differ in IQ score, years of education, occupational status, or number of years of handicapping experience—both groups had been going to the track for about 16 years! Ceci and Liker concluded that expertise in handicapping is not purely dependent on past experience or general intelligence.

The encapsulation model suggests that basic mental capacities and fluid mental abilities become increasingly dedicated to and encapsulated within specific domains of knowledge during the course of adult development. As general processes and abilities become encapsulated within domains, adults' knowledge becomes more differentiated, accessible, usable, and "expert" in nature. The encapsulation model also suggests that the acquisition of new knowledge (knowledge unrelated to that already encapsulated

World-renowned British astrophysicist Stephen Hawking, at age 47, held the Newton Rostrum at Cambridge University. Hawking, who authored the book A Brief History of Time, *suffers from motor neurone disease, cannot walk or talk, and communicates with the help of a voice-equipped computer.*

in specific domains) becomes increasingly less efficient with advances in age. Mastery of new domains is somewhat uncharacteristic of older adults, who are not ideal "learning machines." Childhood and adolescence are periods of the life span characterized by the acquisition of new knowledge in a variety of ever-expanding domains. Adulthood may be a time during which individuals refine and develop a perspective on their knowledge.

The reduced capacity to acquire new knowledge during adulthood may be compensated for by the development of expert knowledge within existing domains and by the development of a postformal perspective on that knowledge. Once adults conceptualize their domain-specific knowledge in a relativistic, dialectic, and open-ended manner, they become capable of solving the ill-defined problems characteristic of real life, finding new problems and new perspectives from which these problems may be solved, and producing creative and sophisticated works within defined areas of expertise.

The encapsulation of thinking and knowing within specific domains seems to represent a necessary and adaptive feature of adult cognitive development. Thus, the age-related loss of general intellectual abilities as reported in psychometric and information-processing research may have little functional significance for most adults in most situations. Although age-related declines in fluid abilities and mental capacities are indeed documented, these findings seem to result from the practice of assessing mental processes apart from the domains in which they have become encapsulated. Age-related differences in the component processes of cognition (memory, attention,

TABLE 9.4

Basic Assumptions of the Encapsulation Model

1. Processing, knowing, and thinking are the three dimensions of cognition that must be addressed in any comprehensive theory of adult cognitive development.
2. The processes associated with the acquisition, utilization, and representation of knowledge become encapsulated within particular domains as one grows older.
3. Mental capacities appear to decline with age when assessed as general abilities but show minimal age-related decline when assessed within encapsulated domains.
4. Adult cognitive development is characterized by the growth of expert knowledge and the emergence of postformal styles of thought. Adult styles of thinking and forms of knowing are the result of the process of encapsulation.

Source: Data from J. M. Rybash, W. J. Hoyer, and P. A. Roodin, Adult Cognition and Aging: Developmental Changes in Processing, Knowing, and Thinking, *Pergamon Press, Inc., Elmsford, New York, 1986.*

etc.) cannot be meaningfully assessed apart from the domain in which these processes are encapsulated. A summary of the encapsulation model is provided in table 9.4.

We can illustrate the basic claims of the encapsulation model by examining two different lines of research. First, we present the results of several studies that have examined the relationship between aging, information processing, and cognitive expertise. Second, we review studies on the growth of wisdom during adulthood.

AGING, INFORMATION PROCESSING, AND COGNITIVE EXPERTISE

The encapsulation model suggests that adults continue to accumulate knowledge, which becomes increasingly refined with age and experience. Accumulated domain-specific knowledge can take on a compensatory function for older adults. This means that older adults can continue to function effectively when given tasks that allow them to draw on their expert knowledge (Clancy-Dollinger & Hoyer, 1995; Hoyer & Rybash, 1992a, 1994; Morrow, Leirer, Alteri, & Fitzsimmons, 1992). This occurs in spite of the significant reduction in the generalized information-processing skills and/or fluid intellectual abilities that accompany the aging process. Evidence for this point of view comes from several sources. Timothy Salthouse (1984, 1990), Neil Charness (1981, 1985, 1988), and Stephanie Clancy-Dollinger and William Hoyer (1988, 1994, 1995) have all shown that expert knowledge can compensate for general losses in processing speed and working memory in older adults.

Typing

Salthouse (1984) conducted an experiment with typists who differed in age (young adults versus older adults) and skill level (novices versus experts). As might be expected, Salthouse discovered that the older typists performed more poorly than younger typists on tasks assessing (1) simple reaction time, (2) the fastest speed at which they could tap their fingers, and (3) digit-symbol substitution. (Remember that the digit-symbol substitution task is a component of the WAIS. In this task, a person is asked to match, as quickly as possible, a series of numbers with a series of abstract geometric patterns.) More important, Salthouse also discovered that the participants' typing speed was uncorrelated with age but was significantly related to the participants' skill level. The expert typists (both young and old) were significantly quicker than the novice typists (both young and old). Through a set of ingenious experiments, Salthouse was able to determine that older expert typists compensated for age-related declines in speed and reaction time by looking farther ahead at printed text, thereby giving themselves more time to plan what their next keystroke should be. Finally, Salthouse's findings illustrate the domain-specific nature of older adults' compensatory mechanisms. Older expert typists did not employ the same look-ahead strategy on any of the other tasks Salthouse administered (e.g., digit-symbol substitution), although the implementation of this strategy would have improved their performance.

Chess

Charness (1981, 1985) reported that older chess experts were found to be as competent as younger chess experts in choosing the best chess move from four possible alternatives. More specifically, older experts were found to search just as many moves ahead as younger experts. But they were also found to entertain fewer possible moves than their younger counterparts, showing even greater efficiency. Charness concluded that older chess experts compensate for general processing and memory deficits by using an elaborate knowledge base acquired over years of practice. The growth of this vast and highly organized knowledge base allows older experts to search for appropriate moves as quickly as (and perhaps even more efficiently than) younger experts.

One thing to consider is that there is difference between maintaining expertise versus maintaining one's best performance. As figure 9.3 shows, the performance of a chess grand master (a very select group indeed) peaks at about age 40. But, the typical 65-year-old grand master play on a par with the average 21-year-old grand master.

Medical Diagnostics

Clancy and Hoyer (1988) conducted an experiment with medical laboratory technologists who differed in both age (young adults versus older adults) and skill level (novices versus experts). Keep in mind that a medical laboratory technologist, as an integral part of his or her job, performs a number of complex visual identification tasks such as looking at slides of tissue or blood under a microscope to identify certain diseases. This experiment consisted of two parts. In the first part, the participants had to identify several unfamiliar visual stimuli (e.g., abstract geometric figures) that were flashed on a video screen for less than a second. As expected, results showed that younger participants scored better on this domain-general task than older participants. Also, the participants' success on this task was unrelated to their skill level within the field of medical laboratory technology.

Figure 9.3 Age and chess performance. *Source: Charness, N., & Bosman, E. (1990). Expertise and aging: Life in the lab. In T. H. Hess (Ed.), Aging and cognition: Knowledge, organization, and utilization (p. 358). Amsterdam: Elsevier.*

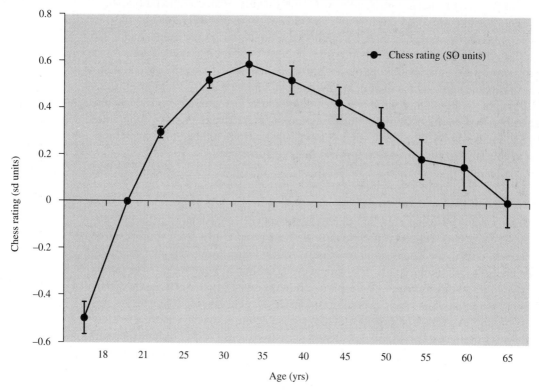

In the second part of the study, the technologists were briefly shown pictures of complex microscopic slides of actual laboratory specimens. Each slide contained a number of clinically significant and clinically insignificant pieces of information. Clinically significant information was defined as a piece of visual information crucial to the diagnosis of a particular disease. On the other hand, clinically insignificant information was defined as visual information that does not serve as an effective diagnostic aid. The participants were shown a single piece of visual information and asked if it was present in the original complex slide. Results indicated that both the younger and older experts were equally quick and accurate in determining if a clinically significant piece of information was present in a previously seen complex slide. Furthermore, the performance of both expert groups on this task was unaffected by having to perform another task concurrently—pressing a button whenever a tone sounded. In contrast, both younger and older novices performed poorly on this microscopic identification task, especially under dual-task conditions (when they were also required to perform the button-pressing task).

Clancy and Hoyer (1994) performed another experiment that examined the effects of age and experience on information processing. They administered domain-general and domain-specific visual search tasks to medical laboratory technologists and control subjects at two age levels (young adulthood and middle adulthood). The domain-general task involved finding a letter of the alphabet in a briefly presented visual display. In the skilled task, participants searched a visual display for a specific type of bacteria specimen. Also, prior to the presentation of the bacteria samples, participants were shown word cues that were informative, noninformative, or neutral with regard to the target they had to search for. Results indicated that middle-aged control participants performed more poorly than younger control individuals on the domain-general and domain-specific tasks. When the data from the experts were analyzed, a different pattern emerged. Middle-aged experts performed worse than younger experts on the domain-general task but not the domain-specific task. And both expert groups benefited to the same extent when informative cue words were presented prior to the domain-specific search task.

Limits of Expertise

Finally, note that cognitive expertise is not powerful enough to compensate for the reductions in the mental capacities and physical abilities that underlie performance in all domains. For example, performance in such sports as golf, tennis, basketball, and football declines with age even among individuals who possess a great deal of expert knowledge about these sports. On the other hand, performance within domains that allow more time for planning and reflection, that demand fewer snap decisions and less physical exertion (e.g., musical composition or visual art), may actually improve because of the cumulative effects of age and experience. In connection with this point, Charness (1985) has commented that "... when people can draw upon domain-specific knowledge and when they have developed appropriate compensatory mechanisms, they can treat us to a memorable performance, whether on the keyboard of a typewriter, a piano, or on the podium of an orchestral stage. When the task environment does not afford the same predictability or opportunity to plan ahead, however, as is the case in fast-moving sports environments, degradation in hardware cannot be compensated for by more efficient software" (p. 23).

Furthermore, for expertise to aid problem solving there needs to be an exact match between the older person's knowledge and the task that he or she is given to solve. In other words, expertise does not enhance (or even maintain) the domain-general abilities upon which the expertise seems to be based. The conclusion is based on the work of Lindenberger, Kliegl, and Baltes (1992) and Salthouse, Babcock, Skovronek, Mitchell, and Palmon (1990). Both of the research groups discovered that older adult experts in architecture and graphic design—occupations that place a premium in visual cognition—displayed significant declines in domain-general visual thinking and mental imagery.

One of the most perplexing questions surrounding the issue of aging and expertise is: "Why does an individual become an expert in a particular area?" See Research Focus 9.3 for a discussion of some of the most current theories of expertise.

What Does It Take to Become an Expert?

What accounts for the extraordinary performance of a musician, the outstanding contribution of a scientist or writer, or the unique feats of an athlete? Sir Francis Galton (1869/1979) was one of the first individuals to examine the development of expertise from a scientific perspective. He argued that excellence within a particular field is due to three factors: innate ability (or talent), a burning desire to become the "best," and extensive and laborious practice. Galton assumed that these last two factors (i.e., motivation and practice) were necessary but not sufficient conditions in achieving exceptional performance. In other words, practice is necessary for greatness (even Michael Jordan has to practice), but extensive practice, by itself, will not guarantee success (extensive practice alone will not turn the most dedicated basketball player into another Michael Jordan). This means that individual variability in optimal performance must, in the final analysis, reflect individual differences in what might be called innate talent, giftedness, or natural ability—or "unmodifiable genetic good luck."

This view has both intuitive appeal and scientific credibility. One of the leading proponents of the talent-based approach to expertise is Howard Gardner (1983, 1993a, 1993b, 1995). As you remember from the chapter on intelligence, Gardner put forth the theory of multiple intelligences. Gardner's theory emphasizes (1) the neurological basis of different symbol systems (e.g., linguistic, musical, visual-spatial, bodily-kinesthetic, etc.), which lay the basis for various human intelligences, and (2) the wide-ranging variability that exists both between (and within) individuals in terms of the inborn strength of these different symbol systems (i.e., the degree to which individual brains differ in the extent to which they are "hardwired" via genetic mechanism to excel at dif-

ferent ways of being intelligent). The biggest selling point of Gardner's theory is the observation that certain individuals—namely, childhood prodigies and idiot savants—display superior performance in a single domain (e.g., music or mathematics) but exhibit average (or below average) performance in all other areas. Most certainly, the psychometric or Piagetian approaches cannot account for this pattern of behavior.

Despite its intuitive appeal, Gardner's talent-based approach is not without its critics. Ericsson and Charness (1994, 1995), for example, do not deny the fact that childhood prodigies and idiot savants exist. However, they point out that the vast majority of prodigies develop their skills because of continued practice in combination with constant support from teachers and parents, that hardly any childhood prodigies become exceptional adult performers (e.g., it is extremely rare to see a childhood prodigy like Mozart become a world-renowned musician during adulthood), and that most exceptional adult performers were not identified as childhood prodigies (e.g., based on his performance relative to his agemates in elementary or high school, there was no basis for the prediction that Michael Jordan would become one of the best basketball players ever). Finally, Ericsson and Charness (1994) argue that it is possible to train "normal" individuals to achieve the high levels of performance displayed by savants in areas such as mental arithmetic, calendar calculation, memory span, and so on, and that the special skills and abilities displayed by prodigies and savants do not develop all at once as suggested by popular myths and stereotypes—their detection may in some case be sudden, but the skill probably took a great time to develop and was fostered by supportive conditions.

WISDOM

Wisdom is a mental characteristic or ability that has long been associated with aging within both Eastern and Western cultural traditions (Clayton & Birren, 1980). Beyond any doubt, the most exciting and provocative work on the topic of wisdom has been conducted by Paul Baltes and his colleagues at the Max Planck Institute in Berlin, Germany. Dittmann-Kohli and Baltes (1988) distinguished between philosophical wisdom and practical wisdom. **Philosophical wisdom** refers to an understanding of the abstract relationship between one's self and the rest of humanity. Alternatively, **practical wisdom** refers to the ability to display superior judgment with regard to important matters of real life. Baltes and Staudinger (1993) defined this latter form of wisdom as ". . . an expert knowledge system in the fundamental pragmatics of life permitting exceptional insight, judgment, and advice involving complex and uncertain matters of the human condition" (p. 76). And they suggested (see figure 9.4) that wisdom may be characterized by a family of dimensions that,

Ericsson and Charness (1994, 1995) have argued for a practice-based model of exceptional performance. They discount the innate abilities position and suggest that expertise is the end result of many years (and thousands of hours) of deliberate practice and hard work under the watchful eye of a coach or teacher. In fact, there is evidence from a number of different sources that approximately 10 years of intense preparation and practice is necessary to achieve an exceptionally high level of performance across a wide range of domains. This 10-year rule seems to apply to such diverse areas such as chess, athletic events, literary achievement, and scientific research. One very important point to consider is that the practice that leads to expertise is both deliberate and tedious. It is not necessarily fun and does not lead to immediate personal, social, or monetary rewards. Ericsson, Krampe, and Tesch-Römer (1993) showed that top-level teenage violinists had practiced, on the average, more than 10,000 hours, which was approximately 2,500 hours more than the next most accomplished group, and 5,000 hours more than those who were categorized at the lowest expert level. Interestingly, Ericsson and Charness (1994) suggest that genetic factors might be responsible for expertise. But they suggest that the genetic mechanisms indirectly affect expertise by having a direct influence on temperament and motivation. Humans might be more likely to inherit genes for hard work and perseverance than for musical talent. This is consistent with Charles Darwin's statement that ". . . men do not differ much in intellect, only in zeal for hard work" (quoted in Galton, 1869/1979, p. 290).

Two other points raised by Ericsson and Charness (1994, 1995) also need to be briefly addressed. Both of the points refute the assumption that the exceptional performance rests upon unmodifiable abilities. First, the basic biological, behavioral, and cognitive capacities of experts do not differ from nonexperts. For example, elite basketball players and boxers do not have simple reaction times and perceptual abilities that differ from the average individual's; chess grand masters have not been found to have out of the ordinary generic memory skills and visual-spatial abilities. Second, the cultural evolution of expertise occurs at pace that certainly exceeds any large-scale biogenetic changes in our basic biological structure. For example, today's high school students are capable of grasping mathematical concepts and procedures (e.g., calculus) that two centuries ago were only understood by the world's most advanced mathematicians. Today's typical elite musicians consider several pieces (e.g., Tchaikovsky's violin concerto) to be part of their standard repertoire, whereas performers at the turn of the century considered these selections to be unplayable. And progress in sporting events has been so fast paced that the winner of the 1896 Olympic marathon running race would just about qualify to be in the field for next year's Boston Marathon.

Given the basic tenets of the talent-based versus practice-based models of exceptional performance, what advice would you give individuals throughout the life span who strive for superior performance? What factors would you look for if you wanted to discover people who would become the "best" at what they do?

over the course of human history, many diverse cultures have identified as important. Note that these characteristics reflect the essential features of knowledge encapsulation and postformal thinking.

Fluid Mechanics and Crystallized Pragmatics

Baltes's research on age-related changes in wisdom is a component of his overarching viewpoint that the human mind possesses two fundamental dimensions (Baltes, 1987). First, the **mechanics of mind** involves the raw, basic operations of our human information-processing system. It represents elementary "mental hardware" such as sensation, perception, and memory. These processes are typically measured by the speed and accuracy with which people can perform simple tasks. In general, mental tasks that reflect the operations of basic cognitive-neural mechanisms are referred to as measures of fluid intellectual abilities. There is a gradual age-related decline in performance on measures of fluid intelligence.

Wisdom-related skills and personal intelligence are characteristics that help determine a successful psychotherapist or counselor.

Figure 9.4 The Berlin model of wisdom as an expert knowledge and behavior system in the fundamental pragmatics of life.

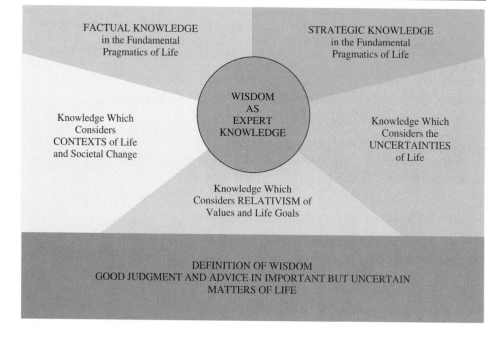

FACTUAL KNOWLEDGE
in the Fundamental
Pragmatics of Life

STRATEGIC KNOWLEDGE
in the Fundamental
Pragmatics of Life

WISDOM
AS
EXPERT
KNOWLEDGE

Knowledge Which
Considers
CONTEXTS of Life
and Societal Change

Knowledge Which
Considers the
UNCERTAINTIES
of Life

Knowledge Which
Considers RELATIVISM of
Values and Life Goals

DEFINITION OF WISDOM
GOOD JUDGMENT AND ADVICE IN IMPORTANT BUT UNCERTAIN
MATTERS OF LIFE

Second, the **pragmatics of mind** refers to the "mental software" that encompasses the general system of factual and strategic knowledge accessible to members of a particular culture, the specialized systems of knowledge available to individuals within particular occupations and avocations, and an understanding of how to effectively activate these different types of knowledge within particular contexts to aid problem solving. Most important, the pragmatic quality of mind allows us to develop a strategy—wisdom—for negotiating the major and minor obstacles of everyday life. Furthermore, since cultural (not biological) factors influence mental pragmatics, it may be the case that aging is accompanied by cognitive growth—a growth in wisdom—not decline or stagnation.

Testing the Limits of Cognitive Reserve

To evaluate his ideas about the mechanics of mind, Baltes and his coworkers (Baltes & Kliegl, 1992; Kliegl, Smith, & Baltes, 1989) have used the technique of **testing the limits** of maximum cognitive reserve. In this methodology, groups of younger adults and older adults are required to recall a list of 30 familiar nouns (plane, chair, etc.) in the order in which they were presented. Then they are taught a mnemonic strategy—the method of loci—to increase their recall. In this memory enhancement procedure, individuals are instructed to create mental images that allow them to associate list items with familiar landmarks. For example, a person may think about driving to work in the morning while visualizing list items. One might imagine an airplane at the end of one's driveway, a chair perched on the top of the stop sign at the end of one's street, and so on. When given a memory test, the person re-creates these images one location after another.

Using this technique, Baltes and Kliegl (1992) gave groups of younger (20-year-olds) and older (70-year-olds) participants 35 training and testing sessions over a period of one year and four months. Across all sessions, each participant performed 4,380 trials of trying to generate a mental image that linked a familiar location to a list item. The results of this research are displayed in figure 9.5.

In the initial testing session, participants remembered about six words, and younger adults performed slightly better than older adults. With extended practice, the memory of both younger and older participants increased in a spectacular fashion. Now, a large proportion of the participants could remember between 20 and 30 words in the correct order. However, the training increased (rather than decreased) the difference in memory performance between the two age groups. In fact, the older adults who displayed the best performance at the end of the experiment seemed to be on a par with the younger adults who displayed the worst performance! And, after all of the training sessions, the older adults did not achieve a level of performance that the younger adults exhibited after just a few sessions. Baltes and Kliegl suggested that older adults do not benefit from practice as much as younger adults because of an age-related deterioration in mental reserve capacity that is similar to the loss of reserve capacity in biological domains such as cardiovascular or respiratory potential.

In an interesting twist on the preceding research, Margaret Baltes and her associates (Baltes, Kühl, & Sowarka, 1992; Baltes, Kühl, Gutzman, & Sowarka, 1995) used the testing-the-limits methodology as a diagnostic strategy for the early identification of Alzheimer's disease (AD). The major idea behind these experiments is that at-risk

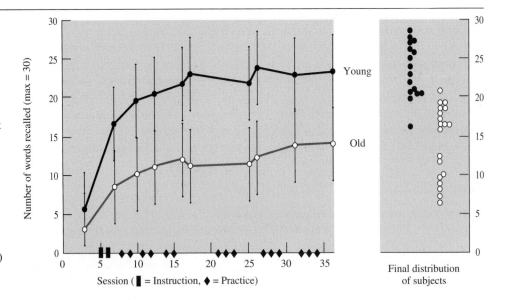

Figure 9.5 Performance by young and old adults in serial recall of lists of words as function of training in the method of loci (left panel). (The bars indicate standard deviations. In the right panel, individual scores are given for the last assessment sessions [36/37]. Max = maximum.)

elderly should possess less reserve capacity than healthy elderly, and therefore should not profit from cognitive training in comparison to healthy elderly. In these experiments, therefore, healthy older adults as well as older adults who were at risk for AD were given several training sessions on various measures of fluid intelligence such as figural relations and inductive reasoning. Results shows that the at-risk group of older adults benefited far less from training than their healthy counterparts. Thus, the testing-the-limits strategy may become an important clinical screening tool.

Wisdom and Aging

Are the inevitable declines in the mechanics of mind offset by positive changes in the pragmatics of mind—in wisdom? This is a rather complex question, because living a long life would seem to be a sufficient condition to produce a decline in basic mental abilities; but, a long life, by itself, does not seem to be a sufficient condition for the growth of wisdom. Consequently, Baltes and his colleagues (Baltes & Staudinger, 1993; Smith & Baltes, 1990; Staudinger, Smith, & Baltes, 1992) hypothesized that wisdom is the end result of a coalition of three factors: (1) advanced chronological age, (2) favorable personality traits such as openness to experience, and (3) specific experiences in matters relating to life planning and the resolution of personal, ethical dilemmas.

Given this orientation, Staudinger et al. (1992) investigated the growth of wisdom via the **age-by-experience paradigm,** a method that possesses a great deal of commonality with the strategy that researchers such as Clancy-Dollinger and Hoyer (1994) have used to assess the role of age and expertise on information processing. Specifically, Staudinger et al. (1992) tried to find groups of individuals who differed in age as well as exposure to life experiences that would be considered facilitative to the development of wisdom. For example, they argued that certain professions such as

TABLE 9.5

Two Life Review Problems

Young Version

Martha, a young woman, had decided to have a family and not to have a career. She is married and has children. One day Martha meets a woman friend whom she has not seen for a long time. The friend had decided to have a career and no family. She is about to establish herself in her career.

Old Version

Martha, an elderly woman, had once decided to have a family and not to have a career. Her children left home some years ago. One day Martha meets a woman friend whom she has not seen for a long time. The friend had decided to have a career and no family. She had retired some years ago.

Standard Probe Questions for Both Versions on the Life Review Problem

This meeting causes Martha to think back over her life.
1. What might her life review look like?
2. Which aspects of her life might she remember?
3. How might she explain her life?
4. How might she evaluate her life retrospectively?

From U. M. Staudinger, J. Smith, and P. B. Baltes, "Wisdom-Related Knowledge in a Life Review Task: Age Differences and the Role of Professional Specialization" in Psychology and Aging, 7: 271–281. Copyright 1992 by the American Psychological Association. Reprinted by permission.

clinical psychology might give rise to a series of life experiences that are more conducive to wisdom than the life experiences associated with a career in a nonhuman services field such as accounting. This research strategy enabled Staudinger et al. (1992) to assess the separate, and interactive, effects of age and experience on wisdom.

Staudinger et al. (1992) selected a subject sample that consisted of younger (average age 32 years) and older (average age 71 years) women who were either clinical psychologists or professionals from outside the area of psychology (e.g., architects, journalists, and natural scientists). All of the participants, regardless of age and professional specialization, were similar in terms of formal education and socioeconomic status and displayed identical scores on a measure of crystallized intelligence. As would be expected, however, younger adults performed better than older adults on a measure of fluid intelligence.

In the main part of the experiment, Staudinger et al. presented the participants with a "life review problem" in which the main character was either a young or an elderly woman who had to reflect on her decision to have a career rather than a family (see table 9.5 for the actual problems and a list of the standard probe questions). Participants' responses to the life review problems were scored on the five different dimensions of wisdom as identified by Baltes and his colleagues. Table 9.6 contains examples of wise responses to the life review problems from the perspective of each of these dimensions.

Results of the Staudinger et al. study were straightforward (see figure 9.6). First, younger and older women did not differ in their overall level of performance. Second, clinical psychologists exhibited a greater amount of wisdom-based responses than the nonclinicians. Third, older adults displayed better performance than younger adults when the life review dilemma involved an elderly woman; but younger and older adults displayed

TABLE 9.6

Illustration of the Characteristics of a Wise Response to the Life Review Tasks

Dimension of Wisdom	Characteristics of an Ideal Wise Response
Factual Knowledge	Knowledge about the human condition as it relates to the life review situation (e.g., achievement motivation, emotions, vulnerability, and societal norms). Knowledge about life events relevant to a mother's versus a professional woman's life.
Strategic Knowledge	Cost-benefit analysis: developing various scenarios of life interpretation. Means-goals analysis: what did/does the woman want and how can she/did she try to achieve it.
Contextualism	Discussion of the life review tasks in age-graded (e.g., timing of childrearing and professional training), culturally graded (e.g., change in woman's roles), and idiosyncratic (e.g., no money for education) contexts. The three contexts are discussed across different domains of life (e.g., family, profession, and leisure) and across time (past, present, future). The contexts are not independent; sometimes their combination creates conflict and tension that can be solved.
Relativism	Life goals differ depending on the individual and the culture. The origins of these differences is understood and the differences are respected. No absolute relativism but a set of "universal" values is acknowledged.
Uncertainty	Plans can be disrupted; decisions have to be taken with uncertainty; the past cannot be perfectly explained nor the future fully predicted (e.g., marriage does not work out, children handicapped, or professional failure). One can work, however, from experience and knowledge-based assumptions and continuously modify those as new information becomes available.

From U.M. Staudinger, J. Smith, & P.B. Baltes, "Wisdom-Related Knowledge in a Life Review Task: Age Differences and the Role of Professional Specialization" in Psychology and Aging, 7: 271–281. Copyright 1992 by the American Psychological Association. Reprinted by permission.

identical performance when the life review problem focused on a young woman. Fourth, when the top 25 percent of the responses to the life review problems were examined, it was found that the older clinicians were the group most likely to generate wise responses. Fifth, participants' performance on standardized measures of fluid and crystallized intelligence accounted for very little of their performance on the life review tasks.

Overall, these findings are important for several reasons. First, unlike fluid mechanics, age differences are eliminated on wisdom-related tasks, and older adults seem to display the "best" levels of performance. Second, life experience and professional specialization seem to interact. The highest level of performance was displayed by older adults who responded to a dilemma involving an older person. Younger adults, on the other hand, were not capable of using knowledge about their own life stage when responding to the dilemma involving a younger person.

Although certainly thought provoking, the findings reported by Staudinger et al. (1992) do not clarify the roles of professional training and life experiences in the development of wisdom. For example, "Would it be possible for older (or younger) adults who were not trained as psychologists to display wisdom?" Clearly, the notion of "wisdom" would lose a great deal of its appeal if it hinged on one's professional training and occupational experiences. See Research Focus 9.4 for more information on this matter.

Figure 9.6 Distribution of the top 25% of responses in a wisdom-related task of life review. Clinical psychologists (a sample case of professionals with exposure to structured tutoring and practice in the meaning and conduct of life) outperformed matched control subjects. In addition, older clinical psychologists contributed a major share to the top performances. *Source: Data from Baltes and Staudinger, 1993.*

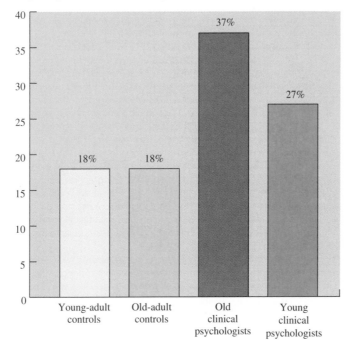

One final observation is that wisdom is not an isolated object or skill to be found within an individual. Rather, wisdom typically manifests within the context of human social interactions. (For example, when faced with a difficult problem we typically ask other people for their opinions. We usually don't act on our own hunches.) This insight led Staudinger and Baltes (1997) to conduct an empirical study in which pairs of individuals between 20 and 70 years of age were assigned to different experimental conditions that varied the degree to which the participants had to interact with each other as they tried to solve various wisdom-related problems. Results showed that experimental manipulations that increased social interactions had a very beneficial effect on wisdom-based responses. More interesting, the older adults in a study benefited much more from this "interactive minds" setting than did the younger adults.

SELECTIVE OPTIMIZATION AND COMPENSATION

Given the results of the research studies that have investigated age-related changes in the mechanics and pragmatics of mind, psychologists should realize that cognitive aging is a dynamic process that involves a changing gain/loss ratio in which decrements in reserve capacity may be offset by the accumulation of expertise. Baltes and Baltes (1990) have developed a strategy for successful aging, termed **selective optimization**

Wisdom and Professional Expertise

Research conducted by Paul Baltes and his associates has contributed to the understanding of wisdom. This team of researchers has shown that wisdom is an attribute of older adults that does not exhibit an age-related decline. Using an age-by-experience paradigm, Staudinger et al. (1992) have shown that older clinical psychologists were more likely to generate high-quality wise responses to a life review problem than were younger clinical psychologists, and that both groups of clinicians performed better than younger and older controls. Despite the intuitive appeal of these findings, the Staudinger et al. (1992) research possesses two drawbacks. First, and foremost, it's unclear if the older clinical psychologists preformed exceptionally well on the wisdom task merely because they were psychologists. Wisdom, in other words, may be a form of expertise that is tied to the profession of psychology. If this is true, it would mean that the concept of wisdom advanced by Baltes is much too limited in scope. Perhaps Baltes and colleagues, because they are psychologists, unconsciously biased their conception of wisdom to make it consistent with psychological principles. Second, the life review problem used in the Staudinger et al. (1992) study may not have been the best task by which to measure wisdom. Perhaps another type of problem could have been constructed that placed a greater premium on generating truly wise responses.

Recently, Baltes, Staudinger, Maecker, and Smith (1995) conducted a study that addressed both of the preceding shortcomings. In their research, they compared younger and older clinical psychologists (along with age-appropriate control subjects) to a group of older adults who were nonpsychologists who were "nominated" to be wise. To select these "wisdom nominees," Baltes et al. contacted 21 top journalists of various political persuasions in West Berlin and asked them to identify citizens of this city who are active in public life and could be cat-

egorized as wise. This procedure yielded a list of 159 names. Then, the journalists were asked to rate all of these individuals via a seven-point scale on three criteria: life knowledge, wisdom, and personal familiarity. Next Baltes et al. only considered those nominees who were well known to each journalist (i.e., scored five or higher on the personal familiarity issue) and scored above average on the life knowledge and wisdom dimensions. This winnowing procedure resulted in a list of 22 persons, 14 of whom were younger than 80 years of age (see table 9.A for details) and were selected as the primary participants in the current research. This group of individuals was characterized by Baltes et al. as ". . . highly regarded citizens who lived extraordinary lives" (p. 157). About half of these people had published autobiographies, and approximately one-third of them had been involved in the resistance movement against the Nazi regime or emigrated during the Third Reich. Based on one's perspective, these individuals represented the "cream of the crop" or a "very biased subsample" of the older adults in Berlin.

Also, Baltes et al. (1995) used two different tasks to assess wisdom (see table 9.B). Most important, they hypothesized that the highest level of wise responses would be given to the existential life management problem rather than the life planning task. This is because issues involving human suffering and death are at the core of the construct of wisdom.

The results of the Baltes et al. research tell a most interesting story. For example, when the overall pattern of results were considered (see box figure 9.A) for individuals between 25 and 80 years of age, it was found that no age differences obtained in wisdom-related performance. However, when the top 20 percent of responses were examined, it was discovered that wisdom nominees and psychologists performed significantly better than controls. This finding reinforces the idea that wis-

TABLE 9.A				
Characteristics of the Research Participants				
Groups of Participants	Number per Group	Mean Age (and Range)	Males	Females
Wisdom nominees	14	64 (41–79)	9	5
Academics/Science	2			
Cultural Life	6			
Media	1			
Political Life	2			
Theology	3			
Old clinical psychologists	15	66 (60–76)	7	8
Young Non-human-service professionals	20	29 (25–35)	10	10
Old Non-human-service professionals	20	68 (60–80)	10	10

dom in older adults is not the outgrowth of a professional specialization in psychology. It is interesting to note, however, that performance among the nominees falls off between 80 and 90 years of age. This is consistent with Baltes and Graf's (1996) speculation that the ninth decade of life, at least under current day cultural conditions, represents a critical threshold point at which losses in cognitive mechanics cannot be offset by gains in the pragmatics of intelligence. Thus, there seems to be a

TABLE 9.B
Wisdom-Related Tasks
Existential Life Management
Somebody gets a phone call from a good friend who says that he/she can't go on anymore and that he/she has decided to commit suicide. What should one do and consider?
Life Planning
Joyce, a widow aged 60 years, recently completed a degree in business management and opened her own business. She has been looking forward to this challenge. However, she has just heard that her son has been left with two small children to care for. Joyce is considering the following options: She could plan to give up her business and live with her son, or she could plan to arrange for financial assistance for her son to cover child-care costs. Formulate a plan that details what Joyce should do and consider the next three to five years. What extra pieces of information are needed?

Figure 9.A Wisdom-related scores for nominees, clinicians, and controls. *Source: Baltes, P. B., Staudinger, U. M., Maeker, A., & Smith, J. (1995). People nominated as wise: A comparative study of wisdom related knowledge.* Psychology and Aging, *10, 155–166.*

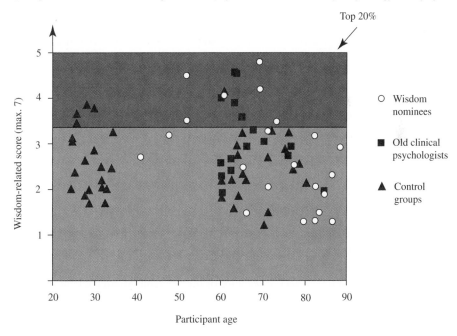

hort
Normal
Long

Figure 9.B Wisdom-related scores for nominees, clinicians, and controls on the life planning and existential life management tasks. *Source: Baltes, P. B., Staudinger, U. M., Maeker, A., & Smith, J. (1995). People nominated as wise: A comparative study of wisdom related knowledge. Psychology and Aging, 10, 155–166*

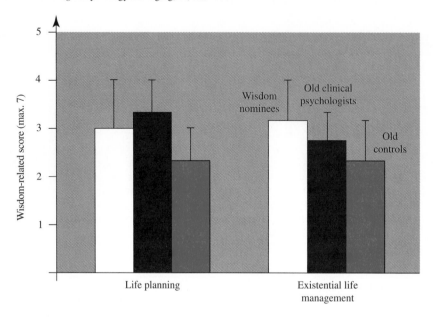

point at which very old individuals may no longer be able to compensate for their declining biological and psychological resources.

Another point to consider is illustrated in box figure 9.B. Namely, the wisdom nominees (but not the clinical psychologists) produced more wise responses to the existential life management task than the control subjects. However, on the life planning task, the clinicians scored higher than both the nominees and the controls. This is important because the existential (i.e., suicide) task seems to be more central to the concept of wisdom than the life planning problem, and because one might assume that the clinicians would excel on the suicide task due

to their professional training. This suggests that wisdom per se may be a more powerful force than professional training when dealing with the resolution of certain life matters.

In summary, the Baltes et al. (1995) research reinforced the point that wisdom is not constrained by age, occupation, and professional training. Beyond any doubt, these are encouraging results. They show that individuals from a wide range of domains may achieve wisdom, and that adults are capable of identifying wise individuals. Do these findings have any bearing on your beliefs about the capability of older individuals to occupy leadership roles in the major political, cultural, and religious institutions of our society?

with compensation, based on the insights gained from this research. The notion of *selection* means that individuals should restrict their life work to fewer intellectual domains because of an age-related loss in adaptive ability and reserve potential. These domains should be selected because of their personal (and societal) importance and relevance. *Optimization* refers to the idea that adults engage in activities that maintain their mental reserves and increase their domain-specific knowledge to maximize their cho-

TABLE 9.7

Illustration of the Principles of Selection, Optimization, and Compensation

Type of Individual	Principle
Nursing Home Resident	Selection—teach resident to become responsible for a few, but important, aspects of his daily life Optimization—offer resident extensive practice in those domains which were selected as important Compensation—give resident access to technological aids and medical interventions that support functions with diminished reserve capacities
Marathon Runner	Selection—instruct the person to give up those activities that take away from running Optimization—have the person increase the quality and quantity of her training and develop better dietary habits Compensation—have the person pay more attention to the running shoes she buys, and new techniques for healing injuries
Musician* **(*comments made** **by the pianist** **A. Rubenstien during** **a TV interview)**	Selection—reduce your repertoire, play fewer pieces Optimization—practice more Compensation—slow down playing speed prior to fast movements, thereby, producing a contrast that gives the impression of "speed" in the fast movement

Source: From P. B. Baltes & M. Baltes, "Psychological Perspectives on Successful Aging: The Model of Selective Optimization with Compensation." In P. B. Baltes and M. Baltes (eds.), Longitudinal Research and the Study of Successful (Optimal) Aging, *Cambridge University Press, Cambridge, England, 1990, pp. 1–49.*

sen life path. The term *compensation* involves the use of a new strategy or technique to adapt to a life task when a long-used psychological (or physical) skill or ability is lost or falls below a critical level. This model, which was originally developed to foster successful "intellectual aging," also offers valuable advice about how nonintellectual facets of development may be maximized across the adult years. For example, table 9.7 provides insights about how nursing home residents, athletes, and musicians might use the principles of selection, optimization, and compensation to maintain (or enhance) their performance upon entry into older adulthood.

Recently, Abraham and Hansson (1995) wanted to determine whether well-educated white-collar working adults between 40 and 69 years of age used, on a natural or spontaneous basis, the principles of "selection," "optimization," and "compensation" (SOC) in their occupational lives. One of the guiding ideas behind this study was that the use of SOC strategies might become more necessary for maintaining high levels of job performance among older adults. This is because older individuals are apt to experience declines in their biological and psychological reserve capacities. The results of this research showed that older adults were just as likely to use SOC strategies as younger individuals. This finding is important since it shows that SOC is applicable to, and used by, individuals across the adult life span. More interestingly, however, Abraham and Hansson (1995) reported that the use of SOC strategies was more highly related to job performance and goal attainment among older than younger workers. Thus SOC strategies seem especially useful for older workers.

SOC may not just apply to behaviors that are physical, artistic, intellectual, or occupational in nature. It may be applicable to many aspects of successful interpersonal and intrapersonal functioning. For example, Baltes and Graf (1996) examined the relationship age, intelligence, and subjective well-being in a group of individuals between 70 and 105 years of age. The results of this study, which took into account a subgroup of adults suspected of suffering from dementia, are displayed in figure 9.7. As would be expected, general intelligence declined with age, especially for demented individuals. However, the most interesting aspect of the data was that there was no relationship whatsoever between age and subjective well-being. What accounts for this highly paradoxical and counterintuitive finding? Why should older adults still experience a strong sense of personal control and self-esteem despite the significant losses they experience in many aspects of biological and psychological functioning? Perhaps these last two questions should be recast in the following manner: How (and why?) have older adults chosen to select and optimize their sense of well-being at the expense of other aspects of their selves? What types of strategies are they using to help them compensate for age-related losses in reserve capacity? Baltes and Graf (1996), suggest that older adults may enhance their sense of subjective well-being in a number of different ways. For example, consider an older individual who has suffered a heart attack and has the intuition that his memory and mental quickness have recently declined. This person may begin to: view himself from the perspective of a "new self" (e.g., he may think of himself as a "lover of music" instead of "as an executive who is an avid golfer"), change

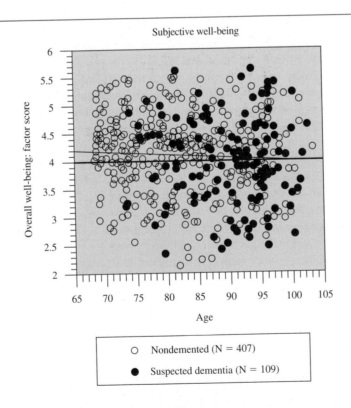

Figure 9.7 Age & subjective well-being. *Source: Baltes, P. B., & Graf, P. (1996). Psychological aspects of aging: Facts and frontiers. In D. Magnusson et al. (Eds.), Individual development over the lifespan: Biological and psychological perspectives (pp. 1–34). New York: Cambridge University Press.*

his goals and aspirations (e.g., he may adopt the primary goal of helping his grown children achieve their life goals—by giving them financial aid, advice, etc.—rather than seeking new work-related challenges for himself), and change the manner by which he compares himself to others (e.g., he may start to compare himself to other retired individuals who have cardiovascular disease rather than healthy, middle-aged executives).

One of the important aspects of the SOC approach is that the principles of selection, optimization, and compensation may be used in a very positive manner by individuals of all ages. But older adulthood is that part of the human life span during which the principles of SOC take on added significance.

RELATIONSHIP BETWEEN WISDOM, BIOLOGY, AND SOCIETY

At the most general level, the work of Baltes and his associates may be viewed as an attempt to understand the relationship between biology, society, and the aging individual. Baltes and Staudinger (1993) have made this point in a very elegant way:

> . . . because of the enriching and compensatory power of culture and knowledge-based factors, we have come to believe that the potential for future enhancement of the aging mind is considerable despite biological limits. Why? From the point of view of civilization, old age is young; it is only during the last century that many people have reached old age. Therefore, there has not been much of an opportunity for the development and refinement of a culture for and of old age. Culture, however, has the power not only to "activate" whatever biological potential is available, but also, within certain limits, to outwit the constraints (losses) of biology.
>
> Our concluding kernel of truth is this: The complete story of old age cannot be told based on the current reality about old age. . . . What also must be considered are the special strengths of *Homo sapiens:* the unrivaled ability to produce a powerful stream of cultural inheritance and cultural innovation and to compensate for biological vulnerability. Searching for a better culture of old age is not only a challenge for the future. It is the future, because the future is not something people enter, it is something people help create. In this sense research on wisdom offers a challenge to look beyond. (p. 80)

SUMMARY

The stage approach to the study of adult cognition offers an important alternative to the psychometric and information-processing perspectives. Genuine cognitive stages must meet a strict set of criteria. These criteria include (1) invariant movement, (2) qualitative restructuring, (3) hierarchical integration, (4) structured wholeness, and (5) universal progression. Jean Piaget developed the most significant stage theory of cognitive development. Originally, Piaget argued for the existence of four different cognitive stages. The fourth stage, formal operations, which Piaget thought emerged during adolescence, was thought to be representative of mature adult cognition. Piaget viewed formal operational thought as a form of scientific thinking, described as hypotheticodeductive, logical, and abstract. Formal thought seems best suited for the solution of well-defined, closed-system problems.

In the mid- to late-1970s, it became clear that Piaget's stage of formal operations did not capture the essential features of mature adult thought. Thus, psychologists began to search for a fifth, postformal stage of cognitive development. Postformal thought allows adults to solve ill-defined, open-system problems as well as to focus on problem finding, not just problem solving. We concluded that postformal development may be best understood as a number of unique styles of thinking that emerge during adulthood, not as a genuine stage of cognitive development. We also concluded that postformal accounts of adult cognition place an emphasis on social cognition. Social cognition refers to reasoning about the social, interpersonal, and ethical problems characteristic of everyday living.

We briefly described the encapsulation model of adult cognition. This model integrates the theory and research stemming from the psychometric, information-processing, cognitive-science, and cognitive-stage perspectives. It suggests that the salient dimensions of cognition are processing, knowing, and thinking. It also suggests that the most important characteristics of adult cognition (the development of domain-specific expert knowledge and postformal thinking) result from the encapsulation of basic cognitive processes and abilities. We illustrated the encapsulation model through a discussion of the relationships between aging, cognitive expertise, and information processing and by a discussion of the growth of wisdom during the adult years.

REVIEW QUESTIONS

1. Describe each of the different criteria that define genuine cognitive stages.
2. Discuss the essential features of formal operations. Describe some of the different problems that may be used to test for the presence of formal thinking.
3. Why did psychologists become disenchanted with Piaget's contention that formal operational thinking was the final stage of cognitive development?
4. Describe the essential features of postformal cognitive development. What aspect of postformal thinking (relativistic thinking, dialectic thinking, or problem finding) do you think has generated the most meaningful and important research? Why?
5. Compare and contrast the psychometric, information-processing, and cognitive-stage approaches to the study of adult cognition. Indicate the focal point as well as the strengths and weaknesses of each approach.
6. Explain the basic tenets of the cognitive-science approach to the study of cognition. What are the implications of the cognitive-science approach for psychologists interested in the study of adult cognition?

7. Explain the basic features of the encapsulation model. Explain the differences between processing, knowing, and thinking.
8. Discuss the research studies that suggest that adults continue to function effectively on tasks within which they have developed cognitive expertise.
9. Explain how psychologists have attempted to examine the concept of wisdom. What insights have psychologists gained about the relationship between the biological and cultural dimensions of aging by studying wisdom?
10. Explain how Baltes's distinction between the mechanics and pragmatics of mind relate to the basic features of the encapsulation model.
11. Give examples of how the concept of *selective optimization with compensation* may be used to help boost the performance of younger and older adults.
12. Explain the significance of research that uses the *age-by-experience paradigm* as well as the technique of *testing the limits* of cognitive reserve.
13. Briefly describe the contrasting approaches that have been put forth to explain the growth of cognitive expertise.
14. What role, if any, does professional training in psychology play in the development of wisdom?

For Further Reading

Baltes, P. B., & Graf, P. (1995). Psychological aspects of aging: Facts and frontiers. In D. Magnusson (Ed.), *Individual development over the lifespan: Biological and psychological perspectives.* New York: Cambridge University Press.

Commons, M. L., Sinnott, J. D., Richards, F. A., & Armon, C. (Eds.). (1989). *Adult development: Vol. 1. Comparisons and applications of developmental models.* New York: Praeger.

Ericsson, K. A., & Charness, N. (1994). Expert performance: Its structure and acquisition. *American Psychologist, 49,* 725–747.

Rybash, J. M., Hoyer, W. J., & Roodin, P. A. (1986). *Adult cognition and aging: Developmental changes in processing, knowing, and thinking.* New York: Pergamon Press.

PERSONALITY DEVELOPMENT

INTRODUCTION

In this chapter we examine the changes as well as the continuities of adult personality. We begin by defining personality, and then we present Erik Erikson's, Jane Loevinger's, and Daniel Levinson's stage theories of adult personality development. Next, we turn to the results of longitudinal studies of personality stability and change. Then, we describe how context or life-events affect adult personality. Last, we examine the development of morality during the adult years. We devote special attention to the relationship between moral development and the ability to cope with significant life events.

WHAT IS PERSONALITY?

Personality refers to a person's distinctive patterns of behavior, thought, and emotion. Sometimes, the term *personality* is used to refer to a person's most unique characteristics. For example, we might notice that someone we know is "shy" and that another person we know is an "extrovert." The concept of personality rests on the assumption that individuals have distinctive qualities that are relatively invariant across situations and over time (Mischel & Shoda, 1995).

Researchers and theorists often differ substantially in their views about how personality develops. Sigmund Freud emphasized the importance of unconscious motives outside the adult's awareness as determinants of personality development. B. F. Skinner (1990), in contrast, stressed the importance of learning and reinforced experiences in understanding personality and how it develops. Skinner suggested that the things a person does—his or her overt behaviors, not unconscious wishes—compose personality.

How do we measure something as complex as an adult's personality? One way is to ask a person about his or her personality. However, people do not always perceive themselves objectively. Another way to assess personality is to observe it directly as it occurs in everyday life or as it occurs under particular conditions. Other ways to assess personality involve administering tests, surveys, or questionnaires.

Regardless of the method of measurement, it is necessary to consider the effects of sociohistorical influences when trying to assess age-related changes. For example, it has been pointed out that the personality characteristics of younger adults today are different from the characteristics of older adults today, and that younger adults will be unlike older adults today when they are old (e.g., Kogan, 1990).

THE STAGE APPROACH TO ADULT PERSONALITY DEVELOPMENT

Some theorists have proposed that personality development can be described as a progression of stages. In this section, we describe the stage theories of Erik Erikson, Jane Loevinger, and Daniel Levinson.

Erik Erikson's "Eight Stages"

One of the earliest and most prominent theories of life-span personality development is Erik Erikson's eight-stage theory of psychosocial development. Freud influenced

Erikson, but unlike Freud, Erikson recognized that personality development takes place in the context of a social system.

Erikson's theory (Erikson 1963, 1968, 1982; Erikson, Erikson, & Kivnick, 1986) is particularly important because it casts a life-span frame of reference on development. Erikson accepted the basic outline of Freud's theory that early **psychosexual development,** the ways in which developing individuals deal with pleasurable body sensations, affects and shapes personality development. At the same time, however, Erikson called attention to the individual's **psychosocial development** across the life span. Erikson placed strong emphasis on the lifelong relationship between developing individuals and the social system of which they are a part. Erikson envisioned a dialectic relationship between the individual and society. Both the society and the individual change each other and are changed by each other.

According to Erikson, the personality of individuals changes or develops in a predictable manner. Erikson's theory is based on the premise that development throughout life is influenced by epigenesis. **Epigenesis** refers to an in-common genetic plan that unfolds with age. However, this genetically programmed unfolding of the personality occurs in a particular social and cultural context and is modified by that context. According to Erikson, human cultures guide or facilitate the emergence of epigenetic development. His theory emphasized the interaction between epigenesis (genetics) and culture (environment) in understanding human development. To quote Erikson:

> The human personality develops in stages predetermined in the growing person's readiness to be driven toward, to be aware of, and to interact with a widening social radius; and society, in principle, tends to be constituted so as to meet and invite this succession of potentialities for interaction and attempts to safeguard and encourage the proper rate and the proper sequence of their unfolding. (Erikson, 1963, p. 270)

Each of Erikson's eight stages centers around a salient and distinct emotional concern stemming from epigenetic pressures within the person and sociocultural expectations outside the person. The concerns or conflicts at each stage are resolved either in a positive and healthy manner or in a negative and unhealthy way. Each conflict offers a polarity that predominates all other concerns for a time. Earlier stage conflicts must be resolved satisfactorily for the successful resolution of conflicts appearing at subsequent stages.

Successful resolution of a stage crisis is not necessarily entirely positive. Exposure to the negative dimensions of conflict is often inevitable and necessary for a healthy solution to a stage crisis.

Erikson's stages of psychosocial development are listed in table 10.1. The table indicates (1) the social sphere within which each conflict occurs, (2) the self-definition that arises during the course of each conflict, and (3) the virtue (psychological strengths) that may evolve if an individual resolves a conflict in a positive manner.

The first stage, *trust versus mistrust,* corresponds to the oral stage in Freud's theory. An infant depends almost entirely on parents for food and comfort. The caretaker is the primary representative of society to the child. And Erikson assumed that the infant is incapable of distinguishing himself from his caregivers. When responsible caretakers meet the infant's needs with warmth, regularity or predictability, and

TABLE 10.1

An Overview of Erikson's Theory of Psychosocial Development

Epoch of the Life Span	Psychosocial Crisis	Sphere of Social Interaction	Self-Definition	Virtue
Early infancy	Trust vs. mistrust	Mother	I am what I am given	Hope—the enduring belief in the attainability of primal wishes in spite of the urges and rages of dependency
Late infancy/ early childhood	Autonomy vs. shame	Parents	I am what I will to be	Will—the unbroken determination to exercise free choice as well as self-restraint in spite of the unavoidable experiences of shame, doubt, and a certain rage over being controlled by others
Early childhood	Initiative vs. guilt	Family	I am what I can imagine	Purpose—the courage to pursue valued goals while guided by conscience and not paralyzed by guilt
Middle childhood	Industry vs. inferiority	Community, school	I am what I learn	Competence—the free exercise of dexterity and intelligence in the completion of a serious task
Adolescence	Identity vs. confusion	Nation	I am who I define myself to be	Fidelity—the ability to sustain loyalties freely pledged in spite of the inevitable contradictions of value systems
Early adulthood	Intimacy vs. isolation	Community, nation	We are what we love	Love—the mutuality of devotion greater than the antagonisms inherent in divided function
Middle adulthood	Generativity vs. stagnation	World, nation, community	I am what I create	Care—the broadening concern for what has been generated by love, necessity, or accident
Late adulthood	Integrity vs. despair	Universe, world, nation	I am what survives me	Wisdom—a detached yet active concern for life bounded by death

affection, the infant will develop a feeling of trust toward the world and in himself. The infant's trust consists of that comfortable feeling that someone will care for his or her needs, even though the caretaker is not always present or available. Alternatively, a sense of mistrust or fearful uncertainty can develop if the caretaker fails to provide for these needs.

Autonomy versus shame and doubt is the second stage and corresponds to the anal stage in Freud's theory. The infant begins to gain control over bowels and bladder. Parents begin to expect the child to conform to socially acceptable methods for eliminating wastes. The child may develop a healthy sense of self-control over his or her actions (not just bowel and bladder) or may develop feelings of shame and doubt because he or she is unsuccessful in self-control.

Initiative versus guilt corresponds to the phallic period in Freud's theory. The child is experiencing an Oedipal conflict or an Electra conflict, represented by competition with one parent for the love of the parent of the opposite sex. The child's exploration and discovery of ways to overcome feelings of powerlessness leads to a self-view of being competent and effective. Alternatively, the child may fail to discover ways to overcome feelings of powerlessness, which leads to feelings of guilt about being dominated by primitive urges.

Industry versus inferiority corresponds roughly to Freud's period of latency. This stage represents the years of middle childhood when the child is involved in learning new cognitive and physical skills. The child is drawn into his or her culture because many of the skills are socially prescribed and occur in interactions with peers or siblings. If children view themselves as basically competent in these activities, feelings of productivity and industry will result. On the other hand, if children view themselves as incompetent, particularly in comparison with peers, the resulting feelings are ones of inferiority.

Identity versus identity confusion is roughly associated with Freud's genital stage. The major focus during this stage is the formation of a stable personal identity. For Freud, the important part of identity formation resided in the adolescent's resolution of sexual conflicts; for Erikson, the central ingredient is the establishment of a sense of mutual recognition or appreciation between the adolescent and key persons in his or her social context. The adolescent comes to view society as decent, moral, and just. And the adolescent comes to the view that his or her existence is valued by society at large. Mutual appreciation of this sort leads to feelings of personal identity, confidence, and purposefulness. Without mutual appreciation, the adolescent feels confused and troubled.

Erikson described three stages of adult personality development. These stages, unlike the earlier ones, do not have parallels in Freud's theory. The first of these adult stages occurs during early adulthood and is termed *intimacy versus isolation*. Young adulthood usually brings opportunities to form a deeply intimate relationship with another person as well as meaningful friendships. A feeling of isolation results from the experience of not forming valued friendships and an intimate relationship.

At the same time that young adults are becoming strongly interested in developing close relationships with others, there is also a strong need for independence and freedom. Development during early adulthood involves a struggle between needs for intimacy and commitment on the one hand and needs for independence and freedom on the other. Although the balance between intimacy and independence is a concern throughout the adults years, Erikson suggested that it was a predominant theme in the early adult years.

The chief concern of middle-aged adults is to resolve the conflict of *generativity versus stagnation.* **Generativity** refers to caring about generations—one's own generation as well as future generations. Generativity could be expressed through parenting or helping others' children, or through working as a caring contributor to society. Thus, generative individuals place themselves in roles that involve caring and giving in meaningful ways.

It is during this stage that adults may experience a midlife crisis. For example, middle-aged adults may feel a sense of stagnation because they perceive that their interpersonal relationships and work have no meaning. Occupations such as teacher, minister, nurse, physician, and social worker appear generative, but builder, artist, entertainer, community volunteer, or any occupation can be generative depending on how it is carried out. The interpretation that each individual gives to his or her actions is the primary determinant of feelings of generativity or stagnation. Consider Erikson's remarks about nongenerativity, as follows:

> The only thing that can save us as a species is seeing how we're not thinking of future generations in the way we live. . . . What's lacking is generativity, a generativity that will promote positive values in the lives of the next generation. Unfortunately, we set the example of greed, wanting a bigger and better everything, with no thought of what will make it a better world for our great-grandchildren. That's why we go on depleting the earth: we're not thinking of the next generations. (quoted in Coleman, 1988)

In one study, McAdams, de St. Aubin, and Logan (1993) examined age differences in generativity among young adults (22 to 27 years), middle-aged adults (37 to 42 years), and older adults (67 to 72 years). McAdams et al. (1993) collected data on four different dimensions of generativity: generative concern—the extent to which an individual feels concerned about the welfare of future generations; generative strivings—the specific things that an individual would like to do that would help and nurture the next generation; generative action—a listing of the specific generative behaviors that one has actually performed; and generative narration—the degree to which salient past memories reflect the basic theme of generativity. Erikson's theory suggests that generativity should peak during middle adulthood and progressively decline throughout old age. Results in the McAdams et al. study were partially supportive of Erikson's position. As expected, younger adults displayed, by far, the lowest levels of generativity. Contrary to expectation, however, the scores of middle-aged adults and older adults were not different. Thus, it would seem as if the daily lives of middle-aged and older adults, much more so than younger adults, are guided by a need to be generative. This finding is illustrated by the responses (see table 10.2) to the open-ended question, "I typically try to . . . " Finally, McAdams et al. (1993) reported that, within each age group, participants who scored the highest on the generativity measures also displayed the greatest amounts of life satisfaction and happiness.

TABLE 10.2

Some of the Strivings Reported by Younger, Midlife, and Older Adults

Age of Participant	Examples of Responses to the Statement "I typically try to . . ."
26-year-old woman	"make my job more interesting" "figure out what I want to do with my life" "be well liked" "make my life more interesting and challenging" "keep up with current events" "make others believe I am completely confident and secure"
40-year-old woman	"be a positive role model for young people" "explain teenage experience to my son and help him work through difficult situations" "provide for my mother to the best of my ability" "be helpful to those who are in need of help"
68-year-old woman	"counsel a daughter who was recently let go from a job due to cutbacks" "help a daughter with her sick child" "help as a volunteer at a nonprofit organization" "offer financial aid to someone, friend or relative, if needed"

From D. P. McAdams, E. de St. Aubin, and R. L. Logan, "Generativity Among Young, Midlife, and Older Adults" in Psychology and Aging, 8:221–230. Copyright 1993 by the American Psychological Association. Reprinted with permission.

In the later years, adults enter the stage of *ego integrity versus despair.* This is a time when individuals face their own deaths by looking back at what they have done with their lives. Some older persons construct a positive view about their past, and see their life as meaningful and satisfying (ego integrity). However, some older persons look back on their lives with resentment, bitterness, or dissatisfaction. Sadly, some older adults feel that they were unable to create the life that they wanted for themselves, or blame others for their disappointment (despair). Erikson's own words best capture the richness of his thoughts about the crisis of ego integrity versus despair:

> A meaningful old age, then . . . serves the need for that integrated heritage which gives indispensable perspective on the life cycle. Strength here takes the form of that detached yet active concern with life bounded with death, which we call wisdom. . . .
>
> To whatever abyss ultimate concerns may lead individual men, man as a psychosocial creature will face, toward the end of his life, a new edition of the identity crisis which we may state in the words, "I am what survives me." (1968, pp. 140–141)

Robert Butler (1963) has given a special name to the older adult's tendency to look back in time and analyze the meaning of his or her life: the **life review.**

Erikson arranged the crises of the life span in a linear manner. Moving through the stages described by Erikson seems like climbing a ladder. The bottom rung is the crisis of trust versus mistrust, and the top rung is the crisis of ego integrity versus despair. This is not the picture of the life span, however, that Erikson tried to paint. Erikson envisioned the life span in a cyclical or circular manner. He thought the individuals who are just beginning life (infants and very young children) may be profoundly influenced by individuals who are about to leave life behind (the elderly). Erikson has stated his thoughts on this matter in the following way: "And it seems

Sex Differences in Well-Being, Personality, and Health

It is puzzling that average life expectancy is longer for women than men, but that women have higher rates of illness (or morbidity). In the United States and in a number of other countries, women experience more acute illnesses and stress than men (as discussed in chapter 6). Helgeson (1994) has suggested that these sex differences in physical well-being are related to sex role differences.

Some of these differences in physical well-being may have to do with sex differences in how men and women are socialized. For example, greater mortality from accidents for men may have to do with greater risk-taking. Women report more "illness behavior" than men, as measured by greater number of days of restricted activities, greater use of health services, and taking more medications. Helgeson suggests that women may be more responsive to stressors that affect friends and others, and that women may be generally more affected by stressors that involve

relationships than men. Evidence for the deleterious effects of having an "other orientation" comes from physiological studies. Women showed greater negative immunological effects than men when discussing marital conflict (Kiecolt-Glaser et al., 1993).

Helgeson examined sex differences in agency and communion. *Agency* and *communion* are considered to be fundamental styles of being. Agency refers to one's existence as an individual, and communion refers to the participation of an individual in relationships, groups, or communities. Helgeson suggested that both agency and communion are required for optimal functioning and well-being. When one exists in the absence of the other, negative health outcomes occur. Possible sex differences in agency and communion may account for sex differences in adverse health and mortality. Sex roles that involve a balance between agency and communion may be associated with optimal health and longer life.

---

possible to paraphrase the relation of adult integrity and infantile trust by saying that healthy children will not fear life if their elders have integrity enough not to fear death" (1963, p. 268).

Research Focus 10.1 presents information about the relationship between early experience with parents and subjective well-being during later adulthood. The research described in this box would seem to be a natural extension of Erikson's nonlinear model of personality development.

Jane Loevinger's Theory of Ego Development

Jane Loevinger's (1976) theory emphasizes that personality development involves an increasingly more differentiated perception of oneself. That is, each person develops a more precise understanding of oneself and of one's relationships to others. The adult stages of her theory are summarized in table 10.3. Several stages precede the ones listed in the table that apply to childhood and adolescent developmental issues. Loevinger states that not everyone will go through all stages. Indeed, attainment of the last two stages is relatively rare. Loevinger also emphasizes that one stage shouldn't be seen as any "better" than another, even though individuals may aspire to higher stages.

Loevinger observed that people seldom back-slide to ways of thinking associated with an early stage once they have attained a particular stage. Loevinger suggested that there is little or no back-sliding because the stages are in a sense *earned* by the individual through struggling with personal feelings and thoughts. Along these lines, Johnson and Barer (1996) and Troll and Skaff (1997) observed that many older individuals, especially individuals over 85 years who had experienced a variety of hardships and

TABLE 10.3	
Loevinger's Six Stages of Ego Development During Adulthood	
Conformist	Obedience to external social rules. Preoccupied with appearance, belongingness, and superficial matters.
Conscientious-Conformist	Increased awareness of one's own emerging personality. Increased realization of the consequences of one's actions on others.
Conscientious	Intense and complete realization of one's own standards. Self-critical.
Individualistic	Recognition that one's efforts and actions on behalf of others are more important than personal outcomes.
Autonomous	Respect for each person's individuality. Acceptance of ambiguity. Continued coping with inner conflicts contributes to feelings of appreciating the actions and approaches of other individuals.
Integrated	Resolution of inner conflicts. Renunciation of the unattainable for oneself. Cherishing the individuality of others.

Adapted from Loevinger (1976). Ego development. *San Francisco: Jossey-Bass.*

disruptive life events, radiated an "aura of survivorship," part of which is demonstrated by greater tolerance, serenity, and acceptance of what life has to offer.

According to Loevinger, people are continually directing their energies toward becoming or achieving their true selves. One's real self, or *ego,* develops slowly toward perfection, the point where there is no discrepancy between who one really is and how one acts. The ego is the chief organizer of our values, goals, and how we view ourselves and others. In her theory, the development of the true self or the *ego* comes about because of (1) basic feelings of responsibility or accountability, (2) the capacity for honest self-criticism, (3) the desire to formulate one's own standards and ideals, and (4) the nonselfish concern and love for others.

Daniel Levinson's "The Seasons of Life"

Daniel Levinson's vision of adult development was first set out in his book *The Seasons of a Man's Life* (1978). His view grew out of his interviews with middle-aged men. He interviewed hourly workers, business executives, academic biologists, and novelists. Though Levinson's major interest was the midlife transition, he described a number of phases, stages, and transitions in the life cycle, as indicated in figure 10.1.

From 1982 to 1992, Daniel Levinson, Judy Levinson, and their colleagues interviewed women regarding adult developmental transitions. The framework shown in figure 10.1 extended to the development of women during the adult years. The work applying the life transitions framework to understanding women's development during the adult years was published in the *Seasons of a Woman's Life,* in 1996.

The most important concept in Levinson's theory is the individual's **life structure.** The term *life structure* refers to the ". . . underlying pattern or design of a person's life at any given time" (Levinson, 1986, p. 41). A person's life structure is revealed by the choices he or she makes and one's relationships with others. For example, a person may choose to devote a significant amount of time and energy to an occupation and forsake relationships with a spouse, children, and fellow coworkers. Another individual

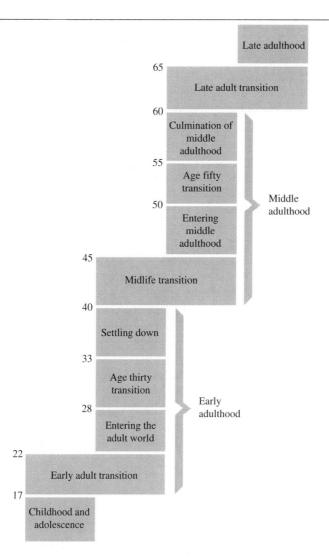

Figure 10.1 The sequence of eras and transitions for personality development during the adult years, according to Levinson (1978, 1996).

may choose to use his or her time and energy to help others acquire new competencies and job skills and to become closer to family members. Levinson reminds us that the choices we make concerning marriage and family and occupation are the two most important facets of our life structure. The relationships we have with others, as well as with our work, ". . . are the stuff our lives are made of. They give shape and substance to the life course. They are the vehicle through which we live out—and bury—various aspects of ourselves and by which we participate, for better or worse, in the world around us" (Levinson, 1986, p. 6). Finally, Levinson argues that the life structure changes and evolves over the different periods of the adult life span.

According to Levinson, the human life cycle consists of four different **eras,** each of which has a distinctive character. Like Robert Havighurst (1972), Levinson emphasizes that developmental tasks must be mastered during each of these eras. The eras partially overlap one another; a new era begins as an old era comes to an end. These periods of overlap are referred to as **transitions** and last for approximately five years. As Levinson notes, "The eras and cross-era transitional periods form the macrostructure of the life cycle, providing an underlying order in the flow of all human lives yet permitting exquisite variations in the individual life course" (1986, p. 5).

The first era, preadulthood, lasts from conception to about 17 years of age. During this time, the individual grows from a highly dependent infant to beginning to be an independent, responsible adult. The years from 17 to 22 compose the early adult transition. It is at this time that the developing person first starts to modify his relationships with family and friends to help build a place in the adult world.

The next era, early adulthood, spans the approximate ages of 22 to 40. This is an era that is characterized by the greatest energy, contradiction, and stress. The major tasks to be mastered are forming and pursuing youthful aspirations (fulfilling a dream), raising a family, and establishing a senior position in the adult world. This period can be immensely rewarding in terms of love, occupational advancement, and the realization of one's major life goals. But, due to the demands of parenthood, marriage, and occupation, this era can also be marked by conflict. One's own ambitions as well as the demands of family, community, and society can be overwhelming.

The midlife transition lasts from about 40 to 45 years of age. By the time many individuals enter this transitional period, they realize they have not accomplished what they set out to do during the early adulthood era. This realization leads to feelings of disappointment and forces the individual to recast earlier life goals. Alternatively, some individuals meet or even exceed their initial dreams. These individuals may soon realize, however, that their outstanding accomplishments did not insulate them from feelings of anxiety and crisis. These negative emotions emerge from several different sources. For example, individuals start to experience themselves as old and physically vulnerable. They become aware of their own aging, as well as the aging (and deaths) of their parents. They begin to view themselves as next in line for death. And they view themselves as the oldest surviving members of their families. Individuals still want to accomplish much, but they feel they have little time left. In essence, these are the characteristics of what other psychologists such as Gould (1972, 1980) and Sheehy (1995) refer to as the *midlife crisis.* The successful resolution of the midlife transition leads men and women to refine their goals and prove themselves while separating themselves from mentors and parents. This process is referred to as "becoming one's own self."

Levinson suggested that the midlife transition is a time of crisis and soul-searching that provides the opportunity to either become more caring, reflective, and loving or more stagnated, depending on how we accept and integrate the following polarities of adult existence: (1) being young versus old, (2) being masculine versus feminine, (3) being destructive versus constructive, and (4) being attached versus separated from others.

The third era, middle adulthood, lasts from about 45 to 60 years of age. This is the time period during which most individuals have the potential to have the most profound and positive impact on their families, their professions, and their world. Individuals no longer concern themselves with their own ambitions. They develop new long-range goals that help them to facilitate the growth of others. This is the time during which adults have the capacity to become mentors to younger individuals. One takes pride in the competence and productivity of younger individuals rather than being threatened by them. Furthermore, as individuals enter middle adulthood, they are more able to reap the benefits of family life. In essence, Levinson's ideas about middle adulthood correspond to Erikson's notion of generativity.

The late adult transition occurs from ages 60 to 65. It is during this time that older adults experience anxiety because of the physical declines they see in themselves and their age-mates, and because they are now "old" in the eyes of their culture. In the late adulthood era (65 years of age to death), the individual must develop a way of living that allows acceptance of the realities of the past, present, and future. During this era, the individual must come to grips with a crisis that is similar to Erikson's idea of ego integrity versus despair.

Levinson (1996) reported that the sequence of eras and transitions just described holds true for women as well as for men from different cultures, classes, and historical epochs. In a review of four doctoral dissertations, Priscilla Roberts and Peter Newton (1987) found that several aspects of Levinson's model applied to the personality development of young and middle-aged women. This was especially true for Levinson's suggestion that a significant transition occurs at about 30 years of age. There was, however, a major sex difference with regard to the type of dreams that were constructed during early adulthood. Recall that a "dream," according to Levinson, refers to a set of aspirations that allows an individual to break away from the preadult world and establish an overarching goal for his/her adult life, and that the dreams of young men focus on career-related issues (e.g., rising to a position of responsibility within a law firm). Roberts and Newton (1987) reported that women's dreams were far more complex. In fact, women were likely to experience a split dream in which they expressed a concern with both interpersonal relationships and occupational accomplishments. Most important, women with split dreams tended to have unstable lives. These women were likely to experience a sense of dissatisfaction with either their family lives, their husbands, or their careers. They took longer to settle into an occupation, and they established fewer mentor relationships. Further work is needed to determine if these observations are cohort-specific or age-related changes.

Conclusions About Stage Theories

The theories of Erikson, Loevinger, and Levinson describe a similar road map of adult development. Adult development begins with a shift away from identity toward intimacy. Next there is a change away from meaningless activity toward generativity in family and interpersonal matters. Last, as a result of searching for meaning in life (in the face of death), comes integrity. Although each theorist labels the stages differently and views the processes responsible for developmental change uniquely, the underlying themes of adult development are similar. (See figure 10.2 for a comparison of Levinson's and Erikson's viewpoints.)

Stage theories have intuitive appeal, but they suffer from four major limitations. First, stage theories are extremely difficult to verify through empirical

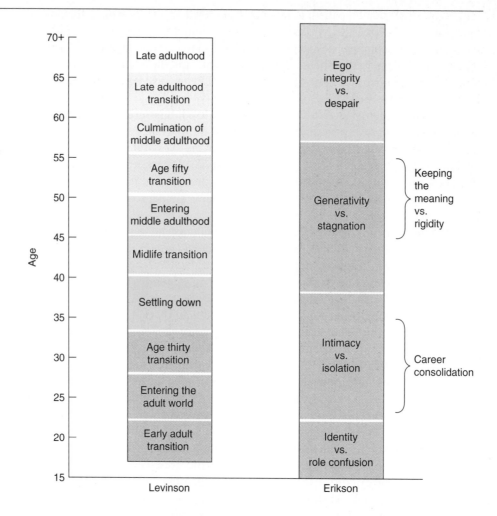

Figure 10.2 A comparison of the adult stages of Levinson and Erikson.

research. How can you determine whether an individual has experienced a particular stage of development? You might follow Erikson's and Levinson's technique of probing the depths of an individual's personality by conducting a series of intensive interviews. Or you might decide to use Loevinger's Sentence Completion instrument to determine the stage level. Or you might decide to use a questionnaire or survey that asks adults how they feel about themselves. The interview method is extremely costly and time-consuming, and information could be collected from a rather small (and perhaps nonrepresentative) number of participants. The sentence completion method is also costly and time-consuming. The survey method is less expensive and less time-consuming and may be used to test large numbers of participants. But could a researcher really capture the essence of the stages and crises using a paper-and-pencil survey or questionnaire? Given these problems, it should come as no surprise that there is considerable debate about whether stage theories can be tested (i.e., confirmed or rejected).

Second, these theorists have a tendency to focus too extensively on stages as crises in development, particularly in the case of the midlife crisis. For example, only a small percentage of the adult population experiences a midlife crisis, and that those individuals who suffer from crisis at midlife have typically experienced traumas and psychological upheavals throughout their entire lives. Ronald Kessler, a noted sociologist, has maintained that middle age is the "best" time of life. Gallagher (1993, p. 51) stated:

> At fifty, in Kessler's view, one does not have to deal with the anxieties and stress of youth and young adulthood or with the physical declines of old age. "Is anyone going to love me? Will I ever get my career off the ground?" Rates of general distress are low—then incidence of depression and anxiety fall at about age thirty-five and don't climb again until the sixties. You're healthy. You're productive. You have enough money to do some of the things you like to do. You have come to terms with your relationships, and the chance of divorce is very low. Midlife is the "it" you have been working toward. You can turn your attention toward being rather than becoming.

Third, there is an increasing tendency for theory and research on adult development to emphasize the importance of personal life events (e.g., a change in occupational or marital status) and major sociocultural factors (e.g., a war or economic depression) rather than using stages or phases to organize development. Alice Rossi (1984) observed that most of the individuals studied by Levinson were born right around the time of the depression. What was true for these individuals when they reached age 40 may not be true for the members of more recent cohorts when they reach 40. Rossi suggests that the men studied by Levinson may have been burned out at a premature age (because of the pressures put upon them by their generation) rather than moving through a normal developmental pattern that all adults go through upon entry into midlife. What events or societal changes do you think have occurred during the latter part of this century that may have led to the birth of the midlife crisis? Do you think that changes in society will heighten or diminish the tendency for members of future cohorts to experience a crisis at midlife?

Fourth, stage theories may focus too much attention on the development of the individual self as well as the self's ability to review and understand its own existence. For example, the mature individual is said "to become a unique person," "to know who she is," and "to be able to accept her life." In contrast, the goal of personality development may be to lose oneself, to become less of a unique individual. See Research Focus 10.2 to learn more about this perspective on adult personality.

THE TRAIT APPROACH TO ADULT PERSONALITY

The degree to which personality is stable or changes is a major issue in adult development. To what extent do childhood personality characteristics predict adult personality characteristics? Does a shy child become a shy adult? Does a high-achieving woman in early adulthood continue to strive hard to succeed at 50. Will an extroverted 25-year-old still be extroverted at the age of 65?

Instead of looking at the stability of a single personality characteristic across time, researchers are frequently interested in predictability across time using combinations of

Beyond Stages: The Development of Gero-Transcendence

According to stage theory, the hallmark of personality development is the attainment of ego integrity. Ego integrity is achieved as the individual looks backward in time and reaffirms his life in the face of his impending death. According to this theory, ego integrity would not occur unless the person developed a well-differentiated self that could draw a fundamental distinction between the present, the past, and the future. Unless the individual had a firm sense of "who he is," and "what types of internal and external forces have shaped his past as well as his present life" the aging adult could not find personal contentment and experience a strong affinity with past and future generations.

Despite the intuitive appeal of the preceding scenario, Lars Tornstan (1994) doubts that it truly describes the personality changes that are characteristic of older adults. Tornstan suggests that the basic distinctions between "self versus other" and "present versus past" reflect an orientation to reality that is representative of younger and middle-aged adults. With advanced old age, Tornstan believes that individuals experience a fundamental paradigm shift. They move from a rational, dualistic, and material view of life to one that is more cosmic and transcendent. Tornstan uses the term **gero-transcendence** to refer to this emergent perspective that characterizes the worldview of the older adult. Some of the most salient features associated with gero-transcendence are listed in box table 10.A.

The construct of gero-transcendence, although it is not explicitly religious in nature, has much in common with the guiding principles of Eastern religions. For example, the overarching goal of the aging Hindu in Indian culture is to become a nonperson, devoid of the need for spirituality, sensuality, psychological bonds, or social dimensions. The individual strives to have no self, no real-world concerns; he waits to die. Death is

BOX TABLE 10.A
Significant Features of Gero-transcendence
Decreased concern for one's personal life and an increased emphasis on the flow of life
Decreased emphasis on the distinctions between self-other and past-present-future
Increased time spent in meditation and decreased interest in social interactions and material objects

blissful liberation. It is the deserved attainment of one who has led a perfect life: having committed time to religious study, having married and produced children, and having offered support and help to those in need. Given these accomplishments, his life should be in total harmony. The emphasis on ego integrity, self-awareness, and personal wisdom in American culture is in sharp contrast to the values of Indian religious culture. The Indian search for connectedness and oneness between self and the cosmos is antithetical to Western notions of personal growth and individual maturity in old age.

To test his notion of gero-transcendence, Tornstan (1994) administered a series of questionnaires to 912 Danish adults between 74 and 100 years of age. Of primary interest was the percentage of participants who expressed agreement with 10 statements that were indicative of two aspects of gero-transcendence: cosmic transcendence and ego transcendence. Results, which are shown in box table 10.B, are consistent with a shift to gero-transcendence with increasing age. Most interestingly, Tornstan found that endorsing statements indicative of cosmic and ego transcendence was positively correlated with

characteristics present at particular points in the life cycle. We might also be interested in how social experiences, family experiences, and work experiences predict personality characteristics later in life.

To the extent that there is consistency or continuity from one period of time to another for some attributes of personality, we usually describe personality as being stable. In contrast, to the extent that there is little consistency from one period of time to another, we refer to change or discontinuity in personality.

Personality theorists are often categorized by whether they stress stability in personality across time as well as across situations. Personality theorists called *personologists,* or **trait theorists,** argue for consistency and stability, whereas contextual, life-events, or stage theorists are likely to maintain that personality changes over time.

Percentage of Participants Who Agreed with Statements Indicative of Gero-transcendence

Statements Indicative of Cosmic Transcendence	(% Agree)
Today I feel that the border between life and death is less striking compared with when I was 50.	60%
Today I feel to a higher degree how unimportant an individual life is, in comparison to the continuation of life.	55%
Today I feel a greater mutual connection to the universe, compared with when I was 50 years of age.	32%
Today I often experience a close presence of persons, even when they are physically elsewhere.	36%
Today I feel that the distance between past and present disappears.	42%
Today I feel a greater state of belongingness with both earlier and coming generations.	49%

Statements Indicative of Ego Transcendence	(% Agree)
Today I take myself less seriously than earlier.	60%
Today material things mean less compared with when I was 50.	74%
Today I am less concerned with superficial social contacts.	53%
Today I have more delight in my inner world compared with when I was 50.	57%

measures of life satisfaction, affirmative coping, and social activity. However, he also discovered that participants who were the most likely to agree with transcendent statements were the least likely to maintain that social interactions were necessary for life satisfaction! Thus gero-transcendence entails a rather paradoxical relationship between the need to be alone and the need to be with others. This is clear evidence that successful aging does not represent a simple disengagement or withdrawal from society.

In conclusion, it seems that if Tornstan's (1994) ideas about gero-transcendence are correct, we face the interest-ing possibility the psychologists (who are typically younger or middle-aged adults) have failed to capture the essence of aging. This is because, by virtue of their age, they have used a worldview to study older adults that is completely antitheti-cal to the perspective by which older adults live their lives. Thus psychologists and health care providers face the chal-lenge of understanding the aging process from a radically dif-ferent point of view. Furthermore, as members of an aging society, we all face the challenge of constructing social roles for older individuals that are consistent with their transcendent orientation.

Characteristics of Traits

What is a trait? What are the major assumptions that underlie the trait approach to personality? To help answer these questions, it may be useful to consider the ideas of Paul Costa and Robert McCrae (1980). These psychologists, two of the most influential researchers studying adult personality, have listed a set of principles underlying the trait approach:

1. Traits may be regarded as generalized dispositions to thoughts, feelings, and behaviors that endure over substantial periods of time.
2. Traits have relatively little to do with the determination of single, specific behaviors. Specific behaviors are usually controlled by situational influences.

(as discussed in chapter 8). Schaie and Willis (1991) examined the scores of 3,442 participants on measures of behavioral rigidity, attitudinal flexibility, and social responsibility in 1956, 1963, 1970, 1977, and 1984. The participants ranged from 22 to 84 years of age and were from 10 different birth cohorts between 1896 to 1959. Given the complex nature of this study, Schaie and Willis were able to examine the separate (and interactive) influences of age and cohort on personality development. As would be expected, cross-sectional analyses showed that individuals became more rigid and inflexible as they aged, whereas the longitudinal data showed that most traits remained stable until the late sixties, and then displayed small negative age changes thereafter. Furthermore, more-sophisticated sequential methods of data analysis indicated that the age differences obtained in the cross-sectional analysis were, in reality, due to cohort or generational influences. This finding led Schaie and Willis (1991) to conclude that, over the last 70 years, there has been a substantial positive change toward more open and flexible behaviors, attitudes, and personality styles in successive generations of individuals. The continuation of this trend would mean that future generations of individuals will be effective in adapting to changes brought on by rapid social change.

Berkeley Older Generation Study

The Berkeley Older Generation Study is a longitudinal study of approximately 420 men and women who were first interviewed in Berkeley, California, in 1928 and 1929. The participants in the study have been tested over a 55-year time span that has encompassed their young adulthood, midlife, and older years. Field and Millsap (1991) analyzed the information gathered from the surviving participants in this study during the years of 1969 and 1983. In 1969 two distinct age groups were interviewed: a group of young-old adults (individuals who averaged 65 years of age), and old-old adults (individuals who averaged 75 years of age). In 1983, a group of 47 old-old adults (average age of 79) and 21 oldest-old (average age of 89) were reexamined. Given this design, Field and Millsap were able to compare the stability of personality for members of two cohorts across a 14-year time span.

All of the participants were administered a rather intensive open-ended interview that assessed the traits of intellect, extraversion, agreeableness, satisfaction, and energetic. These traits, except for energetic (the degree to which a person feels fresh, energetic, restless, etc.) were very similar to the traits of openness to experience, extraversion, agreeableness, and neuroticism that play a dominant role in Costa and McCrae's model of adult personality development.

The results of this study tell an interesting story. When data from all participants were taken as a whole, satisfaction and agreeableness remained stable. In fact, satisfaction was, by far, the most stable trait. With regard to this finding, Field and Millsap (1991) commented that it seems very hard for younger persons to understand the continuing satisfaction that older people derive from life considering the fact that old age is accompanied by significant losses in the interpersonal and physical domains. On the other hand, moderate declines were noted for intellect, energetic, and extraversion. However, as illustrated in figure 10.4, traits of intellect, agreeableness, and

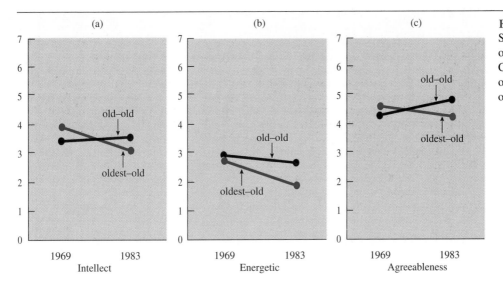

Figure 10.4
Significant change
over time:
Comparing the
old-old and the
oldest-old persons.

energetic changed in a different manner for individuals who, between 1969 and 1983, made the transition from young-old to old-old, and from old-old to oldest-old. Figures 10.4a and 10.4b shows for example, that scores on the dimensions of intellect and energetic declined over time for the people who became the oldest-old but not the old-old. And, figure 10.4c shows that individuals who made the transition to the status of old-old increased in agreeableness, while those who became the oldest-old exhibited stability on this trait. In conclusion, Field and Millsap (1991, p. 307) argued that there is a

> normative developmental increase in agreeableness, accompanied by what may be a normative decline in extraversion, as well as relative stability in two other traits, satisfaction and intellect, in advanced old age. These findings help shatter the common stereotype that personality becomes rigid in old age, or that people become more conservative or cranky as they age.

Overall, the data obtained by Field and Millsap, as well as other personologists mentioned in this section, have shown that adult personality is remarkably stable over the adult years. There may be profound individual differences, however, in the stability (or instability) of personality over time. Research Focus 10.3 presents some rather surprising data about the mortality rates of older adults who exhibit a stable versus unstable pattern of personality.

The Berlin Aging Study

Another important source of information about personality and aging is provided by the Berlin Aging Study. The Berlin Aging Study provides information about the effects of aging on personality development, social relationships, and intellectual functioning

Stability of Personality and Survival Rates in Old Age

Some individuals exhibit significant changes in personality during the adult years, whereas others do not. Hagberg, Samuelsson, Lindberg, and Dehlin (1991) wondered if interindividual differences in the stability of personality were related to survival rates during older adulthood. They suggested that a change in personality could be the end product of a fragile individual personality structure coming into contact with a number of harsh psychological (e.g., loss of a loved one) and/or biological (e.g., illness) stressors. This led them to hypothesize that older adults who displayed stability in personality would live longer than those adults who exhibited a significant change in their personality.

To test their hypothesis, Hagberg et al. employed a unique measure of personality called the Rod and Frame Task (RFT). In the RFT, a participant is asked to look into a darkened chamber that contains an illuminated square-shaped frame inside of which is positioned a straight illuminated glass rod. The frame is tilted, by the experimenter, 20 degrees to the right or the left and the participant is asked to turn a knob so that the rod

rotates to a true vertical position. There are two distinct patterns of performance on the RFT. First, some individuals (see box figure 10.A) are categorized as *field independent*. They are capable of aligning the rod in a true vertical position without being influenced by the tilted frame. Second, other people (see box figure 10.B) are labeled as *field dependent.* They align the rod in a vertical position relative to the tilted frame, but they think they are positioning the rod in a truly vertical manner. In other words, the terms field independent and field dependent signify the degree to which an individual's perceptual judgments are affected by the elements within his visual environment. The perceptual styles of field independence versus field dependence have been found to be related to the personality traits of extroversion, locus of control, and flexibility as well as self-concept and identity status.

Hagberg et al. (1991) conducted a longitudinal design in which they administered the RFT to 113 men and 79 women every second year during a six-year period. Testing began

Figure 10.A A field-independent response on the rod-and-frame task.

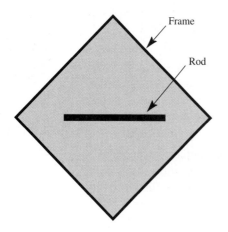

Figure 10.B A field-dependent response on the rod-and-frame task.

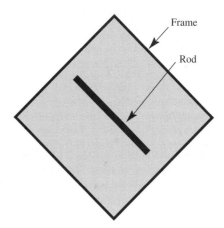

from a systemic-wholistic view (Baltes, Mayer, Helmchen, & Steinhagen-Thiessen, 1993; Baltes & Smith, 1997).

The Berlin Aging Study is distinct in several ways from the other longitudinal data sets just described. First, very old participants (95–103 years) were deliberately included in the study at the outset. In other major studies of aging such as the Berkeley Older Generation Study and the BLSA, the initial data collections did not include

when each participant was 67 years of age. The proportion of survivors was calculated when the participants should have reached 69, 71, 73, 75, 77, 79, 81, and 83 years of age. It was found that about 20 percent of the older adults displayed an unstable pattern of performance on the RFT (i.e., they changed from field independence to field dependence [or vice versa] over the six-year testing period). These "unstable" participants (see box figure 10.C) were less likely to survive than the elderly adults who displayed a consistent pattern of performance on the RFT. This finding held true for both males and females. Finally, whether participants were classified as field independent or dependent was found to be unrelated to survival rates.

Hagberg et al. concluded that human personality is a tremendously intricate system. In fact, personality is probably so complex that various sorts of perturbations (psychological stress, disease, etc.) that accompany the aging processes, as well as aging itself, can have a significant destabilizing effect. This would help explain why personality change is a sensitive predictor of mortality.

Figure 10.C The relationship between stability of performance on the rod-and-frame task and survival rates for older males and females.

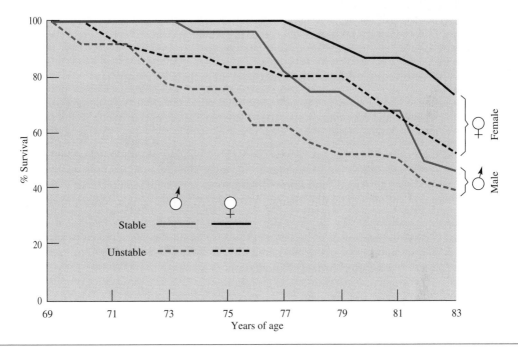

older participants. These studies were begun as investigations of early development and became longitudinal studies of aging as the participants (and investigators) grew old during the course of the study. In the Berlin Aging Study, very old participants were tested at the beginning of the study.

A second unique feature of the Berlin Aging Study is the emphasis on including equal numbers of men and women at each of the selected age groups (70–74, 75–79,

80–84, 85–89, 90–94, and 95–103 years). In most other studies, the samples usually have different numbers of men and women, and fewer and fewer men at later testing occasions because of differential mortality rates for men and women.

A third feature of the study is the wide range of assessment measures used. Approximately 10,000 measures per individual have been taken, including objective and subjective measures of physical health and appearance, mental health, personality and well-being, cognitive and sensory functioning, social and family roles, and economics, work history, and residential situation. The Berkeley Older Generations Study, the BLSA, and several other major longitudinal studies also use a range of physical, psychological, and social measures, but not as many as in the Berlin Aging Study.

In a recent report from the Berlin Aging Study, Smith and Baltes (1997) examined personality and self in relation to measures of intellectual and social functioning. The findings of the study revealed that a number of distinct subgroups of individuals having similar characteristics could be identified. Nine distinct subgroups, called *profiles,* were extracted. More of the very old participants (85–103 years) and more women than men belonged to profiles associated with greater vulnerability to poor health, less successful functioning in social and family matters, and other less positive characteristics. Preliminary reports from the Berlin Aging Study suggest that the profiles observed at initial testing are relatively stable in data collections in 1996.

Conclusions About the Stability of Adult Personality

Costa and McCrae (1986) observed that adult personality is characterized largely by stability and continuity rather than by extensive change or declines and reorganization. The adult personality seems to be an organized system of traits that resists major alteration. Imagine how difficult it would be to adapt to the changing demands of our lives if our core personalities underwent frequent change. Imagine how difficult it would be to know our friends and family members if personality characteristics underwent frequent and unpredictable change. With regard to this matter, Krueger and Heckhausen (1993) have shown that individuals across the adult life span tend to have subjective conceptions about adult personality development that are characterized by the growth and/or stability of personality traits until about 60 years of age, followed by a slight decline thereafter. In fact, Krueger and Heckhausen (1993) found that elderly adults were much more optimistic about late-life personality development than were younger or middle-aged adults.

Ruth and Coleman (1996) pointed out that many of the apparent personality differences between young, middle-aged, and older adults are really caused by generational (cohort) differences rather than by age-related differences. One of the most salient predictors of adult personality is year of birth rather than chronological age.

New theories of personality emphasize that despite the apparent stability of adult personality, there is considerable potential for change. Ruth and Coleman (1996) suggest that research on personality and aging is moving away from looking for average personality descriptions at different ages toward the study of individual lives. Research on ego development by Loevinger (1976) and by Labouvie-Vief and her colleagues, and on life stories by McAdams (1995) and others, exemplify this new approach.

There is also a trend in the measurement of personality away from the use of questionnaires and tests and toward the use of direct observations and interviews. In new research on personality, there is also an emphasis on trying to understand adaptive competence—that is, the individual is effective in using his or her unique resources to change oneself or re-create situations in which to develop optimally, and in using resources to override limitations.

It should be mentioned that the trait approach to adult personality is not totally antagonistic to the stage approaches. For example, it is possible that an individual may go through adulthood with a constellation of stable, enduring personality traits; yet this adult may use these stable traits to tackle the different tasks and psychosocial crises that writers like Erikson and Levinson have identified. A person may deal with an identity crisis in adolescence, a midlife crisis at age 40, and a life review at age 75 with the same stable degrees of openness to experience, introversion-extroversion, and neuroticism. It is reasonable to assume that personality development involves both change and stability.

THE LIFE-EVENTS APPROACH

An alternative to the stage and trait approaches to adult personality development is the life-events framework or contextual model. In the earlier versions of this perspective (e.g., Holmes & Rahe, 1967), it was suggested that major life events produce taxing circumstances for individuals, forcing them to change their personalities. Events such as the death of a spouse, marriage, and divorce were thought to produce increasing degrees of stress and therefore were likely to have an influence on the individual's personality.

More-sophisticated versions of the life-events framework (Brim & Ryff, 1980; Dohrenwend, Krasnoff, Askensay, & Dohrenwend, 1978; Hultsch & Plemons, 1979) emphasize the factors that mediate the influence of life events on adult development—physical health, intelligence, personality, family supports, income, and so forth. Some individuals may perceive a life event as highly stressful whereas others perceive the same event as a challenge.

It is important to consider the sociocultural circumstances within which life events occur. For example, divorce may be more stressful after many years of marriage, when individuals are in their fifties, than when they have only been married a few years and are in their twenties. Also, individuals may be able to cope more effectively with divorce in 1998 than in 1950 because divorce is more common in today's society.

Bernice Neugarten and Nancy Datan (1973) suggested that understanding the nature of adult personality development depends on an analysis of the sociohistorical and personal circumstances within which adult life occurs. They also suggested that chronological age has little, if any, bearing on adult personality. For example, Neugarten (1980a, 1980b, 1989) proposed that the admonition "Act your age" has become progressively less meaningful since the middle part of this century. We are constantly aware of adults who occupy roles that seem out of step with their biological ages (e.g., the 28-year-old mayor, the 60-year-old father of a preschooler, and the 70-year-old college student).

Neugarten also has deep-seated doubts about an increasing number of popular books that emphasize predictable, age-related life crises. People who read such books worry about their midlife crises, apologize if they don't seem to be coping with them properly, and appear dismayed if they aren't having them. These crisis theories, Neugarten maintains, do not really define the typical pattern of adult development. It may be that adults change far more, and far less predictably, than many oversimplified stage theories or crisis theories suggest. As Neugarten (1980b) has asserted:

> My students and I have studied what happens to people over the life cycle. . . . We have found great trouble clustering people into age brackets that are characterized by particular conflicts; the conflicts won't stay put, and neither will the people. Choices and dilemmas do not sprout forth at ten-year intervals, and decisions are not made and then left behind as if they were merely beads on a chain. (p. 289)

Neugarten (1968) argued that the social environment within which the members of a particular generation evolved can alter their **social clock**—the timetable according to which individuals are expected to accomplish life's tasks, such as marrying, establishing a career, and even experiencing a monumental crisis at midlife. Social clocks provide guides for our lives. Sociohistorical events and trends unique to specific cohorts "set" the social clock for that cohort.

In earlier periods in our society, it may have been reasonable to describe life as a series set of discrete, predictable stages or crises. More people seemed to experience the same life events at the same ages. People knew the "right age" for marriage, the first child, the last child, career achievement, retirement, and even death. In the last few decades, however, Neugarten (1989) has argued that chronological age has become nearly irrelevant as an index of such significant events within adult development.

During the latter part of this century, our social time clocks have changed dramatically. New trends in work, family size, health, and education have produced phenomena that are unprecedented in our history. We see, for example, a significantly longer empty nest period after the children leave home that may require major readjustments in the parents' relationship. Also, we see an increase in the numbers of great-grandparents as well as those who start new families, new jobs, and new avocations when they are 40, 50, or 60 years old (Neugarten, 1980a, 1989).

Some of the life tasks that used to be associated with a particular age or stage of development seem to reoccur over the entire course of the adult life span. Neugarten articulated this point as follows:

> Most of the themes of adulthood appear and reappear in new forms over long periods of time. Issues of intimacy and freedom, for example, which are supposed to concern young adults just starting out in marriage and careers, are never settled once and for all. They haunt many couples continuously; compromises are found for a while, then renegotiated. Similarly, feeling the pressure of time, reformulating goals, coming to grips with success (and failure)—these are not the exclusive property of the forty-eight to fifty-two-year-olds, by any means. (Neugarten, 1980a, pp. 289–290)

APPLYING A LIFE-COURSE PERSPECTIVE TO LIFE EVENTS

It is important to make connections between age or life stage, the probability of certain events taking place, and the power of the event as a stressor (Brim & Ryff, 1980). Some events, such as a serious automobile accident, are not necessarily age-linked and have a low probability of occurring. Therefore, we are seldom prepared for such events psychologically. However, other events, such as menopause, retirement, or the death of a parent have stronger ties with age. This allows us to anticipate the events and to develop coping strategies that may help alleviate some of the stress these events engender (Neugarten, 1989; Pearlin & Lieberman, 1977). Figure 10.5 shows how a life-course perspective can be applied to life events (Hultsch & Plemons, 1979). This figure considers variations in the probability of certain events, their timing and sequencing, the motivational factors stimulated by the events, the coping resources available for dealing with them, and adaptive outcomes.

The life-events framework described in figure 10.5 has four main components: antecedent life-event stressors, mediating factors, a social/psychological adaptation process, and consequent adaptive or maladaptive outcomes. From this perspective, all life events, regardless of whether they are positive (marriage, being promoted at work) or negative (divorce, the death of a spouse), are viewed as potentially stressful. Factors that may mediate the effects of life events on the individual can be categorized as internal (physical health or intelligence) or external (salary, social support network). Social-psychological adaptation refers to the individual's coping strategies, which may produce either a positive or negative outcome.

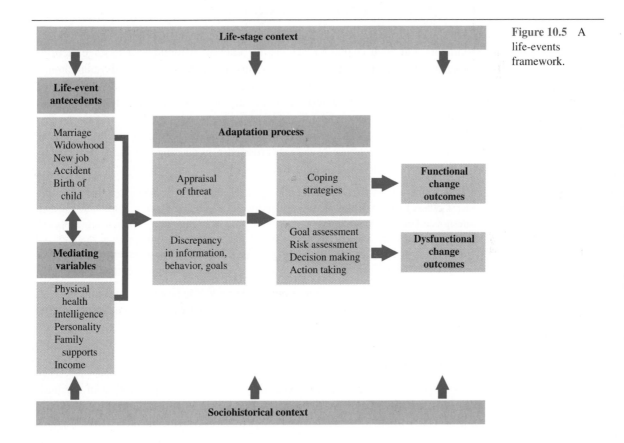

Figure 10.5 A life-events framework.

As indicated in figure 10.5, it is also important to consider both the life stage and the sociohistorical context in which a life event occurs. Two time lines that are important in our lives, then, are **individual time** and **historical time.** An event (such as the death of a spouse) that occurs at age 30 may have a different impact on the individual than if it occurred at age 73. Similarly, an event (such as a woman being promoted over a man at work) would have a different impact if it occurred in 1990 rather than 1950.

The life-events framework provides valuable insights into adult development (Kogan, 1990). Like all the other theories described in this chapter, however, it is not without flaws (Lazarus & DeLongis, 1983; Maddi, 1986). One of the most significant drawbacks of the life-events framework is that it may place too much emphasis on change. It does not recognize the stability that, at least to some degree, characterizes adult development. Another potential drawback is that this perspective may place too much emphasis on major life events as the primary sources of personality change. Enduring a boring and tense job, a dull marriage, or living in poverty do not qualify as major life events. Yet the everyday pounding we take from these types of conditions can add up to a highly stressful life. Some psychologists (e.g., Lazarus & Folkman, 1984) believe that we can gain greater insight into the source of life's stresses by focusing on daily hassles and uplifts rather than focusing so much on the catastrophic experience of major life stressors.

RECOGNIZING INDIVIDUAL VARIATION

Broadly speaking, there are two theoretical approaches to the study of personality development—one focuses on similarities, the other on differences. The stage theories of Erikson and Levinson attempt to describe universal forms of intraindividual change that take place during adult development. The life-events framework, as championed by Neugarten, focuses on the interindividual variability that is characteristic of adult personality change.

In an extensive investigation of a random sample of 500 men at midlife, Michael Farrell and Stanley Rosenberg (1981) discovered a wide range of individual differences in adult personality. They concluded:

> While some studies have found middle age to be the apex of satisfaction and effectiveness, others found it to be a period of identity crisis and discontent. . . . Both our research design and our findings suggest a more complex model [than the universal stage model], one anchored in the idea that the individual is an active agent in interpreting, shaping, and altering his own reality. He not only experiences internal and external changes, he gives meaning to them. The meaning given shows a wide range of variation. (p. 2)

Think about yourself and other people you know. You have certain things in common with others, yet you differ in many ways. Individual variation must be an important aspect of any viable model of adult development.

LEVELS OF PERSONALITY

Theories of personality yield, at the very best, an incomplete description of the individual. Consequently, Dan McAdams (1995) proposed a novel approach that would allow personality theorists to get to know the people they study. The key to McAdams's viewpoint is that a "full description" of an individual entails three different levels of analysis.

Level I is referred to as the *dispositional level.* Here, the individual is described in terms of basic personality traits or dispositions such as extroversion, neuroticism, openness to experience, and so on. For example, say you attend a party and meet a person named George who behaves in a manner that is socially dominant, entertaining, moody, and anxious. It might strike you that your newfound acquaintance scores high on the traits of extroversion and neuroticism. The strength of descriptions offered at Level I is their generality. You may predict that, across a great variety of contexts, George, in relationship to other individuals, will typically behave in an extroverted and anxious manner. The greatest strength of Level I is also its greatest weakness—Level I only provides general, decontextualized information about another person. As McAdams points out, "No description of a person is adequate without trait attributions, but trait attributions, by themselves, yield little beyond a 'psychology of the stranger' " (1995, p. 365).

To gain a better understanding of George, you need to know something about the nuances of his personality. You need to know: What does George want out of life? What's really important to him? How does he go about satisfying his goals and aspirations? How does George cope with the challenges, successes, and disappointments that characterize everyday life? And, more important, you must have an appreciation of how "the answers" to the preceding questions depend on the different social roles that George has to play (he is one person's son, another person's employee, another's lover, etc.) in combination with the different life tasks (identity formation, generativity, etc.) associated with different phases of his adult development. All of these issues are the focal points of Level II—the *personal concerns level.* At this level we could come to understand George by measuring his values and coping styles, as well as the defense mechanisms he uses to reduce anxiety. And we could look to stage theories like Erikson's and Levinson's to get an understanding of how all these aspects of George's personality might change across time and developmental level. For example, the coping style and defense mechanisms that George uses to deal with issues of intimacy in younger adulthood may be different from the ones he uses while establishing a sense of generativity during middle age.

The last, and perhaps most important, piece of information we need to gather in order to know George (and, of course, for George to know himself) is his answer to the most intimate and personal of all questions, "Who am I?" In other words, we need to know something about George's sense of personal identity. Identity formation is the focal point of Level III—the *life story level.* Within McAdams's model of personality, identity is best conceptualized as an internalized and evolving personal myth or life story. According to McAdams,

> Contemporary adults create identity in their lives to the extent that the self can be told in a coherent narrative that integrates the person into society in a productive and generative way and provides the person with a purposeful self-history that explains how the self of yesterday became the self of today and will become the anticipated self of tomorrow. Level III in personality, therefore, is the level of identity as a life story. Without exploring this third level, the personologist can never understand how and to what extent the person is able to find unity, purpose, and meaning in life. (1995, p. 382)

Level III of personality, unlike the preceding levels, does not seem to be knowable by scores on standardized tests. Alternatively, Level III reveals itself through long-term intensive interactions with others. Thus, individuals who share special intimate relationships with each other such as friends, lovers, spouses, siblings, psychotherapists and clients, and so on, have a good chance of knowing each other at the life story level.

It may prove interesting to speculate about the factors that influence personality at each of the levels elaborated upon by McAdams. For example, it could be argued that biological, perhaps even genetic, factors influence personality at the dispositional level. This might account for the remarkable stability of traits over time. At the other end of the spectrum, a myriad of cultural, developmental, and idiosyncratic factors might influence personality at the personal concerns and life story levels. Also it may be informative to consider which levels of personality are most resilient (or fragile). What level of personality is most negatively affected by mental disorder or dementia? One final realization is that McAdams's (1995) model suggests strong links between personality structure and basic cognitive processing. For example, there seems to be a very strong relationship between the notion of personality as a "life story" and the active, reconstructive nature of human autobiographical memory processes as mentioned in chapter 7.

MORAL DEVELOPMENT

Morality is conceptualized in terms of three interrelated aspects. The first component is moral reasoning: How do people think about the rules of ethical conduct? The second issue involves the moral behavior: How do people behave in real-life situations where a moral principle is at stake? The third domain of interest is moral emotion: How do individuals feel after making a moral decision and engaging in a behavior that is ethical (or unethical)? Although Kohlberg's theory of moral development focuses primarily on moral reasoning, it has some implications for how adults adjust to emotionally charged life events and how adults behave in moral contexts.

Kohlberg's Theory

Kohlberg (1958, 1987, 1990) argued that moral development involves a gradual stage-like progression in which the individual passes through three different levels of moral thought with two different stages within each level. Kohlberg maintained that these levels and stages represent an invariant, universal, and qualitatively distinct sequence.

Kohlberg measured moral development by evaluating an individual's response to a number of hypothetical dilemmas. One of his most well-known dilemmas, "Heinz and the Drug," is as follows:

> In Europe a woman was near death from cancer. One drug might save her, a form of radium that a druggist in the same town had recently discovered. The druggist was charging $2,000, ten times what the drug cost him to make. The sick woman's husband, Heinz, went to everyone he knew to borrow the money, but he could only get together about half of what the drug cost. He told the druggist his wife was dying and asked him to sell it cheaper or let him pay later. But the druggist said no. The husband got desperate and broke into the man's store to steal the drug for his wife. Should the husband have done that? Why? (Kohlberg, 1969, p. 379)

Middle-aged and older adults are often in positions associated with the responsibility of making moral and ethical judgments.

A person's stage of moral development is determined by his or her answer to the question "Why?," not to the question about what Heinz should have done. In other words, it is the type of reasoning a person uses to justify his or her judgment that counts; whether the person thinks Heinz should or should not have stolen the drug is unimportant. Put somewhat differently, Kohlberg's theory places primary emphasis on the structure of moral judgment, not the content of moral judgment. The former refers to the underlying rule system that gives rise to a specific moral decision; the latter refers to the decision itself.

The first two stages compose the **preconventional level,** because the individual interprets moral problems from the point of view of physical or material concerns (punishment and reward, the maintenance of power and wealth, etc.) or his own hedonistic wishes. At the preconventional level, then, rules and social expectations are viewed as something external to the self.

The third and fourth stages make up the **conventional level.** Here, the individual's understanding of morality depends on her internalization of the expectations that other individuals such as friends, family, or society have of her. Maintaining these expectations leads to interpersonal trust and loyalty as well as the preservation of the social system of which the individual is a part. At the conventional level, therefore, the person has identified with or internalized the rules and expectations of other individuals or of a more generalized social system.

The **postconventional level** consists of the fifth and sixth stages in Kohlberg's sequence. At this level, the individual becomes capable of distinguishing between basic human rights and obligations, which remain constant over different cultures and historical epochs, versus societal and legal rules, which can change over sociohistorical contexts. In other words, the postconventional reasoner can construct a set of universal moral principles by differentiating his or her moral point of view from the rules and expectations of significant others and society. Table 10.4 provides a more complete description of the different stages and levels that make up Kohlberg's theory. Also, table 10.5 provides examples of the type of moral reasoning generated by an individual at each of Kohlberg's stages.

Age-Related Changes in Moral Reasoning

Kohlberg's initial research (Kohlberg, 1958) led to the conclusion that individuals completed the moral stage sequence by the end of adolescence. However, longitudinal data collected by Kohlberg and Kramer (1969) showed that the adolescents who had attained postconventional morality during high school regressed to a preconventional level in their college years. Such a clear violation of the stage criterion of invariant progression forced Kohlberg and his associates to undertake major changes in the theory and measurement of moral development.

Using a revised and more stringent scoring system, Colby, Kohlberg, Gibbs, and Lieberman (1983) reanalyzed Kohlberg and Kramer's longitudinal data and found no evidence of regressive stage movement. Furthermore, Colby et al. (1983) analyzed the data from a 20-year longitudinal study of moral development that began in the late 1950s. The results of this study are illustrated in figure 10.6. As you can see, there is a clear relationship between age and moral reasoning. Over the 20-year period, reasoning at stages 1 and 2 decreased. Stage 3 peaked in late adolescence or early adulthood and declined thereafter. Reasoning at stage 4 did not appear at all among the 10-year-olds in the study; yet it was reflected in 62 percent of the judgments of the 36-year-olds. Stage 5 moral reasoning did not appear until the age of 20 to 22. Furthermore, it never rose above 10 percent of the total number of the participants' judgments. Similar results have been obtained by Armon (1991).

Based on these results, Kohlberg (1987) suggested that children and young adolescents reason at the preconventional level, most older adolescents and adults reason at the conventional level, and a small percentage of adults (mostly middle-aged and older) reason at the postconventional level. Therefore, it seems as if adulthood (not adolescence, as originally suggested) is marked by the ability to construct a universal set of moral principles. Kohlberg's main discovery was that moral development occurs during all epochs of the life span—childhood, adolescence, and adulthood.

Determinants of Moral Development

What causes a person to move from one moral stage to the next? There is no reason to believe that chronological age, by itself, is a prime determinant of moral change. Some researchers (Kuhn, Langer, Kohlberg, & Haan, 1977; Tomlinson-Keasey & Keasey, 1974) have shown that the attainment of postconventional morality depends on formal operations; however, formal operations, by itself, is not sufficient to automatically produce postconventional morality. Roodin, Rybash, and Hoyer (1984) have suggested that

TABLE 10.4

An Overview of the Levels and Stages That Comprise Kohlberg's Theory of Moral Development

Level and Stage	What Is Right	Reasons for Doing Right	Sociomoral Perspective
Level I— **Preconventional** Stage 1—Heteronomous mortality	To avoid breaking rules backed by punishment, obedience for its own sake, and avoiding physical damage to persons and property.	Avoidance of punishment, and the superior power of authorities.	*Egocentric point of view.* Doesn't consider the interests of others or recognize that they differ from the actor's; doesn't relate two points of view. Actions are considered physically rather than in terms of psychological interests of others. Confusion of authority's perspective with one's own.
Stage 2—Individualism, instrumental purpose, and exchange	Following rules only when it is to someone's immediate interest; acting to meet one's own interests and needs and letting others do the same. Right is also what's fair, what's an equal exchange, a deal, an agreement.	To serve one's own needs or interests in a world where you have to recognize that other people have their interests, too.	*Concrete individualistic perspective.* Aware that everybody has his own interest to pursue and these conflict, so that right is relative (in the concrete individualistic sense).
Level II— **Conventional** Stage 3—Mutual interpersonal expectations, relationships, and interpersonal conformity	Living up to what is expected by people close to you or what people generally expect of people in your role as son, brother, friend, and so on. "Being good" is important and means having good motives, showing concern about others. It also means keeping mutual relationships, such as trust, loyalty, respect and gratitude.	The need to be a good person in your own eyes and those of others. Your caring for others. Belief in the Golden Rule. Desire to maintain rules and authority which support stereotypical good behavior.	*Perspective of the individual in relationships with other individuals.* Aware of shared feelings, agreements, and expectations which take primacy over individual interests. Relates points of view through the concrete Golden Rule, putting yourself in the other guy's shoes. Does not yet consider generalized system perspective.

TABLE 10.4 *(continued)*

An Overview of the Levels and Stages That Comprise Kohlberg's Theory of Moral Development

Level and Stage	What Is Right	Reasons for Doing Right	Sociomoral Perspective
Stage 4—Social system and conscience	Fulfilling the actual duties to which you have agreed. Laws are to be upheld except in extreme cases where they conflict with other fixed social duties. Right is also contributing to society, the group, or institution.	To keep the institution going as a whole, to avoid the breakdown in the system "if everyone did it," or the imperative of conscience to meet one's defined obligations.	*Differentiates societal point of view from interpersonal agreement or motives.* Takes the point of view of the system that defines roles and rules. Considers individual relations in terms of place in the system.
Level III— Postconventional, or Principled Stage 5—Social contract or utility and individual rights	Being aware that people hold a variety of values and opinions, that most values and rules are relative to your group. These relative rules should usually be upheld, however, in the interest of impartiality and because they are the social contract. Some nonrelative values and rights like *life* and *liberty,* however, must be upheld in any society regardless of majority opinion.	A sense of obligation to law because of one's social contract to make and abide by laws for the welfare of all and for the protection of all people's rights. A feeling of contractual commitment, freely entered upon, to family, friendship, trust, and work obligations. Concerns that laws and duties be based on rational calculation of overall utility, "the greatest good for the greatest number."	*Prior-to-society perspective.* Perspective of a rational individual aware of values and rights prior to social attachments and contracts. Integrates perspectives by formal mechanisms of agreement, contract, objective impartiality, and due process. Considers moral and legal points of view; recognizes that they sometimes conflict and finds it difficult to integrate them.
Stage 6—Universal ethical principles	Following self-chosen ethical principles. Particular laws or social agreements are usually valid because they rest on such principles. When laws violate these principles, one acts in accordance with the principle. Principles are universal principles of justice: the equality of human rights and respect for the dignity of human beings as individual persons.	The belief as a rational person in the validity of universal moral principles, and a sense of personal commitment to them.	*Perspective of a moral point of view from which social arrangements derive.* Perspective is that of any rational individual recognizing the nature of morality or the fact that persons are ends in themselves and must be treated as such.

From Lawrence Kohlberg, "Moral Stages and Moralization" in Moral Development and Behavior, *Thomas Lickona (ed.). Copyright © 1976 by Holt, Rinehart and Winston. Reprinted by permission of Thomas Lickona.*

TABLE 10.5

Responses at Each Stage Level to the "Heinz and the Drug" Dilemma

Stage 1

Pro	Con
It's not really bad to steal the drug. It's not like he did not ask to pay for it first. The drug really isn't worth $2,000; at most it costs about $200. Also, letting your wife die would be the same as killing her—and God's commandments say that killing another person is wrong.	Heinz shouldn't steal; he should buy the drug instead. Also, if he steals the drug he'd be committing a big crime and the police would put him in jail for a long time. Finally, God's commandments say that stealing is wrong.

Stage 2

Pro	Con
Heinz should steal the drug because he'd be lonely and sad if his wife dies. He wants her to live more than anything else. Anyway, if he gets sent to jail (that would make him sad), but he'd still have his wife (and that would make him really happy).	Heinz should not steal the drug if he doesn't like his wife a lot. Also, the druggist isn't really a bad person; he just wants to make a profit from all his hard work. That is what you are in business for, to make money.

Stage 3

Pro	Con
If I were Heinz, I'd steal the drug for my wife. Heinz could not be so heartless as to let his wife die. The two partners in a marriage should naturally expect that they will come to each other's aid. Also, you can't put a price on life: and, any decent person should value life above anything else.	Heinz shouldn't steal. If his wife dies, he cannot be blamed. After all, everybody knows that Heinz is not cruel and heartless, he tried to buy the drug legally. The druggist is the selfish one. He deserves to be stolen from.

Stage 4

Pro	Con
When you get married, you take a vow to love and cherish your wife. Marriage is not only love, it's an obligation as well. Marriage is like a legal contract that must be obeyed. Also, by stealing the drug and going to court, Heinz will be able to show the members of his society how dumb the laws about stealing are. This might lead to positive changes in the judicial system.	It's a natural thing for Heinz to want to save his wife, but it is still always wrong to steal. If everybody took the law into their own hands—like Heinz wants to do—his society would be in total chaos. In the long run, nobody in Heinz's society will benefit from this; not even Heinz and his wife!

Stage 5

Pro	Con
The law is not set up to deal with the unique circumstances of the Heinz case. Taking the drug in this situation is not correct from a "legal" point of view. But, there may be a set of basic human rights (such as the right to life) that must be preserved regardless of what the law may happen to say. The law of the land should protect peoples' basic rights. It certainly isn't in this case. Therefore, Heinz should steal the drug.	You cannot completely blame Heinz for stealing; but extreme circumstances do not really justify violating the law. This is because the law represents a commitment that Heinz and the other members of his society have made to one another.

TABLE 10.5 (continued)	
Responses at Each Stage Level to the "Heinz and the Drug" Dilemma	
Stage 6	
Pro	**Con**
Heinz has to act in terms of the principle of preserving and respecting life. It would be both irrational and immoral to preserve the druggist's property right to the drug at the expense of his wife's right to life. After all, people invented the concept of personal property; it is a culturally relative concept. Alternatively, the right of a person to claim their right to life should be absolute.	Heinz is faced with the decision of whether to consider the other people who need the drug just as much as his wife. Heinz ought to act not according to his own feelings toward his wife but on his consideration of all of the lives involved.

Figure 10.6 Age-related changes in moral reasoning.

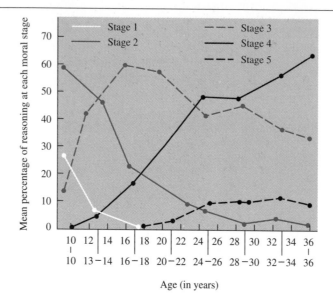

advanced moral reasoning depends on the growth of postformal styles of thinking within the domain of personal knowledge. In fact, it seems that postconventional morality has much in common with Paul Baltes's concept of wisdom discussed in chapter 9.

In addition to logical thinking, psychologists have examined several other factors responsible for the transitions in moral development. After all, if moral development is nothing more than logical thinking applied to moral problems, there should be no need to have a theory of moral development separate from cognitive/intellectual development. Kohlberg (1976) suggested that moral development is heavily dependent on the social perspective a person brings to a moral problem (refer to table 10.4). These stages of perspective taking are actively constructed through the reciprocal interactions that take place between an individual and his or her social environment. Moral development should thus be promoted by social environments that (1) give the individual a broad range of role-taking experiences, so that the person becomes aware of the thoughts, feelings, and attitudes of other people and/or adopts the perspectives of various social institutions; and (2) place the individual in real-life positions of moral responsibility.

The Importance of Moral Development

What is the practical significance of being a postconventional rather than a conventional moral reasoner? Should one try to promote moral development in adults, and if so, how? These important questions can be answered in a variety of ways.

First, as individuals progress through the different moral stages, they should be able to make better or more effective decisions about the moral dilemmas that occur within their own lives. This does not mean that advanced (postconventional) moral reasoners are better people than lower-level moral reasoners. Instead, it means that postconventional reasoners bring a broader, more all-encompassing, and balanced point of view to a moral problem. A postconventional point of view does not have its primary roots in self-centered interests or social/interpersonal expectations. Thus, it allows individuals to more fully consider the conflicting claims that surround a moral dilemma.

Second, it has been shown that a person's level of moral reasoning is related to a person's moral behavior. Kohlberg and Candee (1984) have shown that as individuals progress through the moral stages, they engage in more consistent instances of moral action: honesty, altruism, and political and civil rights activism. Furthermore, they are less likely to comply with immoral orders given by authority figures.

Third, Kohlberg's theory may provide valuable information about how adults comprehend and cope with real-life moral issues. For example, Rybash and Roodin (1989) have discussed the manner by which different moral orientations influence adults' understanding of the right to self-determination in medical contexts (i.e., the right to accept or reject medical treatment for a life-threatening illness). Research Focus 10.4 contains more detailed information about the relationship between coping and moral reasoning.

ALTERNATIVES AND CRITICISMS TO KOHLBERG'S THEORY

A number of studies have supported Kohlberg's claims about the invariance and universality of moral stages (see Colby & Kohlberg, 1987; Demetriou, 1990). However, there are some limitations to Kohlberg's theory.

Kohlberg's view is not as applicable to women as it is to men. Carol Gilligan (1982) pointed out that adult males, on average, score higher (stage 4) than adult females (stage 3) on Kohlberg's measure of moral reasoning. This difference does not mean that men are more moral than women. Instead, Gilligan argues, this sex difference in moral reasoning has its basis in the different orientations that men and women bring to moral problems. A man's orientation toward morality is based in abstract principles of justice, whereas a woman's orientation toward morality is grounded in her relationships with others. These differences have their basis, according to Gilligan (1982), in the socialization of the sexes during childhood. Thus, Gilligan maintains that

Edwai
the re
develc
reform
    Gil
phase
exister
conve
Gibbs
"expec
progre
These
ing an
adults.
tional l
level d
stages
a very
are abs
(2) sub
    Mo
only de
needs
tially id
need to
need to
edness

Life-events theorists believe that personality itself often changes because of the unique life events that individuals experience during adulthood. Bernice Neugarten, one of the major pioneers of the life-events framework, has argued that we need to consider the sociohistorical circumstances in which life events occur. She leaves the impression that sociohistorical influences are more important in the personality equation than chronological age. Life-events theorists believe that too much emphasis has been placed on stages of adult development. Dan McAdams has suggested that a genuine description of personality needs to take place at several different levels: dispositional level, personal concerns level, and life story level.

A person's sense of morality is an important component of his or her personality. At the core of Lawrence Kohlberg's theory of moral development is an analysis of how people reason about and understand complex moral dilemmas. Kohlberg believes that moral development follows a stage sequence. Kohlberg also argued that moral development continues during childhood, adolescence, and adulthood. Most adults reason at the conventional level, although a small percentage of adults attain a postconventional level of morality. Adults who reason at the postconventional level seem to cope with negative life events in a much more affirmative manner than conventional reasoners. Moreover, it appears that postconventional reasoners are more likely to engage in moral action than individuals at lower levels.

Kohlberg's theory is incomplete because it does not use a wide range of measures for assessing moral development. The dilemmas used by Kohlberg are oriented toward approaches that are more common for men than for women. Further, the dilemmas are not typical of ones that adults experience in their everyday lives.

REVIEW QUESTIONS

1. Describe the differences between the views of trait theorists, stage theorists, and life-events theorists.
2. Compare and contrast the stage theories of Erikson, Loevinger, and Levinson.
3. How does the concept of gero-transcendence bear on the fundamental tenets of stage theory?
4. How do the proponents of the life-events framework explain the notion of midlife crisis? Why do life-events theorists attach more importance to sociohistorical influences than stage theorists do?
5. What are personality traits? Briefly describe the three different personality traits that make up Costa and McCrae's five-factor model of personality.
6. What are the findings of the major longitudinal studies of adult personality development?
7. Is there any advantage of having a personality structure that remains stable over time?

8. What aspects of personality do you think are more influenced by a person's year of birth than by age?
9. Describe the three levels of personality that compose McAdams's model of personality. How do these levels complement each other? How can each level be measured?
10. Describe the levels and stages that make up Kohlberg's theory of moral development. What level of moral development is unique to adulthood?
11. According to Kohlberg, what are the factors responsible for moral development?
12. Briefly describe John Gibbs's reformulation of Kohlberg's theory of moral development. Explain how Gibbs's viewpoint may relate both to moral reasoning and coping style.
13. Briefly describe Carol Gilligan's major criticism of Kohlberg's theory.

For Further Reading

Erikson, E. (1963). *Childhood and society* (2nd ed.). New York: Norton.

Gilligan, C. (1982). *In a different voice: Psychological theory and women's development.* Cambridge, MA: Harvard University Press.

Levinson, D. J. (1996). *The seasons of a woman's life.* New York: Ballantine.

McCrae, R. R., & Costa, P. T. (1990). *Personality in adulthood.* New York: Guilford Press.

RELATIONSHIPS AND SEXUALITY

> *Seems like by now I'd find a love, a love who'd care, care just for me*
> *Then we'd go runnin' on faith*
> *All of our dreams would come true*
> *And our world would be right*
> *If love comes over me and you*
> —Eric Clapton
>
> *Love is an irresistible desire to be irresistibly desired.*
> —Robert Frost

INTRODUCTION

In this chapter we explore the personal relationships and emotions of adults. We examine the core dimensions of adult relationships: love, intimacy, and friendship. We discuss marriage and other forms of close relationships, and how these relationships develop and change during the adult years. We discuss sexuality and how sexual relationships change during adulthood. We also examine parenting and grandparenting roles, and the decision to be nonparental.

BUILDING RELATIONSHIPS: LOVE, INTIMACY, AND FRIENDSHIP

It seems that there are mainly two kinds of interpersonal relationships in adulthood—one an emotional, intimate attachment to another person (such as with a partner or spouse); the other, close friendships.

Attachment and Love

Though not easily understood or objectively measured, love is a fundamental aspect of adulthood. Adults seem to want to be loved and to love others. Love stories and romantic songs or poems have been written in all cultures. Often we are touched by love letters, by stories or movies about love, and by the lyrics of songs about love relationships.

A distinction can be made between liking and loving. *Liking* refers to a broad range of positive feelings toward another person. *Loving,* on the other hand, refers to a deep range of feelings. Love is sometimes or often accompanied by feelings of possessiveness.

Meanings of love have changed over time. For example, Allan Bloom (1993) suggested that the distinction between love and sex has become blurred in modern societies. Bloom observed that in earlier times the word *love* was reserved for describing the overwhelming attraction of one individual for another. In modern times, "love" seems to refer to a much broader range of ways of relating to another person. And *sex* is a word that tells us that individuals are acting upon certain bodily needs. Bloom comments that isolation, a sense of lack of contact with others, and loss of human connections seem to be prevalent consequences of modern society.

Berscheid (1988), Davis (1985), and Sternberg (1986) suggested that love is characterized by three themes: (1) emotionality or passion, (2) a sense of commitment or loyalty, and (3) a degree of sharing, openness, or mutual expression of personal identity. These three themes appear in different proportions in each theory. Davis (1985) views loving as composed of intense emotion, a sense of genuine regard and sincere concern for the one who is loved, and also a degree of intimacy unmatched in other relationships (see figure 11.1). Berscheid (1988) suggests that the intensely arousing

Figure 11.1
Davis's conceptualization of the components of love.

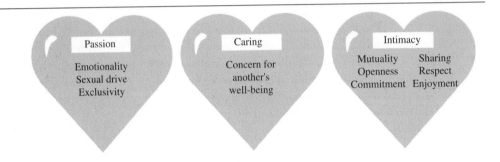

Figure 11.2
Changes in the components of satisfying love relationships across the life span.

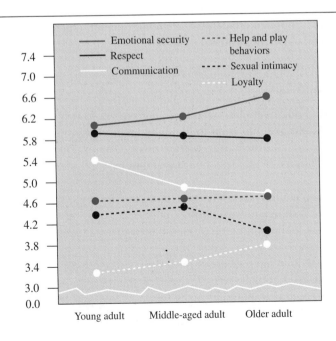

passions we call "being in love" cannot be sustained. Sternberg (1986), who agrees with Berscheid, describes the passionate phase of relationships as predominant in initiating and establishing a love relationship.

Margaret Reedy, James Birren, and K. Warner Schaie (1981) suggested that the passionate fires of youthful love are somehow gradually transformed into the deeper, more serene and tender love. From their perspective, physical attraction, perceived similarity of the loved one, self-disclosure, romance, and passion are important in emerging relationships, whereas security, loyalty, and mutual emotional interest in the relationship sustain love relationships over long periods of time.

To test these hypotheses, Reedy et al. (1981) studied 102 happily married couples in early (average age 28), middle (average age 45), and late adulthood (average age 65). As figure 11.2 shows, the researchers found age-related differences in the nature of satisfying love relationships. Passion and sexual intimacy were more important in early adulthood than late adulthood, whereas tender feelings of affection and loyalty were predominant in later-life love relationships.

In addition to the age-related differences in the nature of the relationships, Reedy et al. observed some striking similarities in the nature of satisfying love relationships in the different age groups. At all ages, emotional security was ranked as the most important factor in love, followed by respect, communication, help and play behaviors, sexual intimacy, and loyalty. Couples today seem to place more emphasis on security, fidelity, trust, and commitment in relationships compared with the 1960s and perhaps other time periods (Hendricks & Hendricks, 1983).

Intimacy

Intimacy becomes an increasingly important factor as love relationships develop and mature. Erik Erikson observed that intimacy is a primary concern in early adulthood. Erikson (1968) suggested that intimacy is only possible after individuals are well on their way toward forming a stable personal identity. Erikson commented:

> As the young individual seeks at least tentative forms of playful intimacy in friendship and competition, in sex play and love, in argument and gossip, he is apt to experience a peculiar strain, as if such tentative engagement might turn into an interpersonal fusion amounting to a loss of identity. . . . Where a youth does not resolve such a commitment, he may isolate himself and enter, at best, only stereotyped and formalized interpersonal relations; or he may, in repeated hectic attempts and dismal failures, seek intimacy with the most improbable of partners. (p. 167)

An inability to develop meaningful relationships with others during young adulthood can be harmful to an individual's personality. It may lead a person to repudiate, ignore, or attack others. Erikson (1968) noted that an inability to form intimate relationships can account for vulnerability to cult figures. Some young adults opt to follow leaders who offer them protection from the harm of an "out-group" world as well as a group identity. When this fails, and Erikson believes that eventually it must, the individual will begin a self-search to discover where he or she went wrong. Such new beginnings are sometimes painful. The experience of having been a naive follower may also lead to feelings of loneliness or mistrust of others.

Friendships

Friendship involves *enjoyment* (spending time with friends); *acceptance* (valuing friends as they are without trying to change them); *trust* (believing that friends act on our behalf); *respect* (knowing that friends have the right to make their own judgments); *mutual assistance* (helping and supporting friends and allowing them to do so for us); *confiding* (sharing experiences and confidential matters with friends); *understanding* (feeling that friends know us well and understand what we are like); and *spontaneity* (doing and saying as we like with friends) (Davis, 1985).

Marjorie Lowenthal and her colleagues suggested that the presence of a *confidant*—an extremely close friend—is a critical aspect of psychological adaptation to aging as measured by morale, avoidance of psychosomatic symptoms, and the ability to cope with stress (Lowenthal et al., 1975). The presence of a close confidant or mentor helps adult males in their twenties and early thirties to become successful in their careers (Levinson, 1986). The mentor serves as coach to those beginning their careers, providing a supervised internship as well as support and encouragement. By contrast, extreme social isolation is associated with psychiatric illness, poor achievement, failure to thrive, and limited job success. Indeed, being embedded in a network of close interpersonal ties is related to general life satisfaction and a sense of belonging, competence, and self-worth (Sarason, Sarason, & Pierce, 1989).

Connidis and Davies (1990b) found that adults are likely to reveal confidences to their relatives but are more likely to seek out spouses and friends as companions. That is, people usually tell their personal secrets and problems to their relatives (e.g., complain about poor health or finances) but do things (e.g., go out to dinner) with their friends. It may come as no surprise, therefore, that Crohan and Antonucci (1989) reported that relationships with friends are more strongly related to psychological well-being than relationships with family.

It has been suggested that female friendships are characterized by more intimacy than male friendships (Antonucci, 1990). Indeed, females are much more likely to disclose themselves to males than vice versa and are much more prone to share their private inner lives than males. Females bring the capacity for intimacy to courtship and then train males to be intimate. The importance of friendship among older women in our society continues to emerge in more recent investigations. In one study, both friendships and family supports were found to be equally effective among married and never-married women in negotiating loneliness and isolation (Essex & Nam, 1987).

Friendships are marked by many of the same characteristics as relationships between spouses or lovers (Davis, 1985). Both share the characteristics of acceptance, trust, respect, confiding, understanding, spontaneity, mutual assistance, and happiness. However, relationships with spouses and lovers, unlike friendships, are marked by strong emotion (passionate love) and strong caring. Sometimes relationships with friends are more stable or reliable than relationships among spouses or lovers (and of course, sometimes not).

Friendships During the Adult Years

In one study of friendships, it was found that newly married young adults have more friends than adolescents, middle-aged adults, or the elderly (Weiss & Lowenthal,

1975). Also, young married couples reported that friendships established in their single days are likely to dissipate. Often friendships among young married adults are based on a four-person relationship (two couples) rather than on a two-person relationship (one couple); the two couples may go out to the movies, or have dinner together, and so forth.

By middle adulthood many friends are "old friends." Closeness and convenience seem less salient in establishing friendships during midlife than in early adulthood. In one investigation of 150 middle-aged adults who had moved within the last five years, a majority of the individuals named someone from their former locale as their best friend (Hess, 1971). This indicates that the friendship role does not need to be filled by someone who is physically present. Many people keep closely connected with friends who are physically distant via electronic mail. For example, e-mail contact with friends and family helps to ease the transitions of moving away from one's hometown to college for a young adult or a disruptive relocation for a middle-aged or older person. What seems to matter is the perception that "there is someone out there who really cares about me."

Antonucci (1990) used the term **social convoy** to describe the network of close relationships that accompany an individual throughout life. The size of the social convoy—most people have somewhere between two to five close relationships— does not seem to change much during adulthood. Of course, the actual members of the convoy may change because of death, illness, or change of residence. Interestingly, younger and middle-aged adults are more likely to perceive the size and emotional intensity of their convoys as inadequate relative to elderly adults.

Throughout the adult years, women seem to have larger social convoys than men, and they maintain their friendships longer than men do (Antonucci, 1990). Women in old age expect friendships to be as reciprocal as they were in middle adulthood, even though they expect their children to provide more for them than previously (Ingersoll-Dayton & Antonucci, 1988; Rook, 1987). Recently, O'Connor (1993) has shown that older women tend to have especially meaningful cross-gender friendships with men. These are typically platonic relationships in which men provide a range of domestic services (e.g., grocery shopping and window washing) as well as closeness and support.

Because women have larger social convoys than men, they are more likely to suffer psychologically because of the negative life experiences that befall their friends, confidants, and spouses (Helgeson, 1994). Furthermore, because women tend to live longer than men, more women than men are faced with adjusting to the loss of a spouse.

Loneliness

According to Robert Weiss (1973) there are two kinds of loneliness: *emotional isolation,* which results from the loss or absence of an emotional attachment; and *social isolation,* which occurs through the loss or absence of social ties. Either type of loneliness is likely to make an individual feel empty and sad. Weiss suggested that one type of relationship cannot easily substitute for another to diminish the loneliness. Consequently, an adult grieving over the loss of a love relationship is likely to still feel very lonely even in the company of friends.

Similarly, people who have close emotional attachments may still feel a great deal of loneliness if they do not also have friends. Weiss described one woman who had a happy marriage but whose husband had to take a job in another state where they knew no one. In their new location she listened to her husband describe all the new friends he was developing on his new job while she was home taking care of the kids. She was bored and miserable. Eventually the family moved to a neighborhood where each was able to develop friendships.

Being alone is different from being lonely. Most of us cherish moments when we can be alone for a while, away from the hectic pace of our lives. Rubin (1979) has commented that for people in high-pressure jobs, aloneness may heal, while loneliness can hurt. In our society we are conditioned to believe that aloneness is to be dreaded, so we develop the expectation that solitude may bring sadness. However, research has revealed that people who choose to live alone are no more lonely than people who live with others (Rubenstein & Shaver, 1981).

An older person's health affects the amount of contact with family and friends, and the amount of closeness (or loneliness) he experiences. Field and colleagues (1993) reported that elderly adults who were in very good health had *more* contacts with relatives and friends than those elderly individuals who were in poor health. Thus the participants who experienced the most loneliness, in reality, should have received the most social support. These results strongly suggest that to maintain closeness with family members and friends, older adults need to possess a certain threshold level of physical vitality. Without health and vitality, it may be difficult, if not impossible, to maintain reciprocal interpersonal relations.

DEVELOPMENT OF MARITAL RELATIONSHIPS

For the vast majority of individuals, the most intense and important relationship they enter during adulthood is marriage. From the time two people marry, an average of two years pass before they have their first child, and the next 25 to 35 years are devoted to parenting. Although this parental period, if it occurs, represents a major part of adulthood, the typical married couple experiences more than one-half of their total years together *after* their last child leaves home. This extended period of shared time is a recent occurrence. Since the turn of the century, due to increased longevity, an average of 10 years has been added to the average length of married life. In the average family of 1900, the last child left home about two years after the death of one parent. Today, both parents are usually alive and healthy when their youngest child becomes independent, and they often live long enough to experience 20 to 30 years of postparental marriage.

Courtship

How do we choose a spouse or partner? Initially, physical appearance is often an important factor. The choice of a mate often entails a selection process based on mutual interests and sharing similar values. As a rule, opposites do not attract. However, being different from your mate in complementary ways is very important in mate selection. For example, if one person tends to be introverted, a socially outgoing spouse may com-

Marriages in which both husband and wife have worked take on a somewhat different pattern of adjustment to retirement, one marked by a simpler transition. In retirement, these couples display more egalitarian and far more cooperative relationships (Tryban, 1985). Among the retired working-class couples interviewed in one study, the dual-career couples derived increased happiness, satisfaction, and involvement in retirement when compared with single-wage-earner families (Tryban, 1985).

Married older adults appear to be happier than those who are single (Lee, 1978). Such satisfaction seems to be greater for women than for men, possibly because women place more emphasis on attaining satisfaction through marriage than men do. However, as more women develop careers, this relationship between satisfaction and marriage may not hold. (See Research Focus 11.1 for a discussion of other research on the sources of conflict and pleasure for middle-aged and elderly couples.)

Of course, not all individuals marry. About 8 percent of people who are age 65 or older have never been married. Never-married older people seem to have the least difficulty coping with loneliness in old age, adapt well to the challenges of growing older, and report high levels of life satisfaction. Many of them learned long ago to live autonomously, sustain friendships, and maintain self-reliance (Essex & Nam, 1987).

Widowhood

As can be seen in figure 11.4, a substantial percentage of the older population of the United States is widowed. Not surprisingly, women are much more likely than men to experience the death of a spouse. In fact, widows outnumber widowers nearly six to one (U.S. Bureau of the Census, 1995).

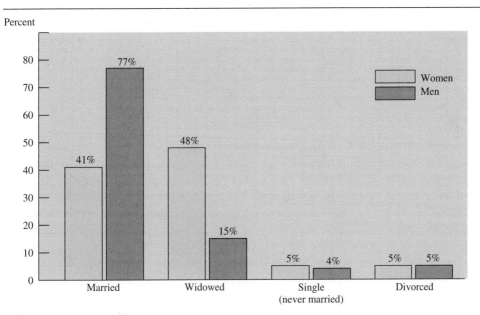

Figure 11.4
Marital status of persons 65 plus.
Source: Data from U.S. Bureau of the Census, 1990.

Sources of Conflict and Pleasure in Middle-Aged and Elderly Couples

Levenson, Carstensen, and Gottman (1993) noted an interesting paradox. Marriage has the potential to be the most long-lasting and intimate of all of the close relationships that we will encounter during our lives. But the vast majority of psychological research on the topic of marriage has focused on young and middle-aged couples, especially those whose marriages end in divorce. Why don't psychologists study long-term marriages that have survived for three or more decades? Do the members of an older marriage experience greater levels of satisfaction and pleasure than the members of a middle-aged marriage? Or, do older married people feel "stuck" and dissatisfied with each other more than middle-aged married people do? These are important issues because as life expectancy increases, the potential for a long-term marriage increases as well.

To examine these issues, Levenson et al. (1993) studied groups of middle-aged and older married couples. The middle-aged and older couples were between 40 and 50 or 60 and 70 years of age and had been married for at least 15 or 35 years, respectively. Overall, couples within these two age groups did not differ in terms of educational background, physical and psychological health status, alcohol consumption, and income. The vast majority of all of the couples had children. And, as would be expected, the children of the older couples (on average, 36 years of age) were older than the children of the middle-aged couples (on average, 17 years of age).

Each spouse, within the 156 pairs of couples in this study, was asked to rate the potential sources of conflict and pleasure he/she perceived in marriage. This was accomplished by presenting the participants with 10 potential conflict domains (e.g., money, communication, sex, children, etc.) and 16 potential areas of pleasure (e.g., vacations, children, watching TV, etc.). Participants rated each of these 26 items on a scale of 0 to 100. The higher the rating, the greater the perceived conflict or pleasure.

The major results of the Levenson et al. research are illustrated in table 11.A. In a very general sense, it seems that older marriages contain lower levels of conflict and higher levels of pleasure than middle-aged marriages, and older and middle-aged couples rank-order sources of conflict and pleasures in a similar way. More specifically, older couples attributed less conflict than middle-aged couples to money, religion, recreation, and children; they attributed more pleasure than middle-aged couples to children, things done together, dreams, and vacations. With regard to the ranking data, it seems as if children become a greater source of pleasure and lesser source of conflict as marriages grow older.

Overall, these results paint a very encouraging picture of long-term marital relationships. The positive state of these marriages could provide a very firm foundation for the increased interdependencies that marriage partners will probably experience in their later years. On another level, the findings obtained by Levenson et al. (1993) are consistent with the concept of selective optimization with compensation as developed by Baltes and Baltes (1990). Namely, as couples age, they may actively seek to narrow their social networks and maximize the amount of satisfaction they experience with each other.

When a spouse dies, the surviving marital partner goes through a period of grieving. The bereavement process of widows or widowers in the year after the death of a spouse is referred to as **grief work** (Parkes, 1972). The individual's structure or model of the world is challenged and disrupted because of the loss of an attachment bond (Bowlby, 1980). Over the course of a year, most individuals come to accept the loss of a spouse and seem to adapt reasonably well. Women seem to adjust better than men to the death of a spouse, and older people seem to adjust better than younger people (Carey, 1977). Most widows and widowers, despite having experienced a deep and close relationship with their spouse, adapt effectively to the loss. Many develop new interests, meet new friends and develop meaningful relationships, and learn new skills

TABLE 11.A

Rankings of Sources of Conflict and Pleasure for Middle-Aged and Older Couples

Middle-aged Couples		Older Couples	
Rank	Topic	Rank	Topic
		Sources of conflict	
1	Children	1	Communication
2	Money	2	Recreation
3	Communication	3	Money
4	Recreation	4	Children
5	Sex	5	Sex
6	In-laws	6	In-laws
7	Friends	7	Friends
8	Religion	8	Religion
9	Alcohol and drugs	9	Jealousy
10	Jealousy	10	Alcohol and drugs
		Sources of pleasure	
1	Good times in the past	1	Children or grandchildren
2	Other people	2	Good times in the past
3	Children or grandchildren	3	Vacations taken
4	Vacations taken	4	Things done together recently
5	Things done together recently	5	Other people
6	Silly and fun things	6	Plans for the future
7	Plans for the future	7	Television, radio, and reading
8	Television, radio, and reading	8	Casual and informal things
9	Casual and informal things	9	Silly and fun things
10	Accomplishments	10	Accomplishments

From: R.W. Levenson, L. L. Carstenson, and J. M. Gottman. "Long-Term Marriage: Age, Gender and Satisfaction." in Psychology and Aging, 8: 301–313. Copyright © 1993 by the American Psychological Association. Reprinted by permission.

in response to the challenges of being alone. Thus, the outcome of grief work may be a new and positive identity for the individual.

PARENTING AND GRANDPARENTING

Usually, the birth of a child quickly transforms a couple into a family, and an adult into a parent. In the United States, the *nuclear family,* consisting of parent(s) and a child or children is the typical form. In other countries, the extended family consisting of parents, grandparents, children, and other relatives is typical. In this section, we examine the parenting and grandparenting roles.

TABLE 11.1
Myths About Parenting

1. The birth of a child will save a failing marriage.
2. Because the child is a possession or extension of the parent, the child will think, feel, and behave as the parents did in their childhoods.
3. Children will always take care of parents in old age.
4. Parents can expect respect and obedience from their children.
5. Having a child means that the parents will always have someone who loves them and who will be their best friend.
6. Having a child gives the parents a second chance to achieve what they should have achieved.
7. If parents learn the right techniques, they can mold their children to be what they want.
8. It's the parents' fault when children fail.
9. Mothers are naturally better parents than fathers.
10. Parenting is an instinct and requires no training.

Parenting

Compared with earlier times, couples today tend to choose to have fewer children, and choose the time for having children. The number of one-child families is increasing. However, even with smaller families, parenting is as much of a time commitment as it has ever been. Frequently, both mothers and fathers are working outside the home. Even with day-care services, most parents find that their life bears little resemblance to what it was like before they became parents.

In the last two decades, three trends in parenting have been observed: (1) women balance the responsibilities of parenthood with work outside the home; (2) men are more invested in parenting compared with previous generations; and (3) parental care in the home is supplemented by care outside the home (e.g., day care).

The parenting role differs from other roles in that it is permanent or irreversible. A person can choose to quit one job and take another. A person can choose to divorce or to end a friendship. However, once children are born, the parent cannot choose to return to being a nonparent. Some adults are relatively prepared for the investment in time, energy, emotion, and money required for parenting, whereas others learn by doing. Table 11.1 summarizes some of the mythical expectations about parenting (Okun & Rappaport, 1980).

To be sure, parents have a significant impact on the psychological health and well-being of their children. Further, the influences of parental practices can be seen during adulthood as well as during childhood! See Research Focus 11.2 for more details.

Grandparenting

Frequently, people who become grandparents say that they did not realize how meaningful the role would be for them. People generally think of grandparents as old, but there is a wide age range for becoming a grandparent. The average ages for first-time grandmothers and grandfathers are 50 and 52 years old, respectively (Tinsley & Parke, 1987). According to Hagestad (1985), with increased life expectancy and

Parental Favoritism and the Quality of Parent-Child Relations in Adulthood

How do children who are disfavored by their parents during childhood relate to their parents during adulthood? This question, which seems relatively straightforward, is much more complex than one would assume. For example, Victoria Bedford (1992) has suggested that a child's self-esteem is threatened if she believes that she is not liked by her parents. To dissipate this threat and reduce feelings of inferiority, a child could develop a profound hatred for her parents. Such a strategy, however, could prove to be very counterproductive, because parents are the primary source of a child's need fulfillment, and it would be unwise to alienate them with signals of resentment. From the perspective of psychoanalytic theory, children might resolve this dilemma by unconsciously displacing feelings of animosity from their parents to their siblings. This would yield two significant accomplishments. First, parents would no longer be perceived as cruel, unfair, or unloving. Second, the child's self-esteem could be maintained. Bedford (1992) has noted that there are several examples of such displacements throughout Western literature, especially in the Bible. For example, "Due to Jacob's preference for Joseph, Joseph's brothers left him to die; because God, the supreme parent figure, preferred Abel's sacrifice to Cain's, Cain murdered Abel . . ." (Bedford, 1992, p. 150).

What happens when these "least favored children" grow older and enter adulthood? Adults are much less dependent on their parents for support than are children. Therefore, given the reasoning described in the previous paragraph, it may be that adults display more resentment toward their parents and less resentment toward their siblings as they age! Bedford (1992) has provided two pieces of evidence in support of this hypothesis. First, she discovered that young and middle-aged adults who felt they had been treated worse than their siblings during childhood experienced less affection for and more conflict with their parents than similarly aged adults who had memories of being favored by their parents. Interestingly, she also reported that the psychological consequences of being a "least favored child" were more pronounced from the perspective of adults who were least favored during adulthood than from the perspective of their parents. Second, Bedford (1992) as well as other researchers found that as siblings age they tend to become much more congenial toward each other.

Bedford (1992) concludes that her psychodynamically inspired research findings have ". . . demonstrated rather convincingly that childhood memories contribute consistently to the perceived quality of the intergenerational bond" (p. 154). She also reminds us that adult children's memories of early parental favoritism may have a significant effect on the degree to which they offer care and support to their elderly parents and siblings during times of crisis.

---

modifications in fertility patterns, the duration and experience of grandparenting has significantly changed in the following ways:

1. More people become grandparents than ever before.
2. The entry into grandparent status typically occurs at midlife, and many people spend four or more decades as grandparents.
3. Multigenerational families are common, and many grandparents also become great- and great-great-grandparents.
4. Parenthood and grandparenthood have become distinct from each other, both as individual life experiences and as two kinds of family status.

It appears that the way in which grandparents and grandchildren interact is partially a function of the age of the grandparents. Younger grandparents are nontraditional in their interactions with their grandchildren. Hagestad believes that our societal definition of the traditional grandparent role is far more likely to be seen among great-grandparents or great-great-grandparents than among grandparents. Thomas (1986a) reports that younger grandparents feel far more responsibility for their grandchildren in terms of discipline, caretaking, and childrearing advice than older grandparents.

Grandparents communicate with their grand-children at many levels, such as direct teaching of skills and cultural traditions.

Thomas (1986b) also observes that most grandparents, by age 70, seek less direct physical intervention and day-to-day care of their grandchildren. "One of the nicest things about being a 72-year-old grandmother," said one woman, "is that you can say good-bye to your grandchildren when they come for a visit."

Regardless of age, grandparenting is a role that has few norms in our society. In one investigation (Neugarten & Weinstein, 1984), 70 pairs of grandparents were interviewed about their relationships with their grandchildren. At least one-third of the grandparents said they had some difficulties with the grandparent role, in terms of thinking of themselves as grandparents, in how they should act as grandparents, and in terms of conflicts with their own children over how to rear the grandchildren.

Kivnick (1983) examined: (1) the meaning of the grandparenting role—*role meaning;* (2) the behavior a grandparent adopts—*role behavior;* and (3) the enjoyment of being a grandparent—*role satisfaction.* For some individuals, the role meaning in being a grandparent was a source of biological renewal and/or continuity. In such cases, feelings of renewal (youth) or extensions of the self and family into the future (continuity) appeared. For others, being a grandparent meant emotional self-fulfillment, generating feelings of companionship, and finding satisfaction from the development of a relationship between adult and grandchild that was often missing in earlier parent-child relationships. For still others, the grandparent role was seen as remote, indicating that the role had little importance in their lives.

In addition to evaluating the meaning of grandparenting, researchers have assessed the behavioral roles exhibited by grandparents in interacting with their grandchildren. In fact, this dimension of grandparent-role behavior is the most frequently studied aspect of grandparenting (Hess, 1988). Kivnick (1983), for example, noted three behavioral roles: formal, fun-seeking, and distant-figure. The *formal role* involved performing what was considered a proper and prescribed role. The *fun-seeking role* was typified by informality and playfulness. Grandchildren were viewed as a source of leisure activity, and mutual satisfaction was emphasized. The *distant-figure role* was characterized by benevolent but infrequent contact between grandparent and grandchild. Two new roles adopted by modern grandparents are that of *surrogate caretaker* (Cherlin & Furstenberg, 1985, 1986) and *family watchdog* (Troll, 1983).

Grandparents often play a significant role in the lives of their grandchildren. In one investigation (Robertson, 1976), 92 percent of young-adult grandchildren indicated that they would have missed some important things in life if there had been no grandparents present when they were growing up; 70 percent said that teenagers do not see grandparents as boring. Such information suggests that the grandparent-grandchild relationship is reciprocal.

Despite the tendency of research investigators to view grandparenting as a generic term, there are real and significant differences between the roles of grandmother and grandfather. Grandmothers, for example, tend to outlive grandfathers, thus occupying their role for a longer time and potentially having a different impact on their grandchildren (Hess, 1988). Grandmothers typically have closer ties to grandchildren of both sexes than grandfathers do (Hagestad, 1982), whereas grandfathers appear to establish closer ties with their grandsons than with their granddaughters (Bengtson, Mangen, & Landry, 1984). Generally, maternal grandparents have more contact with grandchildren than paternal grandparents (Kahana & Kahana, 1970). In times of family crisis, the maternal grandparents are more frequently sought for help and more frequently provide assistance (Cherlin & Furstenberg, 1986).

In a survey of 177 grandmothers and 102 grandfathers, Thomas (1986a) found that grandmothers derived greater satisfaction from their roles than grandfathers. Interestingly, grandmothers are more likely than grandfathers to consider grandparenting a second chance at parenting. And grandmothers appear more willing than grandfathers to accept the role of passing along to grandchildren family traditions, history, and customs. Grandfathers appear more as "secretaries of state" (Troll, 1983) or heads of the family, whereas grandmothers are more "kinkeepers" (Cohler & Grunebaum, 1981), making sure the family stays together and maintains family protocol. Perhaps these factors are responsible for the loss grandparents feel when they witness a divorce (see Research Focus 11.3).

In addition to gender, both cultural diversity and ethnic diversity lead to differences in grandparenting. Black grandmothers, for example, tend to adopt roles that allow them considerable control and authority over their grandchildren. White, Asian, and Hispanic cultures tend to be far more varied in their grandparenting styles (Cherlin and Furstenberg, 1985). In one investigation, Bengtson (1985) reported that Mexican-American grandparenting was marked by many more intergenerational relationships (more children, grandchildren, and great-grandchildren) than black or white families.

The role of *great-grandparent* has emerged with increasing frequency among the elderly. Families composed of four living generations represent a fairly new area for study. There is evidence that younger individuals with living grandparents and great-grandparents maintain very positive attitudes toward the elderly as well as great love and affection for these relatives (Bekker, DeMoyne, & Taylor, 1966; Boyd, 1969). These feelings seem to be reciprocal, in that, in a study of 40 great-grandparents (35 women and 5 men), 93 percent indicated very favorable attitudes toward and emotional significance in their new role (Doka & Mertz, 1988). Most viewed the acquisition of great-grandparenthood as a positive mark of successful aging or longevity.

PARENTAL ABUSE

Parental abuse has become an increasingly visible part of American life. Pillemer and Wolf (1986) believe that elder abuse, like other forms of family violence such as child abuse and spouse abuse, is a reflection of a violent society. Because of varying definitions and state reporting standards, the incidence of elder abuse in the United States is estimated to be in the range of 1 to 10 percent (Pillemer & Wolf, 1986). In a large metropolitan city, a random sampling of incidents of physical violence, verbal aggression, and neglect revealed rates of 32 per 1,000 among older adults (Pillemer & Finkelhor, 1988). Estimates put the incidence of elder abuse at between

Grandparents' Visitation Rights

During the last 10 to 15 years, most states have passed laws granting grandparents the right to petition a court to legally obtain visitation privileges with their grandchildren. Ross Thompson, Barbara Tinsley, Mario Scalora, and Ross Parke (1989) have noted that this is a significant change from traditional laws that gave grandparents visitation rights only if the child's parents consented to such visitation. Now grandparents may be allowed visitation privileges even if parents object.

What made legislators change their minds about grandparents' visitation rights? One of the most important factors is the emerging political influence of older adults. Also, lawmakers seem to believe that grandparent visitation is a way of preserving intergenerational ties within a family, and that grandparents provide their grandchildren with a powerful source of psychological support above and beyond that offered by parents.

Thompson et al. (1989) question whether there is sufficient psychological research to substantiate these beliefs. One of the things psychologists know, however, is that the benefits that children derive from interacting with their grandparents are directly related to the quality of the relationship that exists between the grandparents and the child's parents (Johnson, 1988). For example, if this relationship is typified by ill will and hostility, little, if any, benefits may be derived from grandparent visitation. In fact, children may even suffer from extended contact with their grandparents if significant intergenerational conflict exists. With regard to this issue, Thompson et al. (1989) have commented that

> Grandparents are likely to turn to the courts only if they cannot come to an agreement with the child's parents about visitation with grandchildren. Children are likely to encounter loyalty conflicts during the judicial proceedings, and if a visitation is granted, loyalty conflicts are likely to be maintained as the child remains the focus of intergenerational conflict. Because a child already experiences distress owing to the

triggering conditions linked to a visitation petition (for example, parental divorce or death), it is hard to see how further legal conflict between the family members can assist the child in coping. (p. 1220)

A similar problem may arise, of course, when a child visits a noncustodial parent after a divorce. But Thompson et al. (1989) maintain that the relationship a child shares with a noncustodial parent may be more salient than the relationship he or she shares with grandparents. In fact, it has been shown that children benefit from visiting a noncustodial parent even when there is friction between the custodial and noncustodial parents.

By granting visitation privileges to grandparents, the courts have broadened the degree of "extraparental" parenting to which the child is exposed. This has eroded the traditional notion that parents have virtual autonomy in childrearing matters. Also, grandparent visitation privileges may inadvertently foster changes in how family disputes are resolved. Bargaining between parents and grandparents over visitation privileges now takes place within the shadow of the law. Thompson et al. (1989) suggest that parents could be at a disadvantage in such circumstances because the conditions that allow grandparents to petition for visitation (e.g., divorce or the death of a parent) often render a parent less prepared, both psychologically and financially, for a court battle than the child's grandparents.

Should grandparents have visitation privileges over the objections of a parent? Is court-enforced grandparental visitation really in a child's best interests? Thompson et al. (1989) argue that we do not know enough about grandparenthood to answer these questions. Our ideas about grandparenthood are probably too naive and idealized. We may overestimate the benefits of grandparental visitation and underestimate its costs. Clearly, this is one area where research is needed to help address these basic issues.

700,000 to 1.1 million cases per year (Pillemer & Finkelhor, 1988). A comprehensive definition of elder abuse includes physical, psychological, and financial dimensions (see table 11.2).

Passive forms of neglect are more prevalent than active forms of physical violence. It is estimated that four of every five cases of elder abuse in the United States go unreported and uninvestigated (Church et al., 1988). Furthermore, elder abuse is a repetitive pattern of behavior, not an isolated or single occurrence.

The elderly are most often abused by their own spouses (Pillemer & Finkelhor, 1988). The rates of abuse are nearly equal for older men and women (Pillemer & Finkelhor, 1988). Abusers of the elderly are typically relatives in the role of caregivers (Pillemer & Wolf, 1986). And it appears that abuse is far more likely among the elderly

TABLE 11.2
Forms of Elder Abuse
Physical Abuse: Lack of personal care, lack of supervision, visible bruises and welts, repeated beatings, and lack of food
Psychological Abuse: Verbal assaults, isolation, fear and threats
Financial or Material Abuse: Misuse or theft of money or property
Extremely Unsatisfactory Individual Environment: Dirty and unclean home, urine odor in the home, hazardous living environment
Violation of Constitutional Rights: Reduction of personal freedom, autonomy, involuntary commitment, guardianship, protection, psychiatric "incompetence," false imprisonment

who live with a spouse, child, or another relative than among the elderly who live alone (Quinn & Tomita, 1986).

The causes of elder abuse are varied. Investigators have focused their attention on a recurrent stress pattern found among both abused and abuser (Pillemer & Wolf, 1986). The constant responsibility for the care of an older, frail adult often falls on those who neither choose this relationship nor are able to cope with the financial, interpersonal, and time demands placed upon them. Abusers are frequently those who have experienced marital problems, financial hardships, drug abuse, alcoholism, and child abuse (Church et al., 1988). Pillemer (1986) observed that dependency is commonly a factor in the background of the abused elderly. Initially, researchers focused on the abused's dependency on the perpetrator of abuse (Quinn & Tomita, 1986). However, other data (Pillemer, 1986) suggest that caretakers who abuse the elderly are dependent on those whom they target for abuse. The abuser may be dependent on the elderly victim for housing, for assistance with routine household tasks, or for financial support.

Research also supports the notion that through abuse, the caretaker is able to continue a cycle of abuse that characterized the relationship at earlier periods of development (Steinmetz, 1978, 1981). Resentment over the lack of freedom and free time are also implicated in the development of abusive patterns by those who care for the elderly. The demands of the responsibility of caring for an elderly parent or relative are substantial. The amount of sacrifice and effort required is not sufficiently recognized, which sometimes leads to further cycles of abuse (Myers & Shelton, 1987). In providing care for an elderly parent, for example, adult children in their middle or later adulthood years have to limit or adjust their work and leisure activities. Finally, it should be noted that elderly victims of neglect are generally old, frail, and mentally and/or physically impaired; they view themselves as helpless and dependent (Myers & Shelton, 1987; Pillemer & Wolf, 1986).

NONMARRIAGE

A greater proportion of adults is opting to remain single now than in the past. In 1985, for example, 20.6 million individuals lived alone in the United States, accounting for 11 percent of adults and 25 percent of all households (U.S. Bureau of the Census,

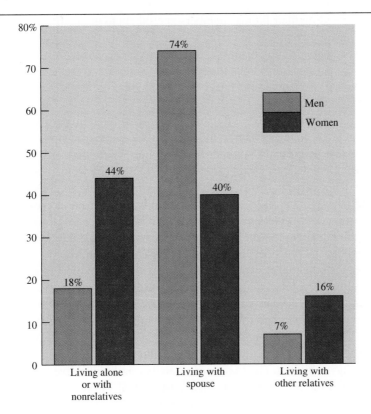

Figure 11.5
Living arrange-
ments of persons
65+: 1990.
*Source: Data from
U.S. Bureau of
Census, 1990 Census
of Population and
Housing.*

1986). In 1990, approximately 44 percent and 18 percent of the women and men in the United States lived alone or with nonrelatives (see figure 11.5).

Single Adults

Some people choose to be single as a preferred lifestyle. For others, being single is associated with circumstances such as the death of a spouse or divorce. At any given time, about 30 percent of all adult males and 37 percent of adult females are unmarried (Macklin, 1980). Kasper (1988) reported that nearly one of every three elderly persons lives alone without a spouse, child, sibling, or friends. Among men 65 to 74 years of age, 79 percent live with their wives as compared with 67 percent over age 75 (Church et al., 1988). Comparable data for women, however, suggest that only 50 percent of those 65 to 74 years of age and less than 25 percent of those over 75 years of age live with a husband. Thus, aging is a different phenomenon depending on one's sex; men typically age with a spouse, whereas many women age alone.

Many myths and stereotypes are associated with being single. These stereotypes range from the swinging-singles lifestyle to the desperately lonely. These stereotypes, of course, do not represent most single adults. Frequently, single adults' concerns center around issues of intimate relationships with other adults, confronting loneliness, and finding a place in a marriage-oriented society. Singles sometimes feel prompted or annoyingly urged by their family members and others to get married. However, individuals see many advantages to remaining single during the early adult years. These include time and opportunity to make one's own decisions about the course of life; time to develop the personal resources to meet goals; freedom to make autonomous decisions and pursue one's own schedule and interests; opportunity to explore new places and try out new things; and availability of privacy.

Choosing a single lifestyle offers flexibility. This freedom partially explains why some adults choose to marry later in life and why the number of single people aged 35 and under is rapidly growing. Another factor in this choice is the change in attitude of many women toward careers and personal fulfillment. Many women (and men) choose to develop their careers before assuming marriage responsibilities. Birth control devices and changing attitudes about premarital sex also make it possible for single adults to explore their sexuality outside the bounds of marriage. However, some psychologists think that adults will limit the range of their sexual partners (as well as the range of their sexual practices) because they fear contracting AIDS.

One of the potential drawbacks associated with a single lifestyle is a lost sense of immortality. In a probing study, Rubenstein, Alexander, Goodman, and Luborsky (1991) found that never-married, childless, elderly women developed close, enduring ties with family members and friends during late life and had led successful generative lives. Yet many of these women felt that something was missing. Specifically, they did not experience the sense of "cultural validation" that is afforded to the members of our society who have children. They saw more than their individual lives ending upon their death. As one of the informants in the Rubenstein et al. study said, "It's hard to think there'll be nothing of you left when you are gone" (1991, p. 276).

Homosexual and Bisexual Adults

The recognition that one is homosexual or bisexual is a challenge that must be confronted throughout the adolescent and early adult years (Remafedi, 1987). Initially, self-acceptance of sexual preferences by gay men and lesbian women may be difficult. In one investigation, males in late adolescence continued to question their sexual orientations despite clear evidence that they were homosexual (Remafedi, 1987). Young homosexual adults, concerned about the attitudes or reactions of parents, straight peers, and coworkers, continue to protect themselves from disclosure of their sexual preferences. Despite legal mandates, homosexuality carries a threat of discrimination in terms of hiring and career advancement.

Short-term relationships seem to be the norm in young adulthood, particularly for gay men up to their mid- to late thirties (Kimmel, 1995). Meaningful long-term relationships are more likely to develop for middle-aged and older lesbians and gay men (Kimmel & Sang, 1997).

Studies of long-term homosexual relationships suggest that commitment emerges after an extended period of time as single dating partners. The period in adulthood in which such commitments are made is often just prior to middle age (in the mid- to late thirties for males). Homosexual couples committed to each other may elect to maintain closed, monogamous relationships or open, nonmonogamous rela-

Gay and lesbian couples experience the positive benefits of long-lasting personal relationships throughout adult life and old age.

tionships. Closed relationships have been found to be associated with greater levels of social support, positive attitudes, and lower anxiety levels than open relationships (Kurdek & Schmitt, 1986).

Concern about the increase in AIDS among the elderly population forces us to focus our attention on aging homosexual and bisexual males. In 1987, these men represented 65.8 percent of all older persons with AIDS (Stall et al., 1988). Other evidence shows that unprotected sexual activity places older homosexual males at risk (Curran et al., 1988; Lifson, 1988). Yet this group is more knowledgeable about safe sex than comparably aged heterosexual males (Catania et al., 1989). AIDS mortality dropped by 26 percent in 1997 from 1996, probably because of new medications as well as reductions in risky sexual behavior (Centers for Disease Control and Prevention, 1997).

In one study, Quam and Whitford (1992) sought to measure how older gay and lesbian women adapted to the aging process. As reported in table 11.3, the majority of older homosexual adults has positive expectations about aging and displayed high levels of life satisfaction. Most of the respondents indicated that being a lesbian woman or gay man helped them adjust to aging. One man commented, "I've been aware of an enhanced psychological and spiritual scope because of the stresses of being in a sexual and a social minority." Similarly, a woman maintained, "My lesbian 'family'—in which I am the oldest—has been a constant source of support. We are learning about

Percent of Aging Gay Men and Lesbians Indicating Different Levels of Life Satisfaction, Loneliness, and Acceptance of Aging

	n = 80 Total	n = 49 <60	n = 31 >60	n = 41 Women	n = 39 Men
Age					
50–59	61.3			74.4	48.8
60+	38.8			25.6	51.2
Gender					
Male	51.3	40.8	67.7		
Female	48.8	59.2	32.3		
Acceptance of Aging Process					
Very accepting	35.0	27.1	48.4	26.3	43.9
Somewhat accepting	42.5	43.8	41.9	55.3	31.7
Neutral	3.8	6.3	0.0	5.3	2.4
Somewhat unaccepting	16.3	20.8	9.7	10.5	22.0
Very unaccepting	1.3	2.1	0.0	2.6	0.0
Life Satisfaction					
First quartile	6.3	6.7	6.1	5.1	7.5
Second quartile	11.4	6.6	14.3	5.2	17.5
Third quartile	31.6	30.0	32.7	25.7	37.5
Fourth quartile	50.6	56.7	46.9	64.0	37.5
Loneliness a Problem					
Yes	20.0	20.4	19.4	10.3	29.3
Sometimes	47.5	49.0	45.2	56.4	39.0
No	31.3	28.6	35.5	30.3	31.7

aging as a group" (Quam & Whitford, 1992, p. 373). The major areas of concern for these aging gay men and lesbian woman are the same as those experienced by most heterosexual adults—loneliness, health, and finances.

Divorced Adults

Divorced and widowed adults experience some of the same emotions. In both situations, the individuals experience the death of a relationship. Next to a death of a spouse, a divorce causes the most trauma in the lives of individuals (Pearlin, 1985). Until recently, divorce was increasing annually by 10 percent, although the rate of increase slowed in the 1990s (Cherlin, 1996). Though divorce rates are high in all socioeconomic groups, people from lower social classes have the highest divorce rates. Among lower socioeconomic classes, factors associated with divorce include marriage at an early age, low levels of education, and low income (Spanier & Glick, 1981; U.S. Bureau of the Census, 1995). Premarital pregnancy is another critical factor. In one investigation, half of the women who were pregnant before marriage lived with their husbands for less than five years (Sauber & Corrigan, 1970). Because the median age for divorce is 38, many divorced people are single parents (Hetherington, Stanley-Hagan, & Anderson, 1989; Kaslow & Schwartz, 1987).

Although divorce rates have declined from 1992 to 1997 by as much as 10 percent (Cherlin, 1996), this might not mean that people are now happier in their marriages. Part of the reduced rate of divorce may have to do with the fact that baby boomers past the "age of divorce" constitute a larger proportion of the married population than previously. The lower divorce rate might also mean that young adults are evaluating the commitments of a long-term relationship more seriously before marrying.

Parenting by Divorced Men and Women

During the first year after a divorce, the quality of parenting that a child in the family experiences is often poor; parents seem to be occupied with their own needs and adjustment. This has a negative impact on parents' ability to respond sensitively to the child's needs. During this period, parents tend to discipline children inconsistently, are less affectionate, and are somewhat ineffective in controlling children. During the second year after a divorce, parents typically become more effective in these matters (Hetherington et al., 1989; Kaslow & Schwartz, 1987).

The parenting capabilities of the father and mother are central to a child's ability to cope with the stress of divorce. It appears that divorced mothers have more difficulty with sons than daughters. Hetherington (1979) reported that divorced mothers and their sons often get involved in what she calls a cycle of coercive interaction. But what about boys growing up in homes in which the father has custody—does the same coercive cycle occur? In one investigation, sons showed more competent social behavior when their fathers had custody, whereas girls were better adjusted when their mothers had custody (Santrock & Warshak, 1979).

Support for Divorced Families

Most information about divorced families emphasizes the role of the loss of one parent on the relationship between the custodial parent and the child. Support systems such as the extended family and school-based and community-based programs are important for assisting children in divorce. Support for single or divorced parents with infant and preschool children can help these persons juggle the demands of work and parenting. Other kinds of support are helpful with feelings, legal matters, and career advice.

Divorce in Later Life

Although the amount of research on divorce has increased in recent years, little attention has been paid to how this critical life event may influence those who have been married a long time (Chiriboga, 1982a; Kaslow & Schwartz, 1987). One view suggests that since middle-aged adults have more maturity and greater resources, divorce in middle age allows the simplification of life patterns and ends an incompatible relationship (Golan, 1986). However, the emotional commitment to a long-term marriage is not easily cast aside. Many middle-aged individuals perceive the divorce as the failure or repudiation of the best years of their lives. The partner initiating the divorce may view it as an escape from an untenable relationship; the divorced partner, however, usually feels betrayal, sadness over the end of a long-standing relationship, and emotional grief over the loss of trust and commitment (Golan, 1986).

David Chiriboga (1982a) evaluated the psychosocial functioning of 310 recently separated men and women ranging in age from 20 to the mid-70s. Included in the analyses were measures of morale, psychiatric symptoms, time perspective, self-reported physical health, social disruption, and divorce-induced upset. People in their fifties were most negatively affected by divorce. With late-age divorce, both men and women feel they lack resources and choices when they compare themselves with the younger population playing the dating game or when they search for an available social group. Thus, older adults seem to have fewer options and a general uncertainty about what to do following divorce. In fact, Uhlenberg, Cooney, and Boyd (1990) found that divorced men over 50 were unable to anticipate what their lives would be like one year into the future.

Remarriage

In the United States remarriage has become less prevalent than it was nearly two decades ago (Glick & Ling-Lin, 1986). Increased mobility and higher rates of cohabitation may account for these data, but remarriage is still a popular choice among those couples who have experienced divorce for the first time (Glick & Ling-Lin, 1986). Approximately 80 percent of all divorced people decide to remarry; yet, of these remarriages, 60 percent will end in divorce (versus a 50 percent rate of divorce for first marriages). In connection with this point, Wallerstein and Blakeslee (1988) remind us that second marriages are highly complex "second chances," with excess baggage such as "his and her small children, lowered income due to alimony, and the ghost of a failed marriage."

The number of remarriages in which children are involved has been steadily growing. Remarried families are usually referred to as stepfamilies, blended families, or reconstituted families. About 10 to 15 percent of all households in the United States are composed of stepfamilies, which represents more than 500,000 families (Prosen & Farmer, 1982). Projections into the first decade of the twenty-first century estimate that approximately 25 to 30 percent of all children in the United States will be part of a stepfamily before their 18th birthday. For better or worse, divorced people seem firmly committed to the institution of marriage.

SEXUALITY

One of the most important elements of adult relationships is sexuality. In this section we discuss several aspects of adult sexuality and focus on age-related changes in sexual functioning.

Sexual Attitudes and Behavior

Some aspects of the expression of sexuality are an outcome of socialization. In many societies, cultural standards concerning *premarital sex* have changed substantially in recent years. For example, consider the data that have been collected on 19-year-old unmarried men and women. During the 1930s and 1940s, 20 percent of females and 45 percent of males within this age group reported having sexual intercourse (Kinsey, Pomeroy, & Martin, 1948). By the mid-1970s, self-reports of premarital sex increased to about 55 percent for females and 60 percent for males (Zelnick & Kanter, 1977). In the mid-1990s, reports suggested that 75 percent of both females and males in this age group had had intercourse (Centers for Disease Control, 1992). During the college years, it has been reported that sexual intercourse increases from 28 percent at the beginning of college to 82 percent during the senior year for men and from 29 to 86 percent for women.

Sex and Marriage

Evidence that sexual intercourse in marriage is a highly satisfying physical experience comes from data reported by more than 2,000 middle-class American married women (Bell & Lobsenz, 1979). Women in their twenties reported that they enjoyed the physical aspects of sex, and women in their thirties reported that they enjoyed the emotional aspects of sex.

It appears that sexual relations follow a predictable pattern depending on how long a couple has been married. For example, intercourse is relatively frequent in the early years of marriage and then decreases over the length of the marriage. Doddridge, Schumm, and Bergen (1987) noted that when married couples reported the preferred frequency of sexual intercourse, the older the couple and the longer the marriage, the lower the preferred frequency. Consistent with these data, Masters, Johnson, and Kolodny (1991) reported that the average American couple has intercourse about two or three times a week during young adulthood, and about once a week after age 50.

The link between frequency of intercourse and marital satisfaction is not the same across marriages. Nonetheless, there is an association between marital satisfaction and sexual activity. The most common reason given for sexual abstinence among married couples is marital conflict. Other reasons include physical illness, loss of interest, and emotional stress. The greatest obstacle to sexual happiness among couples is the level of tension or anxiety in the marriage (Gambert, 1987).

Sexual Attitudes and Behavior at Midlife

Although there is usually little biological decline in a man or woman's ability to function sexually in middle adulthood, middle-aged adults usually engage in sexual activity less frequently than they did when they were younger. Career interests, family concerns, and energy levels may contribute to a decline in sexual activity.

Menopause

A topic of strong interest to researchers studying sexuality in middle adulthood is the range of changes that accompanies menopause. Most of us know something about menopause, but is what we know accurate? Here are some comments made by two women who have experienced menopause.

> "My first sign of menopause was the night sweat. . . . It was a little frightening to wake up in the middle of the night with my sheets all drenched. It was hard not to feel that something was very wrong with me."
>
> "I am constantly amazed and delighted to discover new things about my body, something menstruation did not allow me to do. I have new responses, desires, sensations, freed and apart from the distraction of menses [periods]." (Boston Women's Health Book Collective, 1976, pp. 327, 328)

These comments suggest there is a range of reactions to menopause.

Biologically, **menopause** is defined as the end of menstruation, a marker that signals the cessation of childbearing capacity. Menopause is accompanied by a reduction of **estrogen,** the primary female sex hormone, to one-tenth of earlier levels. Menopause is considered to have occurred when 12 consecutive months have passed without a menstrual period (Block, Davidson, & Grambs, 1981); the average age at menopause in the United States is 50 (Masters et al., 1991). Despite the number of symptoms reported to accompany menopause, only two—hot flashes and the atrophy of the vagina—are believed to be directly related to decreased estrogen levels (Katchadourian, 1987).

The *hot flash,* a feeling of extreme heat that is usually confined to the upper part of the body and often is accompanied by a drenching sweat, is the most commonly experienced symptom of menopause. Hot flashes gradually diminish in frequency and generally disappear completely within a year or two. *Atrophy of the cells of the vaginal walls* means that the vagina becomes drier, the layer of cell walls thinner, and the amount of lubricants secreted during sexual arousal is reduced. These conditions can make sexual intercourse painful for some women. They may require the use of artificial lubrications during intercourse (Gambert, 1987; Masters et al., 1991).

Gambert (1987) identified a large number of physical and psychological effects that may be directly or indirectly associated with menopause (see table 11.4). As mentioned, hot flashes and atrophy of the vaginal walls are the direct results of menopause. On the other hand, *osteoporosis* (thinning of the bones) is directly caused by a woman's inability to uptake calcium to strengthen her bones; this, in turn, is caused by a reduction in available estrogen. Osteoporosis is a common cause of the postural stoop in older people and a contributor to the brittleness of bones, which break easily in old age. None of the psychological effects of menopause identified in table 11.4 are directly related to the physical changes that accompany menopause.

In a recent study, Wilk and Kirk (1995) suggested that menopause is best understood as a developmental stage, as a biological and psychological process, and not as a medical deficiency. Wilk and Kirk reported that most women who are willing to discuss menopause say that menopause means "getting old." Specifically, 70 percent of the women in the Wilk and Kirk study reported that menopause means getting old.

TABLE 11.4
Effects Associated with Menopause

Physical Effects

1. Blood pressure disturbances "hot flashes"
2. Osteoporosis (thinning of the bones, calcium absorption deficiency)
3. Atrophy of the vaginal walls, vaginal shortening, and reduced lubricity
4. Increase in incidence of cardiovascular disease

Psychological Effects (Wide Ranging, Great Degree of Interindividual Variability)

5. Insomnia
6. Anxiety
7. Depression

About 44 percent of the women in this study reported that menopause means a change in sexuality and in feminine identity.

Many middle-aged and older women undergo hysterectomies, a sort of artificial menopause. In a *simple hysterectomy,* the uterus and cervix are surgically removed, while in a *total hysterectomy* the ovaries and fallopian tubes are removed as well. A hysterectomy is performed for various reasons. The most common reason involves the slippage and improper positioning of the uterus. A hysterectomy is also performed to eliminate fibroid tumors; about 25 percent of all women experience fibroid tumors. Such tumors are not cancerous, but they may cause abnormal bleeding. A third common reason for a hysterectomy is cancer, which, if detected early, is not necessarily life threatening (Block et al., 1981; Gambert, 1987).

One of the most controversial aspects of menopause concerns the use of *hormone replacement therapy (HRT).* HRT involves replacing the estrogen that a woman's body no longer produces; physicians usually prescribe it only in severe cases, using the lowest dosage for the shortest possible period of time. Schmitt and his associates (1991) have noted the many benefits and risks of HRT. On the positive side, HRT may be used to reduce hot flashes, relieve vaginal itching and dryness, and prevent osteoporosis. On the negative side, the chances for endometrial, uterine, and breast cancer increase with HRT. To reduce the cancer risk, estrogen is often administered along with a second hormone called *progestin.* Unfortunately, progestin may cause the reoccurrence of cyclical bleeding. And, at present, the risks associated with long-term progestin treatment are unknown. This is important, because much of the danger associated with HRT occurs when the medication is taken for long periods of time. Many women, in fact, receive HRT for 10 years or more.

The Male Climacteric

The **male climacteric** occurs during the sixties and seventies in most men when they experience a decline in sexual potency or fertility. The male climacteric differs in two important ways from menopause: It comes later, and it progresses at a much slower rate. Men experience hormonal changes in their fifties and sixties, but not to the extent that women do. For example, testosterone production declines about 1 percent a year beginning during middle adulthood, but men do not lose their capacity to father children. Consequently, the male climacteric may have less to do with hormonal change than with the psychological adjustments. This conclusion gains credibility when one considers that testosterone therapy does not relieve the symptoms associated with the male climacteric (Burt & Meeks, 1985; Katchadourian, 1987).

The male climacteric manifests itself in many ways. For example, the influence of psychologically erotic stimuli may decline with increasing age. Thus, although physical stimulation remains effective in producing sexual arousal, psychological stimulation loses some of its power. For instance, a spouse's nudity may not arouse as it did in earlier years. Couples often mistakenly view this as evidence that advancing age means waning sexuality (Katchadourian, 1987). Also, the time necessary for erection and ejaculation, as well as the refractory period that follows ejaculation, grows greater with age, while the intensity of orgasm declines with age (Masters et al., 1991).

Sexuality in Late Adulthood

Aging is associated with a gradual reduction of the sexual response for both men and women (Comfort, 1980; Masters et al., 1991). It takes longer for both men and women to become aroused, and to reach climax. Erections are softer and not maintained as long. Climax is less intense, there are fewer spasms, and the volume of ejaculation is diminished in comparison to younger years. For women, there is an age-related reduction in the levels of estrogen, the vaginal walls become thinner and less elastic, and the vagina itself shrinks. However, even when the frequency of intercourse is reduced by infirmity, physical health, or hospitalization, the desire for the intimacy associated with sexuality remains strong. Feelings of closeness, physical touching, emotional intimacy, sensuality, and being valued as a man or a woman continue to be important.

Most elderly adults continue to have meaningful sexual relationships, unencumbered by destructive negative stereotypes. Among people between 60 and 71 years old, almost 50 percent have intercourse on a regular basis. Fifteen percent of those over 78 years old regularly engage in intercourse (Comfort, 1980; Matthias, Lubben, Atchison, & Schweitzer, 1997).

There are no specific or universal limits to sexual activity in later life (e.g., Kaplan, 1974; Masters & Johnson, 1970; Masters et al., 1991). Adults who have always placed a high priority on their sexual lives approach old age with the same values. Healthy older people who want to have sexual activity are likely to be sexually active in late adulthood (Comfort, 1980). Men and women who remain sexually active are more likely to maintain their sexual vigor and interest into their older years.

The results of a 1991 national survey of a large number of married people over 60 years of age provide convincing evidence that older adults maintain their sexual activity (Marsiglio & Donnelly, 1991). As shown in table 11.5, 53 percent of the entire sample and 24 percent of those 76 years old or older had intercourse at least once a month. And most people who are sexually active reported having sex about four times per month. Furthermore, Marsiglio and Donnelly (1991) found that an older person's sense of self-worth and his/her spouse's health status were among the most powerful predictors of sexual activity in their sample.

TABLE 11.5

Descriptive Data on Sexual Frequency Patterns for Married Persons 60 Years of Age and Older

Sociodemographic/Health Variables	Percent Having Sex at Least Once Within the Past Month (N = 807)		Mean Frequency of Sex Among Those Sexually Active Within the Past Month (N = 423)	
	%	N	M	N
Total	53	807	4.26	423
Gender				
Male	54	(427)	4.15	(229)
Female	51	(380)	4.41	(194)
Age				
60–65	65	(340)	4.54	(221)
66–70	55	(206)	4.52	(111)
71–75	45	(140)	3.51	(62)
76 and older	24	(121)	2.75	(29)
Race				
White	53	(711)	4.34	(373)
Black	55	(68)	2.88	(39)
Other	43	(28)	3.54	(11)
Educational Level				
Less than 12 years	46	(288)	4.02	(130)
High school graduate	54	(322)	3.88	(176)
Some college	58	(84)	5.30	(49)
College graduate	62	(113)	4.77	(68)
Personal Health Status				
Excellent/good	58	(524)	4.27	(299)
Fair	45	(202)	4.60	(91)
Poor/very poor	36	(61)	2.97	(24)
Spouse's Health Status				
Excellent	58	(466)	4.29	(271)
Fair	46	(165)	4.90	(76)
Poor/very poor	36	(49)	3.48	(17)

From W. Marsiglio and D. Donnelly. "Sexual Relations in Later Life: A National Study of Married Persons" in Journal of Gerontology: Social Sciences, 46: 338–344. Copyright © 1991 The Gerontological Society of America.

The greatest obstacles to continued sexual expression are the lack of an available partner, interfering health problems, and susceptibility to societal attitudes that discourage sexual intimacy in close relationships in old age. However, societal attitudes are changing, even for elderly living in nursing homes (see Research Focus 11.4).

Sexuality and the Institutionalized Elderly

In most nursing homes and elder care institutions staff generally ignore the sexual needs of the elderly resident. Nursing homes often have sex-segregated floors or wings. Another example is the tendency of institutional personnel to "infantilize" sexual forms of expression. Elderly who express an interest in, genuine caring for, and emotional attachment to each other are often teased, ridiculed, and held up to public scrutiny. For instance, staff might ask a woman how her "date" behaved at the movie shown in the social hall, or they might ask a man to explain his interest in his "girlfriend" or account for her wavering loyalty if she sits next to someone else at mealtime. Adult men and women who display a healthy lifelong interest in their sexuality need *not* be treated as adolescents simply because they reside in an institution. They are entitled to the same privacy and respect that other community-residing elderly receive.

Institutionalization of elderly adults does not necessarily mean the demise of their sexual interest (McCartney, Izeman, Rogers, & Cohen, 1987). Even institutionalized elderly with dementia may maintain the competency to initiate sexual relationships although well-intentioned staff may thwart such interests (Lichtenberg & Strzepek, 1990). Following is one example of guidelines written to help staff determine the competencies of institutionalized elderly to engage in intimate relationships:

1. Patient's awareness of the relationship
   a. Is the patient aware of who is initiating sexual contact?
   b. Does the patient believe that the other person is a spouse and thus acquiesce out of a delusional belief, or are they cognizant of the other's identity and intent?
   c. Can the patient state what level of sexual intimacy they would be comfortable with?
2. Patient's ability to avoid exploitation
   a. Is the behavior consistent with formerly held beliefs/values?
   b. Does the patient have the capacity to say no to any uninvited sexual contact?
3. Patient's awareness of potential risks
   a. Does the patient realize that this relationship may be time limited (placement on unit is temporary)?
   b. Can the patient describe how they will react when the relationship ends (Lichtenberg & Strzepek, 1990, p. 119).

SUMMARY

Our relationships with others are extraordinarily important to us as adults. Those who do not have emotional attachments or social ties often suffer from loneliness. It may be important not only to develop an emotional attachment but also to have a network of social ties to adequately round out one's life as an adult. Emotional attachments give us comfort and security, and social ties provide us with a sense of group identity and integration. In new relationships, physical attraction, perceived similarity of the loved one, self-disclosure, romance, and passion seem to be important; security, loyalty, and mutual emotional interests are more germane to enduring relationships.

Intimacy is a key ingredient in relationships with a spouse, lover, or close friend. Erik Erikson believed that people should develop intimacy after they have developed a stable and successful identity. Intimacy is a part of development in middle and late adulthood as well as early adulthood. Indeed, building a network of close interpersonal ties appears to be closely linked with life satisfaction.

The choice of a spouse or partner may be influenced by similarities and complementary needs and interests. Early communication patterns set the tone in a marital relationship. Couples opting to have children face increased responsibilities and demands. One particularly difficult task is successfully juggling career and parenting demands. Parents often experience mixed emotions when their children leave home, but research suggests that the "empty nest" is associated with increased marital happiness. The time from retirement until the death of a spouse is the final stage of the marriage process. Eventually, one spouse dies and the surviving spouse must adjust to being a widow or widower.

Parenting requires interpersonal skill and emotional sensitivity, responsibility, and substantial commitment. Many young adults have idealized views about what it is like to be a parent. Various meanings have been attributed to the roles, expectations, and emotional fulfillment of grandparenthood. Researchers have identified different interaction styles among grandparents as well as great-grandparents.

The diversity of lifestyles today includes an increase in the number of single adults. Single adults are often concerned with establishing intimate relationships with other adults, confronting loneliness, and finding a place in a marriage-oriented society. Unique issues face homosexual adults, as well as the large number of formerly married adults affected by divorce. Divorce is a process that all family members find complex and emotionally charged. The most stressful impact seems to occur during the period just after the separation, but over the course of several years, the divorced adult seems to adjust to being single. Divorced mothers may be particularly vulnerable to stress because of increased economic and childrearing responsibilities. The effects of divorce on children are mediated by a variety of factors, including postdivorce family functioning and the availability of support systems, particularly for women. Marital separation in later life may be more traumatic than in earlier adulthood because of a greater commitment to the marriage, fewer resources, and more uncertainty about the future. The number of stepfamilies is increasing; it is estimated that in the 1990s, one-fourth to one-third of all children under age 18 will have lived in a stepfamily at some point.

Sexuality consists of biological, behavioral, and attitudinal components. Premarital sex is prevalent among young adults, and sexual activity is a source of great pleasure among young married couples. Menopause—the end of menstruation—is surrounded by many myths. The majority of women cope with menopause without having to undergo medical intervention, and for some women, menopause can be a positive event. Although males do not experience comparable rapid hormonal changes during middle age, they do seem to undergo a climacteric, involving a gradual decline in sexual interest, potency or fertility, and sexual functioning.

Sexual activity and enjoyment may continue among many individuals in late adulthood. However, many elderly adults who have strong sexual interests do not always have the opportunity to fulfill their needs in this important area of life.

REVIEW QUESTIONS

1. Describe Erikson's ideas about intimacy. Discuss why he believed we must go through the intimacy stage in early adulthood.

2. How do close relationships and marriage change with time? What kinds of adjustments are made over the course of marriage?

3. What is the empty nest? Describe the upswing hypothesis.

4. Discuss the challenges associated with widowhood.

5. What are the reasons for choosing to marry or not to marry?

6. Discuss the impact of divorce on men and women.
7. How does adjustment differ when separation or divorce occurs in later life?
8. What are the important characteristics of the grandparenting role? Discuss the meaning of grandparenting to both grandparents and grandchildren from intact families as well as from divorced families.
9. Discuss the biological aspects of sexuality in adulthood. Describe menopause and the male climacteric.
10. Describe the behavioral and attitudinal dimensions of sexuality during the adult years.

FOR FURTHER READING

Coyle, Jean M. (Ed.). (1997). *Handbook on women and aging.* Westport, CT: Greenwood Press.

Johnson, C. L., & Barer, B. M. (1996). *Life beyond 85 years.* New York: Springer.

Jacobowitz, R. S. (1996). *150 most-asked questions about midlife sex, love, and intimacy: What women and their partners really want to know.* New York: Morrow.

Lopata, H. Z. (1995). *Current widowhood: Myths and realities.* Thousand Oaks, CA: Sage.

12

WORK, LEISURE, AND RETIREMENT

A perpetual holiday is a good working definition of hell.
—George Bernard Shaw

Your work is to discover your work, and with all your heart to give yourself to it.
—Buddha

INTRODUCTION

A major part of our waking life is spent working. In most societies, work provides the means for purchasing food, shelter, clothing, and for supporting a family. In addition, work can promote a sense of satisfaction and well-being as adults develop skills, show competence, apply knowledge, and build self-esteem. Sometimes work is interesting and challenging, provides the chance to learn or discover new ideas, meets a desire to be useful or to contribute, and provides opportunity to socialize and develop relationships with people. Adults spend about 40 hours each week doing work of some sort.

In this chapter, we first examine the social and historical contexts of work, then we outline the changes that take place in work across the adult years. Such changes include occupational choice, finding a place in the world of work, adjusting to work, attaining and maintaining occupational satisfaction, and working in late adulthood. We evaluate the varied meanings of work, looking in detail at the achievement motive, intrinsic motivation, the work ethic, and the impact of unemployment. Then we examine perhaps the greatest change in the labor force in the last 40 years: the increasing number of working women. We also pay special attention to the career development of men and women in early adulthood.

Often, to work effectively, one must balance work with leisure; it's been said, "One can work 12 months in 10 months, but one cannot work 12 months in 12 months." We discuss forms of leisure during adulthood and what it is like to leave one's work or to retire. We describe theories of retirement and factors predictive of successful adjustment to retirement.

THE HISTORICAL CONTEXT OF WORK

The society of the United States was preindustrial in the nineteenth century. The majority of families farmed land, worked together, and functioned as a unit. Townspeople also often worked as family units. A son would learn from his father to be a blacksmith or a carpenter, for example. By the end of the nineteenth century, the United States was becoming urbanized and industrialized. By 1910, only one-third of the men were farmers or farm laborers.

The year 1910 is often considered the beginning of the Industrial Revolution in the United States. Factories multiplied, and the labor force changed so dramatically that by 1950 half of all male workers were involved in some form of manufacturing or construction. In an industrial society, machines that operate with mechanical energy substantially increase productivity. Coal, petroleum, and natural gas allowed worker productivity to rise, along with the profits of industrial owners.

By 1990, approximately 65 to 70 percent of all workers were engaged in delivering services. It is estimated that by the year 2000, only 10 percent of the labor force will be involved in manufacturing and producing goods for the other 90 percent. The workplace now requires workers to be highly trained and to continually update their work skills.

The term *services* refers to many different activities. In earlier times, services included mainly domestic work, transportation, and the distribution of goods, whereas in modern society, service jobs are related to providing human services (such as education and health) and professional and technical services—data processing, computer applications, and communication, for example.

WORK OVER THE LIFE CYCLE

In this section, we examine career exploration, planning, and decision making. Then we discuss entry into an occupation as individuals attempt to find their places in the world of work. Subsequently, we evaluate the flexibility of careers in middle adulthood, occupational satisfaction, and work in late adulthood.

Occupational Choice

When you think about choosing a career, you usually think about a single choice and a commitment to a single career throughout your life. Research indicates, however, that more than half of today's workers will experience at least one major career change (Shirom & Mazeh, 1988). Some career changes will challenge and enhance our lives. Other career changes will be forced on us as corporations reduce the size of their workforce and "downsize." In one large-scale national survey, it was found that 42 percent of employees at small, medium, and large companies could identify downsizing and permanent workforce reductions since they had been hired (Galinsky, 1993). Still other career changes are self-imposed. Some occupations are best suited to a particular age, and as we change, a particular occupation may no longer be appropriate or possible. For example, in Research Focus 12.1 we discuss professional athletes who "retire" in their late twenties.

Individuals enter occupations, and begin new careers, at different ages. Although career choices are often accidental, unplanned, or uninformed, such choices are among the most significant decisions of our adult lives (Bolles, 1988). Work decisions have implications for many dimensions of our life. Specifically, your type of work, and how you do your work, is or becomes part of your identity. Your choice of work says something to others about your abilities, motivation, and personality (e.g., aggressive, achieving, independent). Further, your choice of work places you in your community and determines your friendships, lifestyle, and leisure opportunities.

It is wise to explore a variety of occupational alternatives before selecting or changing a career. Current theories of occupational choice also stress the importance of exploration and knowing oneself. We examine the theories of occupational choice proposed by Donald Super, Eli Ginzberg, and John Holland.

The Career of the Professional Athlete: Preparation for Retirement?

Few careers are as intense, emotionally involving, and physically demanding as that of the professional athlete. In the early years of childhood and adolescence, outstanding athletes are advantaged in terms of leadership, autonomy, sense of self, and self-esteem; they are admired, sought by peers, the object of media attention, and recruited by colleges and professional teams (Baillie & Danish, 1992). Yet those who are selected and who participate at the professional level often have a short-lived athletic career. In one study of football players in the National Football League (Pitts, Popovich, & Bober, 1986), the average length of a professional career was 3.2 years. The majority of players end their careers because of an injury, and many experience difficulties in adjusting to retirement and in identifying new career paths (Baillie & Danish, 1992; Shahnasarian, 1992). Many also experience financial, interpersonal, and substance abuse problems. The competitive demands and all-consuming nature of a professional sports career with its focus on each game during lengthy regular season and preseason and post-season games, the competition for a place on the team and a contract, as well as physical conditioning and training during the off-season, mean that there is little opportunity, encouragement, or time for players to devote to other dimensions of personal development and to planning for life after sports. Professional athletes enjoy huge salaries while playing but are often unprepared for the change in lifestyle and loss of earnings that occurs when the playing days are over (Shahnasarian, 1992). Only a handful of professionals in any sport ever realize personal and financial success and a continued career in the same field in upper management or as an announcer, a scout, or coach. In the case of professional football players, Shahnasarian noted that "young men—most retiring in their mid-20s—who have committed a lifetime to pursuing a passion and a dream too often one day find that they are ill-prepared to make the career transition from football" (1992, pp. 300–301).

Retirement from a career as a professional athlete in early adulthood is a difficult life transition leading to predictable stresses. Research studies suggest that a gradual transition for athletes is easier to manage than a precipitous transition to retirement (Baillie & Danish, 1992). There is then more time to prepare and develop career plans beyond the individual's limited but powerful identity as a professional athlete. Retirement is hard not only on the athlete but also on the athlete's family. When retirement is the result of a permanent injury, the stresses are further compounded and life satisfaction indicators are significantly diminished (Baillie & Danish, 1992; Shahnasarian, 1992). Some teams encourage players to participate in counseling programs designed to help individuals plan for retirement (financially, emotionally, and socially).

Super's Theory   Donald Super (1980) has consistently maintained that occupational choices are influenced mostly by self-concept. People select particular careers or vocations that best express their self-concepts. This theory suggests the presence of five stages in vocational development, with each stage reflecting predictable changes in self-concept as one's vocational choice is seen as more or less successful (Super, 1980). Super suggests that occupational choice is a continuous developmental process from adolescence to old age, with the person making modifications, reassessments, and redirection throughout the life span as self-concept becomes clearer and more distinct.

Super refers to the first stage of career development as *implementation*. At this stage, individuals, usually adolescents, simply try out a number of part- or full-time jobs to explore the world of work. Part of the exploration involves finding the boundaries of acceptable work-role behavior: dress, communication, punctuality, social networks, supervisor expectancies, reward structures, and so forth. In this stage, exploration is healthy and a reflection of adolescent self-concept. In one investigation, Super and his colleagues (Super, Kowalski, & Gotkin, 1967) studied young adults after they left high school. The investigators found that more than half of the position changes made between leaving school and the age of 25 involved floundering and unplanned changes. In other words, the young adults were neither systematic nor intentional in their exploration and decision making about careers.

The second stage, the *establishment* stage, involves the transition to a specific career choice. Again, this stage mirrors a young adult's self-concept. Super predicts considerable stability in vocational choice for those at this stage. There will be little movement away from the specific career selected, although some young adults will try to move up the career ladder by changing positions within a company or moving to a different company. If an adult considers a career change, it is usually in midlife that he or she becomes serious about a completely new vocation. Such changes occur after an individual takes stock of the opportunities for self-development within the initially chosen career.

For the majority of people who stay within the career they chose in young adulthood, the *maintenance* stage describes the period from roughly the midforties to the midfifties. This is a time when most people either achieve the levels of occupational success they hoped to attain or recognize that they will not reach these levels. Super describes this decade of vocational development as early preparation for the disengagement expected with retirement. Individuals remain occupationally involved, committed, and focused, but with reduced intensity on personal achievement and success.

About 10 to 15 years prior to actual retirement, Super believes the individual enters the *declaration* stage. This stage reflects an active readiness for retirement as individuals prepare themselves emotionally, financially, and socially. A distance from one's lifelong career begins to emerge. For workers who have made work a central focus in their lives, this stage represents a significant challenge.

The last stage in Super's model is *retirement.* The individual achieves a physical separation from work and begins to function in life without a career or vocation. Super's theory has been criticized for its narrow focus on self-concept as the prime factor responsible for occupational choice. Super largely ignores the role of factors such as social class, education, family, and chance. Moreover, his theory implies that most young adults are articulate, mature, and reflective individuals who are able to reason, evaluate, and rationally compare alternative career pathways. Such assumptions have not been fully tested empirically and rarely are characteristic of women's career development. In fact, one investigation suggests that Super's theory may be irrelevant in accounting for the career development of women (Ornstein & Isabella, 1990). Additionally, Super's approach implies that career choices are stable and predictive throughout adulthood; however, the stages leave no room for the possibility of career change (forced or voluntary), nor for the many entries and exits into the workforce characteristic of women's career pathways (Ornstein & Isabella, 1990).

Ginzberg's Theory Eli Ginzberg (1971, 1972) has also developed a stage theory of occupational choice. The essential principle underlying the *fantasy, tentative,* and *realistic* stages is the emergence of more and more realistic vocational decisions. The fantasy stage occurs as a child imagines and practices various occupations for a few hours, days, or weeks. The tentative stage begins as the early adolescent explores career involvement. Adolescents may closely monitor adults (models) in various careers; they also read about and discuss occupations with family members and friends. The realistic stage begins as the young adult (from high school graduation to the midtwenties) carefully and rationally analyzes career choices. This stage involves a realistic assessment of the necessary education, apprentice period, and personal qualities (values, attitudes, and aptitudes) required to pursue particular careers. The process of realistic assessment is initiated in young adulthood but continues through the life span. Ginzberg's theory has been criticized for being overly rational in its presentation of occupational choice, with too much emphasis placed on cognitive processes. Ginzberg makes no provision for career change in midlife as a part of this theory.

Holland's Theory   Holland's (1985) theory of career choice is quite different from the stage views of Super and Ginzberg. Holland suggests that career selection is based on the best fit between an individual's personality and the demands of the vocation. A good match between an individual's personality and a specific vocation will lead to job satisfaction and stability, whereas a bad match will lead to job dissatisfaction and the search for a different career. In Holland's view, adults look for careers that are most compatible with their personalities. In Holland's theory, psychological tests are used to assess and match personality to particular career categories. Holland has identified six basic personality types along with the kinds of careers that best match these personalities:

1. The *artistic* personality (creative, emotionally expressive, innovative, original, reflective): This personality might enjoy being an architect or a designer, or working in fashion-related industries.
2. The *conventional* personality (concern for conformity, efficiency, somewhat shy and inhibited): This person might become a bookkeeper, secretary, receptionist, or typist.

One change in employment patterns among older adults is the increase in part-time work and volunteering.

3. The *enterprising* personality (high energy and motivation, need to be in control, strong, outgoing, and socially gregarious): This personality thrives in business, management, private companies, and sales work.
4. The *investigative* personality (strong curiosity, intellectual, rational): People of this personality type make good researchers and scientists.
5. The *realistic* personality (concrete, materialistic, mechanical, practical, asocial): This person might be a computer programmer, an engineer, or a mechanic.
6. The *social* personality (cooperative, helpful, social orientation, understanding of human relations): People of this type enjoy being counselors, personnel managers, psychologists, teachers, and social workers.

Some critics of Holland's approach suggest that few adults have the capacity to see themselves, their personalities, and the demands of specific jobs as he suggests. Do adults insightfully, carefully, and deliberately compare potential careers to their own unique personal qualities? Moreover, few people are as accurate in their individual self-assessment as Holland suggests. Critics have also found Holland's theory limited in that it ignores the developmental changes in self-knowledge that occur throughout the life span. Changes in self-knowledge can lead to career changes (Vondareck, Lerner, & Schulenberg, 1986). Yet, for the initial choice of a career, counselors frequently use Holland's approach as a starting point for exploring occupational choices. Many computer-assisted guidance programs employ a Holland-type system (Sampson, Reardon, & Lenz, 1991).

Career Exploration, Planning, and Decision Making

Some individuals prefer to do their own exploration of career options (e.g., by searching the Internet), whereas others seek or receive assistance. Because it is difficult to know what particular careers are really like, often it is useful to have expert guidance and accurate information about career options. College placement centers usually provide assistance with practical matters such as preparing attractive résumés and developing appropriate interview skills.

Career planning is not restricted to any one portion of the adult life span. Discovering and doing one's work is a lifelong developmental process. For some careers, the path or track can be described in four stages: *selection and entry, adjustment, maintenance,* and *retirement* (see figure 12.1). These stages apply to careers that move in an orderly progression. For other careers, the person may be continuously selecting and adjusting, and entering and exiting, different work roles.

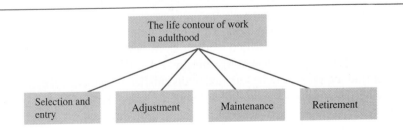

Figure 12.1 The life contour of work in adulthood.

The life contour of work in adulthood

Selection and entry   Adjustment   Maintenance   Retirement

Entering an Occupation

At some point during early adulthood, one usually *enters an occupation.* For the first several years, an occupation may take an inordinate amount of a person's time, so that other aspects of life, such as marriage or starting a family, are put on hold. Of course the demands of getting started in an occupation are different for different career tracks. Valliant and Valliant (1981) interviewed a group of 465 lower-social-class men about their work over a 35-year period. The most industrious participants in childhood remained so in adulthood. Those who were most industrious also reported the greatest enjoyment and success from their work, had the warmest social relationships, and the best overall adjustment to life. Sometimes the workplace provides an escape from some of the inequities of the larger society, and from the demands of children and housework.

Adjustment to the Occupational World

Adjustment is the main concern during the second stage of the occupational cycle (figure 12.1). This is the period that Daniel Levinson (1996) calls the *age-30 transition* in men and women. According to Levinson, once a person has entered an occupation, he or she must develop a distinct occupational identity in the occupational world. Along the way, he or she may fail, drop out, or begin a new career path. The person may stay on a single track or try several directions before settling firmly on one. This adjustment phase lasts several years. Some professional tracks, such as medicine or law, require many years in preparation and apprenticeship, whereas other professional tracks, such as in the business world, require climbing a ladder consisting of a series of lower- or middle-management jobs.

Levinson (1996) reported that women pursuing careers are faced with the same challenges in embarking on a career as men, yet they also give more attention than men do to balancing the competing demands of work and family. Figure 12.2 shows five professions in which women have made sizable gains in employment over a seven-year period (1979–1986). Although women and men are doing the same work, and although there are laws prohibiting sex discrimination in hiring, salary, and promotion, inequities in both opportunity and pay remain (Noble, 1993).

Occupational Satisfaction and Midlife Career Change

In middle adulthood, most men reach their highest status and income levels in their careers; women, if they have been employed without interruption for family responsibilities most of their adult lives, do likewise. Those who remain in their careers from early adulthood to retirement generally become increasingly satisfied with their work through their midsixties (Rhodes, 1983). Satisfied employees are usually somewhat more productive, whereas dissatisfied workers show both decreased productivity and increased absenteeism (Iaffaldano & Muchinsky, 1985; Rhodes, 1983).

What leads employees to be satisfied or dissatisfied with their work? The factors that lead to occupational satisfaction are different for younger and older workers (Warr, 1992). Younger workers seem concerned with salary, job security, opportunity for

Source: New York Times, April 20, 1997.

advancement, and relationships with both supervisors and coworkers (Nord, 1977). By midlife, established workers focus on different factors: autonomy on the job, the opportunity for individual challenge and mastery, personal achievement, freedom to be creative, and the need to see one's work as contributing to a larger whole (Clausen, 1981). These factors emerged in one recent national study of 3,400 workers, when workers

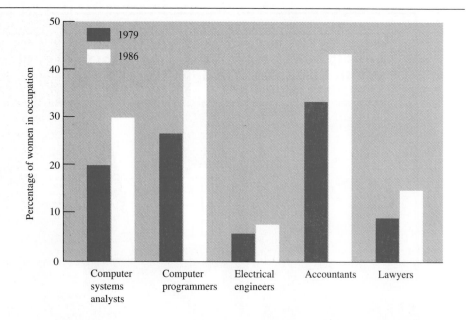

Figure 12.2 Five professions in which women have been historically underrepresented: 1979–1986.
Source: Data from the U.S. Bureau of the Census.

were asked to identify the *most* important reasons in their having selected their current job. Across small, large, and medium-sized companies there was consistency in workers' rankings of those factors that led them to take their current position (Galinsky, 1993). These ratings of importance are summarized in figure 12.3 and show that factors such as salary and fringe benefits are not nearly as important as characteristics of the job that will enable workers to create a balance in their lives at home and in pursuits outside of work. Most workers spend considerable effort to derive a balance between work responsibilities and family responsibilities. We know very little, however, about how this balance is achieved for younger, middle-aged, and older workers (Human Capital Initiative, 1993). Clearly, it is an important concern among workers and apparently important to achieve. Thus, employees were most concerned about flexibility, personal autonomy, and social interaction on the job. It is the quality of the work environment that appears to be of greatest concern to today's workers.

Middle-aged workers find job security and rising to positions of influence—external signs that validate their success—very satisfying. Most older workers are satisfied with their work, have derived recognition for their abilities (enhanced self-esteem), and will not change companies even if offered higher salaries (Havighurst, 1982; Nord, 1977; Tamir, 1989). Middle-aged and older adults are quite reflective and accurate in their assessment of their contributions and the skills necessary for continued occupational success (Fletcher, Hansson, & Bailey, 1992). Middle-aged as well as older employees seem to be able to gauge their own work performance accurately, assess their ability to learn new skills for continued occupational success, and apply their knowledge of the organization to serve their needs far better than younger workers. Thus, middle age becomes a kind of "plateau" for many employees, according to Bardwick (1990).

Figure 12.3 What workers want. Reasons considered to have been "very important" in deciding to take a job with a current employer, from *The National Study of the Changing Workforce.*   *Source: Data from Families and Work Institute.*

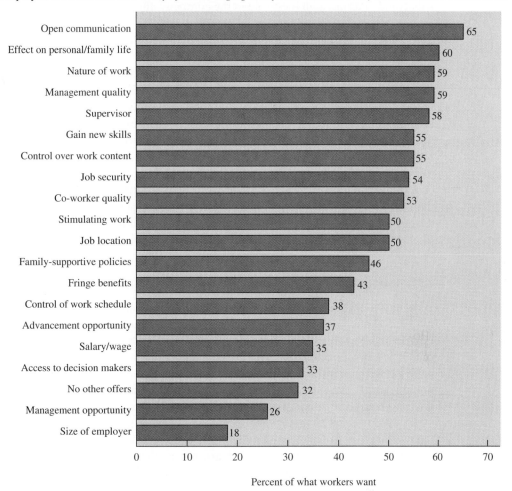

Percent of what workers want

Warr (1992) studied this plateau by examining occupational well-being in relation to age. *Occupational well-being* was operationally defined along two broad parameters: (1) job anxiety versus contentment, and (2) job enthusiasm versus depression. Across a wide variety of different kinds of occupations, those who experienced the highest degree of well-being in their jobs were both young workers and older workers. Middle-aged workers showed the lowest level of occupational well-being; the data reflected a clear U-shaped curve across the 1,686 people studied. In Warr's sample, new workers found occupations both novel and interesting and experienced a sense of belonging with their coworkers. Investigators have speculated that by middle age, people often experience boredom in occupations and recognize some of the limitations of their careers as well as the diminished likelihood of advancement, which together promote diminished job satisfaction (Warr, 1992). By later life, among those workers who remain in their occupations, job satisfaction increases as individuals come to terms with their role in the company, their contributions, and the opportunities afforded to them through work (Warr, 1992).

There are, of course, interesting exceptions to these trends; for instance, some people in middle adulthood start over and select a new career. Many men and women who have had relatively routine jobs deliberately seek change to find work that is more interesting and rewarding. For some, a change is brought about by disappointment in a "dead-end" career; for others, changing jobs represents the need for new challenges, and for still others it is a response to increased job stress. Perhaps this helps describe the shift made by traditional women from housework to careers. At present, just over 50 percent of women aged 40 to 59 are in the workforce, many of them having obtained jobs as they were raising or immediately after raising a family. Approximately 10 percent of men change the nature of their work between the ages of 40 and 60, either for their own reasons or because they lose their jobs (Havighurst, 1982). And some people change jobs because they feel they are not physically fit for the work required of them (e.g., police officers, professional athletes, and armed forces personnel).

Psychological Factors in Midlife Career Change

What are some of the factors that motivate individuals to change their careers at midlife? Daniel Levinson (1978, 1996) suggested that one important challenge in midlife involves adjusting idealistic hopes to realistic possibilities in light of how much time is left in an occupation. Middle-aged adults often focus on how much time they have left before retirement and the speed with which they are reaching their occupational goals. If individuals believe they are behind schedule, or if they now view their goals as unrealistic, then some reassessment and readjustment is necessary. (Levinson, 1978, 1996) observed that people in middle age want to be affirmed in the roles that they value most. At about age 40, Levinson's subjects fixed on some key event in their careers (e.g., a promotion or an award) as carrying the ultimate message of affirmation or devaluation by society.

It is important to consider the deeper meanings of career change during the middle years. Midlife career changes are often linked to changes in attitudes, goals, and values. Though some people hang onto their jobs despite intense dislike for their work, others change careers even when their jobs are still satisfactory. The decision to remain with a career is in itself no guarantee that an individual has not revised personal attitudes, goals, and values. Even if nothing in the individual's external life changes, the individual may change. Middle-aged people begin to see themselves, their life situations, and their careers more introspectively, reflectively, and sensitively. Levinson (1996) and Sheehy (1995, 1998) have noted the importance of these internal psychological changes that give different meanings to life, work, and self.

One additional stress on careers in midlife is the existence of fiscal events that influence career decisions. For example, in some families, midlife is a time of financial strain as children enter college. In other families, a reorientation toward the retirement years causes concerns about financial resources. And, with the advent of the

The Relationship Between Personality Attributes and Upward Occupational Mobility

The California Longitudinal Study compared data collected on the personality attributes of individuals when they were in junior high school with the degree to which the individuals showed upward occupational mobility by the time they reached midlife. Some of the individuals who came from working-class backgrounds ended up with middle-class occupations at midlife. Were there any clues from the personality characteristics of these individuals that were predictive of upward occupational mobility?

John Clausen (1981) found that men who moved from working-class backgrounds into middle-class occupations exceeded their nonmobile peers from comparable backgrounds in dependability, productivity, personal effectiveness, aspiration levels, and intellectual capacities and interests in the junior high school years. The picture that emerged for the working-class mobiles was that of pleasant, dependable, conventional working-class boys who worked productively to get ahead. This contrasted with the more rebellious, self-defensive, less conventional middle-class boys who seemed less pleasant and less dependable. The upwardly mobile working-class boys were also more nurturant and secured more education than their peers who remained in the working class. Further, the upwardly mobile boys continued to increase their intellectual skills and interests as they moved up the occupational ladder. In general, at midlife they more closely resembled men who came from middle-class families than they did their former working-class peers who were employed in blue-collar jobs. Thus, a combination of personality characteristics, the socializing influence of higher education, and the requirements of white-collar jobs differentiated these boys from their peers. Furthermore, it was these upwardly mobile men who were the most satisfied with their occupational success.

---

empty nest, women often embark on new occupations, complete or extend their education, or resume with greater intensity interrupted careers or those in which they were marginally involved through part-time employment (Levinson, 1996).

Of particular interest are the factors related to occupational mobility in adulthood. What factors contribute to the likelihood that an individual from a working-class background will take on a middle-class occupation in adulthood? Data from the California Longitudinal Study (Clausen, 1981) allow us to address this question. See Research Focus 12.2 for information about the relationship between personality attributes in adolescence and middle adulthood and occupational status at midlife.

Work in Late Adulthood

Productivity in old age seems to be the rule rather than the exception. People who have worked hard throughout their lives often continue to do so in old age. Given the changing demographics of the population of the United States, there is and will continue to be a need to invigorate the workforce with older, productive workers (Human Capital Initiative, 1993). With lower birth rates and fewer young workers to support retirees, there will be a need to employ older workers to maintain national productivity. Furthermore, it would be wasteful to have nearly one-third of the adult population out of the workforce (Human Capital Initiative, 1993).

Some older workers keep schedules that would exhaust younger workers, and many continue to be productive and creative, sometimes outperforming their young and middle-aged adult coworkers. Older workers, despite identifiable declines in cognitive functions outside of their work, seem to develop special strategies to maintain or enhance their performance on the job. In some cases, they compensate for declines in motor performance or speed of processing by applying their expertise and acumen developed over many years (Human Capital Initiative, 1993). Corporations have yet to identify the special talents of the older worker and the possibility that such workers could function in new roles to improve overall quality and productivity. Moreover, older workers are less likely to be chosen for training programs since, in the minds of employers, there is minimal "return" on such an investment (Human Capital Initiative, 1993).

In general, there is a modest but positive relationship between age and productivity that favors the older worker. Younger workers have less commitment to their employers than older workers who have invested a lifetime with a company. Older workers have 20 percent less absenteeism than younger workers. Many older workers are more reliable and derive greater satisfaction from their jobs than do younger workers (Human Capital Initiative, 1993). Older workers also have fewer disabling injuries as well as a lower rate of accidents than young adult workers (Sterns, Barrett, & Alexander, 1985). However, fatal injuries or permanently disabling injuries show a U-shaped function across age (Sterns et al., 1985). In addition, older workers are at increased risk for certain safety problems and injuries. When comparable accidents occur on the job, younger workers have a greater possibility of recovery and a smaller likelihood of permanent disability. The older worker experiencing severe injury may become disabled, preventing further employment, or may suffer disability, dysfunction, or even death. Thus, the consequences of accidents and on-the-job injury are far more serious for older than younger workers (Sterns et al., 1985).

Older workers also experience differential levels of stress when compared with younger workers in certain settings. For example, in one investigation, three age groups of workers (19–28, 30–44, and 53–59 years old) were compared on their adjustment to working a night shift (Harma, Hakola, & Laitinen, 1992). The oldest workers in this sample clearly had the most difficulty in adjusting to night shift work (particularly when consecutive night shifts were required), which led to their early retirement (Harma et al., 1992). For those older workers fortunate enough to have sufficient financial resources, early retirement is a predictable outcome (Human Capital Initiative, 1993).

Work Performance and Aging

When does age become a factor in work performance? In a variety of work situations, older individuals frequently hold highly responsible positions. For many kinds of real-world job skills, ranging from routine clerical tasks to artistic and scholarly creativity to executive or professional decision making, management, and leadership, performance is largely unaffected by aging throughout the working years (e.g., Salthouse & Maurer, 1996; Waldman & Avolio, 1986).

Findings from meta-analyses (e.g., McEvoy, & Cascio, 1989; Waldman & Avolio, 1986) show that there is no relationship between age and the quality or effectiveness of work performance. This finding is accurate in general, averaging across many individuals and different kinds of jobs. For specific kinds of work, a more-detailed pattern emerges. That is, with age there are improvements in the skills required for some kinds of work and age-related declines for other kinds of work behavior. Some aspects of work performance, especially speeded performance, show substantial age-related declines for individuals (Salthouse, 1996). Compared with young adults, older adults may experience more difficulty in learning new work tasks such as using new computer systems, and in benefiting from various kinds of job training programs (e.g., Schooler, Caplan, & Oates, 1997; Czaja & Sharit, 1993). Age-related declines are also apparent in physically stressful kinds of work, such as building construction, farming or mining, or professional sports.

Other aspects of work performance, especially the performance of familiar non-speeded tasks, appear to be well maintained for individuals across the adult years. Indeed, observations of age-related impairments in work performance are the exception rather than the rule. When the performance of an older worker is impaired, it is probably due to a change in health and not to normal aging.

The apparent lack of age-associated impairments in work performance is striking, and contrasts with the findings discussed in chapter 7 indicating that there are age-related declines in basic cognitive and perceptual abilities (see e.g., Schaie, 1996). How do older adults maintain effective functioning in their work, despite laboratory research evidence indicative of age-related declines in the basic processes that appear to be requisites?

One explanation has to do with the benefits of experience on how work is performed. Although there are age-related differences in learning new tasks, and in using new technologies (e.g., see Hoyer, 1998, the execution of well-practiced skills is generally unaffected by aging (e.g., Charness & Campbell, 1988; Lincourt et al., 1997; Salthouse & Maurer, 1996). For very demanding kinds of work, effective functioning depends on accumulated knowledge and learned skills. However, work behavior is also affected by age-related declines in the speed and efficiency of information processing. Research concerning job performance and aging is difficult to understand without examining the methods used in research studies. Overall it appears that older workers, despite declining cognitive and sensory processes, are able to maintain high-quality levels of productivity similar to younger workers (Human Capital Initiative, 1993). Many studies suggest that older people perform as well as or even better than younger workers (Salthouse & Maurer, 1996; Waldman & Avolio, 1986).

Decisions About Work

Situational and personal factors influence the amount of energy and effort that individuals give to their work. Job performance and motivation are in part affected by (1) physiological and cognitive aging, (2) personal and work history factors, and (3) prevailing conditions in the workplace and society. These factors then affect the choices individuals make about work and jobs.

Job withdrawal refers to resigning, volunteering to be laid off, and retiring. *Work withdrawal* refers to changes in work behaviors, such as tardiness, absenteeism, leaving work early, and reduced commitment.

Personal decisions about work are usually made thoughtfully, but it is important to recognize that such decisions are influenced by both objective and subjective factors. Individuals carefully evaluate whether they can afford to retire by determining their retirement income and benefits relative to their anticipated expenses. Family caregiving responsibilities and health factors (e.g., increased difficulty in continuing to work or commute) are also considered. However, subjective factors also affect decisions about work. For example, a feeling of being fed up with the annoyances of work could influence the retirement decision.

In a recent study of the factors that lead individuals to make a decision to leave work, Ekerdt, DeViney, and Kosloski (1996) found that individuals frequently attribute their decisions to objective factors. For example, a response to the question "Why did you retire?" might be, "I felt it was time" or "They made me an offer that was too good to refuse." However, further interviewing frequently reveals that the decision to retire was influenced by many events in the everyday work environment. For example, conversations with coworkers at lunch about the demanding new boss, about unfair treatment of a coworker, or about increased job requirements might trigger thoughts that it is time to leave the job. An accumulation of minor unpleasant events, such as having to sit through nonproductive meetings, having to complete more new forms of paperwork, or hearing age-biased derogatory comments from a coworker could be enough of a cause for an individual to reevaluate his or her investment in work. So, like many or all human decisions, decisions about work and retirement are influenced by "comfort level" as well as objective factors.

Capable and energetic older workers often meet with subtle suggestions that it is time to consider retiring. Blatant forms of age discrimination are also prevalent in some work environments. Older workers may find it tiresome to adapt to new methods and technologies. Some older workers may find it difficult to continue facing the pressures and rapid pace of work.

Frequently, older workers are encouraged to quit or retire by employers, even though the worker is performing well. Further, little effort is made to adjust the work situation to make it optimal for older workers. For example, an older worker may want to transfer to a different position within the company, the position may be available, and the person may be perfectly suited to the position, but the company hires someone else. Older workers frequently find it hard to change jobs. In the United States in the 1990s, even highly skilled and highly motivated individuals in their forties and fifties find it difficult to make any sort of job change or to become re-employed in a new job if out of work. Such factors contribute to older workers' feelings of being unwelcome and undervalued.

Antecedents that lead to job withdrawal and work withdrawal include pay inequity, health factors, work dissatisfaction, supervisor dissatisfaction, coworker dissatisfaction, and work stress. Factors such as work history, personal values, family situations, coworker pressures, and personal finances also influence work and job withdrawal.

The effects of such factors on work behavior and attitudes are best understood by observing individual differences (Hanisch, 1995). For example, three individuals, Pat, Kim, and Chris might be equally dissatisfied with their jobs, but each can react by engaging in different behaviors. Pat is unable or unwilling to resign or retire but is frequently absent and arrives late and leaves early as much as possible. Kim actively pursues plans for an early retirement. Chris chooses to work harder within the corporate context to change the sources of her dissatisfaction. Researchers need to consider individual differences in reactions to changes in the workplace. As suggested in the research by Ekerdt, DeViney, and Kosloski (1996), and Maurer and Tarulli (1994), self-appraisals of work behavior may take on new significance for older individuals, and older workers might be particularly sensitive to criticism and negative remarks about aging.

A majority of individuals report that they would continue to work even if they had enough money to live without working (Morse & Weiss, 1968). Sometimes one's work is who one is. For example, at social occasions, people talk about what they do—their work. Thus, work often defines the person's intelligence, personality, motivation, and so on. Work carries a measure of prestige or status, and work brings people into social contact. Work may even determine our friends and leisure choices, to some extent. Table 12.1 presents a list of some of the meanings individuals assign to their jobs and links these meanings with more universal functions of work.

In table 12.2, the data from two studies conducted by Robert Havighurst (Friedmann & Havighurst, 1954; Havighurst, McDonald, Perun, & Snow, 1976) reveal that skilled craftpersons and white-collar groups stress the nonfinancial meanings of work to a much greater degree than workers in heavy industry. The meanings of work vary depending on the type of occupation.

Some individuals love their work and refuse to retire for that reason. The decision to continue to work is certainly also related to health, finances, and job satisfaction. What is emerging, however, are other models of work among older adults. There has been significant growth in part-time employment among older adults. And many productive older workers trade one job for another, as shown in figure 12.4.

TABLE 12.1	
The Relationship Between the Functions and Meanings of Work	
Work Function	**Work Meanings**
Income	Maintaining a minimum sustenance level
	Achieving some higher level or group standard
Expenditure of time and energy	Something to do
	A way of filling the day or passing time
Identification and status	Source of self-respect
	Way of achieving recognition or respect from others
	Definition of role
Association	Friendship relations
	Peer-group relations
	Subordinate-superordinate relations
Source of meaningful life experience	Gives purpose to life
	Creativity, self-expression
	New experience
	Service to others

From E. Friedmann and R. J. Havighurst, The Meaning of Work and Retirement. Copyright © 1954 The University of Chicago Press, Chicago, IL. Reprinted by permission.

TABLE 12.2

Meanings of Work[a]

Meanings	Category of Worker (Percent Choosing)						Social Scientists	
	Steelworkers	Miners	Photoengravers over 65	Salespersons	Senior Physicians	College Administrators	Male	Female
1. Income for my needs	28	18	11	0	0	4	6	5
2. Routine: Makes time pass	28	19	15	21	15	1	1	1
3a. Self-respect				12	7	14	12	8
3b. Prestige 3a + 3b	16	18	24	11	13	11	14	5
4. Association with peers	15	19	20	20	19	11	10	17
5. Self-expression; new experience; creativity	13	11	30	26	15	27	39	41
6. Service to others; useful	N.D.[b]	16	N.D.	10	32	31	17	22

[a]The interview or questionnaire format varied from one group to another, making strict comparisons questionable. The data are reported in percentages within groups, assuming each respondent to have given his/her favored response.
[b]N.D. = No data

Source: Friedmann and Havighurst, 1954 (table 26); Havighurst, McDonald, Perun, and Snow, 1976 (table 7.2); and Havighurst, 1982, p. 782.

Figure 12.4
Reasons for working following retirement. Many people re-enter the workforce after retiring for financial reasons.
Source: Cornell Retirement and Well-Being Study, Phase 1, 1995.

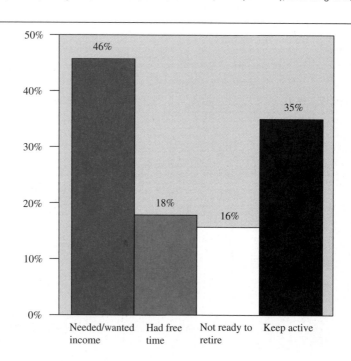

THE CULTURE OF THE WORK ENVIRONMENT

The meaning of work, and the workplace itself, is undergoing rapid change. Likewise, what we do at work is constantly changing. Therefore, quickly adjusting to change, being able to make smooth transitions from one job to another within and across organizations, and having a commitment to continued upgrading of skills and learning are essential requirements for today's workers. Corporations may also value workers' ability to function as a team player in an increasingly diverse workforce (ethnic, racial, gender, and age).

Many of the changes in corporate attitudes and corporate culture serve to ensure strong motivation, organizational commitment, worker satisfaction, and ultimately quality and productivity. There has been considerable emphasis on management innovations such as team building, quality circles, and Total Quality Management (TQM) approaches.

As the nature of work and the work environment change, the meaning and significance of work to employees continues to change. Young workers in organizations tend to be concerned with extrinsic factors such as salary, job security, and continuity in their careers, whereas workers with more seniority focus on intrinsic rewards such as independence, quality and meaning of work, and the authority to set goals and achieve them in line with corporate priorities (Galinsky, 1993; Hall & Rabinowitz, 1988). Those workers who welcome change, those who can manage change, and those who initiate and sustain change derive the highest degree of personal success and pleasure from their careers (Belasco, 1991). Evidence is mounting that today's workers are questioning the value of company loyalty and increasingly placing greater value on personal needs and family concerns (Noble, 1993). Figure 12.3 identifies the major concerns of employees (Galinsky, 1993). The workplace must take into account that nearly 90 percent of all employees live with and care for other family members, and that 50 percent care for dependents including children, elderly parents, or spouses with health problems (Galinsky, 1993).

WORK AND SUCCESSFUL AGING

Models of successful aging describe the positive dimensions of aging, and how these dimensions contribute to carrying out unique work roles. You probably know older individuals who continue to keep up with workplace innovations, or even set the pace, in the workplace. From a successful aging perspective, there is often an optimal match between the changing demands of the work context and the particular abilities, skills, and personal characteristics of individuals at different ages. Workers of all ages can have the potential to make unique and valuable contributions within specific workplace contexts.

Measurement issues must be considered in understanding the apparent discrepancy between real-world job performance and measured age-related declines in basic cognitive abilities. Only about 4 to 25 percent of the variance in job performance can be accounted for by standardized tests of ability. It is better to use assessments consisting of materials and problems typical of actual performance on the job for predicting and evaluating job performance.

The benefits of introducing new technology in the workplace are in terms of helping workers to be more productive or to assist the enhancement of the quality of work in ways that complement the various skills of workers (Hunt, 1993). New technologies can be used to minimize the tedium of repetitive work for the purpose of improving the work context. Unfortunately, more often than not, the introduction of new technology becomes a way of displacing older workers rather than as a means of helping workers to continue on the job.

UNEMPLOYMENT

Unemployment produces stress regardless of whether the job loss is temporary, cyclical, or permanent. The psychological meaning of job loss depends on a number of factors, including the individual's personality, social status, and resources. For example, a 50-year-old married worker with two adolescent children, a high school education, no transferable job skills, and no pension would not react the same way to the shutdown of an automobile assembly plant as a 21-year-old unmarried man.

Being middle-aged and unemployed in the late 1990s may be as bad, or in some cases even worse, than was true in the Great Depression of the 1930s. The unemployed in the 1930s had a strong feeling that their jobs would reopen. Because many of today's workers have been replaced by technology and corporate downsizing, expectations that their jobs will reappear are not very realistic. This suggests that many individuals will experience a number of different jobs during their adult years—not a single occupation, as in the past. The tendency for workers to enter and exit several occupations throughout adulthood means that, in the future, more workers will experience job loss and will need to anticipate the event and its economic, emotional, and social consequences not only for themselves personally but also for their families (McLoyd, 1989).

As noted earlier, to be successful, workers need to view education as a lifelong process, not something completed during two to four years in young adulthood and marked by the receipt of an associate or baccalaureate degree or terminating at the end of a lengthy apprenticeship in the trades. The older, less-educated workers, particularly those with lowest self-esteem, have been reported to have the most difficulty coping with job loss and unemployment (Kinicki, 1989). There are job counseling programs and "executives-out-of-work" self-help groups that meet to assist those for whom the loss of a job is most debilitating. Such interventions take a commonsense approach by offering practical help with writing résumés and interviewing skills; understanding the resources available to assist in job searching, such as networking; identifying the generic skills that workers have acquired and can apply to any work setting; and giving emotional support to help individuals begin to reorganize their personal lives. Successful coping with job loss involves being able to distance oneself from the loss, effectively seek or prepare to seek new employment or activities, and put work in balance with other activities in life.

GENDER AND WORK

The most significant change in labor force participation in the past few decades is in terms of racial, ethnic, and gender diversity. Nearly 70 percent of women with children under the age of 18 currently are employed while more than 50 percent of women with children under the age of 6 are working (Coleman, 1988).

Some of the factors that have increased job opportunities for women are the following:

- Growth of new occupations requiring special technical skills (e.g., in the computer field)
- Penalties for companies that fail to comply with affirmative action policy and negative publicity for companies that fail to make progress toward achieving gender and racial equity
- The increasing availability of technology that reduces the physical strength requirements of jobs
- Greater equality in training and educational opportunities for women and men

Despite new job opportunities, women face a variety of problems in the world of work. For example, women who enter careers in middle age frequently do not have mentors. **Mentors** are experienced, successful workers who help individuals get started in careers. Mentors impart advice, guidance, friendship, and perspective through example.

Tracks for Women and Men

Many young adults today expect to begin work in early adulthood and work more or less continuously until they no longer want to work. Although the majority of college women and men anticipate having both a career and a marriage, it is difficult to do so. The difficulties in combining a family and career seem to result more from role overload than role conflict. Women who cope with time pressures and conflicts by redefining their own and their families' responsibilities are more satisfied than those who attempt to meet all of these demands alone (Osipow, 1983). Galinsky (1993) observed that there is "inequity" among women and men in dual-career families. Figure 12.5 shows that there were four areas in the household in which women assumed a disproportionate share of the work: cooking, cleaning, shopping, and paying the bills. Men only took greater responsibility for household repairs.

Women who return to higher education or careers after marrying and having children show high levels of commitment. Women who are employed have higher levels of life satisfaction and feelings of adequacy and self-esteem than full-time homemakers (Coleman & Antonucci, 1983). However, the psychological benefits of employment are greater for educated middle-class women and the liabilities greater for less well-educated lower-class women.

The most common path for both working-class and middle-class women is to work after finishing high school or college; to marry and cease working when having children; then, when children are a little older, to return to part-time work to supplement

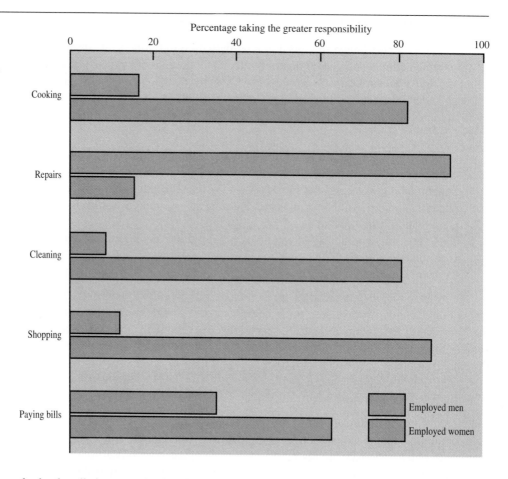

Figure 12.5 A woman's work. Comparison of women and men in dual-earner families with respect to who takes the greater responsibility for household work. *Source: Data from Families and Work Institute.*

Percentage taking the greater responsibility

Cooking
Repairs
Cleaning
Shopping
Paying bills

Employed men
Employed women

the husband's income. As the children begin to leave home, women return to school to update earlier skills or to retrain to better compete for a full-time job. Women in their forties and fifties are relatively free of home and family responsibilities and better able to assume full-time employment.

The picture is different for women who have committed themselves to maintaining professional skills. Researchers have identified four career patterns among professional women (Golan, 1986; Paloma, Pendelton, & Garland, 1982). These patterns include: (1) the *regular career pattern*—the woman who pursued her professional training immediately after graduation and who continued to work with no or minimal interruption throughout the years; (2) the *interrupted career pattern*—the woman who began work in the regular pattern but interrupted her career for several years, usually for childrearing, and then went back to work full-time; (3) the *second career pattern*—the woman who started her professional training near or after the time the children left home or after a divorce; and (4) the *modified second career pattern*—the woman who started her professional training while the children were at home but old enough not to need full-time mothering, then started to work, possibly part-time, until the last child left home, at which time the woman shifted to a full-time career.

It should also be mentioned that there are times when individuals might prefer being at work to being at home (see p. 461). Sometimes the demands of family or home are actually more stressful and chaotic than those of the workplace.

Thus far, we have discussed a number of aspects of work. Individuals must also relax. Let's now look at the nature of leisure in adulthood.

LEISURE

The end of labor is to gain leisure.
—Aristotle

Aristotle recognized the importance of leisure, stressing that we should not only work well but use leisure well. In our society, the idea that leisure is the opposite of work is common. Some see leisure as wasted time and thus antithetical to the basic values of our society: work, motivation, and achievement. John Neulinger (1981), a leading investigator of leisure in the United States, poses this dilemma: Is humanity's ultimate goal a life of leisure? Clearly, most of us would disagree that leisure is what motivates us or is the measure of our life's success. Yet the puzzle remains: What is leisure? How important is it in our lives?

The word **leisure** has usually been used in four different contexts. Burrus-Bammel and Bammel (1985) recognize the *classical* view that leisure is a state of mind. Free time alone is neither a necessary nor sufficient condition for leisure; rather, it is how one chooses to define tasks and situations that is the critical variable (Neulinger, 1981). Thus, some persons define their work as leisure, while others define leisure as activities other than one's work. Generally, the higher one's occupational status and income, the greater the identification with work rather than leisure (Burrus-Bammel & Bammel, 1985; Neulinger, 1981). Viewing work as leisure may also be influenced by the nature of the rewards derived—intrinsic or extrinsic. Intrinsic rewards characterize leisure in that the activity itself is rewarding. Leisure may also depend on *social class*. Historically, only the elite were free to choose and pursue self-selected activities, while those from lower social classes were destined to a life of constant work. Leisure may also lead to particular kinds of *activity* apart from work roles, such as recreation, entertainment, education, or relaxation. Finally, leisure may refer to the availability of *free time* (Burrus-Bammel & Bammel, 1985; Kraus, 1978). For example, our industrial society provides leisure time to retired workers or to employees who choose activities during nonwork hours.

Attitudes toward leisure are becoming more positive in our society (Clebone & Taylor, 1992). For example, among four generations of women within the same family, attitudes were sampled to investigate patterns and transmission of beliefs in a number of areas including leisure. Overall, the results indicated that at each succeeding generation, women displayed increasingly more positive attitudes to a variety of areas and toward leisure specifically.

The Experience of Enjoyment or Flow in Work

In *Finding Flow: The Psychology of Engagement with Everyday Life,* Mihaly Csikszentmihalyi (pronounced "CHICK-sent-me-hi-ee") tells about a letter he received from an 83-year-old man. This man enjoyed the challenges of his young adult years but reported that the next 60 years of his life were uneventful and routine. However, in his eighties, he rediscovered how to experience exhilaration in life. He began to do things that he had always wanted to do but never tried. He took up gardening, actively listening to music, and other activities that revived his enjoyment of life. According to Csikszentmihalyi, individuals are in a state of **flow** when they are doing something that they really enjoy. Flow can be described as having what we want, how we feel, and what we do all on the same page. Any kind of work or leisure activity, no matter how trivial on the one hand or creative and esteemed on the other hand, can produce the experience of flow. Work is onerous and resented only when it is perceived as *pointless.* Individuals work tirelessly when they really enjoy the experience of what they are doing. Working purely for external compensation becomes pointless, unsatisfactory, and eventually impossible to do.

In part, the psychology of flow is about taking steps to enhance the experience of working and leisure by reclaiming ownership of our lives. Absorption and active engagement in what we do are the keys. Csikszentmihalyi's view is based on a substantial amount of research using the Experience Sampling Method (ESM), a behavior sampling tool that individuals use to indicate where they are, what they are doing, what they are thinking, and who they are with immediately when a signal goes off at random times within two-hour segments during the day. Individuals also indicate how happy they are, how much they are concentrating, how strongly they are motivated, and their self-esteem at the time of the signal.

Research using the ESM has revealed that people are happy when they are fully engaged in what they are doing. Athletes and musicians might describe the experience of full engagement or flow as "being in the zone." Flow is reported when the person is doing his or her favorite activity—bowling, gardening, being creative at work, painting, cooking, driving an automobile, rock climbing, sailing, being with one's partner or friend. Flow is rarely reported in passive leisure activities such as watching television or wasting time. For further information, see the web page, http://www.flownetwork.com

The Nature of Leisure Activities

Ninety years ago the average work week was 71 hours. Only in the last several decades has the work week averaged 35 to 40 hours. We have even created flextime so that workers can complete their week's work without being on the job from 9:00 A.M. to 5:00 P.M. For example, some industries give employees the option of working 12-hour shifts for three consecutive days with the next four days off. Other employers allow employees to set the length of their work days as long as they work a specific minimum number of hours each week. Some companies allow employees to take leaves without pay or to choose part-time employment for significant parts of the year. Workers who are given such choices have more free time as well as autonomy than the workers of previous generations. Now the more important question is whether we are enjoying our leisure and work (see Research Focus 12.3).

Watching Television

In American society, watching television and videos is a frequent form of leisure for individuals of all ages. Table 12.3 gives a list of the rankings of preferred leisure-time activities for a representative group of community-dwelling elderly adults (McAvoy, 1979).

Note that a list of preferred leisure activities may not reflect how older adults actually spend their leisure time. Older adults indicate that they actually prefer other activities, including volunteering in meaningful ways, travel, hobbies, gardening, and

TABLE 12.3

Leisure Time Activities of Elderly Community-Residing Adults

Category	Rank
Visiting friends	1
Watching television	2
Reading	3
Gardening	4
Hobbies	5
Driving	6
Walking	7
Indoor games	8
Organization and club meetings	9
Caring for animals	10

From L. McAvoy, "The Leisure Preferences, Problems, and Needs of the Elderly" in Journal of Leisure Research, 11:40–47, Copyright © 1979 National Recreation and Park Association, Alexandria, VA. Reprinted by permission.

driving for pleasure, to watching television (McAvoy, 1979). Yet television watching remains the most common leisure activity for adults next to visiting friends (Moss & Lawton, 1982). According to one estimate, the typical viewing time for older adults is an average of more than 40 hours each week or nearly six hours each day (Bell, 1992).

Recent surveys suggest there are few realistic portrayals of aging and older adults on most television programs (Bell, 1992; Burrus-Bammel & Bammel, 1985). Television presents a highly distorted view of the elderly. Most programs portray older adults living in middle-class settings, without minority representation, free from health concerns, and able to maintain considerable freedom and independence and an active lifestyle.

Positive distortion, which Palmore (1990) has termed an instance of stereotyping or *positive ageism,* ignores the problems of loneliness, poverty, illness, and dependence among the elderly. By ignoring the diversity of ways in which people grow old and the special problems among widows, minorities, or the isolated and lonely elderly, television may be creating in older people the sense that their own aging is largely negative in comparison to what they see.

Sports Participation

Sports play an extremely important role in the leisure activities of Americans, either through direct participation or vicariously through attending sports events, watching televised competitions, reading newspapers or magazines, discussing sports with friends, and so forth. Active participation in physical sports declines somewhat with increasing age (Ostrow, 1980). Thus, in old age, individuals need to make adjustments in sports activities, reducing the intensity but not necessarily the frequency of their participation (Burrus-Bammel & Bammel, 1985; Schmitz-Secherzer, 1976). For example, rather than jogging five miles each day, older adults may reduce the length of their run, the frequency of their run, or both. Research suggests that the more physically active individuals have been in young adulthood and middle age, the more likely they will continue to be involved in physical activities in old age (Bortz, 1980; McAuley, 1992; McAuley, Lox, & Duncan, 1993). Benefits to the individual extend to a variety of psychological domains, including reductions in anxiety (Petruzzello, Landers, Hatfield, Kubitz, & Salazar, 1991), and increases in morale (Hill et al., 1993) and personal efficacy (McAuley, Courneya, & Lettunich, 1991).

Regular physical activity is a way to maintain health during the adult years. Physical exercise improves overall fitness, endurance, muscle tone, flexibility, strength, cardiac output, and respiratory efficiency, no matter what age we begin (Blumenthal et al., 1991; Burrus-Bammel & Bammel, 1985; Hill et al., 1993). Moreover, in some investigations, regular exercise has been related to increases in longevity (Schurr, Vaillant, & Vaillant, 1990), physiological capacity and cardiovascular fitness (Hill et al., 1993), and aerobic capacity (Blumenthal et al., 1991). In one study, the ability to initiate and maintain involvement in a moderate exercise program over a five-month period was found to enhance feelings of self-efficacy and control. Older adults from 45 to 65 years of age enhanced their beliefs about their personal capacity, endurance, and motivation for physical exercise (McAuley et al., 1993). Similar to other research, enhanced self-efficacy leads older adults to engage in more health-promoting behaviors and additional commitments to exercise (McAuley, 1992). Despite the short-term nature of the intervention, the participants continued to demonstrate enhanced self-efficacy perceptions nine months following program completion (McAuley et al., 1993). Physical exercise such as walking has also been found to have beneficial effects on the symptoms of older people with depression, particularly somatic symptoms (McNeil, LeBlanc, & Joyner, 1991).

It is difficult for sedentary adults to turn over a new leaf. Most older adults prefer the leisure activities they have pursued over most of their adult lives and rarely turn to new activities (Cutler & Hendricks, 1990; Schmitz-Secherzer, 1976). Mishra (1992) has found that men with a high level of life satisfaction are more likely to engage in active leisure pursuits and to seek out friends and join volunteer organizations. Sports activities and group participation allow older adults to escape the rigors and pressures of everyday life, even if only for a few hours per week. One critical feature of successful aging is to make the necessary adjustments within physically demanding activities (Burrus-Bammel & Bammel, 1985).

Leisure at Midlife

Middle age is a time for questioning or reassessing priorities. Midlife seems to be a time when adults want more freedom and the opportunity to express their individuality.

Leisure may be a particularly important aspect of middle adulthood because of the many changes experienced at this point in development: physical changes, changes in relationships with spouse and children, changes in self-knowledge, and career changes. With college expenses ended, mortgages paid off, and women embarking on careers, couples find themselves with more spendable income, more free time, and more opportunity for leisure. For many people, midlife is the first time in their adult lives that they have the opportunity to diversify their leisure interests. Neulinger

(1981), in *The Psychology of Leisure,* reminds us that younger adults are more constrained by social and financial pressures and family obligations than middle-aged adults. In midlife, adults may select from a number of intrinsically interesting, exciting, and enjoyable leisure activities. Their participation is largely on their terms, at their pace, and at times they select. Younger adults, by contrast, must often carefully program their leisure activities to match social convention and center them around the "right" people for social and/or career success.

Adults at midlife need to start preparing both financially and psychologically for retirement. Many programs that help workers prepare for retirement (preretirement counseling) begin in middle age and include leisure education (Connolly, 1992; Knesek, 1992). In our society, with its strong work ethic, people need to be educated about how to use their leisure time and to begin to develop leisure pursuits. Constructive and fulfilling leisure activities developed in middle adulthood are important to this preparation. Leisure activities that can be continued at some level into retirement may help to ease the transition.

Leisure Activities in Retirement

What do people do with their time when they retire? Studies reveal that retirees engage in many more activities than they did in their preretired years (Pepper, 1976). Table 12.4 summarizes data across five different investigations of leisure activities in retirement (Harris, 1976; McAvoy, 1979; Nystrom, 1974; Roadberg, 1981; Schmitz-Secherzer, 1976). The most common leisure activities chosen by elderly retirees were reading or writing, television, arts and crafts, games, walking, visiting family and friends, physical activity, gardening, travel or camping, organization and club activities, and outings. Of all the data emerging on older people's retirement activities, perhaps the most interesting are those suggesting that, compared with a decade ago, older people today are choosing activities far more like those of people 20 years younger than themselves (Horn & Meer, 1987).

Cutler and Hendricks (1990) identified gender differences in the choice of leisure activities. Women tend to engage in home-centered and community-centered activities whereas men seem to prefer outdoor activities (fishing, hunting), sports (playing and observing), and travel. When retirees are asked to reflect on their lives and consider things that they might wish to do differently, most people feel that they have adequately balanced and prioritized their lives in terms of leisure as well as friendships, family, work, religion, and health. It is only in the area of education and the development of their intellect that today's retirees feel that they would have liked to have devoted more time if they could live their lives over again (DeGenova, 1992).

Between the ages of 60 and 70, many people retire from their occupations. For a person whose job is the central focus of life, retirement can be a difficult and unwelcome experience. For others, retirement is problematic because it is the result of declining health. And still other retirees relish their new freedom and fill their lives with enjoyable leisure activities, volunteerism, and friendships. One goal for our society is to rethink when and why people retire in view of the increasing retiree/worker ratios (Human Capital Initiative, 1993).

TABLE 12.4

**A Synthesis of Research on Leisure Participation: Percentages
of Respondents Rating Various Leisure Activities as Important**

Activities	A	B	C	D	E
Reading/writing	37	36	55	67	51
Television	28	36	89	69	78
Arts/crafts	26	26	40	46	37
Cards/games	23	—	56	29	16
Walking	16	25	—	31	47
Visiting family/friends	19	47	63	75	56
Physical activity	10	3	—	—	—
Gardening	9	39	40	49	27
Travel/camping	19	—	—	—	29
Organizations/clubs	2	17	51	29	8
Outings/driving	9	—	66	32	29
N	245	2797	65	540	?

A Roadburg, 1981
B Harris, 1976
C Nystrom, 1974
D McAvoy, 1979
E Schmitz-Secherzer, 1979
From The Gerontologist, 21(2): 142–145, 1981. Copyright © The Gerontological Society of America.

RETIREMENT

As shown in figure 12.6, labor force participation for men aged 65 and over has declined steadily during the twentieth century. In 1900, about 60 percent of older men were working. In 1990, less than 20 percent of older men were working. For women aged 65 and over, participation rate has remained about 8 to 10 percent.

Some older individuals who choose to retire report that they were less able to keep pace with the increasing demands of the workplace. Other workers take the view that they have worked long and hard enough, and that they have earned the right to retire while they are still healthy. It is generally the case that people will retire when they either have to or they can afford to. However, the "have to" and "afford to" points are subjective.

In the early part of this century, most individuals did not have a choice between work and retirement. The Social Security system in 1935 established benefits to workers who retired at the age of 65; most private pension plans have adopted a comparable age. Social Security was originally designed to *supplement* a worker's personal savings and investments for retirement (Parnes et al., 1985). However, for many retirees, Social Security income is their only means of support. In 1998, a person who retires at age 65 receives a benefit of between $784 and $1,176, depending on the amount of salary contributions. A person who retires at age 65 with a spouse receives a benefit of between $1,342 and $2,013 (Social Security Administration, 1998).

The development of a retirement option for older workers is a late-twentieth-century phenomenon. It has emerged for two basic reasons: (1) a strong industrial economy

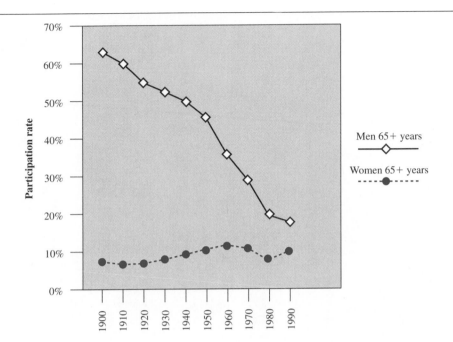

Figure 12.6
Labor force participation of older Americans, 1900–1990, by men and women 65+ years in the United States. *Source: Bronfenbrenner et al., The State of Americans, 1996.*

Legend:
Men 65+ years
Women 65+ years

that provides sufficient funds to support the retirement of older workers and (2) the institutionalization of retirement nationwide through public and private pension systems (Palmore, Burchett, Fillenbaum, George, & Wallman, 1985). Today's workers will spend nearly 10 to 15 percent of their total lives in retirement. In 1967, the Age Discrimination Employment Act (ADEA) made it federal policy to prohibit firing, forcibly retiring, or failing to hire workers strictly on the basis of age. In 1978, Congress further extended the mandatory retirement age from 65 to 70 in business, industry, and the federal government. In 1986, legislation banned mandatory retirement in all but a few specific occupations (Church et al., 1988). These **bona fide occupational qualifications (BFOQ)** permit mandatory retirement only by demonstrating that *all* workers in a specific job classification, because of age, could not continue to function safely and efficiently (Church et al., 1988). Some of the jobs covered by the BFOQ include police officers, firefighters, airline pilots, and foreign service officers (the latter having to retire at age 60 because of the hardship and difficulty encountered in "the rigors of overseas duty"). Employers may not fire older workers who have seniority and higher salaries just to save money. The courts, in vigorously defending workers' rights not to suffer age discrimination, have carefully evaluated the justifications made by employers claiming mandatory retirement in BFOQ jobs (see Research Focus 12.4). Recently, for example, research investigators have questioned whether there are sufficient data to support mandatory retirement at age 60 among airline pilots (Stuck et al., 1992). The authors found no published studies relating declines in cognitive functioning to increases in age among airline pilots. They argued further that there are no validation studies to support a link between tests of cognitive ability and safety performance among experienced airline pilots; that is, there is no evidence that declines on tests of cognitive ability relate

in any way to the job performance of older pilots. With mandatory retirement in our country virtually disappearing, and experts continuing to question the remaining BFOQs, such as airline pilots, Belbin (1983) suggests that most older individuals will be confronted with the decision of *when* to retire rather than being forced to retire (Human Capital Initiative, 1993). In the next section, we look at factors related to retirement and the different phases that people go through when they retire.

Factors Related to Retirement

Several factors influence the decision to retire, including financial security, health status, attitude toward work, job satisfaction, and personal interests (Human Capital Ini-

Police Officers and Mandatory Retirement: Application of the Bona Fide Occupational Qualification

In some jobs, there are compelling reasons for mandatory or forced retirement at specific ages. Such designated jobs are called positions of bona fide occupational qualification (BFOQ). Employers must show, if challenged in court, that a BFOQ job cannot be handled safely and efficiently by older workers. Church et al. (1988) reviewed some of the challenges that have proven successful in demonstrating age discrimination (e.g., when the job was not BFOQ and employers forced retirement to save the company money). Age discrimination is also evidenced by factors such as selective dismissal of or failure to hire qualified older workers. The work of police officers is particularly enlightening in helping us see what the courts accept as a valid BFOQ occupation.

In one case, *Equal Employment Opportunity Commission v. Missouri State Highway Patrol* (748 F.2d 447 1984), an officer challenged the policy mandating forced retirement at age 60 for all officers. The courts ruled in favor of the highway patrol department policy (BFOQ) based on evidence that at age 60, most individuals would not be physically able to keep up with the demanding routine of a police officer. The safety of the public might be jeopardized by continuing to employ police officers over this age. Nearly 90 percent of older police officers, according to experts, would not have the aerobic capacities needed to handle standard emergency situations typically encountered on the job. Further, older officers would be at a disadvantage in terms of vision, auditory response, reaction time, physical endurance, and physical strength. And any person over the age of 60 would be far more at risk for heart attack. The importance of individual differences in such global descriptions was noted in the record; that is, some 60-year-olds are physically fit and capable of meeting the demands of the Highway Patrol officer. However, the court accepted the difficulty faced by the High-

way Patrol in developing, utilizing, and interpreting a battery of tests to measure physical abilities to help them screen which of the 60-year-olds could remain on the job. The policy was justifiable, and the selected age was consistent with expert opinion on the specific behavioral demands and physical requirements of the job of a police officer.

The right of police departments to maintain mandatory retirement policies at similar or even younger ages has been further supported by the courts. A state police officer challenged the right of the Commonwealth of Massachusetts to force his retirement at age 50 (*Massachusetts Board of Retirement v. Murgia* [427 US 307, 1976]). The Supreme Court accepted the retirement policy of Massachusetts as "rationally" based on the performance demands of the job of a police officer, despite the fact that the officer currently was in excellent health, able to handle the requirements of the job on all dimensions, and faced serious psychological and economic hardships due to forced retirement at such a young age. In a similar case, *Equal Employment Opportunity Commission v. Commonwealth of Pennsylvania* (645 F. Supp. 1545, 186), the court accepted that the demanding job of a police officer made mandatory retirement throughout the department appropriate and necessary. All officers had to be prepared to respond to crises, even though such crises materialized infrequently, if at all, for most of the police force. However, the demands that routinely emerged and presented obvious difficulties for older officers included "assisting stranded motorists in snowstorms, pushing disabled vehicles off the roadway, chasing suspects on foot, chasing suspects by vehicle at speeds of seventy to eighty miles per hour, subduing suspects, and removing victims of accidents from wrecked vehicles" (cited in Church et al., 1988, p. 102).

---

tiative, 1993; Palmore et al., 1985). However, it must be recognized that these factors operate in a complex fashion to influence retirement decisions of employees. The factors influencing retirement decisions have been found to overlap one another and to be unique to each individual life situation (Henretta, Chan, & O'Rand, 1992). Table 12.5 summarizes the ratings of "important" and "most important" reasons workers give for having chosen to retire. More than 50 percent of the respondents indicated a single factor led to their retirement decision, 23 percent identified two reasons, 16 percent cited three reasons, and 6 percent cited four or more variables. Social Security benefits and pensions were often mentioned as reasons but rarely identified as the most important factor in a retirement decision; workers cited health and loss of job as the two most important variables (Henretta et al., 1992).

TABLE 12.5

Cross-Classification of "Most Important" and "Important" Reasons for Leaving Last Job

Most Important Reason			Proportion Mentioning Other Reasons								
	N	%	Wanted to Retire	Health	Lost Job	Compulsory	Social Security	Care for Others	Pension	Didn't Like Job	Spouse Retired
Wanted to retire	763	47.4	—	8.0	1.6	6.3	29.5	1.8	34.1	1.7	1.6
Health	401	24.9	25.4	—	2.7	5.5	12.5	4.0	13.2	0.2	0.7
Lost job	160	9.9	9.4	6.9	—	3.1	6.2	0	2.5	0.6	0
Compulsory	139	8.6	21.6	7.9	5.0	—	17.3	3.6	14.4	0	2.7
Social Security	49	3.0	47.0	12.2	2.0	10.2	—	2.0	40.8	0	2.0
Care for others	40	2.5	17.5	5.0	0	0	2.5	—	7.5	0	2.5
Pension	29	1.8	51.7	0	3.4	0	24.1	6.9	—	0	3.4
Didn't like job	24	1.5	54.1	0	4.2	0	8.4	4.2	20.8	—	0
Spouse retired	6	0.4	83.3	0	0	0	33.3	16.6	50.0	—	0
Other	123	7.6	22.0	8.9	4.9	4.1	11.4	2.4	12.2	3.2	0
Percent citing as a reason			56.6	28.5	11.2	12.4	21.8	4.7	23.4	2.5	1.5
Percent most important responses that are *only* response		48.2	59.8	76.2	56.1	30.6	75.0	37.9	37.5	16.7	

From J. C. Henretta, C. G. Chan, and A. M. O'Rand, "Retirement Reason Versus Retirement Process: Examining the Reasons for Retirement Typology" in Journal of Gerontology: Social Sciences, 47:1–7. Copyright © 1992 The Gerontological Society of America.

Workers at all levels engage in some preretirement planning and thinking, and researchers are beginning to explore the possibility of racial and ethnic differences in attitudes toward retirement. Among black professionals, for instance, those who did the least planning were individuals who were highly committed to their work, had few financial investments, and tended to use their work and coworkers as their primary social basis (Richardson & Kilty, 1992). In the case of a fixed age for retirement, evidence has revealed a *preretirement role-exit process* in which men begin to evaluate their jobs as increasingly burdensome (Ekerdt & DeViney, 1993).

It is not uncommon for men and women to retire from one job, and then pursue another job. For example, Frank Baird, a 72-year-old motel manager, found that he could not tolerate the inactivity of retirement:

"They gave me a gold watch—a beautiful thing—six months pay, a new car, and a fabulous pension," Baird explained. "We spent three months traveling, playing golf, fishing, and getting lazy. At first, I thought it was great. You know, for years you look forward to the freedom, the leisure time, the no hassles. But let me tell you, friend, it gets old. After six months I was bored stiff, and my wife, she was getting fed up too. You know, she had her friends and her activities and didn't need me underfoot. Then I found this job, and it's

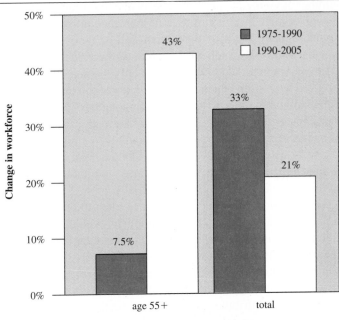

Figure 12.7
Increase in older people in the workplace. In the United States, the number of persons age 55 or older in the workforce is expected to continue to grow faster than any other age group.
Source: Bronfenbrenner et al., The State of Americans, 1996.

great. I love it! New people, people from all over, and I am able to make their stay a little more pleasant. Don't ever retire, friend, if you've got a job, stick with it. Retirement is for the birds. Unless you're a lazy bird." (Van Hoose & Worth, 1982, p. 317)

Still, many individuals look forward to retirement and relish the time when they will no longer have to work long hours. The feelings of Katy Adams, a retired teacher, express this sentiment:

"I don't feel any great loss at all. No, no. I taught math and science for thirty-one years, and if I hadn't taken time out to raise two daughters, I would have made it forty. I loved every minute of it, but now it is time to take a rest. After all that time I have earned it, don't you think? Why would I want to go on teaching? I have my retirement, my insurance, and my health. Now I just want to enjoy it." (Van Hoose & Worth, 1982, p. 317)

In contrast to the trend showing declining numbers of workers aged 65 and over, the numbers of men and women aged 55 and over in the workforce is increasing (see figure 12.7).

Working in the later years is certainly related to a host of factors, among which are health and finances. The 1991 estimate for the United States was that there were 6 million unemployed people over the age of 55 who were ready to join the workforce.

In a study by Teltsch (1991), data were analyzed from three companies (Days Inn of America, Travelers Insurance Corporation, and B & Q, Great Britain's largest do-it-yourself hardware chain) that had policies of hiring people over 50 and were willing to share their business records to evaluate the success of these companies' policies of hiring older workers. Travelers, recognizing demographic trends suggesting that a smaller and smaller number of young people would be available for jobs, began a job bank project for older people, including recruitment of their own retirees for full-time or part-time reemployment. They reported more than 250 of their own former employees elected to come back to work. Such workers proved the value of the rehiring process. And, at Days Inn of America, older workers not only learned their job responsibilities well, they displayed less absenteeism and lower rates of job turnover in comparison to younger workers. Although older workers did take longer to learn new procedures and spent somewhat longer time on the telephone talking with callers, they actually had a higher rate of success in getting customers to commit to a reservation. In the B & Q company, older workers were found to be more familiar with household and construction problems and were better able to direct customers to products that were helpful and sold by the hardware chain (Teltsch, 1991).

When given a choice, most people appear to elect to retire as soon as they can afford it (U.S. Department of Labor, 1989). Curiously, even though older adults in the United States today are healthier and more skilled than ever before, the percentage of individuals age 65 or over in the workforce has continuously declined since the beginning of the twentieth century. In 1900, 67 percent of the workforce was 65 or older. By 1950, 46 percent of workers were older. By 1990, only 19 percent of workers were aged 65 or older. Ekerdt (1998) attributes this decline to financial incentives to retire and to forced exits. In other words, people retire when they have to or when they can afford to.

According to Ekerdt (1998), the decision to retire early is influenced by subjective factors such as self-perceptions of health, attitudes toward work and retirement, and by the adequacy of one's retirement income. Studies show that those who voluntarily leave their careers early for reasons other than ill health enjoy their retirement as long as they have made adequate preparation for their financial needs (Parnes et al., 1985). Elder and Pavalko (1993) studied the pattern of retirement decisions and exit from the work role by studying Terman's original population of gifted individuals as they reached their later years. Nearly half of the men gradually reduced their work time while about 30 percent left the workforce abruptly; only 16 percent of the men returned to their work roles after either a gradual or abrupt retirement decision (Elder & Pavalko, 1993).

Phases of Retirement

Some social scientists believe that many people go through a series of phases before and during retirement. One such perspective has been developed by Robert Atchley (1983). Atchley (1983) reports that people's attitudes toward retirement are generally positive regardless of sex or age. The only group who seem somewhat less enthusiastic about retirement are those who would like to work but because of other factors (forced retirement, adverse labor market, financial needs, or poor health) cannot maintain their jobs (Atchley, 1983; Parnes et al., 1985).

Atchley (1983) suggested that people go through seven phases of retirement: remote, near, honeymoon, disenchantment, reorientation, stability, and termination. The sequence of these phases is shown in figure 12.8.

Most individuals begin work with the vague belief that they will enjoy the fruits of their labor at some point in the distant future. In this *remote phase* of retirement,

Figure 12.8
Seven phases of
retirement.

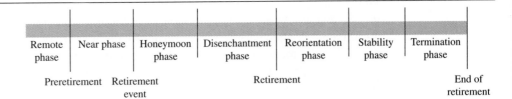

| Remote phase | Near phase | Honeymoon phase | Disenchantment phase | Reorientation phase | Stability phase | Termination phase |

Preretirement   Retirement   Retirement   End of
                 event   retirement

most people do virtually nothing to prepare themselves for retirement. As they age toward possible retirement, they often deny that they will eventually quit working.

Only when workers reach the *near phase* do they sometimes participate in preretirement programs. Preretirement planning programs help workers make the transition to retirement and are becoming more common in American businesses. Preretirement programs may help individuals decide when they should retire by familiarizing them with the benefits and pensions they can expect to receive. These programs also discuss more comprehensive issues, such as physical and mental health. Only about 10 percent of the labor force is involved in such preretirement programs, and these programs have a decided emphasis on benefits, pensions, and health insurance. In one investigation (Atchley, 1983), individuals who had participated in a retirement preparation program had higher retirement incomes, engaged in more activities after retirement, and held fewer stereotyped beliefs about retirement than their counterparts who did not participate in a preretirement program. As indicated in figure 12.8, there are five remaining phases after retirement in this model of the retirement process. Of course, not all people go through all of these phases, nor do they necessarily follow them in the order indicated in the figure. How significant each phase is in the retired person's adjustment depends on such factors as his or her preretirement expectations and the reality of retirement in terms of money, available options, and the ability to make decisions (Williamson, Munley, & Evans, 1980).

It is not unusual for people to initially feel euphoric during the *honeymoon phase* just after their retirement. They may be able to do many things they never had time for before, and they may derive considerable pleasure from leisure activities. However, people who are forced to retire, or who retire because they are angry about their jobs, are less likely to experience the positive aspects of this phase of retirement. The honeymoon phase eventually gives way to a routine. If the routine is satisfying, adjustment to retirement is usually successful. Those whose lifestyles did not entirely revolve around their jobs before retirement are usually able to make the retirement adjustment and develop a satisfying routine more easily than those who did not develop leisure activities during their working years.

Even individuals who initially experience retirement as a honeymoon usually feel some form of letdown or, in some cases, feelings of depression. Preretirement fantasies about the retirement years may be unrealistic. Atchley calls this the *disenchantment phase.* For some, the disenchantment with retirement centers on the experience of loss—loss of power, prestige, status, income, and purpose. Many retired persons also experience the loss of specific work roles (and their own importance) as well as the loss of routine and diminished work-related friendships (Jacobs, 1989).

At some point, most individuals who become disenchanted with retirement begin to reason realistically about how to successfully cope with it. The major purpose of this *reorientation phase* is to explore, evaluate, and make some decisions about the type of lifestyle that will likely lead to life satisfaction during retirement. The *stability phase* of retirement is attained when individuals decide on a set of criteria for evaluating choices in retirement and how they will perform once they have made these choices. For some, this phase may occur after the honeymoon phase, whereas for others the transition is slower and more difficult.

According to Atchley (1983), at some point the retirement role loses its significance and relevance in the eyes of the older person. The autonomy and self-sufficiency developed in the stable phase may begin to give way to dependency on others, both physically and economically. This final phase of retirement is called the *termination phase.* Because people retire at different ages and for a variety of reasons, there is no immutable timing or sequencing to the seven phases of the retirement process described by Atchley.

Some experts question the need for a phase approach. They see retirement, like other life transitions, as a lengthy process of adjustment. Ekerdt, Bosse, and Levkoff (1985), for example, evaluated the adjustment of 293 men to retirement over a three-year period. Examination of life satisfaction and leisure activities at six-month intervals revealed little support for a phase approach to retirement. The men simply took different amounts of time to examine and make choices about this new era in their lives. These authors suggest that retirement is best conceptualized as a process of adjustment.

Retirement Adjustment Styles

Other experts studying retirement consider the importance of factors such as previous lifestyle or the importance of work for the individual. Hornstein and Wapner (1985), for instance, questioned whether all individuals experience retirement in the same fashion suggested by phase theorists such as Atchley. Through in-depth interviews of 24 individuals obtained one month prior to and six to eight months following retirement, Hornstein and Wapner identified four distinctive retirement styles. The first style they called *transition to old age.* Individuals who typified this style felt that retirement was a time to disengage or wind down rather than undertake new activities. One respondent reported it was too late to create new hobbies or interests: "If you've never been a gardener, you're not going to become one now." The adults in this group believed that retirement marked a transition to old age, much like the rites of passage marked transitions at other periods of development. For them, retirement was the shedding of pressure-filled work roles and the adoption of a restful and enjoyable lifestyle as they moved into old age.

A second style, the *new beginning,* viewed retirement as a welcome opportunity, a chance to live life on one's own terms and to have the freedom to devote time and energy to oneself. For individuals in this group, retirement was marked by feelings of renewal, revitalization, enthusiasm, and increased vigor. These individuals responded to retirement enthusiastically: "It's a whole new life. There's so much I want to do that I almost don't know where to start." People with this style view the future positively as a time to gain control over long-overdue goals and pleasures (hobbies, interests, volunteerism, etc.) and to become the person they always wanted to be. Retirement for these individuals is a new beginning and wholly unconnected to becoming old.

Retirement for some means a continuation of mentally challenging skills such as the Japanese board game Go and social participation with friends.

A third style was that of *continuation.* For individuals who adopted this style, retirement carried no major personal impact. These adults were able to continue working, despite having retired. They either changed positions, shifted careers, or devoted greater time to a special skill, hobby, or interest. Thus, work remained a central organizer in their life structure because they voluntarily chose this activity. These individuals differentiated preretirement and retirement not by activity, but by the lessened pace and intensity of the work role. Retirement for people with this style was essentially a nonevent that signified neither an end nor a beginning.

The last retirement style, *imposed disruption,* represented a significant role loss. The people with this style saw retirement in largely negative terms (loss of work, the inability to continue achievement). For the individuals representing this style, work

TABLE 12.6				
Dimensions of the Four Modes of Adaptation to Retirement				
Dimension	**Group 1—Transition to Old Age**	**Group 2—New Beginning**	**Group 3—Continuation**	**Group 4—Imposed Disruption**
Significance or central meaning of retirement	End of working life; time to slow down; beginning of transition to last phase of life (old age)	Beginning of new phase of life; time to live in accordance with *own* needs, not those of others	No major significance except as time to continue preretirement activities in more self-chosen way	Loss of most highly valued activity; period of frustration, lack of focus
Style of making the transition itself	Gradual disengagement from work; transition taken as very meaningful	Rapid disengagement from work; desire to plunge ahead into retirement itself	Minimal sense of transition	Abrupt break with work; "in shock," at a loss for how to proceed
Dominant emotions during the transition period	Reflectiveness; introspection	Excitement; enthusiasm; revitalization; sense of freedom	Quiet satisfaction	Depression; anger; powerlessness
Attitude toward work	Enjoyable but pressured; often frustrating in recent years	In many cases, unsatisfying; in others, satisfying but pressured and draining	Either highly valued and satisfying or not very meaningful, no real investment	Main source of self-definition and identity; allowed time to actualize valued parts of self
Relation of retirement to sense of self	No change—continuity of self before and after	Retirement allows for birth of new part of self	No change—continuity of self before and after	Retirement represents loss of valued part of self
Orientation toward time	Past is satisfying but over; future is constricted; focus is on present	Relief that past is over; future is expanding, filled with opportunity; focus is on actualization of future in present	Future is expanding but based on past; focus is on continuing past in present and future	Past is highly valued; future is constricted; present is "a void," focus is on maintaining past in the present

was a role in which they had invested significant parts of their self-identity; without work, a crucial part of their identity was terminated. Although in time retirement becomes a period in which substitute activities evolve, an underlying sense of frustration and loss remains. Nothing seems to replace work for these individuals and retirement is never truly accepted well. Table 12.6 summarizes these four unique styles of adapting to retirement. Hornstein and Wapner (1985) help us see that the transition to retirement depends on a person's previous orientations to work, to life, and to self.

Braithwaite, Gibson, and Bosly-Craft (1986) have also examined the differential styles of adjusting to retirement. Their research focused on the elderly who really never come to terms with their retirement and continue to have problems coping. Those poorly adjusted to retirement generally showed (1) poor health, (2) negative attitudes

TABLE 12.6 (CONTINUED)

Dimension	Group 1—Transition to Old Age	Group 2—New Beginning	Group 3—Continuation	Group 4—Imposed Disruption
Extent of change in overall life focus	Preretirement focus abandoned	Preretirement focus replaced with new focus	Preretirement focus maintained in slightly changed form	Attempt to maintain preretirement focus despite changed circumstances
General level of activity (postretirement)	Tired, less energy than before; generally passive	Highly active, energetic	Moderately active; no real change	Largely immobilized (in a psychological sense); passive, low activity
Nature of retirement goals and activities	No clear sense of direction; too late to start major new projects; mainly continuation on diminished level of earlier activities and hobbies in satisfying way	Either clearly articulated specific goals for new projects and activities or movement toward articulation of such goals	Clearly articulated goals but no new activities; previously valued activities continued in generally same form	Some goals, but not experienced as satisfying; frustrated attempt to find activities to substitute for work; mainly involved with daily activities, hobbies in nonsatisfying way
Attitude toward old age	Inevitable next stage of life; no choice but to accept it	Denial of connection between retirement and old age; no sense of identification with "old people," "retirees"; feel younger, not older	No particular feelings about it; no clear sense of connection between retirement and old age	Feel as if others see them as old; feel they are not old and should be working; apprehension about idea that retirement is connected to old age

From G. A. Hornstein and S. Wapner, "Modes of Experiencing and Adapting to Retirement" in International Journal of Aging and Human Development, 21(4):302–303. Copyright © 1985 Baywood Publishing Company. Reprinted by permission.

toward retirement, (3) difficulty making transitions and adjustments throughout the life span, and/or (4) inability to confront job loss. The first two traits predicted retirements characterized by low levels of activity and involvement, physical and mental health problems, insufficient income, and low levels of life satisfaction. The latter two traits were problems for the short term only; these individuals usually made more adaptive responses to retirement over time.

Adjustment to Retirement: Activities and Lifestyles

There is no evidence that one single lifestyle will bring about a successful adjustment to retirement. However, it is important that retirees feel that they have choices and control in the way they experience retirement. The fewer choices a person perceives, the greater the dissatisfaction with retirement. If social contacts are sought and maintained, individuals in retirement will be happy. On the other hand, some retirees derive considerable pleasure from having the freedom to spend time alone. Larson, Zuzanek, and Mannel (1985) reported that among retired persons, 50 percent of the waking day was spent alone. Even among married couples in retirement, 40 percent of the waking day was spent in solitude. The investigators hypothesize that the social needs of some older individuals are less intense than those of younger people, since time spent alone was not viewed negatively by the retirees themselves.

In contrast, a study by Hooker and Ventis (1984) reported that satisfaction with retirement among 34 men and 42 women, all between the ages of 53 and 88, was directly proportional to the total number of activities in which they were involved. Moreover, when retirees perceived such activities to be "useful," satisfaction in retirement was enhanced. Hooker and Ventis provide support for the **busy ethic,** a theory of successful retirement developed by Ekerdt (1986). Ekerdt believes that in retirement individuals must transfer or channel the work ethic into productive, useful activities. By keeping busy, retirees remain productive within the freedom provided by retirement. Among the most common busy activities are community service, skill development and enhancement, profitable hobbies, and education. The retiree retains the feeling of being useful and a contributing part of society. In addition, these activities provide justification for taking time out for oneself (e.g., scheduling vacations between volunteer activities or resting after a morning of running errands for a friend). The busy ethic also provides a way to distance oneself from the effects of aging. Recently the impact of continued employment among retirees choosing to engage in work was studied (Mor-Barak, Scharlack, Birba, & Sokolov, 1992). Those who used their retirement to engage in other work roles were able to create significantly larger social networks of friends. Van-Tilburg (1992) reported that among recent retirees who did not work, the size of social networks decreased with the loss of many friends from work. However, those friendships that remained, although smaller in number, became more intensified and emotionally supportive and were sustained through reciprocity.

The importance of work friends in later life is the focus of recent research using a *convoy model* of social support (Antonucci & Akiyama, 1991; Bosse, Aldwin, Levenson, Spiro, & Mroczek, 1993; Francis, 1990). The convoy model suggests that older individuals take with them into aging close friends, family, neighbors, and relatives who define their immediate social support network. Convoys provide one direction for the busy ethic by offering the older person an opportunity to contribute directly to the welfare of others in the social convoy, for example, reciprocity. Morgan, Schuster, and Butler (1991) report that from middle age through age 85 plus, people report giving more support to others than they receive when both instrumental and emotional support are considered. These results have been extended to blacks as well as whites; however, black women were less likely than white women to provide instrumental support to others, but in old age were more likely than white women to receive instrumental support (Silverstein & Waite, 1993). Personal problems are infrequently discussed with former coworkers (Bosse, Aldwin, & Levenson, 1993; Depner & Ingersoll-Dayton, 1988). Convoys allow coworkers to maintain their self-esteem, "provide continuity between past and present and forge an integrated continuous sense of self" and help in adapting to the discontinuities in later life (Francis, 1990). Retired men appear to experience consistent levels of qualitative support from their most trusted coworkers; yet, the overall number of coworkers with whom retirees maintain contact and exchange support is quantitatively smaller in size (Bosse et al., 1993). Ekerdt (1986) and colleagues (Ekerdt & DeViney, 1990) suggest, through the busy ethic, retirees are viewed as still a valuable and contributing part of society. Of course, not all retirees adhere to this ethic (see, e.g., Hornstein & Wapner, 1985), nor should they.

Adjustment to Retirement: Predictive Factors

Who adjusts best to retirement? Overall, older adults who adjust best to retirement are healthy, have adequate incomes, are active, are well educated, have extended social networks including both family and friends, and usually were more satisfied with their lives before they retired (Palmore et al., 1985). Older adults with inadequate incomes, poor health, and other stresses that occur at the same time as retirement, such as the death of a spouse or health concerns, have the most difficult time adjusting to retirement (Stull & Hatch, 1984). Women appear to be more vulnerable than men in making a positive adjustment to retirement given the economic disadvantages that they have experienced throughout their work lives (Perkins, 1992). Increasingly, our society is also encountering women who have been previously married but who enter retirement as single persons, alone, economically disadvantaged, and at greater risk of adjusting poorly to retirement (Hatch, 1992). Like their male counterparts, women may experience retirement as a loss in self-image, productivity, usefulness, and social opportunity. Women who cope best are those with higher levels of education and those with better health status (Szinovacz & Washo, 1992).

Overall, about 15 percent of older people have major difficulties adjusting to retirement. The most frequent difficulties in adjustment are found among workers whose health limitations force a retirement decision (Henretta et al., 1992; Ruchlin & Morris, 1992). In recent years, investigators have also focused their interest on retired workers from the business world, retirees who were college professors, and retired professionals who leave their employment voluntarily (Cude & Jablin, 1992; Dorfman, 1992). Among retired professors, their perception of the importance of their own scholarship, academic work, or creative effort was the most consistent predictor of their adjustment to retirement. For workers in business, however, a paradoxical finding emerged. Those workers who were most strongly committed to their work roles and business organizations, for example, those who had developed a strong identification with the organizational culture and established a deep employee commitment to the company, had the most difficulty in disengaging from work and accepting retirement. Cude and Jablin (1992) suggest that while organizational commitment leads to productive workers with high morale, acceptance of retirement is more difficult for such workers. These individuals may benefit most from preretirement education and attempts to socialize them into acceptable retirement roles.

Not all workers, of course, have such difficulties. Hall and Rabinowitz (1988) distinguished between two broad classes of employees: (1) those for whom work represents indeed an intense commitment (highly involved career track) and (2) those for whom work is less intense, an activity or means to an end (less-involved career track). Based on an analysis of workers at a Motorola assembly plant, Hall and Rabinowitz (1988) charted the likely paths adopted by those highly involved career track workers and those less-involved career track workers. Highly involved workers value job enhancement, increased responsibility, career movement, and phased retirement, whereas those with less-involved career tracks value more extrinsic rewards, reduction in work assignments, and complete retirement. These latter workers would not be predicted to have much difficulty accepting, enjoying, and welcoming retirement (Hall & Rabinowitz, 1988). For some employees, work is an end in itself while for others it is a means to other life opportunities.

Theories of Retirement

There are three types of theories about the effects of retirement on the retiree (Palmore, 1984; Palmore et al., 1985). Some, such as Atchley's, consider retirement to involve a stagelike adjustment process. Other theories consider retirement a "crisis," with retirees experiencing generally negative transitions due to loss (e.g., the loss of occupational role identity). A third class of theories views retirement from the standpoint of continuity or positive adaptation. In continuity theories, one's occupational identity, though important, is not the sole basis for one's self-concept or feelings of worth. In fact, for many older Americans, retirement is a challenge for positive adaptation. New leisure roles, the intensifying of long-standing friendships and the development of new ones, time for self-indulgence, hobbies, family, and travel are positive aspects of retirement. Retirement, in this view, is not a decision or a single event but a long-term process that presents continual opportunities and challenges as retirees structure, define, and construct adaptive responses.

Summary

Work has been an important part of all cultures throughout history. In the last hundred years, substantial changes in the nature of work have taken place. In our postindustrial society we have witnessed a significant increase in jobs related to human services, jobs that usually require extensive training and education. In the future, changes in the nature of work are likely to be influenced by energy costs. Age-related changes in work behavior are best understood in terms of a contextual perspective that describes the relationship between the aging individual and changing work contexts.

Work, to be able to contribute meaningfully, is important to the individual throughout the adult life span. There are both gains and losses associated with individual aging that affect job performance. Generally, there are only minor declines or no declines in many kinds of work performance. The general finding that there is no relationship between age and work performance obscures the description of the unique characteristics of the individual worker at any age.

Virtually all vocational theories stress the importance of the exploration of a wide array of career alternatives. At some point in the late teens or twenties, individuals usually enter an occupation. Doing so signals the beginning of new roles and responsibilities. Career expectations are high and the demands are real; established workers may serve as mentors in socializing new workers to occupational success. In middle adulthood, most men attain the highest status and income in their careers; women do likewise if they have been employed most of their adult years. But there are some interesting exceptions in middle adulthood of people who start over and select a new career for various reasons. One aspect of midlife career change involves adjusting idealistic hopes to realistic possibilities in light of how much time is left in an occupation. Of particular interest are the factors related to occupational mobility in adulthood. Many individuals continue their work into late adulthood, and productivity in old age is often the rule rather than the exception. Work is a way of earning a living, but work has other meanings—prestige, contact with the outside world, and social relationships.

Across types of occupations, the labor force in the United States has become increasingly diverse in terms of racial, ethnic, and gender composition. Though discrimination has been reduced, it has not been eliminated.

Individuals not only need to learn how to work well, they also need to learn how to relax. Although television viewing dominates the leisure time of older adults, many actually prefer a variety of other activities if given a choice. Sports, experienced either directly or vicariously, also play an important role in the leisure activities of many adults. Constructive leisure activities in midlife may be helpful in making the transition from work to retirement.

By 62 years of age, many workers choose to retire—men far more so than women. In a recent analysis of predictors of early retirement, subjective factors such as health, attitudes toward work and retirement, and adequacy of current finances were all significant predictors. With the virtual elimination of mandatory retirement, the roles of health, finances, personality, lifestyle, commitment to work, and the nature of the job become critical predictors of when people choose to retire. Some social scientists believe that we go through a series of phases before and after retirement—the remote, near, honeymoon, disenchantment, reorientation, stability, and termination phases. Others see retirement as a continuous process of adjustment.

REVIEW QUESTIONS

1. Briefly describe how the social and functional contexts of work have changed in the twentieth century.

2. What are the main theories of occupational choice? Describe the roles of exploration, planning, and decision making in occupational choice.

3. Discuss the developmental course of work once one enters an occupation. What is the changing nature of the work environment likely to mean to workers embarking on careers today?

4. What are some of the different meanings of work for men and women?

5. What factors influence the psychological meaning of job loss? How do they operate?

6. Describe the changing role of women in the labor force. Discuss the achievement orientation and career development of females in early adulthood.

7. Describe the importance of leisure in adult life, in particular during the middle adult years. Outline the kinds of leisure activities adults engage in after they retire.

8. What changes would you recommend in social policy regarding work and retirement given the increasing ratios of retirees to workers? Explain.

9. Describe the factors promoting successful retirement. What factors help determine successful adjustment to retirement?

FOR FURTHER READING

Csikszentmihalyi, M. (1997). *Finding flow: The psychology of engagement with everyday life.* NY: Basic Books.

McKenna, E. P. (1997). *When work doesn't work anymore: Women, work and identity.* New York: Delacorte.

Salthouse, T. A., & Maurer, T. J. (1996). Aging, job performance, and career development. In J. E. Birren & K. W. Schaie (Eds.), *Handbook of the psychology of aging* (4th ed., pp. 353–364). San Diego: Academic Press.

Schaie, K. W., Schooler, C. (Eds.). (1997). *Impact of work on older adults.* New York: Springer.

APPROACHING DEATH

To practice death is to practice freedom. A man who has learned how to die has unlearned how to be a slave.
—Montaigne

INTRODUCTION

The quote by Montaigne the philosopher suggests that we can deprive death of its strangeness and its power of surprise over us by getting used to it, thinking and learning about it, and reading about it. We can deprive death of its power over us by being ready for it.

Approaching death raises questions about the meaning of life. Whether we turn to religion, whether we look deep within ourselves, or whether we consider the writings of philosophers, the answers often remain unsatisfactory. Confronting death serves to stimulate personal reflection on the meanings of life. Confronting one's own death is to face with honesty the loss of oneself.

People approaching death may be comforted by a belief that the spirit or soul is immortal. They may believe in spiritual rebirth or in reincarnation (e.g., that the spirit or soul lives in a different physical form). But death is the end of existence. Death makes life meaningful. As we move closer to death we appreciate the preciousness of time and the nature of life (Shneidman, 1992).

People can be anxious about death; they want to know how best to face life's final challenge. Death is absolute, irreversible, and inescapable. There are as many ways to approach death as there are ways to live. Just as each person approaches life in unique ways, each of us approaches death and dying in a unique way.

In this chapter, we consider ways in which death is defined, we consider the sociohistorical and sociocultural contexts of death, and we examine the practice of euthanasia as well as the legal, medical, and ethical issues surrounding end-of-life decisions. We describe attitudes toward death at different points in the life cycle. In our discussion of approaching death, we critically evaluate Elisabeth Kübler-Ross's theory on the stages of dying, and then outline the phases of dying suggested by E. Mansell Pattison. As we examine the transition from denial to acceptance, we emphasize the need for open communication. Next, we turn to the contexts in which people die—in hospitals, at home, and with the assistance of hospice. We examine grief, including stages of grief, impediments to successful grieving, and widowhood. Finally, we detail various forms of mourning, consider the importance of death education, take a critical look at funeral rituals, and consider deaths that are especially difficult to resolve.

DEFINITIONS OF DEATH

Defining death used to be a simple matter. The cessation of biological functioning—the termination of the heartbeat and breathing, the absence of blood pressure, rigidity of the body—was a clear and specific sign of death. With advances in technology in

Current Brain Death Criteria

Guidelines for Brain Death Proposed by Medical Consultants on the Diagnosis of Death to the President's Commission for the Study of Ethical Problems in Medicine and Biomedical and Behavioral Research.

Statement: An individual with irreversible cessation of all functions of the entire brain including the brain stem is *dead*. The determination of death must follow accepted medical standards.

1. *Cessation* is determined by evaluation of a *and* b:
   a. *Cerebral functions are absent*—Deep coma with unreceptivity and unresponsivity; confirmation by flat EEG (no electrical activity) or blood flow analysis/angiography showing no circulating blood to brain for at least ten minutes may be done to confirm evaluation.
   b. *Brainstem functions are absent*—No pupillary reflex to bright light in either eye; no extraocular movements (no eye movements when head turned from side to side or when ear canals are irrigated with ice water); no corneal reflex when the cornea is lightly touched; no gag reflex when a tongue depressor is touched against the back of the pharynx; no cough reflex; no respiratory (apnea) reflexes. Note that some primitive spinal cord reflexes may persist after brain death.

2. *Irreversibility* of death is determined when evaluation discloses a *and* b *and* c:
   a. The cause of coma is determined and is sufficient to account for the loss of brain functions.

   b. The possibility of recovery of any brain function is excluded.
   c. The cessation of all brain functions persists during a reasonable period of observation and/or trial of therapy; and confirmation of this clinical judgment, when appropriate, is made with EEG or blood flow data (cessation of blood flow for at least ten minutes).

Conditions Limiting the Reliable Application of the Above-Mentioned Criteria:
   a. *Drug and metabolic conditions*—If any sedative is suspected to be present, there must be toxicology screening to identify the drug.
   b. *Hypothermia*—Temperature below 32.2 degrees C/90 degrees F.
   c. *Developmental immaturity*—Infants and young children under the age of five have increased resistance to damage and greater potential for recovery despite showing neurologic unresponsiveness for longer periods of time than adults.
   d. *Shock*—Produces significant reduction in cerebral blood flow.

From the *Journal of the American Medical Association*, November 13, 1981:2184–2186. Copyright 1981, American Medical Association.

---

medicine, it has become increasingly difficult to define when death occurs. Death is inherently irreversible. But if a patient's life is interdependent with life-support systems, how can we determine exactly when he or she is no longer really living?

Physicians accept brain death indicators as criteria for death. In the United States, laws define **brain death** as equivalent to cardiopulmonary death (Jonsen, 1989). The criteria for brain death are outlined in Research Focus 13.1. Brain death means that all electrical activity in the brain has ceased for a specified period of time as determined by an electroencephalogram (EEG). The absence of blood flow to the brain, determined by cerebral angiography—monitoring the passage of injectable dye through the arteries—confirms this fact. If an individual's heartbeat has stopped but is restored through cardiopulmonary resuscitation (CPR), then a person who has technically died can be revived. This is because lower brain stem centers (such as the medulla) that monitor heartbeat and respiration may die somewhat later than higher brain centers. However, when the higher brain centers have been deprived of oxygen for more than five or ten minutes, the individual will either never recover mental and motor abilities or will recover them only with severe impairment.

One criticism of the criteria for determining brain death has been that the criteria are difficult to apply in practice. In one investigation of more than 503 neurological patients who were likely brain dead, only 19 actually met all of the criteria completely (Black, 1983a, 1983b). A second criticism is that applying the criteria makes it difficult for medical personnel and families to obtain organs for transplantation. By the time the criteria are met, the organs are often far too damaged for transplantation (Jonsen, 1989). Note that the guidelines for determining brain death presented in Research Focus 13.1 specify that all tests may be repeated in accord with accepted clinical-medical judgment and that the presence of fixed pupils (nonresponsive to bright light) may be differentiated from widely dilated pupils, which may or may not indicate brain death (Hospital Law Manual, 1982). In addition, several specific conditions make the application of brain death criteria invalid: drug or metabolic intoxication, hypothermia, developmental immaturity, or shock.

Others have suggested that qualitative criteria should be used for defining death. For example, minimal electrical brain stem activity sufficient to control respiratory reflexes or heartbeat does not assess or describe quality of life (Veatch, 1981). Questions of ethics, medical responsibility, law, and personal values make the issue of defining death a central concern to society. In at least one state, New Jersey, an exception is made for persons whose religious beliefs are in conflict with the application of the criteria for brain death (Jonsen, 1989).

Physicians and hospital staff have the authority to "pull the plug" and terminate life-sustaining interventions. But family members rarely discuss in advance the situations under which they would like their lives to be continued with life support. Ideally, each person should have a chance to communicate with a physician regarding their status, their chances of survival, and the possibility of recovery. Because people generally, perhaps appropriately, avoid the topic, family members must judge how the person would feel or react to the use of life-sustaining interventions. Physicians may hear a family member say, "Mom was always an active person. For her to simply remain flat in bed, unconscious, hooked to a respirator, is totally contrary to her view of life and living. Please unhook this machine and let her die." Should a physician act in accordance with such statements from the family? What if not all family members agree?

Gaining closure in these debates is difficult. Some believe that the concept of brain death was created mainly to permit the harvesting of donor organs (Kolata, 1997). Even when death of the entire brain occurs (cf. Research Focus 13.1), there is no assurance that all brain functioning has ceased (Halevy & Brody, 1993; Kolata, 1997). Halevy and Brody (1993) reviewed studies showing that despite meeting the criteria of brain death, there remains brain activity in rare instances that includes continuation of neurohormonal functioning, cortical functioning consistent with deep coma and indexed by EEG, and brain stem functioning as revealed through evoked potentials. Based on their analysis, they suggest that any further attempt to try to distinguish between life and death based on brain functioning is "biologically artificial." Kolata (1997) has focused on the growing controversy defining the "exact moment of death" which more and more assumes importance as it relates to the harvesting and transplantation of organs. Brain death is not a fixed, finite event or end point but is best conceptualized as a process with the potential to delay or extend the process through life supports and other medical interventions. It has become as difficult to define scientifically the end of life as the beginning of life (Kolata, 1997).

Halevy and Brody (1993) suggest that we need to consider three questions regarding death and three answers in response: (1) When may organs be harvested?—The answer is when current brain death criteria have been satisfied; (2) When can care be unilaterally withheld?—The answer is when there is irreversible cessation of conscious functioning; (3) When can funeral directors begin their services?—The answer is when there has been no evidence of any blood flow (e.g., absence of any blood pressure). This revises the way we conceptualize life and death and avoids the impossible task of creating a single criterion and a single definition that is satisfying theoretically and speaks practically to each of the three important preceding questions (Halevy & Brody, 1993). For example, accepting only absence of blood flow as a single, certain indicator of death would effectively terminate any transplantation, since tissues and organs at that point would not be viable. And although the loss of conscious functioning would be sufficient grounds for some to withhold extraordinary intervention and life support, it would not be appropriate to call for the services of a funeral director. In contrast with past views of brain death criteria, Halevy and Brody (1993) suggest that how and when we intervene is determined by the nature of the concerns that we bring to the process of death itself. Definitions of death are matters of "policy choice" or consequences: Can organs be transplanted? Can the respirator be disconnected? Can a spouse be permitted to remarry? Regardless of which definitions of death are applied, there will be mistakes. In what direction do we wish to make them: in the direction of protecting the dying individual and family members or maximizing the availability of organs for the living (Kolata, 1997)?

One of the most troubling of interventions occurs when individuals have incurred severe brain damage and coma but also show signs of a "sleep-wakefulness" cycle without any detectable signs of awareness, a condition called persistent vegetative state—PVS (Multi-Society Task Force on PVS, 1994a, 1994b). Karen Ann Quinlan experienced this phenomenon at age 22 when she was brought to a hospital following cardiopulmonary arrest and her breathing was supported by a respirator. She died 10 years later never having regained consciousness and became a classic example of the difficulty families have in removing a relative from a respirator (Kinney, Korein, Panigrahy, Dikkes, & Goode, 1994). Although her family wished to remove her from the respirator after a number of years, the medical staff responsible for her care refused to disconnect the machine. After much legal battling, the New Jersey Supreme Court ruled that the respirator could be stopped. It is often the cost of keeping persons alive with machines that calls the question. Similar legal issues have been raised over tube feeding to other patients in a **persistent vegetative state** (PVS) such as Nancy Cruzan. When her parents asked for the tube feedings to end, the U. S. Supreme Court overruled the state courts, concluding that only patients can choose for themselves to have treatments withdrawn. In the case of a PVS, a patient must have either written evidence regarding such interventions as tube feeding or have corroborative testimony from friends, relatives, and others regarding their wishes. It was the use of corroborative testimony subsequent to the Supreme Court ruling that permitted the family to direct physicians to terminate life-sustaining tube feedings for Nancy Cruzan (Insel et al., 1996).

PVS is a temporary or permanent condition characterized by the absence of ". . . any behaviorally detectable expression of self-awareness, specific recognition of external stimuli, or consistent evidence of attention or intention or learned responses" (Multi-Society Task Force on PVS, 1994a, p. 1500). Individuals are unconscious, completely unaware of the self and environment; yet maintain a sleep-wake cycle and preserve functioning of the autonomic system in the brain-stem as well as function of the hypothalamus (Multi-Society Task Force on PVS, 1994a). Thus individuals such as Nancy Cruzan or Karen Quinlan show no evidence of sustained, reproducible, purposeful, or voluntary behavioral responses to visual, auditory, tactile or noxious stimuli; show no evidence of language comprehension or expression; have bowel and bladder incontinence; and have variably preserved cranial nerve and spinal reflexes (Multi-Society Task Force on PVS, 1994a, p. 1499). PVS is said to be present if such conditions are present one month following acute brain trauma and nontraumatic brain injury or are evident for one month in persons with degenerative or metabolic disorders. Recovery of consciousness from a posttraumatic vegetative state is unlikely after 12 months. Any recovery from a nontraumatic PVS after three months is exceedingly rare; and in cases of trauma unlikely after 12 months (Multi-Society Task Force on PVS, 1994a, 1994b). Survival for more than 10 years is highly unusual.

The distinctions outlined in table 13.1 distinguish PVS from coma and brain death. The decision to withhold or withdraw life support is difficult when the person smiles occasionally, cries, or makes sounds. Because PVS is a new diagnosis, data on the incidence of PVS are unavailable. But it appears that PVS diagnosis will aid decision making about when to provide or withhold life support.

From clinical observation it appears that it is possible to differentiate PVS from **permanent vegetative states.** The latter condition means that an irreversible condition is most likely present, a condition from which the individual will not recover consciousness or, if consciousness were regained, severe disabilities would be present (Multi-Society Task Force on PVS, 1994a). On average children and adults are predicted to live about seven years in a PVS. Life expectancy is reduced due to infection of the lungs or urinary tract, system failure, respiratory failure, or sudden onset deaths. In those cases where tube feedings and water have been removed, patients in a PVS usually die from dehydration or electrolyte imbalance (not malnutrition) within 10 to 14 days (Multi-Society Task Force on PVS, 1994b). The cost of care can be extraordinary with the first three months of care estimated at nearly $150,000, and extended care costs about $100,000 for each year thereafter (Multi-Society Task Force on PVS, 1994b). As a result of the distinction between persistent and permanent vegetative states, the boundaries and outcomes of ethical and legal decisions become more clearly defined.

DECISIONS REGARDING HEALTH CARE: ADVANCE DIRECTIVES

Health care decisions cannot always be made with the full, clear, and unequivocal participation of the dying person. Advance directives refer to the various legally binding medical treatment decisions that are defined as acceptable before they are required.

TABLE 13.1

Characteristics of the Persistent Vegetative State, Coma, and Brain Death

Condition	Self-Awareness	Sleep-Wake Cycles	Motor Function	Experience of Suffering	Respiratory Function	EEG Activity	Cerebral Metabolism	Prognosis For Neurologic Recovery
Persistent vegetative state	Absent	Intact	No purposeful movement	No	Normal	Polymorphic delta or theta, sometimes slow alpha	Reduced by 50% or more	Depends on cause (acute traumatic or nontraumatic injury, degenerative or metabolic condition, or developmental malformation)
Coma	Absent	Absent	No purposeful movement	No	Depressed, variable	Polymorphic delta or theta	Reduced by 50% or more (depends on cause)	Usually recovery, persistent vegetative state, or death in 2 to 4 weeks
Brain death	Absent	Absent	None or only reflex spinal movements	No	Absent	Absent	Absent	No recovery

*From the Multi-Society Task Force on Persistent Vegetative State, "Medical Aspects of the Persistent Vegetative State" in New England Journal of Medicine, 330(21): 1499–1508. Copyright © 1994 The Massachusetts Medical Society, Waltham, MA.

Advanced directives include living wills, medical directives, and durable powers of attorney for health care. Even when older persons are apparently able to communicate effectively, their choice of medical treatments may be influenced by current conditions or context. Cohen-Mansfield, Droge, and Billig (1992), for example, asked 97 hospitalized elderly patients about their views regarding three different hypothetical treatments that might arise under three different conditions, such as, when they were mentally intact, confused, or comatose. Two results are of special interest. First, treatment preferences were influenced by the personal values of the elderly, their religious beliefs, and prior experience with illnesses of others. Second, 12 percent of the respondents showed no consistent pattern in their responses and no systematic approach to resolving these hypothetical dilemmas. Each hypothetical situation for this subset of elderly was interpreted differently depending on the situation (Cohen-Mansfield, Droge, & Billig, 1992). The way in which older persons view themselves and their health care choices is complex, multidimensional, and frequently highly dependent on context.

Living Wills, Medical Directives, and Durable Powers of Attorney for Health Care

The **living will** document helps ensure the right of an individual to choose whether heroic measures will be used to sustain life. This document, (see figure 13.1) allows individuals to state their choice of how, when, and under what circumstances life-sustaining treatments will be provided or withheld. It establishes a contract between the person, the medical community, and close relatives. Individuals are advised to use a living will document specific to their state of residence.

A living will, in principle, is intended to make life-sustaining treatment a less complex decision for physicians and family members. In actual practice, many difficulties may arise. For example, if one relative objects to the wishes outlined in a living will at the time of a medical crisis, the will may not be enforced (Society for the Right to Die, 1987). Another possible complication is that physicians, relatives, and the patient may be at odds regarding treatment outcomes. Sometimes the person's wishes and acceptable medical treatment standards may conflict. For instance, a patient may not want to accept tube feeding to sustain life, yet a physician may be unwilling to withhold nutrients and water knowing the consequences will be death.

The **medical directive** (see figure 13.2) has been proposed to deal with such problems. It anticipates specific conditions not covered in detail in the living will. The medical directive, sometimes called an advance directive, has been seen as empowering the individual to make decisions regarding treatment before special conditions exist, such as brain injury, stroke, or other extreme conditions, rather than having family members or physicians make such choices. Also accepted by the courts is a **durable power of attorney for health care,** which specifies a surrogate decision maker (relative, physician, lawyer, or friend) whom an individual legally designates to elect health care choices if the individual becomes mentally incapacitated. High (1993) noted that within the past 15 years, every state has come to accept ". . . legally binding living wills or powers of attorney for health care decision making in the event of a terminal illness or decisional incapacity necessitating surrogate decision makers" (p. 342). Yet, despite state legislation providing legal

Figure 13.1 Living will document.

FLORIDA LIVING WILL

INSTRUCTIONS

PRINT THE DATE
PRINT YOUR NAME

Declaration made this _____ day of _____, 19_____.

I, _____ ,willfully and voluntarily make known my desire that my dying not be artificially prolonged under the circumstances set forth below, and I do hereby declare:

If at any time I have a terminal condition and if my attending or treating physician and another consulting physician have determined that there is no medical probability of my recovery from such condition, I direct that life-prolonging procedures be withheld or withdrawn when the application of such procedures would serve only to prolong artificially the process of dying, and that I be permitted to die naturally with only the administration of medication or the performance of any medical procedure deemed necessary to provide me with comfort care or to alleviate pain.

It is my intention that this declaration be honored by my family and physician as the final expression of my legal right to refuse medical or surgical treatment and to accept the consequences for such refusal.

In the event that I have been determined to be unable to provide express and informed consent regarding the withholding, withdrawal, or continuation of life-prolonging procedures, I wish to designate, as my surrogate to carry out the provisions of this declaration:

PRINT THE NAME, HOME ADDRESS AND TELEPHONE NUMBER OF YOUR SURROGATE

Name: _____

Address: _____

_____ Zip Code: _____

Phone: _____

©1996
CHOICE IN DYING, INC.

Individuals are advised to use a living will document specific to their state of residence.

I wish to designate the following person as my alternate surrogate, to carry out the provisions of this declaration should my surrogate be unwilling or unable to act on my behalf:

Name: _____

Address: _____

_____ Zip Code: _____

Phone: _____

Additional instructions (optional):

I understand the full import of this declaration, and I am emotionally and mentally competent to make this declaration.

Signed: _____

Witness 1:
   Signed: _____
   Address: _____

Witness 2:
   Signed: _____
   Address: _____

PRINT NAME, HOME ADDRESS AND TELEPHONE NUMBER OF YOUR ALTERNATE SURROGATE

ADD PERSONAL INSTRUCTIONS (IF ANY)

SIGN THE DOCUMENT

WITNESSING PROCEDURE

TWO WITNESSES MUST SIGN AND PRINT THEIR ADDRESSES

©1996
CHOICE IN DYING, INC.

Reprinted by permission of **Choice In Dying, Inc.**   6/96
1035 30th Street, NW Washington, DC 20007 800-989-9455

FLORIDA DESIGNATION OF HEALTH CARE SURROGATE

Name: _____

(Last)   (First)   (Middle Initial)

In the event that I have been determined to be incapacitated to provide informed consent for medical treatment and surgical and diagnostic procedures, I wish to designate as my surrogate for health care decisions:

Name: _____

Address: _____

_____ Zip Code: _____

Phone: _____

If my surrogate is unwilling or unable to perform his duties, I wish to designate as my alternate surrogate:

Name: _____

Address: _____

_____ Zip Code: _____

Phone: _____

I fully understand that this designation will permit my designee to make health care decisions and to provide, withhold, or withhold, or withdraw consent on my behalf; to apply for public benefits to defray the cost of health care; and to authorize my admission to or transfer from a health care facility.

Additional instructions (optional):

I further affirm that this designation is not being made as a condition of treatment or admission to a health care facility. I will notify and send a copy of this document to the following persons other than my surrogate, so they may know who my surrogate is:

Name: _____

Address: _____

Name: _____

Address: _____

Signed: _____

Date: _____

Witness 1:
   Signed: _____
   Address: _____

Witness 2:
   Signed: _____
   Address: _____

PRINT THE NAMES AND ADDRESSES OF THOSE WHO YOU WANT TO KEEP COPIES OF THIS DOCUMENT

SIGN AND DATE THE DOCUMENT

WITNESSING PROCEDURE

TWO WITNESSES MUST SIGN AND PRINT THEIR ADDRESSES

©1996
CHOICE IN DYING, INC.

Courtesy of **Choice In Dying, Inc.**   6/96
1035 30th Street, NW Washington, DC 20007 800-989-9455

The Medical Directive:
An Introduction

As part of a person's right to self-determination, every adult has the freedom to accept or refuse any recommended medical treatment. This is relatively easy when people are well and can communicate. Unfortunately, during severe illness, people are often unable to communicate their wishes at the very time that many critical decisions about medical interventions need to be made.

The Medical Directive states a person's wishes for or against types of medical interventions in several key situations, so that the person's wishes can be respected even when he or she cannot communicate.

A Medical Directive only comes into effect if a person becomes incompetent, or unable to make decisions or to express his or her wishes. It can be changed at any time up until then. Decisions not involving incompetence should be discussed directly with the physician.

The Medical Directive also allows for appointing someone to make medical decisions for a person should he or she become unable to make his or her own; this is a proxy or durable power of attorney. The Medical Directive also allows for a statement of wishes concerning organ donation.

A copy of the completed Medical Directive should be given to a person's regular physician and to his or her family or friend to ensure that it is available when necessary.

Medical Directives should be seen not only as legal protection for personal rights but also as a guide to a person's physician. Discussion of Medical Directives with the physician can help in making plans for health care that suit a person's values.

*   *   *

A person's wishes usually reflect personal, philosophical, and religious views, so an individual may wish to discuss the issues with his or her family, friends, and religious mentor as well.

Before recording a personal statement in the Medical Directive, it may be helpful to consider the following question: What kind of medical condition, if any, would make life hard enough that attempts to prolong life would be undesirable? Some may say none. For others the answer may be intractable pain. For other people the limit may be permanent dependence on others, or irreversible mental damage, or inability to exchange affection.

Under such circumstances as these, the goal of medical treatment may be to secure comfort only, or it may be to use ordinary treatments while avoiding heroic ones, or to use treatments that offer improved function (palliation), or to use all appropriate interventions to prolong life independent of quality. These points may help to clarify a person's thoughts and wishes.

Durable Power of Attorney

I understand that my wishes expressed in these four cases may not cover all possible aspects of my care if I become incompetent. I also may be undecided about whether I want a particular treatment or not. Consequently there may be a need for someone to accept or refuse medical interventions for me in consultation with my physicians. I authorize:

_____

_____

as my proxy(s) to make the decision for me whenever my wishes expressed in this document are insufficient or undecided.

Should there be any disagreement between the wishes I have indicated in this document and the decisions favored by my above-named proxy(s), I wish my proxy(s) to have authority over my Medical Directive/I wish my Medical Directive to have authority over my proxy(s). (Please delete as necessary.)

Should there be any disagreement between the wishes of my proxies,

_____

shall have final authority.

Organ Donation

I hereby make this anatomical gift to take effect upon my death.

I give: _____ my body; _____ any needed organs or parts; _____ the following organs or parts _____ to the following person or institution: _____ the physician in attendance at my death; _____ the hospital in which I die; _____ the following named physician, hospital, storage bank, or other medical institution _____ ; for the following purposes: _____ any purpose authorized by law; _____ transplantation; _____ therapy; _____ research; _____ medical education.

My Personal Statement (use another page if necessary.)

_____

_____

_____

Signed _____ Date _____

Witness _____ Date _____

Witness _____ Date _____

Figure 13.2 The Medical directive. Copyright 1990 by Linda L. Emanuel and Ezekiel J. Emanuel. This form should be completed pursuant to a discussion between the principal and his or her physician, so that the principal can be adequately informed of any pertinent medical information and so that the physician can be apprised of the intentions of the principal and the existence of such a document that may be made part of the principal's records. This form was originally published as part of an article by Linda L. Emanuel and Ezekiel J. Emanuel, "The Medical Directive: A new Comprehensive Advance Care Document" in *Journal of the American Medical Association* June 9, 1989; 261:3290. It does not reflect the official policy of the American Medical Association. Copies of this form may be obtained from the Harvard Medical School Health Publications Group, P.O. Box 380, Boston, MA 02117 at 2 copies for $5 or 5 copies for $10; bulk orders also available.

acceptance of living wills, durable powers of attorney for health care, and advance medical directives, surprisingly few older persons have actually used these options. High's (1993) review of studies showed at most an 18 percent rate among people 60 years of age and older, with usage sometimes as low as 0 to 4 percent. Even with deliberate educational intervention such as free legal assistance and lecture/discussion presentations, elderly individuals were only slightly more willing to complete a living will or advance directive. Among a sample of 293 older people (65–93 years old) living independently and participating in an educational intervention explaining advance directives, the overall percentage increase in the sample was modest—22 percent to 32 percent. Compare this with the 76 percent of this same sample who had filed a legal will directing disposition of their assets. Table 13.2 provides the reasons given for failing to authorize an advance directive (a living will or a surrogate appointment/health care proxy) despite having participated in an educational intervention designed to increase use (High, 1993).

High questioned the assumption underlying living wills, durable powers of attorney for health care, and medical directives, that is, that individual self-determination is better than interdependent decision making among family members. Individual autonomy in our culture has been elevated to the exclusion of family participation (High, 1991, 1993). Some believe that family members' judgments are biased in choosing health care options for relatives. They suggest that families will make poor decisions, be focused on self-interest, or be unwilling to carry out the wishes of loved ones (Zweibel & Cassel, 1989). High (1991) questioned whether "outside" agents such as institutions, lawyers, or medical personnel should be given the power to act on behalf of another person under the illusion that it is the individual's self-determination at work when a decision is made. Outside agents are assumed to be capable of substituted judgments that are closest to those the individual would have made. Is the converse true, however? Are the elderly less well served when family members participate in health care decision making (High, 1991)? There is no evidence for this belief (Horowitz, Silverstone, & Reinhardt, 1991).

Kapp (1991) has summarized the benefits of family-shared decision making regarding medical decisions and concludes that the process (1) is empowering to the

TABLE 13.2

Reasons for Not Executing an Advance Directive

Living Will (n = 151)	n	(%)
Deference to others and putting it off	75	50%
Barriers and difficulties in getting documents executed	30	20
Accept/rely on present arrangements or state of affairs	27	18
Other reasons	19	12
Surrogate Appointment or Health-Care Proxy (n = 63)		
Deference to others and putting it off	31	49
Barriers and difficulties in getting documents executed	07	11
Accept/rely on present arrangements or state of affairs	15	24
Other reasons	10	16

From D. M. High, "Advance Directives and the Elderly: A Study of Intervention Strategies to Increase Use" in The Gerontologist, *33:342–349. Copyright © 1993 The Gerontological Society of America.*

older person, (2) alleviates emotional strain on both the older individual as well as family members, and (3) is helpful to those having to make substituted judgments about health care choices for the older person. Legal remedies, based on property law, exist that could be helpful in mediating those special instances in which family members disagree about health care decisions, when the possibility of coercion has arisen in making treatment choices, or where a conflict of interest appears. Most family relationships permit intimate moral relationships to flourish, and genuine care and concern are communicated in open dialogue (Lambert, Gibson, & Nathanson, 1990). "The family can be presumed to be the best decision maker, not only regarding knowledge about and concern for the relative but because family members embody the social nexus of values shared by the family unit" (High, 1991, p. 617). It is through such dialogue that society will ensure that older individuals preserve their autonomy in governing their health care choices (High, 1991; Jecker, 1990; Kapp, 1991).

DNR ORDERS

Do not resuscitate (DNR) orders in the charts of hospitalized patients specifically direct physicians and hospital staff to not initiate resuscitation measures (such as CPR, electric shock, medication injected into the heart, open chest massage, or tracheotomy) when breathing or heartbeat has stopped. Similar DNR orders apply to nursing home residents for whom transfer to a hospital for these procedures will not be permitted. Hospital and nursing home residents themselves can request and consent to a DNR order orally, provided two witnesses are present, one of whom is a physician. DNR orders can also be made in writing prior to or during hospitalization as long as two adults are present to sign as witnesses (just as a living will provides). Limits on DNR orders can also be established in advance (e.g., do not resuscitate if a terminal illness or irreversible coma exists). The obligations and choices physicians have in following DNR orders are also specified. A physician given a DNR order has three choices: (1) enter the order as given in the chart and follow the specifications; (2) transfer a patient requesting DNR orders to another physician; or (3) bring the DNR order to the attention of a mediation panel in the hospital or nursing home (mediation panels cannot overrule a patient's request for a DNR). For patients who are incapacitated or mentally unable to elect a DNR decision, a list of proxy decision makers may include (1) a person previously designated to make a DNR decision, (2) a court-appointed guardian, (3) the closest relative, or (4) a close friend. The proxy decision must represent the patient's own wishes, religious and moral beliefs, or best interests. Any family disagreements regarding DNR decisions must be mediated. For those with no one to serve as proxy, a DNR decision may be made if two physicians agree that resuscitation would be medically futile. DNR orders may be changed by informing the relevant health care staff of the changes using appropriate notification procedures (New York State Department of Health, 1988).

Compliance with DNR orders, durable powers of attorney for health care, and advance medical directives is not a simple matter for hospitals, nursing homes, and families. Hansot (1996) has documented the difficulty in transmitting this information from one hospital division to another (e.g., from routine care to intensive care or emergency care). Unless medical personnel are directed otherwise by family, hospital staff, or patients, aggressive actions will be taken to save the life of an individual using heroic measures or artificial means (Hansot, 1996). While DNR orders identifying a patient's right to prevent heroic measures from being used are placed in a hospital computer, this does not ensure that hospital personnel will consult the file in an emergency situation. And, a family physician may not be present at the time of hospital admission, particularly during an emergency, to notify medical personnel of a patient's wishes regarding advance directives, especially if a patient enters an unfamiliar hospital (Hansot, 1996). People must actively and aggressively pursue the transmittal of information to medical personnel to ensure that they know the conditions they choose to preserve their integrity and autonomy.

Many DNR directives are disregarded and unwanted interventions initiated because physicians and nurses have not been trained in the clinical aspects of withdrawing life support systems (Brody, Campbell, Faber-Langendoen, & Ogle, 1997; SUPPORT, 1995). Brody et al. (1997) argue that when faced with a decision to implement what they know how to do and for which they have been trained (e.g., intensive intervention and life support) or undertake what they have not received training to do (e.g., withdrawal of life support), physicians and nurses will choose aggressive treatments designed to prolong life. There are few guidelines available for health care professionals and family members regarding withdrawal of life supports. Brody et al. (1997) have focused attention on compassionate care issues in such decisions. The primary recommendation is the identification of strategic goals of both the patient and family members. Strategic goals include promoting the comfort of the patient, preserving the patient's ability to communicate, the withdrawal of burdensome interventions, and permitting death to occur (Brody et al., 1997). The most common treatments that appear to cause patient discomfort when withdrawn are mechanical respirators/ventilators, kidney dialysis, artificial nutrition, and hydration (Asch & Christakis, 1996). Physicians appear more prone to withdraw costly, scarce, or invasive interventions or ones that lead rapidly to death rather than ones that have been in place for a considerable time or are less costly (Asch & Christakis, 1996; Brody et al., 1997). Not all patients die as soon as mechanical respirators are withdrawn; the process can be quick (e.g., minutes) or quite lengthy (days, months, or years). The strategic goal of patient comfort requires frequent monitoring and the administration of drugs including morphine and other opiates when needed. Artificial hydration and nutrition intervention have no unique status as life-sustaining treatments since death after withdrawal is usually comfortable (Brody et al., 1997). By encouraging training in the methods used to eliminate patient discomfort, health care professionals can become more compassionate and offer more legitimate choices to the dying patient and the family.

Emotional support is needed by patients, families, and hospital staff when withdrawing life supports. Attentiveness to the comfort of the patient on a regular and consistent basis will help families see that the decision to withdraw treatment has not led to the abandonment of the patient or that the decision was cruel or in error. Compassionate care requires preparation of the patient, family, and staff for death. All who participate in the experience of dying will need to cope with their individual frustration, anger, emotional exhaustion, loss, and depressive symptoms (Brody et al., 1997).

ORGAN DONATION

The struggle that patients, families, and physicians face in deciding when and how death arrives is made quite clear in the case of organ donation (Hansot, 1996). The number of deaths each year resulting in transplantable organs numbers only 12,000 to 15,000. Although nearly 70 percent of adults in the United States claim that upon their death they would be willing to donate their organs, less than one-third of those eligible to donate organs do so. Usually the failure to make organ donation is the result of family members being unaware of the wishes of a deceased family member or their unwillingness to comply with the wishes of the deceased (Jonsen, 1989; Monmaney & MacIver, 1995). Organ transplantation requires the utmost teamwork following the consent decision and time is critical to maintain the viablity of harvested organs. Doctors have only three to five hours to transplant a heart, up to 12 hours to transplant a liver, and 24 to 48 hours for kidney transplantation, which may account for the kidney being the most commonly transplanted organ (Monmaney & MacIver, 1995). Heart transplantation costs nearly $200,000; currently 75 percent of those receiving a heart transplant survive at least three years given the advances that have occurred in the development of immunosuppressive drugs designed to prevent organ rejection. Using donor matching from national centers across the United States, harvested heart and other organs are rushed to waiting recipients by courier. There are nearly 40,000 Americans waiting for transplants, and 8 to 10 persons die each day awaiting a transplant. Those awaiting transplants are placed on a waiting list with priorities established based on specific criteria such as length of time on the list, urgency, and so on. Only the cornea of the eye, and in some cases bone, can be transplanted without the fear of rejection.

Organ donor cards or signatures permit organ donation under the Anatomical Gift Act. In the event of an automobile accident there are currently 18 state driver's licenses that make it possible for adults' wishes to donate organs for transplantation to be identified. Organ donor cards allow for identification of which specific organs or tissues (heart valves, corneas, kidneys, lungs, liver) may be donated. Cards are available through the United Network for Organ Sharing (1-800-24-Donor). This network is a private, nonprofit corporation with a federal government contract to provide a registry of people needing transplants and a national distribution and procurement system (Jonsen, 1989). The legal status of donor cards has been questioned, and in practice doctors consult with family members about organ donation regardless of signatures on cards and licenses (Monmany & MacIver, 1995). Families may actively participate in life support decisions that are designed to give maximum time to medical personnel to best find a match and a recipient for the donor organs and tissues to be harvested.

As long as there has been no element of force in the decision to donate an organ, ethicists generally support an individual's decision to control the disposition of their bodies since it preserves a person's autonomy even after their death. Traditional Jewish, Buddhist, and Muslim religious practices prohibit mutilation, desecration, or dissection of the dead (Jonson, 1989). Recent developments in Jewish law suggest that organ removal expressly for transplantation is permissible in those cases where the donated organ will save the life of another. Similarly, Buddhist and Islamic practices currently permit organ donation if the explicit consent of the donor has been obtained prior to death (Kimura, 1995; Sachedina, 1995). Japanese cultural practices and public censure permit transplantation of kidneys and corneas, yet other organs are rarely permitted to be harvested (Brannigan, 1992).

Does each person in our society have the right to obtain an organ transplant, and does our society have an obligation to provide this option to all who are in need? On the one hand it would seem responsible for society to restrict the number of transplants to efficiently control the costs of health care and ration services, available organs, and procedures. Yet, on the other hand, who will be granted the right to receive such scarce resources (Buchanan, 1989; Jonsen, 1989)? For example, should younger candidates for organ transplants have higher priority than older candidates because of the greater number of productive years they have left to live? Should older persons receive less than perfect transplantable organs while younger persons receive organs without defects or damage? Should those who can afford to pay for some of the cost of the transplant be granted special priority over those who cannot?

EUTHANASIA

Euthanasia, defined as "the good death," is often identified in the popular press as mercy killing. **Active euthanasia** refers to deliberate, intentional action such as the injection of a deadly drug or the administration of a drug overdose to hasten the death of those with a terminal illness, a massive disability, or an intensely painful disease. **Passive euthanasia** refers to death induced by the failure to act or the withdrawal of a life-sustaining medication or machine. Physicians, in taking the Hippocratic Oath, have vowed to act "to benefit the sick" and to "do no harm" by choosing treatments believed "most helpful to patients." Any form of euthanasia is antithetical to these principles, although some ethicists (Brock, 1989) have argued that there is a difference between killing someone (e.g., taking deliberate action—an act of commission) and allowing them to die (failing to act—an act of omission). Similarly, it is illegal for laypersons to engage in euthanasia in every country worldwide, although the Netherlands exempts a few specific conditions (Cutter, 1991). Cutter (1991) notes that in the Netherlands, a physician may assist in a patient-requested suicide and not be prosecuted as long as the following criteria are met:

1. At least two physicians agree the request by the patient is legitimate and understandable given the current situation.
2. The patient's condition is intolerable and no hope for improvement exists.
3. No relief is apparent or likely to emerge in the immediate future.
4. The patient is competent to make such a request.
5. The patient has made the request repeatedly over an extended period of time.

Euthanasia is neither encouraged nor supported legally in the United States. Yet there may be cases in which euthanasia is justified (Brock, 1989). Could families be spared agonizing decisions, painful memories, guilt, and considerable financial expense if euthanasia were legal? Should hospitals and the health care system use increasingly scarce resources and expensive nursing and medical care for patients with

The Ethics of Prolonging Life

Many clinical, ethical, and legal issues arise when we ask whether it is justifiable to withhold or discontinue aggressive life support to allow severely ill or injured persons to die. In our pluralistic society, the attempt to resolve these issues generates new conflicts within medical ethics, the law, and the general perceptions of the public.

The Refusal to Prolong Life: A Case Study

A 47-year-old woman suffers from a progressive spinal muscular atrophy called Kugelberg-Welander's disease. She has deteriorated to the point where she cannot move or eat by herself. She is intelligent and utterly lucid, knows she has an untreatable fatal disease, realizes she must remain on a respirator with a tracheotomy for the rest of her life, and recognizes that she could live for quite a while. Should a doctor respect this woman's lucid, repeated, and unvacillating demand to disconnect the respirator?

Many would hold to the principle that the will of the patient, not the health of the patient, should be the supreme law. The Vatican Declaration on Euthanasia gives additional support to self-determination. It proposes that

One cannot impose on anyone the obligation to have recourse to a technique which is already in use but which carries a risk or is burdensome. Such a refusal is not the equivalent of suicide; on the contrary it should be considered as an acceptance of the human condition, or a wish

to avoid the application of a medical procedure disproportionate to the results that can be expected, or a desire not to impose excessive expense on the family or community. (Vatican Congregation for the Doctrine of the Faith, 1980)

These clear and reasonable principles may conflict sharply with strongly held clinical perceptions and certain dominant values in our culture. For example, a doctor may be repulsed by the thought of disconnecting a respirator from the intelligent, conscious, and lucid patient described above; particularly when her prognosis is for continued life over an extensive period of time. This reluctance may stem from bonds to this woman forged during preceding fights for life. Distressed family members may also offer sharp dissent when a patient refuses or wants to discontinue life support.

Clinical ethics involve more than the deductive application of principles to cases of this sort. Physicians may experience the "executioner syndrome" when a lucid patient asks to discontinue life support; the physician must weigh the patient's desires against the personal perception that to do so would be to become a killer.

From D. J. Roy, D. Verret, and C. Roberge, "Death, Dying, and the Brain: Ethical Moments in Critical Care Medicine" in *Critical Care Clinics*, 2(1): 168–169. Copyright © W. B. Saunders Co., Philadelphia, PA. Reprinted by permission.

little or no hope of recovery? These decisions are matters of joint concern among patient, physician, and family members (Brock, 1989). Research Focus 13.2 presents one illustration of the ethical difficulties in prolonging life.

In complex situations like the one illustrated in Research Focus 13.2, it appears that physicians, the elderly person, and family members share moral responsibility for treatment decisions (Slomka, 1992). However, it is important to examine the type of decisions that are made and the degree of responsibility accepted by individuals. For example, when a decision is made to withdraw a life-sustaining treatment, such as tube feeding that has already been initiated, and the outcome will be the death of the individual, the moral responsibility is typically shared among family members. Yet, when a decision is made to withhold treatment that could delay a person's death, such as in cases of DNR orders, the moral responsibility appears to be assigned to the right of choice or individual autonomy of the older person (Slomka, 1992). Slomka (1992) raises the possibility that the assignment of moral responsibility in either the case of withdrawing treatment or withholding treatment is designed to assist all participants in an illusion of choice; that is, physicians, family members, and older persons near death negotiate a set of meanings about impending death, share moral responsibility differentially for the failure of medicine, and eventually accept death. Brock (1989) has suggested that there is no moral difference between those circumstances that would justify the failure to initiate life-sustaining treatments and those that would justify stopping it. If families and medical staff are indeed less likely to stop treatments such as respirator support rather than not initiate it at all, then two negative outcomes may occur. First is the likelihood of patient overtreatment (e.g., to provide life support beyond that which benefits the patient or which the patient would want). And, second, some treatments that have some potential, however uncertain, to benefit the patient may not be initiated at all for fear of keeping the patient "stuck on machines" (Brock, 1989).

PHYSICIAN-ASSISTED SUICIDE

The issue of physician-assisted suicide, a form of euthanasia, has been framed as follows: "If competent patients are morally entitled to refuse any life-sustaining treatment, should they also be permitted in similar circumstances to have others, such as their physicians or family members, directly end their lives, or assist them in directly ending their lives by a lethal injection or medication?" (Brock, 1989, p. 381). If we value cooperative responsibility for patient-physician decisions and the right of self-determination by patients to refuse life-support interventions, then how do we argue that physician-assisted suicide and voluntary euthanasia are morally unacceptable? Is the only difference between euthanasia and physician-assisted suicide determined by whether physician or patient actually administers the final lethal drug (Brock, 1989)?

Dr. Jack Kevorkian, a Michigan pathologist, has been an advocate of physician-assisted suicide. He created a device to permit patients to administer an intravenous infusion of an anesthetic (thiopental) followed one minute later by a lethal concentration of potassium chloride (salt) that quickly causes a deadly heart rhythm disorder (Basta, 1996). He has assisted people to commit suicide who were facing terminal cancer, amyotrophic lateral sclerosis (ALS) or Lou Gehrig's disease, multiple sclerosis, Alzheimer's Disease, as well as those coping with severe pain (Basta, 1996; Harvard Health Letter, 1995). Dr. Kevorkian believes that helping others commit suicide is warranted on the basis of meeting patient's goals of self-determination and avoidance of future suffering; his rationale is considered an "argument from mercy" (Brock, 1989). Despite creating his device so that the patient triggers the sequence leading to death, Dr. Kevorkian has been charged with aiding in the suicide of patients, and in 1991 his license to practice medicine was revoked in Michigan. Without a medical license he could not obtain the drugs used in his suicide device; yet this did not deter his assisting with suicides in other ways. Dr. Kevorkian is committed to legalize physician-assisted suicide and bring attention to this issue of "death with dignity." Letting a hopelessly ill patient die, he believes, is humane and defensible; however, there is a significant difference between "letting" a patient die and "making" a patient die (Basta, 1996). In 1997 the United States Supreme Court ruled that states have the right to ban physician-assisted suicide, although they did not establish a federal ban on the practice in all states. In a unanimous opinion they found no constitutional right to physician-assisted suicide. Each of the 12 justices defended the ban differently, leaving room for legal challenges as to how physicians may respect patients' rights to refuse treatment and yet not actively assist in their death.

Brock (1989) noted that there are few conditions which patients face that cause such hardships and pain that suicide becomes the only alternative. There are many newer drugs to alleviate pain and innovative treatments that can provide relief to patients experiencing chronic conditions such as terminal cancer. Dr. Kevorkian has argued that physician-assisted suicide permits a more peaceful, humane, and dignified death. Those opposed to physician-assisted suicide fear the loss of public trust in medicine's commitment to fight disease and death.

Commitments to provide optimal care for those near death might be jeopardized through legalizing physician-assisted suicide. For many years ethicists and physicians have raised the "slippery slope" argument, suggesting that once society endorses as justifiable even a few cases of physician-assisted suicide, it will become easier and easier to permit other instances that are far removed from the specialized cases in which the practice was permitted initially (Brock, 1989). Obviously the positive and the negative consequences of physician-assisted suicide will be debated for some time.

A final issue in the debate over physician-assisted suicide is the role of the physician's intent. Any direct intentional action designed to assist a person to commit suicide is morally unacceptable; however, a physician can take actions that indirectly help to hasten death and may be morally justifiable. The best example of this difference between direct and indirect intention is seen in administration of morphine by physicians to patients in the final stages of coping with cancer (Brock, 1989). The specific levels of morphine needed to control pain must be increased systematically to alleviate severe pain. Physicians recognize that an inherent, but remote, danger in using higher doses of morphine is that patients' respiration is seriously depressed (Brody et al., 1997). The very drug being administered to alleviate pain may actually accelerate a patient's death by suppressing their respiration. A physician can foresee that the patient may experience an earlier death due to respiratory depression, yet still provide convincing evidence that this was not the intended goal (Brock, 1989).

Compare the administration of morphine to a terminal cancer patient on the one hand, and Dr. Kevorkian's assistance in administering potassium chloride on the other hand. Are there differences? Do the physicians in both cases intend to alleviate a patient's suffering? Is there a moral difference in intent? You can see at one level that administering morphine at higher dosages may not with total certainty cause the death of a patient. Yet the outcome of administering potassium chloride is certain and definitive. Are we moving away from intent and into the realm of "risk," for example, the risk of a bad outcome (Brock, 1989)? Such issues are part of society's continual struggle to wrestle with these difficult matters. Will you be able to choose a "graceful exit" and have a painless death at home surrounded by friends and family or will death be uncomfortable as you lie in a high-tech hospital connected to tubes, pumps, and machines (Basta, 1996)?

Sociohistorical and Sociocultural Views of Death

*For certain is death for the born
And certain is birth for the dead
Therefore over the inevitable
Thou shouldst not grieve.*
—Bhagavad Gita

In earlier times, death occurred with roughly equal probability among young infants, young children, adolescents, young adults, and older individuals. As we have advanced in the treatment of disease and improved the likelihood that infants will reach adulthood and old age, growing old has acquired a parallel meaning: Aging means drawing close to death. Over the years, death has become closely associated with old age, although with the increase in AIDS-related death throughout the life span, including infancy and childhood, our society is beginning to recognize that death is not an exclusive old-age phenomenon (Callan, 1990).

Attitudes Toward Death

Just as each person must come to terms with death, each society in history has had to confront death. The ancient Greeks faced death as they faced life—openly and directly. To live a full life and die with glory was the prevailing attitude among the Greeks. Currently, our society largely avoids or denies death. Such denial can take many forms:

- The tendency of the funeral industry to gloss over death and to fashion lifelike qualities in the physical appearance of the dead
- The adoption of euphemistic language for death, such as passing on, passing away, and no longer with us
- The persistent search for the fountain of youth in cosmetics, plastic surgery, vitamins, and exercise
- The rejection and isolation of the aged, who remind us of the inevitability of death
- The appealing concept of a pleasant and rewarding afterlife, suggesting we are immortal
- Emphasis by the medical community on prolonging biological life even among patients whose chances of recovery or quality lifestyle are nil
- The failure to discuss emotional reactions to death with our children
- The attempt to cover up emotions at funerals and afterward as mourners adopt a "stiff upper lip" or are encouraged to "get over it quickly and get on with life"

Though Americans are conditioned from early life to live as though they were immortal, this idea cannot easily be maintained elsewhere in the world. People are more conscious of death in times of natural disaster, plague, and war. Death crowds the streets of Calcutta and poverty-stricken villages of Africa. Children live with malnutrition and disease, mothers lose as many babies as they see survive into adulthood, and it is the rare family that remains intact, insulated from death. Even in geographical areas where life is better and health and maturity may be reasonable expectations, the presence of dying people in the house, the large attendance at funerals, and the daily contact with those who are dying help prepare the young for the realities of death.

In one study conducted in the United States, college students were asked to identify their first experience with death. The average age reported was nearly 8 years and centered on the death of a relative for 57 percent of the sample or the death of a pet for 28 percent of the students. Even years later, students recalled their reactions vividly. Most recalled that they cried, and they remembered the reactions and comments of others, as well as very specific details of the funeral (Dickinson, 1992).

Most societies throughout history have had philosophical or religious beliefs about death, and most societies have some form of ritual that surrounds death. For example, elderly Eskimos in Greenland who could no longer contribute to their society might walk off alone, never to be seen again, or they might be given a departure ceremony at which they are honored, then ritually killed. Freuchen (1961) describes such a departure ceremony among one Eskimo tribe:

> In some tribes, an old man wants his oldest son or favorite daughter to be the one to put the string around his neck and hoist him to his death. This was always done at the height of the party where good things were being eaten, where everyone—including the one who was about to die—felt happy and gay, and which would end with the angakok conjuring and dancing to chase out the evil spirits. At the end of his performance, he would give a special rope made of seal and walrus skin to the "executioner" who then placed it over the beam of the roof of the house and fastened it to the neck of the old man. Then the two rubbed noses, and the young man pulled the rope. Everybody in the house either helped or sat on the rope so as to have the honor of bringing the suffering one to the Happy Hunting Grounds where there would always be light and plenty of game of all kinds. (pp. 194–195)

In most societies, death is not viewed as the end of existence; although the body has died, the spirit is believed to live on. This is true as well in most religions. Ardent Irish Catholics celebrate a wake as the arrival of the dead person's soul in God's heavenly home; the Hindu believes in the continued existence of the person's life through reincarnation; Hungarian gypsies gather at the bedside of a dying loved one to ensure support and make sure that there is always a window open so that the spirit can leave and find its way to heaven. Perceptions of why people die are many and varied. Death may be punishment for one's sins, an act of atonement, or the action of a higher being or deity (Kalish, 1985). In some societies, long life is the reward for having performed many acts of kindness (Cavanaugh, 1997), whereas in other cultures longevity is linked to having wisely conserved one's energy and vitality in youth.

A DEVELOPMENTAL VIEW OF DEATH

In general, we adopt attitudes toward death consistent with our culture, our family values, and our cognitive and emotional maturity (Kastenbaum, 1985). Clearly, attitudes toward death change as we ourselves age.

Children 2 or 3 years old are rarely upset by the sight of a dead animal or by hearing that a person has died. Children at this age really do not easily comprehend the meaning of death. Children may blame themselves for the deaths of those closest to them, illogically believing that they caused the death by disobeying the person who died. For young children, death is equated with sleep. They expect that someone who has died will wake up, return to be with them, and come back to life. Five-year-olds, for example, do not believe that death is final and expect those who have died to come back to life (Speece & Brent, 1984). Although few cross-cultural comparisons of children's understanding of death have been conducted, given the Piagetian cognitive characteristics of preoperational thinking, children up to 7 or 8 years of age do not appear to understand that death is universal, inevitable, and irrevocable. Most preoperational children (those of preschool age) assume that dead people continue to experience the same life processes as they did when they were alive. The dead simply have "moved away" and continue to live in Heaven, working, eating, bathing, shopping, and playing. Preschoolers believe that those who die continue to have concrete needs, feelings, and experiences as they did when they were alive. Children older than 7 or 8 years of age view death as an event that will occur for some people, but not all. Usually by age 9 or so, children recognize both the finality and universality of death. It has also been reported that the majority of young people initially become aware of death sometime between the ages of 5 and 10 (Dickinson, 1992). Most people recall that the death of a relative, typically a grandparent, was their first personal confrontation with death.

The awareness of death increases with age, yet older persons also show a greater acceptance and less fear of death than younger or middle-aged individuals (Woodruff-Pak, 1988). In her review, Woodruff-Pak (1988) confirms that adolescents and young adults are most fearful of death. Adolescents typically deny death, especially the possibility of their own death. The topic is avoided, glossed over, kidded about, neutralized, and controlled as adolescents distance themselves from death. Adolescents do, nonetheless, experience a good deal of anxiety about death.

Older people are most concerned about the circumstances surrounding their death, specifically the context and situation in which they will die (Kastenbaum, 1992). DeVries, Bluck, and Birren (1993) have also reported that in comparison to younger adults, middle-aged respondents tend to focus more detail and attention on the process of dying than on the event of one's death. Kalish (1985) first noted that the elderly show (1) greater knowledge of the limits of their life and a more realistic assessment of their longevity; (2) an awareness that many significant life roles are no longer available; (3) a sense of achievement in being able to live beyond normal life expectancy, or alternatively, a sense of loss if unable to reach expected years of survival; and (4) a sense of sadness, loss, and emptiness as loved ones and close friends die—but also relief and guilt as they continue to escape death.

Fear of death and death anxiety, however, may not represent a single, unidimensional construct for individuals at any age (Gresser, Wong, & Reker, 1987-88). Many adults participate in active denial and avoidance of death. Kastenbaum (1985) found that nearly 25 percent of all patients near the end of life deny that they are dying and Callan (1990) noted a strong belief in invulnerability among gay men with AIDS.

Although it is generally reported that older adults are more accepting of death and dying than younger and middle-aged adults, a person's past experiences and confrontations with death, rather than age, is the better predictor of acceptance of death (Kastenbaum, 1992; Shneidman, 1992). Numerous therapeutic death education programs have recognized the need to provide an opportunity for children and adolescents to discuss their responses to the deaths of people close to them (Attig, 1992). Sandler et al. (1992) provided therapeutic death education for children and remaining family members who had experienced the death of a parent. The education intervention was designed to prevent mental health problems, and results indicated clear support for the program's effectiveness. Through open exchange guided by a mental health professional, children and the remaining family members enhanced the warmth and openness in their relationships despite feelings of loss, sadness, and abandonment. The discussion sessions gave all family members an opportunity to derive mutual social support and provided a forum for exchanging grief-related issues and feelings. Among the older children, reductions in behavioral acting out, depression, and other such problems were noted.

Middle adulthood is a time when men and women begin to think more intensely about how much time is left in their lives. Middle age may be a time for talking with other family members about death as life insurance needs grow, as wills are written or revised, as one's children reach early adulthood, and as one's parents age and die. With middle age comes experience with death and loss, which leads to a greater differentiation between the concept of death and the concept of dying than at younger ages (DeVries et al. 1993). Even in middle age, however, both men and women respondents display far more knowledge and detail in their understanding of death than in their understanding of dying (DeVries et al. 1993).

Kastenbaum (1981) first suggested that the elderly may experience **bereavement overload** from the cumulative effects of having to cope with the deaths of friends, neighbors, and relatives in a short time span. The elderly are forced to examine the meanings of life and death much more often than those in middle age or young adulthood. Bereavement overload has also been reported among gay men coping with the cumulative effects of multiple losses of close friends and lovers (Neugebauer, Rabkin, & Williams, 1992). The greater the number of losses, the more common and intense are bereavement reactions (Neugebauer et al., 1992). There are also, of course, considerable individual differences. Some elderly persons see their lives drawing to a close and readily accept the ending, whereas others cling passionately to life, savoring each activity, personal relationship, and achievement (Kalish, 1987).

Death education programs help friends and family prepare for the death of loved ones. No single approach is more successful than others. In death education programs, whether for children or adults, counselors emphasize honest and open exchange as the best strategy to help people cope with death. In one investigation of the attitudes of 30,000 young adults, more than 30 percent said they could not recall any discussion of death during their childhoods; an equal number said that although death was discussed, the discussion took place in an uncomfortable atmosphere (Shneidman, 1992). Generally, the more freedom to discuss death, the more mature (emotionally and cognitively) are the attitudes toward death. It seems that even religious orientation plays a role. The data suggest a U-shaped pattern. That is, either strong or weak religious beliefs are associated with less fear of death than are moderate levels (Kalish, 1985).

For death education programs to be effective, they must offer individuals an opportunity to personalize the learning that occurs (Attig, 1992). Personally experiencing the death of a friend or loved one makes people especially primed for learning about the event—emotionally and intellectually; however, an immediate personal experience with death is not required for participating in experiential or **person-centered death education** programs. These programs are heavily existential and require participants to share their experiences, inner feelings, and thoughts with methods such as storytelling, to help understand the encounter with death. Participants are taught to use reminiscence, as a way of counteracting the tendency to "intellecutalize" the death event and to personalize the learning that occurs. Skilled death educators help individuals confront death by examining how the experience sheds personal insight into the meaning of life itself (e.g., its finite nature and its uncertainty), what it means to be human (e.g., our vulnerability), and how to respect other persons' lives in leading a humane existence (Attig, 1992).

Other death education programs are far more didactic or instruction-centered in that people enroll as they might for a course and study the subject matter of death; they are not required to involve themselves personally with the material presented. There are formal lectures and discussions, multimedia presentations, and class trips to hospitals, nursing homes, funeral homes, cemeteries, and hospices. However, without some opportunity to reflect on the meaning and experiential component of death, **didactic-centered death education** programs appear to result in minimal change in attitudes about death (Attig, 1992; Durlak & Riesenberg, 1991). In one study (Hutchison & Scherman, 1992), didactic and experiential (person-centered) approaches were compared. At both the conclusion of the programs and at an eight-week follow-up, Hutchison and Scherman (1992) reported that didactic death education with reflection produced lower scores on the Death Anxiety Scale than an experiential approach alone.

There are, as you might imagine, countless problems in evaluating empirical studies in this field. First, those who participate in death education programs represent a sampling bias and control populations are difficult to find for comparative purposes. It is also important to realize that there are multiple indicators of program outcome and success; however, research investigators have relied too heavily on single measures of program effectiveness, most often attitudinal change rather than behavioral change (Durlak & Riesenberg, 1991). In most of the studies, death education effects are evaluated on a short-term basis and little is known about the long-term persistence of any changes. Durlak and Riesenberg (1991), however, suggest that long-term follow-up is particularly needed. What do changes in attitudes among participants in death education programs mean about their future contact with those who are near death? How do program participants approach preparation of their own will, advance medical directive or organ donation?

Swan Songs: Characteristics of Last Compositions

In an article in the journal *Psychology and Aging,* D. K. Simonton from the University of California at Davis reported the results of his analysis of the final musical works of 172 classical composers. He wondered whether there would be any unique characteristics in the very last musical work or "swan song" of each of these composers.

In a series of complex computer analyses performed on these varied pieces, Simonton surprisingly discovered some commonalities in these final musical compositions. Seven basic variables were used to compare earlier works with the last work of the composer: melodic originality and variation, repertoire popularity, aesthetic significance, listener accessibility, performance duration, and thematic size. Unlike earlier investigators' attempts to examine swan songs, Simonton was able to rule out statistically contaminating factors such as the average age at which the last composition was written and individual differences in terms of fame, reputation, and success. In examining each individual composer's last musical work, or swan song, and comparing it to earlier compositions, Simonton found that the last work was somewhat shorter in length. Swan songs were also typically far more simple in their organization or structure. Also, the swan songs have become some of the most enduring, well-recognized, and cherished pieces in the field of classical music. These musical finales are characterized by a degree of aesthetic significance that earlier works do not have. Examples of legendary swan songs include Mozart's *Requiem,* Tchaikovsky's *Sixth Symphony,* and Schubert's *Unfinished Symphony.* As composers near the end of their lives, their musical works seemed to reveal personal contentment, inner harmony, and acceptance rather than depression, sorrow, or tragedy.

The ability of composers to construct such enduring works at the end of their lives remains puzzling. The swan song structure found by Simonton is understated in its aesthetic beauty and simplicity. Yet the simplicity is not that of a country melody or peasant folk tune. What emerges is the elegance of a musical composition that is not too complex, not too simple; music that is "just right." The swan song demonstrates that the composer knew how to produce a work that presented the pure essence of a feeling, mood, or theme in the clearest and most direct fashion. It might be argued that this happened because the composers knew that their lives were nearly over. However, most of the composers did not know they were near death; they did not consciously attempt to produce a final composition. The swan song phenomenon is even more striking when juxtaposed against possible "false alarms"; many of the composers produced musical works against the backdrop of serious disease that brought them to the brink of death. Yet during these near brushes with death, the musical compositions created are similar to those produced at other times throughout their careers. It is only the swan song that contains the unique qualities that separate it from a composer's earlier musical compositions.

FACING DEATH

In his book *The Sane Society,* Erich Fromm (1955) comments, "Man is the only animal that finds his own existence a problem which he has to solve and from which he cannot escape" (p. 24). We know we must die. It is this knowledge that we will someday die that gives meaning to life, that causes us to establish priorities, and that demands that we use our time wisely.

Most dying individuals want the opportunity to make some decisions regarding their death. Some individuals want to complete unfinished business; for example, resolving problems and mending fences in personal relationships. When asked how they would spend their last six months of life, younger adults described activities such as traveling and accomplishing things they previously had not done; older adults, in contrast, described more inner-focused activities such as contemplation and meditation (Kalish & Reynolds, 1981). Research Focus 13.3 describes such a shift in focus among classical musical composers nearing the end of life.

In the next section, we examine the often-cited psychological stages of dying developed by Elisabeth Kübler-Ross and then explore the dying phases or dying trajectories. We also consider the concept of appropriate death, as well as the variety of coping strategies individuals develop to deal with the stress of knowing they are dying.

KÜBLER-ROSS'S THEORY

The most widely cited view of how people cope with death was developed by Elisabeth Kübler-Ross. This view has been applied to many loss experiences, for example, loss of job, loss through miscarriage, or loss through stealing. The stages, however, have received little direct empirical support and have been the subject of much theoretical criticism (Kastenbaum, 1981; Shneidman, 1992). Kübler-Ross's theory, which suggests the existence of stages in dealing with the dying process, helped focus professional concern on death education and counseling—topics that had been largely ignored. In her psychiatric work with hospitalized patients dying from cancer, Kübler-Ross (1969, 1981) first identified and reported the existence of five stages: denial/isolation, anger, bargaining, depression, and acceptance.

In the first stage, a common initial reaction to terminal illness is **denial/isolation.** The individual denies that death is really going to occur, saying, "No, it can't happen to me," "It's not possible," or "There must be a mistake, an error in the laboratory or in the diagnosis." Denial is like shock and is considered a transitory defense. It is eventually replaced with increasing acceptance when the individual confronts such matters as finances, unfinished business, and arrangements for surviving family members.

In the second stage, **anger,** the dying individual recognizes that denial can no longer be maintained; anger, resentment, rage, and envy are expressed directly. Now the issue becomes, "Why me?" At this point, the individual becomes increasingly difficult to care for as anger is displaced and projected onto physicians, nurses, hospital staff, family members, and God. The realization of loss is great, and those who symbolize life, energy, and competent functioning are the targets of the dying individual's resentment and jealousy.

In the third stage, **bargaining,** the individual develops hope that death can somehow be postponed or delayed. Some individuals enter into a brief period of bargaining or negotiation—often with God—as they try to delay their deaths. Psychologically, these people are trying to buy a few more weeks, months, or years in exchange for leading a reformed life or for choosing a life dedicated to God or the service of others.

In the fourth stage, **depression,** the dying individual begins to accept the certainty of his or her death; as she or he recognizes the growing severity of specific symptoms, a period of depression or preparatory grief may appear. The dying individual is often silent, refuses visitors, and spends much of the time crying or grieving. Shneidman (1992) finds individuals at this point mourning their own death, the loss of their special talents and abilities, the loss of their former sense of contentment and well-being, and the loss of their experiences (past, present, and future). Attempts to cheer up dying individuals at this stage should be avoided, says Kübler-Ross, because of the dying person's need to contemplate and grieve over their own impending death.

In the fifth stage, **acceptance,** the individual develops a sense of peace, a unique acceptance of fate, and in many cases, a desire to be left alone. This stage may be devoid of feeling; physical pain and discomfort are often absent. Kübler-Ross describes this stage as the last one before undertaking a long journey and reaching the end of the struggle.

No one has yet been able to provide independent confirmation that people actually go through all five stages in the order described by Kübler-Ross (Kastenbaum, 1981; Shneidman, 1992). Theoretically and empirically, the stages have raised many questions, although Kübler-Ross feels that she has often been misread and misinterpreted. For instance, she maintains that she never intended the stages to represent an invariant sequence of developmental steps toward death. And she has consistently recognized the importance of individual variation in how we face death. Nevertheless, Kübler-Ross still believes that the optimal way to face death lies in the sequence she has proposed. Numerous advocates have seen the stages as prescriptive rather than descriptive and tried to "hurry" dying patients through the individual stages. But the stages are ultimately only descriptive; they make no claim on how all persons should die.

Other investigators have not found the same five stages and many report that a single stage (e.g., depression or denial) dominates the entire dying experience, while others identify dying patients as being in two or three stages simultaneously (Kalish, 1985; Shneidman, 1992). The fact that Kübler-Ross used primarily interview data with many young or middle-aged adults without sophisticated statistical evaluations is yet another criticism of her work. Marsall and Levy (1990) suggest that among her younger and middle-aged respondents, the experience of anger, bargaining, and depression is a far more likely coping response than among older individuals. Even in Kübler-Ross's earliest work, it is clear that many of the cancer patients she studied remained at one of the first stages (denial or anger) and never passed through all five stages of the sequence. And other studies have found that some patients move backward or regress into stages already completed (Shneidman, 1992). We are left with a provocative and historically important theory of dying, but one that has few developmental or stage properties. In the minds of many critics, the theory, other than serving to stimulate interest and research on the topic of death and dying, has had little utility.

AN APPROPRIATE DEATH

In a certain sense, the ways in which people face death may simply reflect how they face life. The concept of an **appropriate death** suggests that individuals should be granted the freedom to face dying as they choose, a death that fits one's expectations and style of coping (Weisman, 1972). An appropriate death permits people to die with dignity on their own terms. There is no mandate to move through a set of stages, no requirement to push to acceptance, no social pressure to face death in a prescriptive way. By permitting individuals an appropriate death, we allow them to maintain a sense of hopefulness. Hopefulness refers to the positive anticipation of the future: birthdays, wedding anniversaries, visits from friends or relatives, seeing the new year arrive.

As studies suggest, hopefulness provides one means of control or mastery over terminal illness and allows the process of living to coexist with the process of dying

(Kalish, 1985; Kastenbaum, 1981). Some dying persons continue to participate in living each day, resisting rather than denying death. Their spirit and hope should not be confused with outright denial; resisting death implies a choice and involves an active decision. With an appropriate death, individuals can maintain their dignity, their self-esteem, their identity, and their individuality. Kalish (1985) identified three factors necessary to permit an appropriate death: (1) a warm, intimate personal relationship with family, friends, or health professionals; (2) an open environment in which emotions, information, and the terminal condition can be discussed by all involved; and (3) a sense of meaning derived from this experience, from one's life, or from religion.

PATTISON'S LIVING-DYING INTERVAL

E. Mansell Pattison (1977) has defined the **trajectory of life** as our anticipated life span and the plan we make for the way we will live out our life. When an illness or serious injury occurs and leads to a revision of our anticipated life span, the life trajectory must be revised because we perceive that we are likely to die much sooner than we had anticipated. Pattison calls the time interval between our discovery that we will die sooner than we had thought and the time when we actually die the *living-dying interval*. The living-dying interval is characterized by three phases: acute, chronic, and terminal. The goal of those who counsel individuals in the living-dying interval is to assist them in coping with the first or acute phase, to help them to live as reasonably as possible through the second, or chronic phase, and to move them into the third or terminal phase (see figure 13.3). Pattison sees a pattern to the phases. Depending on the nature of the illness, different people may spend vastly different periods of time in each phase. For example, some illnesses allow a pattern of chronic living-dying for only a few weeks; others allow a more protracted period of months or even years, such as may occur with a slow, lingering illness or disease or with someone who has a deteriorating heart condition.

Pattison describes each phase in terms of the individual's reactions and coping needs. In the *acute phase,* individuals face what is probably the most severe crisis in

Figure 13.3
Acute, chronic, and terminal phases of the dying process. *From* The Experience of Dying *by E. Mansell Pattison.* © *1977 by Prentice-Hall, Inc. Published by permission of Prentice-Hall, Inc., Englewood Cliffs, NJ.*

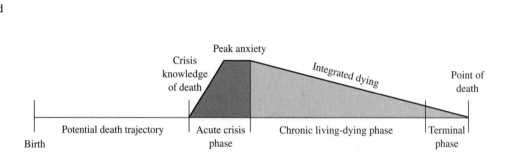

their lives—the realization that they will die sooner than they thought and will not get to accomplish and experience all they had hoped. People in this stage feel immobilized, experience high levels of anxiety, and call into play a number of defense mechanisms to deal with the extreme fear and stress they are confronting. In this phase, people need a great deal of emotional support from others and need help to deal rationally with the fact that they are going to die.

In the *chronic phase,* Pattison believes that individuals begin to confront directly their fear of dying. Fears about loneliness, suffering, separation from loved ones, and the unknown often surface. Health professionals can assist dying people by helping them put life into perspective, working through some of the defense mechanisms, and allowing open discussion of death and basic fears.

In the *terminal phase,* individuals begin to withdraw as their hope of getting better gives way to the realization that they are probably going to get worse. At the end of this phase, individuals turn inward, distancing themselves from people and everyday experience.

Just as Kübler-Ross's stages are neither fixed nor invariant for all people, Pattison's dying phases do not represent a single trajectory descriptive of every person's death; each person spends different amounts of time in each of the three phases. Some have questioned the need to describe the time spent in each phase of Pattison's dying trajectory, preferring to examine the process of dying; for some people dying is rapid and sudden with little time to prepare, for others it is preparation that lasts for years.

Marsall and Levy (1990) have considered that a dying person is involved in a dying career, which begins with the realization that one's time left to live is limited and finite. The dying careers of 17 people (21 to 71 years old) who were coping with AIDS were recently documented by McCain and Gramling (1992). The dying career was marked from the initial diagnosis of being HIV seropositive, through the diagnosis of AIDS, to impending death. McCain and Gramling (1992) identified three processes involved in the dying career: (1) living with dying, (2) fighting the sickness, and (3) getting worn out. Each of us begins his or her dying career from the time that we realize emotionally that we are mortal, like all human beings. As each generation dies before us (i.e., great-grandparents, grandparents, and parents) we come to understand that our own time is drawing closer. With the death of parents, we have no one left to stand before us. We understand that our generation's death is next and our dying career is reaching its end.

COMMUNICATION: LISTENING TO THE DYING PERSON

Often friends and family are unable to listen and communicate with the dying person in an accepting way. This inability to talk honestly isolates the dying person at a time when it would be most helpful to be able to express thoughts and feelings. For Kalish (1985) the advantages of an open-awareness context for dying persons include (1) closing life in accord with their own ideas about proper dying, (2) completing plans and projects, making arrangements for survivors, and participating in decisions about a funeral and burial, (3) conversing and reminiscing with others who have been important in their lives, and (4) having better understanding of what is happening within their

Open Communication with the Dying Person

My 81-year-old aunt was extremely ill and had been for two years; the indications were that she would probably not live for many more weeks. My home was 800 miles away, but I was able to get to visit her and my uncle for a couple of days. It bothered me to see her hooked into a machine that held her life; the ugly wig she had worn during the past couple of years had been discarded, and there were only a few wisps of hair left, but at least they were hers. Her teeth had been placed in the drawer by her bed since she couldn't take solid food and at this point she was not concerned about how she looked.

My uncle and I were in her room talking with her as she moved in and out of awareness. He was standing at the foot of the bed and I was sitting next to her, holding her hand. He began to talk to her about coming to visit me as soon as she could get up and around again, probably next summer. I noticed that she tuned his comments out. Then I found a pretext to get him out of the room.

When we were alone, I stood up and kissed her, I'd like to say that it was easy, but it really wasn't. I told her that I loved her, and I realized that I had never said that to her before, hadn't even thought about it, hadn't even consciously thought that I loved her. I just . . . loved her.

Then I said, "Bea, I have to leave now. I may never see you again, and I want you to know how much I love you." Her eyes were closed and she was breathing strangely, but she winced at my words, and I became frightened that I'd said too much, so I hesitated. "Well, I hope that I'll see you again, but I might not." And I left.

She died before I could visit again, and I always wondered whether I should have said what I did, but it seemed important to say it. Even if it pained her to hear me, she knew it was true, and she had not shrunk from painful situations before. It had been easy for me over many years to talk and write about death and dying, but it was very difficult for me to be in the situation where someone I loved was dying. I did what I have told other people to do, and it wasn't at all natural—I had to force myself. But when I heard, three weeks later, that she had died, I considered myself fortunate to have had the chance to be with her before she died and to have been both caring and honest. (p. 172)

bodies and the treatments being received. It may be easier to die when people we love can converse freely with us about what is happening, even if it entails considerable sadness. Research Focus 13.4 describes a circumstance in which open communication with a dying person occurs and proves beneficial.

For the dying person, external accomplishments and continued achievements become less likely or important. The focus of communication thus needs to be directed more at internal processes, past experiences, endearing memories, and personal successes. A caring relationship is a very important aspect of the dying person's life. But such caring does not have to come from a mental health professional; a concerned nurse, an attentive physician, an interested member of the clergy, a sensitive spouse, or a caring friend all provide important communication resources for the dying person. In such interactions and communications, we want to emphasize the person's strengths and help them prepare for the remainder of life. In one investigation, hospital-based adult volunteers who were assisting families in coping with impending death and subsequent bereavement were surveyed about the care and management dying persons received. The volunteers felt that the illness and the person's death had been very well managed when appropriate caring relationships and open communication had been established among involved family members, health care professionals, and the dying person (Couldrick, 1992).

Likewise, the need for open disclosure of dying is vitally important and has an impact among the institutionalized elderly (Lavigne-Pley & Levesque, 1992). Older individuals who are institutionalized do not want to be kept in the dark regarding the

The Denial of Dying

Denial can be a protective mechanism that enables people to cope with the torturous feelings that accompany the realization that they are going to die. People who are dying can either deny the existence of information about their impending death or they can reinterpret the meaning of the information to avoid its negative implications. There are three forms of denial (Weisman, 1972). The first involves the denial of facts. For example, a woman who has been told by her physician that a scheduled operation is for cancer believes that the operation is for a benign tumor. The second form of denial involves implications. A man accepts the fact that he has a disease but denies that it will end in death. A third form of denial involves extinction, which is limited to people who accept a diagnosis and its implications but still act as if they were going to live through the ordeal. This last form of denial does not apply to people whose deep religious convictions include some form of belief in immortality.

Another classification includes the categories of *brittle* and *adaptive denial*. Brittle denial involves anxiety and agitation. The individual often rejects attempts to improve his or her psychological adaptation to impending death. However, adaptive denial occurs when the individual decides not to dwell on this aspect of his or her life but to emphasize strengths and opportunities during what remains of life. Adaptive deniers want help and support. Such adaptive denial fits well with the ideas of perceived control and the elimination of learned helplessness.

In discussing the role of denial, Richard Kalish (1981) concluded that denial can be adaptive, maladaptive, or even both at the same time. One can call on denial to avoid the destructive impact of shock by delaying the necessity of dealing with one's death. Further, denial can insulate a person from coping with feelings of anger and hurt, emotions that may intrude on other behaviors and feelings because they are so intense.

---

condition of roommates, acquaintances, or friends who reside with them. Of 25 institutionalized elderly in one exploratory investigation, 21 reported that they wanted to be informed of the impending death of a close peer. When asked if the institutional staff had provided or withheld this information in the past, 20 of the 25 residents reported having an experience in which the staff did not communicate with them that a peer was dying (Lavigne-Pley & Levesque, 1992). One of the consequences of withholding information about the impeding death of a close peer is that residents believed that the staff who cared for them were essentially indifferent to the death of an elderly person (Lavigne-Pley & Levesque, 1992).

DENIAL OF DEATH

Not all people close to death can communicate honestly and openly. Denial is characteristic of some individuals' approach to death. In fact, it is not unusual for some dying individuals to continue to deny death right to the end. Denial serves to protect people from the reality that they will soon die and provides a measure of hopefulness. Research Focus 13.5 describes denial in coping with impending death. While some psychologists believe that denying death until the very end may be adaptive, others report a negative relationship between denial and the acceptance of death in a peaceful and dignified way (Shneidman, 1992).

Denial of death takes many forms. Refusing to acknowledge the implications of a disease or a life-threatening situation is one form of denial. For example, a man scheduled for an operation for cancer of the colon denies the facts and may believe that the operation is only for benign polyps. Or a person may accept the presence of a severe kidney disease but deny its life-threatening consequences. Some individuals, while accepting the concept of biological death, deny their own mortality. Many older adults maintain faith in their spiritual immortality. Feifel (1990) suggests that accepting our mortality is a key to self-knowledge.

Denial can be used adaptively to delay dealing with one's death and thus delay the shock, and it can insulate an individual from having to cope with intense feelings of anger and hurt. But denial can have maladaptive features if it is used exclusively or persistently to distort reality. For example, it may keep us from seeking medical diagnosis and treatment when life-threatening symptoms appear, or it may block communication and other forms of adjustment to dying.

The use of denial must be evaluated in terms of its adaptive qualities for the individual. Taylor and her colleagues (1992) have reported that denial and active distortion were characteristic of a group of gay men, all of whom had tested HIV positive. Compared with a group of gay men who had not tested positive for the virus, those who were HIV positive believed that they would not develop AIDS, despite the evidence that they were carrying the virus. Taylor and her colleagues (1992) suggest that such "unrealistic optimism" helped these men cope with the predictable progression of the disease . . . and ultimately death. Denial, avoidance, and active distortion are common among people facing the inevitability of death. Such strategies help people cope and actively manage the stress that is related to the knowledge that their own death is inevitable.

Coping well with dying is not necessarily age-related. It appears that the elderly more frequently must face loss, death, and their own mortality. The elderly are certainly a highly heterogeneous group whose level of comfort with their own death depends on a number of significant variables other than simply age (Feifel, 1990). While coping with death for many involves some elements of denial, there are other older persons who turn to religious beliefs, prayer, and spiritual faith. The homebound elderly are particularly likely to turn to prayer in coping with death, especially when they are uncertain about an afterlife (Fry, 1990). Corr (1992) believes that coping with dying should be approached from a task-based perspective. The coping tasks identified for the dying include coming to terms with four dimensions: the spiritual, the social, the psychological, and the physical. While many find solace, help, and hope through religion and spirituality, there are others who find little comfort in such institutions and beliefs.

WHERE WE DIE

More and more persons in the United States and Canada are dying at home. The majority of individuals, when asked where they would want to die, indicate a preference to be at home; very few young adults asked to imagine their death scene actually visualize themselves dying in a hospital (Kastenbaum & Norman, 1990).

However, dying people do feel they may be a burden at home, recognize the problem of limited space, and know they may place undue stress on family members. Those who are dying also worry about the competency and availability of emergency medical treatment if they remain at home. Hospitals offer certain advantages to the dying person and the family: professional staff members who are available around the clock and access to advanced medical equipment. Yet a hospital may not be the best location for the dying person to engage in meaningful, intimate relationships or to retain autonomy.

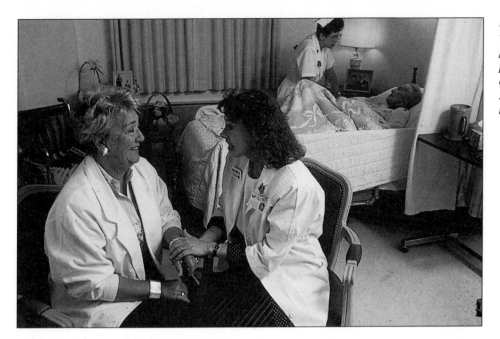

Hospice volunteers and professional staff provide comfort, counseling, and support to family members.

Dying at home, often under the watchful eye of a hospice program, is a choice many elderly individuals elect, despite the requirements for extensive medical care, nursing skills, and their failing condition (Levine, 1995).

HOSPICE PROGRAMS

The hospice provides an alternative to those who are dying. Hospice programs blend institutional care and home care while providing innovations designed to humanize the end-of-life experience for the terminally ill individual and all who interact with this person. Hospice permits the community to face death and for the dying to receive social support directly from those who can add to the remainder of their lives (Kastenbaum, 1993). Hospice programs today increasingly are home-based, although earlier they were largely delivered through hospitals or other institutional environments.

The hospice movement has attracted interest among health care providers in the United States. In 1990 there were nearly 2,000 hospices nationwide and by 1993 more than 200 additional new programs serve more than 1 million people in total (Hanrahan & Luchins, 1995; Levine, 1995). The hospice program emanates from the pioneering work in London, England, of Dr. Cicely Saunders, medical director of St. Christopher's Hospice (Saunders, 1977). Hospices in England are separate inpatient facilities, while 90 percent of those in the United States provide patient services at home (Levine, 1995). When medical treatments are no longer effective and when hospitalization is inappropriate, the hospice may be chosen and medical insurance applied to the cost of care. Medicare-approved hospice coverage has established criteria requiring that two physicians indicate a prognosis of death within six months and written documentation that the patient chooses this care over standard Medicare benefits (Hanrahan & Luchins, 1995; Levine, 1995). Patients who live more than six months must be recertified for eligibility, although the average length of hospice stay is only 64 days (Levine, 1995). Virtually all costs of patient care are covered by Medicare for those who are eligible. In 1994, Medicare provided hospice care benefits of nearly $1.2 billion (Levine, 1995). All hospice patients sign forms indicating that they understand that the treatment they will receive is *palliative,* that is, directed at controlling their pain and physical symptoms, not designed to cure them of their terminal illness. Most hospice patients have cancer (84%) with the remainder suffering from heart disease and AIDS (Levine, 1995).

Hospice programs have two goals: (1) the control of pain for dying individuals, and (2) the creation of an open, intimate, and supportive environment to share the ending of life with loved ones and staff members. Hospice teams consist of health care professionals, lawyers, mental health professionals, members of the clergy, and community volunteers, many of whom have experienced the benefits of hospice programs in their own families. Hospice team members visit patients in their homes and provide helpful services such as assisting with personal care needs, routine household tasks, cooking meals, or listening to the patient and other family members (Levine, 1995). The hospice goal is to maintain the humanity, dignity, independence, and personal identity of each dying individual. Pain control is under the direction of the patient and medications that preserve alertness are used, whenever possible. Patients do not need to wait until they are overwhelmed with pain to receive assistance. Pain medications can be self-administered or self-requested so that the person is kept in control. In one hospice program, pain was managed by the dying person, using standing physician orders for drugs that were self-administered in conjunction with both staff assessments of consciousness and a log or pain diary that was kept (McCracken & Gerdsen, 1991). In the hospice, the dying patient remains an integral part of his or her family. The family is welcomed at any time and the entire staff is trained and skilled in death education and counseling. Staff not only help the patient but also help the family in discussing their feelings over the impending death, the meaning of the loss, and the significance of the dying person in their own lives.

McCracken and Gerdsen (1991) described one hospice program that promotes a "comfortable and satisfying death" by administering care and support tailored to three phases of death: (1) realization of terminal status, (2) imminent death, and (3) **postvention** following death, that is, intervention with survivors up to one year after the person's death. Staff regularly provide psychosocial assessments of the needs of the dying person and the family, paying special attention to their emotional needs and day-to-day problems. All are preparing for the actual death, and staff members provide special support at that time. The formalized postvention bereavement program that extends for up to one year is an important component of this program. Postvention programs help survivors to come to terms with their feelings. Postvention assistance includes conducting a memorial service, providing educational literature, encouraging identification and discussion of feelings, and attending support group meetings (McCracken & Gerdsen, 1991).

Many hospice programs also provide counseling and support to staff members, who themselves need a regular opportunity to share their feelings. Brody et al. (1997) note that dealing with death takes its toll on health care professionals in a variety of settings. Professionals and volunteers experience a range of emotions including frustration, anger, disappointment, and deep feelings of loss and "burnout," which must be dealt with regularly through counseling and intervention. Robbins (1992) found that volunteers in hospice programs derive benefits from the training, support, and experience in managing death. In her investigation, hospice volunteers, compared with controls who were hospital volunteers, displayed strong beliefs that their hospice work made them more capable and competent in dealing with death. Robbins (1992) also found that hospice volunteers who were most experienced (four years or more) were better able to cope with death, as evidenced by their scores on a Coping with Death Scale, than volunteers who had less hospice involvement (two to four years) or recent trainees (less than two years). In a similar vein, nursing home workers have been reported to be more able to manage death and death anxiety as a function of their contact and experience with death and dying than a matched comparison group without such work experience (DePaola, Neimeyer, Lupfer, & Fiedler, 1992).

The hospice program encompasses a philosophy of care for the terminally ill that has already helped to humanize the care of dying patients in all contexts (Hayslip & Leon, 1988; Kastenbaum, 1993; Hanrahan & Luchins, 1995). Despite agreement on the underlying philosophy of hospice care, however, programs may differ substantially in actual practice. For example, some hospice programs will provide services, personnel, and support, as needed, in the dying person's home, while other programs do not offer such support. And within individual programs, hospice staff themselves may not uniformly agree on fundamental issues such as: (1) the appropriateness of hospice treatment for all terminally ill people or (2) the degree to which dying persons should have control over their own lives (Hanrahan & Luchins, 1995; Rinaldi & Kearl, 1990).

Hanrahan and Luchins (1995) recently surveyed nearly 1,700 hospice programs nationwide to determine the extent to which programs were available for persons with end-stage dementia, including Alzheimer's disease. From the responses of 70 percent of the programs it was determined that there were few programs for people with end-stage dementia, unless other terminal illnesses were present. Less than 1 percent of hospice patients were diagnosed with end-stage dementia as the primary condition and only 21 percent of the hospice programs surveyed served these patients. However, 7 percent of hospice patients carried a diagnosis of dementia that was secondary to a terminal illness and 56 percent of the hospice programs served such patients. Survey responses indicated that the major reason for limiting hospice program access to those with end-stage dementia diagnosis was the uncertainty by physicians in making a prognosis of death within six months (Hanrahan & Luchins, 1995). A second reason cited for limited hospice program access to end-stage dementia is the likelihood that needs would be greater than the resources of hospice programs.

To date, only a few research studies have been conducted on the effects of hospice care on recipients, relatives or friends, and hospice staff (Hanrahan & Luchins, 1995; McCracken & Gerdsen, 1991; Rinaldi & Kearl, 1990; Robbins, 1992). Cancer patients receiving hospice care show less anxiety, less depression, less hostility, and more acceptance of the efforts of the staff than patients in traditional treatments in hospitals. Patients appreciate the chance to talk about death, which may help reduce the guilt of family members and lead to more satisfaction with the treatment provided (Lack & Buckingham, 1978). More recently Kazanjian (1997) found wide-ranging individual differences among hospice patients that may mitigate against simple group studies in the future. For example, hospice patients with greater ego strength and spiritual strength were best able to cope with their own death and personal loss than those with lesser strengths. And those hospice patients with both higher ego and spiritual strength showed a greater ability to overcome their basic fear of death. In another investigation, Reese and Brown (1997) reported that spirituality was the most frequently addressed topic of home hospice visits, and death anxiety was the second most common topic. This study highlights the underlying importance of both spiritual and psychosocial concerns of hospice patients and their family members. Volunteers and staff need to be aware and concerned for these dimensions in supporting patients in hospice programs.

Hospice programs are a cost-effective option for insurance providers. Some hospice programs have become physically subsumed within hospitals. It may be possible to provide hospice services on a separate floor or ward of a hospital, but there are risks in maintaining the integrity and distinctiveness of the program (DeSpelder & Strickland, 1992). With hospice treatment covered under Medicare, both hospitals and health maintenance organizations have a strong financial incentive to incorporate these programs into their services.

COPING WITH THE DEATH OF A LOVED ONE

To everything there is a season, and a time to every purpose under heaven. A time to live and a time to die . . .
—Ecclesiastes

Loss comes in many forms in our lives—a divorce, the death of a pet, the loss of a job. No loss, however, is greater than the loss that comes from the death of someone we love—a parent, a sibling, a spouse, a relative, or a friend. In rating life stresses, the death of a spouse is consistently identified as the most stressful life experience.

Significant loss can lead to bereavement, grief, and mourning (Kastenbaum, 1993). The term **bereaved** describes the status of a person who survives the death of a loved one. **Grief** refers to the feelings associated with loss and usually encompasses the deep sorrow, anger, guilt, and confusion that often accompany a loss. The process of grieving is considered essential to full recovery from the loss of a significant person in our life. Grief is one of the most powerful of human feelings and produces intense emotional pain and suffering. **Mourning** is the overt behavioral manifestation of grief by the bereaved as defined by cultural, social, and religious custom. Mourning is expressed in various rituals—how we dress, what burial customs we follow, whether we say prayers, and so forth. Our reactions to death are influenced by a host of demographic factors, including age, gender, culture, family background and social class, as well as a host of dynamic factors, which include faith and religious commitment, physical and emotional health, support networks, and our own personal insight and understanding of grief itself.

The members of this Tibetan family are conducting a ritualistic ceremony as a memorial on the first anniversary of the death of a loved one.

FORMS OF MOURNING AND THE FUNERAL

There are many cultural differences in mourning. For example, **sati** is the ancient and infrequently practiced Hindu ritual of burning a dead man's widow alive to increase his family's prestige, enhance the importance of the village, and create an image of the widow as a goddess in whose memory prayers will be offered at the site of the funeral pyre. Other cultures hold a ceremonial meal for the mourners; in still others, mourners wear black armbands for one year following a death. In the United States, the funeral offers a variety of options through which survivors can express their loss. Table 13.3 describes some of the different religious practices adopted in dealing with death.

The funeral industry has been charged with taking advantage of the bereaved at a time when they are most vulnerable. Undertakers have offered expensive but needless rituals, services, and goods to those who can ill-afford such luxuries. Many states now require "truth in services" at the time funeral arrangements are being made and the Federal Trade Commission in 1994 developed standard definitions for specific funeral practices: (1) a funeral ceremony is a service commemorating the deceased with the body present; (2) a memorial service is a ceremony commemorating the deceased without the body present; and (3) an immediate burial is a disposition of human remains without formal viewing, visitation, or ceremony with the body present, except for a grave-side service. The bereaved must be informed in writing of the exact charges for each specific funeral expense (see table 13.4 for the average funeral costs, goods, and services to understand more completely the range of charges incurred [Federal Trade

TABLE 13.3

Funerals of Different Religions: A Summary of Practices and Customs

At times we all wish to provide comfort and support to friends, coworkers, neighbors, and others in our communities who have experienced a death. We are sometimes unfamiliar with the religious practices or customs to be followed at funerals, concerned about behaving inappropriately, and anxious not to feel out of place. Often our concerns keep us away from the funeral or house of mourning when those who are bereaved would most appreciate our presence. Sweet (1994) has provided a succinct summary of some of the traditions that take place in various religions in hopes of breaking down some of the barriers for those who would like to offer their support and comfort. Knowing some of these funeral customs may make the expression of support more appropriate and consistent with the customs of the mourners. They will be appreciative of your respect and understanding of their faith.

Islam

Traditional Muslim custom is to bury the dead as soon as practically possible and ideally within 24 hours. The brief funeral service occurs in a mosque and is marked by readings from the Koran and ritual chanting by the Imam or religious leader. In the mosque, people will remove their shoes and sit on the floor; women are expected to wear loose-fitting clothes as well as a scarf, veil, or head covering, and the sexes will be physically kept apart from each other in separate sections. At the conclusion of the service each person files past the body and pays their last respects. A brief burial service is conducted at the cemetery and people then return to the mosque for additional prayers and to express condolences to the family. Family members wear black and after burial, at the conclusion of services, a family meal is eaten at the mosque. Sending flowers and sympathy cards is appropriate.

Hindu

Hindu custom is to conduct a funeral service before sundown of the day of the death. This service is held at a funeral home and conducted by the firstborn son. At the funeral service family members will wear white out of respect and others in attendance are expected to wear dark clothes (e.g., without bright colors). Family members may individually place flowers upon the deceased. All Hindus are cremated, and following the cremation a brief service will occur. Family members enter a period of formal grieving for at least 13 days or more depending on their caste. Flowers may be sent to the family in mourning.

Christianity

Protestant faiths conduct a service for the deceased at a funeral home or sometimes at a church. The funeral service usually occurs within three days from the death and is conducted by a minister. The family will hold visiting hours at the funeral home each day and/or evening before the day of the funeral service. The corpse is embalmed and the casket opened during visiting hours. Family members may wear black or dark clothing, but rarely will cover their heads. There is growing participation from family and friends in the funeral service; those at the service are asked in advance of their attendance if they wish to participate. Visitors are not obligated to participate, although there may be a time set aside for personal testimonials and vignettes that reflect on the life of the deceased. Sending flowers, cards, and offering gifts to charities in the name of the deceased is appropriate.

Roman Catholic faith usually conducts a funeral service in the church, although the body may be viewed first in a funeral home before being transported in a hearse for the church service. At the funeral home brief prayers lasting about 15 minutes will be offered by a priest. The body is embalmed, and the casket remains open for viewing the deceased at the funeral home. Visitors present may participate or out of respect simply sit quietly until the service is concluded rather than exiting while prayers are being offered. At the church, mourners and visitors of the Catholic faith will bow at the knee when they enter, a practice that others should not follow. All who are in attendance at the service should stand at appropriate times, kneeling is not obligatory; only those of the Catholic faith will go forward to take communion from the priest. Only family members and those who are extremely close to the family will join the family at the cemetery for burial. Sending flowers, cards, and offering gifts to charities in the name of the deceased is appropriate. And Catholics may purchase mass cards, which may be displayed at the funeral home or the home of the family of the deceased.

TABLE 13.3 (CONTINUED)

Buddhism

Buddhist funerals are conducted in a funeral home and only rarely in a temple. The funeral home is arranged with a low table upon which are candles and incense that burn until the body is moved to the cemetery for burial. Friends and family participate in viewing of the body for one evening only, the night prior to the funeral. The family is seated at the front of the room close by the casket, which is open for viewing. The immediate family wears white to show their grief, and other family members and visitors may wear black to express their respect. After meeting with the immediate family to offer condolences, visitors go directly to the casket and bow before viewing the body. The deceased wears new clothes and shoes (shoes are to be removed only when entering a Buddhist temple). People may stay in the viewing room for a little while, seated or standing, and then quietly depart. The following day a funeral service is conducted by a monk. At the service men and women may sit together and will hear special prayers and chanting; visitors are not expected to participate in the funeral service. As a group, visitors will participate at the end of the service and congregate in front of the casket and bow together in a final show of respect for the deceased.

Judaism

Jewish funerals are expected to be conducted as soon as possible following death, usually within 24 hours. The family of the deceased recognizes support from extended family and visitors through their attendance at the funeral service held at either a Jewish temple or funeral home and at a brief service that occurs at the cemetery. Judaism has three distinct branches, each with somewhat different religious practices at the funeral service. Orthodoxy, for example, requires men and women to sit separately and to wear a head covering (a skullcap called a yarmulke or keppah), Conservative practice is to have men and women sit together and only men cover their heads, and Reform practice is to permit both sexes to sit together and people to choose whether or not to cover their heads.

Appropriate head covering is provided at the funeral and cemetery service for all in attendance appropriate to the branch of Judaism followed. Immediate family members will wear a sign of mourning such as a small piece of black fabric that has been cut and attached to a shirt, blouse, or jacket or will wear some article of clothing that has been similarly cut, such as a tie or collar. Mourners wear dark clothes, and visitors are expected to do the same.

Traditional Jewish practice does not permit an open casket, but this has become more a matter of family choice than a matter of doctrine in recent times. Cremation has generally been frowned upon by traditional Jewish practice, but it is not prohibited.

At the cemetery it is customary that family and close relatives shovel some of the earth on the casket so that each mourner has a share in the burial and a private moment marking their separation from the deceased. Mourners may wash their hands after the burial either at the cemetery or before entering the home to mark the end of one phase of life and the beginning of the next phase (i.e., life without the deceased). The burial service is followed by a meal, prepared and served by friends and extended family to the mourners out of respect to their loss, at the home of an immediate family member. The immediate family also receives visitors during a week of shiva which occurs in the home of a surviving spouse or another member of the immediate family. Regular prayers are to be recited daily in the synagogue or temple for many months by close family members. The family's loss is central, and only after actual burial occurs is it appropriate to visit the family personally or telephone them. It is also not appropriate to send flowers to the family or to the funeral home. To show one's support and respect for the deceased and the family it is acceptable to make a donation to the family's preferred charity in the name of the deceased.

Source: Sweet, L. (1994). In memoriam . . . a user's guide on how to behave at funerals of different faiths. Toronto Star, August 27, p. A10.

Commission, 1994]). An average funeral costs more than $4,287. This estimate does not include the fees and costs for the clergy, limousine, flowers, newspaper notices, cemetery fees or burial plot, and a burial marker (Mulder, 1997). The funeral industry projects increases in costs of 5 percent per year. Figure 13.4 shows these increasing costs for the period from 1992 to 1996; there was 17 percent increase in costs over this four-year period.

TABLE 13.4

Itemization of Funeral Services and Merchandise (1996)

Average Cost of Services and Merchandise

Funeral Home Expenses and Mortician Charges

1. Direct Cremation, $1,320. This charge includes transfer of remains to funeral home, required authorizations, services of funeral director and staff, unfinished wooden box or heavy cardboard container, transportation of the body to local crematory, and return of the remains to the funeral home. The direct cremation charges do not include the crematory charge of approximately $240.
2. Direct Burial Costs, $1,650. This charge includes an immediate burial, transfer of remains to funeral home, required authorizations, funeral services and staff, and transportation of the body to local area cemetery. The charge also includes the least expensive casket @ $675 (cloth-covered hardwood) but does not reflect cemetery charges or preparation-of-remains charges.
3. Preparation of Remains, $920. This includes charges for embalming ($350), use of preparation room ($110), topical disinfectant ($95), hair dressing, casketing, cosmetology ($125), and visitation and viewing ($240).
4. Arrangements and Supervision, $969. Funeral director, staff, equipment, and facilities needed to respond to initial request for service, arrangement conference, coordination of service plan, and final disposition of the deceased. These are nondeclinable professional services provided by the funeral director and staff during visitation (two days), funeral service, and grave-side ceremony.
5. Charge for Facilities, $400. Use of funeral home for visitation (two days) and funeral service.
6. Funeral at Another Facility, $235.
7. Memorial Service, $360.
8. Cemetery or Graveside Service, $600.
9. Hearse (local), $150.
10. Limousine or flower vehicle, (local), $120.
11. Merchandise Charge for select hardwood casket ($1,865–2,897) and charge for outer interment receptacle, liner, or vault ($850).
12. Additional Services and Merchandise, $155. Charges for memorial cards, acknowledgment cards, register book, death notices, and cemetery equipment.
13. Copies of Death Certificate, $20 per copy.

Cemetery Expenses

1. Internment Costs, $425. Opening and closing of grave, rental and setting up chairs, replacement of grass, administrative fees.
2. Cemetery Plot, $200–2,000. Costs vary greatly by location and size (e.g., individual, couple, or family plot).
3. Above-ground mausoleum: Indoor ($2,500 minimum) and outdoor ($1,500 and higher).
4. Perpetual Maintenance, $425. Costs to maintain the cemetery and grave sites (lawnmowing, road upkeep, etc).
5. Marker, Memorial, or Monument $500–6,000. Costs vary depending on size, material, and artwork: bronze marker ($450–500) and upright stone monument ($1,800–6,000).
6. Bronze urn to hold a single cremated remains, $230–1,800.

Source: National Funeral Directors Association. (1997). Average funeral costs rise 17% from 1992 to 1996, *Syracuse Herald American,* June 29, 1997, p. D4.

Because it is difficult for the bereaved to make funeral decisions, some elderly individuals are deciding in advance exactly what funeral arrangements they wish to have. Funeral homes have adopted **prior-to-need (or preneed)** funeral plans so that survivors may be spared the difficulty of making and paying for such services at a time when they are intensely grieving. Cemeteries also have their own preneed plans to cover the cost of burial expenses. More and more people have opted for prior-to-need arrangements. In one study, more than a million people over 65 years of age purchased such arrangements for themselves in 1990 in the United States (American Association of

Funeral costs

The average cost of a funeral for an adult has risen 17 percent in five years.

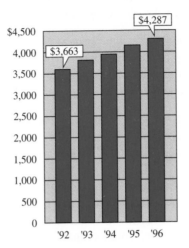

$4,500

4,000 — $3,663

3,500

3,000

2,500

2,000

1,500

1,000

500

0

'92 '93 '94 '95 '96

$4,287

Source: Federated Funeral Directors of America

Figure 13.4
Average funeral costs rise 17% from 1992 to 1996.
Source: Syracuse Herald American Sunday, June 29, 1997. p. 04

Retired Persons [AARP], 1992). Most bodies in the United States are placed in caskets in the ground or in mausoleums; in-ground burial adds about $1,000 to $2,000 in cemetery charges (National Funeral Directors Association [NFDA], 1997). About 20 percent of those who die are cremated, with Florida and California reporting nearly 25 percent (NFDA, 1997). Individuals who are cremated typically have their ashes spread in the crematorium's garden; others have their ashes taken to specific locations. Cremation societies offer to provide all such arrangements for a lesser fee than funeral directors. Some people prefer to donate their bodies to medical schools for research (AARP, 1988, 1992). A viewing of the body occurs in about 84 percent of deaths, a practice that many experts concur helps avoid denial (NFDA, 1997). Obviously, having an open casket is a personal choice for families and raises additional costs as funeral directors must perform such services as embalming, applying facial makeup, and preparing the body. Though the funeral industry has been charged with exploiting the bereaved in the purchase of unnecessary services and merchandise, other factors may also come into play, including a sense of guilt on the part of survivors, their reluctance to ask about various options, and their desire to bury their loved one "in style." Nationwide the funeral industry is undergoing merger and consolidation with four large corporations currently owning about 20 percent of the more than 24,000 individual funeral homes (Mulder, 1997). The largest of these companies is Service Corporation International with annual revenues of $2.29 billion. The companies continue to aggressively purchase independent funeral homes, leaving the local name in place since most families prefer to do business with the same home that they have always used. The companies anticipate continued growth, acquisitions, profitability, and higher revenues as our society enters the "golden age of funeral service" over the next three decades (Mulder, 1997).

THE GRIEVING PROCESS

Researchers have identified several phases of grief. However, validation of each phase has been controversial. One view suggests there are three phases of grief: shock, despair, and recovery (Worden, 1982). Another identifies four phases (Parkes, 1970, 1972):

- Numbness—downplaying the significance of the loss
- Yearning—attempting to recover or search for the person we have lost
- Disorganization and despair—accepting and no longer pining over the loss
- Reorganization—recovery from the loss

It appears that the first phase of grief is marked by feelings of shock, disbelief, numbness, and considerable weeping and agitation. This stage occurs very soon after the death and usually lasts no more than three days. Survivors may experience faint, panic, and even shriek or moan.

During the second phase, survivors feel a painful longing for the dead, and memories and visual images of the deceased are often on their minds. People actually experience hallucinations and report seeing, hearing, being held, kissing, touching, and even talking to the deceased. Survivors feel intense psychological pain. The desire to recover the dead is very strong, and some may even contemplate suicide as a way to rejoin their loved one. Insomnia, compulsive pacing or walking, intense sadness, irritability, and restlessness are common. Private conversations, fantasies, and dreams of the deceased are also characteristic of this phase. If such responses persist and survivors continue to ignore reality, the grief process may be difficult to complete. This phase emerges soon after death, peaks two to four weeks later, and may subside after several months but can persist for as long as one or two years.

The third phase is the realistic appraisal of what the loss means. It is characterized by the separation reaction of survivors, which produces both disorganization and despair as it becomes clear that the deceased is no longer physically close and will never return. Common responses include heightened anxiety and fear for one's safety and protection. Survivors may even express anger toward the deceased for leaving them and making them experience such sorrow, or they may channel their anger (displaced aggression) toward health professionals who cared for the dead. Finally, in this phase, the experience of guilt occurs (Stephenson, 1985). Survivors may regret what they did not do for or say to the deceased. They may even feel that if they had acted more quickly, recognized the signs of serious illness earlier, or found a better physician or hospital, then the death would not have happened. Guilt may also appear in a form of idealization or sanctification (Lopata, 1979), in which a spouse identifies only the most positive image of a mate who has died. The dead spouse's faults are ignored and their strengths overdramatized. The deceased is remembered without flaws or human weaknesses; they are recalled with only positive emotion and wonderful memories.

The last phase (reorganization and recovery) usually occurs within a year after the death. It is marked by a resumption of ordinary activities, a greater likelihood that the deceased will be recalled with pleasant but realistic memories, and the resumption of social relationships—maintaining ongoing friendships as well as establishing new ones. One component of this phase is the survivor's identification with the deceased.

In the case of a young person dying of AIDS, an AIDS quilt serves as a concrete tie between victims and survivors dealing with the grief and sorrow that accompanies such untimely deaths.

Identification involves adopting the personal traits, behaviors, speech, mannerisms, gestures, habits, and concerns of the deceased (Stephenson, 1985). Worden (1982) first noted that through such identification the dead person becomes a part of the mourner, internalized so that the dead person is still a part of the living. This too is a necessary part of grieving and helps to pave the way for continuing life. At this point, survivors realize that they can continue to live without the dead. They recognize the sources of pleasure, love, and support derived from relatives, friends, and community.

Grief is a powerful emotion. Therapists and counselors recognize the immense energy that must be expended to arrive at some resolution of loss. The term *grief work* is an apt description of the intensity and duration of this process. It is difficult, all-consuming, and pervasive work for those who mourn (Worden, 1982). Some experts believe that dying persons grieve as they anticipate their own death. As people begin to face their death from terminal illnesses or chronic conditions, they actually begin to grieve, express sorrow, and feel intense sadness over their own loss, the loss of their self. Family, relatives, and friends often note the depression, hopelessness, and isolation of persons as they anticipate their own death (Shneidman, 1992).

OUTCOMES OF THE GRIEVING PROCESS

Grief can be experienced in many ways—as anger, guilt, or idealization. One of the most common is through **grief pangs.** These feelings include somatic distress occurring in waves and lasting 20 minutes to an hour, a tight feeling in the throat, shortness of breath, the need to sigh, an empty feeling in the stomach, lack of physical strength, tension, sobbing, or crying. The sadness and deep sorrow that grieving people experience are sufficient to meet the criteria for clinical depression or physical illness. Research has shown that the experience of intense grief produces heightened levels of corticosteroids (hormones), which may account, in part, for the psychological and physical symptoms of grief. It has also been reported that among the recently bereaved, the rate of death and the incidence of serious illness are dramatically higher (Stephenson, 1985). Kalish (1985) speculates that this may be the result of psychological stress, the impact of the loss, and the cumulative effects of the physical stress of caretaking and visiting the hospital, all of which lead to inadequate sleep, exercise, and poor nutrition.

Resolution of grief leads to a renewal of interest in living and in the self. Often after a year or so, people come to terms with the death and begin to make major decisions affecting their lives. To emphasize that life must continue, they may repaint a room, buy new furniture, or travel. Regression may also be a consequence of mourning; some people need to return to an earlier stage to gather their resources and try to cope with loss. In addition, grief work may be arrested and remain incomplete as individuals deny their loss, their feelings, and their need to bring resolution to their grief. Experts have reported the existence of **delayed grief reactions** in some personal histories. Delayed grief emerges long after the deaths of those we love. It may emerge as a heightened reaction to the death of someone we barely know, of a relative with whom we were not very close, or even of the loss of a family pet (see Research Focus 13.6).

At special times that remind us of a loss, we may experience an **anniversary reaction.** On birthdays, at family gatherings, on holidays, or on the anniversary date of the person's death, we may feel particularly lonely and yearn for the relationship we have lost. One form of grief, **anticipatory grief,** actually begins prior to death. This form is the anticipation of a death that is virtually guaranteed to occur. The grief work may begin weeks or months in advance of the actual death. Interestingly, there is no evidence that anticipatory grief makes adapting to the actual loss easier (Stephenson, 1985).

MAKING SENSE OUT OF THE WORLD

One of the most important aspects of grieving is that it stimulates many people to try to make sense of their world and to search for new meanings in life (Lieberman & Peskin, 1992). In a study of recently bereaved spouses, 27 percent reported themselves

The Delayed Grief Reaction

John Dacy, psychologist, professor at Boston College, and author has allowed us to share a particularly tragic encounter with delayed grief reaction from his own life. In a discussion of grief, he related the following story:

> I would like to relate an experience of mine that seems relevant to this question about the role of grief. In April 1957, I joined the United States Navy and sailed to the Mediterranean for a six-month tour of duty on an oil supply ship. In early November I returned home to a joyful reunion with my family. After this wonderful weekend at home, I returned to my ship. Two days later I received a telegram informing me of a tragedy: my mother, two younger brothers and two younger sisters had been killed in a fire that had destroyed our house. My father and four other brothers and sisters had escaped with burns.
>
> On the long train ride home from the naval port, I recall thinking that, as the oldest, I should be especially helpful to my father in the terrible time ahead. I was also aware of a curious absence of dismay in myself. In our upstate New York town, the catastrophe was unprecedented, and expressions of grief and condolence were myriad. People kept saying to me, "Don't try to be so brave, it's good for you to let yourself cry." And I tried to, but it just wouldn't come.
>
> At the funeral, the caskets were closed, and I can remember thinking that maybe, just maybe, this was all just a horrible dream. I distinctly remember one fantasy about my brother Mike, who was born on my first birthday and with whom I had recently become especially close. I imagined that he had actually hit his head trying to escape, and wandered off to Chicago with a case of amnesia, and no one was willing to admit that they didn't know where he was. I knew this wasn't true, but I secretly clung to the possibility. After a very difficult period of time, our family gradually began a new life. Many people generously helped us, and eventually the memories faded.
>
> Several times in the years that followed, I went to doctors because of a stomach ache, a painful stiff neck, or some other malady, which couldn't be diagnosed physically. One doctor suggested that I might be suffering from an unresolved subconscious problem, but I doubted it.
>
> Then one night in 1972, fifteen years after the fire, I was watching the original version of *The Waltons* on TV, the episode in which the father is lost at Christmas. Although dissimilar from my own experience, this tragedy triggered an incredible response in me. Suddenly it occurred to me, "My God, half my family is really gone forever!" I began sobbing and could not stop for over three hours. When I finally stopped, I felt weak and empty, relieved of an awful burden. In the days that followed I believe I went through a clear-cut "delayed grief" reaction. Therefore, the answer to the question above, at least in my experience, is clear: grief work really is essential, and we avoid it only at the cost of even greater pain. My father died recently, and my reaction was immediate and intense. I cannot help but feel that my emotional response this time was considerably more appropriate and healthy.

to have grown from the experience as indexed by having created new ways of responding, new methods of completing tasks, thinking about the self differently, and discovering components of their individual identity in the process of grieving. Edmonds and Hooker (1992) published an investigation in which 49 college students, all of whom had recently experienced the death of a close family member, were asked to complete measures assessing their grief-distress as well as the significance of the loss in terms of its personal meaning (existential), its religious meaning, and its meaning in terms of life goals. A significant inverse relationship was found between level of grief and personal or existential meaning. Further, college students indicated a positive change in life goals as well as a correlated change in existential meaning of the loss. The higher the levels of grief experienced, the more likely that students refined their religious beliefs. The authors concluded that bereavement can bring about positive changes in one's life, and grief itself may be an impetus for individual growth in the search for the personal or existential meaning of the loss (Edmonds & Hooker, 1992).

Grief is an overwhelming emotion with which younger individuals have little prior experience. It is particularly difficult to grieve alone or in secrecy. Yet, in recent years, death due to AIDS has led to such private grief, which offers little help, since it often cannot be fully shared with other friends or family (Ascher, 1993). Without the opportunity to talk, experience, and fully explore the range of emotions that are associated with the loss, friends and relatives of those who have died of AIDS remain remorseful over a long period of time. They often ruminate over the years in which a gulf distanced the loved one from themselves. As Ascher (1993) notes, grieving for those who die of AIDS means realizing that it is too late to ever re-create the years of separation and too late to "remedy failed love."

Whether we are young or old, coping with death is difficult. Age itself is of little benefit, as can be seen in the description that Richard Kalish (1981) has written of the process of searching for personal (existential) meaning:

> A common occurrence during the grieving period is to go over, again and again, all the events that led up to the death. This can become a virtual preoccupation with some individuals, but almost all of us partake of it to some extent. In the days and weeks after the death, the closest family members will share experiences with each other—sometimes providing new information and insights into the person who died, sometimes reminiscing over familiar experiences. . . .
>
> When a death is caused by an accident or a disaster, the effort to make sense of it is pursued more vigorously. As added pieces of news come trickling in, they are integrated into the puzzle. The bereaved want to put the death into a perspective that they can understand—divine intervention, a curse from a neighboring tribe, a logical sequence of cause and effect, or whatever it may be. . . .
>
> Eventually each of us finds an adequate "story of the dying and death"—of our father, mother, or of a friend. Versions of the death may differ—whether the physician really did all she could to save the patient, whether Aunt Bella showed up frequently at the hospital or not, whether the operation succeeded or didn't quite succeed, whether Father was ready to die or would have lived longer if possible—but each person's version satisfies him [or her] and that version, with slight modifications, becomes the official version for the teller. (pp. 227–228)

TYPES OF DEATH THAT ARE DIFFICULT TO RESOLVE

Coping with death is never easy. However, some deaths are more difficult to resolve than others. According to Richard Kalish (1985), some of the most problematic deaths include:

- Suicides or deaths due to self-neglect
- Unexpected deaths, such as deaths of young people, those recently married, or those close to achieving significant goals
- Deaths that forced the bereaved to care for the dying person in a manner that proved to be distressing
- Deaths in which the bereaved believes he or she was partly or fully responsible, such as a child's drowning in a swimming pool
- Homicides

- Unconfirmed deaths with no body found
- Deaths so drawn out over time that the survivors become impatient for death to occur

In the remainder of this section, we briefly describe some of the types of deaths that place the greatest burden on our coping skills.

Death of a Young Child

The death of a young child produces such intense grief and is such a devastating loss that parents may not ever recover; local support groups for those who have experienced such a loss (parents, siblings, grandparents, friends, and relatives) are particularly helpful (Rando, 1991). The unexpected death of a child due to accident or the sudden onset of a disease is even more difficult. If the death is due to an accident, parents experience enormous guilt, accepting responsibility far in excess of what is appropriate. When the death is anticipated, parents are encouraged to be honest and open with their child rather than engaging in mutual pretense (Stephenson, 1985). Parents may alleviate the child's fears of loneliness, separation, and pain rather than trying to have the child understand the concept of death itself. Parents are usually encouraged to begin the process of anticipatory grief work.

Death of an Adult Child

The death of an adult child for an elderly parent can also be devastating (DeSpelder & Strickland, 1992; Moss & Moss, 1995; Goodman, Rubinstein, Alexander, & Luborsky, 1991). It is unexpected for a parent to survive a child, and for some older parents it is the most difficult death to accept—generating fears of isolation, insecurity regarding their own care, as well as intense guilt and anger over the loss of a lifetime identity as parent (DeSpelder & Strickland, 1992). The loss of an adult child is at least as intense as that of the loss of a spouse or one's own parent (Moss & Moss, 1995). Some research investigators have found that the death of an adult child leads to more intense grief (e.g., despair, guilt, anger, anxiety and symptoms of physical illness) than the deaths of a spouse or parent. Insurance industry statistics indicate that as many as 25 percent of women over the age of 65 with an adult son will have to cope with the death of their adult child (Moss & Moss, 1995).

Cultural differences in how elderly women (61 to 93 years of age) coped with the death of an adult child were reported by Goodman and colleagues (1991). Jewish women in the study appeared to be more grief-stricken and more depressed than non-Jewish women in having lost a fundamental role, focus, and identity in their lives. Among Protestant and Catholic women, the investigators found somewhat more acceptance and an ability to place the death of their adult child into a larger perspective so that they could move beyond the loss and continue with their own lives (Goodman et al., 1991).

Quantitative indicators of well-being, affect, generativity, and personality showed Jewish women to be far more intense in openly expressing the meaning of the death of an adult child and their personal loss than Protestant or Catholic women.

Perhaps the concept of afterlife among the Christian women served to ease the pain of the loss more than for Jewish women. Clearly culture, ethnicity, and religion play an important role in determining the quality and strength of the mother-child bond, which in turn influences the coping responses to the death of an adult child.

Moss and Moss (1995) have identified six major themes underlying the death of an adult child: (1) the untimeliness of the death and its destruction of parents' world-view; (2) the loss of the bond established between child and parent and the threat to a major component of parental identity (e.g., the protective parent); (3) intense survivor guilt; (4) disequilibrium and strain in the parents' marital relationship and relationships with other children as well as the children of the deceased child; (5) loss of social and instrumental support in old age (e.g., someone to share, help, and provide for the parents especially in times of need) and (6) change in meaning for the future with generativity needs unfulfilled and incomplete.

Death of a Sibling

The death of a sibling is difficult to resolve. Brothers and sisters not only feel the loss deeply, but there may also be cognitive distortions as to the meaning of the loss. Because the parents are intensely grieving, siblings may not have much support to deal with their feelings.

The death of an adult sibling is a normative experience for many elderly persons (Moss & Moss, 1995; Perkins & Harris, 1990), so it is curious that this type of loss has received so little research attention. It appears that neither clinicians, relatives, or friends truly appreciate the significance of the loss, the depth of the attachment bond, or the importance of grief expression among older persons who have lost a sibling (Moss & Moss, 1995). Sibling bonds represent the family bond of longest duration (Bedford, 1995). Following the death of a sibling, brothers and sisters feel a strengthening of the tie to the deceased and reminisce with surviving siblings to build solace, comfort, and renewal. It is as if ties with the deceased sibling are preserved in the relationship with surviving brothers and sisters (Moss & Moss, 1995). In some studies it appears that ties with the children and spouse of a deceased sibling are strengthened. In many cases the deceased sibling has served as a role model or standard of comparison, a major contributor to another brother or sister's sense of self; such losses are hard to accept. Moss and Moss (1995) also note that whenever a same-aged peer or relative dies, the sense of one's own "shortened distance" to death is heightened. Siblings may anticipate similar health patterns, similar life endings, and similar life expectancies.

Death of a Parent

The death of a parent shows persistent long-term effects whether it occurs in childhood, adolescence, or adulthood. Children are faced with separation and loss as well as a reduction in the love, affection, and attention they have received. Parental death often means other significant life changes such as moving, reduction in standard of living, changes in friends, and stepparenting. Krause (1993) has recently identified that early parental loss has lifelong effects persisting well into old age. When young children experience the death of a parent, they often have no one to replace the lost parent; in single-parent families they usually assume adult roles, including work and financial support, far earlier than children from two-parent, intact homes. Krause (1991a, 1991b) has already shown that the financial strain experienced and the increased social isolation have deleterious effects well into late adulthood. Among a sample of 519 older adults participating, Krause (1993) provided support for a model showing that early parental loss was related to lower levels of educational attainment, leading to financial difficulties later in life and ultimately contributing to a reduced sense of personal control in late adulthood.

Even for middle-aged or older adults, the death of a parent is an enormous loss. The way in which survivors cope emotionally following the death of any close relative such as a parent has been studied using depression as the primary outcome variable. However, an index of depression or depressive symptoms is not the same as an index of grief (Moss & Moss, 1995). Grief can involve preoccupation with the parent, intense loneliness, and periods of crying without necessarily indicating depression. In one investigation the relationship between grief expression and social-cultural roles was studied (Klapper, Moss, Moss, & Rubinstein, 1994). A form of **selfish grief** was identified in which daughters were reluctant to display outward, visible signs of emotional expression following the death of their mothers. Rather than expressing their grief, the daughters believed that emotional displays such as crying or sobbing would reflect their personal wish to have their mothers still alive with them, but continuing the physical pain and suffering that their mothers experienced at the end of their lives. This tension between outward emotional expression of grief and the prolonging of a mothers' pain and suffering was experienced as selfish grief by these daughters and resolved by hiding or controlling the feelings that were a natural part of their loss (Klapper et al., 1994).

The death of an elderly parent can be somewhat less stressful than the death of a younger parent. There is some evidence that in the former instance, adult children have an opportunity to prepare themselves for the death as they witness parents becoming older and more frail (Moss & Moss, 1995; Norris & Murrell, 1990). Regardless of circumstances, most adult children believe that a parent who has died did not live long enough (Moss & Moss, 1995). The death of a parent signifies for adult children that there is no other older generation standing between them and death.

Death of a Spouse

The death of a spouse is one of the most common relationship losses among the elderly and leads to overwhelming bereavement and personal challenges (Blieszner & Hatvany, 1996; Lieberman & Peskin, 1992). Statistics suggest that by age 65, roughly 50 percent of the women in the United States are already widowed. By age 75, nearly 67 percent of all females and 25 percent of all males have experienced the death of a spouse (Meyers, 1990). Widows outnumber widowers by a 5:1 ratio (Lund, Caserta, & Dimond, 1993). Experts have begun to recognize that reactions to being widowed are dynamic and change over time. Surviving spouses have many different emotions existing simultaneously in response to being widowed (Blieszner & Hatvany, 1996; Lund et al., 1993). Widows and widowers must begin to confront themselves, their strengths and weaknesses, and their futures, which creates a heightened sense of the closeness of their own death (Lieberman & Peskin, 1992). Bereavement is not always debilitating, as we have discussed, and investigators are beginning to identify the "existential" growth that occurs among some surviving spouses (Lieberman, 1992; Parkes, 1993; Yalom & Lieberman, 1991).

The death of a spouse is usually unpreventable and may shatter a long-standing attachment bond. It requires the pursuit of new roles and status, leads to financial hardship, and leaves the survivor without a major support system (Blieszner & Hatvany, 1996; Lieberman & Peskin, 1992). Following the death of a spouse there is an increased risk of mortality, reduced protection from the immune system, and increased risk of various physical, health, and psychological disorders (Bradsher, Longino, Jackson, & Zimmerman, 1992; Parkes, 1993). Some research suggests that women have more depression and psychological difficulties than men in widowhood, but generally men and women experience similar levels of emotional grief from their loss (Blieszner & Hatvany, 1996). Among older widows who were engaged in continuous long-term care for a spouse, the death of that spouse brings relief from the physical, emotional, and intellectual demands of caretaking. In shedding the role of caregiver, widows may "reclaim" their identity and redefine their lives (Blieszner & Hatvany, 1996). Widows generally have the greatest difficulties in managing new roles, such as finances, insurance, home maintenance, lawn and garden care, and upkeep of the family car, and dealing with unbearable loneliness. Those who were most independent and in control during their marriage had less difficulties in widowhood and in managing their grief than widows who were highly dependent on their spouse for social contacts (Blieszner & Hatvany, 1996).

The loss of a partner for an older person has an impact in virtually every area of life. Parkes (1993) has noted that widowhood means the loss of a recreational partner, loss of a sexual partner, loss of a person to provide protection from danger, loss of a friend and companion, and loss of a reassuring partner who contributed to one's self-worth. Rosenbloom and Whittington (1993) found among recent widows that bereavement reactions and high levels of grief significantly changed the social meaning that eating played in their lives; that is, mealtime was no longer a social, shared, and emotionally satisfying experience. Widows found their loneliness particularly difficult to manage at mealtimes; widows found eating less pleasurable, ate less, and experienced significant reductions in nutrients, and lost weight—an average of 7.6 pounds. As the widows' grief diminished, these trends began to be reversed (Rosenbloom & Whittington, 1993). Bereavement has also been reported to be related to difficulty sleeping and in early morning awakening (Hoch, Buysse, Monk, & Reynolds, 1992). Such symptoms are also associated with depression.

Widows appear to provide considerable social support for each other, whereas widowers are often more isolated (Connidis & Davies, 1990a, 1990b). Note that living alone is not the same thing as being lonely or being socially isolated (O'Bryant & Hansson, 1995). Social support can be helpful in overcoming loneliness, but it cannot replace the loss of a significant interpersonal attachment bond (Levy, Martinkowski, & Derby, 1994).

Most widows experience a significant reduction in income and support following the death of their husbands. Widowers, on the other hand, must cope with new responsibilities in the home: cooking, doing laundry, cleaning, and coping with their personal sense of isolation (Kalish, 1985). Younger surviving spouses experience different kinds of adjustment problems than do surviving older spouses (Lund et al., 1993). Young survivors often deal with childrearing as single parents, cope with the demands of grandparents, and manage a work role as well as the complexities of new relationships. Older survivors must deal with the loss of security and support (physical, emotional, and financial) as well as manage the difficulty in maintaining social contacts. In the early phases of bereavement, younger surviving spouses appear to undergo far more intense grief reactions, whereas older surviving spouses show better earlier adjustment but more intense feelings of grief months later (Lund et al., 1993). Blieszner and Hatvany (1996) note that older widows seem to have fewer close social supports, seek less support, and have more health and adjustment problems than younger widows. Adjustment problems include depression, increasing physician consultations, hospitalization, increases in smoking and drinking, pathological grief reactions, nutritional deficits, and higher mortality rates (Parkes, 1993; Rosenbloom & Whittington, 1993). Among older adults, the loss of a spouse often occurs at the same time as other stressors associated with one's own aging. Surviving spouses may have to focus on multiple stressors during bereavement as families experience multiple losses and threats to their ongoing functioning (Blieszner & Hatvany, 1996).

Widowhood may be experienced in many diverse ways (Blieszner & Hatvany, 1996; Lopata, 1987b). Some widows are unable to reengage in social relations, and those friendships enjoyed with other couples may wane after the death of a spouse; however, others continue and even create new support systems and reimmerse themselves in their families, their neighborhoods, communities, occupations, or volunteer organizations. Generally a widowed spouse continues the pattern of social contact and social supports that have been established at points earlier in the life span, although these relationships may be redefined (Blieszner & Hatvany, 1996; Lieberman, Heller, & Mullan, 1990). Some widows are passive and accept the changes produced by the death of a husband. Others display personal abilities, long dormant, that may blossom in widowhood. Some widows remarry to overcome their loneliness and loss of attachment. Others prefer their new identities and growing independence. They have no interest in marriage and another experience of intense loss or providing care to a seriously ill partner (Blieszner & Hatvany, 1996; Lopata, 1994). Elderly widows will be more likely to change their residence when health and functional disability occur since they do not have the additional support from a spouse to manage the routine tasks of the household and chores of daily living (Bradsher et al., 1992).

Perhaps there is no predictable time period or orderly progression that governs widows' adjustment and grief (Blieszner & Hatvany, 1996). Grief appears to diminish in time. There is some evidence to suggest that adaptation to the death of a spouse generally occurs between one and four years after the loss (Blieszner & Hatvany, 1996). Survivors who had the most difficulty at the beginning of widowhood took longer to adjust (Blieszner & Hatvany, 1996). Research investigators believe that widows who derive significant social support, develop mastery over the social context in which they live, who are positive copers, and who have adjusted to life crises successfully in the past are the ones who actively manage the loss of a spouse in the most effective manner (Lieberman & Peskin, 1992; Parkes, 1993).

However, current interest is being directed at some results that challenge this conventional wisdom. In one study widows and widowers were evaluated who showed little grieving at the time of the death of a spouse (Lieberman & Peskin, 1992). This group showed no grief reactions either at the time of death or 12 months later, yet they were able to adapt successfully to the loss of a spouse. And they were the most well-adjusted widows when compared with others who grieved primarily at the time of death, throughout the 12-month period, or who showed delayed grief (Lieberman & Peskin, 1992).

Suicide

The impact of suicide on survivors is enormous, particularly for a surviving spouse. In many investigations, the impact of suicide on middle-aged and younger spouses appears to produce heightened, intense bereavement reactions such as denial, major depression, uncontrollable grief, physical symptoms requiring medical examination, and even hospitalization (Farberow, Gallagher-Thompson, Gilewski, & Thompson, 1992). These studies have focused on the immediate reaction to the suicide in short-term follow-ups and have not typically included older surviving spouses. Farberow et al. (1992) completed a two-and-a-half-year longitudinal investigation examining the impact of suicide among surviving spouses (55 years of age and older), similar-aged respondents who were coping with the natural death of their spouse, and married older persons who were still living. The longitudinal nature of the study confirmed that older surviving spouses experience lengthy and intense feelings of bereavement when compared with previous investigations of younger surviving spouses of suicide. Survivors of the natural death of their spouse showed gradual decline and relief from grief both 6 months following death and then again after 18 months. Grief reactions among those whose spouse had committed suicide, however, remained high consistently throughout the first year and did not show any appreciable decline until 18 months had passed. This extended period of grief was also seen in spousal survivors' negative ratings of their mental health, depression, and distress, which showed little improvement until a year after the suicide (Farberow et al., 1992). At the end of the 30 months of the study, both bereaved groups of older spouses were functioning at nearly similar levels and reported continued feelings of loss, isolation, and sadness as well as bereavement reactions such as grief, depression, anxiety, and alienation.

SUMMARY

Despite the inevitability of death, it remains an uncomfortable topic in our culture. Recent medical advances have made the determination of death complex. For example, brain death can occur even though critical organs like the heart and lungs continue to function. Today we are faced with ethical questions concerning the practice of euthanasia, physician-assisted suicide, and when we should prolong a person's life. Several states have enacted laws to determine when a dying person may not be resuscitated, the use of living wills, durable powers of attorney, health care proxy, and advance medical directives. Controversy continues over the definition of brain death and its relation to the process of death. Depending on what policy decisions need to be made about the process of death, competing definitions may be entirely acceptable.

It is important to consider the sociohistorical and sociocultural contexts of death. There is more avoidance and denial of death in American culture than in many other cultures. Experience and contact with death and dying may contribute to cultural differences and individual differences in attitudes toward death and dying. A growing emphasis on the importance of death education is emerging to help those facing death as well as those who have experienced the death of someone close to them.

Elisabeth Kübler-Ross suggested five psychological stages of dying: denial and isolation, anger, bargaining, depression, and acceptance. Researchers have been unable to verify that dying people go through the stages in the prescribed sequence; however, Kübler-Ross has contributed significantly to society's emphasis on humanizing the dying process. E. Mansell Pattison has suggested three phases of what he calls the living-dying interval: acute, chronic, and terminal. The dying process is multifaceted and involves much more than descriptive stages or phases; some have explored the dying career. Denial is an important aspect of the coping process for the dying person. For many dying people, denial may be helpful to their coping. An open system of communication with the dying is an optimal strategy for the dying person, staff, and family members. It is important to try and avoid stereotypes about dying and the aged. The dying person is a unique individual, with strengths and ongoing challenges to face. For those people near death and with limited ability to participate in their environment, it may be best to emphasize their own inner personal resources.

The contexts in which people die are also important to understand. Hospitals ensure medical expertise and sophisticated equipment, but more intimacy and autonomy is usually possible at home. Hospice represents a humanizing approach to those facing death. Hospice blends the benefits of home and hospital care. The hospice movement stresses patient control and management of pain as well as a philosophy based on open communication, family involvement, and extensive support services.

The loss of someone with whom we have developed enduring attachment bonds is among the most stressful of life events. Coping with the death of a loved one has been described in terms of bereavement—the state of loss—and mourning, the overt, behavioral expression of bereavement and grief—the most powerful of human emotions. Mourning takes many forms, depending on one's culture, ethnicity, and religious practices. In the United States, the mourning process usually involves a funeral, which is followed by burial or cremation. In recent years, controversy has arisen about the funeral industry, and steps have been taken to improve consumer understanding of its services, charges, and products.

Grief may be seen as a series of phases—shock, despair, and recovery. However, people do not have to go through each phase to cope adaptively with grief. One of the most common ways of experiencing grief is through grief pangs. Denial is also part of grief, just as it is part of the dying process. One aspect of grief is existential and involves making sense out of the world and trying to solve the puzzle of death. One of the most intense losses we can suffer is the death of a spouse. Longitudinal studies of bereavement in older surviving spouses shows how lengthy the process can be. Other difficult deaths to resolve include the death of a young child, the death of an adult child, the death of a sibling, and the death of a parent. Suicide has an immense impact on survivors, and bereavement among widows and widowers is both more intense and more extended than when death is self-inflicted.

REVIEW QUESTIONS

1. What is the definition of death?
2. Explain the difference between death and the process of dying.
3. In your view, in what situations should euthanasia be permitted?
4. Discuss the sociohistorical contexts of death.
5. What are common attitudes and beliefs about death in young childhood, adolescence, and early, middle, and late adulthood?
6. Describe and critically evaluate Kübler-Ross's five psychological stages of dying. Are these stages prescriptive or descriptive?
7. Describe how denial can affect the dying person.
8. What are some of the characteristics of bereavement? Discuss the role of funeral practices and rituals for the bereaved.
9. Describe the contexts in which people die—in hospitals, hospices programs, and at home—and include the benefits and disadvantages of each.
10. Outline the phases of grief that people go through. Discuss how people try to adapt to the loss of a loved one.
11. Discuss various forms of mourning and the practices of the modern funeral industry.

FOR FURTHER READING

Burnell, G. M. (1993). *Final choices: To live or die in an age of medical technology.* New York: Plenum Press.

Buckingham, R. W. (1996). *The Handbook of hospice care.* Amherst, NY: Prometheus Books.

Irish, D. P., Lundquist, K. F., & Nelson, V. K. (1993). *Ethnic variations in dying, death, and grief: Diversity in universality.* Bristol, PA: Taylor & Francis.

Johnson, C. L., & Barer, B. M. (1997). *Life beyond 85 years: The aura of survivorship.* New York: Springer.

Keyes, W. N. (1995). *Life, death, and the law: A sourcebook on autonomy and responsibility in medical ethics.* Springfield, IL: Charles C. Thomas.

King, N. M. P. (1996). *Making sense of advanced directives, revised edition.* Washington, DC: Georgetown University Press.

Lopata, H. Z., & Prosterman, A. C. (1996). *Current widowhood: Myths and realities.* Thousand Oaks, CA: Sage.

DEVELOPMENTAL RESEARCH METHODS

INTRODUCTION

Imagine that you are a researcher studying whether creativity declines with age. How should you proceed? You suspect that many opinions about aging and the decline of creativity are rooted in negative prejudices and stereotypes of the aged or that they are based on socially accepted behavior standards for people of different ages. You are interested in obtaining objective, scientific evidence on creativity across the life span. How should you proceed?

One approach might be simply to ask people of different ages to rate their creativity (using a seven-point scale, e.g.). But your goal is to gather objective, scientific data on creativity, not subjective impressions that doubtlessly are influenced by conventional wisdom as well as the egos of your participants. Another approach might be to collect ratings on people's creativity from friends and relatives. This might solve the ego problem, but conventional wisdom and subjective judgments would remain troublesome factors. Moreover, how well can friends and relatives judge a person's creativity? (Do your friends and relatives know exactly how creative you are?) Another approach might be to use a questionnaire or structured interview. Rather than simply asking people about their creativity, you might ask them about a variety of items such as lifestyle (are they unconventional?), work habits (do they waste many idle hours until spurred by a creative burst?), and motivations (do they enjoy following orders and being told what to do, or do they prefer to set their own tasks and goals?). Responses could be scored or weighted for creativity, and a total creativity score derived. Unfortunately, participants might guess the purpose of your study and try to produce answers that appear creative.

Perhaps it would be better to test people's ability to find creative solutions to problems rather than to ask them about creativity. Indeed, it might be useful to find a standardized test of creative problem solving that many samples of people have taken. This approach seems promising, but you must ensure the reliability and validity of your creativity test. Does the test give consistent estimates of creativity if the same individual is tested twice? This demonstrates *reliability*. Does the test truly measure creativity, or simply intelligence? This question involves *validity*.

Even if a test shows high reliability and validity with young adults, the test might not be as reliable and valid for elderly people. Further, age differences in creative problem solving might not reflect age per se, but, rather, extraneous factors such as educational background or health. Some of these factors might be controlled by a longitudinal design, testing the same individuals every 10 years from ages 20 to 70. But do you have 50 years to complete your study? And how many of the participants you test today will still be available 50 years from now?

The problem of extraneous factors and the difficulty of conducting longitudinal designs might lead you to use archival or historical data. For example, you might investigate the typical ages at which people have produced great artistic or scientific achievements. Unfortunately, the evidence provided by archival investigations is highly indirect; many factors in addition to creativity determine at what age someone might produce a great artistic or scientific accomplishment. (Indeed, it is arguable that many social and cultural factors, including conventional wisdom about aging and creativity, may influence the time course of creative achievement in adults.) Further, the accuracy and completeness of archival data are always concerns.

Faced with all of these problems, you might wish to use animal models in your research. With animals, it is possible to control many factors (diet, experiences in infancy, etc.) that cannot be controlled in humans. Also, many animals have a relatively brief life span, making longitudinal research more feasible. But how do you devise a creativity test that animals can complete? And can results obtained with animals be generalized to humans?

What, then, should you do to investigate aging and creativity? There is no one right answer—only alternative approaches with varying advantages and disadvantages. Furthermore, there is ample room for your own creativity in selecting, combining, and even modifying approaches to suit your own research goals. Indeed, the need for creativity in science is an integral part of its challenge and appeal.

Since the fundamental task of science is measurement (Shaughnessy & Zechmeister, 1996), we begin this chapter with a discussion of two basic issues involved in measurement: the reliability of measurements and the validity of measurements. Then we discuss several basic techniques used for collecting observations: the structured interview and questionnaire, standardized tests, and behavioral research. Next, we'll consider some of the basic ways to describe and interpret measurements. Then we'll explore the topic of research design, considering first simple correlational designs and then more powerful experimental designs. We also discuss the role played by quasi-experimental designs in developmental research. The appendix closes with a section on sampling, a critical problem in all psychological research but particularly important in research on adult development and aging.

BASIC ISSUES OF MEASUREMENT

Measurement—a major task of science—sounds simple. However, to make accurate and meaningful measurements is far from simple. Let's look at two basic issues we must consider when making scientific measurements.

Reliability of Measures

Suppose you are assisting on a research project focusing on age changes in **reaction time,** the amount of time it takes to respond to a simple stimulus. You are asked to construct a task that will measure the reaction times of all the adults participating in this research study. After a great deal of thought, you develop the following reaction-time task. You ask participants to sit individually at tables and you place a set of earphones on each of their heads. Directly in front of each participant on the table is a telegraph key. You tell the participants that every now and then they will hear a beeping sound delivered to both ears via the earphones. You instruct the participants to press the telegraph key as quickly as possible whenever they hear a beep. Within this context, you define reaction time as the amount of time it takes a participant to press the key after the beep has initially sounded. Furthermore, you decide to measure the participants' reaction times by using a handheld stopwatch that measures time in hundredths of seconds. You plan to start the watch when the participant hears the beep (you will also wear a pair of earphones connected to the same sound source as those worn by each participant). And you plan to stop the watch when the participant presses the key.

Suppose that you tell the principal investigator of the research project about your plan to measure reaction time. You assume that she will be very impressed with the task you have developed. However, she seems very concerned about the reliability of your measure. What exactly is the principal investigator worried about? How can you reassure her? Essentially, the concept of **reliability** refers to the degree to which measurement is consistent, stable, and accurate over time. Given your inexperience at measuring reaction time, there are many reasons why the measurements you collect might be inconsistent and unstable. For example, were all of the participants instructed to press the button by using the index finger on their preferred hand? Did some of the participants position their fingers directly on top of the telegraph key before some of the trials but place their fingers on the table before some of the other trials? If the participants positioned their fingers in different locations before each trial, you would collect very unreliable data. (Remember, you want to measure the time it takes to press the key, not the time it takes to move your finger to the key and then press the key!) Also, when did you plan to begin measuring the participants' response times—as soon as they begin to perform the reaction-time task or after several practice trials? Until a participant becomes familiar with the experimental task and apparatus, his or her reaction times could vary considerably from trial to trial. Finally, the principal investigator may wonder how accurately you can measure reaction time by using a hand-held stop watch. Is it possible for you to start your watch at the exact split-second the beep sounds and stop the watch at the exact instant the participant depresses the telegraph key? Even if you could accurately measure reaction time at the beginning of the experimental session (which is extremely doubtful), might you become increasingly tired, bored, and/or absent-minded as you measured more and more reaction times. As you can now see, there are several points to consider in measuring reaction time reliably. Other types of measurement can pose much greater problems of reliability. Suppose, for example, that you were asked to determine an adult's IQ or measure the life satisfaction of an elderly adult using a (standardized measure of life satisfaction). How reliable would your estimations be? How many sources of measurement error would exist? Obviously, reliability of measurement can frequently be questioned in behavioral research.

Assessing Reliability   How can we assess the reliability of various measures? There are a variety of techniques, but all are based on the assumption that reliable observations are repeatable.

Test-retest reliability can be assessed by obtaining the same set of measurements on two different occasions. The question is whether measurements (frequently numerical scores of some kind) on occasion 2 are predictable from observations gathered on occasion 1. Thus, after a familiarization period, we could administer 100 reaction-time trials to participants on day 1 and 100 trials on day 2; if the test is reliable, we should be able to compute the reliability of the participants' reaction times. Of course, test-retest reliability is meaningful only when the variable we are measuring is assumed to be stable over time. Were we observing the momentary moods of individuals, we probably would not wish to assess test-retest reliability. For example, if a person were judged to be happy on day 1 and sad on day 2, this need not imply low test reliability. It could simply mean that the person's mood had changed.

Interrater reliability should be assessed whenever measurements involve a subjective, judgmental component. This is frequently the case in studies where observational data are collected. The technique is simply to use two or more observers independently, then assess the agreement among these observers. High agreement implies high reliability.

Interitem reliability can be examined whenever measurements entail multiple items. A common procedure for assessing interitem reliability is to divide the items into halves (for instance, the odd-numbered items versus the even-numbered items) and to determine the extent to which measurements (average scores) on one half are predictable from measurements on the other half. High predictability implies high reliability.

Ways of Improving Reliability   How do we improve the reliability of measurements? One method is to take many different measures of the same individual or behavior. However, an even better way is to refine and standardize the procedures and tools used for measurement. In our initial example of measuring reaction time, we could improve reliability by making multiple assessments of reaction time, particularly if the assessments were made by different research assistants. It obviously would also be helpful to use a carefully planned and standardized set of procedures for assessing reaction time (e.g., instructing participants to place the index finger of their preferred hand on the telegraph key). Finally, the use of high-precision equipment would be beneficial (a computer with an internal clock could be programmed to record the exact time—in milliseconds—between the onset of the beep and the depression of the key). Future scientific advances should ultimately provide the refinements and standardization needed to produce truly reliable measures of physical, intellectual, and social behaviors.

Reliability is a concern in all psychological research. However, reliability problems are particularly bothersome in developmental research, especially when individual differences are at issue. If a group of people is given an IQ test at age 18 and again at age 45, it is probable that some individuals will show gains from the first test to the second, whereas others will show losses. Are there true differences between the gainers and the losers in intelligence, or are we simply seeing the effects of an unreliable measuring instrument? Although statistical methods can be applied to this problem, reliability remains questionable. Furthermore, envision a situation where every person tested at age 45 scores exactly 10 points higher on the IQ test than they scored at age 18. Since we could exactly predict a person's IQ at age 45 from his or her IQ at age 18, we would conclude that the test used to measure IQ is highly reliable—it possesses a perfect level of test-retest reliability. However, it is obvious that not one of our participants has the same IQ score at both times of testing, making the test's stability questionable. Therefore, since the concept of reliability entails both the predictability and the stability of measurements, separate measures of predictability and stability should be developed and used.

Validity of Measurement

In our example of measuring reaction time, the principal investigator questioned the reliability (essentially, the repeatability) of the measurement. What if she also doubted the **validity** of the measure itself? A measure is valid if it actually measures what it purports to measure. The measure of reaction time, therefore, is valid if it really measures the amount of time it takes adults to make a simple motor response once they hear a sound. The principal investigator might suggest that the task you developed to measure reaction time could actually measure how well participants can hear the beep rather than react to it. If older adults have trouble hearing, they will have difficulty reacting to the beep. Thus, to make certain that the measure of reaction time is valid, all of the prospective participants in the study will have to be screened for auditory sensitivity.

Although there are many different types of validity, the type we are currently addressing is **construct validity.** Constructs are abstract entities that cannot be directly observed but are presumed to influence observable phenomena. Intelligence is a construct; so are anxiety, creativity, memory, self-esteem, and other aspects of personality and cognition. We often attempt to observe phenomena that we believe might reflect these constructs. The question of whether the observed phenomena actually do reflect the constructs is the issue of construct validity.

Even when observations are highly reliable, they do not necessarily imply high construct validity. Were we to devise a test of creativity, we might be able to demonstrate high test-retest reliability as well as high interitem reliability. However, the test could still be vulnerable to the charge that it really measures intelligence, not creativity—or to the charge that creativity may not even truly exist.

Students of adult development and aging must consider whether a given test or measurement might have reasonable construct validity for young adults but not for elderly people. For example, a test of long-term memory might be reasonably valid for college students who are accustomed to memory tests. But the same test might be intimidating to elderly people who might not have taken a memory test for decades. Hence, the performance of elderly people might reflect anxiety more than memory per se.

Basic Techniques Used for Collecting Measurements

Psychologists collect data in a number of ways to test hypotheses about adult development. In this section, we discuss the salient features of these different techniques.

Interviews and Questionnaires

Many inquiries on adult development have been based on the techniques of interview and questionnaire. An **interview** is a set of questions asked face-to-face. The interview can range from being very structured to very unstructured. For example, a very unstructured interview might include open-ended questions such as, "Tell me about some of the things you do with your friends," or "Tell me about yourself." On the other hand, a very structured interview might question whether the respondent highly approves, moderately approves, moderately disapproves, or highly disapproves of his friends' use of drugs. Highly unstructured interviews, while often yielding valuable clinical insights, usually do not yield information suitable for research purposes. However, unstructured interview questions can be helpful in developing more focused interview questions for future efforts.

Structured interviews conducted by an experienced researcher can produce valuable data. However, structured interviews are not without problems. Perhaps the most critical of these problems involves the response bias of social desirability. In a face-to-face situation, where anonymity is impossible, a person's responses may reflect social desirability rather than her actual feelings or actions. In other words, a person may respond to gain the approval of the interviewer rather than say what she actually thinks. When asked about sexual relationships, for example, a person may not want to admit having had sexual intercourse on a casual basis. Skilled interviewing techniques and built-in questions designed to help eliminate such defenses are critical in obtaining accurate information in an interview.

Researchers are also able to question adults through surveys or questionnaires. A **questionnaire** is similar to a highly structured interview except that adults read the questions and mark their answers on a sheet of paper rather than responding orally to the interviewer. One major advantage of questionnaires is that they can easily be given to a very large number of people. A sample of responses from five thousand to ten thousand people is possible to obtain. However, a number of experts on measurement (Shaughnessy & Zechmeister, 1996) have pointed out that surveys and questionnaires have been badly abused instruments of inquiry. For example, survey items should be concrete, specific, and unambiguous; often they are not.

Another problem with both interviews and surveys or questionnaires is that some questions may be retrospective in nature; that is, they may require the participant to recall events or feelings that occurred at some point in the past. It is not unusual, for example, to interview older adults about experiences they had during adolescence or young adulthood. Unfortunately, retrospective interviews may be seriously affected by distortions in memory. It is exceedingly difficult to glean accurate information about the past from verbal reports. However, because of the importance of understanding retrospective verbal reports, 1978 Nobel Prize winner Herbert Simon and others are developing better ways to gain more accurate verbal assessments of the past (Ericsson & Simon, 1984).

Behavioral Research

Regardless of advances in our understanding of verbal reports, they probably will never be adequate, by themselves, as a basis for psychological research. Apart from problems of response set or memory, verbal reports obviously depend on conscious awareness. Yet many aspects of cognition, personality, and social behavior apparently are subconscious. Thus we must go beyond what people tell us about themselves and examine how they behave.

Behavioral research does not depend on participants' verbal reports regarding the issue under study. For example, a questionnaire might be based on verbal reports of memory problems as experienced by the elderly. In contrast, a behavioral study of memory might actually assess the accuracy of verbal recall by the elderly. (For instance, the researcher might present a list of words, followed by a test of verbal recall for these words.) Both approaches involve verbalization on the part of participants, but only the questionnaire involves verbalization about memory itself. Interestingly, evidence exists that indicates that reports of memory problems are not strongly associated with true deficits in performance on memory tasks. Marion Perlmutter has collected both questionnaire and performance data on memory in young and elderly adults. Overall, she found that older adults report more memory problems on a questionnaire and that they also perform more poorly on some (but not all) memory tasks. But reported memory problems have proved to be a poor basis for predicting actual memory performance in this type of research (Perlmutter, 1986). For example, a person reporting many memory problems might actually perform very well on a memory test, and vice versa.

Behavioral Research in Laboratory Versus Field Settings

In behavioral research, it is frequently necessary to control certain factors that might determine behavior but are not the focus of the inquiry. For example, if we are interested in studying long-term memory in different age groups, we might want to control motivation as well as the conditions of learning (study time, distracting noises, etc.). Even extraneous factors such as temperature and time of day might be important. Laboratories are places that allow considerable control over many extraneous factors. For this reason, behavioral research is frequently conducted in laboratories.

However, costs are also involved in conducting laboratory research, and some of these costs are especially high when developmental issues are being addressed. First, it is impossible to conduct research in a laboratory without letting the participants know they are in an experiment. This creates problems of reactivity. **Reactivity** occurs when participants think they should behave in a specific manner because they are in an experimental setting. Second, the laboratory setting is unnatural and might cause unnatural behavior on the part of participants. This problem can be particularly severe with elderly participants, who may find the laboratory setting even more unnatural than young adults do. Finally, certain phenomena, particularly social phenomena, are difficult if not impossible to produce in the laboratory. The effects of "job-related stress on marital satisfaction," for example, might be difficult (and unethical) to investigate in a laboratory setting.

Because of these problems with laboratory research, many psychologists are beginning to conduct field or observational research in real-world settings. Such settings can include job sites, shopping malls, senior citizen centers, nursing homes, or any other place where appropriate observations can be made. The main drawback of field research is limited control over extraneous factors. However, this drawback is frequently outweighed by the benefits of low reactivity, natural contexts, and access to interesting phenomena that are difficult to observe in the laboratory.

Though they are often presented as dichotomous, laboratory and field research are really two points on a continuum, a continuum that can be labeled naturalism versus control. If some laboratory experiments employ conditions or tasks of a decidedly natural character, these experiments belong in the middle area of the continuum. For example, a laboratory study of memory might examine recall of events from one's past. A laboratory study of social behavior might bring middle-aged parents and their adolescent offspring together to discuss problems in their family. Researchers find that many benefits of field studies can be enjoyed in the laboratory if the activities of the participants are to some degree natural. This is an important lesson for psychologists interested in adult development and aging. It is frequently necessary to collect data in a laboratory-like context (perhaps a simple room with few distracting stimuli). This does not mean that the tasks performed by participants must be unnatural and uninteresting. Such tasks might put elderly people who are unaccustomed to performing artificial and irrelevant tasks at an unfair advantage.

Laboratory Research with Animal Models

Although laboratory and field research can be thought of as two points on a continuum, laboratory research with human participants is not the end point of this continuum. The end point is laboratory research with animal participants, because such research allows far more control than is possible with humans. We can control an animal's genetic endowment, diet, experiences during infancy, and countless other factors that cannot be controlled when humans are studied. We can also investigate effects of treatments (e.g., brain lesions or restricted diet) that would be unethical to attempt with humans. Moreover, with some animals it is possible to track the entire life course in a very short period of time. (Laboratory mice live at most a few years.)

A major disadvantage of animal research is, of course, that it may well not generalize to humans. Indeed, many aspects of human development—language, for example—are simply impossible to study except with humans. Nevertheless, some aspects of animal development do generalize to humans and promise to teach us much about development across the life span. For example, there is an amazing degree of similarity in the structure and function of the brain in humans and rats. Furthermore, a team of researchers (Selkoe, Bell, Podlisny, Price, & Cork, 1987) have discovered that the same brain changes that accompany normal aging in humans (and abnormal aging such as Alzheimer's disease) occur in a wide variety of animals (e.g., rats, dogs, and polar bears) as well. This suggests that researchers may be able to construct animal models that will shed a great deal of light on both normal and pathological age-related changes in the human nervous system.

Standardized Tests

Standardized tests attempt to measure an individual's characteristics or abilities as compared with those of a large group of similar individuals. Such tests may take the forms of questionnaires, interviews, or behavioral tests. To maximize reliability, a good test should have a reasonably large number of items and should be given in an objective, standardized manner. The **standardization** of tests actually refers to two different qualities: the establishment of fixed or standard procedures for administration and scoring, and the establishment of norms for age, grade, race, sex, and so on. Norms are patterns or representative values for a group. Hence, the performance of an individual can be assessed relative to that of a comparison group (people of the same age, sex, etc.).

Many standardized tests have good reliability but their construct validity can be questioned. IQ tests, for example, show impressive reliability, but there is considerable uncertainty about what such tests actually measure. The problem is compounded by the possibility that a single test might measure different things at different ages—for example, an IQ test might measure intellectual ability in young adulthood but anxiety in old age. This possibility is critical in interpreting developmental research that shows that IQ performance can change with age.

There are standardized tests for intellectual functioning, for psychopathology or mental illness, for life satisfaction, creativity, and many other aspects of personality and cognition. Such tests are used for a wide variety of purposes and are invaluable in developmental research. However, when using any test, it is important to consider construct validity. That is, does the standardized test truly measure the construct in question, whether it is intelligence, creativity, or schizophrenia?

Physiological Research

There is no question that a biological level of analysis offers a great deal of information about adult development and aging. This is not to say that psychological and sociocultural factors are unimportant; indeed, there is good reason to believe that there are multiple determinants of adult development. Moreover, physiological factors and sociocultural factors interact during the course of adult development. Biological research frequently suggests strategies to remove or reverse certain types of behavioral change, which is sometimes desirable.

BASIC STRATEGIES FOR DESCRIBING AND INTERPRETING MEASUREMENTS

In most scientific studies, a vast number of measurements allow researchers to collect considerable amounts of raw data. For these data to be understood, they must be described and interpreted objectively. In this section, we summarize some of the statistical techniques that researchers use to make sense of raw data.

Measures of Central Tendency and Variability

Most people are familiar with the procedure of averaging. Given a set of n scores (where n refers to the total number of scores in a data set), we add their values and divide by n. The result is called the **mean,** which is by far the most common—but not the only—measure of **central tendency.** Another such measure is the **median,** which is a value in the middle of the distribution of scores (so that as many scores fall above the median as fall below it). The **mode** is the most frequently appearing score in the set.

Measures of central tendency such as the mean provide important but incomplete information. Reporting the mean score is like telling another person that the score of a baseball game is 3–1 but failing to tell the person which team is ahead and which inning it is. For this reason, we often need information on the variability of scores as well as their mean.

The simplest measure of **variability** is the **range,** which is a comparison between the lowest and highest scores in a data set. A much more meaningful measure of variability is the **standard deviation.** The standard deviation is a mathematical index of the degree to which every score in a distribution of scores differs from the mean score. The more the scores in a distribution vary from the mean, the larger the standard deviation. The less the scores in a distribution differ from the mean, the smaller the standard deviation.

Means and standard deviations are reported frequently in research on adult development. There are several reasons for this, but none is more important than the relevance of these measures to individual differences in the course of adult development. For example, it is possible that a group of young adults and a group of older adults would both remember the same mean number of items on a test of memory ability (each group could recognize, on average, 20 words from a list of 35). However, we might discover that the standard deviation for the older group was 7.4, while the standard deviation for the younger group was 3.1. These results would suggest that there is much more variability in the performance of older persons than in that of the younger persons. This important point would be obscured if the investigator only reported the mean score.

Correlation Between Variables

To understand the concept of correlation, one must first understand the meaning of the term **variable.** A variable is something that can vary—that is, take on different levels or values. Age, for example, is a variable because it can take on values between 0 and 100 years or more. Other common variables are IQ, height, weight, and years of education. Some variables can take only two different values (biological sex, e.g., can take on only male or female).

A **correlation** is a measure of the relationship or strength of association between two variables. During adulthood, for example, there is usually a correlation between a person's age and the number of grandchildren he or she has—generally, the older the adult, the greater the number of grandchildren.

Correlations can be either positive or negative. A **positive correlation** exists when high values of one variable are associated with high values of the other. During the adult years, the variables of age and onset of chronic illness are positively correlated—the older a person is, the more likely she is to develop a chronic illness such as arthritis. A **negative correlation** exists when high values of one variable are associated with low values of the other. In contemporary American society, there is a negative correlation between age and years of education; young adults in their thirties, on the average, have completed more years of formal education than older adults in their seventies and eighties. This is because of the relative lack of educational opportunity available to many individuals during the early part of the twentieth century. Remember that a positive correlation is not necessarily reflective of a "good" finding, nor is a negative correlation reflective of a "bad" finding. For example, there is obviously nothing "good" about the finding that as individuals grow older they are more likely to encounter a greater number of health problems.

Whether positive or negative, correlations can vary from weak to strong. A correlation is strong if the values of one variable are predictable from the values of the other. A perfect correlation exists when the values of one variable are perfectly predictable from the values of the other. The strength of a correlation can be measured quantitatively by computing the **Pearson product moment correlation coefficient,** which is abbreviated as r. A perfect correlation will yield an r of either $+1.0$ or -1.0, depending on whether the association between the variables is positive or negative. As the association becomes weaker, the r score drops in absolute value from 1.0 to .90, .60, .40, and so on, to 0.00. A correlation of 0.0 indicates that there is no relationship between the measures. Perfect correlations (1.0) are seldom obtained, but even moderate correlations (say, those with r values of .30 to .60) can be very meaningful.

An example should help illustrate the importance of correlations and how they can be interpreted. One study involved measurement of IQ on individuals at two points in their lives, once in late adolescence and again in middle age (Eichorn et al., 1981). The striking result was that IQ in late adolescence and IQ in middle age were strongly correlated, with r values of about $+.80$. Despite these high correlations, it was also true that about half of the participants showed changes of at least 10 points in IQ between the two testings. These IQ changes are at least as important as the stability in IQ implied by the high correlation.

To be sure, a strong correlation implies significant predictability of scores on one variable (IQ in middle age) from scores on another (IQ in adolescence). But significant predictability is not perfect stability. Even strong correlations allow for interesting discrepancies between the values on two variables.

Two final points need to be made about correlational analyses. First, measures of correlation, such as Pearson's r, reflect the strength of the **linear** association between variables. This is fine in many cases, but sometimes there are **curvilinear** associations between variables. For example, it doubtlessly is true that most people have little personal income in childhood but that their income increases and then falls again as they grow older. Such a curvilinear association between age and income cannot be measured by Pearson's r. Second, correlational techniques are typically used to measure the relationship between two variables at a time. Thus, we could examine the correlation between: IQ and income, income and years of education, and IQ and years of education. Correlational analyses are not usually called upon to examine how income and years of education, taken together, predict IQ scores.

Multiple Regression

Multiple regression is a powerful statistical method that allows an investigator to go beyond correlational analyses. Using this technique, a researcher can set up a complex model to determine whether a number of variables, in combination with one another (or independent of one another), predict another variable. For example, a psychologist could determine how age, years of education, social class, gender, and need for achievement predict IQ scores. And the psychologist could also find out whether age predicts IQ independent of years of education, social class, gender, and need for achievement. Finally, multiple regression may be used to measure curvilinear relationships. Thus, a regression model could be developed that describes the finding that marital satisfaction progressively declines as children move through adolescence but begins to increase once children leave home and attend college.

Factor Analysis

To understand adult development, it is sometimes necessary to examine many variables and to assess the pattern of correlations between these variables. For example, we might be interested in examining the variables of age with mathematical ability, creativity, health, income, occupational status, and life satisfaction. That would give us seven variables in all, among which there are 21 possible correlations. How do we make sense of so many correlations? How do we get a view of the forest, not just the trees?

Factor analysis can be useful for producing a kind of summary of many correlations. The goal is simply to reduce a large number of correlations to a smaller number of independent sets called factors. Put somewhat differently, the purpose of this procedure is to discover what variables are significantly correlated with one another but totally uncorrelated with all the other variables. For example, if health, exercise, life satisfaction, and income all correlated with one another but were mathematically independent of all of the other variables, we might want to say that these variables make up a factor that we could label as "general well-being" or "vigor." Through this process, we would replace four original variables with a single derived factor.

A potential problem with factors derived from patterns of correlations is their meaning. Once we identify and label a factor as representing x (well-being or vigor, e.g.), there is a tendency to believe that x truly exists (that there is, in fact, a separate "trait" of well-being or vigor and that people differ on this trait). In reality, a factor is only a summary of a pattern of correlations among variables. Our label for a factor is just that, a label. It can be wrong or misleading.

Significance Tests

Suppose we conducted a study to determine whether early retirement results in high levels of life satisfaction. We might ask a group of adults who opted for early retirement and a group of their age-mates who are still working to complete a standardized measure of life satisfaction. After collecting the data, we discover that the mean scores for the early retirees versus the workers were 101 and 77, respectively. At this point we might wonder if there is a significant difference between the two groups on the measure of life satisfaction. Or we might wonder if there is a significant relationship between the participants' work status (working versus retired) and their scores on the measure of life satisfaction.

To determine the **statistical significance** of the results of a research study, it is first necessary to determine the probability of obtaining the observed results by pure chance alone. This is accomplished by using any of a number of sophisticated statistical techniques. It is possible to determine mathematically the probability of getting the results we obtained in our study by chance. Although it is not within the scope of this text to show you how to obtain these probability estimates, you should know how these probability estimates are interpreted. If a researcher determined that the probability of obtaining the observed results by pure chance is 5/100 or less, she would conclude that the two groups in her study reflected differences so great that they are unlikely to have occurred by chance alone. Thus, differences this substantial would be viewed as "significant." Conversely, if the researcher determined that the probability of obtaining the observed results by chance is high (say 80/100 or more), she would conclude that the differences between the groups in her study were "not significant" and that the two groups responded in much the same way. Specifically, psychologists consider probabilities of 5/100 or less as indicative of statistical significance. To return to our original example, if we discovered that the probability of obtaining the observed differences between the workers and early retirees on the life satisfaction measure by pure chance was 1/100 or less, we would conclude that (1) the two groups differ significantly on their responses to the life satisfaction measure, and (2) there is a significant relationship between work status and life satisfaction.

BASIC STRATEGIES FOR RESEARCH DESIGN

In preparing to conduct a research project, it is especially important to consider design principles. The research design will determine the relationships assessed and/or the comparisons made. It will also determine how valid our conclusions can be. In general, there are two types of research designs: correlational and experimental designs.

Correlational Versus Experimental Strategies

It often is said that the experiment is the principal tool of any research scientist. Yet the vast majority of studies on adult development and aging are not true experiments; rather, they are correlational studies. What is the difference between the two? Why are correlational strategies so often used to study development? Do developmental researchers pay a price for not performing true experiments?

A **correlational study** is one in which associations among variables are merely observed. An **experimental study** also assesses associations among variables; but, in an experiment, a distinction is made between dependent variables, which are measured or observed, and independent variables, which the experimenter manipulates. Thus, both the manipulation of independent variables and the observation of dependent variables are the critical features of experiments.

A concrete example may help to clarify the differences between a correlational versus an experimental study. Suppose we develop the hypothesis that living in a dull, nondemanding social environment causes a deterioration in the memories of older adults, whereas living in a stimulating, demanding social environment causes older adults to maintain their memories. We could investigate this hypothesis by conducting a correlational study. This might entail administering a standardized test of memory to two groups of older adults who live in two different types of environments: a nondemanding environment (perhaps a nursing home), and a demanding environment (living independently at home and being actively involved in a senior citizens center, doing volunteer work, etc.). From this study we might discover that the level of demand or challenge in the social environment is positively correlated with memory performance—that is, as the demands of the environment increase, participants' scores on the memory test increase. Regardless of the strength of this correlation, however, we could not conclude that changes in the environment cause differences in memory. It may be that older people who remember and think well are likely to choose to live at home, while people who have more difficulty remembering and who are not self-sufficient wind up in nursing homes. Thus, it could be that the ability to remember determines the type of environment in which a person lives, rather than vice versa. The real purpose of a correlational study is to make accurate predictions (not to determine cause-effect relationships). For example, from this study we could predict that people who live in nursing homes often have poor memories, but we would not know why they have poor memories.

To determine cause-and-effect relationships, it is necessary to perform an experimental study. To conduct an experimental study, it is necessary to manipulate an **independent variable.** Ellen Langer and her associates (Langer, Rodin, Beck, Weinman, and Spitzer, 1979) conducted an experimental study that bears on the hypothesis described in the preceding paragraph. The investigators randomly divided a sample of the residents of a nursing home into different groups or conditions. In the contingent condition, residents were told that they would be visited several times during the next few weeks and would be asked a number of questions such as, "What did you have for breakfast two days ago?" These residents were given a poker chip for each memory question they answered correctly. The poker chips could be exchanged for gifts at a later date. The participants in the contingent condition thus lived in a demanding social environment. In the noncontingent condition, residents were asked the same memory questions over the same time period. At the end of each questioning session, these residents were given some poker chips as a "momento." (Care was taken to equate the number of chips given to members of the contingent and noncontingent groups.) Residents in the noncontingent group were told that the number of chips they received did not depend on the accuracy of their memory. They were also allowed to exchange their chips for gifts. The participants in the noncontingent condition, therefore, lived in a nondemanding social environment. After three weeks of treatment, all participants were administered a number of memory tests. Results indicated that the residents from the demanding environment (the contingent condition) performed significantly better on the memory tests than those from the nondemanding environment (the noncontingent condition). Thus, the initial hypothesis was confirmed. In this experiment the manipulated independent variable was whether participants received poker chips under contingent or noncontingent conditions. The observed or measured **dependent variable** was the way the participants scored on the memory tests. But could other factors besides the conditions to which the participants were assigned account for the results of this experiment? How do we actually know that it was the independent variable that produced the differences between the participants in the two conditions?

One approach to this problem is to match the two groups on **extraneous variables** that are suspected to be important. For example, we could give IQ tests to all participants, making sure that the groups were matched with respect to IQ. Such matching can be useful; but **random assignment** is a much more powerful technique. In an experiment, individuals are always assigned to a specific group on a random basis. If assignment to groups is random and if the number of participants is reasonably large, we can assume that all extraneous factors will be randomly distributed in the two groups. This includes extraneous factors that we could never have thought of in advance, as well as the more obvious factors that might be handled through matching.

Manipulations Between and Within Research Participants

Random assignment of participants to different groups is one way to manipulate an independent variable. Such manipulations are **between-subject manipulations.** There are also within-subject manipulations, which involve observing each participant in an experiment under two or more conditions. For example, if we suspect that a certain drug improves memory in patients with Alzheimer's disease, we might measure memory ability in each individual after administration of this drug and also after administration of a placebo. Each individual then could be examined under the drug condition and later under the placebo condition to determine the effect of the drug. Counterbalancing would be advisable in such an experiment—we would test one half of the sample first in the drug condition and later in the placebo condition, and we would test the remaining sample first in the placebo condition and later in the drug condition. Counterbalancing controls the effects of the time at which variables are manipulated within subjects.

Quasi-Experimental Strategies in Developmental Research

All "true" experiments involve the manipulation of variables. Unfortunately, some variables are difficult if not impossible to manipulate. Age is one of these variables. Since we cannot manipulate a person's age, we cannot perform true experiments to examine the effects of age on a person's behavior. Despite the fact that most studies involving age are not true experiments, they often resemble true experiments in the ways in which they are designed or analyzed; age is treated as an independent variable even though it is not actually manipulated. Thus, we look for effects of age—actually, effects related to age—on one or more dependent variables. Because they are similar to true experiments, but also because the independent variable—age—is not truly manipulated, such studies are called **quasi-experiments.**

Let's consider what it means to say that a person's age cannot be manipulated. Suppose we are conducting a study on adult development and succeed in finding individuals who are willing to serve as participants. We can observe their behavior under a variety of conditions that are under our control. For example, we might present one of several different types of instruction, or administer several different types of drugs. It is up to us, the experimenters, to decide which conditions or treatments each participant will receive. But we can't decide each participant's age; we cannot alter the number of years each person has lived.

Of course, we can assign any one participant to a group of similarly aged individuals and compare this group to another group of younger or older individuals. We can also plan to test our participants not only today but again several years from now. Using these strategies, we can compare functioning at different ages and gather evidence about effects and phenomena that are related to age. But clearly these strategies do not entail the actual manipulation of age. They simply allow us to take advantage of differences and changes in age that occur independently of our study and that are beyond our control.

The Problem of Internal Validity   Perhaps you feel that the difference between an experiment and a quasi-experiment is rather subtle and has no practical importance. If so, you are right about the subtlety but wrong about the importance. The difference is critical, and it is clarified by the concept of internal validity.

The concept of **internal validity** concerns the role played by an independent variable in an experiment (or quasi-experiment). An experiment possesses internal validity if the results of the experiment reflect the influence of the independent variable rather than the influence of any extraneous or uncontrolled variables.

Internal validity is a concept that was developed by Donald Campbell and Julian Stanley in their classic book *Experimental and Quasi-Experimental Designs for Research* (1963). Campbell and Stanley enumerate several threats to internal validity and show that quasi-experimental studies, which include most studies of adult development and aging, are much more vulnerable to these threats than are true experiments.

One of the most serious threats to internal validity is **selection.** This threat is especially troublesome when different-aged groups are compared. In such cases, the procedures used to select groups can result in many extraneous differences among these groups, differences that do not pertain to age per se. For example, a young-adult group and an elderly group might differ with respect to years of education, health status, and so on. These differences between the members of these different cohorts may make the results of a research study very difficult to interpret.

A second threat to internal validity is **history.** This is especially serious when we test the same individuals at different ages. The problem is that between one time of testing and another, many events can have a profound effect on the person's behavior; also, of course, the person is growing older between testings. Possible historical effects include attitudinal changes (e.g., social attitudes toward aging), economic events (increases in Social Security), and social changes (the development of new senior citizen's centers), among others. These changes might have a positive effect on an aging population if, as individuals grow older, they (1) are looked on more positively, (2) have more money to spend, and (3) have more opportunities for social and intellectual stimulation. Thus, these individuals are likely to function in a more adaptive psychological manner not because they are getting older, but because of positive sociohistorical changes.

A third threat to internal validity is **testing.** Taking a test on one occasion can affect test performance on a subsequent occasion. Obviously, the testing threat can accompany the history threat whenever we test the same individuals at different ages. However, the testing threat is especially serious when we are measuring some type of behavior that can change as an individual practices. (Many types of intellectual performance can change with practice.)

Suppose that we had a machine that could make someone 20 years old, or even 90 years old, by turning a switch (and that we could bring the person back to his or her original age with no harm done). We could take a sample of individuals and randomly assign half of them to a 20-year-old condition and the other half to a 90-year-old condition, and then compare them on many different dependent measures (e.g., creativity). Random assignment would take care of all extraneous differences between the two age groups (the selection threat). History would not be a factor because we could test all participants on the same day. Further, we would test each person only once, thus avoiding the threat of testing. Under these ideal conditions, we could solve all problems of internal validity. Unfortunately, we have no ideal situation. In developmental research we must live with threats to internal validity and compensate for them as best we can.

Next we consider several different types of quasi-experimental designs that are used in research on adult development and aging. We will see that different designs compensate for different internal validity threats. We will also see that the time span of a research design is a critical factor in determining what kinds of threats it can handle.

QUASI-EXPERIMENTAL DESIGNS FOR THE STUDY OF ADULT DEVELOPMENT AND AGING

Discussion of quasi-experimental research designs can be complicated. Let's start with the simplest designs: the cross-sectional and longitudinal designs, which are the basis for all developmental research. Then we'll describe more complex designs called sequential designs, which are actually further elaborations of the basic cross-sectional and simple longitudinal designs. There are ways in which all of these designs compensate, or fail to compensate, for the various threats to internal validity. Table A.1 provides a summary of each design, its susceptibility to internal validity threats, and other distinguishing features. It may be helpful to consult this table throughout the discussion that follows.

Cross-Sectional and Longitudinal Designs

Consider two different ways in which we might attempt to examine the impact of aging on behavior. First, we might perform a **cross-sectional study,** comparing groups of people in different age ranges. A typical cross-sectional study might include a group of 18- to 20-year-olds and a group of 65- to 70-year-olds. A more comprehensive cross-sectional study might include groups from every decade of life from the twenties through the nineties. The investigators could compare the different groups on a variety of dependent variables, such as IQ performance, memory, and creativity. They could collect data in a very short time; even a large study can be completed within a few

TABLE A.1

Summary of Quasi-Experimental Designs and in Adult Development and Aging

Design	Description	Threats to Internal Validity	Other Properties
Simple-Cross Sectional	Two or more age groups are compared at one time of testing	Selection, especially cohort effects; differences between groups might reflect differences in time of birth	Easy to conduct; can be useful as a pilot study
Simple Longitudinal	A single group of subjects is tested repeatedly at different points in time	Time-of-testing (history) effects: historical changes might product effects that appear to be age-related changes; repeated testing might influence measures (testing effects)	Time-consuming; subjects may drop out of study prior to completion—selective dropout (this threatens generalizability of findings); allows assessment of individual differences in developmental change
Cohort-Sequential	Two or more longitudinal comparisons are made on different cohorts	Time-of-testing and testing effects as for simple longitudinal (can remove testing effects with independent samples)	Extremely time-consuming; requires two time periods to examine change over one time period; allows separate examination of age-related effects and cohort effects
Time-Sequential	Two or more cross-sectional comparisons are made at different times of testing	Cohort effects, since every cross-sectional comparison is possibly influenced by cohort as well as age	Time-consuming, but not as time-consuming as cohort-sequential designs; allows separate examination of age effects and time-of-testing (history) effects
Cross-Sequential	Two or more cohorts are compared at two or more times of testing	Neither time-of-testing nor cohort effects are independent of age-related changes	Time-consuming; provides no clear information on age-related changes

months. The major purpose of a cross-sectional study is to measure age-related differences. As we shall see, a cross-sectional study allows us to determine whether one age group of individuals differs from other age groups. Cross-sectional studies, however, do not allow us to measure age-related change (i.e., the extent to which age-graded factors, by themselves, cause developmental change).

Another way we might explore the effects of aging on behavior is to perform a **longitudinal study.** In this case, we would take a single group of individuals, all the same age, and test them today and on one or more occasions in the future. For example, we might decide to examine creativity at ages 50, 57, 64, and 71. Longitudinal studies clearly take a long time to complete. Furthermore, the purpose of a longitudinal study is to measure age-related changes, not age differences. As we shall see, simple longitudinal studies are not always successful in measuring such changes.

One advantage of cross-sectional designs, then, is time efficiency. Further, cross-sectional designs are virtually free of two important internal validity threats. There is no history threat because all participants are tested at the same time. There is no testing threat because it is necessary to test each individual only once. For these reasons, cross-sectional designs are enormously popular. However, as mentioned earlier, cross-sectional designs are highly susceptible to the internal validity threat of selection. We often do not know the extent to which the results of a cross-sectional study reflect the effects of age versus the effects of countless extraneous factors.

Many extraneous factors involved in cross-sectional designs pertain to **cohort effects.** Cohort effects are caused by a person's time of birth or generation but not actually to her or his age. For example, cohorts can differ with respect to years of education, childrearing practices, health, and attitudes on topics such as sex and religion. These cohort effects are important because they can powerfully influence the dependent measures in a study concerned with age. Cohort effects can look like age effects, but they are not.

Since cross-sectional designs do not allow random assignment of individuals to age groups, there is no way to control cohort effects or other extraneous variables. Our only approach to controlling these variables is through matching. For example, if our young participants are all college students, we might make sure that all our elderly participants are also college students. Unfortunately, matching for extraneous variables is sometimes impossible. (We may be unable to find an adequate number of elderly college students who are willing to participate in our study.) Further, we can only match for the extraneous variables whose importance we recognize. Finally, matching can have the unwanted side effect of producing unusual or nonrepresentative groups—elderly people in college may differ in many ways from the average person of their age. Selection poses a serious threat to cross-sectional studies, and matching is not truly adequate to remove it.

Figure A.1 contains a diagram of a simple cross-sectional study that addresses the issue of whether IQ changes from 50 to 60 to 70 years of age. This study, if it were con-

Figure A.1 A cross-sectional design measures age-related differences between different cohorts.

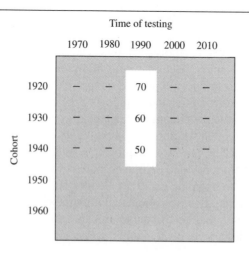

ducted in the year 1990, would employ participants of different ages (50, 60, and 70) representing different cohorts according to the year in which they were born (1920, 1930, and 1940). Interpreting the data obtained in this study would be impossible because changes in age are confounded (i.e., confused with) changes in cohort. For example, we might find that 70-year-olds have lower IQ scores than 50-year-olds. But we would not know if this is because of the ages of the participants, the amount of education received by individuals born in 1920 versus those born in 1940, or some other extraneous factor.

Although longitudinal studies are time-consuming, they are valuable because they remove the threat of selection, or cohort effects. This is because individuals from a single cohort form the participant pool for a longitudinal study. Further, longitudinal studies have the great advantage of allowing us to track changes that take place within individuals over a long time interval. If one's primary concern is the study of intraindividual change over the course of development, longitudinal designs are indispensable.

Unfortunately, the threats of history, testing, and selective dropout are especially troublesome in longitudinal designs. Selective dropout refers to the possibility that over the course of a longitudinal study, participants who either perform poorly on a particular test, or are unmotivated or ill, will be less likely to undergo repeated testing. To illustrate, consider the longitudinal study diagrammed in figure A.2. This study measures IQ changes in individuals from the 1920 birth cohort as they move from 50 to 60 to 70 years of age. The study begins in the year 1970 and concludes in the year 1990. The same participants are retested at 10-year intervals. Interpreting the data obtained in this study would be very difficult. For example, we might find that the participants display higher IQ scores at age 70 than age 50. This finding might be due to any number of facts; for example, it could be true that (1) people actually become more intelligent as they age; (2) between 1970 and 1990 our society has changed so that life has become more stimulating, enriching, and enjoyable for the typical older person; (3) the participants became more familiar with the IQ test each time they were tested; or (4) at

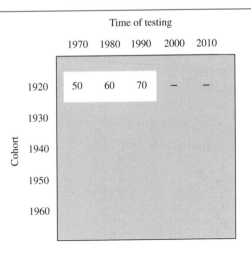

Figure A.2 A longitudinal design measures age-related changes for a selected cohort.

the end of the study in 1990, we were left with a very biased group of participants—those who were exceptionally bright, motivated, healthy, and so on.

It may be possible to remove the threats of testing and selective dropout by adding new or independent samples of participants at each testing. For example, we could collect data on a group of randomly selected 60-year-olds in 1980 and compare their IQ performance to those participants tested for the second time in 1980. And we could also add another group of randomly selected 70-year-olds in 1990. This procedure, however, would still not remove the history threat.

Cohort-Sequential Designs

Sequential research designs may be used to correct some of the inadequacies of cross-sectional and longitudinal research. A **cohort-sequential design** entails two or more longitudinal studies, each covering the same range of ages, conducted over differing lengths of time. An example of a simple cohort-sequential design is shown in figure A.3. Three different cohorts are selected—a cohort born in 1920, a second cohort born in 1930, and a third born in 1940. A sample from each cohort is tested on three different occasions—first when the participants are 50 years old, again when they are 60 years old, and a third time when they are 70 years old. As in the simple longitudinal design, independent samples could also be drawn at the different times of testing to control the threats of testing and selective dropout.

The cohort-sequential design corrects for the major drawback associated with the simple cross-sectional design; that is, by conducting a cohort-sequential study, we can estimate the relative importance of age effects in comparison to cohort effects. For example, we can compare performance by the 1920 versus 1930 versus 1940 cohorts by looking across the rows in figure A.3. This tells us something about how cohort-related factors might influence our measure. We can also compare the performance of individuals from each of the three age groups. This is accomplished by looking at the diagonals in figure A.3—we could calculate the average score of all of the 50-year-olds

Figure A.3 A cohort-sequential design involves two or more longitudinal studies covering the same age ranges over different time eras.

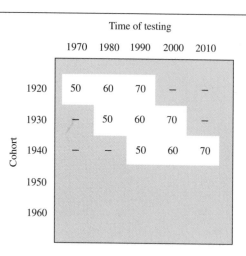

and compare it with the average score for all groups of 60-year-olds, and so on. This tells us how age influences our measure independently of cohort. Further, the design allows us to assess interactions between cohort and age. We can see if the age effect is constant across the two cohorts, or if it varies between the cohorts. This can obviously be very important if there are different rates of aging in different cohorts.

The main weakness of cohort-sequential design is that it doesn't compensate for the history threat. We would have no understanding, in other words, of how the historical changes that occurred from 1970 to 2010 affected the behavior of our participants. Another weakness of the design is that it takes a great deal of time to complete. As you can see from figure A.3, to study aging and cohort effects on IQ at 50, 60, and 70 years of age, we need 40 years to collect the data.

Time-Sequential Designs

The **time-sequential design** corrects for the major limitation of the longitudinal design. This design is capable of differentiating age effects from historical changes (or time-of-testing effects). Time-sequential designs involve two or more cross-sectional studies, each covering the same range of ages, conducted at different times. An example is shown in figure A.4. According to this figure, in 1970, we examine performance of three age groups: 50-, 60-, and 70-year-olds. In 1980 and also in 1990, we again examine the performance of individuals at these three age levels (these are, of course, entirely new samples of participants).

The strength of the time-sequential design is that history effects—or time-of-testing effects—can be examined explicitly, in addition to differences related to age. That is, looking at the columns in figure A.4, we can examine differences between performance in 1970, 1980, and 1990; this tells us directly about history effects. Independent of history, we can look at the diagonals to examine differences between the 50-, 60-, and 70-year-olds; this gives us information relevant to aging. Furthermore, we can examine the interactions between age and time of testing. If age-related differences in 1980 are

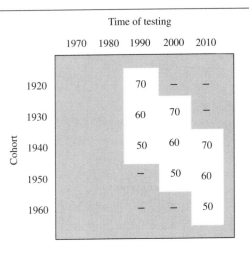

Figure A.4 A time-sequential design differentiates age effects from historical changes.

smaller than age-related differences in 1970 and 1990, it might support some interesting conclusions about history-related changes in the course of adult development.

Another advantage of the time-sequential design is that it is more time efficient than the cohort-sequential design. In our example (figure A.4), age and history effects can be studied over a 20-year span (compared with a 40-year span for the cohort-sequential design). Also, note that the time-sequential design (figure A.4) takes the same length of time to conduct as the longitudinal design (figure A.2)!

The disadvantage of the time-sequential design is that it does not consider cohort effects. At each time of measurement, we must be concerned with the possibility that differences between our age groups may, in part, reflect differences in their respective cohorts.

Cross-Sequential Designs

Cross-sequential designs are a kind of hybrid combination of cross-sectional and longitudinal designs. They are not fundamentally relevant to adult development and aging because they do not separate age effects from either cohort or history effects. Rather, cross-sequential designs separate cohort and history effects from each other.

The technique used in a cross-sequential design, illustrated in figure A.5, is to examine two (or more) cohorts, covering different age ranges, at each of two (or more) times of testing. Differences among cohorts can be examined independently of differences among times of measurement. Unfortunately, neither of these differences can be separated from age. The cohorts differ on an age dimension, and participants must obviously be older at the second testing than the first.

Perhaps this is a good time for you to stop and review the various quasi-experimental designs in adult development and aging. Going over them once or even twice probably won't be enough. Take some time to study the material in table A.1, which summarizes the main characteristics of each of these quasi-experimental designs.

Figure A.5 A cross-sequential design combines the cross-sectional and longitudinal designs.

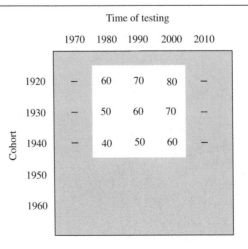

Schaie's Most Efficient Design

We can summarize the preceding discussion by saying that the cohort-sequential design is a useful extension of simple longitudinal designs and that the time-sequential design is a useful extension of cross-sectional designs. Furthermore, we could conclude that these sequential designs are far superior to the simple cross-sectional and longitudinal studies from which they are derived. However, the various sequential designs are still less than perfect. History or time-of-testing effects threaten the internal validity of cohort-sequential designs. Cohort effects threaten the internal validity of time-sequential designs. So what are we to do to ensure the internal validity of our research?

One answer is to use both the cohort-sequential and time-sequential designs, and then even to add the cross-sequential design for good measure. Incorporating all of these designs at once is more difficult than performing one of them alone. K .W. Schaie, an authority on sequential designs, has developed the **most efficient design** to combine the best features of the other designs.

The most efficient design is illustrated in figure A.6. Individuals in five different cohorts are studied: 1900, 1910, 1920, 1930, and 1940. Measurements are made at five different times: 1950, 1960, 1970, 1980, and 1990. Finally, it is necessary to collect data from new, independent samples of each cohort at each of the different times of testing (though retesting of the original samples is also recommended). If all this is accomplished, it is possible to perform a cohort-sequential analysis, a time-sequential analysis, and a cross-sequential analysis all at once, as shown in figure A.6.

Such analyses provide a wealth of interesting comparisons. Certain patterns can reveal strong evidence for age-related changes, cohort differences, and history effects. Consider the following possible outcome in a study of creativity: The cohort-sequential analysis may suggest a strong effect of cohort but only a weak effect of age. The time-sequential analysis supports only weak effects of time of testing and age. Finally, the cross-sequential analysis supports, again, a strong effect of cohort but only a weak effect of time of measurement. In this hypothetical case, we would have clear indications that cohort is an important variable but that age and time of measurement are not.

We must always be mindful of the tremendous difficulty of collecting the data that permit such complex analyses. Faced with this difficulty, it may frequently be advisable to first conduct simple cross-sectional studies, controlling as much as possible for extraneous, cohort-related variables known to be important. Examining the effects of different treatments in such designs can also help isolate the specific ways in which younger groups differ from older groups at a particular time in history. Subsequently, once important differences between younger and older groups have been isolated, longitudinal and even sequential strategies can be carried out, allowing a much more complete understanding of the causes of these differences.

Stated somewhat differently, cross-sectional studies seem to be the logical starting point in developmental research. If this type of research establishes reliable age differences in behavior, then other types of designs should be carried out to determine the underlying causes of the apparent age difference.

Figure A.6
Schaie's "most efficient" design.

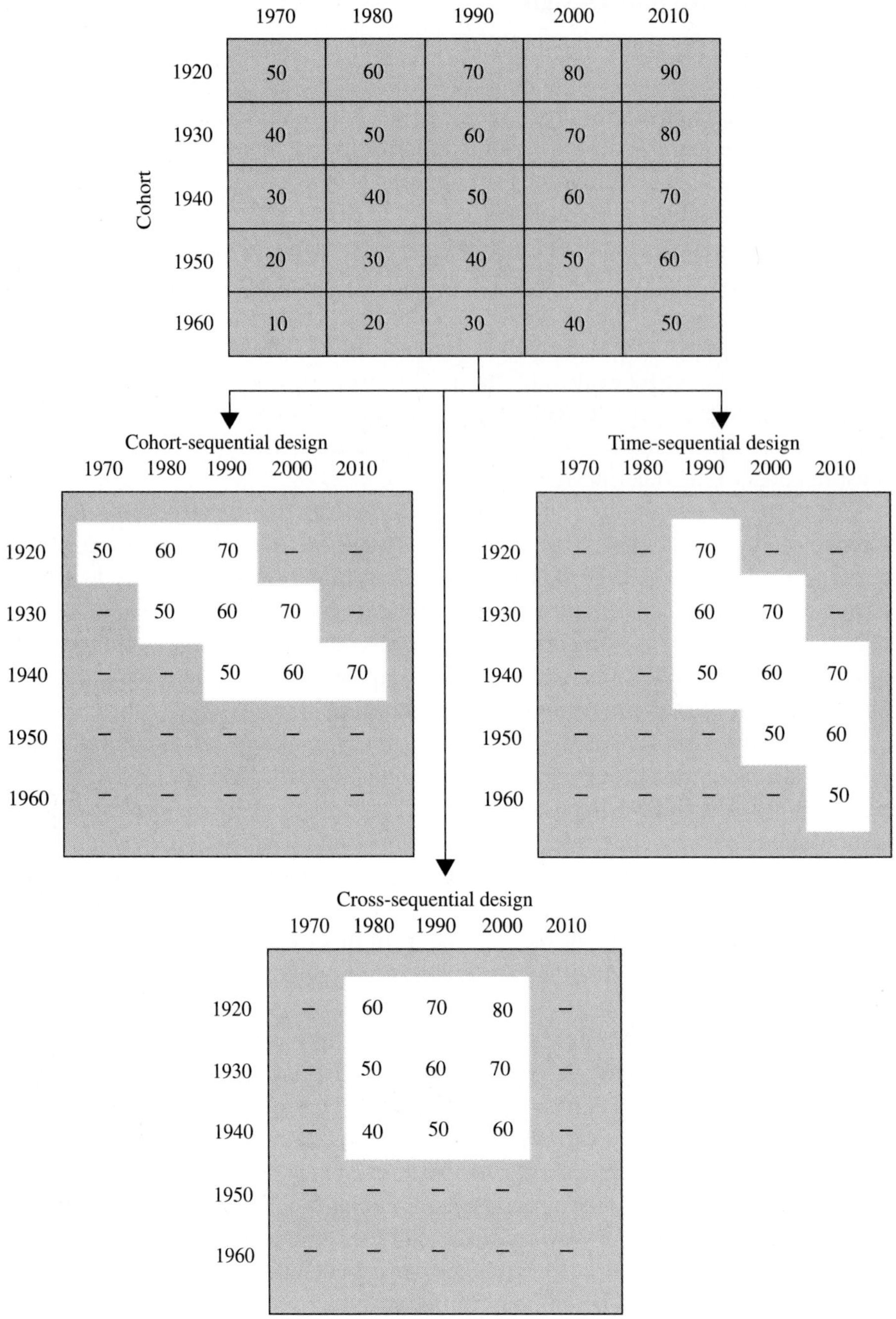

Appendix

META-ANALYSIS

As you have seen from reading this chapter, there are a vast number of ways to engineer a research study. It is possible to use a correlational, experimental, or quasi-experimental research design. One drawback associated with any particular research study, no matter how elegant its design, is the fact that it is a *single* study. As scientists, we want to get the "big picture" on a particular topic. This is accomplished by putting together the results of a number of individual studies.

The problem faced by researchers about *how* they should interpret the results of several different experiments is similar to the one they experience when they interpret a single experiment. Namely, should they come to some personal or subjective conclusion about the results of an array of studies? Or should they use some sort of *objective* methodology to reach a conclusion? The technique of **meta-analysis** was developed to provide an objective account of the results of several studies that are taken as a whole.

When a researcher conducts a meta-analysis she examines each individual research study to determine: the number of individuals within particular groups, group performance means, and group performance standard deviations. All these variables are used to estimate the effect size of a certain independent variable on a particular dependent variable. Then, all of the estimates of effect size from the individual studies are grouped together via a mathematical procedure to determine the overall effect size for all of the studies, and to determine whether this overall effect size is statistically significant.

The utility of the meta-analytic technique is illustrated by the following example. Say we want to determine whether a particular training program improves the memory performance of patients with AD. We begin by reading 30 different experiments that have been conducted on this topic. Ten of the studies show that the training program has a statistically significant beneficial effect on the patients' memory. Another 10 of the studies indicate that the training program had a slightly positive impact on the patients' memory, but this beneficial effect just missed attaining statistical significance. And the remaining 10 studies reveal that the program had no beneficial effect on patients' memory whatsoever. If we just "eyeballed" all of these data we'd most likely become confused and conclude that no firm conclusions may be drawn. A meta-analysis of all of these studies, however, might lead to a definitive conclusion that the training program did (or did not) boost the memory of the AD patients.

Note that a meta-analysis is an extremely handy tool when the individual studies one is examining have extremely small sample sizes (as is usually the cases in experiments that use groups of demented patients). This is because the smaller the number of individuals within different groups, the larger the mean difference in group difference needs to be in order to achieve statistical significance.

PROBLEMS OF SAMPLING IN DEVELOPMENTAL RESEARCH

When we decide to study a certain group of individuals (say, 70-year-olds who have recently retired), we obviously cannot collect measurements on everyone in that group. Rather, we must study a sample of the entire population of individuals in the class. Although we study only a sample, we want to generalize our findings to the rest of the population. Thus, the sampling procedures form a very important aspect of research methodology.

A **representative sample** has the same characteristics as the larger population to which we want to generalize our findings. The best way to achieve a representative sample is through the technique of random sampling, a technique in which every member of the population has an equal chance of being in the sample that we study. For example, the ideal way to find a representative sample of recently retired 70-year-olds would be to compile a list of every such individual in the world and then to pick randomly a number of these individuals to be in our study. Obviously, truly random sampling can rarely be employed. Indeed, we often must struggle to find people with certain characteristics who are willing to participate in our studies.

Investigators of adult development seldom can be sure that their samples are representative. This fact produces two consequences, one pertaining primarily to cross-sectional designs and the other primarily to longitudinal designs.

Nonrepresentative Samples in Cross-Sectional Designs

In cross-sectional designs, the problem of nonrepresentative samples adds to problems of internal validity. Specifically, selection threats may be due partially to nonrepresentative sampling. If we find differences between a group of young persons and a group of elderly persons but do not know whether either sample is representative, it is difficult to be sure if either age or cohort is responsible for the differences. Perhaps these differences occurred because we selected a group of young adults with below-average intelligence for individuals of their age and a group of older persons with above-average intelligence for individuals of their age. The solution to this problem is to measure various extraneous variables (e.g., IQ) that are suspected to be important. We must measure the IQs of the two groups and relate them to the norms for their age groups. Though not ideal, this approach is much better than ignoring these issues.

Nonrepresentative Samples in Longitudinal Designs

The problem of sampling in longitudinal studies is not just a hypothetical problem; it has been shown to occur. It frequently takes the form of selective dropout. As we have already mentioned, selective dropout refers to the fact that some participants drop out of a longitudinal study before all of the testings are complete. The problem is that those who drop out of a study are likely to differ significantly from those who continue until the end. Indeed, it has been shown that people who return for testing in a longitudinal study often have greater intellectual abilities than those who do not (Riegel & Riegel, 1972). Further, longitudinal declines in intellectual ability are more likely to occur among those who drop out of a study after several testings than among those who remain. Finally, Cooney, Schaie, and Willis (1988) have shown that participants who leave a longitudinal study for health reasons are largely responsible for producing the selective dropout effect. As a result, the data collected in a longitudinal study may reflect aging among adults of superior ability and good health, not aging among adults of average or below-average ability and health.

At another level, sampling problems can threaten the external validity of longitudinal research (Campbell & Stanley, 1963). **External validity** refers to the degree to which we may generalize the results of a scientific study. When we use nonrepresentative samples, we often do not know whether age trends observed in one longitudinal study are representative of age trends in the population at large. The external validity of cross-sectional designs, of course, may be threatened for the same reason.

SUMMARY

Two basic problems of measurement are reliability and validity. Although the problem of reliability is serious, effective methods for assessing reliability (e.g., the test-retest method) and for increasing reliability (e.g., collecting data on multiple items) do exist. The problem of validity is more troublesome because many psychological concepts, such as creativity and self-concept, are highly abstract. When we attempt to evaluate such abstract concepts, it is often arguable that we are not truly measuring what we think we are measuring.

Among the basic measures used for collecting observations are the interview and questionnaire, behavioral research, standardized tests, and physiological research. Each has strengths and weaknesses. Interview and questionnaire studies can often be conducted when other sorts of studies are impossible or, at best, impractical. However, these types of studies are especially susceptible to the problem of reactivity, particularly the problem of response bias. Moreover, interviews and questionnaires are highly dependent on the participants' conscious impressions of themselves, and these impressions can be at variance with actual behavior.

Behavioral measures are many and varied. They can be collected in laboratory settings or in the field. Behavioral studies in the laboratory allow impressive control over many extraneous variables. However, they often can be artificial, even anxiety provoking, to individuals. Further, laboratory studies produce problems of reactivity, and they cannot be used to study certain kinds of real-world phenomena. Field studies allow fewer controls, but they can be very naturalistic, can reduce problems of reactivity, and can reveal real-life phenomena that are not reproducible in the laboratory. Standardized tests are useful for comparing a particular sample of individuals to representative samples of individuals tested previously. However, the validity of such tests is often questionable. Further, it is frequently the case that no previously developed test can measure exactly what we want to measure. Physiological measures can be invaluable for an increased understanding of behavioral data, and they can suggest ways to reduce or remove age-related differences in behavior when this is desirable.

Among the basic strategies for summarizing data are measures of central tendency and variability. Correlations are used to determine the degree to which two variables are related to each other. However, many studies produce so many correlations that interpretation is difficult. In these cases, factor analysis can be useful for reducing many correlations to a smaller number of factors. Significance tests are used to determine if the results of a study are due to chance.

In terms of research design, correlational studies must be distinguished from true experiments. Experiments involve the manipulation of independent variables and actually provide evidence for cause-effect relationships between independent and dependent variables. Quasi-experiments are similar to true experiments, but quasi-experiments do not involve the actual manipulation of independent variables. Since age cannot be manipulated, studies of this variable are considered to be quasi-experimental. Three threats to internal validity, threats that are problematic in such quasi-experimental studies, are selection, history, and testing.

Several types of quasi-experiments are used to study adult development and aging. Simple cross-sectional and longitudinal designs are limited in their usefulness. Cross-sectional designs suffer from cohort effects, whereas longitudinal designs suffer from both testing and history effects. Among the sequential designs, the cohort-sequential design allows independent assessment of age and cohort effects but does not solve the problem of history effects. The time-sequential design allows independent assessment of age and history effects but does not solve the problem of cohort effects. The use of both designs together, along with the cross-sequential design as well, can in principle allow us to distinguish age, cohort, and history effects. A greater investment of time and resources is necessary to use all these designs together, however.

Researchers must frequently sample their participants from different age groups (cohorts), and this sampling can introduce bias; samples may be nonrepresentative. The problem of sampling is unavoidable, but we must keep it in mind when we are interpreting the data in studies of adult development and aging. Particularly vexing is the problem of selective dropout or experimental mortality, which occurs when participants drop out of a longitudinal study. Those who drop out are likely to differ systematically from those who remain. This can threaten the generalizability of longitudinal studies.

REVIEW QUESTIONS

1. How can we assess reliability? How can we improve the methods we use to assess reliability?
2. What are the central issues involved in the validity of measurement?
3. Describe the basic types of measures used for collecting information about adults. Include the advantages and disadvantages of each type.
4. What are the basic strategies for summarizing measurements?
5. Explain the logic behind the technique of factor analysis.
6. Provide an overview of correlational and experimental strategies in research design.

Include in your answer information about manipulations between and within individuals.

7. Discuss quasi-experimental designs and the problem of internal validity.
8. Compare and contrast the simple quasi-experimental designs (cross-sectional and longitudinal) with the complex quasi-experimental designs (sequential designs) used to study adult development and aging.
9. What are some of the main sampling problems in conducting research with adults?

GLOSSARY

Abortive coping A form of adjustment to life events which is predominantly negative, nonproductive, and limiting to human growth. (p. 414)

Acceptance The fifth and final stage of Kübler-Ross's psychological stages of dying; in this stage of dying, patients end their struggle against death and show acceptance of their end, peacefulness, and solitude. (p. 525)

Accommodation The process of eye muscle adjustments that allows the eye to have the greatest clarity of image (resolution); the ability to focus and maintain an image on the retina. (p. 65)

Accommodative processes Processes involved in helping older persons adjust to cumulative losses and threats to self-esteem by disengagement and the lowering of aspiration from goals that are unattainable. (p. 131)

Acetylcholine A neurotransmitter necessary for brain activation, responsiveness, and communication. Composed essentially from choline, it travels from the axon across the synaptic cleft and to the dendrites of another cell. (p. 79)

Acetylcholinesterase The substance responsible for the deactivation of acetylcholine; limits the length of time a neuron is stimulated. (p. 93)

Acquired immunodeficiency syndrome (AIDS) The failure of the body's immune system that leaves afflicted individuals vulnerable to a variety of diseases and ultimately leads to death. (p. 96)

Active euthanasia Inducing death in an incurably ill person by some direct action, such as injecting a lethal dose of a drug. (p. 504)

Active mastery A style of relating to the environment that changes with age in different ways for men and women. It allows the adult more direct control over the environment. (p. 44)

Activities of daily living (ADL) The basic functions necessary for individuals to maintain independent living, which include feeding, meal preparation, bathing, dressing, toileting, and general health/hygiene. The long-term needs of the elderly are assessed through these activities, which serve as a guide for appropriate intervention. (p. 123, 199)

Affirmative coping A form of adjustment to life events which is positive, productive, and enhancing to human growth. (p. 414)

Age-by-experience paradigm A methodology used to assess the role of age and expertise on some aspect of cognitive ability. (p. 364)

Age structure The percentage of males and females within various age intervals in a given society. (p. 25)

Ageism The unwarranted assumption that chronological age is the primary determinant of human traits, abilities, and characteristics and that one age is superior to another. (p. 39)

Agnosia The inability to visually recognize familiar objects. (p. 76)

AIDS dementia complex (ADC) A set of cognitive dysfunctions associated with brain infection caused by the HIV virus. (p. 96)

Alpha rhythm The dominant rhythm displayed by the brain that is linked with alert wakefulness. (p. 81)

Alternative resource theory The search by ethnic minority families for help first from family and the church rather than secondary community resources such as government sponsored programs; accounts for underutilization of services such as community mental health. (p. 141)

Alzheimer's disease (AD) Irreversible dementia characterized by progressive deterioration in memory, awareness, and body functions, eventually leading to death. (p. 81)

Amyloid precursor protein (APP) The chemical substance that underlies the manufacture of amyloid, which is the core material of senile plaques. (p. 87)

Androgynous Having and accepting both male and female characteristics in one person. (p. 42)

Anger The second of Kübler-Ross's stages of dying; in this stage of dying, persons realize that denial of death cannot be maintained, causing them to become angry, resentful, and envious. (p. 524)

Anniversary reaction Feelings of loneliness that occur on holidays, birthdays, etc. following the death of a loved one. (p. 542)

Anticipatory grief Feelings of grief, loneliness, and despair that precede the death of a loved one. (p. 542)

Aphasia A breakdown or loss of an individual's language abilities. (p. 76)

Apparent memory deficits Memory losses that can be attributed to faulty encoding and retrieval processes; these are potentially reversible through intervention or instruction. (p. 295)

Appropriate death A mode of coping with death that approximates the wishes and ideals of the dying person (e.g., to be given the freedom to die as one has been given the freedom to live). (p. 525)

Ascending reticular activation system (ARAS) A brain system that controls levels of awareness or consciousness. (p. 74)

Assimilative processes Processes that help to direct older adults to specific activities and goals that are personally derived and that effectively reduce the cumulative impact of developmental losses central to self-esteem and personal identity. (p. 131)

Assisted living Similar to apartment style residences, elderly receive individual services to maximize their independence such as prepared meals, help with dressing, bathing, or administration of medications. (p. 207)

Atherosclerosis Coronary artery disease caused by the accumulation of fatty deposits (e.g., plaque) on the arterial walls of vessels supplying blood to the heart. (p. 238)

Automatic information processing Information processing that does not draw on limited attentional resources. (p. 288)

Axon The part of the neuron that transmits information. (p. 76)

Bargaining The third of Kübler-Ross's stages of dying; in this stage of dying, patients hope that death can be postponed by negotiating with God. (p. 524)

Barrier theory An explanation for the underutilization by Hispanic, black, and Asian minorities of government health and mental health programs, which are seen as large bureaucratic organizations that are impersonal, inaccessible, and distant with few professional staff from historically underrepresented groups. (p. 150)

Behavior therapy The application of positive rewards for appropriate behavior and nonrewards for inappropriate behavior. (p. 187)

Behavioral research Research that obtains the direct observation and recording of behavior, including experimental approaches. (p. 560)

Benign senescent forgetfulness The normal, nonpathological memory loss associated with aging. (p. 294)

Bereaved The status of a person or family who has survived the death of a loved one. (p. 534)

Bereavement overload The inability to work through the deaths of loved ones that occur close to one another in time. (p. 521)

Beta rhythm Fast brain rhythm that characterizes an attentive, alert state. (p. 81)

Beta-amyloid A protein that makes up senile plaques. (p. 78)

Between-subjects manipulations The random assignment of subjects to groups in an experiment. (p. 568)

Biological age The relative condition of an individual's organ and body system. (p. 13)

Biological approach The idea that age-related memory deficits may be traced to the deterioration of the brain. (p. 290)

Biomarker A physiological measure that is a valid indicator of the speed of the primary aging process. (p. 56)

Bona fide occupational qualifications (BFOQ) Legislation that mandates that workers in selective job classifications retire at a specific age due to the abilities or traits demanded for successful performance, e.g., police or airline traffic controllers. (p. 481)

Brain death That point at which all electrical activity has ceased in the brain as determined by an EEG. (p. 499)

Brain stem The primitive part of the lower brain that controls the basic biological processes associated with respiration and heartbeat. (p. 74)

Busy ethic A theory of successful retirement developed by Ekerdt. (p. 492)

Cancer A group of different diseases characterized by rapid, uncontrollable growth of abnormal cells that forms a malignant tumor. (p. 227)

Caregiver burden The intense reactions common to those adults caring for the emotional, social, intellectual, and physical needs of an elderly relative in their own home. (p. 117)

Cataracts Opacity in the lens of the eye that can cause blindness if not corrected. (p. 65)

Central tendency The manipulation of a given set of scores to determine the mean, median, or mode. (p. 562)

Cerebellum A primitive part of the brain that controls balance and motor programming, and simple conditioning. (p. 75)

Cerebrum The largest and evolutionarily most recent part of the brain. (p. 75)

Chronic exercise Regular, consistent, and sustained exercise over an extended period of time. (p. 225)

Chronological age The number of years since a person's birth. (p. 13)

Clinical depression A constellation of behaviors, thoughts, and emotions characterized by intense loneliness and isolation, extreme sadness, crying, feelings of worthlessness, perfectionism, guilt, anxiety, dread, and being unloved. (p. 153)

Cochlea The primary neural receptor for hearing. (p. 66)

Codicils Changes or amendments made to a will that has already been legally filed or recorded. (p. 192)

Cognitive model of coping A model of coping and adaptation development by Lazarus that emphasizes the person's subjective perception of potentially stressful life events; cognitive processes underlie subjective perception through primary and secondary appraisal. (p. 111)

Cohort A group of people born in the same time period; the shared or distinctive characteristics of a generation. (p. 10)

Cohort effects Differences in behaviors that are found among people born at different times in history. (p. 313)

Cohort-sequential design A complex research design that allows a research investigator to distinguish between age effects and cohort effects. (p. 574)

Competence A legal term informed by professional input from a psychiatrist or clinical psychologist that describes an older person's capacity to make independent decisions affecting their care, medical treatment, and disposition of assets through a will. (p. 190)

Computerized axial tomography (CT scan) A radiological technique that yields a three-dimensional representation of the structure of the brain. (p. 80)

Concrete-operational stage The third stage of Piaget's theory of mental development that highlights a type of thinking limited to concrete ideas and experiences. (p. 340)

Construct validity The extent to which a psychological test or assessment measures a hypothetical entity, e.g., intelligence. (p. 558)

Contextual approach The viewpoint that suggests that the effectiveness of a person's memory depends on the context or setting within which the person is required to learn and remember information. (p. 293)

Contextual paradigm The model that suggests that adults, like historical events, are ongoing, dynamic, and not directed toward an ideal or end-state. (p. 16)

Continuity The notion that the same processes control development. (p. 6)

Contrast sensitivity An individual's ability to perceive visual stimuli that differ in terms of both contrast and spatial frequency. (p. 65)

Conventional level The third and fourth stages of Kohlberg's theory of moral development in which moral thought is based on the desire to preserve good interpersonal relations (stage 3) and to comply with formalized rules that exist in society (stage 4). (p. 407)

Convergent thinking A type of thinking that is designed to reveal a single correct answer for a problem. (p. 330)

Coronary arteries The vessels that provide blood directly to the heart muscle. (p. 238)

Corpus callosum A band of nerve fibers that connects the brain's two hemispheres. (p. 76)

Correlation A relationship or association between two variables that can be either positive or negative and vary from weak to strong. (p. 563)

Correlational study A type of research in which associations between variables are merely observed. (p. 566)

Cortex The outer covering of the cerebrum. (p. 76)

Crossover effect Black Americans at higher risk for death at earlier ages and who reach old age represent a select, hardy group of survivors whose life expectancies are higher (i.e., cross over) relative to those of similar age from other races. (p. 163)

Cross-sectional study A study in which individuals of different ages are observed at different times to obtain information about some variable, usually contaminated by cohort effects. (p. 570)

Cross-sequential designs A complex research design that allows an investigator to distinguish time of testing effects from cohort effects. (p. 576)

Crystallized intelligence The type of intelligence that involves skills, abilities, and understanding gained through instruction and observation. (p. 302)

Cultural paranoia The suspicion, hostility, and distrust that African Americans have toward white middle-class community-based programs such as mental health programs; limits willingness to seek services when needed. (p. 176)

Curvilinear The reflection of the association of variables that is represented by a curved line when plotted on a graph. (p. 564)

Daily hassles The little irritating annoyances that punctuate our daily

lives (e.g., the broken shoelace syndrome). (p. 112)

Declarative memory The conscious recollection of the past. (p. 268)

Delayed grief reaction A delayed and heightened reaction to the death of a loved one that is elicited in response to the death of someone to whom the individual is not emotionally attached. (p. 542)

Delta rhythm The brain wave associated with deep sleep. (p. 81)

Dementia An organically based disorder of late adulthood characterized by a deterioration of intelligence and behavior. (p. 81)

Dendrites The component of a neuron that receives information. (p. 76)

Denial/isolation The first of Kübler-Ross's psychological stages of dying; in this stage of dying, persons react to terminal illness with shock, denial, and withdrawal. (p. 524)

Dependency ratio A reflection of the number of workers relative to the number of people deriving support from these workers, most typically children under the age of 15 and elderly persons 65 years of age and older. (p. 34)

Dependent variables The values that are measured as a result of experimental manipulations. (p. 567)

Depletion syndrome A form of "minor" depression among the elderly characterized by lack of interest and the feeling that everything requires enormous effort, even the simplest of daily tasks. (p. 154)

Depression The fourth of Kübler-Ross's stages of dying; in this stage of dying, persons become silent, spend much time crying, and want to be alone in an effort to disconnect themselves from objects of love. (p. 524)

Depressive pseudodementia Depression that mimics dementia. (p. 97)

Development Refers to a form of change that is organized and adaptive (positive) in nature. (p. 4)

Developmental psychology The study of age-related interindividual differences and age-related intraindividual change. (p. 3)

Diagnostic related group (DRG) National health care definitions of specific medical conditions to permit construction of average costs and lengths of treatment in a hospital for insurance reimbursement purposes. (p. 206)

Dialectical view The view that individuals are constantly changing organisms in a constantly changing world. (p. 17)

Diathesis-stress model Descriptive account of the relationship between a person's current level of vulnerability or frailty (diathesis) and the capacity to manage challenging life events (stressors). (p. 146)

Didactic-centered (instruction-centered) death education Helping people understand death through their enrollment in a specific course with formal lectures, discussion, instruction and tutoring, multimedia presentations, and visits to hospitals, cemeteries, funeral homes, nursing homes, and hospice. (p. 522)

Discontinuity The idea that development is abrupt and controlled by different processes. (p. 5)

Divergent thinking A type of thinking closely related to creativity that produces many different answers to a single question. (p. 330)

Divided attention The ability to simultaneously attend to two different pieces of environmental information. (p. 287)

Do not resuscitate (DNR) Specific orders that direct physicians not to initiate heroic measures (e.g., electric shock, drugs to restart a stopped heart) when breathing or heartbeat has stopped. (p. 571)

Dopamine A neurotransmitter implicated in Parkinson's disease and schizophrenia. (p. 79)

Dual-processing (tasks) A person's ability to attend to and perform two tasks at once; this ability declines with advancing age. (p. 135)

Durable power of attorney Legal appointment of a surrogate (relative, friend, physician, lawyer) designated to make health care choices in the event a person becomes decisionally incompetent or incapacitated; the surrogate is legally authorized to accept or refuse any medical interventions not specified in advance by the person. (p. 192, 504)

Early-onset alcoholism The development of alcohol addiction through adolescence to middle age. (p. 168)

Effortful information processing Information processing that draws on limited attentional resources. (p. 288)

Ego mastery styles The style adopted in coping with self and others that reflects the underlying organization of values and beliefs that govern external behavior. (p. 43)

Electroencephalogram (EEG) A machine used to measure the electrical activity of the cortex. (p. 81)

Emotional intelligence The ability to be aware of the needs, feelings, and motives that operate in one's self and in others. (p. 328)

Emotion-focused coping Behavioral and cognitive strategies designed to help manage the emotional tensions produced by stressful life situations. (p. 116)

Empty nest syndrome A group of symptoms typified by anxiety and depression thought to be experienced by parents associated with their children's leaving home. (p. 428)

Encapsulation model A model of adult cognitive development designed to explain age-related changes in processing, knowing, and thinking. (p. 352)

Encoding deficit A memory failure that may be traced to the inability to acquire to-be-remembered information. (p. 291)

Epigenesis In Erikson's theory, the belief that all growth has an underlying structure that determines the occasions during which specific psychosocial crises may occur. (p. 378)

Episodic memory The memory for the details of personally experienced events, such as the ability to accurately recall details about the source or the context of remembered information. (p. 268)

Eras Major portions of the life span according to Daniel Levinson. (p. 385)

Error catastrophe theory The theory that errors occur in the RNA responsible for the production of enzymes that are essential to metabolism, resulting in a reduction of cell functioning and possible death. (p. 53)

Estrogen The primary female sex hormone, the depletion of which is associated with menopause. (p. 446)

Ethnic elderly A dimension of culture reflective of the older adult's nationality, heritage, race, religion, and language. (p. 148)

Ethnic gloss The tendency to make ethnic groups (e.g., Asian, Latino, Blacks) appear more homogeneous than they actually are. (p. 171)

Ethnic identity A person's membership in an ethnic group based on shared customs, heritage, values, history, language, and race. (p. 149)

Ethnic matching Identification of a mental health professional with similar ethnic characteristics as those of a client; facilitates mental health treatment and continuity of treatment. (p. 176)

Euthanasia The act of painlessly putting to death people who are suffering from incurable diseases or severe disability. (p. 514)

Exceptional creativity Another term for creative genius. (p. 329)

Existential phase The term Gibbs uses to describe the last two stages in Kohlberg's theory of moral development. (p. 414)

Experimental study A study in which an independent variable is manipulated and a dependent variable is observed. (p. 566)

Explicit memory A task in which a subject is directly instructed to consciously remember a previous event or experience. (p. 282)

External validity The extent to which one may generalize the results of an experiment. (p. 581)

Extraneous variables Variables that are not measured nor manipulated but are suspected to be important. (p. 568)

Extroversion One of the dimensions of Costa and McCrae's five-factor model of personality. (p. 394)

Factor analysis A statistical technique that produces a summary of many correlations. (p. 306)

Filial maturity Adults' growing ability to view their parents as separate persons and personalities. (p. 427)

Filial piety The cultural belief in Eastern society that the elderly possess a higher status and command a higher respect than younger people. (p. 40)

Filial responsibility The obligation felt by adult children to provide care and assistance as their parents become older. (p. 116)

Five-factor model Costa and McCrae's theory that adult personality consists of five stable and independent personality traits: neuroticism, extroversion, openness-to-experience, agreeableness, and conscientiousness. (p. 394)

Flashbulb memories Vivid, detailed, and long-lasting mental representations of personally experienced events. (p. 276)

Flexibility The range of motion in a joint or group of joints; directly related to muscle length. (p. 248)

Flow Refers to the experience of being fully engaged in an activity. (p. 476)

Fluid intelligence The basic information-processing abilities of the mind independent of life experience and education; measured by relational thinking tasks such as block design and digit-symbol substitution. (p. 302)

Flynn Effect The tendency for IQ scores to increase over time. (p. 314)

Folk systems In Hispanic cultures the assumption that mental and physical disorders may be resolved by bringing balance between the person, the environment and the spirits/cosmos (life forces) through informal, community-based healers. (p. 150)

Formal operations The fourth stage in Piaget's theory of intellectual development in which individuals are capable of abstract, hypothetical thinking. (p. 340)

Free radical theory A theory that suggests that aging is due to deleterious and short-lived chemical changes occurring within the cells of the body. (p. 53)

Free radicals By-products of incomplete or inefficient cellular metabolism and characterized by a free, unpaired electron. (p. 237)

Frontal lobe A portion of the cortex that controls higher-order executive processes. (p. 76)

Functional age An individual's level of capacity relative to other people of the same age for functioning in a given environment. (p. 13)

Functional assessment The determination of an older person's basic abilities necessary for adequate functioning including physical dimensions, mental health status, social skills, and intellect; used to determine whether intervention services, if any, are needed. (p. 86, 197)

Functional Assessment Staging System (FAST) Reisberg's conceptualization of the predictable, progressive declines in patients with AD. (p. 86)

G factor Spearman's term for general intelligence. (p. 300)

Gait speed/velocity The rate at which a person normally walks; normative changes occur in walking speed with age. (p. 253)

Gender consistency model The assumption of caregiving roles and responsibilities by adult daughters of their elderly mothers and the reverse by sons for their fathers. (p. 117)

Generativity Refers to caring about future generations of people, and to a concern about contributing to society. (p. 381)

Genetic mutation theory The idea that aging is caused by changes, or mutations, in the DNA of the cells in vital organs of the body. Eventually, the number of mutated cells in a vital organ would increase to the point that the efficacy of the cell's functioning is significantly impaired. (p. 53)

Genetic switching theory A theory or proposal that attributes biological aging to the cessation of operation of selected genes. (p. 53)

Genuine memory deficits Memory impairment that is due to the brain's inability to store new information. (p. 295)

Geriatric care managers Master's-level professionals, usually social workers, who are hired by families to identify appropriate services, level of independence, and level of functioning for an older person having medical, social, emotional, nutritional, or physical problems. (p. 206)

Gero-transcendence Refers to a view of the world that is characterized by decreased concern with personal and material interests, and greater concern with the deeper meaning of life. (p. 390)

Glare The reflection of light that has the capacity to limit vision begins in middle age. (p. 65)

Glaucoma An increase in pressure within the eye that may lead to blindness if left untreated. (p. 65)

Global Deterioration Scale A method used to describe the stages of AD. (p. 86)

Grief The sorrow, anger, guilt, and confusion that usually accompany a significant loss. (p. 534)

Grief pangs The somatic experience of grief, which includes tightness in the throat, nausea, difficulty in breathing, and sobbing. (p. 542)

Grief work The process of arriving at resolution of the loss of a loved one. (p. 430)

Guardian A court-appointed designee who makes substituted judgments on behalf of an older adult who has been judged not competent to make certain kinds of decisions for himself or herself. (p. 192)

Hemispheres The division of the cerebrum into two halves. (p. 76)

Hidden poor Those individuals who could be classified as poor on the basis of their own income but who reside with friends or relatives who are not poor. (p. 36)

Hierarchical integration One of the criteria used to identify cognitive stages; current stages incorporate (and extend) the characteristics of preceding stages. (p. 339)

Hippocampus A portion of the limbic system involved with memory processes. (p. 75)

Historical time The sociohistorical context within which a life-event occurs. (p. 404)

History A potential threat to the internal validity of a quasi-experiment; it is most likely to occur when the same individuals are tested at different times. (p. 569)

Hypertension High blood pressure, the cause of which is often the narrowing of arterial walls, familial, or unknown (idiopathic) cause. (p. 238)

Hypothetical construct A process or entity that is inferred from observation. (p. 304)

Idiosyncratic change Development that is unique to individuals. (p. 11)

Implicit memory A memory task that does not require a subject to consciously remember a previous event. (p. 282)

Independent variables The variables that are manipulated within an experimental study. (p. 567)

Individual time The time in an individual's life at which an event occurs. (p. 404)

Infantalizing the elderly Treating older persons as if they were children; seeing them as helpless, dependent, immature, and cute. (p. 134)

Infantile amnesia The inability to remember events from the first three and one-half years of life. (p. 275)

Information-processing approach The idea that age-related memory deficits are caused by the inefficient encoding, storage, and retrieval of information. (p. 291)

Instrumental activities of daily living Basic personal self-care and complex dimensions of daily living: preparation of meals, shopping, money management, telephone use, light housework, and heavy housework; used in assessment of older adults to determine appropriate intervention and services. (p. 200)

Interindividual differences The different patterns of developmental change that may be observed between different adults. (p. 3)

Interitem reliability The extent to which measurements on one-half of the items on a test are predictable from the measurements of the other half. (p. 557)

Internal validity The extent to which an independent variable determines the outcome of an experiment. (p. 569)

Interrater reliability The assessed amount of agreement between two or more observers who make independent observations in behavioral studies. (p. 557)

Interview A method of data collection in which individuals have a verbal conversation with each other. (p. 558)

Intraindividual change Different patterns of developmental change observed within individual adults. (p. 3)

Invariant movement A criteria of developmental stages; suggests that individuals must progress through developmental stages in an unchangeable manner. (p. 339)

K response An item on a memory test that a subject "knows" was presented at study. (p. 271)

Kinesthesis The ability to sense the position of one's body parts in space. (p. 70)

Korsakoff's syndrome A disorder manifested by chronic alcoholics typified by severe memory loss. (p. 168)

Late-onset alcoholism Emerging in middle to late life it is usually a response to multiple stressors such as the loss of loved ones, reaction to retirement or chronic conditions; currently underdiagnosed. (p. 168)

Leisure Descriptive account of a person's activities during free time and may include work for some people, recreation for others, or a state of mind for others. (p. 475)

Life dreams   Levinson's construct that young adolescents and adults create an idealized view of the life they will lead including the nature of their work, their lifestyles, their partners, children, families, and friends. (p. 179)

Life expectancy   How long, on the average, one is expected to live. (p. 25)

Life management   The integration and application of both assimilative and accommodative processes used to protect the aging self in the face of the cumulative effects of developmental change and to preserve positive self-evaluation and well-being. (p. 132)

Life review   A looking-back process that is set in motion by nearness to death and that potentially proceeds toward personality reorganization; the attempts to make sense of one's own life and experiences through reflection. (p. 382)

Life structure   Levinson's theoretical construct that defines the context in which adult development occurs, including the people, the places, the work, and the situations through which people choose to define themselves. (p. 384)

Life-events model   A view that suggests that some life events produce taxing circumstances for individuals, forcing them to change their personality and value orientation; it is important to consider the sociohistorical circumstances in which those events occur. (p. 109)

Limbic system   A part of the brain that controls memory and emotional responsiveness. (p. 75)

Linear   A straight line relationship between two variables. (p. 564)

Lipofuscin   A pigment that accumulates in progressive fashion with age in specific organ systems of the body. (p. 79)

Living will   A document in which an individual identifies for a physician and/or family members the specific conditions under which life-sustaining measures may be implemented or withdrawn. (p. 504)

Lobes   A name used to describe different areas of the cortex of the brain. (p. 76)

Longevity   The theoretical upper limit of the life span that is genetically fixed and species-specific. (p. 29)

Longevity difference   The difference between the number of years individuals live when compared with the number of years they are expected to live based on their age, race, and sex. (p. 32)

Longitudinal study   A research design in which data are collected from the same group of individuals on multiple occasions. (p. 571)

Long-term care   Intervention (medical, social support, personal care, health care, etc.) designed to assist the chronically ill elderly or disabled in meeting their daily needs; may be home-based or delivered in specialized centers offering rehabilitation, respite care, adult day care, or nursing care. (p. 208)

Long-term memory   A test of long-term memory in which an individual is asked to recall as many items as possible from a given list. (p. 262)

Magnetic resonance imaging (MRI)   A powerful radiological technique in which various regions of the brain are surrounded by a strong magnetic field. MRI yields a much more detailed three-dimensional representation of the brain than does the CT scan. (p. 80)

Male climacteric   The decline of sexual potency that usually begins when men are in their sixties and seventies and progresses at a much slower rate than female menopause. (p. 447)

Mammography   A procedure used to screen for breast cancer using low radiation X-ray imaging. (p. 232)

Mastectomy   Removal of the breast and associated lymph nodes under the arm. (p. 232)

Maximal oxygen uptake (VO$_2$max)   One of the standard methods for establishing a person's overall aerobic capacity; the higher the oxygen consumption per minute per kilogram of body weight, the better one's cardiovascular system and the greater one's overall endurance. (p. 245)

Mean   The statistical procedure used to determine the arithmetic average. (p. 562)

Mechanics of mind   The basic operations of our human information-processing system. Mental hardware such as sensation, perception, and memory. (p. 361)

Mechanistic paradigm   The model that suggests that adults are passive machines that merely react to environmental events. (p. 16)

Median   The value in the exact middle of a distribution of scores. (p. 562)

Medicaid   Federal- and state-supported health care program for low-income persons. (p. 210)

Medical directive   An explicit written statement of a person's wish to accept or reject particular forms of medical intervention that might arise in key situations; it preserves the rights of persons to self-determination when they become incompetent or are unable to make decisions or express their wishes. (p. 504)

Medicare   Federal health insurance for adults 65 and older and the disabled (regardless of age) that provides short-term in-patient hospital care and limited skilled care at home or in a nursing home. (p. 211)

Medigap policies   Health care insurance designed to meet the shortfall between actual medical treatment costs and that provided by Medicare. (p. 213)

Melatonin   A hormone produced by the pineal gland that binds with free radicals. (p. 56)

Menopause   The permanent cessation of menstruation and the ability to bear children. (p. 446)

Mental health   A psychological state marked by the absence of mental disorders and the ability to cope effectively with life events. (p. 145)

Mental imagery   The process of forming mental images as a means of enhancing memory performance. (p. 272)

Mentor   An adult who guides or advises another, typically younger, adult about personal, social, or occupational goals. (p. 473)

Meta-analysis   A method that provides an objective account of the results of several studies that are taken as a whole. (p. 579)

Metabolism   A measure of the rate at which an individual burns calories. (p. 236)

Metamemory   Knowing about one's own memory abilities. Being able to accurately assess your own memory abilities and to accurately report what you know are examples. (p. 260)

Milieu therapy   Improving the quality of an institutional environment by modifying physical, social, cognitive, and emotional dimensions to maximize the needs of its residents. (p. 188)

Mitochondria   Structure of the cell responsible for producing energy through breakdown of nutrients into basic elements. (p. 237)

Mode   The most frequently appearing score in a distribution of scores. (p. 562)

Most efficient design   The complex design that allows investigators to separate out the specific effects of age, time of testing, and cohort. (p. 577)

Mourning   The overt, behavioral expression of grief and bereavement that is heavily influenced by cultural patterns. (p. 534)

Multidirectionality   The idea that there are intraindividual differences in the patterns of development and aging. (p. 7)

Multiple regression   A statistical method by which a researcher can determine if a number of variables, in combination with each other (or independent of each other), predict another variable. (p. 564)

Mutual help   A significant value in Hispanic culture that sustains intergenerational patterns of care through an obligatory norm biased on guilt and gratitude. (p. 149)

Myocardial infarction   Blockage of one of the coronary arteries sufficient to cause the heart to be deprived of blood, causing irreversible damage to the heart muscle (e.g., heart attack). (p. 238)

Near poor   Those individuals with incomes between the poverty level and 125 percent of this level. (p. 36)

Negative correlation   A pattern of association between two variables in which higher scores on one variable are related to lower scores on another. (p. 563)

Neurofibrillary tangles   Intertwined fibers that interfere with normal neuronal functioning. (p. 78)

Neuron   A nerve cell that is the basic unit of the nervous system. (p. 76)

Neuroticism   One of the personality traits in Costa and McCrae's Five-Factor Model of adult personality. (p. 394)

Neurotransmitters   Chemical substances used to send messages across a synapse. (p. 79)

Nondeclarative memory   The influence that past events have on a person's current behavior. (p. 268)

Nonnormative life events   Influences on development that do not follow a prescribed social or biological order. (p. 8)

Normative age-graded factors   Influences on developmental change that are closely related to an individual's chronological age. (p. 8)

Normative history-graded factors   Influences on development that are closely related to societal events. (p. 8)

Obese   Body weight defined as more than 20% higher than ideal or average as established by normative data. (p. 236)

Objective caregiver burden   The disruption of an adult's routine or expected lifestyle (e.g., finances, travel, friendships, family interactions) caused by having to care for an older parent or close relative. (p. 117)

Occipital lobe   The portion of the cortex involved in visual perception. (p. 76)

Oldest-old   The fastest growing segment of the population in the United States, those 85 years of age and older. (p. 109)

Oncologists   Physicians who specialize in the diagnosis and treatment of cancer. (p. 228)

Ontogeny   The study of maturation of the individual. The term ontogeny can be contrasted with phylogeny, which refers to the study of species development. (p. 3)

Openness to experience   One of the personality traits that comprises Costa and McCrae's Five-Factor Model of adult personality. (p. 394)

Optimization   A goal of the field of gerontology to understand how to best preserve a positive life for all adults (e.g., independence, freedom, personal autonomy, dignity) in keeping with an age-irrelevant view of society. (p. 197)

Ordinary creativity   Creativity exhibited by "ordinary adults" in everyday situations. (p. 330)

Organ of Corti   The organ in the inner ear that transforms sound vibrations into nerve impulses. (p. 66)

Organismic paradigm   The model that views development as genetically programmed and following a set progression of qualitatively discontinuous stages. (p. 16)

Organization   A strategy useful in enhancing memory performance. (p. 271)

Osteoporosis   The thinning and weakening of the bones due to calcium deficiency in older people, especially women. (p. 59)

P300 brain wave   A unique pattern of brain activity associated with the identification of novel stimuli. (p. 81)

Palliative treatments   A treatment that focuses on the symptoms rather than the cause of a disease. (p. 93)

Paradigm   Refers to a theoretical approach or perspective that helps researchers organize and interpret their observations. (p. 15)

Parental imperative   Refers to the tendency of the birth of a child to trigger heightened sex-role differentiation between mother and father in order to assist with the division of labor. (p. 44)

Parietal lobe   A portion of the cortex involved in short-term memory and the representation of spatial relationships. (p. 76)

Passive accommodative mastery style (passive mastery)   A style of coping in which individuals fit themselves to the environment rather than try to change the external environment. (p. 44)

Passive euthanasia   Inducing a natural death by withdrawing some life-sustaining therapeutic effort such as turning off a respirator or heart-lung machine. (p. 514)

Pearson product moment correlation coefficient   Abbreviated as *r*, this computes the quantitative strength of a correlation on a scale of -1.00 to $+1.00$. (p. 564)

Permanent vegetative state   An irreversible clinical condition from which the individual will not regain consciousness, awareness of self or the environment; or, if consciousness were regained, permanent and severe disabilities would be present. (p. 502)

Persistent vegetative state   A clinical condition of complete unawareness of the self and the environment, accompanied by sleep-wake cycles but no evidence of purposeful or voluntary behavioral responsiveness to environmental stimuli, no language comprehension or expression, no bowel or bladder control. It lasts for at least one month following degenerative or metabolic disorders. (p. 501)

Personality   The distinctive patterns of behavior, thought, and emotion that characterize each person's adaptation to the situations of his/her life. (p. 377)

Person-centered death education   An existential approach to helping people understand death—cognitively and emotionally, by focusing on the personal meaning of the loss and sharing the experience: the feelings, reactions, and intellectual dimensions that are so intense and yet rarely communicated to others. (p. 522)

Pet therapy   Regular contact with domestic animals encourages older persons sense of autonomy, responsibility, well-being, control, and improves their general social responsiveness. (p. 188)

Philosophical wisdom   Refers to an understanding of the abstract relationship between one's self and the rest of humanity. (p. 360)

Physical competence   A basic concept of exercise physiology used to assess the impact of physical training and exercise relative to baseline measurements. (p. 224)

Physiological or system-based theories   The position that aging is caused by changes, or mutations, in the DNA of the cells in vital organs of the body. (p. 14, 52)

Plasticity   Refers to the range of function that can be observed in individuals; frequently used to refer to the extent to which cognitive or physical performance can be improved by practice or training. (p. 6)

Positive correlation   An association between variables such that high scores on one variable are related to high scores on another variable. (p. 563)

Positron-emission tomography (PET scan)   A noninvasive method of measuring the metabolic activity of the brain. (p. 80)

Postconventional level   The last two stages within Kohlberg's theory of moral development; at this level, individuals are capable of generating moral rules that are based on universal principles of justice. (p. 407)

Postformal operational thought   Generic term used to describe the qualitative changes in thinking beyond Piaget's stage of formal operations; characterized by an acceptance of relativity, dialectic thinking, and problem finding. (p. 141)

Postformal operations   The generic term used to describe qualitative changes in thinking beyond Piaget's stage of formal operations, characterized by an acceptance of

relativity, dialectic thinking, and problem finding. (p. 346)

Postvention program   Yearlong hospice program providing survivors counseling, home visits, and peer support groups following the death of a loved one to help them cope with their loss. (p. 532)

Potential life span   The maximum age that could be attained if the individual were able to avoid illness and accidents. (p. 31)

Practical wisdom   Refers to the ability to display superior judgment with regard to important matters of real life. (p. 360)

Pragmatics of mind   The mental software that encompasses the general system of factual and strategic knowledge accessible to members of a particular culture, the specialized systems of knowledge available to individuals within particular occupations and avocations, and an understanding of how to effectively activate these different types of knowledge within particular contexts to aid problem solving. (p. 363)

Preconventional level   The first two stages in Kohlberg's theory of moral development; characterized by the construction of moral rules that are based on the fear of punishment and the desire for pleasure. (p. 407)

Preoperational stage   The second stage in Piaget's theory of cognitive development; characterized by illogical thinking that is marked by irreversibility as well as the inability to distinguish fantasy from reality. (p. 340)

Presbycusis   The general term used to describe age-related problems in hearing, especially hearing high-pitched sounds. (p. 66)

Presbyopia   The reduction in the efficacy of near vision; usually first observed during middle adulthood. (p. 64)

Primary appraisal   The process of choosing whether an event is stressful and requires the implementation of coping strategies. (p. 111)

Primary mental abilities   Thurstone's belief that intelligence consisted of the following mental abilities: verbal comprehension, word fluency, number, space, associative memory, perceptual speed, and induction. (p. 301)

Priming task   An implicit memory task in which subjects are asked to identify

or make judgments about stimuli that were (or were not) presented during an earlier phase of an experiment. (p. 281)

Prior to need (or preneed)   The practice of arranging funeral expenses long before the need arises, when the individual is healthy and well. (p. 538)

Probable causes   The use of ex post facto analysis of treatment success to determine the source of a psychological problem such as clinical depression; successful intervention indicates the likely source of the problem. (p. 181)

Problem finding   The identification and construction of sophisticated problems to resolve. (p. 335)

Problem-focused coping   The determination that a stressful life event requires changing the event or obtaining additional information about the event in order to cope successfully. (p. 116)

Process dissociation procedure (PDP)   A method of estimating the degree to which conscious and unconscious (or automatic) factors independently contribute to performance on a memory test. (p. 284)

Progressive overload   Training principle establishing a level of intervention sufficient to increase stress on the body to cause adaptations that improve fitness; too much stress can cause damage and too little will be insufficient to enhance fitness. (p. 242)

Prostatic specific antigen (PSA)   Blood test used to screen males for prostate cancer. (p. 234)

Psychological age   An individual's ability to adapt to changing environmental demands in comparison to the adaptability of other individuals of identical chronological age. (p. 14)

Psychometric approach   An approach to adult intellectual development that involves the administration of standardized adult intelligence tests such as the WAIS and PMA. (p. 300)

Psychomotor slowing   The age-related slowing of behavior. (p. 71)

Psychoneuroimmunology   The study of the multifaceted changes in the central nervous system and immune system in response to life events, stressors, and special challenges that heighten or reduce a persons's susceptibility to disease. (p. 226)

Psychopharmacology   The administration of prescription drugs to alter a person's biological state to attain a desirable goal, e.g., modification of behavioral, affective, or physiological states. (p. 184)

Psychosexual development The study of how individuals of different ages deal with pleasurable body sensations. (p. 378)

Psychosocial development The study of the lifelong relationship between the developing individual and the social system of which she or he is a part. (p. 378)

Qualitative change Abrupt, stagelike differences rather than differences in amount that occur in development. (p. 5, 339)

Quantitative change The differences in amount rather than kind that occur in development. (p. 5)

Quasi-experiments Studies that resemble true experiments in design and analysis but contain an independent variable that cannot be manipulated. (p. 568)

Questionnaire A method of data collection in which an individual responds to a standardized list of questions. (p. 559)

R response An item on a memory test that a subject "remembers" was presented at study. (p. 271)

Random assignment The technique of assigning individuals to exposure conditions on a random basis in order to evenly distribute extraneous factors. (p. 568)

Range of motion The full motion possible in a joint. (p. 248)

Range The simplest measure of variability; revealed by the lowest and the highest score in a set. (p. 563)

Reaction time Experimental assessments of the time elapsed between the appearance of a signal and a person's responding movement. (p. 555)

Reactivity The way in which an individual reacts to being tested/observed within a psychological study; a threat to the internal validity of an experiment or quasi-experiment. (p. 560)

Reality orientation Providing elderly regular reminders of where they are and of their present situation (e.g., day, date, residence). (p. 188)

Recall A type of memory task in which individuals must remember

information without the aid of any external cues or supports. (p. 270)

Recognition A basic strategy for assessing memory ability. (p. 270)

Reliability The consistency of the results of a test in the same person(s) from one time to another. (p. 556)

Reminiscence bump The tendency for older adults to remember a disproportionately large number of memories from late-adolescence and early adulthood. (p. 277)

Reminiscence therapy The encouragement of older persons to recall their past reflect on their memories and bring closure to personal-family conflicts, e.g., resolution of "unfinished business." (p. 188)

Representative sample A sample of a population that has the same characteristics as the entire population. (p. 580)

Reserve capacity The amount of resources available to the individual for responding to physical or psychological challenges. The amount of reserve capacity, or the range of plasticity, of particular physiological systems may become limited with aging. (p. 6)

Respite care Temporary assistance to relieve family members from the physical, emotional, and social demands of caring for an older person at home. Such assistance is often provided by volunteers, friends, relatives, or through community agencies including adult day care programs. (p. 103)

Retrieval deficit Memory impairment due to the inability to successfully access stored information. (p. 292)

Reversibility of fitness The loss of fitness and conditioning that occurs when people curtail their training. (p. 242)

Rheumatoid arthritis An autoimmune disease marked by swelling of the joints and, over time, degeneration of cartilage in affected joints and resultant loss of joint function. (p. 226)

Sarcopenia Atrophy of skeletal muscle mass; one of the most predictable consequences of aging. (p. 248)

Sati The ancient Hindu practice of burning a dead man's widow to increase his family's prestige and establish her image as a goddess in his memory. (p. 535)

Schaie-Thurstone Adult Mental Abilities Test A standardized test of adult intelligence, which is adapted from Thurstone's Primary Mental Abilities Test. (p. 301)

Search for meaning Existential quest for understanding the human condition and one's purpose in life. (p. 133, 138)

Secondary appraisal When facing a life event determined to be stressful a person's assessment of the range of available resources and the "cost" of implementing such resources. (p. 111)

Selection A threat to internal validity when the procedures used to select individuals for research result in extraneous or unintended differences in the groups selected for study, e.g., young vs. old subjects may differ not only on education but also in terms of health. (p. 569)

Selective attention A type of attention in which we ignore irrelevant information while focusing on relevant information (e.g., ignoring a television program while listening to a friend). (p. 287).

Selective dropout The tendency for particular individuals to drop out of longitudinal studies, e.g., the infirm, the less able, those who move from the area, and thus skew the results in a biased fashion. (p. 315)

Selective optimization with compensation A technique by which older adults alter their behavior in such a way as to preserve (and perhaps enhance) specific cognitive, behavioral, or physical abilities. (p. 367)

Selfish grief The conflict experienced by daughters who fear that overt expression of grief over the loss of their mothers would mean that they wished to prolong the suffering and pain that their mothers experienced; they suppress their emotional reactions to the loss of their mothers, appearing to readily accept their death. (p. 547)

Semantic elaboration A strategy used to enhance memory. (p. 27)

Semantic memory Use of acquired knowledge about the world; thinking about the meanings of words or concepts without reference to when or how we acquired such knowledge. (p. 269)

Senescence All of the changes that are associated with the normal process of aging. (p. 51)

Senile plaques The accumulation of spherical masses of amyloid surrounded by degenerating axons and dendrites; senile plaques prevent normal communication between neurons. (p. 78)

Senility An outdated term referring to abnormal deterioration of mental functions in old people. (p. 82)

Sensation The reception of physical stimuli at a sense organ and the translation of this stimulation to the brain. (p. 64)

Sensorimotor stage The first stage in Piaget's theory of cognitive development in which the child discovers the world using the senses and motor activity. (p. 340)

Service delivery An intervention designed to provide substitute assistance for activities that individuals normally provide for themselves. (p. 176)

Sex role The behaviors that are expected of individuals because they are either male or female. (p. 42)

Short-term memory Information that is stored and retained for a brief period, usually less than 60 seconds. (p. 262)

Social age Refers to the social roles and social expectations people have for themselves as well as those imposed by others in society. (p. 14)

Social clock The internalized sense of timing that tells people whether they are experiencing predictable/normative life events on-time or off-time (e.g., too fast or too slow). (p. 113, 402)

Social cognition Cognitive development that is focused on the individual's reasoning about social and interpersonal matters. (p. 351)

Social comparisons Evaluation of one's current status and function using other social groups for normative comparisons; social comparisons can result in upward or downward contrasts vs. one's own status. (p. 132)

Social convoy The network of close relationships that accompany an individual throughout life. (p. 423)

Social Security A federal program designed to provide benefits to adults who become disabled or retire. Comprised of four separate trust funds: (1) Old Age Survivors Insurance, (2) Disability Insurance, (3) Hospital Insurance Trust Fund–Medicare part A, (4) Supplementary Medical Insurance–Medicare part B. (p. 203)

Soma The cell body of a neuron. (p. 76)

Source memory The ability to remember the context in which a particular piece of information has been learned. (p. 272)

Spending down Depletion of an individual's income and assets to meet the eligibility requirements for Medicaid. (p. 211)

Spirituality The motivational and emotional source of an individual's search for a personally defined relationship with a higher being; leads to enhanced feelings of well-being, inner peace, and life satisfaction. (p. 138)

Stage theory A theory that suggests that development consists of a series of abrupt changes in psychological functions and processes, marked by qualitative change at each stage. (p. 6)

Standard deviation A common measure of variability that reveals the extent to which the individual scores deviate from the mean of a distribution. (p. 563)

Standard phase Gibbs's term that refers to the first four stages in Kohlberg's theory of moral development. (p. 44)

Standardization The establishment of fixed procedures for administration, scoring, and norms for age, grade, race, sex and so on. (p. 562)

Statistical significance A mathematical procedure to determine the extent to which differences in performance between groups of subjects are due to chance factors or the independent variable. (p. 566)

Strength training Directed physical activity requiring resistance against a mass or load to produce muscle contraction. (p. 247)

Stress-buffering effect The reduction in the impact of stressful events due to moderating influences of social supports (family, peers, neighbors, and community), which lead to decreased likelihood of depression in older adults. (p. 157)

Stroke Blockage of one of the arteries supplying blood to the brain causing destruction of associated areas and corresponding loss of function; e.g., loss of language center leads to various speech disorders such as aphasia, loss of certain motor centers leads to paralysis, etc. (p. 238)

Structured wholeness A criteria for determining developmental stages; implies that individuals' cognitions are consistent with their current stage of development. (p. 339)

Subjective caregiver burden The emotional reactions of adults providing care for an older parent or relative that include embarrassment, shame, guilt, resentment, and social exclusion. (p. 117)

Successful aging Refers to avoiding disease and disability, and continued active engagement in life. (p. 14)

Sundowning Heightened incidence of wandering, pacing, and generalized restlessness found among elderly with dementia, which occurs in the early evening (e.g., 7–10 P. M.). (p. 220)

Syncope Temporary loss of consciousness ("blackouts") often due to medical conditions, prescription drugs, or special physical conditions. (p. 137)

Temporal lobe The portion of the cortex involved in audition, language, and long-term memory. (p. 76)

Tension-reduction hypothesis The use of alcohol to manage the tension and anxieties associated with negative life events and chronic stress. (p. 168)

Terminal drop A decline in psychological functioning, revealed in standardized tests, that precedes death by about five years. (p. 317)

Testamentary capacity Having the mental capacity and judgment necessary to create a will directing disposition of one's assets (real estate, valuables, stocks, bonds, jewelry, clothes, etc.). (p. 192)

Testing the limits The technique used to measure age differences in maximum cognitive reserve. (p. 363)

Testing A threat to internal validity that is based on the readministration of the same instrument on more than one occasion. (p. 570)

Test-retest reliability The degree of predictability that measurements taken on one test on one occasion will be similar to those taken on another occasion. (p. 556)

Theory of Multiple Intelligences The position that there are several neurologically based types of human intelligences. (p. 328)

Time-sequential design A complex research design that allows an investigator to disentangle age effects from time-of-testing effects. (p. 575)

Tinnitus A constant high-pitched or ringing sound in the ears reported in about 10 percent of older adults. (p. 66)

Trait theorists Personality theorists who believe that there is some consistency and stability to human personality over time. (p. 390)

Trajectory of life According to Pattison, our anticipated life span and the plan we make for the way in which we will live out our life. (p. 526)

Transient ischemic attack (TIA) A temporary, reversible minor stroke. (p. 94)

Transitions According to Levinson, the periods that overlap one era with another; transitions last for approximately five years. (p. 386)

Triarchic Theory of Intelligence The theory that suggests that intelligence consists of three independent facets: analytic, creative, and practical. (p. 328)

Type A behavior style Behavior reflecting excessive competitiveness, accelerated pace of normal activities, time-urgency, hostility, and aggressiveness. (p. 238)

Type B behavior style Behavior reflective of the absence of Type A behavior style, behavior indicative of a relaxed, less hurried, and less preoccupied lifestyle. (p. 238)

Unfinished business Resolution, where possible, of the interpersonal problems created in social relationships; the desire by dying persons to bring closure to the different dimension of their lives. (p. 188)

Unidirectional change The idea that developmental change in a given function follows the same trajectory in all individuals. (p. 7)

Universal progression A criteria for the presence of developmental stages; the belief that all individuals in all cultures progress through all stages in the same invariant sequence. (p. 339)

Uplifts The small positive experiences we encounter in daily living that counterbalance the hassles that occur in everyday life. (p. 112)

Upswing hypothesis The contention that there is an increase in marital satisfaction when children leave home. (p. 428)

Validity The soundness of measurements in terms of measuring what they are intended to measure. (p. 558)

Variability The statistical description of distribution scores; includes range and standard deviation. (p. 563)

Variable Anything that may change and influence behavior. (p. 563)

Wear-and-tear theory The idea that aging occurs because of physical wear and tear on the body caused by hard work. (p. 51)

Wechsler Adult Intelligence Scale (WAIS) A standard test of adult intelligence that provides both a verbal IQ and performance IQ as well as an overall IQ score. (p. 305)

White matter Another name for the fatty myelin sheath that surrounds and insulates long axons. (p. 78)

Wisdom An expert knowledge system in the fundamental pragmatics of life permitting exceptional insight, judgment, and advice involving complex and uncertain matters of the human condition. (p. 338)

Within-subject manipulations Experimental design in which each subject is administered each level of an independent variable. (p. 568)

Working memory The active manipulation of information in short-term memory. (p. 263)

REFERENCES

Abraham, J. D., & Hansson, R. O. (1995). Successful aging at work: An applied study of selection, optimization, and compensation through impression management. *Journal of Gerontology: Psychological Sciences, 50,* P94–103.

Adams, S. L., & Waskel, S. A. (1993). Late onset alcoholism: Stress or structure. *Journal of Psychology, 127* (3), 329–334.

Adler, T. (1992, February). For depressed elderly, drugs advised. *American Psychological Association Monitor,* pp. 16–17.

Adrain, M.J. (1981). Flexibility in the aging adult. In E.L. Smith & R.C. Serfass (Eds.), *Exercise and aging: The scientific basis.* Hillsdale, NJ: Enslow.

Albert, M. (1993). Neuropsychological and neurophysiological changes in healthy adult humans across the age range. *Neurobiology of Aging, 14,* 623.

Albert, M., & Moss, M. B. (in press). Neuropsychology of aging: Findings in humans and monkeys. In E. Schneider & J. W. Rowe (Eds.), *Handbook of the biology of aging* (4th ed.). San Diego: Academic Press.

Albert, M. S., & Stafford, J. L. (1988). Computed tomography studies. In M. S. Albert & M. B. Moss (Eds.), *Geriatric neuropsychology* (pp. 211–227). New York: Guilford.

Albert, S. M. (1991). Cognition of caregiving tasks: Multidimensional scaling of the caregiver task domain. *The Gerontologist, 31,* 726–734.

Aldridge, D., & Aldridge, G. (1992). Two epistemologies: Music therapy and medicine in the treatment of dementia. *Arts in Psychotherapy, 19,* 243–255.

Aldwin, C. (1995). The role of stress in aging and adult development. *Adult Development and Aging News, 23,* 3, 7, 16.

Aldwin, C. M., Spiro, A., Bosse, R., & Levenson, M. R. (1989). Longitudinal findings from the normative aging study: 1. Does mental health change with age? *Psychology and Aging, 4,* 295–306.

Aldwin, L. M. (1994). *Stress, coping, and development: An integrative perspective.* New York: Guilford.

Alpaugh, P., & Birren, J. E. (1977). Variables affecting creative contributions across the life span. *Human Development, 20,* 240–248.

Altman, L. K. (1992). Alzheimer's dilemma: Whether to tell people they have the disease. *New York Times,* April 7, p. C3.

American Association of Retired Persons. (1992). *A profile of older Americans.* Washington, DC.

American Association of Retired Persons. (1993a). *Understanding senior housing.* (D13899). Washington, DC.

American Association of Retired Persons. (1993b). *A perfect fit.* (D14823). Washington, DC.

American Cancer Society. (1997). *Cancer Facts and Figures, 1997.* Atlanta, GA: American Cancer Society.

American Cancer Society. Guidelines (1996). Cancer Society warns about red meat, alcohol consumption. Burros, M. New York Times, September 17, 1996.

American Heart Association. (1992). *Silent epidemic: The truth about women and heart disease.* Dallas: American Heart Association.

American Heart Association. (1995). *Heart and stroke facts: 1995 statistical supplement.* Dallas: American Heart Association.

American Psychiatric Association. (1994). *Diagnostic and Statistical Manual of Mental Disorders-Fourth Edition.* Washington, DC: American Psychiatric Association.

Anastasi, A. (1988) *Psychological testing–Sixth Edition.* New York: Macmillan.

Anders, T. R., Fozard, J. L., & Lillyquist, T. D. (1972). Effects of age upon retrieval from short-term memory. *Developmental Psychology, 6,* 214–217.

Anderson, S. A., Russell, C. S., & Schumm, W. R. (1983). Perceived marital quality and family life-cycle categories: A further analysis. *Journal of Marriage and the Family, 45,* 127–139.

Angel, J. L., Angel, R. J., McClellan, J. L. & Markides, K. S. (1996). Nativity, declining health, and preferences in living arrangements among elderly Mexican Americans: Implications for long-term care. *Gerontologist, 36,* 464–473.

Angel, R. S., & Angel, J. L. (1995). Mental and physical comorbidity among the elderly: The role of culture and social class. In D. K. Padgett (Ed.), *Handbook on ethnicity, aging, and mental health* (pp. 47–70). Westport, CT: Greenwood Press.

Anthony, J. C., & Aboraya, A. (1992). The epidemiology of selected mental disorders in later life. In J. E. Birren, R. B. Sloane, G. D. Cohen, N. R. Hooyman, B. Leibowitz, M. H. Wykle, & D. E. Deutchman, *Handbook of mental health and aging* (2nd ed.). San Diego: Academic Press.

Antonucci, T. C. (1990). Social supports and social relationships. In R. H. Binstock & K. K. George (Eds.), *Handbook of aging and the social sciences* (3rd ed.). New York: Academic Press.

Antonucci, T. C., & Akiyama, H. (1991a). Social relationships and aging well. *Generations, 15,* 39–44.

Antonucci, T. C., & Akiyama, H. (1991b). Convoys of social support: Generational issues. *Marriage and Family Review, 16,* 103–123.

Aponte, J. F., & Barnes, J. M. (1995). Impact of acculturation and moderator variables on the intervention and treatment of ethnic groups. In J. F. Aponte, R. Y. Rivers, & J. Wohl. (Eds.), *Psychological interventions and cultural diversity* (pp. 19–39). Boston: Allyn & Bacon.

Aponte, J. F., & Crouch, R. T. (1995). The changing ethnic profile of the United States. In J. F. Aponte, R. Y. Rivers, & J. Wohl. (Eds.), *Psychological interventions and cultural diversity.* Boston: Allyn & Bacon.

Aponte, J. F., Rivers, R. Y., & Wohl, J. (1995). *Psychological interventions and cultural diversity.* Boston: Allyn & Bacon.

Applebaum, P. S., & Grisso, T. (1988). Assessing patient's capacities to consent to treatment. *New England Journal of Medicine, 319,* 1635–1638.

Argyle, M. (1994). *The psychology of social class.* New York: Routledge.

Arlin, P. K. (1975). Cognitive development in adulthood: A fifth stage. *Developmental Psychology, 11,* 602–606.

Arlin, P. K. (1984). Adolescent and adult thought: A structural interpretation. In M. L. Commons, F. A. Richards, & C. Armon (Eds.), *Beyond formal operations: Late adolescent and adult cognitive development.* New York: Praeger.

Arlin, P. K. (1989). Problem solving and problem finding in young artists and young scientists. In M. L. Commons, J. D. Sinnott, F. A. Richards, & C. Armon (Eds.), *Adult development, Vol. 1: Comparisons and applications of developmental models.* New York: Praeger.

Armon, C. (1991). *The development of reasoning about the good life.* Paper presented at the Sixth Adult Development Symposium of the Society for Research in Adult Development, Boston, MA, July.

Asch, D. A., & Christakis, N. A. (1996). Why do physicians prefer to withdraw some forms of life support over others? Intrinsic attribute of life-sustaining treatments are associated with physicians preferences. *Medical Care, 34,* 103–111.

Ascher, B. (1993). *Landscape without gravity.* New York: Delphinivar Books.

Atchley, R. C. (1983). *Aging: Continuity and change.* Belmont, CA: Wadsworth.

Atkinson, R. M., Ganzini, L., & Bernstein, M. J. (1992). Alcohol and substance-use disorders in the elderly. In J. E. Birren, R. B. Sloane, and G. D. Cohen (Eds.), *Handbook of mental health and aging* (2nd ed.). San Diego, CA: Academic Press.

Attig, T. (1992). Person-centered death education. *Death Studies, 16,* 357–370.

Ausubel, D. P. (1968). *Educational psychology.* New York: Holt, Rinehart & Winston.

Backman, L., Mantyla, T., & Herlitz, A. (1990). Psychological perspectives on successful aging: The optimization of episodic remembering in old age. In P. B. Baltes & M. M. Baltes (Eds.), *Successful aging* (pp. 118–163). New York: Cambridge University Press.

Baddeley, A. (1986). *Working memory.* Oxford: Oxford University Press.

Baddeley, A. (1994). Working memory: The interface between memory and cognition. In D. L. Schacter & E. Tulving (Eds.), *Memory systems 1994* (pp. 351–368). Cambridge, MA: MIT Press.

Baer, D. M. (1970). An age-irrelevant concept of development. *Merrill Palmer Quarterly of Behavior and Development, 16,* 238–245.

Bahrick, H. P., Bahrick, P. O., & Wittlinger, R. P. (1975). Fifty years of memory for names and faces: A cross-sectional approach. *Journal of Experimental Psychology: General, 104,* 54–75.

Baillie, P. H., & Danish, S. J. (1992, March). Understanding the career transition of athletes. *Sport Psychologist, 6,* 77–98.

Balch, D. W. (1997). Long term healthcare: A family crisis. *Maturity Focus, Eagle Newspapers Supplement,* p. 7.

Baltes, M. M., Kühl, K. P., Gutzmann, H., & Sowarka, D. (1995). Potential of cognitive plasticity as a diagnostic instrument: A cross-validation and extension. *Psychology and Aging, 10,* 167–172.

Baltes, M. M., Kühl, K. P., & Sowarka, D. (1992). Testing for limits of cognitive reserve capacity: A promising strategy for early diagnosis of dementia? Journal of Gerontology: *Psychological Sciences, 47,* P165–P167.

Baltes, M. M., Neumann, E., & Zank, S. (1994). Maintenance and rehabilitation of independence in old age: An intervention program for staff. *Psychology and Aging, 9,* 179–188.

Baltes, P. B. (1987). Theoretical propositions of life-span developmental psychology: On the dynamics between growth and decline. *Developmental Psychology, 23,* 611–626.

Baltes, P. B. (1993). The aging mind: Potential and limits. *The Gerontologist, 33,* 580–594.

Baltes, P. B. (1997). On the incomplete architecture of human ontogeny: Selection, optimization, and compensation as foundations of developmental theory. *American Psychologist, 52,* 366–380.

Baltes, P. B., & Baltes, M. (1990). Psychological perspectives on successful aging: The model of selective optimization with compensation. In P. B. Baltes & M. Baltes (Eds.), *Longitudinal research and the study of successful (optimal) aging* (pp. 1–49). Cambridge England: Cambridge University Press.

Baltes, P. B., & Graf, P. (1996). Psychological aspects of aging: Facts and frontiers. In D. Magnusson (Ed.), *The life span development of individuals: Behavioral, neurobiological, and psychosocial perspectives* (pp. 427–459). Cambridge: Cambridge University Press.

Baltes, P. B., & Kliegl, R. (1986). On the dynamics between growth and decline in the aging of intelligence and memory. In K. Poeck, H. J. Freund, & H. Ganshirt (Eds.), *Neurology.* Heidelberg, West Germany: Springer-Verlag.

Baltes, P. B., & Kliegl, R. (1992). Further testing of limits of cognitive plasticity: Negative age differences in a mnemonic skill are robust. *Developmental Psychology, 28,* 121–125.

Baltes, P. B., & Lindenberger, U. (1997). Emergence of a powerful connection between sensory and cognitive functions across the adult lifespan: A new window to the study of cognitive aging? *Psychology and Aging, 12,* 410–432.

Baltes, P. B., & Smith, J. (1997). A systemic-wholistic view of psychological functioning in very old age: Introduction to a collection of articles from the Berlin Aging Study. *Psychology and Aging, 12,* 396–409.

Baltes, P. B., & Staudinger, U. (1993). The search for a psychology of wisdom. *Current Directions in Psychological Science, 2,* 75–80.

Baltes, P. B., Lindenberger, U., & Staudinger, U. M. (1998). Life-span theory in developmental psychology. In R. M. Lerner (Ed.), *Handbook of child psychology: Vol. 1. Theoretical models of human development* (5 ed.). New York: Wiley.

Baltes, P. B., Sowarka, D., & Kliegl, R. (1989). Cognitive training research on fluid intelligence in old age: What can older adults achieve by themselves? *Psychology and Aging, 4,* 217.

Baltes, P. B., Mayer, K. U., Helmchen, H., & Steinhagen-Thiessen, E. (1993). The Berlin Aging Study (BASE): Overview and design. *Aging and Society, 13,* 483–515.

Baltes, P. B., Staudinger, U. M., Maeker, A., & Smith, J. (1995). People nominated as wise: A comparative study of wisdom related knowledge. *Psychology and Aging, 10,* 155–166.

Bandura, A. (1982). Self-efficacy in human agency. *American Psychologist, 37,* 122–137.

Bandura, A. L. (1989). Human agency in social cognitive theory. *American Psychologist, 44,* 1175–1184.

Bardwick, J. (1990). Where we are and what we want: A psychological model. In R. A. Nemiroff & C. A. Colarusso (Eds.), *New dimensions in adult development* (pp. 186–213). New York: Basic Books.

Barney, D. D. (1995). Use of mental health services by American Indians and Alaska Native elders. In D. K. Padgett (Ed.), *Handbook of ethnicity, aging, and mental health* (pp. 203–214). Westport, CT: Greenwood.

Barron, S. A., Jacobs, L., & Kirkei, W. R. (1976). Changes in size of normal lateral ventricles during aging determined by computerized tomography. *Neurology, 26,* 1011–1013.

Bartoshuk, L. M., Rifkin, B., Marks, L. E., & Bars, P. (1986). Taste and aging. *Journal of Gerontology, 41,* 51–57.

Bashore, T. R. (1993). Differential effects of aging on the neurocognitive functions subserving speeded mental processing. In J. Cerella, J. M. Rybash, W. J. Hoyer, & M. L. Commons (Eds.), *Adult information processing: Limits on loss* (pp. 37–76). San Diego: Academic Press.

Basseches, M. (1984). *Dialectic thinking.* Norwood, NJ: Ablex.

Basta, L. L. (1996). *A graceful exit: Life and death on your own terms.* New York: Insight Books-Plenum Press.

Bastida, E. (1987). Sex-typed age norms among older Hispanics. *The Gerontologist, 27,* 59–65.

Baum, C., Edwards, D. F., & Morrow-Howell, N. (1993). Identification and measurement of productive behaviors in servile dementia of the Alzheimer type. *Journal of Gerontology, 33,* 403–408.

Baum, M., & Page, M. (1991). Caregiving and multi-generational families. *The Gerontologist, 31,* 762–769.

Baumgartner, R. N., Stauber, P. M., McHugh, D., Koehler, K. M., & Garry, P. J. (1995). Cross-sectional age differences in body composition in persons 60 years or older. *Journal of Gerontology, 50A,* M307–M316.

Beach, D. L. (1997). Family caregiving: The positive impact on adolescent relationships. *Gerontologist, 37,* 233–238.

Bearon, L., & Koenig, H. G. (1990). Religious cognitions and use of prayer in health and illness. *Gerontologist, 30,* 249–253.

Beckman, A. T. F., Kriegsman, D. M. W., Deeg, D. J. H., & Van Tilburg, W. (1995). The association of physical health and depression in the older population: Age and sex differences. *Social Psychiatry and Psychogeriatric Epidemiology, 30,* 32–38.

Bedford, V. H. (1992). Memories of parental favoritism and the quality of parent-child ties in adulthood. *Journal of Gerontology: Social Sciences, 47,* S149–S155.

Bedford, V. H. (1995). Sibling relationships in middle and old age. In R. Blieszner & V. H. Bedford (Eds.), *Handbook of aging and the family* (pp. 201–222). Westport, CT: Greenwood Press.

Begley, S. (1993). The puzzle of genius. *Newsweek,* June 28, 46–50.

Bekker, L., DeMoyne, L., & Taylor, C. (1966). Attitudes toward the aged in a multigenerational sample. *Journal of Gerontology, 21,* 115–118.

Beland, F. (1987). Living arrangement preferences among elderly people. *The Gerontologist, 27,* 797–803.

Belasco, J. A. (1991). *Teaching the elephant to dance: The manager's guide to empowering change.* New York: Plume & Penguin Books.

Belbin, R. M. (1983). The implications of gerontology for new work roles in later life. In J. E. Birren et al. (Eds.), *Aging: A challenge to science and society.* New York: Oxford University Press.

Bell, J. (1992). In search of a discourse on aging. The elderly on television. *The Gerontologist, 32,* 305–311.

Bell, R. R., & Lobsenz, N. (1979, September). Married sex: How uninhibited can a woman dare to be? *Redbook,* pp. 75–78.

Belsky, J. (1981). Early human experience: A family perspective. *Developmental Psychology, 17,* 3–23.

Bem, S. L. (1974). The measurement of psychological androgyny. *Journal of Consulting and Clinical Psychology, 42,* 155–162.

Bem, S. L. (1977). On the utility of alternative procedures for assessing psychological androgyny. *Journal of Consulting and Clinical Psychology, 45,* 196–205.

Bem, S. L. (1981). Gender schema theory: A cognitive account of sex typing. *Psychological Review, 88,* 354–364.

Bengtson, V. L. (1985). Diversity and symbolism in grandparental roles. In V. L. Bengtson & J. Robertson (Eds.), *Grandparenthood.* Beverly Hills, CA: Sage.

Bengtson, V. L., Mangen, D. G., & Landry, T. J., Jr. (1984). Multigenerational family: Concepts and findings. In V. Garmsholova, E. M. Horning, & D. Schaffer (Eds.), *Intergenerational relationships.* Lewiston, NY: Hogrefe.

Bengtson, V. L., Reedy, M., & Gordon, C. (1985). Aging self conceptions: Personality processes and social context. In J. E. Birren & K. W. Schaie (Eds.), *Handbook of the psychology of aging* (2nd ed.). New York: Van Nostrand Reinhold.

Ben-Sira, Z. (1991). *Regression, stress, and readjustment in aging.* New York: Praeger.

Benson, M. (1997). Healthy life often determined by socioeconomic status. *Syracuse Post Standard,* August 18, p. A-4.

Berg, C. A., & Sternberg, R. J. (1992). Adults' conceptions of intelligence across the adult life span. *Psychology and Aging, 7,* 221–231.

Berkelman, R. L., & Hughes, J. M. (1993). The conquest of infectious diseases: Who are we kidding? *Annals of Internal Medicine, 119,* 426–427.

Berry, J. W., & Kim, V. (1988). Acculturation and mental health. In P. R. Dasen, J. W. Berry, & N. Satorius (Eds.), *Health and cross-cultural psychology: Toward applications* (pp. 207–236). Newbury Park, CA: Sage.

Berscheid, E. (1988). Some comments on love's anatomy: Or whatever happened to old-fashioned lust? In R. J. Sternberg & M. L. Barnes (Eds.), *Anatomy of love.* New Haven: Yale University Press.

Berzonsky, M. D. (1978). Formal reasoning in adolescence: An alternative view. *Adolescence, 13,* 279–290.

Biegel, D. E., & Blum, A. (Eds.). (1990). *Aging and caregiving: Theory, research and policy.* Newbury Park, CA: Sage.

Biegel, D. E., Bass, D. M., Schulz, R., & Morycz, R. (1993). Predictors of in-home and out-of-home service use by family caregivers of Alzheimer's disease patients. *Journal of Aging and Health, 5,* 419–438.

Black, P. M. (1983a). Clinical problems in the brain death standards. *Archives of Internal Medicine, 143,* 121–123.

Black, P. M. (1983b). Guidelines for the diagnosis of brain death. In A. H. Ropper, S. K. Kennedy, & N. T. Zervas (Eds.), *Neurological and neurosurgical intensive care.* Baltimore: University Park Press.

Black, S. A., & Markides, K. (1994). Americans, Cuban Americans, and Mainland Puerto Ricans. *International Journal of Aging and Human Development, 39,* 97–103.

Blanchard-Fields, F,. & Hess, T. H. (Eds.) (1996). *Perspectives on cognitive change in adulthood and aging.* New York: McGraw-Hill.

Blanchard-Fields, F., & Irion, J. C. (1988). The relation between locus of control and coping in two contexts: Age as a moderator variable. *Psychology and Aging, 3,* 197–203.

Blanchard-Fields, F., & Robinson, S. L. (1987). Age differences in the relation between controllability and coping. *Journal of Gerontology, 42,* 497–501.

Blazer, D. (1994). Epidemiology of late-life depression. In L. Schneider, C. F. Reynolds, B. Lebowitz, & A. Friedhoff (Eds.), *Diagnosis and treatment of depression in late life* (pp. 9–19). Washington, DC: American Psychiatric Press.

Blazer, D. G. (1993). *Depression in late life* (2nd ed.). St. Louis, MO: C. V. Mosby.

Blazer, D. G., Burchett, B., Service, C., & George, L. K. (1991). The association of age and depression among the elderly: An epidemiologic exploration. *Journals of Gerontology, 46* (6), M20–M215.

Blieszner, R., & Hatvany, L. E. (1996). Diversity in the experience of late-life widowhood. *Journal of Personal and Interpersonal Loss, 1,* 199–211.

Block, M. R., Davidson, J. L., & Grambs, J. D. (1981). *Women over forty.* New York: Springer.

Bloom, A. (1993). The death of eros. *New York Times Magazine,* May 23, p. 26.

Blumenthal, J. A., Emery, C. F., Madden, D. J., Schniebolk, S., Walsh-Riddle, M., George, L. K., McKee, D. C., Higgenbotham, M. B., Cobb, F. R., & Coleman, R. E. (1991). Long-term effects of exercise on psychological functioning in older men and women. *Journal of Gerontology: Psychological Science, 46,* P352–361.

Bodnar, J. C., & Kiecolt-Glaser, J. K. (1994). Caregiver depression after bereavement: Chronic stress isn't over when it's over. *Psychology and Aging, 9* (3), 372–380.

Bolger, N., Foster, M., Vinokur, A. D., & Ng, R. (1997). Close relationships and adjustments to a life crisis: The case of breast cancer. *Journal of Personality and Social Psychology, 70,* 283–294.

Bolles, R. N. (1988). *What color is your parachute?* Berkeley, CA: Ten Speed Press.

Bondi, M. W., Monsch, A. U., Galasko, D., Butters, N., Salmon, D. P., & Delis, D. C. (1994). Preclinical cognitive markers for dementia of the Alzheimer's type. *Neuropsychology, 8,* 374–384.

Bookwala, J., & Schulz, R. (1996). Spousal similarity in subjective well-being: The cardiovascular health study. *Psychology and Aging, 11,* 587–590.

Booth-Kewley, S., & Friedman, H. (1987). Psychological predictors of heart disease: A quantitative review. *Psychological Bulletin, 101,* 343–362.

Bortz, W. M. (1980). Effects of exercise on aging—effects of aging on exercise. *Journal of the American Geriatric Society, 28,* 49–51.

Bortz, W. M., & Bortz, W. M. (1996). How fast do we age? Exercise performance over time as a biomarker. *Journal of Gerontology: Medical Sciences, 51A,* M223–M225.

Borup, J. H. (1983). Relocation mortality research: Assessment, reply, and the need to refocus on the issues. *The Gerontologist, 23,* 235–242.

Bosse, R., Aldwin, C. M., Levenson, M. R., Spiro, A., & Mroczek, D. K. (1993). Change in social support after retirement: Longitudinal findings from the normative aging study. *Journal of Gerontology: Psychological Sciences, 48,* P210–P217.

Boston Women's Health Book Collective. (1976). *Our bodies, ourselves* (2nd ed.). New York: Simon & Schuster.

Botwinick, J. (1977). Intellectual abilities. In J. E. Birren & K. W. Schaie (Eds.), *Handbook of the psychology of aging.* New York: Van Nostrand Reinhold.

Botwinick, J., & Storandt, M. (1974). *Memory-related functions and age.* Springfield, IL: Charles C. Thomas.

Bould, S., Sanborn, B., & Reif, L. (1989). *Eighty-five plus: The oldest old.* Belmont, CA: Wadsworth.

Bowlby, J. (1980). Loss: Sadness and depression. In J. Bowlby (Ed.), *Attachment and loss (Vol. 6).* New York: Basic Books.

Boyd, P. (1969). The valued grandparent: A changing social role. In W. Donahue, J. Kornbluth, & B. Powers (Eds.), *Living in the multigenerational family.* Ann Arbor, MI: Institute of Gerontology.

Bradsher, J. E., Longino, C. F., Jackson, D. J., & Zimmerman, R. S. (1992). Health and geographic mobility among the recently widowed. *Journal of Gerontology: Social Sciences, 47,* S261–S268.

Brainerd, C. J. (1978). The stage question in cognitive developmental theory. *Behavioral and Brain Sciences, 1,* 173–214.

Braithwaite, V. A., Gibson, D. M., and Bosly-Craft, R. (1986). An exploratory study of poor adjustment styles among retirees. *Social Science and Medicine, 23,* 493–499.

Bram, S. (1987). Parenthood or nonparenthood: A comparison of intentional families. *Lifestyles, 8,* 69–84.

Branch, L. G. (1987). Continuing care retirement communities: Self-insuring for long-term care. *The Gerontologist, 27,* 4–8.

Branch, L. G., Friedman, D. J., Cohen, M. A., Smith, N., & Socholitzky, E. (1988). Impoverishing the elderly: A case study of the financial risk of spending down among Massachusetts' elderly. *The Gerontologist, 28,* 648–658.

Brandtstadter, J., & Renner, G. (1992). Coping with discrepancies between aspirations and achievements in adult development: A dual-process model. In L. Montada, S. H. Filipp, & M. Lerner (Eds.), *Crises and experiences of loss in adulthood* (pp. 301–319). Hillsdale, NJ: Erlbaum.

Brandtstadter, J., Wentura, D., & Greve, W. (1993). Adaptive resources of the aging self: Outlines of an emergent perspective. *International Journal of Behavioral Development, 16,* 323–350.

Brannigan, M. (1992). A chronicle of organ transplant progress in Japan. *Transplant International, 5,* 180–186.

Breast imaging: Today and tomorrow. (1995). *Harvard Women's Health Watch,* January, p. 2.

Brennan, P. L., Moos, R. H. (1992). Life stressors, social resources and late life problem drinking. *Psychology and Aging, 7*(4), 653.

Brickel, C. M. (1985). Initiation and maintenance of the human-animal bond: Familial roles from a learning perspective. *Marriage and the Family Review, 8,* 31–48.

Brickel, C. M. (1986). Pet-facilitated therapies: A review of the literature and clinical implementation considerations. *Clinical Gerontologist, 5,* 309–332.

Brim, G. (1992). *Ambition: How we manage success and failure throughout our adult lives.* New York: Basic Books.

Brim, O. G., Jr., & Ryff, C. D. (1980). On the properties of life events. In P. B. Baltes & O. G. Brim, Jr. (Eds.), *Life-span development and behavior* (Vol. 3). New York: Academic Press.

Brink, S. (1993). Elderly empowerment. *U.S. News and World Report,* April 26, 65–70.

Brock, D. (1989). Death and dying. In R. M. Veatch (Ed.). *Medical ethics* (2nd ed., pp. 363–394).

Brody, H., Campbell, M. L., Faber-Langendoen, K., & Ogle, K. (1997). Withdrawing intensive life sustaining treatment. Recommendations for compassionate clinical management. *New England Journal of Medicine, 336,* 652–657.

Bronfenbrenner, U., McClelland, P., Wethington, E., Moen, P., & Ceci, S. J. (1996). *The State of Americans.* New York: Free Press.

Brown, M., Sinacore, D. R., & Host, H. H. (1995). The relationship of strength to function in the older adult. *Journal of Gerontology, 50A,* 55–59.

Bruner, J. (1986). *Actual minds, possible worlds.* Cambridge, MA: Harvard University Press.

Buchanan, A. (1989). Healthcare delivery and resource allocation. In R. M. Veatch (Ed.), *Medical ethics* (2nd ed., pp. 321–362). Sudbury, MA: Jones and Bartlett.

Buchner, D. M., Cress, M. E., Esselman, P. C., Margherita, A. J., Delateur, B. J., Campbell, A. J., & Wagner, E. H. (1996). Factors associated with changes in gait speed in older adults. *Journal of Gerontology: Medical Sciences, 51A,* 297–302.

Burgio, L. D., Cotter, E. M., & Stevens, A. B. (1996). Treatment in residential settings. In M. Hersen, V. Van Hasselt (Eds.), *Psychological treatment of older adults: An introductory text.* New York: Plenum Press.

Burker, E. J., Wong, H., Sloane, P. D., Mattingly, D., Preisser, J., & Mitchell, C. M. (1995). Predictors of fear of falling in dizzy and nondizzy elderly. *Psychology and Aging, 10,* 104–110.

Burkhauser, R. V., & Salisbury, D. L. (Eds.). (1993). *Pensions in a changing economy.* Employee Benefit Research Institute, Washington, DC and Syracuse University.

Burkhauser, R. V., Couch, K. A., & Phillips, J. W. (1996). Who takes early social security benefits? The economic and health characteristics of early beneficiaries. *The Gerontologist, 36,* 789–799.

Burrus-Bammel, L. L., & Bammel, G. (1985). Leisure and recreation. In J. E. Birren & K. W. Schaie (Eds.),

Handbook of the psychology of aging (2nd ed.). New York: Van Nostrand Reinhold.

Burt, J. J., & Meeks, L. B. (1985). *Education for sexuality: Concepts and programs for teaching* (3rd ed.). Philadelphia: Saunders College.

Burton, L. C., German, P. S., Rovner, B. W., Brant, L. J., & Clark, R. D. (1992). Mental illness and the use of restraints in nursing homes. *The Gerontologist, 32,* 164–170.

Burwell, B. (1996). *Medicaid long term care expenditures in fiscal year 1995.* Cambridge, MA: The Medstat Group.

Butler, R. N. (1963). The life review: An interpretation of reminiscence in the aged. *Psychiatry, 26,* 65–76.

Butler, R. N., Lewis, M., & Sunderland, T. (1991). *Aging and mental health* (4th ed.). New York: Macmillan.

Cabeza, R., Grady, C. L., Nyberg, L., McIntosh, A. R., Tulving, E., Kapur, S., Jennings, J. M., Houle, S., & Craik, F. I. M. (1997). Age-related differences in neural activity during memory encoding and retrieval: A positron emission tomography study. *The Journal of Neuroscience, 17,* 391–400.

Caine, E. D., & Grossman, H. (1992). Neuropsychiatric assessment. In J. E. Birren, R. B. Sloane, & G. D. Cohen (Eds.), *Handbook of mental health and aging* (2nd ed., pp. 603–641). San Diego: Academic Press.

Cairl, R. E., & Kosberg, J. I. (1993). The interface of burden and level of task performance in caregivers of Alzheimer's disease patients: An examination of clinical profiles. *Journal of Gerontological Social Work, 19,* 133–151.

Callahan, C. M., & Wolinsky, F. D. (1995). Hospitalization for major depression among older Americans. *Journal of Gerontology, 50A,* M196–M202.

Callan, M. (1990). *Surviving AIDS.* New York: HarperCollins.

Callan, V. J. (1984). Childlessness and marital adjustment. *Australian Journal of Sex, Marriage, and the Family, 5,* 210–214.

Callan, V. J. (1987). Personal and marital adjustment of voluntary and nonvoluntary childless wives. *Journal of Marriage and the Family, 49,* 847–856.

Camp, C. J., Foss, J. W., O'Hanlon, A. M., & Stevens, A. B. (1996). Memory interventions for persons with dementia. *Applied Cognitive Psychology, 10,* 193–210.

Campbell B. A., & Gaddy, J. R. (1987). Rate of aging and dietary: Sensory and motor function in the Fischer 344 rat. *Journal of Gerontology, 42,* 154–159.

Campbell, D. T., & Stanley, J. C. (1963). *Experimental and quasi-experimental designs for research.* Chicago: Rand McNally.

Campbell, M. K., Bush, T. L., & Hale, W. E. (1993). Medical conditions associated with driving cessation in community-dwelling ambulatory elders. *Journal of Gerontology: Social Sciences, 48,* S230–S234.

Caracci, G., & Miller, N. S. (1991, July). Epidemiology and diagnosis of alcoholism in the elderly (A review). *International Journal of Geriatric Psychiatry, 6,* 511–515.

Carey, R. G. (1977). The widowed: A year later. *Journal of Counseling Psychology, 24,* 125–131.

Carstensen, L. L. (1993). Motivation for social contact across the life span: A theory of socioemotional selectivity. In J. E. Jacobs (Ed.), *Nebraska Symposium on Motivation* (pp. 209–254). Lincoln: University of Nebraska Press.

Carstensen, L. L. (1995). Evidence for a life-span theory of socio-emotional selectivity. *Current Directions in Psychological Science, 4,* 151–156.

Carstensen, L. L., Gottman, J. M., & Levenson, R. W. (1995). Emotional behavior in long term marriage. *Psychology and Aging, 10,* 140–149.

Carver, C. S., Scheier, M. F., & Weintraub, J. K. (1989). Assessing coping strategies: A theoretically based approach. *Journal of Personality and Social Psychology, 56,* 267–283.

Catania, J. A., Turner, H., Kegeles, S. M., Stall, R., Pollack, L., & Coates, T. J. (1989). Older Americans and AIDS transmission risks and primary prevention research needs. *The Gerontologist, 29,* 373–381.

Cavanaugh, J. C. (1997). *Adult development and aging* (2nd ed.). Pacific Grove, CA: Brooks Cole.

Ceci, S. J. (1991). How much does schooling influence general intelligence? A reassessment of the evidence. *Developmental Psychology, 27,* 703–722.

Ceci, S. J., & Liker, J. K. (1986). A day at the races: A study of IQ, expertise, and cognitive complexity. *Journal of Experimental Psychology: General, 115,* 255–266.

Centers for Disease Control. (1992, January 3). Sexual behavior among high school students—United States, 1990. *Morbidity and Mortality Weekly Report, 40,* 885–888.

Centers for Disease Control. (1997). *Report on AIDS mortality statistics.*

Cerella, J. (1985). Age-related decline in extrafoveal letter perception. *Journal of Gerontology, 40,* 727–736.

Cerella, J., Poon, L., & Fozard, J. L. (1981). Mental rotation and age reconsidered. *Journal of Gerontology, 38,* 447–454.

Chalke, H. D., Dewhurst, J. R., & Ward, C. W. (1958). Loss of sense of smell in old people. *Public Health, 72,* 223–230.

Chappell, N. L., & Novak, M. (1992). The role of support in alleviating stress among nursing assistants. *The Gerontologist, 32,* 351–359.

Charness, N. (1981). Search in chess: Age and skill differences. *Journal of Experimental Psychology: Human Perception and Performance, 7,* 467–476.

Charness, N. (1985). *Age and expertise: Responding to Talland's challenge.* Paper presented at the George A. Talland Memorial Conference on Aging and Memory, Cape Cod, MA.

Charness, N. (1988). Expertise in chess, music, and physics: A cognitive perspective. In L. K. Obler & D. A. Fein (Eds.), *The neuropsychology of talent and special abilities.* New York: Guilford Press.

Charness, N., & Bosman, E. A. (1992). Human factor and age. In Fergus I. M. Craik & Timothy A. Salthouse (Eds.), *Handbook of aging and cognition* (pp. 495–551). Hillside, NJ: Lawrence Erlbaum.

Charness, N., & Campbell, J. I. D. (1988). Acquiring skill at mental calculation in adulthood: A task decomposition. *Journal of Experimental Psychology: General, 117,* 115–129.

Chase, W. G., & Simon, H. A. (1973). Perception in chess. *Cognitive Psychology, 4,* 55–81.

Chen, Y. P. (1987). Making assets out of tomorrow's elderly. *The Gerontologist, 27,* 410–416.

Cherlin, A. (1996). *Public and private families: An introduction.* New York: McGraw-Hill.

Cherlin, A., & Furstenberg, F. (1985). Styles and strategies of grandparenting. In V. L. Bengtson & J. Robertson (Eds.), *Granparenthood.* Beverly Hills, CA: Sage.

Cherlin, A., & Furstenberg, F. (1986). Grandparents and family crisis. *Generations, 10,* 26–28.

Chiriboga, D. A. (1982a). Adaptations to marital separation in later and earlier life. *Journal of Gerontology, 37,* 109–114.

Chiriboga, D. A. (1982b). An examination of life events as possible antecedents to change. *Journal of Gerontology, 37,* 595–601.

Church, D. K., Siegel, M. A., & Foster, C. D. (1988). *Growing old in America.* Wylie, TX: Information Aids.

Cicirelli, V. G. (1992). *Family caregiving* (Vol. 186). Newbury Park, CA: Sage Library of Social Research.

Clancy, S. M., & Hoyer, W. J. (1994). Age and skill in visual search. *Developmental Psychology, 30,* 545–552.

Clancy-Dollinger, S. M., & Hoyer, W. J. (1988). Effects of age and skill on domain specific search. In V. L. Patel & G. J. Groen (Eds.), *Proceedings of the tenth conference of the Cognitive Science Society* (pp. 398-404). Hillsdale, NJ: Earlbaum.

Clancy-Dollinger, S.M., & Hoyer, W. J. (1995). Skill differences in medical laboratory diagnostics. *Applied Cognitive Psychology, 9,* 235–248.

Clausen, J. A. (1981). Men's occupational careers in the middle years. In D. H. Eichorn, J. A. Clausen, N. Haan, M. Honzik, & P. Mussen (Eds.), *Present and past in middle life.* New York: Academic Press.

Clayton, V., & Birren, J. E. (1980). Age and wisdom across the life-span: Theoretical perspectives. In P. B. Baltes & O. G. Brim, Jr. (Eds.), *Life-span development and behavior: Vol. 3.* New York: Academic Press.

Clebone, B. L., & Taylor, C. M. (1992, February). Family and social attitudes across four generations of women or maternal lineage. *Psychological Reports, 70,* 268–270.

Clipp, E. C., & George, L. K. (1990). Psychotropic drug use among caregivers of patients with dementia. *Journal of the American Geriatrics Society, 38,* 227–235.

Cohen, C. I., Teresi, J. A., Holmes, D., & Roth, E. (1988). Survival strategies of older homeless men. *The Gerontologist, 28,* 58–65.

Cohen, D., & Eisdorfer, C. (1986). *The loss of self.* New York: Norton.

Cohen, D., & Eisdorfer, C. (1989). Depression in family members caring for a relative with Alzheimer's Disease. *Journal of the American Geriatrics Society, 36,* 385–389.

Cohen, F., Bearison, D. J., & Muller, C. (1987). Interpersonal understanding in the elderly: The influence of age-integrated and age-segregated housing. *Research on Aging, 9,* 79–100.

Cohen, G. D. (1988). *The brain in human aging.* New York: Springer.

Cohen, G., & Faulkner, D. (1989). Age differences in source forgetting: Effects of reality monitoring on eyewitness testimony. *Psychology & Aging, 4,* 10–17.

Cohen, G., Conway, M. A., & Maylor, E. A. (1994). Flashbulb memories in older adults. *Psychology and Aging, 9,* 454–463.

Cohen, M. A., Tell, E. J., Batten, H. L., & Larson, M. J. (1988). Attitudes toward joining continuing care retirement communities. *The Gerontologist, 28,* 637–643.

Cohen, S., & Herbert, T. B. (1996). Health psychology: Psychological factors and physical disease from the perspective of human psychneuro-immunology. *Annual Review of Psychology, 47,* 113–142. Palo Alto, CA: Annual Reviews.

Cohen-Mansfield, J., Werner, P., Marx, M. S., & Freedman, L. (1991). Two studies of pacing in the nursing home. *Journal of Gerontology, 46,* 77–83.

Cohler, B. J. (1992). The myth of successful aging. *Readings: A Journal of Reviews and Commentary in Mental Health,* p. 18–22.

Cohler, B. J., & Grunebaum, H. V. (1981). *Mothers, grandmothers, and daughters: Personality and child-care in three-generation families.* New York: John Wiley.

Colby, A., & Kohlberg, L. (Eds.). (1987). *The measurement of moral judgment, Vol. 1: Theoretical foundations and research validation.* New York: Cambridge University Press.

Colby, A., Kohlberg, L., Gibbs, J. C., & Lieberman, M. (1983). A longitudinal study of moral development. *Monographs of the Society for Research in Child Development, 48 (4),* 1–124.

Coleman, J. (1988). *Intimate relationships, marriage, and families.* New York: Macmillan.

Coleman, L., & Antonucci, T. (1983). Impact of working women at midlife. *Developmental Psychology, 19,* 290–294.

Comfort, A. (1980). Sexuality in later life. In J. E. Birren & R. B. Sloane (Eds.), *Handbook of mental health and aging.* New York: Van Nostrand Reinhold.

Commons, M. L., Sinnott, J. D., Richards, F. A., & Armon, C. (1989). *Adult development, Vol. 1: Comparisons and applications of developmental models.* New York: Praeger.

Conger, R. D., Lorenz, F. O., Elder, G. H., Simmons, R. L., & Xiaojia, G. (1993). Husband and wife differences in response to undesirable life events. *Journal of Health and Social Behavior, 34,* 71–88.

Conley, J. J. (1985). Longitudinal stability of personality traits. *Journal of Personality and Social Psychology, 54,* 1266–1282.

Connelly, S. L., & Hasher, L. (1993). Aging and inhibition of spatial location. *Journal of Experimental Psychology: Human Perception and Performance, 19,* 1238–1250.

Connidis, I. A., & Davies, L. (1990a). *Family ties and aging.* Toronto: Butterworths.

Connidis, I. G., & Davies, L. (1990b). Confidants and companions in later life: The place of friends and family. *Journal of Gerontology: Social Sciences, 45,* S141–S149.

Connolly, J. (1992). Participatory versus lecture/discussion preretirement education: A comparison. *Educational Gerontology, 18,* 365–379.

Conrad, P. (1990). Qualitative research on chronic illness: A commentary on method and conceptual development. *Social Science Medicine, 30,* 1257–1263.

Conwell, Y. (1994). Suicide and aging: Lessons from the nursing home. *Crisis, 15* (4), 153–154.

Conwell, Y. (1995). Suicide among elderly people. *Psychiatric Services, 46* (6), 563–564.

Cool, L., & McCabe, J. (1983). The "scheming hag" and the "dear old thing": The anthropology of aging women. In J. Sokolovsky (Ed.), *Growing old in different societies: Cross cultural perspectives.* Belmont, CA: Wadsworth.

Cooney, T. M., Schaie, K. W., & Willis, S. L. (1988). The relationship between prior functioning on cognitive and personality dimensions and subject attrition in longitudinal research. *Journal of Gerontology: Psychological Science, 43,* P12–P17.

Corder, E. H., Saunders, A. M., Strittmatter, W. J., Schmechel, D. E., Gaskell, P. C., Small, G. W., Roses, A. D., Haines, J. L., & Pericak-Vance, M. A. (1993). Gene dose of apolipoprotein E type 4 allele and the risk of Alzheimer's disease in late onset families. *Science, 261,* 921–926.

Cornelius, S. W., & Capsi, A. (1987). Everyday problem solving in adulthood and old age. *Psychology and Aging, 2,* 144–153.

Coronel, S., & Fulton, D. (1995). *Long term care insurance in 1993.* Washington, DC: Health Insurance Association of America.

Corr, C. A. (1992). A task-based approach to coping with dying. *Omega, 24,* 81–94.

Corso, J. F. (1977). Auditory perception and communication. In J. E. Birren & K. W. Schaie (Eds.), *Handbook of the psychology of aging* (2nd ed.). New York: Van Nostrand Reinhold.

Corso, J. F. (1981). *Aging, sensory systems, and perception.* New York: Praeger.

Costa, P. T., Jr. (1986). *The scope of individuality.* Paper presented at the meeting of the American Psychological Association, Washington, DC.

Costa, P. T., Jr., & McCrae, R. R. (1977). Age differences in personality structure revisited: Studies in validity, stability, and change. *Aging and Human Development, 8,* 261–275.

Costa, P. T., Jr., & McCrae, R. R. (1978). Objective personality assessment. In M. Storandt, I. C. Siegler, &

M. P. Elias (Eds.), *The clinical psychology of aging.* New York: Plenum.

Costa, P. T., Jr., & McCrae, R. R. (1980). Still stable after all these years: Personality as a key to some issues of adulthood and old age. In P. B. Baltes & O. G. Brim, Jr. (Eds.), *Life-span development and behavior* (Vol. 3). New York: Academic Press.

Costa, P. T., Jr., & McCrae, R. R. (1982). An approach to the attribution of aging: Period and cohort effects. *Psychological Bulletin, 92,* 238–250.

Costa, P. T., Jr., & McCrae, R. R. (1985). Personality as a lifelong determinant of well-being. In C. Malatesta & C. Izard (Eds.), *Affective processes in adult development and aging.* New York: Sage.

Costa, P. T., Jr., & McCrae, R. R. (1986). Cross-sectional studies of personality in a national sample: I. Development and validation of survey measures. *Psychology and Aging, 1,* 140–143.

Costa, P. T., Jr., & McCrae, R. R. (1988). Personality in adulthood: A six-year longitudinal study of self reports and spouse rating in the NEO personality inventory. *Journal of Personality and Social Psychology, 54,* 853–863.

Cotrell, M., & Schulz, R. (1993). The perspective of the patient with Alzheimer's disease: A neglected dimension of dementia research. *The Gerontologist, 33,* 205–211.

Couldrick, A. (1992). Optimizing bereavement outcome: Reading the road ahead. *Social Science and Medicine, 35,* 1521–1523.

Covey, H. C. (1988). Historical terminology used to represent older people. *The Gerontologist, 28,* 291–297.

Cowgill, D., & Holmes, L.D. (1972). *Aging and modernization.* New York: Appleton-Century-Crofts.

Cox, H. (Ed.). (1997). *Aging* (11th ed.) Guilford, CT: Dushkin Press. On Aging, Reprinted from Administrative Aging, (1991), #362, pp. 37–40. Washington, D.C.

Coyne, J. C., & Fiske, V. (1992). Couples coping with chronic health and catastrophic illness. In T. J. Akamatsu, S. C. Crowther, S. E. Hobfil, & M. A. P. Stevens (Eds.), *Family health psychology* (pp. 129–149). Washington, DC: Hemisphere.

Craik, F. I. M. (1977). Age differences in human memory. In J. E. Birren & K. W. Schaie (Eds.), *Handbook of the psychology of aging.* New York: Van Nostrand Reinhold.

Craik, F. I. M., & Jennings, J. (1992). Human memory. In F. I. M. Craik & T. A. Salthouse (Eds.), *Handbook of aging and cognition* (pp. 51–110). Hillsdale, NJ: Erlbaum.

Craik, F. I. M., Byrd, M., & Swanson, J. M. (1987). Patterns of memory loss in three elderly samples. *Psychology and Aging, 2,* 79–86.

Craik, F. I. M., Govoni, R., Naveh-Benjamin, M., & Anderson, N. A. (1996). The effects of divided attention on encoding and retrieval processes in human memory. *Journal of Experimental Psychology: General, 125,* 159–180.

Craik, F. I. M., Morris, L. W., Morris, R. G., & Loewen, E. R. (1990). Relations between source amnesia and frontal lobe functioning in older adults. *Psychology and Aging, 5,* 148–151.

Cristofalo, V. J. (1986). The biology of aging: An overview. In M. J. Horan, G. M. Steinberg, J. B. Dunbar, & E. C. Hadley (Eds.), NIH, *Blood pressure regulation and aging: Proceedings from a symposium.* New York: Biomedical Information Corporation.

Crohan, S. E., & Antonucci, T. C. (1989). Friends as a source of social support in old age. In R. Adams & R. Blieszner (Eds.), *Older adult friendship: Structure and process.* Beverly Hills, CA: Sage.

Csikszentmihalyi, M. (1997). *Finding flow: The psychology of engagement with everyday life.* NY: Basic Books.

Cude, R. L., & Jablin, F. M. (1992). Retiring from work: The paradoxical impact of organizational commitment. *Journal of Managerial Issues, 4*(1), 31–45.

Cunningham, W. R., & Owens, W. A., Jr. (1983). The Iowa study of the adult development of intellectual abilities. In K. W. Schaie (Ed.), *Longitudinal studies of adult psychological development.* New York: Guilford Press.

Curran, J., Jaffe, H., Hardy, A., Morgan, W., Selik, R., & Dondero, T. (1988). Epidemiology of HIV infection and AIDS in the United States. *Science, 239,* 610–616.

Curtis, J. R., Geller, G., Stokes, E. J., & Levine, D. M. (1989). Characteristics, diagnosis, and treatment of alcoholism in elderly patients. *Journal of American Geriatrics Society, 37* (4), 310–316.

Cutler, S. J., & Hendricks, J. (1990). Leisure time use across the life course. In R. H. Binstock, & L. K. George (Eds.), *Handbook of aging and social sciences* (3rd ed.). New York: Academic Press.

Cutter, M. A. G. (1991). Euthanasia: Reassessing the boundaries. *Journal of National Institute of Health Research, 3,* 59–61.

Czaja, S. J., & Sharit, J. (1993). Age differences in performance of computer-based work. *Psychology and Aging, 8,* 59–67.

Dannefer, D., & Perlmutter, M. (1990). Development as a multidimensional process: Individual and social constraints. *Human Development, 33,* 108–137.

Davies, R. M., Sieber, K. O., & Hunt, S. L. (1994). Age-cohort differences in treating symptoms of mental illness: A process approach. *Psychology and Aging, 9,* 446–453.

Davis, K. E. (1985). Near and dear: Friendship and love compared. *Psychology Today, 19,* 22–30.

de Groot, A. (1965). *Thought and choice in chess: The Hague:* Mouton.

de la Rochefordiere, A., Asselain, B., & Campena, F. (1993). Age as a prognostic factor in premenopausal breast carcinoma. *Lancet, 341* (8852), 1039–1043.

DeAngelis, T. (1989). Mania, depression, and genius: Concert, talks inform public about manic-depressive illness. *APA Monitor, 20*(1), 1, 24.

Deeg, J. H. D., Kardaun, P. F., & Fozard, J. L. (1996). In J. E. Birren & K. W. Schaie (Eds.), *Handbook of the psychology of aging* (4th ed., pp. 129–149). San Diego, CA: Academic Press.

DeGenova, M. K. (1992). If you had your life to live over again: What would you do differently? *International Journal of Aging and Human Development, 34,* 135–143.

DeLongis, A., Coyne, J. C., Dakof, S., Folkman, S., & Lazarus, R. S. (1982). Relationship of daily hassles, uplifts, and major life events to health status. *Health Psychology, 1,* 119–136.

Demaris, A. (1984). A comparison of remarriages with first marriages on satisfaction in marriage and its relationship to prior cohabitation. Special Issue: Remarriage and stepparenting. *Family Relations Journal of Applied Family and Child Studies, 33,* 443–449.

Demetriou, A. (1990). Structural and developmental relations between formal and postformal capacities: Towards a comprehensive theory of adolescent and adolescent cognitive development. In M. L. Commons, C. Armon, L. Kohlberg, F. A. Richards, T. A. Groetzer, & J. D. Sinnott (Eds.), *Adult development, Vol. 2: Models and methods in the study of adolescent and adult thought.* New York: Praeger.

Denney, N. W. (1984). A model of cognitive development across the life span. *Developmental Review, 4,* 171–191.

Dennis, W. (1966). Creative productivity between the ages of twenty and eighty years. *Journal of Gerontology, 21,* 1–18.

Dennis, W. (1968). Creative productivity between the ages of twenty and eighty years. In B. L. Neugarten (Ed.), *Middle age and aging.* Chicago: University of Chicago Press.

DePaola, S. J., Neimeyer, R. A., Lupfer, M. B., & Fiedler, J. (1992, Nov./Dec.). Death concern and attitudes toward the elderly in nursing home personnel. Special issue: Death attitudes. *Death Studies, 16,* 537–555.

Department of Health and Human Services. (1990). *Program announcement: Research on the prevention of alcohol abuse in the older population* (RFP). Catalog of Federal Domestic Assistance No. 13, 273, p. 2, Washington, DC: U.S. Superintendent of Documents.

Depner, C. E., & Ingersoll-Dayton, B. (1988, December). Supportive relationships on later life. *Psychology and Aging, 3,* 348–357.

DeSpelder, L. A., & Strickland, A. L. (1992). *The last dance: Encountering death and dying* (3rd ed.). Mountain View, CA: Mayfield.

deVries, B., Bluck, S., & Birren, J. E. (1993). The understanding of death and dying in a lifespan perspective. *The Gerontologist, 33,* 366–372.

Dewji, N. N., & Singer, J. S. (1996). Genetic clues to Alzheimer's Disease. *Science, 271,* 159–160.

Dick, L. P., & Gallagher-Thompson, D. (1996). Late-life depression. In M. Hersen & V. B. Van Hasselt (Eds.), *Psychological treatment of older adults: An introductory text* (pp. 181–208). New York: Plenum Press.

Dickinson, G. E. (1992). First childhood death experiences. *Omega Journal of Death and Dying, 25,* 169–182.

Diehl, M., Willis, S. L., & Schaie, K. W. (1995). Everyday problem solving in older adults: Observational assessment and cognitive correlates. *Psychology and Aging, 10,* 478–491.

Dinges, N. G., & Cherry, D. (1995). Symptom expression and the use of mental health services among American ethnic minorities. In J. E. Aponte, R. Y. Rivers, & J. Wohl (Eds.), *Psychological interventions and cultural diversity* (pp. 40–56). Boston: Allyn & Bacon.

Dittmann-Kohli, F., Lachman, M. E., Kliegl, R., & Baltes, P. B. (1991). Effects of cognitive training and testing on intellectual efficacy beliefs in elderly adults. *Journal of Gerontology: Psychological Sciences, 46,* P162–P164.

Dittmann-Kohli, F., & Baltes, P. B. (1988). Toward a neofunctionalist conception of adult intellectual development: Wisdom as a prototypical case of intellectual growth. In C. Alexander, E. Langer, & R. Oetzel (Eds.), *Higher stages of human development.* New York: Oxford University Press.

Dixon, R. A., & Baltes, P. B. (1986). Toward life-span research on the functions and pragmatics of intelligence. In R. J. Sternberg & R. K. Wagner (Eds.), *Practical intelligence: Origins of competence in the everyday world.* New York: Cambridge University Press.

Dixon, R. A., Kurzman, D., & Friesen, I. C. (1993). Handwriting performance in younger and older adults: Age, familiarity, and practice effects. *Psychology and Aging, 8,* 360–370.

Doddridge, R., Schumm, W. R., & Bergen, M. B. (1987). Factors related to decline in preferred frequency of sexual intercourse among young couples. *Psychological Reports, 60,* 391–395.

Dohrenwend, B. S., Krasnoff, L., Askensay, A., & Dohrenwend, B. P. (1978). Exemplification of a method of scaling life events: The PERI life-events scale. *Journal of Health and Social Behavior, 19,* 205–229.

Doka, K. J., & Mertz, M. E. (1988). The meaning and significance of great-grandparenthood. *Gerontologist, 28,* 192–197.

Donaldson, G. (1981). Letter to the editor. *Journal of Gerontology, 36,* 634–636.

Dorfman, L.T. (1992, June). Academics and the transition to retirement. *Educational Gerontology, 18,* 343–363.

Douglas, K. W., & Arenberg, D. (1978). Age changes, cohort differences, and cultural change on the Guilford-Zimmerman temperament survey. *Journal of Gerontology, 33,* 737–747.

Downton, J. H., & Andrews, K. (1990). Postural disturbance and psychological symptoms amongst elderly people living at home. *International Journal of Geriatrics Psychiatry, 5,* 93–98.

Duncan, G.J., & Smith, K.R. (1989). The rising affluence of the elderly: How far, how fair, and how frail? *Annual Review of Sociology, 15,* 261–28.

Dupree, L. W., & Schonfeld, L. (1996). Substance abuse. In M. Hersen & V. B. Van Hasselt (Eds.), *Psychological treatment of older adults: An introductory text* (pp. 281–297), New York: Plenum Press.

Durlak, J. A., & Riesenberg, L. A. (1991). The impact of death education. *Death Studies, 15,* 39–58.

Dywan, J., & Jacoby, L. (1990). Effects of aging on source monitoring: Differences in susceptibility to false fame. *Psychology and Aging, 5,* 379–387.

Eberling, J. L., & Jagust, W. J. (1995). Imaging studies of aging, neurodegenerative disease, and alcoholism. *Alcohol World Health and Research, 19,* 279–286. U.S. Public Health Service, National Institute of Health.

Edmonds, S., & Hooker, K. (1992). Perceived changes in life meaning following bereavement. *Omega Journal of Death and Dying, 25,* 307–318.

Eichorn, D., Clausen, J., Haan, N., Honzik, M., & Mussen, P., (Eds.) (1981). *Past and present in middle life.* New York: Academic Press.

Eisdorfer, C. (1993). Three overviews of mental health and aging. *The Gerontologist, 33* (4), 570–571.

Ekerdt, D. J. (1986). The busy ethic: Moral continuity between work and retirement. *The Gerontologist, 26,* 239–244.

Ekerdt, D. J. (1998). Workplace norms for the timing of retirement. In K. W. Schaie & C. Schooler (Eds.), *Impact of work on older adults.* New York: Springer.

Ekerdt, D. J., & DeViney, S. (1990). On defining persons as retired. *Journal of Aging Studies, 4,* 211–229.

Ekerdt, D. J., & DeViney, S. (1993). Evidence for a preretirement process among older male workers. *Journal of Gerontology: Social Sciences, 48,* S535–S543.

Ekerdt, D. J., Bosse, R., & Levkoff, S. (1985). An empirical test for phases of retirement: Findings from the normative aging study. *Journal of Gerontology, 40,* 95–101.

Ekerdt, D. J., DeViney, S., & Kosloski, K. (1996). Profiling plans for retirement. *Journal of Gerontology: Social Sciences, 51B,* S140–S149.

Ekstrom, R. B., French, J. W., & Harman, M. H. (1979). *Cognitive factors: Their identification and replication.* Multivariate Behavior Research Monographs (No. 79.2).

Elder, G. (1981). *Present and past in middle life.* San Diego: Academic Press.

Elder, G. H. (1997). Life-course theory. In R. M. Lerner (Ed.), *Handbook of child psychology: Vol. 1. Theoretical models of human development* (5th edition). New York: Wiley.

Elder, G. H., & Pavalko, E. K. (1993). Work careers in men's later years: Transitions, trajectories, and historical change. *Journal of Gerontology: Social Sciences, 48,* S180–S191.

Elder, G. H., Shanahan, M. J., & Clipp, E. C. (1994). When war comes to men's lives: Life-course patterns in family, work, and health. *Psychology and Aging, 9,* 5–16.

Elias, M. F., Elias, J. W., & Elias, P. K. (1990). Biological and health influences on behavior. In J. E. Birren & K. W. Schaie (Eds.), *Handbook of the psychology of aging* (3rd ed., pp. 80–102). San Diego: Academic Press.

Ellison, C. G. (1991). Religious involvement and subjective well-being. *Journal of Health and Social Behavior, 32,* 80–99.

Ellison, C. G. (1994). Religion, the life stress paradigm, and the study of depression. In S. J. Levin (Ed.), *Religion in aging and health: Theoretical foundations and methodological frontiers* (pp. 78–121). Thousand Oaks, CA: Sage.

Engen, T. (1977). Taste and smell. In J. E. Birren & K. W. Schaie (Eds.), *Handbook of the psychology of aging* (2nd ed.). New York: Van Nostrand Reinhold.

Ericsson, K. A., & Charness, N. (1994). Expert performance: Its structure and acquisition. *American Psychologist, 49,* 725–747.

Ericsson, K. A., & Charness, N. (1995). Abilities: Evidence for talent or characteristics acquired through engagement in relevant activities? *American Psychologist, 50,* 803–804.

Ericsson, K. A., & Crutcher, R. J. (1990). The nature of exceptional performance. In P. B. Baltes, D. L. Featherman, & R. Lerner (Eds.), *Life-span development and behavior* (Vol. 10, pp. 187–217). New York: Academic Press.

Ericsson, K. A., & Simon, H. A. (1984). *Protocol analysis.* Cambridge, MA: Harvard University Press.

Ericsson, K. A., Krampe, R. T., & Tesch-Römer, C. (1993). The role of deliberate practice in the acquisition of expert performance. *Psychological Review, 100,* 363–406.

Erikson, E. H. (1963). *Childhood and society* (2nd ed.). New York: Norton.

Erikson, E. H. (1968). *Identity, youth and crisis.* New York: Norton.

Erikson, E. H. (1982). *The life cycle completed: A review.* New York: Norton.

Erikson, E. H., Erikson, J. M., & Kivnick, H. Q. (1986). *Vital involvement in old age.* New York: Norton.

Essex, M.J., & Nam, S. (1987). Marital status and loneliness among older women: The differential importance of close family and friends. *Journal of Marriage and the Family, 49,* 93–106.

Esterling, B. A., Kiecolt-Glaser, J. K. Bodnar, J. C., & Glaser, R. (1994). Chronic stress, social support, and persistent alterations in the natural killer response to cytokinesin older adults. *Health Psychology, 13,* 291–298.

Evans, W. (1992). Body building for the nineties. *Nutrition Action Health Letter, 19,* 5–8. Washington, DC: Center for Science in the Public Interest.

Evans, W. J. (1995a). What is sarcopenia. *Journal of Gerontology, 50A* (Special Issue), 5–10.

Evans, W. J. (1995b). Effects of exercise on body composition and functional capacity of the elderly. *Journal of Gerontology, 50A* (Special Issue), 147–150.

Evans, W., Rosenberg, I. H., with Thomson, J. (1991). *Biomarkers—The 10 determinants of aging you can control.* New York: Simon & Schuster.

Fahey, T. D., Insel, P. M., & Roth, W. T. (1997). *Fit and well: Core concepts in physical fitness and wellness* (2nd ed.). Mountain View, CA: Mayfield.

Farberow, N. L., Gallagher-Thompson, D., Gilewski, M., & Thompson, L. (1992). Changes in grief and mental health. *Journal of Gerontology: Psychological Sciences, 47,* P357–P366.

Farran, C. J. (1997). Theoretical perspectives concerning positive aspects of caring for elderly persons with dementia: Stress, adaptation, and existentialism. *Gerontologist, 37,* 250–257.

Farrell, M. P., & Rosenberg, S. D. (1981). *Men at midlife.* Boston: Auburn House. Industry practices. Washington, DC: U.S. Superintendent of Documents.

Federal Trade Commission, Bureau of Consumer Protection. (1994). Funeral industry practices. Washington, DC: U.S. Superintendent of Documents.

Feifel, H. (1990). Psychology and death: Meaningful re-discovery. *American Psychologist, 45,* 537–543.

Field, D., & Millsap, R. E. (1991). Personality in advanced old age: Continuity or change. *Journal of Gerontology: Psychological Sciences, 46,* P299–P308.

Field, D., & Minkler, M. (1988). Continuity and change in social support between young-old and old-old or very-old age. *Journal of Gerontology: Psychological Sciences, 43,* P100–P106.

Field, D., Minkler, M., Falk, R. F., & Leino, E. V. (1993).The influences of health and family contacts and family feelings in advanced old age: A longitudinal study. *Journal of Gerontology: Psychological Sciences, 48,* P18–P28.

Fischer, K. W. (1980). A theory of cognitive development: The control and construction of hierarchies of skills. *Psychological Review, 87,* 477–531.

Fisher, L., & Lieberman, M. A. (1994). Alzheimer's disease: The impact of the family on spouses, offspring, in-laws. *Family Process, 33,* 305–325.

Fisk, A. D., & Rogers, W. (1991). Toward an understanding of age-related memory and visual search effects. *Journal of Experimental Psychology: General, 120,* 131–149.

Fisk, A. D., Cooper, B. P., Hertzog, C., Anderson-Garlach, M., & Lee, M. D. (1995). Understanding performance and learning in consistent memory search: An age-related perspective. *Psychology and Aging, 10,* 255–268.

Fisk, A. D., Hertzog, C., Lee, M. D., Rogers, W. A., & Anderson-Garlach, M. (1994). Long-term retention of skilled visual search: Do young adults retain more than old adults? *Psychology and Aging, 9,* 206–215.

Fiske, M.L. (1980). Changing hierarchies of commitment in adulthood. In N. J. Smelser & E. Erikson (Eds.), *Theories of love and work in adulthood.* Cambridge, MA: Harvard University.

Fitzgerald, J. M. (1988). Vivid memories and the reminiscence phenomenon: The role of a self-narrative. *Human Development, 31,* 260–270.

Fitzgerald, J. M. (1996).The Distribution of Self-Narrative Memories in Younger and Older Adults: Elaborating the Self-Narrative Hypothesis. *Aging, Neuropsychology, and Cognition, 3,* 229–236.

Fitzgerald, J. M., & Lawrence, R. (1984). Autobiographical memory across the life-span. *Journal of Gerontology, 39,* 692–699.

Flavell, J. H. (1977). *Cognitive development.* Englewood Cliffs, NJ: Prentice-Hall.

Flavell, J. H. (1985). *Cognitive development* (2nd ed.). Englewood Cliffs, NJ: Prentice-Hall.

Fletcher, W. L., Hansson, R. O., & Bailey, L. (1992, December). Assessing occupational self-efficacy among middle-aged and older adults. *Journal of Applied Gerontology, 11,* 489–501.

Flynn, J. R. (1984). The mean IQ of Americans: Massive gains 1932 to 1978. *Psychological Bulletin, 95,* 29–51.

Flynn, J. R. (1987). Massive IQ gains in 14 nations: What IQ tests really measure. *Psychological Bulletin, 101,* 171–191.

Flynn, J. R. (1996). What environmental factors affect intelligence: The relevance of IQ gains over time. In D. K. Detterman (Ed.), *Current topics in Human intelligence,* Vol. 5 (pp. 17–29), Norwood, NJ: Ablex.

Folkman, S. L., & Lazarus, R. S., (1980). An analysis of coping in a middle-aged community sample. *Journal of Health and Social Behavior, 21,* 219–239.

Folkman, S. L., Lazarus, R. S., Dunkel-Schetter, C., DeLongis, A., & Gruen, R. J. (1986). The dynamics of a stressful encounter: Cognitive appraisal, coping, and encounter outcomes. *Journal of Personality and Social Psychology, 50,* 992–1003.

Folkman, S. L., Lazarus, R. S., Gruen, R., & DeLongis, A. (1986). Appraisal, coping, health status, and psychological symptoms. *Journal of Personality and Social Psychology, 50,* 571–579.

Folkman, S. L., Lazarus, R. S., Pimley, S., & Novacek, J. (1987). Age differences in stress and coping processes. *Psychology and Aging, 2,* 171–184.

Fowler, J. W. (1981). *Stages of faith.* San Francisco: Harper & Row.

Fozard, J. L. (1990). Vision and hearing in aging. In J. E. Birren & K. W. Schaie (Eds.), *Handbook of the psychology of aging* (3rd ed., pp. 150–170). San Diego: Academic Press.

Franceschi, C., & Fabris, N. (1993). Human longevity: The gender difference. *Aging: Clinical and Experimental Research, 5,* 333–335.

Francis, D. (1990). The significance of work friends in late life. Special Issue: Process, change, and social support. *Journal of Aging Studies, 4,* 405–424.

Franks, M. M., & Stephens, M. A. P. (1992). Multiple roles of middle-generation caregivers: Contextual effects and psychological mechanisms. *Journal of Gerontology: Social Sciences, 47,* S123–S129.

Freeman, E. (1992). The use of storytelling techniques with young African American males: Implications for substance abuse prevention. *Journal of Intergroup Relations, 19,* 53–72.

Freuchen, P. (1961). *Book of the Eskimos.* Cleveland: World Press.

Friedman, H. S., & Booth-Kewley, S. (1987). The disease-prone personality: A meta-analytic view of the construct. *American Psychologist, 42,* 539–555.

Friedman, M., & Rosenman, R. M. (1974). *Type A behavior and your heart.* New York: Knopf.

Friedmann, E., & Havighurst, R.J. (1954). *The meaning of work and retirement.* Chicago: University of Chicago Press.

Friedmann, E., Katcher, A. H., Lynch, J. J., & Thomas, S. A. (1980). Animal companions and one-year survival of patients after discharge from a coronary care unit. *Public Health Reports, 95,* 307–312.

Fries, J. F. (1997). Can preventive gerontology be on the way? [Editorial.] *American Journal of Public Health, 87,* 1591–1593.

Fries, J. F., & Crapo, L. M. (1981). *Vitality and aging.* San Francisco: Freeman.

Frieswick, K. (1997). In health: The battle against breast cancer. *Boston Magazine, 84,* 79–91.

Frisoni, G. B., Franzoni, S., Rozzini, R., Ferrucci, L., Boffelli, S., & Trabucchi, M. (1995). Food intake and mortality in the frail elderly. *Journal of Gerontology, 50A,* M203–M210.

Fromm, E. (1955). *The sane society.* New York: Fawcett Books.

Fry, P. S. (1990). A factor analytic investigation of home-bound elderly individuals' concerns about death and dying and their coping responses. *Journal of Clinical Psychology, 46,* 737–748.

Fuller-Jonap, F., & Haley, W. E. (1995). Mental and physical health of male caregivers of a spouse with Alzheimer's disease. *Journal of Aging and Health, 7,* 99–118.

Fuster, J. M. (1991). Prefrontal cortex and bridging of temporal gaps in the perception-action cycle. *Annals of the New York Academy of Sciences, 608,* 318–329.

Futterman, A., Thompson, L. W., Gallagher-Thompson, D., & Ferris, R. (1995). Depression in later life: Epidemiology, assessment, etiology and treatment. In E. E. Beckham & W. R. Leber (Eds.), *Handbook of depression* (2nd ed., pp. 495–525). New York: Guilford Press.

Galinsky, E. (1993). *National study of the changing work force.* New York: Families and Work Institute.

Gallagher, W. (1993). Midlife myths. *The Atlantic Monthly, 271,* 51–68.

Gallagher-Thompson, D., & Thompson, L. W. (1995). Psychotherapy with older adults. In B. M. Bodgar & L. E. Beutler (Eds.), *Comprehensive textbook of psychotherapy: Theory and practice.* New York: Oxford Press.

Gallo, J. J., Anthony, J. C., & Muthen, B. O. (1994). Age differences in the symptoms of depression: A latent trait analysis. *Journal of Gerontology, Psychological Sciences, 49,* 251–254.

Galton, F. (1979). *Heredity and genius: An inquiry into its laws and consequences.* London: Julian Freeman (Original work published 1869).

Gambert, S. R. (Ed.). (1987). *Handbook of geriatrics.* New York: Plenum Medical Book Company.

Gardner, H. (1983). *Frames of mind: The theory of multiple intelligences.* New York: Basic Books.

Gardner, H. (1985). *The mind's new science.* New York: Basic Books.

Gardner, H. (1993a). *Creating minds.* New York: Basic Books.

Gardner, H. (1993b). *Multiple intelligences: The theory in practice.* New York: Basic Books.

Gardner, H. (1995). Why would anyone become an expert? *American Psychologist, 50,* 802–803.

Gardnier, J. M. & Java, R. I. (1990). Recollective experience in word and nonword recognition. *Memory and Cognition, 16,* 309–313.

Gardnier, J. M. & Parkin, A. J. (1990). Attention and recollective experience in recognition memory. *Memory and Cognition, 18,* 23–30.

Garret, H. E. (1957). *Great experiments in psychology* (3rd ed.). New York: Appleton-Century-Crofts.

Gatz, M., Bengtson, V. L., & Blum, M. J. (1990). Caregiving families. In J.E. Birren & K.W. Schaie (Eds.)., *Handbook of the psychology of aging* (3rd ed., pp. 404–426). New York: Academic Press.

Gatz, M., Kasl-Godley, J. E., & Karel, M. I. (1996). Aging and mental disorders. In J. E. Birren & K. W. Schaie (Eds.), Handbook of the psychology of aging (4th ed., pp. 365–382). San Diego, CA: Academic Press.

Gavin, R. (1997). Medicare changes would put CNY hospitals under the knife. *Post-Standard,* July 25, pp. 1–2.

Gelman, R. (1979). Preschool thought. *American Psychologist, 34,* 900–904.

George, L. K. (1980). *Role transition in later life.* Belmont, CA: Wadsworth.

George, L. K. (1990a). Social structure, social processes, and social-psychological states. In R. H. Binstock & L. K. George (Eds.), *Handbook of aging and the social sciences,* (3rd ed., pp. 186–204). San Diego, CA: Academic Press.

George, L. K. (1990b). Caregiver stress studies: There really is more to learn. *The Gerontologist, 30,* 580–581.

George, L. K. (1992). Community and home care for mentally ill older adults. In J. E. Birren, R. B. Sloane, & G. D. Cohen (Eds.), *Handbook of mental health and aging* (2nd ed., pp.793–813). San Diego, CA: Academic Press.

Gerhardt, V. (1990). Qualitative research on chronic illness: The issue and the story. *Social Science Medicine, 30,* 1149–1159.

Gescheider, G. A. (1997). *Psychophysics: The fundamentals.* Mahwah, NJ: Erlbaum.

Gescheider, G. A., Bolanowski, S. J., Verillo, R. T., Hall, K. L., & Hoffman, K. E. (1994). The effects of aging on information processing channels in the sense of touch: I period absolute sensitivity. *Somatasensory and Motor Research, 11,* 345–357.

Gibbons, F. X., & Gerrard, M. (1991). Downward comparisons and coping with threat. In J. Suls & T. A. Wills (Eds.), *Social comparison: Contemporary theory and research* (pp. 317–346). Hillsdale, NJ: Lawrence Erlbaum.

Gibbs, J. C. (1977). Kohlberg's stages of moral development: A constructive critique. *Harvard Educational Review, 47,* 43–61.

Gibbs, J. C. (1979). Kohlberg's moral stage theory: A Piagetian revision. *Human Development, 22,* 89–112.

Gibbs, J. C., Arnold, K. D., & Burkhart, J. E. (1984). Sex differences in the expression of moral judgment. *Child Development, 55,* 1040–1044.

Gignac, M. A. M., & Gottlieb, B. H. (1996). Caregivers appraisals of efficacy in coping with dementia. *Psychology and Aging, 11,* 214–225.

Gilley, D. W., Wilson, R. S., Bennett, D. A., Stebbins, G. T., Bernard, B. A., Whalen, M. E., & Fox, J. H. (1991). Cessation of driving and unsafe motor vehicle operation by dementia patients. *Archives of Internal Medicine, 15,* 941–946.

Gilligan, C. (1977). In a different voice: Women's conceptions of self and morality. *Harvard Educational Review, 47,* 481–517.

Gilligan, C. (1982). *In a different voice: Psychological theory and women's development.* Cambridge, MA: Harvard University Press.

Gilligan, C., & Belenky, M. F. (1980). A naturalistic study of abortion decisions. *New directions for child development* (No. 7, pp. 69–90). San Francisco: Jossey-Bass.

Ginzberg, E. (1971). *Career guidance.* New York: McGraw-Hill.

Ginzberg, E. (1972). Toward a theory of occupational choice: A restatement. *Vocational Guidance Quarterly, 20,* 169–176.

Glass, T. A., Prigerson, H., Kasl, S. V., & Mendes de Leon, C. F. (1995). The effects of negative life events on alcohol consumption among older men and women. *Journal of Gerontology, 50B,* S205–S216.

Glick, P. C., & Ling-Lin, S. (1986). Recent changes in divorce and remarriage. *Journal of Marriage and the Family, 48,* 737–747.

Golan, N. (1986). *The perilous bridge: Helping clients through midlife transitions.* New York: Free Press.

Goleman, D. (1987). Personality: Major traits found stable through life. *New York Times,* March 24, pp. C1, C14.

Goleman, D. (1995). *Emotional intelligence.* New York: Bantam Books.

Goodman, M., Rubinstein, R. L., Alexander, B. B., & Luborsky, M. (1991). Cultural differences among elderly women in coping with the death of an adult child. *Journal of Gerontology: Social Sciences, 46,* S321–S329.

Gorman, D. G., Benson, F., Vogel, D. G., & Vinters, H. V. (1992, February). Creutzfeldt-Jakob disease in a pathologist. *Neurology, 42,* 463.

Gottlieb, G. L. (1992). Economic issues and geriatric mental health. In J. E. Birren, R. B. Sloane, & G. D. Cohen (Eds.), *Handbook of mental health and aging* (2nd ed). (pp. 873–890). San Diego, CA: Academic Press.

Gould, R. L. (1972). *Transformations: Growth and change in adult life.* New York: Simon & Schuster.

Gould, R. L. (1980). Transformation tasks in adulthood. *In the course of life, Vol. 3: Adulthood and aging process.* Bethesda, MD: National Institute of Mental Health.

Grady, C. L., McIntosh, A. R., Horwitz, B., Maisog, J. M., Ungerleider, L. G., Mentis, M. J., Pietrini, P., Schapiro, M. B., & Haxby, J. V. (1995). Age-related reductions in human recognition memory due to impaired encoding. *Science, 269,* 218–221.

Grams, A., & Albee, G. W. (1995). Primary prevention in the service of aging. In L. A. Bond, S. J. Cutler, & A. Grams (Eds.), *Promoting successful and productive aging* (pp. 5–35). Thousand Oaks, CA: Sage.

Grant, R. W. (1995). Interventions with ethnic minority elderly. In J. F. Aponte, R. Y. Rivers, & J. Wohl. (Eds.), *Psychological interventions and cultural diversity* (pp. 199–214). Boston: Allyn & Bacon.

Greene, V. L., & Monahan, D. J. (1987). The effects of a professionally guided caregiver support and education group on institutionalization and care receivers. *The Gerontologist, 27,* 716–721.

Greer, S. (1991). Psychological response to cancer and survival. *Psychological Medicine, 21,* 43–49.

Gresser, G., Wong, P. T., & Reker, G. T. (1987-88). Death attitudes across the life span: The development and validation of the death attitude profile. *Omega: Journal of Death and Dying, 18* (2), 113–128.

Grober, E., & Buschke, H. (1987). Genuine memory deficits in dementia. *Developmental Neuropsychology, 3,* 13–36.

Group for the Advancement of Psychiatry, Committee on Cultural Psychiatry. (1989). *Suicide and ethnicity in the United States.* Washington, DC: Author.

Gubrium, J. F. (1993). *Speaking of life.* New York: deGruyter.

Guilford, J. P. (1959). Three faces of intellect. *American Psychologist, 14,* 469–479.

Guilford, J. P. (1967). *The nature of human intelligence.* New York: McGraw-Hill.

Gurland, B. J. (1981). The borderlands of dementia: The influence of sociocultural characteristics on the rates of dementia occurring in the senium. In N. E. Miller & G. D. Cohen (Eds.), *Aspects of Alzheimer's disease and senile dementia* (pp. 61–80). New York: Raven Press.

Gutmann, D. L. (1975). Parenthood, key to the comparative study of the life cycle. In N. Datan & L. Ginsberg (Eds.), *Life-span developmental psychology: Normative life crises.* New York: Academic Press.

Gutmann, D. L. (1977). The cross-cultural perspective: Notes toward a comparative psychology of aging. In J. E. Birren & K. W. Schaie (Eds.), *Handbook of the psychology of aging* (1st ed.) New York: Van Nostrand Reinhold.

Gutmann, D. L. (1987). *Reclaimed powers: Toward a new psychology of men and women in later life.* New York: Basic Books.

Gutmann, D. L. (1992). Culture and mental health in later life. In J. E. Birren, R. B. Sloane, and G. D. Cohen (Eds.), *Handbook of mental health and aging* (2nd ed., pp. 75–97). San Diego: Academic Press.

Gwyther, L. P. (1992). Proliferation with pizzazz. *The Gerontologist, 33,* 865–867.

Haber, P. A. L. (1987). Nursing homes. In G.L. Maddox (Ed.), *Encyclopedia of aging.* New York: Springer.

Habermas, J. (1971). *Knowledge and human interests.* Boston: Beacon Press.

Hafen, B. Q., & Hoeger, W. W. K. (1994). *Wellness: Guidelines for a healthy lifestyle.* Englewood, CO: Morton Publishing.

Hagberg, B., Samuelsson, G., Lindberg, B., & Dehlin, O. (1991). Stability and change of personality in old age and its relation to survival. *Journal of Gerontology: Psychological Sciences, 46,* P285–P291.

Hagberg, J. M. (1987). Effects of training on the decline of VO_2 max with aging. *Federation Proceedings, 46,* 1830–1833.

Hagestad, G. O. (1985). Continuity and connectedness. In V. L. Bengtson & J. Robertson (Eds.), *Grandparenthood.* Beverly Hills, CA: Sage.

Haier, R. J., Siegel, A. V., Nuechterlein, K. H., Hazlett, E., Wu, J. C., Pack, J., Browning, H. L., & Buchsbaum, M. S. (1988). Cortical glucose metabolic rate correlates of abstract reasoning and attention studied with positron emission tomography. *Intelligence, 12,* 199–217.

Haldipur, C. V., & Ward, M. S. (1996). Competence and other legal issues. In M. Hersen & V. B. Van Hasselt (Eds.), *Psychological treatment of older adults: An introductory text.* New York: Plenum Press.

Halevy, A., & Brody, B. (1993). Brain death reconciling definitions, criteria, and tests. *Annals of Internal Medicine, 119,* 519–525.

Haley, W. E. (1991). Caregiver intervention programs: The moral equivalent of free haircuts. *The Gerontologist, 31,* 7–8.

Hall, D. T., & Rabinowitz, S. (1988). Maintaining employee involvement in a plateaued career. In M. London & E. Mone (Eds.), *Career management and human resources.* New York: Quorum.

Hall, G. S. (1922). *Senescence: The last half of life.* New York: Appleton.

Hanisch, K. A. (1995). Behavioral families and multiple causes: Matching the complexity of responses to the complexity of antecedents. *Current Directions in Psychological Science, 4,* 156–162.

Hanrahan, P., & Luchins, D. J. (1995). Access to hospice programs in end-stage dementia: A national survey of hospice programs. *Journal of the American Geriatric Society, 43,* 56–59.

Hansot, E. (1996). A letter from a patient's daughter: *Analysis of Internal Medicine, 125,* 149–151.

Harada, N. D., & Kim, L. S. (1995). Use of mental health services by older Asian and Pacific Islander Americans. In D. K. Padgett (Ed.), *Handbook of ethnicity, aging, and mental health* (pp. 184–202). Westport, CT: Greenwood.

Harel, Z., & Biegel, D. E. (1995). Aging, ethnicity, and mental health services: Social work perspectives on need and use. In D. K. Padgett (Ed.), *Handbook of ethnicity, aging, and mental health* (pp. 217–241). Westport, CT: Greenwood.

Harkins, S. W., Price, D. D., & Martinelli, M. (1986). Effects of age on pain perception. *Journal of Gerontology, 41,* 58–63.

Harma, M. I., Hakola, T., & Laitinen, J. (1992). Relation of age of circadian adjustment to night work. Fifth US-Finnish Joint Symposium on Occupational Safety and Health: Occupational epidemics of the 1990s. *Scandinavian Journal of Work, Environment and Health, 18,* Suppl. 2, 116–118.

Harris, L. (1976). *The myth and reality of aging in America.* Washington, DC: National Council on Aging.

Harris, P. B. (1993). The misunderstood caregiver? A qualitative study of the male caregiver of Alzheimer's disease victims. *The Gerontologist, 33,* 551–556.

Harris, P. B. (1995). Differences among husbands caring for their wives with Alzheimer's disease: Qualitative findings and counseling implications. *Journal of Clinical Geropsychology, 1,* 9–106.

Hart, R. P., Kwentus, J. A., Hamer, R. M., & Taylor, J. R. (1987). Selective reminding procedures in depression and dementia. *Psychology and Aging, 2,* 111–115.

Hartley, A. A. (1992). Attention. In F. I. M. Craik and T. A. Salthouse (Eds.), *The handbook of aging and cognition* (pp. 3–49). Hillsdale, NJ: Lawrence Erlbaum.

Harvard Health Letter. (1995). *The final chapter.*

Harvard Mental Health Letter (1995a). *Update on Alzheimer's disease, 2.*

Harvard Mental Health Letter (1995b). *Update on Alzheimer's disease,* Part II, 11 (#9).

Hasher, L., & Zacks, R. T. (1988). Working memory, comprehension, and aging: A review and a new view. In G. H. Bower (Ed.), *The psychology of learning and motivation* (Vol. 22, pp. 193–225). Orlando: Academic Press.

Hasher, L., Stoltzfus, E. R., Zacks, R. T., & Rypma, B. (1991). Age and inhibition. *Journal of Experimental Psychology: Learning, Memory and Cognition, 17,* 163–169.

Hashimoto, A. (1996). *The gift of generations: Japanese and American perspectives on aging and the social contract.* New York: Cambridge University Press.

Hatch, L. R. (1992). Gender differences in orientation toward retirement from paid labor. *Gender and Society, 6,* 66–85.

Haughie, E., Milne, D., & Elliot, V. (1992). An evaluation of companion pets with elderly psychiatric patients. *Behavioral Psychotherapy, 20,* 367–372.

Havighurst, R. J. (1972). *Developmental tasks and education* (3rd ed.). New York: David McKay.

Havighurst, R. J. (1982). The world of work. In B. J. Wolman (Ed.), *Handbook of developmental psychology.* Englewood Cliffs, NJ: Prentice-Hall.

Havighurst, R. J., McDonald, W. J., Perun, P. J., & Snow, R. B. (1976). *Social scientists and educators: Lives after sixty. Chicago: Committee on Human Development,* University of Chicago.

Hawkes, K., O'Connell, J. F., & Blurton Jones, N. G. (1998). Hadza Women's time allocation, offspring provisioning, and the evolution of long post-menopausal life spans. *Current Anthropology, 38,* 551–557.

Hawkes, K., O'Connell, J. F., Blurton Jones, N. G., Alvarez, H., & Charnov, E. L. (1998). *Proceedings of the National Academy of Sciences, 95,* 1336–1339.

Hayflick, L. (1980). The cell biology of human aging. *Scientific American, 242,* 58–65.

Hayflick, L. M. (1996). *How and why we age.* New York: Ballantine Books.

Hayslip, B., Jr., & Leon, J. (1988). *Geriatric case practice in hospice settings.* Beverly Hills, CA: Sage.

Health Care Financing Administration. (1996). *Your medicare handbook, 1996.* Washington, DC: Department of Health and Human Services, U.S. Government Printing Office.

Heckhausen, J., Dixon, R. A., & Baltes, P. B. (1989). Gains and losses in development throughout adulthood as perceived by different adult age groups. *Developmental Psychology, 25,* 109–121.

Heidrich, S. M., & Ryff, C. D. (1993). The role of social comparisons. Processes in the psychological adaptation of elderly adults. *Journal of Gerontology: Psychological Sciences, 48,* P127–P136.

Helgeson, V. S. (1994). Relation of agency and communion to well-being: Evidence and potential explanations. *Psychological Bulletin, 116,* 412–428.

Henderson, J. N., Gutierrez-Mayka, M., Garcia, J., & Boyd, S. (1993). A model for Alzheimer's disease support group development in African-American and Hispanic populations. *The Gerontologist, 33,* 409–414.

Hendricks, C. D., & Hendricks, S. (1983). *Living, loving, and relating.* Monterey, CA: Brooks/Cole.

Henretta, J. C., Chan, C. G., & O'Rand, A. M. (1992). Retirement reason versus retirement process: Examining the reasons for retirement typology. *Journals of Gerontology: Social Sciences, 47*

Herrnstein, R. J., & Murray, C. (1994). *The bell curve: Intelligence and class structure in American life.* New York: The Free Press.

Hertzog, C., & Schaie, K. W. (1988). Stability and change in adult intelligence: 2. Simultaneous analysis of longitudinal means and covariance structures. *Psychology and Aging, 3,* 122–130.

Hertzog, C., Cooper, B. P., & Fisk, A. D. (1996). Age and individual differences in the development of skilled memory search. *Psychology and Aging, 11,* 497–520.

Hess, B. (1971). *Amicability.* Unpublished doctoral dissertation. New Brunswick, NJ: Rutgers University.

Hess, L. A. (1988). *The depiction of grandparents and their relationships with grandchildren in recent children's literature: Content analysis.* Unpublished master's thesis. State College, PA: Penn State University.

Hess, T. M., & Pullen, S. M. (1996). Memory in context. In F. Blanchard-Fields, & T. H. & Hess, (Eds.), *Perspectives on cognitive change in adulthood and aging.* NY: McGraw-Hill.

Heston, L. L., & White, J. A. (1983). *Dementia: A practical guide to Alzheimer's disease and related illnesses.* New York: W.H. Freeman.

Hetherington, E. M. (1979). Divorce: A child's perspective. *American Psychologist, 34,* 851–858.

Hetherington, E. M., Stanley-Hagan, M., & Anderson, E. R. (1989). Marital transitions: A child's perspective. *American Psychologist, 44,* 303–312.

Hickey, T., Akiyama, H., & Rakowski, W. (1991). Daily illness characteristics and health care decisions of older people. *Journal of Applied Gerontology, 10,* 169–184.

High, D. M. (1991). A new myth about families of older people. *The Gerontologist, 31,* 611–618.

High, D. M. (1993). Advance directives and the elderly: A study of intervention strategies to increase use. *The Gerontologist, 33,* 342–349.

Hill, R. D., Storandt, M., & Malley, M. (1993). The impact of long-term exercise training on psychological function in older adults. *Journal of Gerontology: Psychological Sciences, 48,* P12–P17.

Hinrichsen, G. A., & Ramirez, M. (1992). Black and white dementia caregivers: A comparison of their adaptation, adjustment and service utilization. *The Gerontologist, 32,* 375–381.

Hirsch, C. H., Davies, H. D., Boatwright, F., & Ochango, G. (1993). Effects of a nursing-home respite admission on veterans with advanced dementia. *The Gerontologist, 33*(4), 523–528.

Hoch, C. C., Buysse, D. J., Monk, T. H., & Reynolds, C. F., III. (1992). Sleep disorders and aging. In J. E. Birren, R. B. Sloane, & G. D. Cohen (Eds.), *Handbook of mental health and aging* (2nd ed., pp. 557–581). San Diego, CA: Academic Press.

Hoeger, L. W., & Hoeger, W. W. K. (1995). *Lifetime: Physical fitness and wellness.* Englewood, CO: Norton.

Hoffman, L. W. (1982). Social change and its effects on parents and children: Limitations to knowledge. In P. W. Berman & E. R. Ramey (Eds.), *Women: A developmental perspective.* Washington, DC: U.S. Department of Health and Human Services, Public Health Services, National Institute of Health Publication No. 82-2298.

Holland, J. L. (1985). *Making vocational choices: A theory of vocational personalities and work environments* (2nd ed.). Englewood Cliffs, NJ: Prentice-Hall.

Holmes, E. R., & Holmes, L. D. (1995). *Other cultures, elder years: An introduction to cultural gerontology* (2nd ed.). Thousand Oaks, CA: Sage.

Holmes, T. H., & Rahe, R. H. (1967). The social readjustment rating scale. *Journal of Psychosomatic Research, 11,* 213–218.

Hooker, K., & Kaus, C. R. (1992). Possible selves and health behaviors in later life. *Journal of Aging and Health, 4,* 390–411.

Hooker, K., & Kaus, C. R. (1994). Health-related possible selves in young and middle adulthood. *Psychology and Aging, 9,* 126–133.

Hooker, K., & Ventis, G. (1984). Work ethic, daily activities and retirement satisfaction. *Journal of Gerontology, 39,* 478–484.

Horn, J. C., & Meer, J. (1987). The vintage years. *Psychology Today, 21,* 76–84.

Horn, J. L. (1982). The theory of fluid and crystallized intelligence in relation to concepts of cognitive psychology and aging in adulthood. In F. I. M. Craik & S. Trehub (Eds.), *Aging and cognitive processes* (Vol. 8). New York: Plenum.

Horn, J. L., & Donaldson, G. (1976). On the myth of intellectual decline in adulthood. *American Psychologist, 31,* 701–709.

Horn, J. L. & Noll, J. (1994). A system for understanding cognitive capabilities: A theory and the evidence upon which it is based. In D. K. Detterman (Ed.), *Current topics in human intelligence* (Vol. 4.), Norwood, NJ: Ablex.

Hornstein, G. A., & Wapner, S. (1985). Modes of experiencing and adapting to retirement. *International Journal of Aging and Human Development, 21,* 291–315.

Horowitz, A., Silverstone, B. H., & Reinhardt, J. P. (1991). A conceptual and empirical exploration of personal autonomy issues within family caregiving relationships. *Gerontologist, 31* (1), 23–31.

Horvath, T. B., & Davis, K. L. (1990). Central nervous system disorders in aging. In E. L. Schneider & J. W. Rowe (1990). *Handbook of the biology of aging* (3rd ed., pp. 306–329). San Diego: Academic Press.

Hospital Law Manual. (1982). Dying, death and dead bodies (pp. 39–41). Gaithersburg, MD: Aspen Systems Corporation.

Howard, D. V. (1996). The aging of implicit and explicit memory. In F. Blanchard-Fields & T. M. Hess (Eds.), *Perspective on cognitive change in adulthood and aging* (pp. 221–254). New York: McGraw-Hill.

Howe, M. L., & Courage, M. L. (1993). On resolving the enigma of infantile amnesia. *Psychological Bulletin, 113,* 305–326.

Hoyer, W. J. (1998). The older individual in a rapidly changing work context: developmental and cognitive issues. In K. W. Schaie & C. Schooler (Eds.), *Impact of work on older adults.* New York: Springer.

Hoyer, W. J., & Lincourt, A. E. (1998). Aging and the development of learning. In M. A. Stadler & P. A. Frensch (Eds.), *Handbook of implicit learning* (pp. 445–470). Thousand Oaks, CA: Sage.

Hoyer, W. J., & Rybash, J. M. (1992a). Knowledge factors in everyday visual perception. In R. L. West & J. D. Sinnott (Eds.), *Everyday memory and aging: Current research and methodology* (pp. 215–222). New York: Springer-Verlag.

Hoyer, W. J. & Rybash, J. M. (1992b). Age and visual field differences in computing visual-spatial relations. *Psychology and Aging, 7,* 339–342.

Hoyer, W. J., & Rybash, J. M. (1994). Characterizing adult cognitive development. *Adult Development, 1,* 7–12.

Hoyer, W. J., & Rybash, J. M. (1996). Life-span theory. In J. E. Birren (Ed), *Encyclopedia of gerontology* (pp. 65–71). San Diego: Academic Press.

Hultsch, D. F. (1971). Adult age differences in free classification and free recall. *Developmental Psychology, 4,* 338–342.

Hultsch, D. F., & Plemons, J. K. (1979). Life events and life-span development. In P. B. Baltes & O. G. Brim, Jr. (Eds.), *Life-span development and behavior* (Vol. 2). New York: Academic Press.

Hultsch, D. F., Hammer, M., & Small, B. J. (1993). Age differences in cognitive performance in later life: Relationship to self-reported health and activity life style. *Journal of Gerontology: Psychological Sciences, 48,* P1–P11.

Human Capital Initiative. (1993). *Vitality for life: Psychological research for productive aging.* Washington, DC: American Psychological Society.

Hunt, E. (1993). What we need to know about aging. In J. Cerella, J. Rybash, W. Hoyer, & M. L. Commons (Eds.), *Adult information processing: Limits on loss* (pp. 587–589). San Diego, CA: Academic Press.

Hunt, E. (1995). The role of intelligence in modern society. *American Scientist, 83,* 356–368.

Hutchison, T. D., & Scherman, A. (1992). Didactic and experiential death and dying training: Impact upon death anxiety. *Death Studies, 16* (4), 317–330.

Huyck, M. H. (1990). Gender differences in aging. In J. E. Birren & K. W. Schaie (Eds.), *Handbook of the psychology of aging* (3rd ed., pp. 124–132). San Diego: Academic Press.

Iaffaldano, M. T., & Muchinsky, P. M. (1985). Job satisfaction and job performance: A meta-analysis. *Psychological Bulletin, 97,* 251–271.

Ingersoll-Dayton, B., & Antonucci, T.C. (1988). Reciprocal and nonreciprocal social support: Contrasting sides of intimate relationships. *Journal of Gerontology: Social Sciences, 43,* 565–573.

Ingram, D. K., Weindruch, R., Spangler, E. L., Freeman, J. R., Walford, R. L. (1987). Dietary restriction benefits learning and motor performance of aged mice. *Journal of Gerontology, 42,* 78–81.

Inhelder, B., & Piaget, J. (1958). *The growth of logical thinking from childhood to adolescence.* New York: Basic Books.

Insel, P. M., Roth, W. T., Rollins, L. M., & Peterson, R. A. (1996). *Core concepts in health* (7th ed.) Mountain View, CA: Mayfield.

Insurance Institute for Highway Safety. (1992). *Status Report 12,* 1–7. Arlington, VA.

Jackson, J. S. (1988). *The black American elderly.* New York: Springer.

Jacobs, J. A. (1989). *Revolving doors: Sex segregation in women's careers.* Stanford, CA: Stanford University Press.

Jacoby, L. L. (1991). A process dissociation framework: Separating automatic from intentional uses of memory. *Journal of Memory and Language, 30,* 513–541.

Jacoby, L. L., Jennings, J. M., & Hay, J. F. (1996). Dissociating automatic from consciously-controlled processes: Implications for the diagnosis and treatment of memory disorders. In D. J. Herrmann, C. L. McEvoy, C. Hertzog, P. Hertrel, & M. K. Johnson (Eds.), *Basic and applied memory research: Theory in context* (Vol. 1, pp. 161–193). Hillsdale, NJ: Erlbaum.

Jacoby, L. L., Yonelinas, A. P., & Jennings, J. M. (1996). The relation between conscious and unconscious (automatic) influences: A declaration of independence. In J. D. Cohen & J. W. Schooler (Eds.), *Scientific approaches to consciousness.* (pp. 13–48), Mahwah, NJ: Erlbaum.

Jacoby, L. L., Kelley, C., Brown, J., & Jasechko, J. (1989). Becoming famous overnight: Limits on the ability to avoid unconscious influences of the past. *Journal of Personality and Social Psychology, 56,* 326–338.

James, W. (1890). *Principles of psychology.* New York: Henry Holt.

Jansari, A. J., & Parkin, A. J. (1996). Things that go bump in your life: Explaining the reminiscence bump in autobiographical memory. *Psychology and Aging, 11,* 85–91.

Jarvik, L. (1987). *The aging of the brain: How to prevent it.* Paper presented at the annual meeting of the Gerontological Society of America, Washington, DC.

Jasen, G. (1993). When crisis strikes: Caring for an elderly parent. *Wall Street Journal,* May 28, pp. C1, C14–C15.

Jecker, N. S. (1990). The role of intimate others in medical decision-making. *The Gerontologist, 30,* 65–71.

Jennings, J. M., & Jacoby, L. L. (1993). Automatic versus intentional uses of memory: Aging, attention, and control. *Psychology and Aging, 8,* 283–293.

Jennings, J. M., & Jacoby, L. L. (1997). An opposition procedure for detecting age-related deficits in recollection: Telling effects of repetition. *Psychology and Aging, 12,* 352–361.

Johnson, C. L. (1988). Grandparenting options in divorcing families: An anthropological perspective. In V. L. Bengtston & J. Robertson (Eds.), *Grandparenthood.* Beverly Hills, CA: Sage.

Johnson, C. L., & Barer, B. M. (1993). Coping and a sense of control among the oldest old: An explanatory analysis. *Journal of Aging Studies, 7,* 67–80.

Johnson, C., & Barer, B. (1996). *Life beyond 85 years: The aura of survivorship.* New York: Springer.

Johnson, C., Lahey, P. P., & Shore, A. (1992). An exploration of creative arts therapeutic group work on an Alzheimer's unit. *Arts in Psychotherapy, 19,* 269–277.

Johnson, S. J., & Rybash, J. M. (1993). A cognitive neuroscience perspective on age-related slowing: Developmental changes in the functional architecture. In J. Cerella, J. M. Rybash, W. J. Hoyer, & M. L. Commons (Eds.), *Adult information processing: Limits on loss* (pp. 143–175). San Diego, CA: Academic Press.

Jones, H. E., & Conrad, H. S. (1933). The growth and decline of intelligence: A study of a homogeneous group between the ages of ten and sixty. *Genetic Psychology Monographs, 13,* 223–294.

Jones, N. S. (1990). Black-white issues in psychotherapy: A framework for clinical practice. *Journal of Social Behavior and Personality, 5,* 305–322.

Jonsen, A. R. (1989). Ethical issues in organ transplantation. In R. M. Veatch (Eds.), Medical ethics (2nd ed., pp. 239–274). Sudbury, MA: Jones & Bartlett.

Judge, J. O., Davis, R. B., & Ounpuu, S. (1996). Step length reductions in advanced aging: The role of ankle and hip kinetics. *Journal of Gerontology: Medical Sciences, 51A,* 303–312.

Jung, C. G. (1933). *Modern man in search of a soul.* New York: Harcourt, Brace, & World.

Kübler-Ross, E. (1969). *On death and dying.* New York: Macmillan.

Kübler-Ross, E. (1981). *Living with dying.* New York: Macmillan.

Kahana, B. (1992). Theoretical and methodological issues in the study of extreme stress in later life. In M. Wykle (Ed.), *Stress and health among the aged* (pp.151–171). New York: Springer.

Kahana, B., & Kahana, E. (1970). Grandparenting from the perspective of the developing grandchild. *Developmental Psychology, 3,* 98–105.

Kahana, E., Stange, K., & Kahana, B. (1993). Stress and aging: The journey from what, to how, to why. *The Gerontologist, 33,* 423–426.

Kalish, R. (1981). *Death, grief, and caring relationships.* Monterey, CA: Brooks-Cole.

Kalish, R. (1985). The social context of death and dying. In R.H. Binstock & E. Shanas (Eds.), *Handbook of aging and the social sciences* (2nd ed.). New York: Van Nostrand Reinhold.

Kalish, R. (1987). Death. In G. L. Maddox (Ed.), *Encyclopedia of aging.* New York: Springer.

Kalish, R. A., & Reynolds, D. K. (1981). *Death and ethnicity: A psychosocial study.* Farmingdale, New York: Baywood. (Original work published 1976).

Kaplan, H. S. (1974). *The new sex therapy.* New York: Brunner/Mazel.

Kaplan, M. S., Adamek, M. E., & Geling, O. (1996). Sociodemographic predictions of firearm suicide among older white males. *Gerontologist, 36,* 530–533.

Kapp, M. B. (1991). Health care decision-making by the elderly: I get by with a little help from my family. *The Gerontologist, 31,* 619–623.

Karoly, P. (1993). Mechanisms of self-regulation. *Annual Review of Psychology, 44,* 23–52.

Kart, C. S., Metress, E. K., & Metress, S. P. (1992). *Human aging and chronic disease.* London: Jones & Bartlett.

Kasch, F. W., Boyer, J. L., VanCamp, S. P., Verity, L. S., & Wallace, S. P. (1990). The effect of physical activity and inactivity on aerobic power in older men. (a longitudinal study). *Journal of Sports Medicine, 18,* 73–83.

Kaslow, F. W., & Schwartz, L. I. (1987). *The dynamics of divorce: A life cycle perspective.* New York: Brunner/Mazel.

Kasper, J. D. (1988). Aging alone: Profiles and projections. *Report of the Commonwealth Fund Commission: Elderly People Living Alone.* Baltimore: Commonwealth Fund Commission.

Kastenbaum, R. (1981). *Death, society, and human experience* (2nd ed.). Palo Alto, CA: Mayfield.

Kastenbaum, R. (1985). Death and dying: A life-span approach. In J. E. Birren & K. W. Schaie (Eds.), *Handbook of the psychology of aging* (2nd ed.). New York: Van Nostrand Reinhold.

Kastenbaum, R. (1992). *The psychology of death* (2nd ed.). New York: Springer.

Kastenbaum, R. (1993). Re-constructing death in postmodern society. *Omega, 27,* 75–89.

Kastenbaum, R., & Norman, C. (1990). Deathbed scenes imagined by the young and experienced by the old. *Death Studies, 14,* 201–217.

Kastenbaum, R., Feifel, H., Rosenberg, C. D., & Lule, J. (1995). Confronting death. In L. S. DeSpelder & A. L. Strickland. *The path ahead: Readings in death and dying.* Mountain View, CA: Mayfield.

Katchadourian, H. (1987). *Fifty: Midlife in perspective.* New York: W.H. Freeman.

Katon, W., & Sullivan, M. D. (1990). Depression and chronic mental illness. *Journal of Clinical Psychiatry, 51,* 3–11.

Katz, I. R. (1997). Late life suicide and the Euthanasia debate: What should we do about suffering in terminal illness and chronic disease? *Gerontologist, 37,* 269–271.

Katzman, R. (1986). Alzheimer's disease. *New England Journal of Medicine, 314,* 964–973.

Katzman, R., Terry, R., DeTeresa, R. F., Brown, T., Davies, P., Fuld, P., Renbing, X., & Peck, A. (1988). Clinical pathological, and neurochemical changes in dementia: A subgroup with preserved mental status and numerous neocortical plaques. *Annals of Neurology, 23,* 138–144.

Kausler, D. H. (1994). *Learning and memory in normal aging.* San Diego: Academic Press.

Kausler, D. H., & Kausler, B. C. (1996). *The graying of America: An encyclopedia of aging, health, mind, and behavior.* Champaign, IL: University of Illinois Press.

Kazanjian, M. A. (1997). The spiritual and psychological explanations for loss experience. *The Hospice Journal, 12,* 17–27.

Kazdin, A. E., & Kagan, J. (1994). Models of dysfunction in developmental psychopathology. *Clinical Psychology: Science and Practice, 1* (1), 35–52.

Keith, P. M., & Wacker, R. (1993). Is it hard to guard the aged: Role strain of male and female guardians. *Journal of Gerontological Social Work, 21* (1–2), 41–58.

Keith, P. M., & Wacker, R. R. (1995). *Older wards and their guardians.* Westport, CT: Praeger.

Kemp, B. (1985). Rehabilitation and the older adult. In J.E. Birren & K.W. Schaie (Eds.), *Handbook of the psychology of aging* (2nd ed.). New York: Van Nostrand Reinhold.

Kemp, B. J., & Mitchell, J. M. (1992). Functional assessment in geriatric mental health. In J.E. Birren, R.B. Sloane, & G.D. Cohen (Eds.). *Handbook of mental health and aging* (2nd ed., pp. 671–719). San Diego, CA: Academic Press.

Kemper, T. L. (1994). Neuroanatomical and neuropathological changes during aging and in dementia. In M. L. Albert & E. J. E. Knoepfel (Eds.), *Clinical neurology of aging,* 2nd edition. (pp. 3–67). NY: Oxford University Press.

Kennedy, G. I. (1996). *Suicide and depression in late life: Critical issues in treatment, research, and public policy.* New York: John Wiley & Sons.

Kenshalo, D.R. (1977). Age changes in touch, vibration, temperature, kinesthesis, and pain sensitivity. In J. E. Birren & K. W. Schaie (Eds.), *Handbook of the psychology of aging* (2nd ed.). New York: Van Nostrand Reinhold.

Kerlikowske, K., Grady, D., Barclay, J., Sickles, E.A., Eaton, A., & Ernster, V. (1993). Positive predictive value of screening mammography by age and family history of breast cancer. *Journal of the American Medical Association, 270,* 2444–2450.

Kessler, R. C., Foster, C., Webster, P. S., & House, J. S. (1992). The relationship between age and depressive symptoms in two national surveys. *Psychology and Aging, 7,* 119–126.

Kiecolt-Glaser, J. K., Malarkey, W. B., Chee, M., Newton, T., Cacioppo, J. T., Mao, H., & Glaser, R. (1993). Negative behavior during marital conflict is associated with immunological down-regulation. *Psychosomatic Medicine, 55,* 395–409.

Kiesler, C. A. (1992). U.S. mental health policy: Doomed to fail. *American Psychologist, 47,* 1077–1081.

Kiloh, L. G. (1961). Pseudodementia. *Acta Psychiatrica Scandanavica, 37,* 336–351.

Kimmel, D. (1995). Lesbians and gay men grow old. In L. A. Bond, S. J. Cutler, & A. Grams (Eds.), *Promoting successful and productive aging.* Thousand Oaks, CA: Sage.

Kimmel, D., & Sang, B. E. (1997). Lesbians and gay men at midlife. In C. J. Patterson & A. R. D'Augelli (Eds.), *Lesbian and gay identities across the lifespan: Psychological perspectives.* New York: Oxford University Press.

Kimura, R. (1995). Medical ethics; History of subsection: Contemporary Japan. In W. T. Reich (Ed.), *Encyclopedia of Bio-Ethics* (revised ed., pp. 1496–1505). New York: Simon & Schuster/Macmillan.

Kindleberger, R. (1996). Priced out: Assisted living tackles how to make services available to poor and middle-class elderly. *Boston Globe,* November 10, pp. F1–F6.

King, P. M., Kitchener, K. S., Davison, M. L., Parker, C. A., & Wood, P. K. (1983). The justification of beliefs in young adults: A longitudinal study. *Human Development, 26,* 106–116.

Kingson, E. R., & O'Grady-LeShane, R. (1993). The effects of caregiving on women's social security benefits. *The Gerontologist, 33,* 230–239.

Kington, R., Rogowski, J., & Lillard, L. (1995). Dental expenditures and insurance coverage among older adults. *Gerontologist, 35,* 436–443.

Kinicki, A. J. (1989). Predicting occupational role choices after involuntary job loss. *Journal of Vocational Behavior, 35,* 204–218.

Kinney, H. C., Korein, J., Panigrahy, A., Dikkes, P., & Goode, R. (1994). Neuropathological findings in the brain of Karen Ann Quinlan. *New England Journal of Medicine, 330* (21), 1469–1475.

Kinoshita, Y., & Kiefer, C.W. (1993). *Refuge of the honored: Social organization in a Japanese retirement community.* Berkeley, CA: University of California Press.

Kinsey, A. C., Pomeroy, W. B., & Martin, C. (1948). *Sexual behavior in the human male.* Philadelphia: W. B. Saunders.

Kitchener, K. S., & King, P. M. (1981). Reflective judgment: Concepts of justification and their relationship to age and education. Journal of *Applied Developmental Psychology, 2,* 89–111.

Kitchener, K. S., & Wood, P. K. (1987). Development of concepts of justification in German university students. *International Journal of Behavioral Development, 10,* 171–186.

Kivnick, H. Q. (1983). Dimensions of grandparental meaning: Deductive conceptualization and empirical derivation. *Journal of Personality and Social Psychology, 44,* 1056–1068.

Klapper, J., Moss, S., Moss, M. S., & Rubinstein, R. (1994). The social context of grief among adult daughters who have lost a parent. *Journal of Aging Studies, 8,* 29–43.

Kleemeier, R. W. (1972). Intellectual change in the senium. *Proceedings of the Social Statistics Section of the American Statistical Association, 1,* 290–295.

Kliegl, R., Smith, J., & Baltes, P. B. (1989). Testing-the-limits and the study of adult age differences in cognitive plasticity of a mnemonic skill. *Developmental Psychology, 25,* 247–256.

Kline, D. W. & Scialfa, C. T. (1996). Visual and auditory aging. In J. E. Birren, K. W. Schaie, R. P. Abeles, M. Gatz, & T. A. Salthouse (Eds.), *Handbook of the psychology of aging* (4th edition). San Diego: Academic Press.

Kline D. W., Kline, T., Fozard, J. L., Kosnik, W., Scheiber, F. & Sekular, R. (1992). Vision, aging and driving: The problems of older drivers. *Journal of Gerontology: Psychological Sciences, 47,* P27–P34.

Kline, T. J. B., Ghali, L. M., Kline, D. W., & Brown, S. (1990). Visibility distance of highway signs among young, middle-aged, and older observers. *Human Factors, 32,* 609–619.

Knesek, G. E. (1992). Early versus regular retirement: Differences in measures of life satisfaction. *Journal of Gerontological Social Work, 19,* 3–34.

Knight, B. G., Lutzky, S. M., & Macofsky-Urban. (1993). A meta-analytic review of interventions for caregiver distress: Recommendations for future research. *The Gerontologist, 33,* 240–248.

Koenig, H. G. (1995). Religion as a cognitive schema. *International Journal for the Psychology of Religion, 5,* 31–37.

Koenig, H. G., & Blazer, D. G. (1992). Mood disorders and suicide. In J. E. Birren, R. B. Sloane, & G. D. Cohen (Eds.), *Handbook of mental health and aging* (2nd ed., pp. 380–409). San Diego, CA: Academic Press.

Kogan, N. (1990). Personality and aging. In J. E. Birren, & K. W. Schaie (Eds.), *Handbook of the psychology of aging* (3rd ed., pp. 330–346). San Diego, CA: Academic Press.

Kohlberg, L. (1958). *The development of mode of moral thinking and choice in the years ten to sixteen.* Unpublished doctoral dissertation, University of Chicago.

Kohlberg, L. (1969). Stage and sequence: The cognitive-developmental approach to socialization. In D. Goslin (Ed.), *Handbook of socialization theory and research.* Chicago: Rand McNally.

Kohlberg, L. (1976). Moral stages and moralization: The cognitive-developmental approach. In T. Lickona (Ed.), *Moral development and behavior: Theory, research, and social issues.* New York: Holt, Rinehart & Winston.

Kohlberg, L. (1987). The development of moral judgment and moral action. In L. Kohlberg (Ed.), *Child development and childhood education: A cognitive-developmental view.* New York: Longman Press.

Kohlberg, L. (1990). Which postformal levels are stages? In M. L. Commons, C. Armon, L. Kohlberg, F. A. Richards, T. A. Groetzer, & J. D. Sinnott (Eds.), *Adult development, Vol. 2: Models and methods in the study of adolescent and adult thought.* New York: Praeger.

Kohlberg, L., & Candee, D. (1984). The relationship of moral judgment to moral action. In W. M. Kurtines & J. L. Gewirtz (Eds.), *Morality, moral behavior, and moral development.* New York: Wiley.

Kohlberg, L., & Kramer, R. B. (1969). Continuities and discontinuities in childhood and adult moral development. *Human Development, 12,* 93–120.

Kolata, G. (1997). When death begins. *New York Times,* April 20, pp. 1–3.

Kolb, B. & Whishaw, I. Q. (1995). *Fundamentals of human neuropsychology* (3rd ed.). New York: W. H. Freeman.

Koplowitz, H. (1984). A projection beyond Piaget's formal operations stage: A general system stage and a unitary stage. In M. L. Commons, F. A. Richards, & C. Armon (Eds.), *Beyond formal operations: Late adolescent and adult cognitive development.* New York: Praeger.

Kosik, K. S. (1992). Alzheimer's disease: A cell biological perspective. *Science, 256,* 780–783.

Kosnik, W. D., Sekuler, R., & Kline, D.W. (1990). Self-reported visual problems of older drivers. *Human Factors, 32,* 597–608.

Kosnik, W., Winslow, L., Kline, D., Rasinski, K., & Sekuler, R. (1988). Visual changes in daily life throughout adulthood. *Journal of Gerontology: Psychological Sciences, 43,* P63–P70.

Koss-Chioino, J. D. (1995). Traditional and folk approaches among ethnic minorities. In J. F. Aponte, R. Y. Rivers, & J. Wohl (Eds.), Psychological interventions and cultural diversity, (pp. 145–163). Boston: Allyn & Bacon.

Kostyk, D., Lindblom, L., Fuchs, D., & Tabisz, E. (1994). Chemical dependency in the elderly. *Journal of Gerontological Social Work, 22,* 175–191.

Kotary, L., & Hoyer, W. J. (1995). Age and the ability to inhibit distractor information in visual selective attention. *Experimental Aging Research, 21,* 159–171.

Kramer, B. (1997a). Gain in the caregiving experience: Where are we? What next? *Gerontologist, 37,* 218–232.

Kramer, B. (1997b). Differential predictors of strain and gain among husbands caring for wives with dementia. *Gerontologist, 37,* 239–249.

Kramer, B. J. (1993a). Expanding the conceptualization of caregiver coping: The importance of relationship-focused coping strategies. *Family Relations, 42,* 383–391.

Kramer, B. J. (1993b). Marital history and the prior relationship as predictors of positive and negative outcomes among wife caregivers. *Family Relations, 42,* 367–375.

Kramer, D. A. (1983). Postformal operations: A need for further conceptualization. *Human Development, 26,* 91–105.

Kramer, D., Kahlbaugh, P. E., & Goldston, R. B. (1992). A measure of paradigm beliefs about the social world. *Journal of Gerontology: Psychological Sciences, 47,* P180–P189.

Kraus, R. (1978). *Recreation and leisure in modern society* (2nd ed.). Santa Monica, CA: Goodyear.

Krause, N. (1991a). Stress and isolation from close ties in later life. *Journal of Gerontology: Social Sciences, 46,* S183–S194.

Krause, N. (1991b). Stress, religiosity, and abstinence from alcohol. *Psychology and Aging, 6,* 134–143.

Krause, N. (1993). Early parental loss and personal control in later life. *Journal of Gerontology: Psychological Sciences, 48,* P100–P108.

Krause, N. (1995a). Religiosity and self-esteem among older adults. *Journal of Gerontology: Psychological Sciences, 50B,* 236–246.

Krause, N. (1995b). Stress, alcohol use, and depressive symptoms in late life. *Gerontologist, 35,* 296–307.

Krueger, J., & Heckhausen, J. (1993). Personality development across the adult life span.: Subjective conceptions vs cross-sectional constraints. *Journal of Gerontology: Psychological Sciences, 48,* P100–P108.

Kuhn, D., Langer, J., Kohlberg, L., & Haan, N. (1977). The development of formal operations in logical and moral thought. *Genetic Psychology Monographs, 95,* 97–188.

Kuhn, T. S. (1962). *The structure of scientific revolutions.* Chicago: University of Chicago Press.

Kumagai, F. (1996). *Unmasking Japan today. The impact of traditional values on modern Japanese society.* Westport, CT: Greenwood Press.

Kurdek, L. A., & Schmitt, J. P. (1986). Relationship quality of gay men in closed or open relationships. *Journal of Homosexuality, 12,* 85–99.

Labouvie-Vief, G. (1982). Dynamic development and mature autonomy. *Human Development, 25,* 161–191.

Labouvie-Vief, G. (1984). Logic and self-regulation from youth to maturity. In M. L. Commons, F. A. Richards, & C. Armon (Eds.), *Beyond formal operations: Late adolescent and adult cognitive development.* New York: Praeger.

Labouvie-Vief, G. (1985). Intelligence and cognition. In J. E. Birren & K. W. Schaie (Eds.), *Handbook of the psychology of aging* (2nd ed.), New York: Van Nostrand Reinhold.

Labouvie-Vief, G., & Schell, D. A. (1982). Learning and memory in later life. In B. B. Wolman (Ed.), *Handbook of developmental psychology.* Englewood Cliffs, NJ: Prentice-Hall.

Lachman, M. E. (1986). Personal control in later life: Stability change, and cognitive correlates. In M. M. Baltes & P. B. Baltes (Eds.), *Aging and the psychology of control.* Hillsdale, NJ: Erlbaum.

Lachman, M. E., & Burak, O. R. (1993). Planning and control processes across the lifespan: An overview. *International Journal of Behavioral Development, 16,* 131–143.

Lack, S., & Buckingham, R. W. (1978). *First American hospice: Three years of home care.* New Haven, CT: Hospice, Inc.

Lamberson, S. D., & Fischer, K. W. (1988). Optimal and functional levels in cognitive development: The individual's developmental range. *Newsletter of the International Society for the Study of Behavioral Development, 2,* 1–4.

Langer, E. J., & Rodin, J. (1976). The effects of choice and enhanced personal responsibility for the aged: A field experiment in an institutionalized setting. *Journal of Personality and Social Psychology, 34,* 191–198.

Langlois, J. A., Keyl, P. M., Guralnick, J. M., Foley, D. J., Marottoli, R., & Wallace, R. B. (1997). Characteristics of older pedestrians who have difficulty crossing the street. *American Journal of Public Health, 87,* 393–397.

Larsen, M. E. (1973). Humbling cases for career counselors. *Phi Delta Kappan, 54,* 374.

Larson, E. B. (1993). Illnesses causing dementia in the very elderly. *New England Journal of Medicine, 328,* 203–205.

Larson, R., Zuzanek, J. & Mannel, R. (1985). Being alone versus being with people: Disengagement in the daily experience of older adults. *Journal of Gerontology, 40,* 375–381.

LaRue, A., Dessonville, C., & Jarvik, L. F. (1985). Aging and mental disorders. In J. E. Birren & K. W. Schaie (Eds.), *Handbook of the psychology of aging* (2nd ed.). New York: Van Nostrand Reinhold.

Lavigne-Pley, C., & Levesque, L. (1992). Reactions of the institutionalized elderly upon learning of the death of a peer. *Death Studies, 16,* 451–461.

Lawlor, B. A. (1994). Non-cognitive disturbances in Alzheimer's disease. *Human Psychopharmacology, 9,* 393–396.

Lawton, M. P. (1977). The impact of the environment on aging and behavior. *Handbook of the psychology of aging.* New York: Van Nostrand Reinhold.

Lawton, M. P., Brody, E. M., & Saperstein, A. R. (1991). *Respite care for caregivers of Alzheimer patients: Research and practice.* New York: Springer.

Lawton, M. P., Moss, M., Kleban, M. H., Glicksman, A., & Rovine, M. (1991). A two-factor model of caregiving appraisal and well-being. *Journal of Gerontology: Psychological Sciences, 46,* P181–P189.

Lawton, M. P., Rajogopal, D., Brody, E., & Kleban, M. (1992). The dynamics of caregiving for a demented elder among black and white families. *Journal of Gerontology: Social Sciences, 47,* S156–S164.

Lazarus, R. S., & DeLongis, A. (1983). Psychological stress and coping in aging. *American Psychologist, 38,* 245–254.

Lazarus, R. S., & Folkman, S. (1984). *Stress, appraisal, and coping.* New York: Springer.

Lebowitz, B. D., & Niederehe, G. (1992). Concepts and issues in mental health and aging. In J. E. Birren, R. B. Sloane, & G. D. Cohen, *Handbook of mental health and aging* (2nd ed.) San Diego, CA: Academic Press.

Lee, G. R. (1978). Marriage and morale in late life. *Journal of Marriage and the Family, 40,* 131–139.

Lee, G. R., Dwyer, J. W., & Coward, R. T. (1993). Gender factors in parent care: Demographic factors and same-gender preferences. *Journal of Gerontology: Social Sciences, 48,* S9–S16.

Lehman, H. C. (1953). *Age and achievement.* Princeton, NJ: Princeton University Press.

Lehman, H. C. (1960). The age decrement in outstanding scientific creativity. *American Psychologist, 15,* 128–134.

Lentzner, H. R., Pamuk, E. R., Rhodenhiser, E. P., Rothberg, R., & Powell-Griner, E. (1992). The quality of life in the year before death. *American Journal of Public Health, 82,* 1093–1098.

Lerner, M. J., Somers, D. G., Reid, D., Chiriboga, D., & Tierney, M. (1991). Adult children as caregivers: Egocentric biases in judgments of sibling contributions. *Gerontologist, 31,* 746–755.

Lerner, R. M. (1984). *On the nature of human plasticity.* New York: Cambridge University Press.

Lerner, R. M. (1991). Changing organism-context relations as the basic process of development: A developmental contextual perspective. *Developmental Psychology, 27,* 27–32.

Letzelter, M., Jungeman, R., & Freitag, K. (1986). Swimming performance in old age. *Zeitschrift fur Gerontologie, 19,* 389–395.

Levenson, R. W., Carstensen, L. L., & Gottman, J. M. (1993). Long-term marriage: Age, gender, and satisfaction. *Psychology and Aging, 8,* 301–313.

Leventhal, E. A., Leventhal, H., Schaefer, P., & Easterling, D. (1993). Conservation of energy, uncertainty reduction and swift utilization of medical care among the elderly. *Journal of Gerontology: Psychological Sciences, 48,* P78–P86.

Leventhal, H., Leventhal, E., & Schaefer, P. M. (1992). Vigilant coping and health behavior. In M. G. Ory, R. P.

Abeles, & P. D. Lipman (eds.), Aging, Health and Behavior, (pp. 109–140). Newbury Park, CA: Sage.

Leventhal, H., Leventhal, E., & Schaefer, P. M. (1993). Conservation of energy, uncertainty reduction, and swift utilization of medical care among the elderly. *Journal of Gerontology: 48* (2), 78–86.

Levin, J. S., Chatters, L. M., & Taylor, R. J. (1995). Religious effects on health status and life satisfaction among Black Americans. *Journal of Gerontology: Social Sciences, 50B,* S154–S163.

Levin, J. S., Markides, K. S., & Ray, L. A. (1996). Religious attendance and psychological well-being in Mexican Americans: A panel analysis of three generations data. *Gerontologist, 36,* 454–463.

Levine, D. (1995). Choosing a nursing home: *American Health,* June, 82–84.

Levinson, D. J. (1978). *The seasons of a man's life.* New York: Knopf.

Levinson, D. J. (1986). A conception of adult development. *American Psychologist, 41,* 3–13.

Levinson, D. J. (1996). *Seasons of a woman's life.* New York: Alfred Knopf.

Levy, L. H., Martinkowski, K. S., & Derby, J. F. (1994). Differences in patterns of adaptation to conjugal bereavement: Their sources and potential significance. *Omega, 29,* 71–87.

Liberto, J. G., Oslin, D. W., & Ruskin, P. E. (1992). Alcoholism in older persons: A review of the literature. *Hospital and Community Psychiatry, 43,* 975–984.

Lichtenberg, P. A. (1994). *A guide to psychological practice in geriatric long term care.* Binghamton, NY: Haworth.

Lichtenberg, P. A., & Strzepek, D. M. (1990). Assessments of institutionalized dementia patients' competencies to participate in intimate relationships. *The Gerontologist, 30,* 117–120.

Lieberman, M. A. (1992). A re-examination of the adult life crises: Spousal loss in mid and late life. In G. H. Pollock (Ed.), *The course of life.* New York: International Press.

Lieberman, M. A., & Fisher, L. (1995). The impact of chronic illness on the health and well-being of family members. *Gerontologist, 35,* 94–102.

Lieberman, M. A., & Peskin, H. (1992). Adult life crises. In J.E. Birren, R.B. Sloane, & G.D. Cohen (Eds.), *Handbook of mental health and aging* (2nd ed., pp.119–143). San Diego: Academic Press.

Lieberman, M. A., Heller, K., & Mullan, J. (1990). *Predicting the effects of social network and social supports on adaptation.* Unpublished manuscript.

Liebman, B. (1995). Exercise: Use it or lose it. *Nutrition Health Letter, 22,* 9–17. Center for Science in the Public Interest: Washington, DC.

LifePlans. (1990). *Financing long-term care: The impact of alternative government programs and the potential of private insurance.* Boston University, Department of Economics (June).

Lifson, A. (1988). Do alternative models for transmission of HIV exist? *Journal of the American Medical Association, 259,* 1353–1356.

Light, E., Niederehe, G., & Lebowitz, B. (Eds.). (1994). *Stress effects on family caregivers of Alzheimer's patients: Research and interventions.* New York: Springer.

Lillard, L., Rogowski, J., & Kington, R. (1997). Long term determinants of patterns of health insurance coverage in the Medicare population. *Gerontologist, 37,* 314–323.

Lincourt, A. E., & Hoyer, W. J. (1996, November). *Aging and attention in memory-based automaticity.* Paper presented at the Psychonomic Society Meetings. Chicago.

Lincourt, A. E., Hoyer, W. J. & Cerella, J. (1997, November). Aging and the development of instance-based automaticity. *Psychonomic Society meetings,* Philadelphia, PA.

Lindenberger, U., & Baltes, P. B. (1994). Sensory functioning and intelligence in old age: A strong connection. *Psychology and Aging, 9,* 339–355.

Lindenberger, U., Kliegl, R., & Baltes, P. B. (1992). Professional expertise does not eliminate age differences in imagery-based memory performance during adulthood. *Psychology and Aging, 7,* 585–593.

Lindenberger, U., Mayr, U., & Kliegl, R. (1993). Speed and intelligence in old age. *Psychology and Aging, 8,* 207–220.

Liska, D., Obermaier, K., Lyons, B., & Long, P. (1995). *Medicaid expenditures and beneficiaries: National and state profiles and trends, 1984–1993.* Washington, DC: Kaiser Commission on the Future of Medicaid.

Loevinger, J. (1976). *Ego development.* San Francisco: Jossey-Bass.

Loftus, E. F., & Ketcham, K. (1994). *The myth of repressed memories.* New York: St. Martin's Press.

Lonky, E., Kaus, C., & Roodin, P. A. (1984). Life experience and mode of coping: Relation to moral judgment in adulthood. *Developmental Psychology, 20,* 1159–1167.

Lopata, H. Z. (1979). *Widowhood in an American city.* Cambridge, MA: Schenkman.

Lopata, H. Z. (1987b). *Widows: The Middle East, Asia, and the Pacific.* Durham, NC: Duke University Press.

Lopata, H. Z. (1994). *Circles and settings.* Albany: State University of New York Press.

Lopez-Bushnell, F. K., Tyra, P. A., & Futrell, M. (1992). Alcoholism and the Hispanic older adult. Special Issue: Hispanic aged mental health. *Clinical Gerontologist, 11*(3-4), 123–130.

Loveridge-Sanonmatsu, J. (1994, April). *Personal communication.* Oswego, NY: SUNY College at Oswego, Department of Communication.

Lowenthal, M., Thurnher, M., & Chiriboga, D. (1975). *Four stages of life: A comparative study of women and men facing transitions.* San Francisco: Jossey-Bass.

Lubomudrov, S. (1987). Congressional perceptions of the elderly: The use of stereotypes in the legislative process. *The Gerontologist, 27,* 77–81.

Ludwig, A. M. (1996). Mental disturbance and creative achievement. *Harvard Mental Health Letter,* March 4–5.

Lund, D. A., Caserta, M. S., & Dimond, M. F. (1993). The course of spousal bereavement in later life. In M. S. Streobe, W. Stroebe, & R. Hansson (Ed.), Handbook of bereavement: *Theory, research, and intervention* (pp. 240–254). New York: Cambridge University Press.

Lyons, N. (1983). Two perspectives: On self, relationships, and morality. *Harvard Educational Review, 53,* 125–145.

Mace, N., & Rabins, P. (1991). *The 36 hour day.* Baltimore, MD: Johns Hopkins University Press.

Macklin, E. (1980). Nontraditional family forms: A decade of research. *Journal of Marriage and the Family, 42,* 905–922.

Madden, D. J., & Plude, D. J. (1993). Selective preservation of selective attention. In J. Cerella, J. Rybash, W. Hoyer, & M. Commons (Eds.), *Adult information processing: Limits on loss* (pp. 273–300) San Diego, CA: Academic Press.

Maddi, S. (1986). *The great stress-illness controversy.* Paper presented at the meeting of the American Psychological Association, Washington, DC.

Majerovitz, S. D. (1995). Role of family adaptability in the psychological adjustment of spouse caregivers to patients with dementia. *Psychology and Aging, 10,* 447–557.

Malfetti, J. (Ed.) (1985). *Drivers 55 plus.* Falls Church, VA: AAA Foundations of Traffic Safety.

Manley, A. F. (1996). *U.S. Surgeon General Report: Commonplace exercise.* USPHS.

Mannix, M. (1993). The case for homecare. *U.S. News and World Report,* April 26, pp. 71–72.

Manton, K. G., Corder, L. S., & Stallard, E. (1993). Estimates of change in chronic disability and institutional incidence and prevalence rates in the U.S. elderly population from the 1982, 1984, and 1989 National Long Term Care Survey. *Journal of Gerontology: Social Sciences, 48,* S153–S166.

Marcoen, A. (1994). Spirituality and personal well-being in old age. *Aging and Society, 14,* 521–536.

Marion, T. R., & Stefanik-Campisi, C. (1989). The elderly alcoholic: identification of factors that influence the giving and receiving of help. *Perspectives in Psychiatric Care, 25,* 32–35.

Markus, H., & Nurius, P. (1992). Possible selves. In R. H. Roth (Ed.), *Personality structures and functions.* Needham, MA: Ginn Press.

Marottoli, R. A., Ostfeld, A. M., Merrill, S. S., Perlman, G. D., Foley, D. J., & Cooney, L. M. (1993). Driving cessation and changes in mileage drivers among elderly individuals. *Journal of Gerontology: Social Sciences, 48,* S255–S260.

Marsiglio, W., & Donnelly, D. (1991). Sexual relations in later life: A national survey of married persons. *Journal of Gerontology: Social Sciences, 46,* S338–S344.

Marsiske, M., Klumb, P., & Baltes, M. M. (1997). Everyday activity patterns and sensory functioning in old age. *Psychology and Aging, 12,* 444–457.

Martino-Saltzman, D., Blasch, B. B., Morris, R. D., & McNeal, L. W. (1992). Travel behavior of nursing home residents perceived as wanderers and non-wanderers. *The Gerontologist, 31,* 666–672.

Marx, J. (1996). Searching for drugs that combat Alzheimer's disease. *Science, 273,* 50–53.

Mason, S. E., & Smith, A. D. (1977). Imagery and the aged. *Experimental Aging Research, 3,* 17–32.

Masoro, E. J. (1984). Food restriction in the aging process. *Journal of the American Geriatrics Society, 32,* 296–300.

Masoro, E. J. (1988). Food restriction in rodents: An evaluation of its role in the study of aging. *Journal of Gerontology: Biological Sciences, 43,* B59–B64.

Masters, H. H., & Johnson, V. E. (1970). *Human sexual inadequacy.* Boston: Little, Brown.

Masters, H. H., Johnson, V. E., & Kolodny, R. C. (1991). *Human sexuality.* Boston: Little, Brown.

Matson, N. (1995). Coping in context: Strategic and tactical coping in careers of stroke survivors and careers of older confused people. *Journal of Community and Applied Social Psychology, 5,* 89–104.

Matsushima, N. M., & Tashima, N. (1982). Mental health treatment modalities of Pacific/Asian-American practitioners. San Francisco: Pacific Asian Mental Health Research Project. As cited in L. Uba (1994), *Asian Americans: Personality Patterns, Identity, and Mental Health.* New York: Guilford Press.

Matthias, R. E., Lubben, J. E., Atchison, K. A., & Schweitzer, S. O. (1997). Sexual activity and satisfaction among very old adults: Results from a community-dwelling medicare population survey. *The Gerontologist, 37,* 6–14.

Maurer, T., & Tarulli, B. (1994). Perceived environment, perceived outcome, and person variables in relationship to voluntary development activity by employees. *Journal of Applied Psychology, 79,* 3–14.

McAdams, D. P. (1995). What do we know when we know a person? *Journal of Personality, 63,* 365–396.

McAdams, D. P., de St. Aubin, E., & Logan, R. L. (1993). Generativity among young, midlife and older adults. *Psychology and Aging, 8,* 221–230.

McAuley, E. (1992). Understanding exercise behavior: A self-efficacy perspective. In G. C. Roberts (Ed.), *Understanding motivation in exercise and sport* (pp. 107–128). Champaign, IL: Human Kinetics.

McAuley, E., Courneya, K. S., & Lettunich, J. (1991). Effects of acute and long-term exercise on self-efficacy responses in sedentary, middle-aged males and females. *The Gerontologist, 31,* 534–542.

McAuley, E., Lox, L., & Duncan, T. E. (1993). Long-term maintenance of exercise, self-efficacy, and physiological change in older adults. *Journal of Gerontology: Psychological Sciences, 48,* P218–P224.

McAvoy, L. (1979). The leisure preferences, problems, and needs of the elderly. *Journal of Leisure Research, 11,* 40–47.

McCain, N. L., & Gramling, L. F. (1992). Living with dying: Coping with HIV disease. *Issues in Mental Health Nursing, 13,* 271–284.

McCartney, J., Izemen, H., Rogers, D., & Cohen, N. (1987). Sexuality in the institutionalized elderly. *Journal of the American Geriatrics Society, 35,* 331–333.

McCay, C. M., & Crowell, M. F. (1934). Prolonging the life span. *Scientific Monthly, 39,* 405–414.

McCracken, A. L., & Gerdsen, L. (1991, December). Sharing the legacy: Hospice care principles for terminally ill elders. *Journal of Gerontological Nursing, 17* (12), 4–8.

McCrae, R. R., & Costa, P. T. (1990). *Personality in adulthood.* New York: Guilford Press.

McCrae, R. R., & Costa, P. T., Jr. (1984). *Emerging lives and enduring dispositions: Personality in adulthood.* Boston: Little, Brown.

McCrae, R. R., & Costa, P. T., Jr. (1987). Validation of the five-factor model of personality across instruments and observers. *Journal of Personality and Social Psychology, 52,* 81–90.

McCrae, R. R., Arenberg, D., & Costa, P. T., Jr. (1987). Declines in divergent thinking with age: Cross-sectional, longitudinal, and cross-sequential analyses. *Psychology and Aging, 2,* 130–137.

McDowd, J. M., & Birren, J. E. (1990). Attention and aging. In J. E. Birren & K. W. Schaie (Eds.), *Handbook of the psychology of aging* (3rd ed., pp. 222–233). San Diego, CA: Academic Press.

McDowd, J. M., & Craik, F. I. M. (1988). Effects of aging and task difficulty on divided attention performance. *Journal of Experimental Psychology: Human Perception and Performance, 14,* 267–280.

McEvoy, G. M., & Cascio, W. F. (1989). Cumulative evidence of the relationship between employee age and job performance. *Journal of Applied Psychology, 74*(1), 11–17.

McFadden, S. H. (1996). Religion, spirituality, and aging. In J. E. Birren & K. W. Schaie (Eds.), *Handbook of the psychology of aging* (4th ed., pp. 162–177). San Diego, CA: Academic Press.

McGowin, D. F. (1993). *Living in the labyrinth: A personal journey through Alzheimer's disease.* New York: Delacorte Press.

McIlroy, W. E., & Maki, B. E. (1996). Age-related charges in compensatory stepping in response to unpredictable perturbations. *Journal of Gerontology: Medical Sciences, 51A,* 289–296.

McIntosh, J. L. (1995). Suicide prevention in the elderly (65–99). *Suicide and Life-Threatening Behavior, 25,* 180–192.

McIntosh, J. L., Santos, J. F., Hubbard, R. W., & Overholser, J. C. (1994). *Elder suicide: Research, theory, and treatment.* Washington, DC: American Psychological Association.

McIntyre, J. S., & Craik, F. I. M. (1987). Age differences in memory for item and source information. *Canadian Journal of Psychology, 41,* 175–192.

McKee, R. D., & Squire, L. R. (1993). On the development of declarative memory. *Journal of Experimental Psychology: Learning, Memory, and Cognition, 19,* 397–404.

McKibben, B. (1998). *Maybe one: A personal and environmental argument for single-child families.* New York: Simon & Schuster.

McLay, P. (1989). The Parkinsonian and driving. *International Disability Studies, 11,* 50–51.

McLeod, B. W. (1997). Author alters society's image of aging. *Syracuse Post Standard,* June 4, p. D–8.

McLoyd, V. C. (1989). Socialization and development in a changing economy: The effects of paternal job and income loss on children. *American Psychologist, 44*(2), 293–302.

McNeil, J. K., LeBlanc, E. M., & Joyner, M. (1991). The effects of exercise on depressive symptoms in the moderately depressed elderly. *Psychology and Aging, 6,* 487–488.

Meyer, B. J. F., Russo, C., & Talbot, A. (1995). Discourse comprehension and problem-solving decisions about the treatment of breast cancer by women across the life-span. *Psychology and Aging, 10,* 84–103.

Meyers, G. C. (1990). Demography of aging. In R. H. Binstock & L. K. George (Eds.), *Handbook of aging and the social sciences (3rd ed.).* San Diego, CA: Freeman Press.

Miles, S. H., & Irvine, P. (1992). Deaths caused by physical restraints. *The Gerontologist, 32* (6), 762–766.

Miller, B., & Lawton, M. P. (1997). Introduction: Finding balance in caregiver research. *Gerontologist, 37,* 216–217.

Miller, D., Staats, S. R., & Partlo, C. (1992, December). Discriminating positive and negative aspects of pet interaction: Sex differences in the older population. *Social Indicators Research, 27,* 363–374.

Miller, F. S. (1992). Network structural support: Its relationship to the psychosocial development of black females. In A. K. H. Burlew, W. C. Banks, H. P. McAdoo, & D. A. Azibo (Eds.), *African-American psychology: Theory, research, and practice* (pp. 105–126). Newbury Park, CA: Sage.

Miller, G. A. (1956). The magical number seven, plus or minus two: Some limits on our capacity to process information. *Psychological Review, 86,* 93–118.

Mirowsky, J., & Ross, C. E. (1992). Age and depression. *Journal of Health and Social Behavior, 33,* 187–205.

Mischel, W., & Shoda, Y. (1995). A cognitive-affective system theory of personality: Reconceptualizing situations, dispositions, dynamics, and invariance in personality structure. *Psychological Review, 102,* 246–268.

Mishra, S. (1992). Leisure activities and life satisfaction in old age: A case study of retired government employees living in urban areas. *Activities, Adaptation and Aging, 16,* 7–26.

Mittleman, M. S., Ferris, S. H., Shulman, E., Steinberg, G., Ambinder, A., Mackell, J. A., & Cohen, J. (1995). A comprehensive support program: Effect on depression in spouse-care givers of AD patients. *Gerontologist, 35,* 729–802.

Monat, A., & Lazarus, R. S. (Eds.). (1985). *Stress and coping* (2nd ed.). New York: Columbia University.

Monmaney, T., & MacIver (1995). Marty's gift. *American Health, 14,* 64–69.

Montgomery, R. J. V., Kosloski, T., & Borgatta, E. (1990). Service use and the caregiving experience: Does Alzheimer's disease make a difference? In D. E. Biegel and A. Blum (Eds.), *Aging and caregiving: Theory, research, and policy.* Newbury Park, CA: Sage.

Moos, R. H., Mertens, J. R., & Brennan, P. L. (1993). Patterns of diagnosis and treatment among late middle-aged and older substance abuse patients. *Journal of Studies on Alcohol, 54*(4), 479–487.

Moos, R. H., Brennan, P. L., Fondacara, M. R., & Moos, B. S. (1990). Approach and avoidance coping responses among older problems and non-problem drinkers. *Psychology and Aging, 5* (1), 31–40.

Mor-Barak, M. E., Scharlach, A. E., Birba, L., & Sokolov, J. (1992). Employment, social networks, and health in the retirement years. *International Journal of Aging and Human Development, 35,* 145–159.

Morgan, D. G. (1992). Neurochemical changes with aging: Predisposition toward age-related mental disorders. In J. E. Birren, R. B. Sloane, & G. D. Cohen (Eds.), *Handbook of mental health and aging* (2nd ed., pp. 175–199). San Diego, CA: Academic Press.

Morgan, D. L., Schuster, T. L., & Butler, E. W. (1991). Role reversals in the exchange of social support. *Journal of Gerontology: Social Sciences, 46,* S278–S287.

Morrow, D., Leirer, V., Alteri, P., & Fitzsimmons, C. (1992). *When expertise reduces age differences in performance.* Annual Meeting of the Psychonomics Society, St. Louis, MO.

Morse, W. C., & Weiss, R. S. (1968). The function and meaning of work and the job. In D. G. Zytowski (Ed.), *Vocational behavior.* New York: Holt, Rinehart & Winston.

Moscovitch, M. (1986). Memory from infancy to old age: Implications for theories of normal and pathological aging. *Annals of the New York Academy of Sciences, 444,* 78–96.

Moscovitch, M. M. (1994). Memory and working with memory: Evaluation of a component process model and comparison with other models. In D. L. Schacter & E. Tulving (Eds.), *Memory systems 1994.* Cambridge, MA: MIT Press.

Moscovitch, M., & Winocur, G. (1992). The neuropsychology of memory and aging. In F. I. M.

Craik & T. A. Salthouse (Eds.), *The handbook of aging and cognition* (pp. 315–372). Hillsdale, NJ: Erlbaum.

Moss, M. S., & Moss, S. Z. (1995). Death and bereavement. In R. Blieszner & V. H. Bedford (Eds.), *Handbook of aging and the family* (pp. 422–439). Westport, CT: Greenwood Press.

Moss, M. S., Lawton, M. P., Kleban, M. H., & Duhamel, L. (1993). Time use of caregivers of impaired elders before and after institutionalization. *Journal of Gerontology: Social Sciences, 48,* S102–S111.

Moss, M., & Lawton, M. P. (1982). Time budgets of older people: A window on four lifestyles. *Journal of Gerontology, 37,* 115–123.

Mulder, J. T. (1997). Death care giant tightens grip on central New York. *Syracuse Herald American,* June 29, pp. D4–D9.

Multi-Society Task Force on PVS. (1994a). Medical aspects of the persistent vegetative state. *New England Journal of Medicine, 330,* 1499–1508.

Multi-Society Task Force on PVS (1994b). Medical aspects of the persistent vegetative state. *New England Journal of Medicine, 330,* 1572–1579.

Mumford, M. D., & Gustafson, S. B. (1988). Creativity syndrome: Integration, application, and innovation. *Psychological Bulletin, 103,* 27–43.

Must, A., Jacques, P. F., Dallal, G. E., Bajema, C. J., & Dietz, W. H. (1992). Long-term morbidity and mortality of overweight adolescents. *New England Journal of Medicine, 327,* 1350–1355.

Mutchler, J. E., Burr, J. A., Pienta, & Massagli, M. P. (1997). Pathways to labor exit: Work transitions and work instability. *Journal of Gerontology: Social Sciences, 52B,* S4–S12.

Myers, J. E., & Shelton, B. (1987). Abuse and older persons: Issues and implications for counselors. *Journal of Counseling and Development, 65,* 376–380.

Namazi, K. H. (1994). Research Brief: Management of wandering behavior. *Respite Report: Partners in Caregiving: The Dementia Services Program, 6,* 6.

National Academy on Aging. (1995). Facts on Medicare: Hospital insurance and supplementary medical insurance. *Gerontology News,* October, 9–10.

National Academy on Aging. (1996). Facts on social security: The old age and survivors trust fund. *Gerontology News,* July, 5–6.

National Advisory Mental Health Council (1993). Health care reform for Americans with severe mental illnesses:

Report of National Advisory Mental Health Council. *American Journal of Psychiatry, 150* (10), 1447–1465.

National Association of Insurance Commissioners. (1993). A shoppers guide to long-term care insurance. Kansas City.

National Center for Health Statistics. (1987a). *Characteristics of the populations below the poverty level.* (Current Population Reports, Series P–60, No. 152). Washington, DC: U.S. Government Printing Office.

National Center for Health Statistics. (1987b). *Use of nursing homes by the elderly: Preliminary data from the national nursing home survey.*

National Center for Health Statistics. (1992). *Chartbook on health data on older Americans: United States, 1992.* Series 3–29.

National Center for Health Statistics. (1993). *Common beliefs about the rural elderly: What do national data tell us?* Series 3 (No. 28) PHS 93-1412. Washington, DC: U.S. Govt. Printing Office.

National Center for Health Statistics. (NCHS) 1993. Healthy people 2000: National health promotion and disease prevention objectives. PHS93-12311, Washington, D.C.: U. S. Government Printing Office.

National Funeral Directors Association. (1997). *Funeral services and expenses.* Office of Public Affairs. Northbrook, Illinois.

National Institutes of Health. (1988, September). *Health benefits of pets.*

National Research Council. (1992). *Committee for the study of improving mobility and safety for older persons. Transportation in an aging society (Vol. 1).* Washington, DC: Transportation Research Board.

Neisser, U. Boodoo, G., Bouchard, T. J., Boykin, A. W., Brody, N., Ceci, S. J., Halpern, D. F., Loehlin, J. C., Perloff, R., Sternberg, R. J., & Urbina, S. (1996). Intelligence: Knows and unknowns. *American Psychologist, 51,* 77–101.

Nelson, K. (1993). The psychological and social origins of autobiographical memory. *Psychological Science, 4,* 7–13.

Nelson, M. E., Fiatarone, M. A., Morganti, C. M., Trice, I., Greenberg, R. A., & Evans, W. J. (1994). Positive effects of high intensity strength training on the multiple risk factors for osteoporotic fractures. *Journal of American Medical Association, 272,* 1909–1914.

Nesselroade, J. R. (1991). The warp and the woof of the developmental fabric. In R. Downs, L. Liben, & D. Palermo (Eds.), *Visions of aesthetics, the environment, and development: The legacy of Joachim F. Wohlwill* (pp. 213–240). Hillsdale, NJ: Erlbaum.

Neugarten, B. L. (1968). *Personality in middle and late life* (2nd ed.). New York: Atherton Press.

Neugarten, B. L. (1973). Personality change in late life: A developmental perspective. In C. Eisdorfer & M. P. Lawton (Eds.), *The psychology of adult development and aging.* Washington, DC: American Psychological Association.

Neugarten, B. L. (1977). Personality and aging. In J. E. Birren & K. W. Schaie (Eds.), *Handbook of the psychology of aging.* New York: Van Nostrand Reinhold.

Neugarten, B. L. (1980a). Act your age: Must everything be a midlife crisis? *In Annual editions: Human development, 1980/1981* (pp. 289–290). Guilford, CT: Dushkin Publishers.

Neugarten, B. L. (1980b, February). *Must everything be a midlife crisis? Prime Time.*

Neugarten, B. L. (1989). Policy issues for an aging society. *The psychology of aging.* Washington, DC: American Psychological Association.

Neugarten, B. L., & Datan, N. (1973). Sociological perspectives on the life cycle. In P. B. Baltes & K. W. Schaie (Eds.), *Life-span developmental psychology.* New York: Academic Press.

Neugarten, B. L., & Neugarten, D. A. (1987). The changing meanings of age. *Psychology Today, 21,* 29–33.

Neugarten, B. L., & Weinstein, K. K. (1984). The changing American grandparent. *Journal of Marriage and the Family, 26,* 199–204.

Neugebauer, R., Rabkin, J. G., & Williams, J. B. (1992). Bereavement reactions among homosexual men experiencing multiple losses in the Aids epidemic. *American Journal of Psychiatry, 149* (10), 1374–1379.

Neulinger, J. (1981). *The psychology of leisure.* Springfield, IL: Charles C Thomas.

New York State Department of Health. (1988). *Do-not-resuscitate orders: A guide for patients and families.* Albany, NY: New York State Department of Health.

Newmann, J. P., Engel, R., & Jensen, J. E. (1991). Age differences in depressive symptom experiences. *Journal of Gerontology, 46* (5), P224–P235.

Newsom, J. T., & Shulz, R. (1996). Social support as a mediator in the relation between functional status and quality of life in older adults. *Psychology and Aging, 11,* 34–44.

Niederehe, G. (1986). Depression and memory impairment in the aged. In L. W. Poon (Ed.), *Handbook for clinical memory assessment of older adults* (pp. 226–237). Washington, DC: American Psychological Association.

Noble, B. P. (1993). Dissecting the '90's workplace. *New York Times,* Sunday, September 19, p. F21.

Nord, W. R. (1977). Job satisfaction reconsidered. *American Psychologist, 32,*

Nordin, B. E. C., & Need, A. G. (1990). Prediction and prevention of osteoporosis. In M. Berener, M. Ermini, & H. B. Stahelin (Eds.), *Challenges of aging.* New York: Academic Press.

Norris, F. H., & Murrel, S. A. (1990). Social support, life events, and stress as modifiers of adjustment to bereavement by older adults. *Psychology and Aging, 5,* 429–436.

Nyberg, L., Cabeza, R., & Tulving, E. (1996). Pet studies of encoding and retrieval: The HERA Model. *Psychonomic Bulletin & Review, 3,* 135–148.

Nystrom, E. P. (1974). Activity patterns and leisure concepts among the elderly. *American Journal of Occupational Therapy, 28,* 337–345.

O'Bryant, S. L., & Hansson, R. O. (1995). Widowhood. In R. Blieszner & V. H. Bedford (Eds.), *Handbook of aging and the family* (pp. 440–458). Westport, CT: Greenwood Press.

O'Connor, P. (1993). Same gender and cross-gender friendships among the frail elderly. *The Gerontologist, 33,* 24–30.

Okun, B. F., & Rappaport, L. J. (1980). *Working with other families: An introduction to family therapy.* North Scituate, MA: Duxbury.

Olshansky, S. J., Carnes, B. A., & Cassel, C. K. (1993). The aging of the human species. *Scientific American, 268,* 46–52.

Orgel, L. E. (1973). Aging of clones of mammalian cells. *Nature, 243,* 441–445.

Ornstein, R., & Thompson, R. F. (1984). *The amazing brain.* Boston: Houghton Mifflin.

Ornstein, S., & Isabella, L. (1990). Age vs. stage models of career attitudes of women: A partial replication and extension. *Journal of Vocational Behavior, 36,* 1–19.

Ory, M. G., Schechtman, K. B., Miller, J. P., Hardley, E. C., Fiatarone, M. A., Province, M. A., Arfken, C. L., Morgan, D., Weiss, S., Kaplan, M., & the FICSIT Group. (1993). Fraility and injuries in later life: The FICSIT Trials. *Journal of American Geriatrics Society, 41,* 283–296.

Oser, F. K. (1991). The development of religious judgment. In F. K. Oser & W. G. Pearlin, L. I., Mullan, J. T., Semple, S. J., & Skaff, M. M. (1990). The effects of alternate support strategies on family caregiving. *Gerontologist, 29,* 457–464.

Oser, F. K., & Gmunder, P. (1991). Religious judgment: A developmental approach. Birmingham, Ala.: Religious Education Press.

Osipow, S.H. (1983). *Theories of career development.* Englewood Cliffs, NJ: Prentice-Hall.

Ostrow, A. C. (1980). Physical activity as it relates to the health of the aged. In N. Data & N. Lohmann (Eds.), *Transitions of aging.* New York: Academic Press.

Over, R. (1989). Age and scholar impact. *Psychology and Aging, 4,* 222–225.

Owens, W. A., Jr. (1966). Age and mental abilities: A second adult follow-up. *Journal of Educational Psychology, 51,* 311–325.

Owsley, C., Sekuler, R., & Siemsen, D. (1983). Contrast sensitivity throughout adulthood. *Vision Research, 23,* 689–699.

Padgett, D. K. (1995). Concluding remarks and suggestions for research and service delivery. In D. K. Padgett (Ed.), *Handbook of ethnicity, aging, and mental health* (pp. 304–319). Westport, CT: Greenwood Press.

Padgett, D. K., Patrick, C., Burns, B. J., & Schlesinger, H. J. (1995). Use of mental health services by black and white elderly. In D. K. Padgett (Eds.), *Handbook of ethnicity, aging, and mental health* (pp. 145–164). Westport, CT: Greenwood Press.

Paffenbarger, R. S. (1993). The association of changes in physical activity level and other lifestyle characteristics with mortality among men. *New England Journal of Medicine, 328,* 538–545.

Palmore, E. B. (1982). Predictors of the longevity difference: A twenty-five year follow-up. *The Gerontologist, 22,* 513–518.

Palmore, E. B. (1984). Consequences of retirement. *Journal of Gerontology, 39,* 109–116.

Palmore, E. B. (1990). *Ageism: Negative and positive.* NY: Springer.

Palmore, E. B, & Maeda, D. (1985). *The honorable elders revisited: A revised cross-cultural analysis of aging in Japan.* Durham, NC: Duke University Press.

Palmore, E. B., Burchett, B. M., Fillenbaum, G. C., George, L. K., & Wallman, L. M. (1985). *Retirement: Causes and consequences.* New York: Springer.

Palmore, E. B., George, L. K., & Fillenbaum, G. G. (1982). Predictors of retirement. *Journal of Gerontology, 37,* 733–742.

Paloma, M., Pendelton, B. F., & Garland, T. N. (1982). *Reconsidering the dual-career marriage: A longitudinal approach.* In J. Aldous (Ed.), Two paychecks: Life in dual-earner families. Beverly Hills, CA: Sage.

Parkes, C. M. (1970). Seeking and finding a lost object. *Social Science and Medicine, 4,* 187–201.

Parkes, C. M. (1972). *Bereavement: Studies of grief in adult life.* New York: International University Press.

Parkes, C. M. (1993). Bereavement as a psychosocial transition: Processes of adaptation to change. In M. S. Stroebe, W. Stroebe, and R. O. Hansson (Eds.), *Handbook of bereavement: Theory, research, and intervention* (pp. 91–101). New York: Cambridge University Press.

Parkin, A. J., & Walter, B. M. (1992). Recollective experience, normal aging, and frontal dysfunction. *Psychology and Aging, 7,* 290–298.

Parmelee, P. A., Katz, I. R., & Lawton, M. P. (1991). The relation of pain to depression among institutionalized aged. *Journal of Gerontology: Psychological Sciences, 46,* P15–P21.

Parnes, H. W., Crowley, J. E., Haurin, R. J., Less, L. J., Morgan, W. R., Mott, F. L., & Nestel, G. (1985). *Retirement among American men.* Lexington, KY: Lexington Books.

Patala, F., & Winter (1990). Assessment of balance control in the elderly: Major issues. *Physiotherapy Canada, 42,* 89–97.

Pattison, E. M. (1977). *The experience of dying.* Englewood Cliffs, NJ: Prentice-Hall.

Pearlin, L. I. (1985). *Life strains and psychological distress among adults.* In A. Monat & R. S. Lazarus (Eds.), Stress and coping: An anthology (2nd ed.). New York: Columbia University Press.

Pearlin, L. I., & Lieberman, M. A. (1977). *Social sources of emotional distress.* In R. Simmons (Ed.), Research in community mental health. Greenwich, CT: J.A.I. Press.

Pearlin, L. I., Mullan, J. T., Semple, S. J., & Staff, M. M. (1990). Caregiving and the stress process: An overview of concepts and their measures. *The Gerontologist, 30,* 583–594.

Pepper, L. G. (1976). Patterns of leisure and adjustment to retirement. *The Gerontologist, 16,* 441–446.

Perkins, K. (1992). Psychosocial implications of women and retirement. *Social Work, 37,* 526–532.

Perkins, W. H., & Harris, L. B. (1990). Familial bereavement and health in adult life course perspective. *Journal of Marriage and the Family, 52,* 233–241.

Perlmutter, M. (1980). *An apparent paradox about memory aging.* In L. W. Poon, J. L. Fozard, L. S. Cermak, D. Arenberg, & L. W. Thompson (Eds.), New directions in memory and aging. Hillsdale, NJ: Erlbaum.

Perlmutter, M. (1986). A life-span view of memory. In P. B. Baltes, D. Featherman, & R. Lerner (Eds.), *Advances in life-span development and behavior* (Vol. 7). Hillsdale, NJ: Erlbaum.

Perry, W. B. (1968). *Forms of intellectual and ethical development in the college years: A scheme.* New York: Holt, Rinehart & Winston.

Persson, D. (1993). The elderly driver deciding when to stop. *The Gerontologist, 33,* 88–91.

Peters, K. (1996). Carrier hopes fancy new fitness center pumps up financial wellness. *Syracuse Post-Standard,* September 29, p. D5.

Petruzzello, S. J., Landers, D. M., Hatfield, B. D., Kubitz, K. A., & Salazar, W. (1991). A meta-analysis on the anxiety-reducing effects of acute and chronic exercise. *Sports Medicine, 11,* 143–182.

Pettibone, W. H., Van Hasselt, V. B., & Hersen, M. (1996). Social adaption in older adults. In M. Hersen & V. B. Hasselt (Eds.), *Psychological treatment of older adults* (pp. 11–34). New York: Plenum.

Piaget, J. (1954). *The construction of reality in the child.* New York: Basic Books.

Piaget, J. (1970). Piaget's theory. In P. H. Mussen (Ed.), *Carmichael's manual of child psychology* (3rd ed., Vol. 1). New York: Wiley.

Piaget, J. (1972). Intellectual evolution from adolescence to adulthood. *Human Development, 15,* 1–12.

Piaget, J., & Inhelder, B. (1969). *The psychology of the child.* (H. Weaver, trans.). New York: Basic Books (Original work published 1932).

Pierpaoli, W., & Regelson, W. (1995). *The melatonin miracle.* New York: Pocket Books.

Pillemer, K. A. (1986). The dangers of dependency: New findings on domestic violence against the elderly. *Social Problems, 33,* 147–156.

Pillemer, K. A., & Finkelhor, D. (1988). The prevalence of elder abuse: A random sample survey. *The Gerontologist, 28,* 51–57.

Pillemer, K. A., & Wolf, R. S. (1986). *Elder abuse.* Dover, MA: Auburn House.

Pitts, B. J., Popovich, M. N., & Bober, A. T. (1986). Life after football: A survey of former NFL players. (Unpublished manuscript). Cited in M. Shahnasarian (1992). Career development after professional football. *Journal of Career Development, 18,* 299–304.

Plude, D. J., & Hoyer, W. J. (1985). Attention and performance: Identifying and localizing deficits. In N. Charness (Ed.), Aging and human performance (pp. 47–99). London: Wiley.

Plude, D. J., & Hoyer, W. J. (1986). Age and the selectivity of visual information processing. *Psychology and Aging, 1,* 4–10.

Plude, D. J., Kaye, D. B., Hoyer, W. J., Post, T. A., Saynisch, M., & Hahn, M. V. (1983). Aging and visual search under varied and consistent mapping. *Developmental Psychology, 19,* 508–512.

Ponds, R. W., Brouwer, W. H., & van Wolffelaar, P. C. (1988). Age differences in divided attention in a simulated driving task. *Journal of Gerontology, 43,* P151–156.

Posner, M. C., & Wolmark, N. (1994). Indication for breast-preserving surgery and therapy in early breast cancer. *International Surgery (GUP), 79,* 43–47.

Post, G. (1992). Aging and meaning: the Christian tradition. In T. R. Cole, D. D. Van Tassel, & R. Kastenbaum (Eds.), *Handbook of the humanities and aging* (pp. 127–146). New York: Springer.

Price, R. W., Sidtis, J., & Rosenblum, M. (1988). The AIDS dementia complex: Some current questions. *Annals of Neurology 23* (Suppl), S27–S33.

Priest, R. (1991). Racism and prejudice as negative impacts on African American clients in therapy. *Journal of Counseling and Development, 70,* 213–215.

Princeton Religion Research Center. (1994). Importance of religion. *Princeton Religion Research Center Emerging Trends, 16,* 4.

Prosen, S., & Farmer, J. (1982). Understanding stepfamilies: Issues and importance for counselors. *Personnel and Guidance Journal, 60,* 393–397.

Pruchno, R. A., Smyer, M. A., Rose, M. S., Hartman-Stein, P. E., & Henderson-Laribee, D. L. (1995). Competence of long-term care residents to participate in decisions about their medical care: A brief objective assessment. *Gerontologist, 35* (5), 622–629.

PSA debate continues. (1995). *Johns Hopkins Medical Letter (February),* 2–3.

Pushkar, D., Arbuckle, T., Conway, M., Chaikelson, J., & Maag, U. (1997). Everyday activity parameters and competence in older adults. *Psychology and Aging, 12,* 600–609.

Quam, J. K., & Whitford, G. S. (1992). Adaptation and age-related expectations of older gay and lesbian adults. *The Gerontologist, 32,* 367–374.

Quinn, J. F., & Smeeding, T. M. (1993). *The present and future economic well-being of the aged.* In D. Salisbury & R. Burkenhauser (Eds.), Pensions in a changing economy. Washington, DC: Employee Benefit Research Institute.

Quinn, M., & Tomita, S. (1986). *Elder abuse and neglect: Causes, diagnosis, and intervention strategies.* New York: Springer.

Rabbitt, P. A., & Abson, V. (1990). "Lost and found." Some logical and methodological limitations of self-report questionnaires as tools to study cognitive aging. *British Journal of Psychology, 81,* 1–16.

Rabbitt, P., & McInnis, L. (1988). Do clever older people have earlier and richer first memories? *Psychology and Aging, 3,* 338–341.

Rakfedlt, J., Rybash, J. M., & Roodin, P. A. (1996). *Affirmative coping as a marker of success in adult therapeutic intervention.* In M. L. Commons, C. Goldberg, & J. Demick (Eds.), Clinical approaches to adult development (pp. 295–310). Norwood NJ: Ablex Publishers.

Rando, T. A. (1991). Parental reaction to the loss of a child. In D. Papadatos and C. Papadatos (Eds.), *Children and death.* New York: Hemisphere Publishers.

Raskind, M. A., & Peskind, E. R. (1992). Alzheimer's disease and other dementing disorders. In J. E. Birren, R. B. Sloane, & G. D. Cohen (Eds.), *Handbook of mental health and aging* (2nd ed., pp. 477–513). San Diego, CA: Academic Press.

Raz, N. (1996). Neuroanatomy of the aging brain observed in vivo: A review of structural MRI findings. In E. D. Bigler (Ed.), *Neuroimaging II. Clinical applications* (pp. 153–182). New York: Plenum.

Raz, N., Gunning, F. M., Head, D., Dupuis, J. H., McQuain, J. M., Briggs, S. D., Loken, W. J., Thornton, A. E., & Acker, J. D. (1997). Selective aging of human cerebral cortex observed in vivo: Differential vulnerability of the prefrontal gray matter. *Cerebral Cortex, 7,* 268–282.

Read, D. E. (1987). Neuropsychological assessment of memory in the elderly. *Canadian Journal of Psychology, 41,* 158–174.

Rebok, G. W. (1987). *Life-span cognitive development.* New York: Holt, Rinehart & Winston.

Reedy, M. N., Birren, J. E., & Schaie, K. W. (1981). Age and sex differences in satisfying love relationships across the adult life span. *Human Development, 24,* 52–66.

Reese, D. J., & Brown, D. R. (1997). Psychosocial and spiritual care in hospice: Differences between nursing, social work, and cleary. *Hospice Journal, 12,* 29–41.

Regnier, V., & Pynoos, J. (1992). Environmental intervention for cognitively impaired older persons. In J. E. Birren, R. B. Sloane, & G. D. Cohen (Eds.),

Handbook of mental health and aging (2nd ed., pp. 763–792). San Diego, CA: Academic Press.

Reifler, B. V. (1994). Depression: Diagnosis and Comorbidity. In L. S. Schneider, C. F. Reynolds, III, B. D. Lebowitz, & A. J. Friedhoff (Eds.), *Diagnosis and treatment of depression in late life* (Vol. 2, pp. 55–59). Washington, DC: American Psychiatric Press.

Reisberg, B. (1987, October). Classification of the various stages of Alzheimer's disease. *Paper presented at the conference on Alzheimer's Update: Translating Theory into Practice,* Utica, NY.

Reisberg, B., & Bornstein, J. (1986). Clinical diagnosis and assessment. *Drug Therapy, 16,* 43–59.

Reisberg, B., Ferris, S. H., & Franssen, E. (1985). An ordinal functional assessment toll for Alzheimer's-type dementia. *Hospital and Community Psychiatry, 36,* 593–595.

Remafedi, G. (1987). Adolescent homosexuality: Psychosocial and medical implications. *Pediatrics, 79,* 331–337.

Reynolds, P., & Kaplan, G. A. (1990). Social connections and risk for cancer: Prospective evidence from the Alameda County Study. *Behavior Medicine, 16,* 101–110.

Rhodes, S. L. (1977). A developmental approach to the life cycle of the family. *Social Casework, 58,* 301–311.

Rhodes, S. R. (1983). Age-related differences in work attitudes and behavior: A review and conceptual analysis. *Psychological Bulletin, 93,* 328–367.

Richardson, V., & Kilty, K. M. (1992). Retirement intentions among black professionals: Implications for practice with older black adults. *The Gerontologist, 32,* 7–16.

Riegel, K. F. (1976). The dialectics of human development. *American Psychologist, 31,* 689–700.

Riegel, K. F., & Riegel, R. M. (1972). Development, drop, and death. *Developmental Psychology, 6,* 306–319.

Rikli, R., & Busch, S. (1986). Motor performance of women as a function of age and physical activity level. *Journal of Gerontology, 41,* 645–649.

Riley, M. W. (1985). Age strata and social systems. In R. H. Binstock & E. Shanas (Eds.), *Handbook of aging and the social sciences* (Vol. 3, pp. 369–411). New York: Van Nostrand Reinhold.

Riley, M. W. (1997). *The hidden age revolution: Emergent integration of all ages.* Policy Brief: Center for Policy Research, Syracuse University.

Riley, M. W., & Riley, J. W. (1994). Age integration and the lives of older people. *The Gerontologist, 34,* 110–115.

Rinaldi, A., & Kearl, M.C. (1990). The hospice farewell: Ideological perspectives of its professional practitioners. *Omega Journal of Death and Dying, 21*(4), 283–300.

Rivers, P. C., Rivers, L. S., & Newman, D. L. (1991). Alcohol and aging: A cross-gender comparison. *Psychology of Addictive Behaviors, 5,* 41–47.

Rivers, R. Y. (1995). Clinical issues and intervention with ethnic minority women. In J. F. Aponte, R. Y. Rivers, & J. Wohl (Eds.), Psychological interventions and cultural diversity (pp. 181–198). Boston: Allyn & Bacon.

Roadberg, A. (1981). Perceptions of work and leisure among the elderly. *The Gerontologist, 21,* 142–145.

Robbins, L. N., Locke, B. Z., & Reiger, D. A. (1991). An overview of psychiatric disorders in America. In L. N. Robbins & D. A. Reiger (Eds.), *Psychiatric disorders in America: The Epidemiologic Catchment Area Study* (pp. 328–366). New York: Springer.

Robbins, R. A. (1992). Death competency: A study of hospice volunteers. *Death Studies, 16* (6), 557–569.

Roberts, P., & Newton, P. M. (1987). Levinsonian studies of women's adult development. *Psychology and Aging, 2,* 154–163.

Robertson, J. (1976). Significance of grandparents: Perceptions of young adult grandchildren. *The Gerontologist, 16,* 137–140.

Robinson, K., & Yates, K. (1994). Effects of two caregiver training programs on burden and attitude towards help. *Archives of Psychiatric Nursing, 8,* 312–319.

Rockstein, M., & Sussman, M. (1979). *Biology of aging.* Belmont, CA: Wadsworth.

Rodin, J. (1986). Aging and health: Effects of the sense of control. *Science, 233,* 1271–1276.

Rodin, J. (1990). Control by any other name: Definitions, concepts, and processes. In J. Rodin, C. Schooler, & K.W. Schaie (Eds.), *Self-directedness cause and effects throughout the life course* (pp. 1–17). Hillsdale, NJ: Lawrence Erlbaum.

Rodin, J., & McAvay, G. (1992). Determinants of change in perceived health in a longitudinal study of older adults. *Journal of Gerontology, 47,* P373–P384.

Rodriguez, O. (1987). *Hispanics and human services help-seeking in the inner city.* Monograph 14. Bronx, NY: Hispanic Research Center, Fordham University.

Rodriguez, O., & O'Donnell, R. M. (1995). Help-seeking and use of mental health services by the Hispanic elderly. In D. K. Padgett (Ed.), *Handbook of ethnicity, aging, and mental health* (pp. 165–184). Westport, CT: Greenwood.

Roediger, H. L. & McDermott, K. B. (1995). Creating false memories: Remembering words not presented in lists. *Journal of Experimental Psychology: Learning, Memory, and Cognition, 21,* 803–814.

Rogaev, E. I., Sherrington, R., Rogaev, E. A., Levesque, G., Ikeda, M., Laing, Y., Chi, H., Lin, C., Holman, K., Tsuda, T., Mar, L., Sorbl, S., Macmias, B., Placentil, S., Amaducci, L., Chumakor, I., Cohen, D., Lannfelt, L., Fraser, P. E., Rommens, J. M., & St. George: Hyslop, P.H. (1995). Familial Alzheimer's disease in kindreds with missense mutations in a gene on chromosome 1 related to the Alzheimer's disease type 3 gene. *Nature, 375,* 775–778.

Rogers, R., Meyer, J., & Mortel, K. (1990). After reaching retirement age physical activity sustains cerebral perfusion and cognition. *Journal of the American Geriatrics Society, 38,* 123–128.

Rogler, L. H., Malgady, R. G., & Rodriguez, O. (1989). Hispanics and mental health: A framework research. Malabar, Florida: R. E. Krieger.

Rogler, L., & Cortes, D. (1993). Help-seeking pathways: A unifying concept in mental health care. *American Journal of Psychiatry, 150,* 554–561.

Rollins, B. C., & Feldman, H. (1970). Marital satisfaction over the life cycle. *Journal of Marriage and the Family, 32,* 20–28.

Rollins, B. C., & Gallagher, R. (1978). The developing child and marital satisfaction. In R. Lerner & G. Spanier (Eds.), *Child influences on marital interaction: A life-span perspective.* New York: Academic Press.

Romaniuk, J. G., & Romaniuk, M. (1981). Creativity across the life span: A measurement perspective. *Human Development, 24,* 366–381.

Roodin, P. A., Rybash, J. M., & Hoyer, W. J. (1984). *Affect in adult cognition: A constructivist view of moral thought and action.* In C. Malatesta & C. Izard (Eds.), The role of affect in adult development and aging. Beverly Hills, CA: Sage.

Rook, K. S. (1987). Reciprocity of social exchange and social satisfaction among older women. *Journal of Personality and Social Psychology, 52,* 145–154.

Rosenbloom, C. A., & Whittington, F. J. (1993). The effects of bereavement on eating behaviors and nutrient intakes in elderly widowed persons. *Journal of Gerontology, 48,* S223–S229.

Rosenthal, C. J., Martin-Matthews, A., & Matthews, S. A. (1996). Caught in the middle? Occupancy in multiple roles and help to parents in a national probability sample of Canadian adults. *Journal of Gerontology: Social Sciences, 51B,* 274–283.

Ross, C. E. (1990). Religion and psychological distress. *Journal for the Scientific Study of Religion, 29,* 236–245.

Rossi, A. (1984). Gender and parenthood. *American Sociological Review, 49,* 1–19.

Rowe, J. W., & Kahn, R. L. (1987). Human aging: Usual and successful. *Science, 237,* 143–149.

Rowe, J. W. & Kahn, R. L. (1997). Successful aging. *The Gerontologist, 37,* 433–440.

Rubenstein, C., & Shaver, P. (1981). The experience of loneliness. In L. A. Peplau & D. Perlman (Eds.), *Loneliness: A source book of current theory, research, and therapy.* New York: Wiley Interscience.

Rubenstein, R. L., Alexander, B. B., Goodman, M., & Luborsky, M. (1991). Key relationships of never married, childless older women: A cultural analysis. *Journal of Gerontology: Social Sciences, 46,* S270–S277.

Rubin, R. M., & Koelln, K. (1993). Out-of-pocket health expenditure differentials between elderly and nonelderly households. *The Gerontologist, 33,* 596–602.

Rubin, Z. (1979, October). Seeking a cure for loneliness. *Psychology Today, 13,* 82–91.

Ruchlin, H. S., & Morris, J. N. (1992, February). Deteriorating health and the cessation of employment among older workers. *Journal of Aging and Health, 4,* 43–57.

Rudberg, M. A., Parzen, M. I., Leonard, L. A., & Cassel, L. K. (1996). Functional limitation pathways and transitions in community-dwelling older persons. *Gerontologist, 36,* 430–440.

Rusting, R. L. (1992). Why do we age? *Scientific American, 267,* 130–141.

Ruth, J. E., & Birren, J. E. (1985). Creativity in adulthood and old age: Relations to intelligence, sex, and mode of testing. *International Journal of Behavioral Development, 8,* 99–109.

Ruth, J. E., & Coleman, P. (1996). Personality and aging: Coping and management of the self in later life. In J. E. Birren & K. W. Schaie (Eds.), *Handbook of the psychology of aging* (4th ed., pp. 308–322). San Diego: Academic Press.

Rybash, J. M. (1996). Aging and implicit memory: A cognitive neuropsychological perspective. *Developmental Neuropsychology, 12,* 127–178.

Rybash, J. M. & Hoyer, W. J. (1996a). Brain reserve capacity and aging: Some unanswered questions. *Brain and Cognition, 30,* 320–323.

Rybash, J. M., & Hoyer, W. J. (1996b). Process dissociation procedure reveals age differences in conscious and unconscious influences on memory for possible and impossible objects. *Aging, Neuropsychology, and Cognition, 3,* 1–13.

Rybash, J. M., & Hrubi, K. L. (1997). Psychometric and psychodynamic correlates of first memories in younger and older adults. *The Gerontologist, 37,* 581–587.

Rybash, J. M., & Roodin, P. A. (1989). *A comparison of formal and post formal modes of health care decision-making competence.* In M. L. Commons, J. D. Sinnott, F. A. Richards, & C. Armon (Eds.), Adult development: Vol. 1. Comparisons and applications of developmental models (pp. 217–235). New York: Praeger

Rybash, J. M., DeLuca, K. L., & Rubenstein, L. (1995). Conscious and unconscious influences on remembering information from the near and distant past. *Journal of Adult Development, 2,* 15–21.

Rybash, J. M., Hoyer, W. J., & Roodin, P. A. (1986). *Adult cognition and aging: Developmental changes in processing, knowing, and thinking.* New York: Pergamon.

Rybash, J. M., Roodin, P. A., & Hoyer, W. J. (1983). Expressions of moral thought in later adulthood. *The Gerontologist, 23,* 254–260.

Rybash, J. M., Roodin, P. A., & Hoyer, W. J. (1986). *Adult cognition and aging: Developmental changes in processing, knowing, and thinking.* New York: Pergamon.

Rybash, J. M., Rubenstein, L., & DeLuca, K. L. (1997). How to become famous but not necessarily recognizable: Encoding processes and study-test delays dissociate source monitoring from recognition. *American Journal of Psychology, 110,* 93–114.

Rybash, J. M., Santoro, K. E., & Hoyer, W. J. (in press). Adult age differences in conscious and unconscious influences on memory for novel associations. *Aging, Neuropsychology, and Cognition.*

Ryff, C. D. (1991). Possible selves in adulthood and old age: A tale of shifting horizons. *Psychology and Aging, 6,* 286–295.

Ryff, C. D. (1995). Psychological well-being in adult life. *Current Directions in Psychological Science, 4,* 99–104.

Ryff, C. D., & Essex, M. J. (1991). Psychological well-being in adulthood and old age: Descriptive markers and explanatory processes. In K.W. Schaie & M. Powell Lawton (Eds.), *Annual review of gerontology and geriatrics* (Vol. 11, pp. 144–171). New York: Springer.

Ryff, C. D., & Keyes, C. L. M. (1995). The structure of psychological well-being revisited. *Journal of Personality and Social Psychology, 69,* 719–727.

Sachedina, A. (1995). Islam. In W. T. Reich (Ed.), Encyclopedia of bio-ethics (revised ed., Vol. 1. pp. 1289–1297). New York: Simon & Schuster/Macmillan.

Salthouse, T. A. (1984). Effects of age and skill in typing. *Journal of Experimental Psychology: General, 113,* 345–371.

Salthouse, T. A. (1985). Spread of behavior and its implications for cognition. In J. E. Birren & K. W. Schaie (Eds.), *Handbook of the psychology for aging* (2nd ed.). New York: Van Nostrand Reinhold.

Salthouse, T. A. (1990). Speed of behavior and its implications for cognition. In J. E. Birren & K. W. Schaie (Eds.), *The handbook of the psychology of aging* (2nd ed., 400–426). New York: Van Nostrand Reinhold.

Salthouse, T. A. (1992). Shifting levels of analysis in the investigation of cognitive aging. *Human Development, 35,* 321–342.

Salthouse, T. A. (1996). Constraints on theories of cognitive aging. *Psychonomic Bulletin & Review, 3,* 287–299.

Salthouse, T. A. (1997). The processing speed theory of adult age differences in cognition. *Psychological Review, 103,* 403–429.

Salthouse, T. A., & Maurer, T. J. (1996). Aging, job performance, and career development. In J. E. Birren & K. W. Schaie (Eds.), *Handbook of the psychology of aging* (4th ed., pp. 353–364). San Diego: Academic Press.

Salthouse, T. A., & Somberg, B. L. (1982). Skilled performance: The effects of age and experience on elementary processes. *Journal of Experimental Psychology: General, 111,* 176–207.

Salthouse, T. A., Babcock, R. L., Skovronek, E., Mitchell, D., & Palmon, R. (1990). Age and experience effects in spatial visualization. *Developmental Psychology, 26,* 128–136.

Salzman, C., & Nevis-Olesen, J. (1992). Psychopharmacologic treatment. In J. E. Birren, R. B. Sloane, & G. D. Cohen (Eds.), *Handbook of mental health and aging* (2nd ed., pp. 722–763). San Diego, CA: Academic Press.

Sampson, J. P., Jr., Reardon, R. C., & Lenz, J. G. (1991). Computer assisted career guidance: Improving the design and use of systems. *Journal of Career Development, 17,* 185–190.

Sandler, I. N., West, S. G., Baca, L., Pillov, D. R., et. al. (1992, Aug.). Linking empirically based theory and evaluation: The Family Bereavement Program. *American Journal of Community Psychology, 20,* 491–521.

Sands, L. P., & Meredith, W. (1992). Blood pressure and intellectual function in late midlife. *Journal of Gerontology: Psychological Sciences, 47,* 81–84.

Sandvik, L., & Erikssen, J. (1993). Physical fitness as a predictor of mortality among healthy middle-aged Norwegian men. *New England Journal of Medicine, 328,* 533–537.

Santrock, J. W., & Warshak, R. A. (1979). Father custody and social development in boys and girls. *Journal of Social Issues, 35,* 112–125.

Sarason, I. G., Sarason, B. R., & Pierce, G. R. (1989). *Social support: An interactional view.* NY: Wiley.

Satz, P. (1993). Brain reserve capacity on symptom onset after brain injury: A formulation and review of evidence for threshold theory. *Neuropsychology, 7,* 273–295.

Sauber, M., & Corrigan, E. M. (1970). *The six-year experience of unwed mothers as parents.* New York: Community Council of Greater New York.

Saunders, C. (1977). Dying to live: St. Christopher's Hospice. In H. Feifel (Ed.), *New meanings of death.* New York: McGraw-Hill.

Schacter, D. L. (1994). *Priming and multiple memory systems: Perceptual mechanisms of implicit memory.* In D. L. Schacter, & E. Tulving, (Eds.). Memory systems 1994. Cambridge, MA: MIT Press.

Schacter, D. L. (1996). *Searching for memory.* NY: Basic Books.

Schacter, D. L., & Buckner, R. L. (1998). Priming and the brain. *Neuron, 20,* 185–195.

Schacter, D. L., & Tulving, E. (1994). (Eds.), *Memory systems 1994.* Cambridge, MA: MIT Press.

Schacter, D. L., Kasniak, A., Kihlstrom, J., & Valdiserri, M. (1991). The relation between source memory and aging. *Psychology and Aging, 6,* 559–568.

Schacter, D. L., Savage, C. R., Alpert, N. M., Rauch, S. L., & Albert, M. S. (1996). The role of hippocampus and frontal cortex in age-related memory changes: A PET study. *NeuroReport, 7,* 1165–1169.

Schafer, E. P. (1982). Neural adaptivity: A biological determinant of behavioral intelligence. *International Journal of Neuroscience, 17,* 183–191.

Schaie, K. W. (1979). *The primary mental abilities in adulthood: An exploration in the development of psychometric intelligence.* In P. B. Baltes & O. G. Brim, Jr. (Eds.), Life-span development and behavior (Vol. 2). New York: Academic Press.

Schaie, K.W. (1983). *Consistency and changes in cognitive functioning of the young-old and old-old.* In M. Bergner, U. Lehr, E. Lang, & R. Schmidt-Scherzer (Eds.), Aging in the eighties and beyond. New York: Springer.

Schaie, K. W. (1985). *Manual for the Schaie-Thurstone Adult Mental Abilities Test (STAMAT).* Palo Alto, CA: Consulting Psychologists Press.

Schaie, K. W. (1990). The optimization of cognitive functioning in old age: Prediction based on cohort-sequential and longitudinal data. In. P. B. Baltes & M. Baltes (Eds.), *Longitudinal research and the study of successful (optimal) aging* (pp. 94–117). Cambridge, England: Cambridge University Press.

Schaie, K. W. (1991). Adult personality and psychomotor performance: Cross-sectional and longitudinal analyses. *Journal of Gerontology: Psychological Sciences, 46,* P275–P284.

Schaie, K. W. (1993). The Seattle longitudinal studies of adult intelligence. *Current Directions in Psychological Science, 2,* 171–174.

Schaie, K. W. (1994). The course of adult intellectual development. *American Psychologist, 49,* 304–313.

Schaie, K. W. (1996). *Intellectual development in adulthood: The Seattle longitudinal study.* New York: Cambridge University Press.

Schaie, K. W., & Hertzog, C. (1983). Fourteen-year cohort-sequential studies of adult intelligence. *Developmental Psychology, 19,* 531–543.

Schaie, K. W., & Hertzog, C. (1985). *Toward a comprehensive model of adult intellectual development: Contributions of the Seattle longitudinal study.* In R. J. Sternberg (Ed.), Advances in human intelligence (Vol. 3). New York: Academic Press.

Schaie, K. W., & Labouvie-Vief, G. (1974). Generational versus ontogenetic components of change in adult cognitive behavior: A fourteen-year cross-sequential study. *Developmental Psychology, 10,* 305–320.

Schaie, K. W., & Willis, S. L. (1993). Age difference patterns of psychometric intelligence in adulthood: Generalizability within and across ability domains. *Psychology and Aging, 8,* 44–55.

Schaie, K. W., & Willis, S. L. (1996). *Psychometric intelligence and aging.* In F. Blanchard-Fields, & T. H. & Hess, (Eds.), Perspectives on cognitive change in adulthood and aging. NY: McGraw-Hill.

Schaie, K. W., Willis, S. L., Hertzog, C., & Schulenberg, J. E. (1987). Effects of cognitive training on primary mental ability structure. *Psychology and Aging, 2,* 233–242.

Scharff, V. (1991). *Taking the wheel: Women and the coming of the motor age.* New York: Free Press.

Scheibel, A. B. (1996). Structural and functional changes in the aging brain. In J. E. Birren, K. W. Schaie, R. P. Abeles, M. Gatz, & T. A. Salthouse (Eds.), *Handbook of the psychology of aging* (4th edition). San Diego: Academic Press.

Scheibel, A. B., & Wechsler, A. F. (Eds.). (1986). *The biological substrates of Alzheimer's disease.* New York: Academic Press.

Scheidt, R. J. (1985). The mental health of the aged in rural environments. In R. T. Coward & G. R. Lee (Eds.), *The elderly in rural society.* New York: Springer.

Schieber, F. (1992). Aging and the senses. In J. E. Birren, R. B. Sloane, & G. D. Cohen (Eds.), *Handbook of mental health and aging* (second edition, pp. 252–306). San Diego: Academic Press.

Schiffman, S. (1977). Food recognition by the elderly. *Journal of Gerontology, 32,* 586–592.

Schmidt, W. C. (Ed.) (1995). *Guardianship: The court of last resort for the elderly and disabled.* Durham, NC: Carolina Academic Press.

Schmitt, N. Gogate, J., Rothert, M., Rovner, D., Holmes, M., Talarcyzk, G., Given, B., & Kroll, J. (1991). Capturing and clustering women's judgment policies: The case of hormonal therapy for menopause. *Journal of Gerontology: Psychological Sciences, 46,* S92–S101.

Schmitz-Secherzer, R. (1976). Longitudinal change in leisure behavior of the elderly. *Contributions to Human Development, 3,* 127–136.

Schnelle, J. F., McNees, P., Crooks, V., & Ouslander, J. G. (1995). The use of a computer-based model to implement an incontinence management program. *Gerontologist, 35,* 656–665.

Schonfield, A. E. D., & Robertson, B. A. (1966). Memory storage and aging. *Canadian Journal of Psychology, 20,* 228–236.

Schooler, C., Caplan, L., & Oates, G. (1998). *Aging and work: An overview.* In K. W. Schaie & C. Schooler (Eds.), Impact of work on older adults. New York: Springer.

Schroots, J. J. F., & Birren, J. E. (1990). Concepts of time and aging in science. In J. E. Birren & K. W. Schaie (Eds.), *Handbook of the psychology of aging* (3rd ed., pp. 45–64). New York: Academic Press.

Schuckit, M. A., Morrissey, E. R., & O'Leary, M. R. (1979). Alcohol problems in elderly men and women. In D. M. Peterson (Ed.), *Drug use among the aged.* New York: Spectrum.

Schultz, N. R., Jr., Elias, M. F., Robbins, M. A., Streeten, D. P. H., & Blakeman, N. (1986). A longitudinal comparison of hypertensives and normotensives on the Wechsler Adult Intelligence Scale: Initial findings. *Journal of Gerontology, 41,* 169–175.

Schulz, R., & Curnow, C. (1988). Peak performance and age among superathletes: Track and field, swimming, baseball, tennis, and golf. *Journal of Gerontology: Psychological Sciences, 43,* 1113–1120.

Schulz, R., & Williamson, G. M. (1994). Health effects of caregiving: Prevalence of mental and physical illness in Alzheimer's disease caregivers. In E. Light & G. Niederehe (Eds.), *Stress effects on family caregivers of Alzheimer's patients: Research and intervention* (pp. 38–63). New York: Springer.

Schulz, R., Musa, D., Staszewski, J., & Siegler, R. S. (1994). The relation between age and major league baseball performance: Implications for development. *Psychology and Aging, 9.*

Schulz, R., Bookwala, J., Knapp, J. E., Scheier, M., & Williamson, G. M. (1996). Pessimism, age and cancer mortality. *Psychology and Aging, 11,* 304–309.

Schurr, P., Vaillant, C. O. & Vaillant, G. E. (1990). Predicting exercise in late middle life from young adult personality. *International Journal of Aging and Human Development 30(2),* 153–160.

Schwartzman, A. E., Gold, D., Andres, D., Arbuckle, T. Y., & Chiakelson, J. (1987). Stability of intelligence: A forty-year follow-up. *Canadian Journal of Psychology, 41,* 244–256.

Seeman, T. W., Bruce, M. L., & McAvay, G. J. (1996). Social network characteristics and onset of ADL disability: MacArthur studies of successful aging. *Journal of Gerontology: Series B: Psychological Sciences and Social Sciences, 51B,* S191–S200.

Selkoe, D. J. (1992). Aging, brain, and mind. *Scientific American, 267,* 134–143.

Selkoe, D. J. (1995). Missense on the membrane. *Nature, 375,* 734–735.

Selkoe, D. J., Bell, D. S., Podlisny, M. B., Price, D. L., & Cork, I. C. (1987). Conservation of brain amyloid proteins in aged mammals and humans. *Science, 235,* 873–877.

Sell, D. R., Lane, M. A., Johnson, W. A., Masoro, E. J., Mock, O. B., Reiser, K. M., Fogarty, J. F., Cutler, R. G., Ingram, D. K., Roth, G. S., & Monnier, V. M. (1996). Longevity and the genetic determination of collagen glycoxidation kinetics in mammalian senescence. *Proceedings of the National Academy of Science, 93,* 485–490.

Seltzer, B. J., Vasterling, J. J., Yoder, J., & Thompson, K. A. (1997). Awareness of deficit in Alzheimer's disease: Relation to caregiver burden. *Educational Research, 37,* 120–124.

Seltzer, M. M., Greenberg, J. S., & Krauss, M. W. (1995). A comparison of coping strategies of aging mothers of adults with mental illness or mental retardation. *Psychology and Aging, 10,* 64–75.

Selye, H. (1956). *The stress of life.* New York: McGraw-Hill.

Selye, H. (1980). *Selye's guide to stress research.* New York: Van Nostrand.

Shahnasarian, M. (1992). Career development after professional football. *Journal of Career Development, 18,* 299–304.

Shanan, J. (1991). Who and how: Some unanswered questions in adult development. *Journal of Gerontology: Psychological Sciences, 46,* P309–P316.

Shaughnessy, J. J., & Zechmeister, E. B. (1996). *Research methods in psychology* (3rd ed.). New York: McGraw-Hill.

Sheehy, G. (1995). *New passages.* New York: Ballantine Books.

Sheehy, G. (1998). *Men's passages.* New York: Ballantine Books.

Sheridan, C. (1993). *Failure-free activities for the Alzheimer's patient.* San Francisco: Elder Books.

Sherrington, R., Rogaev, E. I., Laing, Y., Rogaeva, E. A., Levesque, G., Ikeda, M., Chi, H., Lin, C., Li, G., Holman, K., Tsuda, T., Mar, L., Foncin, J. F., Bruni, A. C., Montesi, M. P., Sorbl, S., Rainero, I., Pinessi, L., Nee, L., Chumakov, I., Pollen, D., Brookes, A., Sanseau, P., Polinsky, R. J., Wasco, W., DaSilva, H. A. R., Haines, J. L., Pericak-Vancer, M. A., Tansi, R. E., Roses, A. D., Fraser, P. E., Rommens, J. M., & St. George-Hyslop, P. H. (1995). Cloning of a gene bearing missense mutations in early-onset familial Alzheimer's Disease. *Nature, 375,* 754–760.

Shi, L. (1993). Family financial and household support exchange between generations: A survey of Chinese rural elderly. *The Gerontologist, 33,* 468–480.

Shirom, A., & Mazeh, T. (1988). Periodicity in seniority-job satisfaction relationship. *Journal of Vocational Behavior, 33,* 38–49.

Shneidman, E. (1992). *Death: Current perspectives* (3rd ed.). Mountain View, CA: Mayfield.

Siegler, I. C. (1983). Psychological aspects of the Duke longitudinal studies. In K. W. Schaie (Ed.), *Longitudinal studies of adult psychological development.* New York: Guilford Press.

Siegler, I. C., & Costa, P. T., Jr. (1985). Health behavior relationships. In J. E. Birren & K. W. Schaie (Eds.), *Handbook of the psychology of aging* (2nd ed.). New York: Van Nostrand Reinhold.

Silverstein, M., & Waite, L. J. (1993). Are blacks more likely than whites to receive and provide social support in middle and old age? Yes, no, and maybe so. *Journal of Gerontology: Social Sciences, 48,* S212–S222.

Simms, L. M., Jones, S. J., & Yoder, K. K. (1982). Adjustment of older persons in nursing homes. *Journal of Gerontological Nursing, 8,* 383–386.

Simoneau, G. G., & Leibowitz, H. W. (1996). Posture, gait, and falls. In J. E. Birren & K. W. Schaie (Eds.), *Handbook of the psychology of aging* (4th ed., pp. 204–235). San Diego: Academic Press.

Simons-Morton, B. G., Greene, W. H., & Gottlieb, N. H. (1995). *Introduction to health education and health promotion* (2nd ed.) Prospect Heights, IL: Wavelength Press.

Simonton, D. K. (1988). Age and outstanding achievement: What do we know after a century of research? *Psychological Bulletin, 104,*251–267.

Simonton, D. K. (1990). Creativity and wisdom in aging. In. J. E. Birren & K.W. Schaie (Eds.), *Handbook of the psychology of aging* (3rd ed., pp. 320–329). San Diego, CA: Academic Press.

Simonton, D. K. (1997). Creative productivity: A predictive and explanatory model of career trajectories and landmarks. *Psychological Review, 104,* 66–89.

Sinnott, J. D. (1981). The theory of relativity: A metatheory for development? *Human Development, 24,* 293–311.

Sinnott, J. D. (1984). Postformal reasoning: The relativistic stage. In M. L. Commons, F. A. Richards, & C. Armon (Eds.), *Beyond formal operations: Late adolescent and adult cognitive development.* New York: Praeger.

Sinnott, J. D. (1989). A model for solution of ill-structured problems: Implications for everyday and abstract problem-solving. In J. D. Sinnott (Ed.), *Everyday problem-solving: Theory and Application* (pp. 72–99). New York: Praeger.

Sinnott, J. D. (1994). Development and yearning: Cognitive aspects of spiritual development. *Journal of Adult Development, 1,* 91–99.

Sinnott, J. D., & Cavanaugh, J. C. (Eds.). (1991). *Bridging paradigms: Positive development in adulthood and cognitive aging.* New York: Praeger.

Skaff, M. M., Pearlin, L. I., & Mullan, J. T. (1996). Transitions in the caregiving career. Effects on sense of mastery. *Psychology and Aging, 11,* 247–57.

Skinner, B. F. (1990). Can psychology be a science of mind? American *Psychologist, 45,* 1206–1210.

Slomka, J. (1992). The negotiation of death: Clinical decision making at the end of life. *Social Science and Medicine, 35,* 251–259.

Smith, A. D. (1977). Adult age differences in cued recall. *Developmental Psychology, 13,* 326–331.

Smith, A. D., & Earles, J. K. L. (1996). Memory changes in normal aging. In F. Blanchard-Fields & T. M. Hess (Eds.), *Perspective on cognitive change in adulthood and aging* (pp. 192–220). New York: McGraw-Hill.

Smith, B. B. (1992, Summer). Treatment of dementia: Healing through cultural arts. *Pride Institute Journal of Long Term Home Health Care, 11,* 37–45.

Smith, J. S., & Kiloh, I. G. (1981). The investigation of dementia: Results in 200 consecutive admissions. *The Lancet, 1,* 824–827.

Smith, J., & Baltes, P. B. (1990). Wisdom-related knowledge: Age/cohort differences in response to life-planning problems. *Developmental Psychology, 26,* 494–505.

Smyer, M. A. (1993). Aging and decision-making capacity. *Generations, 17,* 51–56.

Smyer, M. A. (1995). Formal support in later life: Lessons for prevention. In L. A. Bond, S. J. Cutler & A. Grams (Eds.), *Promoting successful and productive aging* (pp. 186–202). Thousand Oaks, CA: Sage.

Snowdon, D. A. (1997). Aging and Alzheimer's Disease: Lessons from the Nun Study. *The Gerontologist, 37,* 150–156.

Snyder, D. C. (1993). The economic well-being of retired workers by race and Hispanic origin. In D. Salisbury & R. B. Burkenhauser (Eds.), *Pensions in a changing economy* (pp. 67–78). Washington DC: Employee Benefit Research Institute.

Soares, C. J. (1985). The companion animal in the context of the family system. *Marriage and the Family Review, 8,* 49–62.

Social Security Administration. (1998). *A summary of benefits, 1998.*

Society for the Right to Die. (1987). *A living will.* New York: Society for the Right to Die.

Sohal, R. S., & Weindruch, R. (1996). Oxidative stress, colaric restriction, and aging, *Science, 273,* 59–63.

Sokolovsky, J. (1986). *Growing old in different societies: Cross-cultural perspectives.* Belmont, CA: Wadsworth.

Soldo, B. J. (1996). Cross-pressures on middle-aged adults: A broader view. *Journal of Gerontology: Psychological Sciences and Social Sciences, 51B,* S271–S273.

Soldo, B. J., & Agree, E. M. (1988). America's elderly population. *Population Bulletin, 43,* 1–53.

Somers, S., & Beatrice, D. (1994). What's happening with healthcare reform? *Partners in Caregiving: The Dementia Services Program, Respite Report, 10,* 1–2.

Sommers, I., Baskin, D., Specht, D., & Shively, M. (1988). Deinstitutionalization of the elderly mentally ill: Factors affecting discharge to alternate living arrangements. *The Gerontologist, 28* (5), 653–658.

Souza, P. E., & Hoyer, W. J. (1996). Age-related hearing loss: Implications for counseling. *Journal of Counseling and Development, 74,* 652–655.

Spanier, G., & Glick, P. (1981). Marital instability in the United States: Some correlates and recent changes. *Family Relations, 31,* 329–338.

Speare, A., & Avery, R. (1993). Who helps whom in older parent-child families. *Journal of Gerontology, 48,* 564–573.

Spearman, C. (1927). *The abilities of man.* New York: Macmillan.

Speece, M. W., & Brent, S. B. (1984). Children's understanding of death: A review of three components of a death concept. *Child Development, 55,* 1671–1686.

Speechly, M., & Tinetti, M. (1990). Assessment of risk and prevention of falls among elderly persons: Role of the Physiotherapist. *Physiotherapist Canada, 42,* 75–87.

Spence, J. T., & Helmreich, R. L. (1978). *Masculinity and femininity: Their psychological dimensions.* Austin, TX: University of Texas Press.

Spina, R. J., Miller, T. R., Bogenhagen, W. H., Schechtman, K. B., & Ehsani, A. A. (1996). Gender-related differences in left ventricular filling dynamics in older subjects after endurance exercise training. *Journal of Gerontology: Biological Sciences, 51A* (3), B232–B237.

Squire, L. R. (1987). *Memory and brain.* New York: Oxford University Press.

Squire, L. R. (1994). Declarative and non-declarative memory: Multiple brain systems supporting learning and memory. In D. L. Schacter, & E. Tulving, (Eds.). *Memory systems 1994* (pp. 203–232). Cambridge, MA: MIT Press.

Squire, L. R., & Knowlton, B. J. (1995). The organization of memory. In H. Horowitz & J. Singer (Eds.), *The mind, the brain and the CAS: SFI studies in the Sciences of complexity,* Vol XXII, (pp. 63–77) NY: Addison Wesley.

St. George-Hyslop, P. H., Tanzi, R. E., Polinsky, R. J., Haines, J. L., Nee, L., Watkins, P. C., Myers, R. H., Feldman, R. G., Pollen, D., Drachman, D., Growdon, J., Bruni, A., Foncin, J. F., Salmon, D., Frommelt, P., Amaducci, L., Sorbi, S., Piacentini, S., Steward, G. D., Hobbs, W. J., Conneally, P. M., & Gusella, J. F. (1987). The genetic defect causing familial Alzheimer's disease maps on chromosome 21. *Science, 235,* 885–889.

Stall, R., Catania, J., & Pollack, L. (1988). AIDS as an age-defined epidemic. The social epidemiology of HIV infection among older Americans. *Report to the National Institute of Aging.* Unpublished document.

Starrett, R. A., Todd, A. M., & DeLeon, L. (1989). A comparison of the social services utilization behavior of the Cuban and Puerto Rican elderly. *Hispanic Journal of Behavioral Sciences, 11,* 341–353.

Staudinger, U. M. & Baltes, P. B. (1996). Interactive minds: A facilitative setting for wisdom related performance. *Journal of Personality and Social Psychology, 71,* 746–762.

Staudinger, U. M., Smith, J., & Baltes, P. B. (1992). Wisdom-related knowledge in a life review task: Age differences and the role of professional specialization. *Psychology and Aging, 7,* 271–281.

Stein, S., Linn, M. W., & Stein, E. M. (1985). Patient's anticipation of stress in nursing home care. *The Gerontologist, 25,* 88–94.

Stein, S., Linn, M. W., & Stein, E. M. (1986). *Patient's perceptions of nursing home stress related to quality of care.* Unpublished report, VA Health Services Research Grant (#547). Miami, FL: University of Miami Medical School.

Steinmetz, S. (1978). Battered parents. *Society, 15,* 54–55.

Steinmetz, S. (1981). *Elder abuse.* Aging, January/February, 6–10.

Ste-Marie, D. M., Jennings, J. M., & Finlayson, A. J. (1996). Process dissociation procedure: memory testing in populations with brain damage. *The Clinical Neuropsychologist, 10,* 25–36.

Stephens, M. A. P., Norris, V. K., Kinney, J. M., Ritchie, S. W., & Grotz, R. C. (1988). Stressful situations in caregiving: Relations between caregiver coping and well-being. *Psychology and Aging, 3,* 208–209.

Stephenson, J. S. (1985). *Death, grief, and mourning: Individual and social realities.* New York: Free Press.

Sternberg, R. J. (1985). *Beyond IQ: A triarchic theory of human intelligence.* New York: Cambridge University Press.

Sternberg, R. J. (1988). *Intelligence applied: Understanding and increasing your intellectual skills.* New York: Harcourt Brace Jovanovich.

Sternberg, R. J., Wagner, R. K., Williams, W. M., & Horvath, J. A. (1995). Testing common sense. *American Psychologist, 50,* 912–927.

Sterns, H. L., Barrett, G. V., and Alexander, R.A. (1985). Accidents and the aging individual. In J. E. Birren and K. W. Schaie (Eds.), *Handbook of the psychology of aging* (2nd ed.). New York: Van Nostrand Reinhold.

Sticht, J. P., & Hazzard, W. R. (1995). Weight control and exercise: Cardinal features of successful preventative gerontology. *Journal of the American Medical Association, 274,* 1964–1965.

Stones, J. J., & Kozma, A. (1996). Activity, exercise, & behavior. In J. E. Birren & K. W. Schaie (Eds.), *Handbook of the psychology of aging* (4th ed., pp. 338–364). San Diego, CA: Academic Press.

Stones, M. J., & Dawe, D. (1993). Acute exercise facilitates semantically cued memory in nursing home residents. *Journal of American Geriatrics Society, 41,* 531–534.

Stratton, J. R., Levy, W. C., Cerqueira, M. D., Schwartz, R. S., & Abrass, I. B. (1994). Cardiovascular responses to exercise: effects of aging and exercise training in healthy men. *Circulation, 89,* 1648–1655.

Strawbridge, W. J., Camacho, T. C., Cohen, R. D., & Kaplan, G. A. (1993). Gender differences in factors associated with change in physical functioning in old age: A 6–year longitudinal study. *The Gerontologist, 33,* 603–609.

Stuck, A. E., Van Gorp, W. G., Josephson, K. R. & Morgenstern, H. (1992). Multidimensional risk assessment versus age as criterion for retirement of airline pilots. *Journal of the American Geriatrics Society, 40,* 526–532.

Stull, D. E., & Hatch, L. R. (1984). Unraveling the effects of multiple life changes. *Research on Aging, 6,* 560–571.

Sue, S. (1981). Programmatic issues in the training of Asian-American psychologists. *Journal of Community Psychology, 9* (4), 293–297.

Sue, S. (1998). In search of cultural competence in psychotherapy and counseling. *American Psychologist, 53* (4), 440–448.

Sue, S., Zane, N., & Young, K. (1994). Research on psychotherapy with culturally diverse populations. In A. E. Bergin & S. L. Garfield (Eds.), *Handbook of psychotherapy and behavior change* (4th ed. pp. 783–820). NY: John Wiley.

Sue, S., Fujino, D., Hu, L., Takeuchi, D. T., & Zane, N. W. S. (1992). Community mental health services for ethnic minority groups: A test of the cultural sensitivity hypothesis. *Journal of Consulting and Clinical Psychology, 59,* 533–540.

Suitor, J., & Pillemer, K. (1993). Support and interpersonal stress in the social networks of married daughters caring for parents with dementia. *Journal of Gerontology, 48*(1), S1–S8.

Sullivan, M. (1995). Depression and disability from chronic medical illness. *European Journal of Public Health, 5,* 40–45.

Summers, R., Majowski, L. V., Marsh, G. M., Tachiki, K., & Kling, A. *315* (#20), (1986). Oral tetrahydroaminoacridine in long-term treatment of senile dementia, Alzheimer's type. *New England Journal of Medicine, 315,* 1241–1245.

Super, D. E. (1980). A life-span, life-space approach to career development. *Journal of Vocational Behavior, 16,* 282–298.

Super, D. E., Kowalski, R., & Gotkin, E. (1967). *Floundering and trial after high school.* Unpublished manuscript, Columbia University, New York.

SUPPORT Principal Investigators. (1995). A controlled study to improve care for seriously ill hospitalized patients: The study to understand prognosis and preferences for outcomes and risks of treatments. *Journal of American Medical Association, 274,* 1591–1598.

Sweet, L. (1994). In memorium a user's guide on how to behave at funerals of different faiths. *Edmonton Journal,* Aug. 27, p. A10.

Szinovacz, M., & Washo, C. (1992). Gender differences in exposure to life events and adaptation to retirement. *Journals of Gerontology, 47,* S191–S196.

Taking the "Iliad" on the road. (1994). *Chronicle of Higher Education, 40,* 34.

Takman, A. (1992). Nonpharmacologic treatment of behavioral symptoms. *Acta Neurologica Scandinavica, 85* (Suppl): 81–83.

Tamir, L. M. (1989). *Modern myths about men at mid-life: An assessment.* Newbury Park, CA: Sage.

Tang, M., Jacobs, D., Stern, Y., Marder, K., Schofield, P., Gurland, B., Andrews, H., & Mayeux, R. (1996). Effect of estrogen during menopause on risk and age at onset of Alzheimer's disease. *Lancet, 348,* 492–432.

Tanzi, R. E., Gusella, J. F., & Watkins, P.C. (1987). Amyloid B protein gene: cDNA, mRNA distribution, and genetic linkage near the Alzheimer locus. *Science, 235,* 880–884.

Taylor, R. J., & Chatters, L. M. (1988). Correlates of education, income, and poverty among aged blacks. *The Gerontologist, 28,*

Taylor, S. E. (1983). Adjustment to threatening events: A theory of cognitive adaptation. *American Psychologist, 38,* 1161–1173.

Taylor, S. E. (1990). Health psychology: The science and the field. *American Psychologist, 45,* 40–50.

Taylor, S. E., & Lobel, M. (1989). Social comparison activity under threat: Downward evolution and upward contacts. *Psychology Review, 96,* 569–575.

Taylor, S. E., Kemeny, M. E., Aspinwall, L. G., Schneider, S. G., Rodriguez, R., & Heubert, M. (1992). Optimism, coping, psychological distress, and high-risk sexual behavior among men at risk for Acquired

Immunodeficiency Syndrome (AIDS). *Journal of Personality and Social Psychology, 63,* 460–473.

Taylor, S. E., Repetti, R. L., & Seeman, T. (1997). Health psychology: What is an unhealthy environment and how does it get under the skin? *Annual Review of Psychology, 58,* 411–447.

Teachers Insurance and Annuity Association. *Teachers Long Term Care: Policy Benefits and Features Guide. (1996).* New York, NY.

Tell, E. J., Cohen, M. A., Larson, M. J., & Batten, H. L. (1987). Assessing the elderly's preferences for life-care retirement options. *The Gerontologist, 27,* 503–509.

Teltsch, K. (1991). New study of older workers finds they can become good investments. *New York Times,* May 21, p. A16.

Teri, L. (1996). Depression in Alzheimer's disease. In M. Hersen & V. B. Van Hasselt (Eds.), *Psychological treatment of older adults: An introductory text* (pp. 209–222). New York: Plenum Press.

Thomae, H. (1992). Emotion and personality. In J. E. Birren, R. B. Sloane, & G. D. Cohen (Eds.), *Handbook of mental health and aging* (2nd ed., pp. 355–375). San Diego, CA: Academic Press.

Thomas, J. (1986a). Gender differences in satisfaction with grandparenting. *Psychology and Aging, 1,* 215–219.

Thomas, J. (1986b). Age and sex differences in perceptions of grandparenting. *Journal of Gerontology, 41,* 417–423.

Thomas, L. E., & Eisenhandler, S. A. (1994). Introduction: A human science perspective on aging and the religious dimension. In L. E. Thomas & S. A. Eisenhandler (Eds.), *Aging and the religious dimension* (pp. xvii–xxi). Westport, CT: Auburn House.

Thompson, E. H., Futterman, A. M., Gallagher-Thompson, D., Rose, J. M., & Lovett, S. B. (1993). Social support and caregiving burden in family caregivers of frail elders. *Journal of Gerontology: Social Sciences, 48,* S245–S254.

Thompson, J. W., Walker, R. D., & Silk-Walker, P. (1993). Psychiatric care of American Indians and Alaska Natives. In A. C. Gaw (Ed.), *Culture, ethnicity, and mental illness* (pp. 189–243). Washington, DC: American Psychiatric Press.

Thompson, L. W., Gallagher-Thompson, D., Hauser, S., Gantz, F., & Steffen, A. (1991, August). Comparison of desipramine and cognitive/behavioral therapy for the treatment of depression in the elderly. San Francisco, CA: The American Psychological Association.

Thompson, M. G., Heller, K., & Rody, C. A. (1994). Recruitment challenges in studying late life depression: Do community samples adequately represent depressed older adults. *Psychology and Aging, 9,* 121–125.

Thompson, R. A., Tinsley, B. R., Scalora, M. J., & Parke, R. D. (1989). Grandparents' visitation rights. *American Psychologist, 44,* 1217–1222.

Thorndike, E. L., Bregman, E. O., Tilton, J. W., & Woodyard, E. (1928). *Adult learning.* New York: Macmillan.

Thurstone, L. L. (1938). *Primary mental abilities.* Chicago: University of Chicago Press.

TIAA (1992). *Long term care.* New York: Teachers Insurance and Annuity Association.

Tideiksaar, R. (1989). *Falling in old age: Its preventions and treatment.* New York: Springer-Verlag.

Tiffany, D. W., & Tiffany, P. G. (1996). Control across the life span: A model for understanding self-direction. *Journal of Adult Development, 3,* 93–108.

Tinetti, M. E. (1990). In C. K. Cassel, D. E., Risenberg, L. B. Sorenson, & J. R. Walsh (Eds.). *Geriatric medicine* (2nd ed., pp. 528–534). New York: Springer-Verlag.

Tinsley, B. J., & Parke, R. D. (1987). *Grandparents as interactive and socialization agents.* In M. Lewis (Ed.), Beyond the dyad. New York: Plenum.

Tobin, J. J. (1987). The American idealization of old age in Japan. *The Gerontologist, 27,* 53–58.

Tobin, S. S. (1991). *Personhood in advanced old age: Implications for practice.* New York: Springer.

Tobin, S. S., & Lieberman, M. (1976). *Last home for the aged.* San Francisco: Jossey-Bass.

Tomlinson-Keasey, C., & Keasey, C. B. (1974). The mediating role of cognitive development in moral judgment. *Child Development, 45,* 291–298.

Tornstan, L. (1994). Gero-transcendence: A theoretical and empirical exploration. In L. E. Thomas & S. A. Eisenhandler (Eds.), *Aging and the religious dimension.* Westport, CT: Greenwood.

Trimble, J. E. (1989). *The enculturation of contemporary psychology.* Paper presented at the annual meetings of the American Psychological Association, New Orleans, August.

Troll, L. E. (1983). Grandparents: The family watchdogs. In T. Brubaker (Ed.), *Family relationships in later life.* Beverly Hills, CA: Sage.

Troll, L. E. & Skaff, M. M. (1997). Perceived continuity of self in very old age. *Psychology and Aging, 12,* 162–169.

Tryban, G. M. (1985). Effects of work and retirement within long-term marital relationships. *Lifestyles, 7,* 207–223.

Tucker, J. S., Friedman, H. S., Tsai, C. M., & Martin, L. R. (1995). Playing with pets and longevity among older persons. *Psychology and Aging, 10,* 3–7.

Tulving, E. (1989). Remembering and knowing the past. *American Scientist, 77,* 361–367.

Tulving, E. (1993). Varieties of consciousness and levels of awareness in memory. In A. Baddeley & L. Weiskrantz (Eds.), *Attention: Selection, awareness, and control. A tribute to Donald Broadbent* (pp. 283–299). London: Oxford University Press.

Tulving, E., Hayman, C. A. G., & MacDonald, C. A. (1991). Long-lasting priming in amnesia: A case experiment. *Journal of Experimental Psychology: Learning, Memory, and Cognition, 17,* 595–617.

Turnbull, J. E., & Mui, A. C. (1995). Mental health status and needs of black and white elderly: Differences in depression. In D. K. Padge (Ed.), *Handbook on ethnicity, aging, and mental health.* Westport, CT: Greenwood Press.

U.S. Bureau of the Census. (1985). *Statistics.* Washington, DC: U.S. Government Printing Office.

U.S. Bureau of the Census. (1986). *Statistics.* Washington, DC: U.S. Government Printing Office.

U.S. Bureau of the Census. (1990a). *Household and family characteristics.* (Current Population Reports) Washington, DC: U.S. Government Printing Office.

U.S. Bureau of the Census. (1995). *Statistics.* Washington, DC: U.S. Government Printing Office.

U.S. Bureau of the Census. *Statistical Abstract of the United States: 1997* (117th ed.). National Data Book. Washington, DC: U.S. Government Printing Office.

U.S. Department of Agriculture, Human Nutrition Information Service. (1992). *Food Guide Pyramid.* Bulletin 249.

U.S. Department of Health and Human Services (1992). *Income of the aged chartbook, 1990.* (Social Security Administration Publication No. 13–11727). Washington, DC: U.S. Government Printing Office.

U.S. Department of Labor. (1989, January). Labor market problems of older women. *Report of the Secretary.* Washington, DC: United States Department of Labor.

U.S. House of Representatives. (1992). *Alcohol abuse and misuse among the elderly. A report by the chairman of the subcommittee on aging.* House of Representatives, 102nd Congress; second session.

Uba, L. (1994). *Asian Americans: Personality patterns, identity, and mental health.* New York: Guilford Press.

Uhlenberg, P., Cooney, T., & Boyd, R. (1990). Divorce for women after midlife. *Journal of Gerontology, 45,*

Usher, J. A., & Neisser, U. (1993). Childhood amnesia and the beginnings of memory for four early life events.

Journal of Experimental Psychology: General, 122, 155–165.

U.S. News & World Report. (1993). Grief re-examined. June 14, 81–87.

Valliant, G. (1977). *Adaptation to life.* Boston: Little, Brown.

Valliant, G. E., & Valliant, C. O. (1981). Natural history of male psychological health, X: Work as a predictor of positive mental health. *American Journal of Psychiatry, 138,* 1433–1440.

Van Hoose, W. H., & Worth, M. (1982). *Adulthood in the life cycle.* Dubuque, IA: Wm C. Brown.

Van-Tilburg, T. (1992). Support networks before and after retirement. Special issue: Social networks. *Journal of Social and Personal Relationships, 9,* 433–445.

Vasquez, M. J., & Han, A. L. (1995). Group interventions and treatment with ethnic minorities. In J. F. Aponte, R. Y. Rivers, & J. Wohl (Eds.), *Psychological interventions and cultural diversity* (pp. 109–127). Boston: Allyn & Bacon.

Veatch, R. M. (1981). *A theory of medical ethics.* New York: Basic Books.

Veevers, J. E. (1980). *Children by choice.* Toronto, Canada: Butterworth.

Verbrugge, L. M., & Jette, A. M. (1994). The disablement process. *Journal of Social Science and Medicine, 38,* (1), 1–14.

Verhaeghen, P., Marcoen, A., & Goossens, L. (1992). Improving memory performance in the aged through mnemonic training: A meta-analytic study. *Psychology and Aging, 7,* 242–251.

Vitaliano, P. P., Young, H. M., & Russo, J. (1991). Burden: A review of measures used among caregivers of individuals with dementia. *Gerontologist, 31,* 67–75.

Vitaliano, P. P., Russo, J., Young, H. M., Teri, L., & Maivro, R. D. (1991). Predictors of burden in spouse caregivers of individuals with Alzheimer's disease. *Psychology and Aging, 6,* 392–402.

Vondareck, F. W., Lerner, R. M., & Schulenberg, J. E. (1986). *Career development: A life-span developmental approach.* Hillsdale, NJ: Erlbaum.

Waldemar, G. (1995). Functional brain imaging with SPECT in normal aging and dementia: Methodological, pathophysiological, and diagnostic aspects. *Cerebrovascular Brain Metaboloic Review, 7,* 89–130.

Waldman, D. A., & Avolio, B. J. (1986). A meta-analysis of age differences in job performance. *Journal of Applied Psychology, 71,* 33–38.

Waldrop, M. M. (1984). The necessity of knowledge. *Science, 223,* 1279–1283.

Walker, A. J., Martin, S. S. K., & Jones, L. L. (1992). *Journal of Gerontology: Social Sciences, 47,* S130–S139.

Walker, J. E., & Howland, J. (1990). Falls and fear of falling among elderly persons living in the community: Occupational therapy interventions. *American Journal of Occupational Therapy, 15,* 119–122.

Walker, L. J. (1986). Experiential and cognitive sources of moral development in adulthood. *Human Development, 29,* 113–124.

Walker, L. J., deVries, B., & Trevethan, S. D. (1987). Moral stages and moral orientations in real-life and hypothetical dilemmas. *Child Development, 58,* 842–858.

Walker, P. F. (1991). The older driver. *Human Factors, 33,* 499–505.

Wallerstein, J. S., & Blakeslee, S. (1988). *Second chances: Men, women, and children a decade after divorce.* Boston: Ticknor & Fields.

Ward, R., Logan, J., & Spitze, G. (1992). The influence of parent and child needs on co-residence in middle and later life. *Journal of Marriage and the Family, 54,* 209–221.

Warr, P. (1992). Age and occupational well-being. *Psychology and Aging, 7,* no. 1, 37–45.

Weale, R. A. (1986). Aging and vision. *Vision Research, 26,* 1507–1512.

Webster, J. D., & Cappeliez, P. (1993). Reminiscence and autobiographical memory: Complementary contexts for cognitive aging research. *Developmental Review, 13,* 54–91.

Wechsler, D. (1939). *Measurement of adult intelligence.* Baltimore: Williams & Wilkins.

Wechsler, D. (1958). *The measurement and appraisal of adult intelligence.* Baltimore: Williams & Wilkins.

Wechsler, D. (1972). "Hold" and "don't hold" tests. In S. M. Chown (Ed.), *Human aging.* New York: Penguin.

Weinberger, D. A., & Schwartz, G. E. (1990). Distress and restraint on superordinate dimensions of adjustment: A typological perspective. *Journal of Personality, 58*(2), 381–417.

Weindruch, R. (1996). Caloric restriction and aging. *Scientific American, 274,* 46–52.

Weiner, J. (1996). Can medicaid long term care expenditures for the elderly be reduced? *Gerontologist, 36,* 800–811.

Weiner, M. B. (1992). Treating the older adult: A diverse population. Special issue: Psychoanalysis of the mid-life and older patient. *Psychoanalysis and Psychotherapy, 10,* 66–76.

Weisberg, R. W. (1986). *Creativity.* New York: W.H. Freeman.

Weisman, A. T. (1972). *On dying and denying: A psychiatric study of terminality.* New York: Behavioral Publications.

Weiss, L., & Lowenthal, M. (1975). Life course perspectives on friendship. In M. Lowenthal, M. Turnher, & D. Chiriboga (Eds.), *Four stages of life.* San Francisco: Jossey-Bass.

Weiss, R. S. (1973). *Marital separation.* New York: Basic Books.

Welte, J. W., & Mirand, A. L. (1995). Drinking, problem drinking, and life stressors in the elderly general population. *Journal of Studies on Alcoholism, 51,* 67–73.

Wertheimer, M. (1945). *Productive thinking.* New York: Harper & Row.

Westermeyer, J. J. (1993). Cross-cultural psychiatric assessment. In A. C. Gaw (Ed.), *Culture, ethnicity and mental illness* (pp. 125–144). Washington, DC: American Psychiatric Press.

Wheeler, M., Stuss, D. T., & Tulving, E. (1997). Toward a theory of episodic memory: The frontal lobes and autonoetic consciousness. *Psychological Bulletin, 121,* 331–354.

Whitbourne, S. K. (1996). *The aging individual: Physical and psychological perspectives.* NY: Springer Pub. Co.

White, N., & Cunningham, W. R. (1988). Is terminal drop pervasive or specific? *Journal of Gerontology: Psychological Sciences, 44,* P141–P144.

Whitehouse, P. J. (1993). Autopsy. *The Gerontologist, 33,* 436–437.

Whitehouse, P. J., Price, D. L., Clark, A. W., Coyle, J. T., & DeLong, M. R. (1981). Alzheimer's Disease: Evidence for the selective loss of cholinergic neurons in nucleus basalis. *Annals of Neurology, 10,* 122–126.

Whitten, P. (1992). Just how much do we decline with age? *APA Monitor* (July-August), 17–20.

Wilber, K. H. (1997). Choice, courts, and competency: The coming of age of protective services research. *Gerontologist, 37,* 272–274.

Wilber, K. H., & Reynolds, S. L. (1995). Re-thinking alternatives to guardianship. *Gerontologist, 35* (2), 248–257.

Wilk, C. A., & Kirk, M. A. (1995). Menopause: A developmental stage, not a deficiency disease. *Psychotherapy, 32,* 233–241.

Wilkelgren, I. (1996). For the cortex, neuron loss may be less than thought. *Science, 273,* 48–50.

Wilkie, F., & Eisdorfer, C. (1971). Intelligence and blood pressure in the aged. *Science, 172,* 959–962.

Willerman, L., Schultz, R., Rutledge, J. N., & Bigler, E. D. (1994). *Brain structure and cognitive function.* In C. R. Reynolds (Ed.), Cognitive assessment: A multidisciplinary perspective (pp. 35–55). New York: Plenum Press.

Willett, W. C., Stampfer, M. J., Coditz, G. A., Rosner, B. A., & Speizer, F. E. (1990). Relation of meat, fat, and fiber intake to the risk of colon cancer in a prospective study among women. *New England Journal of Medicine, 323,* 1664–1672.

Williamson, D. F., Kahn, H. S., Remington, P. L., & Anda, R. F. (1990). A 10 year incidence of overweight and major weight gain in U.S. adults. *Archives of Internal Medicine, 150,* 665–672.

Williamson, G. M., & Schulz, R. (1991). Pain, activity restriction, and symptoms of depression among community-residing elderly adults. *Journal of Gerontology, 46,* 367–372.

Williamson, G. M., & Schulz, R. (1993). Coping with specific stressors in Alzheimer's disease. *Gerontologist, 33,* 747–755.

Williamson, J. B., Munley, A., & Evans, I. (1980). *Aging and society: An introduction to social gerontology.* New York: Holt, Rinehart and Winston.

Willis, S. L. (1985). Towards an educational psychology of the adult learner. In J. E. Birren & K. W. Schaie (Eds.), *Handbook of the psychology of aging* (2nd ed.). New York: Van Nostrand Reinhold.

Willis, S. L. (1996). Everyday cognitive competence in elderly persons: Conceptual issues and empirical findings. *The Gerontologist, 36,* 595–601.

Willis, S. L., & Schaie, K.W. (1985). Practical intelligence in later adulthood. In R. J. Sternberg & R. K. Wagner (Eds.), *Intelligence in the everyday world.* New York: Cambridge University Press.

Willis, S. L., & Schaie, K. W. (1986). Training the elderly on the ability factors of spatial orientation and inductive reasoning. *Psychology and Aging, 2,* 239–247.

Wise, P. M. (1993, June). Hormone regulation during aging. *Paper presented at the NIA Conference on Experimental Psychology of Aging.* University of Michigan.

Wohl, J. (1995). Traditional individual psychotherapy and ethnic minorities. In J. F. Aponte, R. Y. Rivers, & J. Wohl (Eds.), *Psychological interventions and cultural diversity.* Boston: Allyn & Bacon.

Wohlwill, J. F. (1973). *The study of behavioral development.* New York: Academic Press.

Wolfson, C., Handfield-Jones, R., Glass, K.C., McClaran, J., & Keyserlingk, E. (1993). Adult children's perception of their responsibility to provide care for their elderly parents. *The Gerontologist, 33,* 315–323.

Wolfson, L., Judge, J. Whipple, R., & King, M. (1995). Strength is a major factor in balance, gait, and the occurrence of falls. *Journal of Gerontology, 50A,* 64–67.

Wood, J. V., Taylor, S. E., & Lichtman, R. R. (1985). Social comparison in adjustment to breast cancer. *Journal of Personality and Social Psychology, 49,* 1169–1183.

Woodruff-Pak, D. (1988). *Psychology and aging.* Englewood Cliffs, NJ: Prentice-Hall.

Woodruff-Pak, D. (1993). Neural plasticity as a substrate for cognitive adaptation in adulthood and old age. In J. Cerella, J. M. Rybash, W. J. Hoyer, & M. C. Commons (Eds.), *Adult information processing: Limits on loss* (pp. 13–35). San Diego: Academic Press.

Worden, J. W. (1982). *Grief counseling and grief therapy: A hardbook for the mental health practioner.* New York: Springer.

Wurtman, R. J. (1985). Alzheimer's disease. *Scientific American, 252,* 62–74.

Yalom, I. D., & Lieberman, M. A. (1991). Bereavement and heightened existential awareness. *Psychiatry, 54*(4), 334–345.

York, K. L., & John, O. P. (1992). The four faces of Eve: A typological analysis of women's personality at midlife. *Journal of Personality and Social Psychology, 63,* 494–508.

Zarit, S. H., & Zarit, J. M. (1983). Cognitive impairment. In P. M. Lewinsohn & L. Teri (Eds.), *Clinical geropsychology: New directions in assessment and treatment.* New York: Pergamon Press.

Zarit, S. H., Eiler, J., & Hassinger, M. (1985). Clinical assessments. In J. E. Birren & K. W. Schaie (Eds.), *Handbook of the psychology of aging* (2nd ed.). New York: Van Nostrand Reinhold.

Zarit, S. H., Orr, N. K., & Zarit, J. M. (1985). *The hidden victims of Alzheimer's disease: Families under stress.* New York: New York University Press.

Zeiss, A. M., Lewinsohn, P. M., Rohde, P., & Seeley, J. R. (1996). Relationship of physical disease and functional impairment to depression in older people. *Psychology and Aging, 11,* 572–581.

Zelnick, M., & Kanter, J. (1977). Sexual and contraceptive experience of young unmarried women in the United States. *Family Planning Perspectives, 9,* 55–71.

Zweibel, N. R., & Cassel, C. K. (1989). Treatment choices at the end of life: A comparison of decisions by older patients and their physician-selected proxies. *The Gerontologist, 29,* 615–621.

CREDITS

Line Art

Chapter 2

Fig. 2.1: Data from the United States Census Bureau, Washington, DC. 1990.
Fig. 2.5: Reprinted by permission from L. Hayflick (1980). Cell biology of human aging. *Scientific American,* 242, 58-65.

Chapter 3

Fig. 3.1: Osteoporosis: Reducing the risk. From Stevens-Long and M. Commons (1992). *Adult life.* Reprinted with permission from Mayfield Publishing Company, Mountainview, CA.
Fig. 3.3: Average declines in biological systems. From J. Fries and L. M. Crapo (1981). *Vitality and aging.* Reprinted by permission of the W. H. Freeman Company, New York.
Box Fig. 3a: (Examples of spatial frequency gratings) and Box Figure 3b (Changes in contrast sensitivity). From C. Owsley, R. Sekuler, & D. Siemsen (1983). Contrast sensitivity throughout adulthood. *Vision Research,* 23, 689-699.
Box Fig. 3c: Best race times for swimmers. From M. Letselter, R. Jungeman, and K. Freitag (1986). Swimming performance in old age. *Zeitschrift fur Gerontologie,* 19, 389-395. Reprinted by permission.
Box Fig. 3d: Changes in average race times. From M. Letselter, R. Jungeman, and K. Freitag (1986). Swimming performance in old age. *Zeitschrift fur Gerontologie,* 19, 389-395. Reprinted by permission.
Fig. 3.6: The illustration of brain structures is adapted from previous edition of Adult development and aging (Rybash, Roodin, & Hoyer, 1995) and from D. J. Selkoe (1992). Aging, brain, aging mind. *Scientific American,* 267, 134-143.
Fig. 3.8: Data describing a relationship between age brain weight, and cell counts is adapted from the previous edition of this text (Rybash, Roodin, & Hoyer, 1995), and from D. J. Selkoe (1992). Aging, brain, aging mind. *Scientific American,* 267, 134-143.

Chapter 4

Fig. 4.2: From S. K. Whitbourne (1985). The psychological construction of the life span. In J. E. Birren and K. W. Schaie (Eds.). *Handbook of the psychology of aging.* VanNostrand Reinhold Company.
Fig. 4.3: From B. J. Kramer (1997). Gain in caregiving experience. *The Gerontologist,* 37, 218-232. Reprinted with permission of The Gerontological Society of America.
Box Fig. 4a: From B. J. Kramer (1997). Differential predictors of strain and gain among husbands caring for wives with dementia. *The Gerontologist,* 37, 239-249. Reprinted with permission of The Gerontological Society of America.

Chapter 4

Fig. 4.5: From J. Brandtstadter, D. Wentura, and W. Greve (1993). Adaptive resources of the aging self. *International Journal of Behavioural Development,* 16, 323-349. Reprinted by permission.
Fig. 4.6: From D. W. Kline, T. Kline, J. L. Fozard, W. Kosnick, F. Scheiber, and R. Sekuler (1992). Vision, aging and driving: the problems of older drivers. *Journal of Gerontology: Psychological Sciences,* 47, 27-34. Reprinted by permission.

Chapter 6

Fig. 6.7: From V. Regnier and J. Pynoos (1992). Environmental intervention for cognitively impaired persons. In J. E. Birren, R. B. Sloane, G. D. Cohen (Eds.), *Handbook of mental health and aging.* Reprinted by permission of Academic Press.

Chapter 7

Fig. 7.2: Response times, age, and set size. From J. L. Fozard, T. Anders, and T. D. Lilyquist (1972). Retrieval from short-term memory. *Developmental Psychology,* 6, 214-217. Reprinted by permission of the American Psychological Association.
Fig. 7.3: (examples of figure rotations) and **Fig. 7.4:** (Mean decision latencies for figure rotations). From L. W. Poon and J. L. Fozard (1981). Mental rotation and age reconsidered. *Journal of Gerontology,* 36, 620-624. Reprinted by permission of the Gerontological Society of America.
Fig. 7.6: Reprinted by permission from A. E. D. Schonfield and B. A. Robertson (1966). Memory storage and aging. *Canadian Journal of Psychology,* 20, 228-236.
Fig. 7.7: From H. P. Bahrick, P. O. Bahrick, and R. P. Wittlinger. (1975). Fifty years of memory for names and faces. *Journal of Experimental Psychology: General,* 104, 54-75. Reprinted by permission of the American Psychological Association.
Fig. 7.8: From J. Fitzgerald and Lawrence. (1984). Autobiographical memory across the life span. *Journal of Gerontology,* 39, 692-699. Reprinted by permission of the Gerontological Society of America.

Chapter 8

Fig. 8.3: From K. W. Schaie & S. L. Willis (1993). Age differences in patterns of psychometric intelligence in adulthood. *Psychology and Aging,* 8, 44-55. Reprinted by permission of the Gerontological Society of America.
Fig. 8.8: From U. Lindenberger, U. Mayr, and R. Kliegl (1993). Speed and intelligence in old age. *Psychology and Aging,* 8, 207-220. Reprinted by permission of the American Psychological Association.

Chapter 9
Fig. 9.1: From M. Berzonsky (1978). Formal reasoning in adolescence: An alternative view. *Adolescence,* 13, 279-290. Reprinted by permission.
Fig. 9.2: Number of absolute relativistic, and dialectical items chosen by age. From D. Kramer, P. E. Kahlbaugh, and R. B. Goldston (1992). A measure of paradigm beliefs about the social world. *Journal of Gerontology: Psychological Sciences,* 47, 180-189. Reprinted by permission of the Gerontological Society of America.
Fig. 9.4: From P. B. Baltes and U. Staudinger (1993). The search for the psychology of wisdom. Current directions in *Psychological Science,* 2, 75-80. Reprinted by permission.
Fig. 9.5: From P. B. Baltes and R. Kliegl (1992). Further testing of limits of cognitive plasticity. *Developmental Psychology,* 28, 121-125. Reprinted by permission of the American Psychological Association.
Research Focus Box Table 9.A: From P. B. Baltes, U. Staudinger, A. Macker, and J. Smith (1995). People nominated as wise: A comparative study of wisdom-related knowledge. *Psychology and Aging,* 10, 155-166. Reprinted by permission of the American Psychological Association.

Chapter 10
Fig. 10.1: Adapted from D. J. Levinson, The seasons of a man's life by permission from Knopf, 1978, and from D. J. Levinson, The season's of a woman's life by permission from Ballantine 1996.
Fig. 10.3: Illustration of Costa and McCrae's 5-factor model, reproduced by permission of the publisher, Psychological Assessment Resources, from the NEO PI-R Professional Manual, copyright 1992 by PAR, Inc. Further reproduction prohibited without written permission from the publisher.
Fig. 10.4: From D. Field and R. E. Millsap, Personality in advanced old age: Continuity or change in the *Journal of Gerontology: Psychological Sciences,* 46, 299-308. Copyright 1991 Gerontological Society of America.
Research Focus Box Fig. 10.3A, Fig. 10.3B, and Fig. 10.3C: From B. Hagberg, G. Samuelson, B. Lindberg, and O. Dehlin. Stability and change of personality in old age and its relation to survival. In *Journal of Gerontology: Psychological Sciences,* 46, 285-291. Copyright 1991 Gerontological Society of America.
Fig. 10.5: From D. F. Hultsch and J. K. Plemmons, Life events and life span development. In P. B. Baltes and O. G. Brim (Eds.), *Life span development and behavior.* Copyright 1979 Academic Press. Reprinted by permission.
Fig. 10.6: Age-related changes in moral reasoning. Adapted from A. Colby, L. Kohlberg, J. C. Gibbs, and M. Lieberman (1983). A longitudinal study of moral development. *Monographs of the Society for research in child development,* 48, 1-24.

Chapter 11
Fig. 11.2: Changes in the components of satisfying love relationships. From M. N. Reedy, J. E. Birren, and K. W. Schaie. Age and sex differences in satisfying love relationships across the life span. *Human Development,* 24, 52-66. Reprinted by permission from S. Karger, Switzerland.
Fig. 11.3: Marital satisfaction and stage of marriage. Adapted from S. Anderson, C. S. Russell, W. R. Schumm (1983). Perceived marital quality and family life-cycle categories: A further analysis. *Journal of Marriage and the Family,* 45, 127-139.

Chapter 12
Fig. 12.8: Phases of retirement. Adapted from R. C. Atchley (1977). The social forces of later life. An introduction to social gerontology, with permission from the Wadsworth Publishing Company, Belmont, CA.

Photo

Chapter 1
Opener: © Gail Meese/Meese Photo Research;
p. 10: © Allen Zak/Meese Photo Research;
p. 13, both: © Gail Meese/Meese Photo Research:
p. 15: AP/Wide World Photos.

Chapter 2
Opener: © Quiel Begonia/Meese Photo Research;
p. 29: © Toni Michaels/The Image Works;
p. 30: © Martha Tabor/Meese Photo Research;
p. 44 both: © Gail Meese/Meese Photo Research;
p. 46: Courtesy Patricia M. Peterson.

Chapter 3
Opener: © Earl Dotter/Meese Photo Research;
p. 57: © Allen Zak/Meese Photo Research;
p. 59, both; **p. 68, both:** AP/Wide World Photos;
p. 69: © Gail Meese/Meese Photo Research;
figure 3.10: © CNRI/SPL/Photo Researchers, Inc.

Chapter 4
Opener: © Owen Franken/Stock, Boston;
p. 108: AP/Wide World Photos;
p. 126: © Rebecca Bryant Lockridge/Meese Photo Research.

Chapter 5
Opener: © Alan Oddie/PhotoEdit;
p. 175: © Jim Pickerell/The Image Works;
p. 190: © Elizabeth Crews/The Image Works.

Chapter 6
Opener: © Gail Meese/Meese Photo Research;
p. 207: © David Strickler/Meese Photo Research;
p. 217: © Martha Tabor/Meese Photo Research;
p. 225: © David Young-Wolff/PhotoEdit.

Chapter 7
Opener: © Bob Daemmrich/The Image Works;
p. 261: © Cathy Watterson/Meese Photo Research;
p. 264: © Allen Zak/Meese Photo Research;
p. 289: © Gail Meese/Meese Photo Research.

Chapter 8
Opener: © Martha Tabor/Meese Photo Research;
p. 320, top: © Martha Tabor/Meese Photo Research;
p. 320, bottom: © James Shaffer;
p. 324: © Allen Zak/Meese Photo Research;
p. 329: AP/Wide World Photos.

Chapter 9
Opener: © Bedrich Grumzweig/Photo Researchers, Inc.;
p. 343: © Gail Meese/Meese Photo Research;
p. 353: © Tim Davis/Photo Researchers, Inc.;
p. 355: AP/Wide World Photos;
p. 362: © Jose Galvez/PhotoEdit.

Chapter 10
Opener: © David Young-Wolff/PhotoEdit;
p. 392, left: © David Grossman/Photo Researchers, Inc.;

p. 392, right: © Dion Ogust/The Image Works;

p. 393: © Karen Preuss/The Image Works;

p. 407: © Billy Barnes/PhotoEdit.

Chapter 11

Opener: © Allen Zak/Meese Photo Research;

p. 426: © Merritt Vincent/PhotoEdit;

p. 427: © J. Nourok/PhotoEdit;

p. 434: © Peter A. Silva/Meese Photo Research;

p. 435: courtesy William and Joan Hoyer and Alexandra Bebko;

p. 441: © Gail Meese/Meese Photo Research.

Chapter 12

Opener: © Catherine Green/Meese Photo Research;

p. 458: © Bob Daemmrich/The Image Works;

p. 482: © Gary Walts/The Image Works;

p. 489: © Rick Yamda-Lapides/Meese Photo Research.

Chapter 13

Opener: © Jim Mahoney/The Image Works;

p. 531: © A. Ramey/PhotoEdit;

p. 535: © Etter/Anthro-Photo;

p. 541: © Gail Meese/Meese Photo Research.

NAME INDEX

SUPPORT, 512
Sussman, M., 67
Swanson, J. M., 293
Sweet, L., 536–537
Syracuse Herald American, 539
Szinovacz, M., 493

T

Tabisz, E., 170
Taeuber, C. M., 25, 26
Takeuchi, D. T., 172, 176
"Taking the Iliad on the Road," 286
Takman, A., 105
Talbot, A., 232
Tamir, L. M., 462
Tang, M., 91
Tanzi, R. E., 87
Tarulli, B., 469
Tashima, N., 173
Taylor, C., 436
Taylor, C. M., 475
Taylor, J. R., 295
Taylor, R. J., 36, 140
Taylor, S. E., 109, 113, 114, 115, 121, 131, 133, 134, 239, 530
Teachers Insurance and Annuity Association (TIAA), 204, 209, 213, 215
Tell, E. J., 39
Teltsch, K., 485, 486
Teresi, J. A., 38
Teri, L., 117, 120, 158
Tesch-Römer, C., 361
Thomae, H., 128
Thomas, L. E., 139
Thomas, S., 433, 434, 436
Thomas, S. A., 190
Thompson, E. H., 120, 121
Thompson, J., 249
Thompson, J. W., 152
Thompson, K. A., 117, 119
Thompson, L., 550
Thompson, L. W., 153, 160
Thompson, M. G., 154
Thompson, R. A., 437
Thompson, R. F., 76
Thorndike, E. L., 288
Thurstone, L. L., 301, 306
TIAA. *See* Teachers Insurance and Annuity Association
Tideiksaar, R., 252
Tierney, M., 118
Tiffany, D. W., 180, 239
Tiffany, P. G., 180, 239
Tilton, J. W., 288
Tinetti, M. E., 251, 252
Tinsley, B. B., 437
Tinsley, B. J., 432
Tobin, J. J., 41
Tobin, S. S., 105, 140
Todd, A. M., 149

Tomita, S., 438
Tomlinson-Keasey, C., 408
Tornstan, L., 390, 391
Trevethan, S. D., 414
Trimble, J. E., 171
Troll, L. E., 47, 383, 435, 436
Tryban, G. M., 429
Tsai, C. M., 189, 190
Tucker, J. S., 189, 190
Tulving, E., 262, 268–269, 270, 282, 292
Turnbull, J. E., 163, 183
Turnher, M., 43, 422
Tyra, P. A., 170

U

Uba, L., 172, 173–174, 176
Uhlenberg, P., 444
University of Michigan Fitness Research Center, 244
U.S. Bureau of the Census, 24, 36, 37, 196, 429, 438–439, 443, 462
U.S. Department of Agriculture, 240
U.S. Department of Health and Human Services, 36
U.S. Department of Labor, 486
U.S. House of Representatives, 166, 167, 211
U.S. News and World Report, 113
U.S. Public Health Service, 27, 38, 55, 163, 223, 241
Usher, J. A., 275

V

Valdiserri, M., 273
Valliant, C. O., 460, 478
Valliant, G. E., 42, 115, 460, 478
VanCamp, S. P., 246, 247
Van Hasselt, V. B., 181
Van Hoose, W. H., 485
Van-Tilburg, T., 492
Van Tilburg, W., 158
Van Wolffelaar, P. C., 287
Vasquez, M. J., 150, 151, 174
Vasterling, J. J., 117, 119
Vatican Congregation for the Doctrine of the Faith, 515
Veatch, R. M., 500
Veevers, J. E., 425
Ventis, G., 492
Verbrugge, L. M., 223
Verhaeghen, P., 15
Verillo, R. T., 69
Verity, L. S., 246, 247
Verret, D., 515
Vinokur, A. D., 121
Vinters, H. V., 95
Vitaliano, P. P., 117, 120
Vital Statistics of the United States, 229, 230

Vogel, D. G., 95
Vondareck, F. W., 459

W

Wacker, R., 192
Wagner, R. K., 328
Waite, L. J., 493
Waldemar, G., 81
Waldman, D. A., 466, 467
Waldrop, M. M., 352, 354
Walford, R., 56
Walker, J. E., 251
Walker, L. J., 414
Walker, P. F., 134
Walker, R. D., 152
Wallace, S. P., 246, 247
Wallerstein, J. S., 444
Walter, B. M., 270
Wapner, S., 488, 490–491, 493
Ward, C. W., 69
Ward, M. S., 191, 192
Ward, R., 117–118
Warr, P., 460, 463, 464
Warshak, R. A., 443
Washo, C., 493
Waskel, S. A., 167
Watkins, P. C., 87
Weale, R. A., 65
Webster, J. D., 275
Webster, P. S., 153, 156
Wechsler, A. F., 86
Wechsler, D., 307
Weinberger, D. A., 115
Weindruch, R., 56, 58, 237
Weiner, M. B., 155, 156, 211, 213, 215
Weinstein, K. K., 434
Weintraub, J. K., 116
Weisberg, R. W., 330
Weisman, A. T., 525, 529
Weiss, L., 422–423
Weiss, R. S., 423, 469
Welte, J. W., 168, 169
Wentura, D., 131, 132
Werner, P., 220
Wertheimer, M., 346
West, S. G., 521
Westermeyer, J. J., 176
Wethington, E., 24, 27, 34, 481, 485
Wheeler, M., 268–269
Whipple, R., 250, 252
Whishaw, I. Q., 75, 76
Whitbourne, S. K., 60, 68, 69
White, J. A., 86
White, N., 317
Whitehouse, P. J., 86
Whitford, G. S., 441, 442
Whitten, P., 247
Whittington, F. J., 548, 549
Wilber, K. H., 192
Wilk, C. A., 446

Wilkelgren, I., 78
Wilkie, F., 316
Willerman, L., 82
Willett, W. C., 241
Williams, J. B., 521
Williams, W. M., 328
Williamson, D. F., 236
Williamson, G. F., 127, 128, 157
Williamson, G. M., 127, 227, 233
Williamson, J. B., 487
Willis, S. L., 10, 15, 127, 131, 307, 310, 311, 316, 319, 322, 323, 396, 580
Winch, R. F., 424
Winocur, G., 75
Winslow, L., 65
Wise, P. M., 63, 64
Wisewell, R. A., 72
Wittlinger, R. P., 276
Wohl, J., 148, 149, 167
Wohlwill, J. F., 6
Wolf, R. S., 436, 437, 438
Wolfson, C., 117, 252
Wolfson, L., 250, 252
Wolinsky, F. D., 154
Wolmark, N., 232
Wong, P. T., 520
Wood, J. U., 113, 114
Wood, P. K., 348
Woodruff-Pak, D., 75, 520
Woodyard, E., 288
Worth, M., 485
Wurtman, R. J., 83

X

Xiaojia, G., 169

Y

Yalom, I. D., 548
Yates, K., 105, 117
Yoder, J., 117, 119
Yoder, K. K., 105
Yonelinas, A. P., 284
York, K. L., 43
Young, H. M., 117, 120
Young, K., 172, 176

Z

Zacks, R. T., 287, 288
Zane, N. W. S., 172, 176
Zank, S., 256
Zarit, J. M., 86, 94, 95, 96, 97, 98, 102
Zarit, S. H., 86, 94, 95, 96, 97, 98, 102
Zechmeiter, E. B., 555, 559
Zeiss, A. M., 157, 158
Zelnick, M., 445
Zimmerman, R. S., 548, 549
Zuzanek, J., 492
Zweibel, N. R., 510

SUBJECT INDEX

Memory—*Cont.*
  priming tasks and, 281–282,
    283–284
  reminiscence bump and, 277–278
  role of hippocampus, 75
  source memory, 272–274
  three-stage model of, 262–263
  tool-like properties of, 281
  See also Attention; Learning
Memory enhancement procedures,
  363–364
Memory loss
  biological approach to,
    290–291, 297
  contextual approach to,
    293–294, 297
  information-processing approach
    to, 291–293, 297
  memory search and, 265–266
  normal *vs.* pathological, 294–295
  short-term *vs.* long-term memory,
    262–267
  spatial processing and, 266–267
  working memory, 263–265
Memory search, 265–266
Memory set utilization, 290
Menopause
  as developmental change,
    446–447
  longevity and, 30
  race and, 35
  sexuality and, 446–447
Mental age, classifying, 306–307
Mental exercise, 319, 321–323
Mental health
  aging and, 145–147
  ethnicity and, 148–151
  utilization of mental health
    services, 147–152
  See also Psychological disorders
Mental health services
  access to, 151–152
  cultural values and, 149
  ethnicity and, 148–151
  utilization of, 147–152
Mental imagery, 272
Mentors, 422, 473
Meta-analysis, 579
Metabolism, 236
Metamemory, 260
Method of loci, 363–364
Middle adulthood
  assessment of career success, 462
  friendships in, 423
  leisure and, 478–479
  marriage in, 430
  preparation for retirement, 479
  sexual attitudes and behavior, 445
  therapeutic interventions in, 179
Middle adulthood era, 386–387
Midlife career change, 464–465
Midlife crises, 381, 386, 389
Midlife transitions, 179, 386
Milieu therapy, 188
Mini-Mental Status Exam, 90, 91
Minor depression, 154

Mitochondria, 237
Mixed dementia, 94
Mode, 562
Modified second career pattern, 474
Moral development
  age-related changes in, 408
  criticisms of Kohlberg's theory,
    413–415
  determinants of, 408, 412–413
  importance of, 413
  Kohlberg's theory, 406–412
  phases of, 414
Moral reasoning, coping and, 414
Moral responsibility for medical
  decisions, 515–516
Morbidity, 28
Morphine, 517
Mortality, 28, 399
Most efficient design, 577–578
Mourning, 534
MRI (magnetic resonance
  imaging), 80
Multidirectionality of
  development, 7
Multi-infarct dementia, 94, 95
Multiple intelligences, 328
Multiple memory systems, 262,
  267–268
Multiple regression, 564–565
Muscle atrophy. *See* Sarcopenia
Muscle mass, loss of, 248–249
Muscle tissue, 60
Musculoskeletal system, 72
Music, final compositions, 523
Mutual help, 149
Myocardial infarction, 237, 238

N

Native Americans, 151–152,
  163–164
Near phase of retirement, 487
Near poor, 36
Necessary subjectivity, 348–349
Negative correlation, 563–564
Neglect (elder abuse), 437
Neurofibrillary tangles, 78, 82,
  90–91, 290
Neuronal aging, 76–79
Neurons, 76–79, 99
Neuroticism, 394
Neurotransmitters, 79, 90, 290
New beginning (retirement style),
  488, 490–491
Noetic awareness, 269
Nondeclarative memory, 268,
  280–282
Nonnormative life events, 8,
  11–12, 20
Nonrepresentative samples, 580
Normalization, 255
Normative age-graded factors, 8,
  12, 20
Normative history-graded factors,
  8, 9–10, 12, 20
Nuclear family, 431
Number skills, 301

Numbness phase (grief), 540
Nun study, 90–91, 92
Nursing homes, 39
  accreditation of, 215
  autonomy and control in, 134
  common medical conditions
    treated, 206
  costs of, 206
  long-term care in, 210
  sexuality and, 450
  use of restraints in, 222
Nurturance, 46

O

Obesity, 236, 248
Objective caregiver burden, 117
Observational (field) research,
  560–561
Occipital lobe, 76
Occupational choice
  Ginzberg's theory of, 457–458
  Holland's theory of, 458–459
  Super's theory of, 456–457
Occupational goals, 464
Occupational satisfaction, 460–464
Occupational success, 326
Occupational well-being, 463–464
Occupations, cognitively oriented,
  315, 326
Old-Age and Survivors Insurance,
  203–204
Oldest-old, 109, 397
Old-old, 24, 37, 397
Omnibus Budget Reconciliation
  Act (1987), 187, 191, 222
Oncologists, 228
Ontogeny, 3–4
Openness to experience, 394
Optimal level of cognition, 351
Optimally exercised ability, 321–322
Optimism, 239
Optimization, 197, 370–371
Optimization of development, 18
Ordinary creativity, 333–334
Organ donation, 500, 501, 513–514
Organ donor cards, 513
Organismic paradigm, 16, 18
Organization of information,
  271–272
Organ of corti, 66
Osteoporosis, 59, 60, 446
Overweight, 28
Oxidative damage, 58

P

Pain, 157, 532
Pain sensitivity, 70
Palliative treatments for AD, 93
Paradigms, 15, 20–21
Parental favoritism, 433
Parental imperative, 44–45, 425
Parent-child relations, 433
Parenting, 425–427, 432, 443, 451
Parents
  death of, 546–547
  longevity and, 33

Parietal lobe, 76
Parkinson's disease, 96–97
Passive accommodative mastery, 44
Passive euthanasia, 514
Pattison's living-dying interval,
  526–527, 551
Pearson product moment
  correlation coefficient, 564
Pendulum task, 342, 345
Pensions, 204–205
Perceived health, 201–202
Perceptual-motor skills, 280
Perceptual Representation System
  (PRS), 282, 291
Perceptual speed, 301
Performance scale (WAIS), 305, 307
Permanent vegetative state, 502
Persistent vegetative state (PVS),
  501–502
Personal concerns level of
  personality, 405
Personality, 377
  career choice and, 458–459
  levels of, 404–406
  relationships and, 421
  stability of, 389–390, 394–395,
    400–401
  survival rates and, 398–399
  upward occupational mobility
    and, 465
Personality change, sex roles
  and, 46
Personality development
  individuality and, 404
  levels of personality and,
    404–406
  life-events framework,
    401–404, 416
  moral development, 406–415
  sex roles and, 45
  stage approach to, 377–389
  trait approach, 389–401
Personality domain, 19
Person-centered death
  education, 522
Personologists, 390
Person X Situation, 392
PET scan (positron-emission
  tomography), 80–81, 269,
  291, 292
Pet therapy, 188–190
Philosophical wisdom, 360
Physical ability, 71–72
Physical activity
  benefits of, 237
  longevity and, 33
  public health and, 243
  See also Exercise
Physical appearance, 58–61
Physical competence, 224–225
Physical health
  adjustment to retirement and,
    493–494
  behavior and, 223–239, 257
  cognitive impairments. *See*
    Cognitive impairments